CATO HANDBOOK FOR CONGRESS

FOR

105TH CONGRESS

CATO
INSTITUTE
Washington, D.C.

Cato Institute
1000 Massachusetts Avenue, N.W.
Washington, D.C. 20001

Contents

1. Introduction

According to President Clinton, the era of big government is over. Oddly enough, it is, everywhere but in his policy proposals. Around the world, the coercive mechanisms of government have been tried and found wanting. Countries from Russia to South Africa to Argentina to Great Britain are trying to limit political society and allow civil society to reemerge and flourish.

Here in the United States, however, governments at all levels continue to grow. Governments now raise in taxes and spend some $2.6 trillion a year, money that is withdrawn from civil society and spent according to the dictates of politics rather than the choices of those who earned it. Disillusionment with the fruits of big government has grown along with its ambitions. To the question, ''Which do you favor, a smaller government with fewer services or a larger government with many services?'' the percentage responding ''smaller government'' rose from 49 in 1984 to 60 in 1993 to 68 in 1995. Note that the question doesn't even remind people that more services mean more taxes. Another regular poll question is, ''How much of the time do you think you can trust the government in Washington to do what is right?'' In 1964, 14 percent said ''always'' and 62 percent said ''most of the time.'' By 1994 ''always'' had virtually disappeared, and ''most of the time'' was down to 14 percent. ''Only some of the time'' had risen 22 percent to 73 percent, while 9 percent *volunteered* the response of ''never.''

Some commentators would argue that the enthusiasm for limiting government, evident in the 1994 election, had receded by 1996, when incumbents were generally reelected. But it would have been hard for voters disillusioned with big government to identify the party of smaller government in 1996. President Clinton declared that ''the era of big government is over,'' while the Republican Congress moved the country a giant step toward socialized medicine. When the presidential candidate of the presumably small-government party says that the crucial difference in the election is whether government will grow by 14 percent or 20 percent, a voter can hardly express a preference for "smaller government with fewer services" at the ballot box.

The initiatives placed before the voters in 1996 gave a clearer picture of popular opinion. Term limits and tax limits passed in many states; California voters endorsed racial equality under the law and turned down the latest anti-business ploy; and the voters of both trend-setting California and conservative Arizona endorsed alternatives to the futile war on drugs. The "less government, more freedom" message may have been difficult to send via the candidates, but it was clear in the realm of direct democracy.

The Costs of Big Government

As we've seen, however, a popular desire for less government is always difficult to translate into substantive reform. It seems to be the nature of democracy that those who seek power and privilege from government are more energetic in the political arena than those who seek only to be left alone. That reality has been described many times over the years. Thomas Jefferson wrote, "The natural progress of things is for liberty to yield and government to gain ground." The public-choice economists have explained how every government program provides benefits to a few people while diffusing the costs over all taxpayers or consumers. Congress is more likely to hear from those who receive the concentrated benefits than from those who pay the diffused costs.

In *The Culture of Spending,* James L. Payne quantified the situation in which members of Congress find themselves: At 14 randomly selected appropriations hearings, there were 1,060 witnesses, 1,014 of whom supported the program in question, while only 7 opposed it. Even members of Congress committed to limited government will find it difficult to remember their commitment after such a barrage of pleas for government services.

Milton and Rose Friedman argued in *The Tyranny of the Status Quo* that Congress typically debates a new program at some length. But after the program is implemented, subsequent Congresses debate only the amount by which its budget should be increased. And in the case of an "entitlement" program, members of Congress tend only to wring their hands about its "uncontrollable" growth.

The nature of government is to grow. Only rarely can a sustained assault by the nonpolitical forces of civil society present a successful challenge to the entrenched interests of political society. But the absence of a truly reprehensible state against which to rebel, as in Eastern Europe and South

Africa, or a looming fiscal collapse, such as those that fostered reform in New Zealand and Argentina, should not blind us to the real costs of excessive government.

One obvious cost of our gargantuan government is reduced economic growth. In a world of global markets and rapid technological progress, we struggle along with annual growth rates far below what we achieved from World War II until the mid-1970s. With less taxation and less regulation, we could be far wealthier. That's not a great loss to Bill Gates or probably to many of the readers of this *Handbook*, but higher economic growth would mean a great deal to middle-class Americans and those who have the least.

Another cost is the loss of our freedom. We still live in one of the freest countries in the world, but each new government program takes away just a little of that freedom—the freedom to spend our money as we choose, to go into the businesses we choose, to negotiate with our employers over compensation and benefits. Some government programs, of course, take away large parts of our freedom—such as the freedom to choose how much to invest for our retirement and where to invest it, or the freedom to choose the schools that are right for our children, or the freedom of doctors and patients to choose appropriate medicines.

A related cost of big government, but one not often recognized, is the harm it does to morality and responsibility. Expansive government undermines the moral character necessary to both civil society and liberty under law. The "bourgeois virtues" of work, thrift, sobriety, prudence, fidelity, self-reliance, and a concern for one's reputation developed and endured in part because they are the virtues necessary for survival and progress in a world where wealth must be produced and people are responsible for their own flourishing. Government can't do much to instill those virtues in people, but it can do much to undermine them. As David Frum writes in *Dead Right,*

> Why be thrifty when your old age and health care are provided for, no matter how profligately you acted in your youth? Why be prudent when the state insures your bank deposits, replaces your flooded-out house, buys all the wheat you can grow, and rescues you when you stray into a foreign battle zone? Why be diligent when half your earnings are taken from you and given to the idle? Why be sober when the taxpayers run clinics to cure you of your drug habit as soon as it no longer amuses you?

Frum sums up government's impact on individual character as "the emancipation of the individual from the restrictions imposed on it by limited

3

resources, or religious dread, or community disapproval, or the risk of disease or personal catastrophe.'' David Boaz notes in his new book *Libertarianism: A Primer,* ''One might suppose that the very aim of libertarianism is the emancipation of the individual, and so it is—but the emancipation of the individual from artificial, coercive restraints on his actions. Libertarians never suggested that people be 'emancipated' from the reality of the world, from the obligation to pay one's own way and to take responsibility for the consequences of one's own actions.'' People should be free to make their own decisions and to succeed or fail according to their own choices. When we try to limit that freedom, when we shield people from the consequences of their actions, we get a society characterized not by thrift, sobriety, diligence, self-reliance, and prudence but by profligacy, intemperance, indolence, dependency, and indifference to consequences.

By taking away money, liberty, and responsibility, the growth of government necessarily shrinks civil society. Civil society is that whole network of relationships among people, from families to businesses to charities and nonprofit associations, that are formed on the basis of consent. It is contrasted with political society, or government, the distinguishing characteristic of which is coercion. When government spends more money, assumes new functions, or forbids peaceful private actions, it narrows the realm of civil society and thus reduces the ability of people to come together in civil society to accomplish their mutual goals. Communitarians who deplore the decline of community and cooperation should look to big government for an explanation.

Controlling Government

The Constitution of the United States is the best device ever created for limiting government. It was designed by remarkably wise men to solve the problem that had vexed lovers of freedom for centuries: how to establish a government that could protect individuals from each other without giving it the power to take away their freedom. The Constitution provided for a federal government that would protect the United States from foreign enemies, guarantee the citizens of every state a republican form of government, issue a common currency, and do very little else. The basic functions of punishing criminals and enforcing contracts were left to state and local governments, and the infinite variety of social needs was left to individuals and civil society. The challenge was to create a federal government strong enough to accomplish the tasks for which it was intended but constrained by the Constitution from assuming additional powers.

Over the years, however, we have let the federal government exceed the bounds that the Founders wisely placed on it. We have moved from James Madison's statement on the floor of Congress in 1794 that he could not "undertake to lay his finger on that article of the Federal Constitution which granted a right to Congress of expending, on objects of benevolence, the money of their constituents" to Franklin Roosevelt's 1935 plea to the House Ways and Means Committee, "I hope your committee will not permit doubts as to constitutionality, however reasonable, to block the suggested legislation." Today, Congress has gotten into the habit of hardly bothering to search the Constitution for authority before passing legislation.

If we wish once again to live under limited government—and we believe the American people do—then the Constitution is our guide to getting there. Congress should examine every proposed piece of legislation and every existing agency and law in the light of the delegated, enumerated, and thus limited powers granted it by the Constitution. Instead of getting caught up in partisan battles, in ephemeral and essentially minor issues, it is important to step back, get a sense of perspective, and begin to conform American public policy to the Constitution and its design for limited government.

Although this is not a Handbook for the Supreme Court, we urge the Court as well to remain mindful of its obligation under the Constitution to protect the liberties of the people from intrusion by the political branches. As Alexander Hamilton wrote in the *Federalist* no. 78,

> Where the will of the legislature, declared in its statutes, stands in opposition to that of the people, declared in the Constitution, the judges ought to be governed by the latter rather than the former. The prior act of a superior ought to be preferred to the subsequent act of an inferior and subordinate authority; and that accordingly, whenever a particular statute contravenes the Constitution, it will be the duty of the tribunals to adhere to the latter and disregard the former.

If members of Congress conclude that the powers granted to them under the Constitution are inadequate to undertake the tasks that ought to be performed by the federal government on the eve of the 21st century, they should abide by the rule of law and propose amendments to the Constitution granting them those new powers. Believing that the strength of a federal system is that it divides power and offers a natural scope for experimentation, we would likely oppose such a request for new powers; but the debate over Congress's power would be in keeping with the amendment process established in the Constitution.

An Agenda for Reform

The Constitution is the blueprint for limited government. This *Handbook* is offered as a more detailed guide to a reform agenda. The chapters of the *Handbook* proceed logically through the vast expanses of the federal government with suggestions for comprehensive change. In Chapter 3, Roger Pilon expands on the need for adherence to the Constitution. Then two fundamental structural reforms are suggested: an end to the delegation of legislative powers to unelected, unaccountable bureaucrats and limits on the terms of members of Congress.

The next section of the *Handbook* looks at ways to solve an immediate problem: the inexorable growth of federal taxing and spending. Chapter 6 focuses on the domestic budget and thus of necessity touches on issues covered in other chapters. It has in some instances assumed a less ambitious reduction of federal programs than outlined in other chapters in order to present a more immediate case for legislative reform. Adopting the recommendations made in subsequent chapters would allow further reduction in taxes and spending.

The third section, for instance, offers an "abolition agenda." When the federal government has so far exceeded its constitutional bounds, the goal of members of Congress should not be to simply trim federal spending but to abolish those agencies and departments that are not authorized in the Constitution, or have failed in their purpose, or have outlived their usefulness, or are an unwarranted expense.

The chapters in the fourth section deal with a troubling trend in contemporary policy: a growing infringement on civil liberties in America. From the Communications Decency Act to proposed "anti-terrorism" measures, from the restrictions on election-related speech to intrusions on our privacy, from the frightening assaults at Waco and Ruby Ridge to the narrowing of protections for criminal defendants, the federal government is restricting too many of our traditional freedoms. Both liberals and conservatives should be concerned about the intrusion of federal power into every corner of society.

In the next few sections, Cato's scholars recommend reforms in the whole range of domestic policy—Social Security, welfare, regulation, the environment, and more. Finally, we return to the main constitutional function of the U.S. government—foreign and defense policy—and offer some recommendations for keeping Americans at peace and safe from foreign threats.

House Republicans have drawn up a "Framework" similar to the mission statements that corporations are increasingly adopting. As Rep. John A. Boehner of Ohio, chairman of the Republican Conference, says, "In any good company today, all the employees have a good idea what the goals are, where they're heading and why. I don't think we should operate any differently." The Constitution of the United States serves as an excellent mission statement for the federal government and for Congress, and we respectfully submit this *Handbook* as an agenda for carrying out that mission in 1997–98.

Conclusion

For those who go into government to improve the lives of their fellow citizens, the hardest lesson to accept may be that often there is no good reason for Congress to "do anything" about a problem—such as education, crime, or church burning. The advice given here may seem negative. Critics will object, do you want the government just to stand there and do nothing while this problem continues? Sometimes that is exactly the best thing for Congress to do. The Chinese philosopher Lao-tzu urged the ruler ("the sage") to refrain from acting, to accept the good with the bad, to let the people pursue their own actions. Among the advice offered in the *Tao Te Ching* is the following:

Exterminate the sage [the ruler] and discard the wisdom [of rule],
And the people will benefit a hundredfold. . . .
The more prohibitions there are,
The poorer the people will be.
The more laws are promulgated,
The more thieves and bandits there will be.
Therefore a sage has said:
So long as I "do nothing" the people will of themselves be transformed.
So long as I love quietude, the people will of themselves go straight.
So long as I act only by inactivity the people will of themselves become prosperous.

Members of Congress must recognize, understand, and then defend the limited role of the federal government. It isn't just the Supreme Court that is enjoined to enforce the Constitution; the president and members of Congress also take an oath to uphold the Constitution, and they should also take care to see that the government's actions are not just prudent but constitutional. We are all tempted from time to time to demand something of government, whether limits on speech we find offensive, a subsidy for our business, compensation for a failed investment, or whatever. That's why we agree at the constitutional level that none of us will be able to use government in that way. There is no higher duty for members of Congress than to remind us of the constitutional limits on government when we forget them.

Suggested Readings

Boaz, David. *Libertarianism: A Primer.* New York: Free Press, 1997.

Boaz, David, and Edward H. Crane, eds. *Market Liberalism: A Paradigm for the 21st Century.* Washington: Cato Institute, 1993.

Crane, Edward H. "Defending Civil Society." *Cato's Letter* no. 8. Washington: Cato Institute, 1994.

Epstein, Richard. *Simple Rules for a Complex World.* Cambridge, Mass.: Harvard University Press, 1995.

Friedman, Milton. *Capitalism and Freedom.* Chicago: University of Chicago Press, 1962.

Friedman, Milton, and Rose D. Friedman. *The Tyranny of the Status Quo.* San Diego: Harcourt Brace, 1984.

—Prepared by David Boaz and Edward H. Crane

2. Restoring Civil Society

Congress should

- before trying to institute a government program to solve a problem, investigate whether there is some other government program that is causing the problem in the first place and, if such a program is identified, begin to reform or eliminate it;
- ask by what legal authority in the Constitution Congress undertakes an action, thereby subjecting itself to the rule of law;
- recognize that when government undertakes a program, it displaces the voluntary efforts of others and makes voluntary association in civil society appear redundant, with significant negative effects; and
- begin systematically to abolish or phase out those government programs that do what could be accomplished by voluntary associations in civil society, whether business enterprises, self-help groups, or charities, recognizing that accomplishment through free association is morally superior to coercive mandates and almost always generates more efficient outcomes.

Thomas Jefferson observed in 1788 that "the natural progress of things is for liberty to yield and government to gain ground." The truth of his observation has been amply demonstrated in recent decades. As political society—government—grows, civil society retreats. It is in civil society—the realm of liberty—that mankind flourishes. It is from civil society that industry, civility, rectitude, science, and prosperity arise.

If civil society is to be restored, the members of the 105th Congress must reexamine the relationship between political society and civil society, replacing edicts and mandates with the rule of law and substituting voluntary cooperation for coercion.

No challenge is more serious today than the restoration of civil society. Pundits cite violent crime; family breakdown; the waning of some traditional institutions; blighted inner cities; and a decline in civility, honesty, and trust as evidence of a crisis in civil society. And few topics have received as much attention in recent years as this one. Politicians and pundits on both left and right have attempted to exploit the theme for their own purposes, which often hinge on expanding governmental powers to manipulate citizens in order to attain whatever outcomes the manipulators desire. The impulse to do so, however, is fundamentally at odds with civil society, as it has been commonly understood for centuries. As the distinguished historian of civil society Antony Black has noted, "We may identify the central ideal of civil society as personal independence, and its central imperative as respect for persons."

What Is Civil Society?

Civil society can be difficult to understand; it is individualistic without being atomistic and is made up of associations without being collectivist. Civil society is a spontaneous order, a complex network of relationships and associations based on the freedom of the individual, who voluntarily assumes obligations and accepts responsibility for his or her behavior.

Some people define civil society to encompass only nonprofit organizations and to exclude entirely commercial organizations, contractual relationships, and other forms of voluntary cooperation. But dividing the world into the separate spheres of for-profit business enterprises, the institutions of the state, and "everything else" (called "civil society") makes little sense. It is far more fruitful to distinguish institutions on the basis of some shared characteristic; "everything else" does not denote an essential and therefore truly distinguishing characteristic. The thoughtful conservative Don Eberly of the Civil Society Project considers civil society a "third sector" made up of associations "that operate neither on the principle of coercion, nor entirely on the principle of rational self-interest." But, in attempting to set out a third sector, he has contrasted government and the market on the basis of principles as different in kind as apples and triangles. Coercion is a characteristic of actions toward people, not a motivation; "rational self-interest" is a kind of motivation, not a characteristic of action. Self-interested persons can act coercively or in accordance with the principles of voluntarism, just as persons acting coercively can be motivated by altruism or by self-interest. What distinguishes government from the market is coercive force, present in the one case and absent in the other. Eberly's attempt to create a third category of everything other than business and government fails.

10

The clearest and most relevant characteristic to use to distinguish among institutions is whether people interact voluntarily or coercively. Civil society is based on voluntary participation, whereas the state, or political society, is based on coercion. Thus, civil society includes families, businesses, self-help groups, religious institutions, charities, trade associations, Girl Scout troops, and an infinite variety of other kinds of associations. No one is coerced into joining them, and they have no coercive power to force their desires on the unwilling. Political society encompasses those institutions that exercise coercion, whether in their financing (e.g., taxation), their participation (e.g., conscription), or their activities (e.g., economic intervention in or prohibition of peaceful activity). Government is the institutionalization of coercion. Some amount of political society is necessary to protect civil society from even more coercive predators, whether domestic or foreign. But political society always presents the danger of overstepping its bounds and must be kept in check by the Constitution.

Restraining Political Society

As Thomas Paine noted at the very founding of our new nation, "Society in every state is a blessing, but government, even in its best state, is but a necessary evil; in its worst state an intolerable one." Thomas Jefferson stated in the 1798 Kentucky Resolutions (protesting the Alien and Sedition Acts), "Free government is founded in jealousy, not in confidence; it is jealousy and not confidence which prescribes limited constitutions, to bind down those whom we are obliged to trust with power." The mission of protecting civil society and restraining political society is at the very foundation of our Republic.

The Founding Fathers had good reasons for restraining government and subjecting the state itself to the rule of law. Coercive intervention creates conflict and sets citizen against citizen. As Adam Ferguson noted in his 1767 *Essay on the History of Civil Society,* "Men, in general, are sufficiently disposed to occupy themselves in forming projects and schemes; but he who would scheme and project for others, will find an opponent in every person who is disposed to scheme for himself."

Coercion allows some people to shift responsibility for the consequences of their acts to others; it disrupts the normally expected relationship between cause and effect. At the same time, it enervates the citizens, as they come to see their fates determined, not by their own voluntary acts, but by the holders of power.

11

A few examples illustrate the dangers presented by replacing voluntary interaction among free and responsible persons with coercion.

- Social Security has made the middle classes dependent on the state for their retirement income; they have been forced to finance a pay-as-you-go system that cannot keep its promises. Not surprisingly, taxpayers have failed to save and invest adequately, as the responsibility of saving for their retirement was lifted from their shoulders, just as their money was lifted from their wallets. If Social Security is not privatized, there will be massive intergenerational struggles, as payroll taxes on working people will have to rise by nearly 50 percent over current levels simply to meet the obligations of the present system. (That projection is based on moderate assumptions concerning inflation, demographics, and unemployment; the scenario is bleaker if we introduce less optimistic assumptions and catastrophic if we include Medicare in the equation.) Returning Social Security, in some form, to civil society is an imperative.
- The many transfer programs of the welfare state have made the poor dependent on the state and have made the most basic of all forms of association, the family, seem redundant. The numbers have fallen slightly in the past year, but the long-term trend over the past two decades is disturbing; there has been nearly a doubling in the rate of out-of-wedlock births to teenagers. Today nearly a third of all births in America are to unmarried mothers, and the proportion is over two-thirds among African-Americans, the most seriously affected population. Individuals no longer need fear the full consequences of their behavior, as the responsibility for the consequences of unwise choices can be shifted to others. The result is a rise of irresponsibility. Out-of-wedlock birth is the single most significant factor in the growth of poverty in America today. The consequences have been disastrous for everyone, except, of course, for political society's poverty industry: the welfare bureaucracies. Irresponsibility and restrictions on the poor that make it more difficult for them to better their own lives (e.g., onerous licensing laws and minimum wage laws) have led to the institutionalization of dependency. If poverty is to be ameliorated or eliminated, political society must give way to self-help, mutual aid, and charity, which is to say, to civil society.
- Intervention by the federal government into voluntary economic enterprises costs the American people $500 billion in lost wealth every year and has generated enormous investment in the negative-sum

game of lobbying, influence seeking, and corruption. As political society's redistributive powers have grown, more and more trade associations have relocated to Washington, D.C.—where wealth is redistributed rather than created—and more and more business firms have invested in Washington lawyers and lobbyists rather than in engineers and factory workers. The process will continue unabated until we restore incentives to invest in production of wealth rather than in its redistribution.

- The war on drugs costs the taxpayers $15 billion per year in taxes and is responsible for about half of the violent crime in major cities today, for the enriching of organized crime syndicates, for the glorification of the life of the violent drug dealer over that of the honest shop clerk or factory worker, and for the militarization of inner-city gang warfare. By attempting to take responsibility for personal virtue from individuals, the clumsy mechanisms of political society have had disastrous consequences for all. In order to realize a society of responsible and virtuous individuals, responsibility for virtue must be removed from political society and returned to the families, churches, synagogues, neighborhoods, and mutual aid associations that make up civil society.

A primary reason for the negative consequences of the replacement of civil society by political society is that the link between rights and responsibility, between cause and effect, has been broken. The exercise of rights leads to social harmony and personal virtue only when the consequences cannot be shifted to unwilling parties. Any disjunction between rights and responsibility affects, not only the poor, but all of society. To take but one high-profile example from recent years, when the federal government insured savings-and-loan deposits, wealthy depositors sought the highest rates of return, ignoring the riskiness of the institutions' loan portfolios and thereby shifting responsibility for bad investments onto the shoulders of the taxpayers. The result of that off-budget loan guarantee system was the transfer of nearly $150 billion in taxpayers' money to depositors and an implosion of America's savings-and-loan system. Similar examples can be found in almost every field of endeavor, affecting all income groups, races, religions, and areas of the country.

The Condition of Civil Society

Restoring civil society is a moral imperative. There is no more important issue on the political agenda today. The picture, however, is not an entirely bleak one, for the retreat of civil society in the face of advancing political society has been uneven. In some areas, civil society has even advanced, as political society has been restrained and pushed back; notable examples are the partial but progressive deregulation in recent decades of telecommunications, which has opened up so many opportunities for people to communicate and form new communities, and of financial services, which has allowed individuals and families greater control over their own investments. Despite all the advances of political society in recent decades, America still has a vigorous and robust civil society that provides employment for nearly 130 million persons, generates $7.5 trillion in annual production, and brings forth technological innovation on a daily basis. And charity and mutual aid are also growing in civil society; Americans gave $125 billion to private charities last year, and mutual aid organizations from Alcoholics Anonymous to the Promise Keepers to shelters for battered women offer mutual support to help individuals become stronger and more virtuous and to resist the temptations of irresponsible or self-destructive behavior.

Still, a better measure would be, not how numerous or how big those institutions and practices are relative to 10, 20, or 50 years ago, but how robust and vigorous they are compared to what they *would* be if they were not so hampered by political society. Between 1970 and 1975 the number of pages printed annually in the *Federal Register*—a fairly good index of regulatory intervention in the economy—tripled over the annual average since 1947, and the average has remained in the higher range since 1975. It is instructive to compare economic growth rates during the period between 1947 and 1973 with those of the period since 1973. The average annual rate of economic growth from 1947 to 1973 was 3.7 percent, but it was only 2.5 percent from 1974 to 1995. Compounded over a period of 22 years, the difference between actual economic growth and what it *would* have been had growth rates not declined (the growth deficit) is staggering, representing an enormous sum that could have been saved and invested, spent on education, or used to finance a higher standard of living. And that larger base, combined with the higher rate of economic growth, would be multiplied greatly in the future. Another and perhaps more telling measure of the difference between current wealth and what we could produce is the sagging rate of productivity growth, which was 2.25 percent for the first three-quarters of this century but began a long-term tumble in the mid-1970s; since 1992 the rate of productivity growth has been a paltry 0.3 percent per year, perilously close to the zero productivity growth rate in the period before the Industrial Revolution. That is far, far below the rate that led to a doubling of personal income per generation in the first several decades after World War II. (The story of what has happened in the years since 1973 is a complex one, with an enormous rise in some kinds of regulation, a decline in the rate of growth of the adult population, a dramatic decline in the net national savings rate, and a roughly 5 percentage point rise in taxes as a share of gross domestic product compared to the late 1960s, but the rise in economic intervention and in taxation undoubtedly bears most of the blame for declining economic growth and lagging productivity growth.)

Reviving Civil Society

Recently, various programs and projects have been initiated to "revive" civil society through government subsidization or fiat. E. J. Dionne Jr. of the Brookings Institution describes the Brookings research agenda on civil society as studying "government's role in promoting civic life." That assumes that government's role is positive rather than negative. And 19 bills to "renew America," most of which involve the federal government directly in conservative social engineering, have been introduced in the Senate by Sen. Dan Coats (R-Ind.) and in the House by Rep. John Kasich (R-Ohio); those bills include the Role Model Academy Act, the Character Development Act, and the Family Reconciliation Act. But such efforts are likely to fail, not only because of the flawed concept of civil society ("everything else") on which they rest, but also because of the mismatch between principles, between the coercive principle of political society and the voluntary principle of civil society. Political society may exercise coercion to protect individual rights from predators and thus protect the institutions of civil society, but coercion cannot call free associations into being, nor are subsidies administered by political agents likely to solve any more problems than they cause. Indeed, such subsidization carries the danger that with it will come strings, that civil society will be absorbed into or reduced to merely an extension of political society. That is not merely fatalism; it can be observed in practice. The so-called Volunteers of America organization gets 96 percent of its funding from government. Catholic Charities, which relies on government for 65 percent of its budget, has emerged as a significant voice defending the welfare state that funds it. Such institutions have been captured by political society.

Social and political processes are dynamic—one change leading to another—rather than static. As political society captures one form of association after another, it leaves in its wake one problem after another, each of which calls for another government agency or power to solve it. But such a dynamic process can go in the other direction as well. As one form of association after another is liberated from political society, social problems are ameliorated or solved, entailing less demand for political authority to solve them. One example would be the repeal of the prohibition of alcohol, which was followed by a dramatic decline in violent crime and the rise of Alcoholics Anonymous and other associations that help people deal with the temptations of drink. Another would be the deregulation of trucking that has led, not only to lower prices, but to the development of the just-in-time delivery system that has saved billions of dollars in inventory costs and made the economy far more competitive, efficient, and responsive. And looking into the future, we should anticipate the initiation of a similar dynamic process following the repeal of restrictions on self-help, such as licensing laws, and the elimination of welfare handouts, so that unskilled people could obtain employment—and with employment both skills and wealth—and escape the dependency of the welfare state, thereby moving up the economic ladder of success.

The statist ideologue sees nothing *except* political society. To eliminate a coercively financed subsidy or a coercive mandate is, he believes, to eliminate altogether the activity subsidized or mandated. Thus, when it is proposed that we end state funding for the arts and return art to civil society, the ideologue foresees, not art being produced and appreciated in civil society, but the elimination of art. Hillary Clinton exemplified that attitude when she said recently, "This is an ominous time for those of us who care for the arts in America. A misguided, misinformed effort to eliminate public support for the arts not only threatens irrevocable damage to our cultural institutions but also to our sense of ourselves and what we stand for as a people." The historical record indicates otherwise. Authentic American cultural institutions such as jazz, bluegrass, and rock music do not owe their origin or their flourishing to "public" support—if by public one means support from government. And it is not only music that flourishes in civil society, but theater, the plastic and visual arts, and much more. The 17th-century flourishing of painting owed more to Europe's first extended experiment in limited government and civil society, the Dutch Republic, than to political society. As historian Jonathan Israel notes in his new and authoritative work on the Dutch Republic, by 1650 "there were approximately two and a half million paintings in Holland, most admittedly copies, or pictures of poor quality, but a sizable proportion, some 10 percent, pictures of quality." That was due to the growth of civil society, not royal (or presidential) patronage.

Hillary Clinton's error is not a new one. In 1850 the French economist Frederic Bastiat accurately described the statist mentality: "When we oppose subsidies, we are charged with opposing the very thing that it was proposed to subsidize and of being the enemies of all kinds of activity, because we want these activities to be voluntary and to seek their proper reward in themselves. Thus, if we ask that the state not intervene, by taxation, in religious matters, we are atheists. If we ask that the state not intervene, by taxation, in education, then we hate enlightenment. If we say that the state should not give, by taxation, an artificial value to land or to some branch of industry, then we are the enemies of property and of labor. If we think that the state should not subsidize artists, we are barbarians who judge the arts useless." But to insist that an activity not be carried on coercively is not to oppose the activity per se, but only the coercion. If shoe production and sales were a state monopoly, advocates of privatization would undoubtedly be accused of being "against shoes," when in fact civil society produces more and better shoes than political society.

Conclusion

The genius of the Founders of this nation was to establish a political society for the primary purpose of protecting civil society. The former was to be carefully structured and explicitly limited, while the latter was understood to be unlimited, experimental, and able to grow and change in response to the needs or wishes of its members. Article I, section 8, of the Constitution provides a short but exhaustive list of the powers of Congress, concluding with the power "to make all Laws which shall be necessary and proper for carrying into Execution the foregoing Powers, and all other Powers vested by this Constitution in the Government of the United States, or in any Department or Officer thereof." Not only must laws passed by Congress be "proper," they must be *"necessary"* (not merely "sufficient," "expedient," or "politically popular") to carry out the carefully enumerated powers of government. "Necessary" means that, without the power or law, the purpose could not be achieved. If the purpose can be achieved in some other way, such as through the voluntary mechanisms of civil society, the proposed power fails the test of necessity.

The Founders envisioned an island of political society surrounded by a vast sea of civil society, not, as some see matters today, the other way around. With the notable exception of the very uncivil institution of slavery, the system worked relatively well, with limited government providing the legal framework and protection for the American experiment in liberty. But political society emerged with a vengeance in the 20th century, in a variety of malignant forms. It is a moral imperative for Americans to reclaim their heritage as a free people and their right to live in a civil society.

The revival of civil society can only take place when political society is restrained and reduced to its rightful role: protecting the lives and liberties of the people. Political society can do no more than provide the framework for virtue, industry, and responsible behavior; it cannot mandate them. The moral awakening that is necessary will come, not from the corrupted centers of political society, but from the remaining healthy sectors of civil society.

Suggested Readings

Bastiat, Frederic. *Selected Essays on Political Economy.* Edited by George B. de Huszar. Irvington-on-Hudson, N.Y.: Foundation for Economic Education, 1964.

Black, Antony. *Guilds and Civil Society.* Ithaca, N.Y.: Cornell University Press, 1984.

Boaz, David. *Libertarianism: A Primer.* New York: Free Press, 1997.

Crane, Edward H. "Defending Civil Society." *Cato's Letter,* no. 8. Washington: Cato Institute, 1994.

Epstein, Richard. *Simple Rules for a Complex World.* Cambridge, Mass.: Harvard University Press, 1995.

Ferguson, Adam. *An Essay on the History of Civil Society.* 1767. Cambridge: Cambridge University Press, 1995.

Gellner, Ernest. *Conditions of Liberty: Civil Society and Its Rivals.* New York: Penguin Books, 1994.

Green, David G. *Reinventing Civil Society.* London: Institute of Economic Affairs, 1993.

Hayek, F. A. *The Road to Serfdom.* Chicago: University of Chicago Press, 1944.

Israel, Jonathan. *The Dutch Republic: Its Rise, Greatness, and Fall, 1477–1806.* Oxford: Clarendon Press of the Oxford University Press, 1995.

Locke, John. *Two Treatises of Government.* 1690. Cambridge: Cambridge University Press, 1988.

Pilon, Roger. "Freedom, Responsibility, and the Constitution: On Recovering Our Founding Principles." *Notre Dame Law Review* 68 (1993): 507–47.

Shipman, William G. "Retiring with Dignity: Social Security vs. Private Markets." Cato Institute Social Security Privatization Paper no. 2, August 14, 1995.

Tanner, Michael. *The End of Welfare: Fighting Poverty in the Civil Society.* Washington: Cato Institute, 1996.

—Prepared by Tom G. Palmer

3. Congress, the Courts, and the Constitution

Congress should

- encourage constitutional debate in the nation by engaging in constitutional debate in Congress, as urged by the House Constitutional Caucus during the 104th Congress;
- enact nothing without first consulting the Constitution for proper authority and then debating that question on the floors of the House and the Senate;
- move toward restoring constitutional government by carefully returning power wrongly taken over the years from the states and the people; and
- reject the nomination of judicial candidates who do not appreciate that the Constitution is a document of delegated, enumerated, and thus limited powers.

Introduction

Following the elections of 1996, many political commentators concluded that the American people were deeply divided on the basic question of whether we should have more or less government in our lives. Focus groups and exit polls aside, the truth, of course, is that a large group of Americans will almost always vote for more government, a large group will almost always vote for less, while a group in the middle—the so-called swing voters—will come down at different times on different sides of the basic question.

Those electoral categories, which have long been understood, do not change. What does change is the size and composition of the three groups. And on that question, whether judged by the evolving political debate or by the electoral trends of the past 20 years and more, the evidence is unmistakable: the group of Americans calling for less government is growing. However successful some politicians may be from time to time at expanding government by packaging government programs in nongovernment language, the larger trends make it clear that the era of big government is indeed over.

Thus, as we move from a world in which government is expected to solve our problems to a world in which individuals, families, and communities assume that responsibility—indeed, take up that challenge—the basic questions now, at least among a growing number of Americans, are how much and how fast to reduce government. Those are not questions about how to make government run better—government will always be plagued by waste, fraud, and abuse—but, more deeply, about the fundamental role of government in this nation.

How Much to Reduce Government

The first of those questions—how much to reduce government—would seem on first impression to be a matter of policy; yet in America, if we take the Constitution seriously, it is not for the most part a policy question, a question about what we may or may not want to do. For the Founding Fathers thought long and hard about the proper role of government in our lives, and they set forth their thoughts in a document that explicitly enumerates the powers of the federal government.

Thus, setting aside for the moment all practical concerns, the Constitution tells us as a matter of first principle how much to reduce government by telling us, first, what powers the federal government in fact has and, second, how governments at all levels must exercise their powers—by respecting the rights of the people.

That means that if a federal power or federal program is not authorized by the Constitution, it is illegitimate. At this point in the 20th century, that is a stark conclusion, to be sure. But it flows quite naturally from the Tenth Amendment, the final statement in the Bill of Rights, which says, "The powers not delegated to the United States by the Constitution, nor prohibited by it to the States, are reserved to the States respectively, or to the people." In a nutshell, the Constitution establishes a government of delegated, enumerated, and thus limited powers. As the *Federalist Papers* make clear, the Constitution was written not simply to empower the federal government but to limit government as well.

Unfortunately, we have moved a long way from that vision of constitutionally limited government, especially over the course of this century.

20

Today, many Americans not only expect government to solve their problems but believe that government has all but unlimited authority to do so. Why should they not? Since the Progressive Era, the politics of government as problem solver has dominated our public discourse. And since the collapse of the Supreme Court during the New Deal, following President Roosevelt's notorious Court-packing scheme, the Court has abetted that view by standing the Constitution on its head, turning it into a document of effectively unenumerated and hence unlimited powers. (For a fuller discussion of the Constitution and the history of its interpretation, see Chapter 3 of *The Cato Handbook for Congress: 104th Congress.*)

Indeed, limits on government today come largely from political and budgetary rather than from constitutional considerations. It has not been because of any perceived lack of constitutional authority that government in recent years has failed to undertake a program, when that has happened, but because of practical limits on the power of government to tax and borrow. That is not the mark of a limited, constitutional republic. It is the mark of a parliamentary system, limited only by periodic elections.

The Founding Fathers could have established such a system, of course. They did not. But we have allowed the defining marks of a parliamentary system to supplant the system they gave us. To restore truly limited government, therefore, we have to do more than define the issues as political or budgetary. We have to go to the heart of the matter and raise the underlying constitutional questions. In a word, we have to ask the most fundamental question of all: does the government have the authority, the constitutional authority, to do what it is doing?

How Fast to Reduce Government

As a practical matter, however, before Congress or the courts can relimit government as it was meant to be limited by the Constitution, they need to take seriously the problems posed by the present state of public debate on the subject. It surely counts for something that a large number of Americans—to say nothing of the organs of public opinion—have little apprehension of or appreciation for the constitutional limits on activist government. Thus, in addressing the question of how fast to reduce government, we have to recognize that the Court, after 60 years of arguing otherwise, is hardly in a position, by itself, to relimit government in the far-reaching way a properly applied Constitution requires. But neither does Congress at this point have sufficient moral authority, even if it wanted to, to end tomorrow the vast array of programs it has enacted over the years with insufficient constitutional authority.

For either Congress or the Court to be able to do fully what should be done, therefore, a proper foundation must first be laid. In essence, the climate of opinion must be such that a sufficiently large portion of the American public stands behind the changes that are undertaken. When enough people come forward to ask—indeed, to demand—that government limit itself to the powers it is given in the Constitution, thereby freeing individuals, families, and communities to solve their own problems, we will know we are on the right track.

Fortunately, a change in the climate of opinion on such basic questions is already under way. The debate today is very different than it was only a few years ago, much less 20 years ago. But there is a good deal more to be done before Congress and the courts are able to move in the right direction in any far-reaching way, much less say that they have restored constitutional government in America. To continue the process, then, Congress should do the following things.

Encourage Constitutional Debate in the Nation by Engaging in Constitutional Debate in Congress, As Urged by the House Constitutional Caucus during the 104th Congress

Under the leadership of House freshmen like J. D. Hayworth (R-Ariz.), John Shadegg (R-Ariz.), Sam Brownback (R-Kans.), and Bob Barr (R-Ga.) together with a few senior congressmen like Richard Pombo (R-Calif.), an informal Constitutional Caucus was established in the 104th Congress, the purpose of which was to encourage constitutional debate in Congress and the nation and, in time, to restore constitutional government. The work of the caucus, barely begun, needs to continue and expand.

Some 100 members strong by the end of the 104th Congress, the caucus was created in response to the belief that the nation had strayed very far from its constitutional roots and that Congress, absent leadership from elsewhere in government, should begin addressing the problem. By itself, of course, neither the caucus nor the entire Congress can solve the problem. To be sure, in a reversal of all human experience, Congress in a day could agree to limit itself to its enumerated powers and then roll back the countless programs it has enacted by exceeding that authority. But it would take authoritative opinions from the Supreme Court, reversing a substantial body of largely post–New Deal decisions, to embed those restraints in "constitutional law"—even if they have always been embedded in the Constitution, the Court's modern readings of the document notwithstanding.

The Goals of the Constitutional Caucus

The ultimate goal of the caucus and Congress, then, should be to encourage the Court to reach such decisions. But history teaches, as noted above, that the Court does not operate entirely in a vacuum, that to some degree public opinion is the precursor and seedbed of its decisions. Thus, the more immediate goal of the caucus should be to influence the debate in the nation by influencing the debate in Congress. To do that, it is not necessary or even desirable, in the present climate, that every member of Congress be a member of the caucus—however worthy that end might ultimately be—but it is necessary that those who join the caucus be committed to its basic ends. And it is necessary that members establish a clear agenda for reaching those ends.

To reduce the problem to its essence, every day Congress is besieged by requests to enact countless measures to solve endless problems. Indeed, listening to much of the recent campaign debate, one might conclude that no problem is too personal or too trivial to warrant the attention of the federal government. Yet most of the "problems" Congress spends most of its time addressing—from health care to day care to retirement security to economic competition—are simply the personal and economic problems of life that individuals, families, and firms, not governments, should be addressing. What is more, as a basic point of constitutional doctrine, under a constitution like ours, interpreted as ours was meant to be interpreted, there is little authority for government at any level to address such problems.

Properly understood and used, then, the Constitution can be a valuable ally in the efforts of the caucus and Congress to reduce the size and scope of government. For in the minds and hearts of most Americans, it remains a revered document, however little it may be understood by a substantial number of them.

The Constitutional Vision

If the Constitution is to be thus used, however, the principal misunderstanding that surrounds it must be recognized and addressed. In particular, the modern idea that the Constitution, without amendment, is an infinitely elastic document that allows government to grow to meet public demands of whatever kind must be challenged. More Americans than presently do must come to appreciate that the Founding Fathers, who were keenly aware of the expansive tendencies of government, wrote the Constitution precisely to check that kind of thinking and that possibility. To be sure,

23

the Founders meant for government to be our servant, not our master, but they meant it to serve us in a very limited way—by securing our rights, as the Declaration of Independence says, and by doing those few other things that government does best, as spelled out in the Constitution.

In all else, we were meant to be free—to plan and live our own lives, to solve our own problems, which is what freedom is all about. Some may characterize that vision as tantamount to saying, "You're on your own," but that kind of response simply misses the point. In America individuals, families, and organizations have never been "on their own" in the most important sense. They have always been members of communities, of civil society, where they could live their lives and solve their problems by following a few simple rules about individual initiative and responsibility, respect for property and promise, and charity toward those few who need help from others. Massive government planning and programs have upset that natural order of things—less so in America than elsewhere, but very deeply all the same.

Those are the issues that need to be discussed, both in human and in constitutional terms. We need, as a people, to rethink our relationship to government. We need to ask not what government can do for us but what we can do for ourselves and, where necessary, for others—not through government but apart from government, as private citizens and organizations. That is what the Constitution was written to enable. It empowers government in a very limited way. It empowers people—by leaving them free—in every other way.

To proclaim and eventually secure that vision of a free people, the Constitutional Caucus should reconstitute itself and rededicate itself to that end at the beginning of the 105th Congress and the beginning of every Congress thereafter. Standing apart from Congress, the caucus should nonetheless be both of and above Congress—as the constitutional conscience of Congress. Every member of Congress, before taking office, swears to support the Constitution—hardly a constraining oath, given the modern Court's open-ended reading of the document. Members of the caucus should dedicate themselves to the deeper meaning of that oath. They should support the Constitution the Framers gave us, as amended by subsequent generations, not as "amended" by the Court through its expansive interpretations of the document.

Encouraging Debate

Acting together, the members of the caucus could have a major impact on the course of public debate in this nation—not least, by virtue of their numbers. What is more, there is political safety in those numbers. As Benjamin Franklin might have said, no single member of Congress is likely to be able to undertake the task of restoring constitutional government on his own, for in the present climate he would surely be hanged, politically, for doing so. But if the caucus hangs together, the task will be made more bearable and enjoyable—and a propitious outcome more likely.

On the agenda of the caucus, then, should be those specific undertakings that will best stir debate and thereby move the climate of opinion. Drawn together by shared understandings, and unrestrained by the need for serious compromise, the members of the caucus are free to chart a principled course and employ principled means, which they should do.

They might begin, for example, by surveying opportunities for constitutional debate in Congress, then making plans to seize those opportunities. Clearly, when new bills are introduced, or old ones are up for reauthorization, an opportunity is presented to debate constitutional questions. But even before that, when plans are discussed in party sessions, members should raise constitutional issues. Again, the caucus might study the costs and benefits of eliminating clearly unconstitutional programs, the better to determine which can be eliminated most easily and quickly.

Above all, the caucus should look for strategic opportunities to employ constitutional arguments. Too often, members of Congress fail to appreciate that if they take a principled stand against a seemingly popular program—and state their case well—they can seize the moral high ground and prevail ultimately over those who are seen in the end to be more politically craven.

All of that will stir constitutional debate—which is just the point. For too long in Congress that debate has been dead, replaced by the often dreary budget debate. This nation was not established by men with green eyeshades. It was established by men who understood the basic character of government and the basic right to be free. That debate needs to be revived. It needs to be heard not simply in the courts—where it is twisted through modern "constitutional law"—but in Congress as well.

Enact Nothing without First Consulting the Constitution for Proper Authority and Then Debating That Question on the Floors of the House and the Senate

It would hardly seem necessary to ask Congress, before it enacts any measure, to cite its constitutional authority for doing so. After all, is that not simply part of what it means, as a member of Congress, to swear to

25

support the Constitution? And if Congress's powers are limited by virtue of being enumerated, presumably there are many things Congress has no authority to do, however worthy those things might otherwise be. Yet so far have we strayed from constitutional thinking that such a requirement is today treated perfunctorily—when it is not ignored altogether.

The most common perfunctory citations—captured ordinarily in constitutional boilerplate—are to the general welfare and commerce clauses of the Constitution. It is no small irony that both those clauses were written as shields against overweening government; yet today they are swords of federal power.

The General Welfare Clause

The general welfare clause of article I, section 8, of the Constitution was meant to serve as a brake on the power of Congress to tax and spend in furtherance of its enumerated powers or ends: the spending that attended the exercise of an enumerated power had to be for the *general* welfare, not for the welfare of particular parties or sections of the nation.

That view, held by Madison, Jefferson, and many others, stands in marked contrast to the view of Hamilton—that the Constitution established an *independent* power to tax and spend for the general welfare. But as South Carolina's William Drayton observed on the floor of the House in 1828, Hamilton's view would make a mockery of the doctrine of enumerated powers, the centerpiece of the Constitution, rendering the enumeration of Congress's other powers superfluous: whenever Congress wanted to do something it was barred from doing by the absence of a power to do it, it could simply declare the act to be serving the "general welfare" and get out from under the limits imposed by enumeration.

That, unfortunately, is what happens today. In 1936 the Court came down, almost in passing, on Hamilton's side, declaring that there is an independent power to tax and spend for the general welfare. Then in 1937, in upholding the constitutionality of the new Social Security program, the Court completed the job when it stated the Hamiltonian view not as dicta but as doctrine, then reminded Congress of the constraints imposed by the word "general," but added that the Court would not police that restraint; rather, it would leave it to Congress, the very body that was distributing money from the Treasury with ever greater particularity, to police itself. Since that time the relatively modest redistributive schemes that preceded the New Deal have grown exponentially until today they are everywhere—except in the Constitution.

The Commerce Clause

The commerce clause of the Constitution, which grants Congress the power to regulate "commerce among the states," was also written primarily as a shield—here, against overweening *state* power. Under the Articles of Confederation, states had erected tariffs and other protectionist measures that impeded the free flow of commerce among them. Indeed, the need to break the logjam that resulted was one of the principal reasons for the call for a convention in Philadelphia in 1787. To address the problem, the Framers gave *Congress* the power to regulate—or "make regular"— commerce among the states. It was thus meant to be a power primarily to facilitate free trade.

That functional account of the commerce power is consistent with the original understanding of the power, the 18th-century meaning of "regulate," and the structural limits entailed by the doctrine of enumerated powers. Yet today the functional account is all but unknown. Following decisions by the Court in 1937 and 1942, Congress has been able to regulate anything that even "affects" interstate commerce, which in principle is everything. Far from regulating to ensure the free flow of commerce among the states, much of that regulation, for all manner of social and economic purposes, actually frustrates the free flow of commerce.

As the explosive growth of the modern redistributive state has taken place almost entirely under the general welfare clause, so too the growth of the modern regulatory state has occurred almost entirely under the commerce clause. That raises a fundamental question, of course: if the Framers had meant for Congress to be able to do virtually anything it wanted under those two simple clauses alone, why did they bother to enumerate Congress's other powers, or bother to defend the doctrine of enumerated powers throughout the *Federalist Papers*? Had they meant that, those efforts would have been pointless.

Lopez and Its Aftermath

Today, as noted above, congressional citations to the general welfare and commerce clauses usually take the form of perfunctory boilerplate. When it wants to regulate some activity, for example, Congress makes a bow to the doctrine of enumerated powers by claiming that it has made findings that the activity at issue "affects" interstate commerce—say, by preventing interstate travel. Given those findings, Congress then claims it has authority to regulate the activity under its power to regulate commerce among the states.

Thus, when the 104th Congress was pressed in the summer of 1996 to do something about what looked at the time like a wave of church arsons in the South, it sought to broaden the already doubtful authority of the federal government to prosecute those acts by determining that church arsons "hinder interstate commerce" and "impede individuals in moving interstate." Never mind that the prosecution of arson has traditionally been a state responsibility, there being no general federal police power in the Constitution. Never mind that church arsons have virtually nothing to do with interstate commerce, much less with the free flow of goods and services among the states. The commerce clause rationale, set forth in boilerplate language, was thought by Congress to be sufficient to enable it to move forward and enact the Church Arson Prevention Act of 1996— unanimously, no less.

Yet only a year earlier, in the celebrated *Lopez* case, the Supreme Court had declared, for the first time in nearly 60 years, that Congress's power under the commerce clause has limits. To be sure, the Court raised the bar against federal regulation only slightly: Congress would have to show that the activity it wanted to regulate "substantially" affected interstate commerce, leading Justice Thomas to note in his concurrence that the Court was still a good distance from a proper reading of the clause. Nevertheless, the decision was widely heralded as a shot across the bow of Congress. And many in Congress saw it as confirming at last their own view that the body in which they served was simply out of control, constitutionally. Indeed, when it passed the act at issue in *Lopez*, the Gun-Free School Zones Act of 1990, Congress had not even bothered to cite any authority under the Constitution. In what must surely be a stroke of consummate hubris—and disregard for the Constitution—Congress simply assumed that authority.

But to make matters worse, despite the *Lopez* ruling and similar rulings from lower courts in its wake, Congress in September 1996 passed the Gun-Free School Zones Act again. This time, of course, the boilerplate was included—even as Sen. Fred Thompson (R-Tenn.) was reminding his colleagues from the floor of the Senate that the Supreme Court had recently told them that they "cannot just have some theoretical basis, some attenuated basis" under the commerce clause for such an act. The prosecution of gun possession near schools—like the prosecution of church arsons, crimes against women, and much else—is very popular, as state prosecutors well know. But governments can address problems only if they have authority to do so, not from good intentions alone. Indeed, the road to constitutional destruction is paved with good intentions.

Congressional debate on these matters is thus imperative: it is not enough for Congress simply to say the magic words—"general welfare clause" or "commerce clause"—to be home free, constitutionally. Not every debate will yield satisfying results, as the examples above illustrate. But if the Constitution is to be kept alive, there must at least be debate. Over time, good ideas tend to prevail over bad ideas, but only if they are given voice. The constitutional debate must again be heard in the Congress of the United States as it was over much of our nation's history, and it must be heard before bills are enacted. The American people can hardly be expected to take the Constitution and its limits on government seriously if their elected representatives do not.

Move toward Restoring Constitutional Government by Carefully Returning Power Wrongly Taken over the Years from the States and the People

If Congress should enact no new legislation without grounding its authority to do so securely in the Constitution, so too should it begin repealing legislation not so grounded, legislation that arose by assuming power that rightly rests with the states or the people. To appreciate how daunting a task that will be, we need simply reflect on Madison's observation in *Federalist* no. 45 that the powers of the federal government are "few and defined." Federal programs today, most of which are unauthorized by the Constitution, are anything, of course, but few and defined.

But the magnitude of the task is only one dimension of its difficulty. Let us be candid: there are many in Congress who will oppose any efforts to restore constitutional government for any number of reasons, ranging from the practical to the theoretical. Some see their job as one primarily of representing the interests of their constituents, especially the short-term interests reflected in the phrase "bringing home the bacon." Others simply like big government, whether because of an "enlightened" Progressive Era view of the world or because of a narrower, more cynical interest in the perquisites of enhanced power. Still others believe sincerely in a "living constitution," the most extreme form of which imposes no limit whatsoever on government, save for periodic elections. Finally, there are those who understand the unconstitutional and hence illegitimate character of much of what government does today but believe it is too late in the day to do anything about it. All of those people and others will find reasons to resist the discrete measures that are necessary to begin restoring

29

constitutional government. Yet, where necessary, their views will have to be accommodated as the process unfolds.

Maintaining Support for Limited Government

Given the magnitude of the problem, then, and the practical implications of repealing federal programs, a fair measure of caution is in order. As the nations of Eastern Europe and the former Soviet Union have learned, it is relatively easy to get into socialism—just seize all property and labor and place it under state control—but much harder to get out of it. It is not simply a matter of returning what was taken, for much has changed as a result of the taking. People have gone and come. Public law has replaced private law. And new expectations and dependencies have arisen and become settled over time. The transition to freedom that many of those nations are experiencing is what we and many other nations around the world today are facing, to a lesser extent, as we too try to reduce the size and scope of our governments.

As programs are reduced or eliminated, then, care must be taken to do as little harm as possible—for two reasons at least. First, there is some sense in which the federal government today, vastly overextended though it is, stands in a contractual relationship with the American people. That is a very difficult idea to pin down, however, for once the genuine contract—the Constitution—has broken down, the ''legislative contracts'' that arise to take its place invariably reduce, when parsed, to programs under which some people have become dependent upon others, although neither side had a great deal to say directly about the matter at the outset. Whatever its merits, that contractual view is held by a good part of the public, especially in the case of so-called middle-class entitlements.

That leads to the second reason why care must be taken in restoring power to the states and the people, namely, that the task must be undertaken, as noted earlier, with the support of a substantial portion of the people— ideally, at the urging of those people. Given the difficulty of convincing people—including legislators—to act against their relatively short-term interests, it will take sound congressional judgment about where and when to move. More important, it will take keen leadership, leadership that is able to frame the issues in a way that will communicate both the rightness and the soundness of the decisions that are required.

In exercising that leadership, there is no substitute for keeping ''on message'' and for keeping the message simple, direct, and clear. The aim, again, is both freedom and the good society. We need to appreciate how the vast government programs we have created over the years have actually reduced the freedom and well-being of all of us—and have undermined the Constitution besides. Not that the ends served by those programs are unworthy—few government programs are undertaken for worthless ends. But individuals, families, private firms, and communities could bring about most of those ends, voluntarily and at far less cost, if only they were free to do so—especially if they were free to keep the wherewithal that is necessary to do so. If individual freedom and individual responsibility are values we cherish—indeed, are the foundations of the good society—we must come to appreciate how our massive government programs have undermined those values and, with that, the good society itself.

Redistributive Programs

Examples of the kinds of programs that should be returned to the states and the people are detailed elsewhere in this *Handbook*, but a few are in order here. Without question, the most important example of devolution to come from the 104th Congress was in the area of welfare. However flawed the final legislation may be from both a constitutional and a policy perspective, it was still a step in the right direction. Ultimately, as will be noted below in a more general way, welfare should not be even a state program. Rather, it should be a matter of private responsibility, as it was for years in this nation. But the process of getting the federal government out of the business of charity, for which there is no authority in the Constitution, has at least begun.

Eventually, that process should be repeated in every other "entitlement" area, from individual to institutional to corporate, from Social Security and Medicare to the National Endowment for the Arts to the Department of Agriculture's Market Access Program and on and on. Each of those programs was started for a good reason, to be sure, yet each involves taking from some to give to others—means that are both wrong and unconstitutional, to say nothing of monumentally inefficient. Taken together, they put us all on welfare in one way or another, and we are all the poorer for it.

Some of those programs will be harder to reduce, phase out, or eliminate than others, of course. Entitlement programs with large numbers of beneficiaries, for example, will require transition phases to ensure that harm is minimized and public support is maintained. Other programs, however, could be eliminated with relatively little harm. Does anyone seriously doubt that there would be art in America without the National Endowment for the Arts? Indeed, without the heavy hand of government grantmaking, the arts would likely flourish as they did long before the advent of the NEA—and no one would be made to pay, through his taxes, for art he abhorred.

It is the transfer programs in the "symbolic" area, in fact, that may be the most important to eliminate first, for they have multiplier effects reaching well beyond their raw numbers, and those effects are hardly neutral on the question of reducing the size and scope of government. The National Endowment for the Arts; the National Endowment for the Humanities; the Corporation for Public Broadcasting; the Legal Services Corporation; the Department of Education, especially its Goals 2000 project, have all proceeded without constitutional authority—but with serious implications for free speech and for the cause of limiting government. Not a few critics have pointed to the heavy hand of government in those symbolic areas. Of equal importance, however, is the problem of compelled speech: as Jefferson wrote, "To compel a man to furnish contributions of money for the propagation of opinions which he disbelieves is sinful and tyrannical." But on a more practical note, if Congress is serious about addressing the climate of opinion in the nation, it will end such programs not simply because they are without constitutional authority but because they have demonstrated a relentless tendency over the years in only one direction—toward even more government. Indeed, one should hardly expect those institutions to be underwriting programs that advocate less government when they themselves exist through government.

Regulatory Redistribution

If the redistributive programs that constitute the modern welfare state are candidates for elimination, so too are many of the regulatory programs that have arisen under the commerce clause. Here, however, care must be taken not simply from a practical perspective but from a constitutional perspective as well, for some of those programs may be constitutionally justified. When read functionally, recall, the commerce clause was meant to enable Congress to ensure that commerce among the states is regular, especially against state actions that might upset that regularity. Think of the commerce clause as an early North American Free Trade Agreement, without the heavy hand of "managed trade" that often accompanies the modern counterpart.

Thus conceived, the commerce clause clearly empowers Congress, through regulation, to override state measures that may frustrate the free flow of commerce among the states. But it also enables Congress to take such affirmative measures as may be necessary and proper for facilitating free trade, such as clarifying rights of trade in uncertain contexts or regulating the interstate transport of dangerous goods. What the clause does not authorize, however, is regulation for reasons other than to ensure the free flow of commerce—the kind of "managed trade" that is little but a thinly disguised transfer program designed to benefit one party at the expense of another.

Unfortunately, most modern federal regulation falls into that final category, whether it concerns employment or health care or insurance or whatever. In fact, given the budgetary constraints in recent years on the ability of government to tax and spend—to take money from some, run it through the Treasury, then give it to others—the preferred form of transfer today is through regulation. That puts it "off budget." Thus, when an employer, an insurer, a lender, or a landlord is required by regulation to do something he would otherwise have a right not to do, or not do something he would otherwise have a right to do, he serves the party benefited by that regulation every bit as much as if he were taxed to do so, but no tax increase is ever registered on any public record.

The temptation for Congress to resort to such "cost-free" regulatory redistribution is of course substantial, but the effects are both far-reaching and perverse. Natural markets are upset as incentives are changed; economies of scale are skewed as large businesses, better able to absorb the regulatory burdens, are advantaged over small ones; defensive measures, inefficient from the larger perspective, are encouraged; and general uncertainty, anathema to efficient markets, is the order of the day. Far from facilitating free trade, redistributive regulation frustrates it. Far from being justified by the commerce clause, it undermines the very purpose of the clause.

Federal Crimes

In addition to misusing the commerce power for the purpose of regulatory redistribution, Congress has misused that power to create federal crimes. Thus, a great deal of "regulation" has arisen in recent years under the commerce power that is nothing but a disguised exercise of a police power that Congress otherwise lacks. As noted earlier, the Gun-Free School Zones Act and the Church Arson Prevention Act are examples of legislation passed nominally under the power of Congress to regulate commerce among the states; but the acts prohibited by those statutes—gun possession and church arson, respectively—are ordinarily regulated under *state* police power, the power of states, in essence, to "police" or secure our rights. The ruse of regulating them under Congress's commerce power is made necessary because there is no federal police power enumerated in the Constitution—except as an implication of federal sovereignty over federal territory.

That ruse should be candidly recognized. Indeed, it is a mark of the decline of respect for the Constitution that when we sought to fight a war on liquor earlier in the century we felt it necessary to do so by first amending the Constitution—there being no power otherwise for such a federal undertaking. Today, however, when we engage in a war on drugs—with as much success as we enjoyed in the earlier war—we do so without as much as a nod to the Constitution.

The Constitution lists three federal crimes: treason, piracy, and counterfeiting. Yet today there are over 3,000 federal crimes and perhaps 300,000 regulations that carry criminal sanctions. Over the years, no faction in Congress has been immune, especially in an election year, from the propensity to criminalize all manner of activities, utterly oblivious to the lack of any constitutional authority for doing so. We should hardly imagine that the Founders fought a war to free us from a distant tyranny only to establish a tyranny in Washington, in some ways even more distant from the citizens it was meant to serve.

Policing the States

If the federal government has often intruded upon the police power of the states, so too has it often failed in its responsibility under the Fourteenth Amendment to police the states. Here is an area where federal regulation has been, if anything, too restrained—yet also unprincipled, oftentimes, when undertaken.

The Civil War Amendments to the Constitution changed fundamentally the relationship between the federal government and the states, giving citizens an additional level of protection, not against federal but against state oppression—the oppression of slavery, obviously, but much else besides. Thus, the Fourteenth Amendment prohibits states from abridging the privileges or immunities of citizens of the United States; from depriving any person of life, liberty, or property without due process of law; and from denying any person the equal protection of the laws. By implication, section 1 of the amendment gives the courts the power to secure those guarantees. Section 5 gives Congress the "power to enforce, by appropriate legislation, the provisions of this article."

As the debate that surrounded the adoption of those amendments makes clear, the privileges or immunities clause was meant to be the principal source of substantive rights in the Fourteenth Amendment, and those rights were meant to include the rights of property, contract, and personal security—in short, our "natural liberties," as Blackstone had earlier understood that phrase. Unfortunately, in 1872, in the notorious *Slaughter-House* cases, a bitterly divided Supreme Court essentially eviscerated the privileges or immunities clause. There followed, for nearly a century, the era of Jim Crow in the South and, for a period stretching to the present, a Fourteenth Amendment jurisprudence that is as contentious as it is confused.

Modern liberals have urged that the amendment be used as it was meant to be used—against state oppression; but they have also urged that it be used to recognize all manner of "rights" that are no part of the theory of rights that stands behind the amendment as understood at the time of ratification. Modern conservatives, partly in reaction, have urged that the amendment be used far more narrowly than it was meant to be used—for fear that it might be misused, as it has been.

The role of the judiciary under section 1 of the Fourteenth Amendment will be discussed below. As for Congress, its authority under section 5— "to enforce, by appropriate legislation, the provisions of this article"— is clear, provided Congress is clear about those provisions. And on that, we may look, again, to the debates that surrounded not only the adoption of the Fourteenth Amendment but the enactment of the Civil Rights Act of 1866, which Congress reenacted in 1870, just after the amendment was ratified.

Those debates give us a fairly clear idea of what it was that the American people thought they were ratifying. In particular, all citizens, the Civil Rights Act declared, "have the right to make and enforce contracts, to sue, be parties and give evidence; to inherit, purchase, lease, sell, hold, and convey real personal property, and to full and equal benefit of all laws and proceedings for the security of persons and property." Such were the privileges and immunities the Fourteenth Amendment was meant to secure.

Clearly, those basic common law rights, drawn from the reason-based classical theory of rights, are the stuff of ordinary state law. Just as clearly, however, states have been known to violate them, either directly or by failure to secure them against private violations. When that happens, appeal can be made to the federal courts, under section 1, or to Congress, under section 5. The Fourteenth Amendment gives no power, of course, to secure modern "entitlements" that are no part of the common law tradition of life, liberty, and property: the power it grants, that is, is limited by the rights it is meant to secure. But it does give a power to reach even intrastate matters when states are violating the provisions of the amendment. The claim of "states' rights," in short, is no defense for state violations of individual rights.

Thus, if the facts had warranted it, the Church Arson Prevention Act of 1996 might have been authorized not on commerce clause grounds but on Fourteenth Amendment grounds. If, for example, the facts had shown that arsons of white churches were being prosecuted by state officials whereas arsons of black churches were not, then we would have had a classic case of the denial of the equal protection of the laws. With those findings, Congress would have had ample authority under section 5 of the Fourteenth Amendment "to enforce, by appropriate legislation, the provisions of this article."

Unfortunately, in the final version of the act, Congress removed citations to the Fourteenth Amendment, choosing instead to rest its authority entirely on the commerce clause. Not only is that a misuse of the commerce clause, inviting further misuse; but, assuming the facts had warranted it, it is a failure to use the Fourteenth Amendment as it was meant to be used, inviting further failures. To be sure, the Fourteenth Amendment has itself been misused, both by Congress and by the courts. But that is no reason to ignore it. Rather, it is a reason to correct the misuses.

In its efforts to return power to the states and the people, then, Congress must be careful not to misunderstand its role in our federal system. Over the 20th century, Congress has assumed vast powers that were never its to assume, powers that belong properly to the states and the people. Those need to be returned. But at the same time, Congress and the federal courts do have authority under the Fourteenth Amendment to ensure that citizens are free from state oppression. However much that authority may have been underused or overused, it is there to be used; and if it is properly used, objections by states about federal interference in their "internal affairs" are without merit.

Reject the Nomination of Judicial Candidates Who Do Not Appreciate That the Constitution Is a Document of Delegated, Enumerated, and Thus Limited Powers

As noted earlier, Congress can relimit government on its own initiative simply by restricting its future actions to those that are authorized by the

Constitution and repealing those past actions that were taken without such authority; but for those limits to become "constitutional law," they would have to be recognized as such by the Supreme Court, which essentially abandoned that view of limited government during the New Deal. Thus, for the Court to play its part in the job of relimiting government constitutionally, it must recognize the mistakes it has made over the years, especially following Roosevelt's Court-packing threat in 1937, and rediscover the Constitution—a process it began in *Lopez*, however tentatively, when it returned explicitly to "first principles."

But Congress is not powerless to influence the Court in that direction: as vacancies arise on the Court and on lower courts, it has a substantial say about who sits there through its power to advise and consent. To exercise that power well, however, Congress must have a better grasp of the basic issues than it has shown in recent years during Senate confirmation hearings for nominees for the Court. In particular, the Senate's obsession with questions about "judicial activism" and "judicial restraint," terms that in themselves are largely vacuous, only distracts it from the real issue—the nominee's philosophy of the Constitution. To appreciate those points more fully, however, a bit of background is in order.

From Powers to Rights

The most important matter to grasp is the fundamental change that took place in our constitutional jurisprudence during the New Deal and the implications of that change for the modern debate. The debate today is focused almost entirely on rights, not powers. Indeed, the principal concern during recent Senate confirmation hearings has been with a nominee's views about what rights are "in" the Constitution. That is an important question, to be sure, but it must be addressed within a much larger constitutional framework, a framework too often missing from recent hearings.

Clearly, the American debate began with rights—with the protests that led eventually to the Declaration of Independence. And in that seminal document, Jefferson made rights the centerpiece of the American vision: rights to life, liberty, and the pursuit of happiness, derived from a premise of moral equality, itself grounded in a higher law discoverable by reason— all to be secured by a government of powers made legitimate through consent.

But when they set out to draft a constitution, the Framers focused on powers, not rights, for two main reasons. First, their initial task was to create and empower a government, which the Constitution did once it was ratified. But their second task, of equal importance, was to limit that government. Here, there were two main options. The Framers could have listed a set of rights that the new government would be forbidden to violate. Or they could have limited the government's powers by enumerating them, then pitting one against the other through a system of checks and balances—the idea being that where there is no power there is, by implication, a right, belonging to the states or the people. They chose the second option, for they could hardly have enumerated all of our rights, but they could enumerate the new government's powers, which were meant from the outset to be, again, "few and defined." Thus, the doctrine of enumerated powers became our principal defense against overweening government.

Only later, during the course of ratification, did it become necessary to add a Bill of Rights—as a secondary defense. But in so doing, the Framers were still faced with a pair of objections that had been posed from the start. First, it was impossible to enumerate all of our rights, which in principle are infinite in number. Second, given that problem, the enumeration of only certain rights would be construed, by ordinary methods of legal construction, as denying the existence of others. To overcome those objections, therefore, the Framers wrote the Ninth Amendment: "The enumeration in the Constitution of certain rights shall not be construed to deny or disparage others retained by the people."

Constitutional Visions

Thus, with the Ninth Amendment making it clear that we have both enumerated and unenumerated rights, the Tenth Amendment making it clear that the federal government has only enumerated powers, and the Fourteenth Amendment later making it clear that our rights are good against the states as well, what emerges is an altogether libertarian picture. Individuals, families, firms, and the infinite variety of institutions that constitute civil society are free to pursue happiness however they wish, in accord with whatever values they wish, provided only that in the process they respect the equal rights of others to do the same; and governments are instituted to secure that liberty and do the few other things their constitutions make clear they are empowered to do.

That picture is a far cry from the modern liberal's vision, rooted in the Progressive Era, which would have government empowered to manage all manner of economic affairs. But it is a far cry as well from the modern conservative's vision, which would have government empowered to manage all manner of social affairs. Neither vision reflects the true constitutional scheme. Both camps want to use the Constitution to promote their own substantive agendas. Repeatedly, liberals invoke democratic power for ends that are nowhere in the Constitution; at other times they invoke "rights" that are no part of the plan, requiring government programs that are nowhere authorized. For their agenda, conservatives rely largely on expansive readings of democratic power that were never envisioned, thereby running roughshod over rights that were meant to be protected.

From Liberty to Democracy

The great change in constitutional visions took place during the New Deal, when the idea that galvanized the Progressive Era—that the basic purpose of government is to solve social and economic problems—was finally instituted in law through the Court's radical reinterpretation of the Constitution. As noted earlier, following the 1937 Court-packing threat, the Court eviscerated our first line of defense, the doctrine of enumerated powers, when it converted the general welfare and commerce clauses from shields against power into swords of power. Then in 1938 a cowed Court undermined the second line of defense, our enumerated and unenumerated rights, when it declared that henceforth it would defer to the political branches and the states when their actions implicated "nonfundamental" rights like property and contract—the rights associated with "ordinary commercial affairs." Legislation implicating such rights, the Court said, would be given "minimal scrutiny" by the Court, which is tantamount to no scrutiny at all. By contrast, when legislation implicated "fundamental" rights like voting, speech, and, later, certain "personal" liberties, the Court would apply "strict scrutiny" to that legislation, probably finding it unconstitutional.

With that, the Constitution was converted, without benefit of amendment, from a libertarian to a largely democratic document. The floodgates were now open to majoritarian tyranny, which very quickly became special-interest tyranny, as public-choice economic theory amply demonstrates should be expected. Once those floodgates were opened, the programs that poured through led inevitably to claims from many quarters that rights were being violated. Thus, the Court in time would have to try to determine whether those rights were "in" the Constitution—a question the Constitution had spoken to indirectly, for the most part, through the now-discredited doctrine of enumerated powers; and if it found the rights in question, the

Court would then have to try to make sense of its distinction between "fundamental" and "nonfundamental" rights.

Judicial "Activism" and "Restraint"

It is no accident, therefore, that the modern debate is focused on rights, not powers. With the doctrine of enumerated powers effectively dead, with government's power essentially plenary, the only issues left for the Court to decide, for the most part, are whether there might be any rights that would limit that power and whether those rights are or are not "fundamental."

Both liberals and conservatives today have largely bought into this jurisprudence. As noted above, both camps believe the Constitution gives a wide berth to democratic decisionmaking. Neither side any longer asks the first question, the fundamental question: do we have authority, constitutional authority, to pursue this end? Instead, they simply assume that authority, take a policy vote on some end before them, then battle in court over whether there are any rights that might restrict their power.

Modern liberals, fond of government programs, call upon the Court to be "restrained" in finding rights that might limit their redistributive and regulatory schemes, especially "nonfundamental" rights like property and contract. At the same time, even as they ignore those rights, liberals ask the Court to be "active" in finding other "rights" that were never meant to be among even our unenumerated rights.

But modern conservatives are often little better. Reacting to the abuses of liberal "activism," many conservatives call for judicial "restraint" across the board. Thus, if liberal programs have run roughshod over the rights of individuals to use their property or freely contract, the remedy, conservatives say, is not for the Court to invoke the doctrine of enumerated powers—that battle was lost during the New Deal—nor even to invoke the rights of property and contract that are plainly in the Constitution— that might encourage judicial activism—but to turn to the democratic process to overturn those programs. Obvious to the fact that restraint in finding rights is tantamount to activism in finding powers, and ignoring the fact that it was the democratic process that gave us the problem in the first place, too many conservatives offer us a counsel of despair amounting to a denial of constitutional protection.

No one doubts that in recent decades the Court has discovered "rights" in the Constitution that are no part of either the enumerated or unenumerated rights that were meant to be protected by that document. But it is no answer to that problem to ask the Court to defer wholesale to the political branches, thereby encouraging it, by implication, to sanction unenumerated *powers* that are no part of the document either. Indeed, if the Tenth Amendment means anything, it means that there are no such powers. Again, if the Framers had wanted to establish a simple democracy, they could have. Instead, they established a limited, constitutional republic, a republic with islands of democratic power in a sea of liberty, not a sea of democratic power surrounding islands of liberty.

Thus, it is not the proper role of the Court to find rights that are no part of the enumerated or unenumerated rights meant to be protected by the Constitution, thereby frustrating authorized democratic decisions. But neither is it the proper role of the Court to refrain from asking whether those decisions are in fact authorized and, if authorized, whether their implementation is in violation of the rights guaranteed by the Constitution, enumerated and unenumerated alike.

The role of the judge in our constitutional republic is thus profoundly important and oftentimes profoundly complex. "Activism" is no proper posture for a judge, but neither is "restraint." Judges must apply the Constitution to cases or controversies before them, neither making it up nor ignoring it. They must appreciate especially that the Constitution is a document of delegated, enumerated, and thus limited powers. That will get the judge started on the question of what rights are protected by the document; for where there is no power there is, again, a right, belonging either to the states or to the people: indeed, we should hardly imagine that, before the addition of the Bill of Rights, the Constitution failed to protect most rights simply because most were not "in" it. But reviving the doctrine of enumerated powers is only part of the task before the Court; it must also revive the classical theory of rights if the restoration of constitutional government is to be completed correctly.

Those are the two sides—powers and rights—that need to be examined in the course of Senate confirmation hearings for nominees for the courts of the United States. More important than knowing a nominee's "judicial philosophy" is knowing his philosophy of the Constitution. For the Constitution, in the end, is what defines us as a nation.

If a nominee does not have a deep and thorough appreciation for the basic principles of the Constitution—for the doctrine of enumerated powers and for the classical theory of rights that stands behind the Constitution—then his candidacy should be rejected. In recent years, Senate confirmation hearings have become extraordinary opportunities for constitutional debate throughout the nation. Those debates need to move from the ethereal realm of "constitutional law" to the real realm of the Constitution. They are extraordinary opportunities not simply for constitutional debate but for constitutional renewal.

Conclusion

America is a democracy in the most fundamental sense of that idea: authority, or legitimate power, rests ultimately with the people. But the people have no more right to tyrannize each other through democratic government than government itself has to tyrannize the people. When they constituted us as a nation by ratifying the Constitution and the amendments that have followed, our ancestors gave up only certain of their powers, enumerating them in a written constitution. We have allowed those powers to expand beyond all moral and legal bounds—at the price of our liberty and our well-being. The time has come to restore those powers to their proper bounds, to reclaim our liberty, and to enjoy the fruits that follow.

Suggested Readings

Bailyn, Bernard. *The Ideological Origins of the American Revolution.* Cambridge, Mass.: Belknap, 1967.

Barnett, Randy E., ed. *The Rights Retained by the People: The History and Meaning of the Ninth Amendment.* Fairfax, Va.: George Mason University Press, 1989.

Corwin, Edward S. *The "Higher Law" Background of American Constitutional Law.* Ithaca, N.Y.: Cornell University Press, 1955.

Dorn, James A., and Henry G. Manne, eds. *Economic Liberties and the Judiciary.* Fairfax, Va.: George Mason University Press, 1987.

Epstein, Richard A. "The Proper Scope of the Commerce Power." *Virginia Law Review* 73 (1987).

———. *Simple Rules for a Complex World.* Cambridge, Mass.: Harvard University Press, 1995.

———. *Takings, Private Property and the Power of Eminent Domain.* Cambridge, Mass.: Harvard University Press, 1985.

Hamilton, Alexander, James Madison, and John Jay. *The Federalist Papers.* New York: Mentor, 1961.

Lawson, Gary. "The Rise and Rise of the Administrative State." *Harvard Law Review* 107 (1994).

Lawson, Gary, and Patricia B. Granger. "The 'Proper' Scope of Federal Power: A Jurisdictional Interpretation of the Sweeping Clause." *Duke Law Journal* 43 (1993).

Locke, John. "Second Treatise of Government." In *Two Treatises of Government.* Edited by Peter Laslett. New York: Mentor, 1965.

Miller, Geoffrey P. "The True Story of Carolene Products." *Supreme Court Review* (1987).

Pilon, Roger. "A Court without a Compass." *New York Law School Law Review* 40 (1996).

―――. "Freedom, Responsibility, and the Constitution: On Recovering Our Founding Principles." *Notre Dame Law Review* 68 (1993).

―――. "Restoring Constitutional Government." *Cato's Letter* no. 9. Washington: Cato Institute, 1995.

Reinstein, Robert J. "Completing the Constitution: The Declaration of Independence, Bill of Rights and Fourteenth Amendment." *Temple Law Review* 66 (1993).

Siegan, Bernard H. *Economic Liberties and the Constitution.* Chicago: University of Chicago Press, 1980.

Sorenson, Leonard R. *Madison on the "General Welfare" of America.* Lanham, Md.: Rowman & Littlefield, 1995.

Warren, Charles. *Congress as Santa Claus: Or National Donations and the General Welfare Clause of the Constitution.* 1932. Reprint, New York: Arno Press, 1978.

Yoo, John Choon. "Our Declaratory Ninth Amendment." *Emory Law Journal* 42 (1993).

—Prepared by Roger Pilon

4. The Delegation of Legislative Powers

Congress should

- require all "lawmaking" regulations to be affirmatively approved by Congress and signed into law by the president, as the Constitution requires for all laws; and
- establish a mechanism to force the legislative consideration of existing regulations during the reauthorization process.

Separation of Powers: The Bulwark of Liberty

When the legislative and executive powers are united in the same person, or in the same body of magistrates, there can be no liberty.
—Montesquieu, *The Spirit of the Laws*

Article I, section 1, of the U.S. Constitution stipulates, "All legislative powers herein granted shall be vested in the Congress of the United States, which shall consist of a Senate and House of Representatives." Article II, section 3, stipulates that the president "shall take care that the laws be faithfully executed." Thus, as we all learned in high school civics, the Constitution clearly provides for a separation of powers between the various branches of government.

The alternative design—concentration of power within a single governmental body—was thought to be inimical to a free society. John Adams wrote in 1776 that "a single assembly, possessed of all the powers of government, would make arbitrary laws for their own interest, and adjudge all controversies in their own favor." James Madison in *Federalist* no. 47 justified the Constitution's separation of powers by noting that it was a necessary prerequisite for "a government of laws and not of men." Further, he wrote, "The accumulation of all powers, legislative, executive, and judiciary, in the same hands, whether of one, a few, or many, and whether hereditary, self-appointed, or elective, may justly be pronounced the very definition of tyranny.''

For the first 150 years of the American Republic, the Supreme Court largely upheld the original constitutional design, requiring that Congress rather than administrators make the law. The suggestion that Congress could broadly delegate its lawmaking powers to others—particularly the executive branch—was generally rejected by the courts. And for good reasons. First, the Constitution was understood to be a document of enumerated and thus limited powers, and nowhere was Congress either explicitly or even implicitly given the power to delegate. Second, the fear of power concentrated in any one branch still animated both the Supreme Court and the legislature. Third, Americans believed that those who make the law should be directly accountable at the ballot box.

The upshot was that the separation of powers effectively restrained federal power, just as the Founders had intended. As Alexis de Tocqueville observed, ''The nation participates in the making of its laws by the choice of its legislators, and in the execution of them by the choice of agents of the executive government.'' He also observed that ''it may also be said to govern itself, so feeble and so restricted is the share left to the administrators, so little do the authorities forget their popular origins and the power from which they emanate.''

The New Deal: "Delegation Running Riot"

The sense of political crisis that permeated the 1930s effectively buried the nondelegation doctrine. In his first inaugural address, Franklin Roosevelt compared the impact of the ongoing economic depression to a foreign invasion and argued that Congress should grant him sweeping powers to fight it.

Shortly after taking office, Congress in 1933 granted Roosevelt virtually unlimited power to regulate commerce through passage of the Agricultural Adjustment Act (which authorized the president to increase agricultural prices via administrative production controls) and the National Industrial Recovery Act (known as the NIRA), which authorized the president to issue industrial codes to regulate all aspects of the industries they covered.

The Supreme Court, however, temporarily arrested the tide in 1935 in its unanimous opinion in *A.L.A. Schechter Poultry Corp. v. United States*. The Court overturned the industrial code provisions of the NIRA, and, in a separate opinion, Justice Benjamin Cardozo termed the NIRA—and thus the New Deal—"delegation running riot." That same year, the Court struck down additional NIRA delegations of power in *Panama Refining Co. v. Ryan.*

Largely because of the *Schechter* and *Panama Refining* decisions, President Roosevelt decried the Court's interference with his political agenda and proposed legislation enlarging the size of the Court so that he could appoint additional justices—the so-called Court-packing plan. He lost that battle but won the war. Although the Court never explicitly reversed its 1935 decisions and continues to articulate essentially the same verbal formulas defining the scope of permissible delegation—indeed, *Schechter* and *Panama Refining* theoretically are good law today—it would be nearly 40 years before the Court again struck down business regulation on delegation grounds.

As long as Congress articulates some intelligible standard (no matter how vague or arbitrary) to govern executive lawmaking, courts are prepared today to allow delegation, in the words of Justice Cardozo, to run riot. John Locke's admonition that the legislature "cannot transfer the power of making laws to any other hands, for it being but a delegated power from the people, they who have it cannot pass it over to others" is a forgotten vestige from an era when individual liberty mattered more than administrative convenience. As Federal District Court Judge Roger Vinson wrote in *United States v. Mills* in 1989, "A delegation doctrine which essentially allows Congress to abdicate its power to define the elements of a criminal offense, in favor of an un-elected administrative agency such as the [Army] Corps of Engineers, does violence to this time-honored principle. . . . Deferent and minimal judicial review of Congress' transfer of its criminal lawmaking function to other bodies, in other branches, calls into question the vitality of the tripartite system established by our Constitution. It also calls into question the nexus that must exist between the law so applied and simple logic and common sense. Yet that seems to be the state of the law."

Delegation: The Corrosive Agent of Democracy

The concern over congressional delegation of power is not simply theoretical and abstract, for delegation does violence, not only to the ideal construct of a free society, but also to the day-to-day practice of democracy itself. Ironically, delegation does not help to secure "good government"; it helps to destroy it.

Delegation Breeds Political Irresponsibility

Congress delegates power for much the same reason that Congress continues to run budget deficits. With deficit spending, members of Congress can claim credit for the benefits of their expenditures yet escape blame for the costs. The public must pay ultimately, of course, but through taxes levied at some future time by some other officials. Likewise, delegation allows legislators to claim credit for the benefits that a regulatory statute airily promises yet escape the blame for the burdens it will impose, because they do not issue the laws needed to achieve those high-sounding benefits. The public inevitably must suffer regulatory burdens to realize regulatory benefits, but the laws will come from an agency that legislators can then criticize for imposing excessive burdens on their constituents.

Just as deficit spending allows legislators to appear to deliver money to some people without taking it from others, delegation allows them to appear to deliver regulatory benefits without imposing regulatory costs. It provides, in the words of former Environmental Protection Agency deputy administrator John Quarles, ''a handy set of mirrors—so useful in Washington—by which politicians can appear to kiss both sides of the apple.''

Delegation Is a Political Steroid for Organized Special Interests

As Stanford law professor John Hart Ely has noted, ''One reason we have broadly based representative assemblies is to await something approaching a consensus before government intervenes.'' The Constitution was intentionally designed to curb the ''facility and excess of law-making'' (in the words of James Madison) by requiring that statutes go through a bicameral legislature and the president. Differences in the size and nature of the constituencies of representatives, senators, and the president—and the different lengths of their terms in office—increase the probability that the actions of each will reflect a different balance of interests. That diversity of viewpoint, plus the greater difficulty of prevailing in three forums rather than one, makes it far more difficult for special-interest groups or bare majorities to impose their will on the totality of the American people. Hence, the original design effectively required a supermajority to make law as a means of discouraging the selfish exercise of power by well-organized but narrow interests.

Delegation shifts the power to make law from a Congress of all interests to subgovernments typically representative of only a small subset of all interests. The obstacles intentionally placed in the path of lawmaking disappear, and the power of organized interests is magnified.

That is largely because diffuse interests typically find it even more difficult to press their case before an agency than before a legislature. They often have no direct representation in the administrative process, and effective representation typically requires special legal counsel, expert witnesses, and the capacity to reward or to punish top officials through political organization, press coverage, and close working relationships with members of the appropriate congressional subcommittee. As a result, the general public rarely qualifies as a ''stakeholder'' in agency proceedings and is largely locked out of the decisionmaking process. Madison's desired check on the ''facility and excess of law-making'' is thus smashed.

Delegation Breeds the Leviathan State

Perhaps the ultimate check on the growth of government rests in the fact that there is only so much time in a day. No matter how many laws Congress would like to pass, there are only so many hours in a session to do so. Delegation, however, dramatically expands the realm of the possible by effectively ''deputizing'' tens of thousands of bureaucrats, often with broad and imprecise missions to ''go forth and legislate.'' Thus, as columnist Jacob Weisberg has noted in the *New Republic*, ''As a labor-saving device, delegation did for legislators what the washing machine did for the 1950s housewife. Government could now penetrate every nook and cranny of American life in a way that was simply impossible before.''

The Threadbare Case for Delegation

Although delegation has become so deeply embedded in the political landscape that few public officials even recognize the phenomenon or the issues raised by the practice, political observers are becoming increasingly aware of the failure of delegation to deliver its promised bounty of good government.

The Myth of Technical Expertise

It was once maintained that delegation produces more sensible laws by transferring lawmaking from elected officials, who are beholden to concentrated interests, to experts, who can base their decisions solely on a cool appraisal of the public interest. Yet most agency heads are not scientists, engineers, economists, or other kinds of technical experts; they are political operatives. Since the EPA's inception in 1970, for example, seven of its eight administrators and seven of its nine assistant administrators for air pollution have been lawyers. As MIT professor Michael Golay wrote in a recent issue of *Science,* "Environmental protection policy disagreements are not about what to conclude from the available scientific knowledge; they represent a struggle for political power among groups having vastly differing interests and visions for society. In this struggle, science is used as a means of legitimizing the various positions . . . science is a pawn, cynically abused as may suit the interests of a particular protagonist despite great ignorance concerning the problems being addressed." Perhaps that's why the EPA's own Science Advisory Board was forced to concede in a 1992 report that the agency's science "is perceived by many people both inside and outside the agency to be adjusted to fit policy."

We should not necessarily bemoan the lack of agency expertise, for it is not entirely clear that government by experts is superior to government by elected officials. As political scientist Robert Dahl has pointed out, there is no reason to believe that experts possess superior moral knowledge or a better sense of what constitutes the public good. Indeed, specialization often impairs the capacity for moral judgment and often breeds professional zealotry. Likewise, specialized expertise provides too narrow a base for the balanced judgments that intelligent policy requires.

Although both agency administrators and legislators often lack the expertise to evaluate technical arguments by themselves, they can get help from agency and committee staff, government institutes (like the Centers for Disease Control or the General Accounting Office), and private sources such as medical associations, think tanks, and university scientists. After all, that is what the hearings process is supposed to be all about.

And only someone naive about modern government would seriously allege today that the winds of politics blow any less fiercely in administrative meeting rooms than they do in the halls of Congress. As Nobel laureate economist James Buchanan and others have observed, public-choice dynamics provide a multitude of incentives for public officials to pursue both private and political ends that often have little to do with their ostensible mission.

Is Congress Too Busy?

New Dealers once argued that "time spent on details [by Congress] must be at the sacrifice of time spent on matters of the broad public policy." Congress today spends little time on "matters of broad public policy," largely because delegation forces Congress to spend a large chunk of its time constructing the legislative architecture—sometimes over a thousand pages of it—detailing exactly how various agencies are to decide important matters of policy. Once that architecture is in place, members of Congress find that a large part of their job entails navigating through those bureaucratic mazes for special interests jockeying to influence the final nature of the law. Writing such instructions and performing agency oversight to ensure that they are carried out would be unnecessary if Congress made the rules in the first place.

Moreover, delegation often works to prolong disputes and keep standards of conduct murky because pressures from legislators and the complicated procedures imposed upon agencies turn lawmaking into an excruciatingly slow process. Agencies typically report that they have issued only a small fraction of the laws that their long-standing statutory mandates require. Competing interests devote large sums of money and many of their best minds to this seemingly interminable process. For example, it took the EPA *16 years* to ban lead in gasoline despite the fact that the 1970 Clean Air Act explicitly gave them the authority to do so. Simply making the rules the first time around in the legislative process would take less time than the multiyear regulatory sausage machine requires to issue standards.

Complex Rules for a Complex World

Perhaps the most widely accepted justification for some degree of delegation is the complex and technical nature of the world we live in today. As the Supreme Court argued in 1989, "Our jurisprudence has been driven by a practical understanding that in our increasingly complex society, replete with ever changing and more technical problems, Congress simply cannot do its job absent an ability to delegate power under broad general directives."

Yet the vast majority of decisions delegated to the executive branch are not particularly technical in nature. They are instead hotly political, for the reasons mentioned above. If Congress must regulate, it could (and probably should) jettison micromanagerial command-and-control regulations that make up the bulk of the *Federal Register* and instead adopt regulations that are less prescriptive and more performance based or market oriented. Most regulatory analysts on both the left and the right agree that this would also have the happy consequences of decreasing regulatory costs, increasing regulatory efficiency, and decreasing the burden on regulators. In addition, a Congress not skewed toward regulation by delegation would rediscover practical reasons for allowing many matters to be left to state and local regulators.

Conclusion

Forcing Congress to vote on each and every administrative regulation that establishes a rule of private conduct would prove the most revolutionary change in government since the Civil War—not because the idea is particularly radical, but because we are today a nation governed, not by elected officials, but by unelected bureaucrats. The central political issues of the 105th Congress—the complex and heavy-handed array of regulations that entangle virtually all manner of private conduct, the perceived inability of elections to affect the direction of government, the disturbing political power of special interests, the lack of popular respect for the law, the sometimes tyrannical and self-aggrandizing exercise of power by government, and populist resentment of an increasingly unaccountable political elite—are but symptoms of a disease largely caused by delegation.

"No regulation without representation!" would be a fitting battle cry for the 105th Congress if it is truly interested in fundamental reform of government. It is a standard that both the left and the right could comfortably rally around, given that dozens of prominent constitutional scholars, policy analysts, and journalists—from Nadine Strossen, president of the American Civil Liberties Union, to former judge Robert Bork—have expressed support for the end of delegation. Several pieces of legislation (H.R. 47, H.R. 2727, and H.R. 2990, with a total of nearly 100 cosponsors) were introduced in the 104th Congress to accomplish exactly that.

Of course, forcing Congress to take full and direct responsibility for the law would not prove a panacea. The legislature, after all, has shown itself to be fully capable of violating individual rights, subsidizing special interests, writing complex and virtually indecipherable law, and generally making a hash of things. But delegation has helped to make such phenomena, not the exception, but the rule of modern government. No more crucial—and potentially popular—reform awaits the attention of the 105th Congress.

Suggested Readings

Breyer, Stephen. "The Legislative Veto after *Chadha.*" Thomas F. Ryan lecture. *Georgetown Law Journal* 72 (1984): 785–99.

Lawson, Gary. "The Rise and Rise of the Administrative State." *Harvard Law Review* 107 (1994): 1231–54.

Schoenbrod, David. *Power without Responsibility: How Congress Abuses the People through Delegation.* New Haven, Conn.: Yale University Press, 1993.

Schoenbrod, David, and Gene Healy. "Regulation without Representation: The Case against the Administrative State." Cato Institute Policy Analysis, forthcoming.

Smith, Nick. "Restoration of Congressional Authority and Responsibility over the Regulatory Process." *Harvard Journal on Legislation* 33 (1996): 323–37.

—Prepared by David Schoenbrod and Jerry Taylor

5. Term Limits and the Need for a Citizen Legislature

Congress should

- pass a constitutional amendment limiting the terms of representatives to three and of senators to two, providing states the option of increasing the limits on representatives to six terms; and
- absent such a constitutional amendment, voluntarily limit their own terms to three if a representative and to two if a senator, consistent with the overwhelming desire of the American people.

Introduction

The term-limits movement is alive and well in the United States. Opponents of term limits, the most vociferous of whom live inside the Beltway, had assumed the issue would go away following the Supreme Court's narrow five-to-four decision in *U.S. Term Limits v. Thornton* (1995) that said the states do not have the authority to limit the terms of their respective congressional delegations. As Justice Clarence Thomas pointed out in a brilliant dissent, the majority in *U.S. Term Limits* simply ignored the clear meaning of the Tenth Amendment. There being no explicit denial of such power to the states in the Constitution, the right to do so "is reserved to the states respectively, or to the people."

Indeed, the people had spoken loudly and clearly on term limits in virtually all of the initiative states that provided them with an opportunity to do so. Twenty-two states representing nearly half of Congress had passed term limits on their delegations by 1994. The great majority of them had opted to limit their representatives to three terms, and all of them had limited their senators to two terms. Only 2 of the 22 states chose

55

six terms for the House. That initiative process accurately reflected the views of the American people who support three-term limits for the House over six-term limits by a margin of five to one, according to a recent Luntz poll.

So intense is public support for a "citizen Congress" brought about through term limits—national polls have consistently put the number at 75 to 80 percent—that rather than give up after the Supreme Court's *U.S. Term Limits* decision, the movement instead intensified its efforts and adopted a new strategy. In November 1996 voters in nine states approved initiatives that instruct their congressional delegation to vote for term limits (defined as three terms in the House and two terms in the Senate) or face having placed next to their name on the ballot the words, "Disregarded voters' instructions on term limits."

The precedent for that ballot-language approach comes from the early 20th-century movement to end indirect election of senators by state legislatures. It worked, and in 1912 Congress complied with the will of the people by passing a constitutional amendment that called for the direct election of senators by the people. The parallels between the two movements are striking in that both were overwhelmingly popular throughout the nation, yet Congress had a clear conflict in terms of its own interests.

Given that precedent and the Supreme Court's reversal of the Arkansas Supreme Court's 1996 decision to remove a ballot-language initiative from its state ballot (the initiative, put back on the ballot by the Supreme Court, passed with 61 percent of the vote), it is very likely that ballot-language initiatives will be upheld as constitutional. And they will have an impact on candidates who do not support real term limits. In 1998 a dozen more states, including California and Florida, will have ballot-language term-limit initiatives to consider.

It is definitely in the interest of the 105th Congress to vote out a constitutional amendment on its own, before ballot-language term-limit initiatives start restructuring Congress in a major way.

Why Three Terms for the House?

It is important for Congress to address not just the issue of term limits but the nature of those limits. While those in Congress who purport to support term limits overwhelmingly favor six terms in the House, as noted above, the American people have stricter limits in mind. As Michael Kramer wrote in the January 23, 1995, issue of *Time*, "The dissonance between the people and their leaders on term limits is deafening." One possible compromise on this division, suggested by David Keating of the National Taxpayers Union, would be for Congress to vote out an amendment calling for a three-term limit for the House, but providing states with the option of increasing the House limit to six terms. U.S. Term Limits, the leading national term-limits organization, has indicated that such a compromise would be acceptable, thus potentially ending the long-standing split between the grassroots term-limits movement and term-limit supporters in Congress.

It is worth reviewing the reasons why the term-limits movement has been so adamant in supporting short, three-term limits for the House of Representatives, because the debate over three terms versus six terms is not mere quibbling over a technical issue. It is significant and substantive. It is a question of the people's term limits versus the politicians' disingenuous limits.

The political energy behind the term-limit movement is predicated on the need for a citizen legislature. Americans believe that career legislators and professional politicians have created a gaping chasm between themselves and their government. For democracy to work, it must be *representative* democracy—a government of, by, and for the people. That means a citizen legislature.

To achieve a citizen legislature it is imperative that our representatives in Congress—particularly in the House, which the Framers clearly intended to be the arm of government closest to the people—be not far removed from the private sector, which, after all, they are elected to represent. As Rhode Island's Roger Sherman wrote at the time of our nation's founding, "Representatives ought to return home and mix with the people. By remaining at the seat of government, they would acquire the habits of the place, which might differ from those of their constituents." In the era of year-round legislative sessions, the only way to achieve that objective is through term limits.

Three terms for the House is preferable to six terms for a variety of reasons. The most important one, however, deals with the question of who seeks to become a member of Congress in the first place. The fact is that America is best served by a Congress populated with members who are there out of a sense of civic duty, but who would rather live their lives in the private sector, holding productive jobs in civil society, outside the governmental world of political society. Such individuals might be willing to spend two, four, or even six years in Washington, but not if the legislative agenda is being set by others, who've gained their authority through seniority. Twelve-year "limits," which these days amount to a mini-career, do little to remove this major obstacle to a more diverse and representative group of Americans seeking office.

We already have hard evidence that short, three-term limits will enhance the democratic process: Proposition 140 in California, which was passed by the voters there in 1990 and limited the state Assembly to three two-year terms. The 1992 Assembly elections witnessed a sharp increase in the number of citizens seeking office, with a remarkable 27 freshmen elected in the 80-member lower house of the California legislature. In an article on that freshman class, the *Los Angeles Times* wrote, "Among the things making the group unusual is that most of them are true outsiders. For the first time in years, the freshman class does not include an abundance of former legislative aides who moved up the ladder to become members.... Among the 27 are a former U.S. Air Force fighter pilot, a former sheriff-coroner, a paralegal, a retired teacher, a video store owner, a businesswoman-homemaker, a children's advocate, an interior designer, a retired sheriff's lieutenant, and a number of businessmen, lawyers, and former city council members."

A 1996 scholarly study of the California legislature by Mark Petracca of the University of California at Irvine found that the strict term limits Californians passed in 1990 had had the following consequences:

- Turnover in both legislative chambers had increased markedly.
- The number of incumbents seeking reelection had dropped sharply.
- The percentage of elections in which incumbents won reelection had dropped significantly.
- The number of women in both houses had increased.
- The number of uncontested races had declined.
- The number of candidates seeking office in both chambers had increased.
- The winning margin of incumbents had declined.

All of those developments, while perhaps not attractive to those seeking to be career politicians, are consistent with the goals of the great majority of Americans who favor a return to a citizen legislature.

Similarly, a three-term limit for the U.S. House of Representatives will return control of the House—not just through voting, but through participation—to the people. We must make the possibility of serving in Congress a more attractive option for millions more Americans.

A second major reason for the need for a three-term limit is that it ensures that the majority of those serving in the House will not be far removed from their experiences in the private sector. They will bring to the policy issues of the day the common sense and practical experience of living in the real world that will lead to decisions that are truly in the public interest.

Many people reason that it has been the experienced legislators who have brought us the huge deficit and such undesirable episodes as the $300 billion savings-and-loan bailout. The latter incident is a good example of why the common sense of Americans rooted in the private sector is needed in Congress. It's likely a Congress picked by lottery would have refused to expand federal deposit insurance as part of the necessary move to deregulate the thrift industry. "Inexperienced" legislators would have said, in effect, yes, do deregulate, but for goodness sake don't ask the American taxpayer to pay for any bad investments the thrift institutions make—that's a license to speculate. But our experienced legislators apparently thought they could repeal the laws of economics, raising the level of federal deposit insurance and extending it to the deposit rather than the depositor, thus allowing the wealthiest people in the nation to spread their deposits around with utter indifference to the financial soundness of the institutions in which they invested. We are still paying the price for such legislative hubris.

A third reason for the shorter limits is related to the second. And that is that the longer one is in Congress, the more one is exposed to and influenced by the "culture of ruling" that permeates life inside the Beltway. Groups like the National Taxpayers Union have documented the fact that the longer people serve in Congress, the bigger spenders and regulators they become. That is just as true of conservatives as it is of liberals. It is also understandable. Members of Congress are surrounded at work and socially by people whose jobs are to spend other people's money and regulate their lives. It is the unusual individual—although such people do exist—who is not subtly but surely affected by that culture.

A fourth reason to support three terms over six terms is that the shorter limits are an antidote to the growing "professionalization" of the legislative process. As Mark Petracca has written, "Whereas representative government aspires to maintain a proximity of sympathy and interests between representative and represented, professionalism creates authority, autonomy, and hierarchy, distancing the expert from the client. Though this distance may be necessary and functional for lawyers, nurses, physicians, accountants, and social scientists, the qualities and characteristics associated with being a 'professional' legislator run counter to the supposed goals of a representative democracy. Professionalism encourages an independence of ambition, judgment, and behavior that is squarely at odds with the inherently dependent nature of representative government.''

Finally, the shorter limits for the House are guaranteed to enhance the competitiveness of elections and, as noted above, increase the number and diversity of Americans choosing to run for Congress. As Paul Jacob of U.S. Term Limits has pointed out, the most competitive races (and the ones that bring out the largest number of primary candidates) are for open seats. At least a third of all House seats will be open each election under three-term limits, and it is probable that as many as half will not feature an incumbent seeking reelection. We also know from past experience that women and minorities have greater electoral success in races for open seats.

The incentives for a citizen legislature are significantly stronger under the shorter limits. Six-term limits are long enough to induce incumbents to stick around for the entire 12 years. Three-term limits are short enough to prompt incumbents to return to the private sector before spending six years in the House. Under a three-term limit we will witness a return to the 19th-century norm of half the House being freshmen—a true citizen legislature.

In addition, the next most competitive races are incumbents' first attempts at reelection and the races just before retirement. Thus, under a three-term limit virtually all races for the House of Representatives will be more competitive than is the case today or would be the case under six-term limits.

In order for the concept of a citizen legislature to have meaning, it is imperative that those serving in the legislature literally view their time in office as a leave of absence from their real jobs or careers. That is the key to a successful citizen legislature. The incentives facing a member of Congress should never include concern about what other legislators might do in retaliation, or what special interests might do to the member's *political* career.

In the introductory essay in *The Politics and Law of Term Limits*, coauthors Ed Crane and Roger Pilon wrote, ''Stepping back from these policy arguments, however, one sees a deeper issue in the term-limits debate, an issue that takes us to our very foundations as a nation. No one can doubt that America was dedicated to the proposition that each of us is and ought to be free—free to plan, and live his own life, as a private individual, under a government instituted to secure that freedom. Thus, implicit in our founding vision is the idea that most human affairs take place in what today we call the private sector. That sector—and this is the crucial point—is primary: government comes from it, not the other way around. When we send men and women to Congress to 'represent' us, therefore, we want them to understand that they represent us, the overwhelming number of Americans who live our daily lives in that private sector. Moreover, we want them to remember that it is to that private world that they must return, to live under the laws they have made as our representatives. That, in essence, is the message implicit in the growing call for term limits. It is not simply or even primarily a message about 'good government.' Rather, it is a message about the very place of government in the larger scheme of things. Government is meant to be our servant, to assist us by securing our liberty as we live our essentially private lives. It is not meant to be our master in some grand public adventure.''

The term-limits movement is not motivated by disdain for the institution of Congress. It is motivated by a sincere desire on the part of the American people to regain control of the most representative part of the federal government. The people want term limits and for good reasons. Resistance to this movement on the part of elected federal legislators only underscores the image of an Imperial Congress. The 105th Congress should secure an honorable place in American history by passing a ''three and two'' term-limits constitutional amendment and thereby return the American government to the American people.

Suggested Readings

Crane, Edward H., and Roger Pilon, eds. *The Politics and Law of Term Limits.* Washington: Cato Institute, 1994.

Bandow, Doug. ''The Political Revolution That Wasn't: Why Term Limits Are Needed Now More Than Ever.'' Cato Institute Policy Analysis no. 259, September 5, 1996.

—Prepared by Edward H. Crane

CONTROLLING THE BUDGET

6. Downsize the Domestic Budget and Cut Taxes

Congress should

- enact a balanced-budget amendment to the Constitution;
- establish a federal spending freeze at $1.65 trillion through 2002;
- pass a "peace dividend" tax cut by reducing income or payroll tax rates, or both;
- cancel all foreign aid—including Pentagon "peacekeeping" operations unrelated to protecting America's national security;
- eliminate corporate welfare spending programs;
- transform Medicare into a catastrophic coverage plan by gradually raising the deductible;
- allow medical savings accounts for all workers to reduce public and private health care inflation;
- increase the retirement age for Medicare and Social Security by three months per year for the next 24 years;
- end the federal role in welfare by devolving all public assistance programs to the states and private charities;
- terminate more than 100 major federal programs and agencies;
- terminate the U.S. Department of Transportation and repeal the federal gasoline tax, thus leaving highway, road, and transit responsibilities to the states and the private sector; and
- privatize at least $100 billion worth of federal assets and use the proceeds to lower the national debt and interest payments.

Introduction

In 1995 and 1996 the Republicans and moderate Democrats in the 104th Congress fought—at times valiantly—but ultimately lost the battle of the federal budget.

Despite hopeful rhetoric from the Republican majorities about balancing the budget by 2002 and despite impressive—though temporary—progress in reducing the 1996 deficit to $107 billion, the long-term prognosis for the budget of the U.S. government remains depressingly bleak. Federal expenditures, which took more than 200 years to surpass the $1 trillion mark 10 years ago, will have doubled to $2 trillion by 2002. The deficit is expected to gallop in the wrong direction in the coming years, hurdling the $200 billion mark by 2002 and the $300 billion mark by 2005.

Clearly, a new fiscal strategy must be employed if the budget is to be balanced and the U.S. economy restored to its full potential. That new strategy must recognize an unfortunate political reality: *in the absence of a balanced-budget amendment to the Constitution, Congress will never summon the political will power to balance the federal budget, or even come close to balancing the budget.*

For that reason, the crusade in recent years to balance the budget by 2002 without an amendment has been honorable but futile. The unilateral effort by the GOP and moderate Democrats to balance the budget by 2002 without a balanced-budget amendment has been a political trap—used by the spending lobbies all too successfully to block tax and spending cuts without having to propose a serious alternative deficit reduction agenda of their own. The mantra of "balanced budget by 2002" has also diverted public attention from the real fight of consequence, which is over the amendment itself. In other words, establish the rules of the game before making a move.

The 105th Congress should concentrate on cutting taxes and vulnerable spending programs wherever and whenever possible. The larger the spending reductions, and the larger the tax cuts that can be enacted, the better. The aim should be to halt the relentless expansion of the size of the federal empire. Public enemy number 1 in Washington, D.C., is *not* $110 billion of government borrowing; it is $1.65 trillion (and rising) of government spending.

Is the Era of Big Government Over?

In his January 1996 state of the union address, Bill Clinton issued his memorable proclamation that "the era of big government in America is over." One month later the White House released its fiscal 1997 budget proposal, which called for a six-year *increase* in federal spending of roughly $300 billion. The Clinton administration has requested a total six-year budget of $11.2 trillion. That is twice as much money in constant dollars as the combined cost of fighting World War I and World War II. It is more money than the federal government spent cumulatively from 1800 to 1980.

The relentless media coverage of a "revolutionary" GOP budget with "massive and draconian budget cuts" conceals the reality of America's current fiscal predicament. The unreported truth is that the U.S. government is much larger today than was even imaginable in previous eras.

Figure 6.1 shows the expansion of the federal budget since 1800. Real federal outlays climbed from $100 million in 1800 to $8.3 billion in 1900 to $235 billion in 1950 to $1,510 billion in 1995 ($1.31 trillion in 1990 dollars). The federal government now takes 23 percent of gross domestic product, up from 18 percent in 1960 and 4 percent in 1930. Today's massive federal government no longer resembles in any way that established by the Founders, which gave Congress very limited spending authority.

Figure 6.1
Real Federal Outlays, 1800–1996

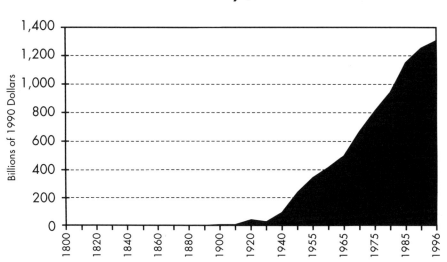

SOURCES: *Historical Tables: Budget of the United States Government, Fiscal Year 1997* (Washington: Government Printing Office, 1996), Table 1.1; and Bureau of the Census, *Historical Statistics of the United States, Colonial Times to 1970,* part 2, p. 1104, Series Y336.

The price tag for government has not risen just in Washington; it has risen at all levels—state, county, and city hall. Total government expenditures today exceed $2.6 trillion. That is roughly $25,000 in spending for every household in America. When the $6,000 per household cost of regulation is added to the price tag for the direct expenditures of the state, the government now reduces average household income by more than $30,000 per year. That is more than half of the income of the typical middle-income family.

No matter how we measure it, and notwithstanding Bill Clinton's proclamation to the contrary, the nanny state in America has never been bigger or better funded.

Where Did All the Money Go?

Table 6.1 highlights the tremendous growth rate of federal programs over just the last 45 years. Entitlements, no surprise, have been the real race horses of the budget. A federal entitlement, simply defined, is any program that says that Peter is entitled to Paul's money. The three major entitlements are Social Security, health care, and welfare.

- Social Security's budget has swelled from $25 billion to $336 billion. But mention the program in the context of budget downsizing and Reagan Republicans are the first to stampede for the exits.
- Federal health care outlays have catapulted from $2 billion to $272 billion—a 16,000 percent increase in spending.
- Welfare spending is up from $30 billion to $225 billion—even though poverty rates are no lower now than before the War on Poverty started.

What Washington refers to as "discretionary spending" has also experienced a surge in funding over the past four decades. Despite the rhetoric about Ronald Reagan's assault on social programs, virtually every civilian program has a far more bloated budget today than it did 10, 20, or 40 years ago. Since the 1950s, education and social services programs have grown from $2.5 billion to $56 billion. Community development is up 1,600 percent, science and technology are up 4,000 percent, and transportation is up 500 percent.

Here is one way of conceptualizing the expansion of the government. If nondefense spending had risen at only the pace of defense spending over the past 40 years, total expenditures would have been $800 billion— or about half the amount that has actually been spent. America would now have a $600 billion budget surplus rather than a $110 billion deficit.

Table 6.1
Federal Spending Growth by Function, 1950–96

	1950	1996	
	(millions of 1987 dollars)		Change (%)
National defense	83,990	197,675	135.4
Veterans benefits and services	54,064	28,099	−48.0
International affairs	28,599	11,039	−61.4
Income security	25,073	169,973	577.9
Agriculture	12,540	5,745	−54.2
Energy, natural resources, and environment	10,006	18,436	84.2
Commerce and housing credit	6,334	−7,998	−226.3
General government	6,034	10,116	67.6
Transportation	5,918	29,603	400.2
Social Security	4,780	261,221	5,365.2
Health and Medicare	1,640	222,418	13,460.9
Education, training, employment, and social services	1,475	40,294	2,632.0
Administration of justice	1,181	13,968	1,082.5
General science, space, and technology	337	12,563	3,632.3
Community and regional development	184	9,586	5,121.2
Net interest	29,449	179,439	509.3
Undistributed offsetting receipts and allowances	11,120	−31,707	185.1
Total outlays	260,477	1,170,471	349.4

SOURCE: *Historical Tables: Budget of the United States Government, Fiscal Year 1997* (Washington: Government Printing Office, 1996), Tables 3.1 and 10.1.

Lessons Learned in the Bush-Clinton Era

America has now completed eight years of what may be described as the "Bush-Clinton era." The defining domestic policy events of George Bush's and Bill Clinton's presidencies were the 1990 and 1993 budget deals, respectively. Budget analysts across the political spectrum agree that the major components of those two five-year budget packages with large tax increases were nearly indistinguishable. Both were dramatic departures from the economic strategy of the 1980s, which included cutting tax rates, preventing new regulations, and restraining domestic spending.

We should have learned the following fiscal lessons from the Bush-Clinton fiscal-economic strategy.

Tax Hikes to Balance the Budget Are Counterproductive

The top marginal income tax rate has risen by 50 percent—from 28 percent in 1989 to 42 percent this year. Yet, as Table 6.2 shows, overall tax receipts grew at a faster rate (24 percent) in the seven years (1982–89) following the Reagan tax cuts than they will have (19 percent) in the seven years following the Bush-Clinton tax hikes (1990–97). In fact, if tax revenues had continued to rise in the 1990s at the pace they did in the 1980s, the deficit would be $50 billion lower this year. Even receipts from the income tax (rates were cut in the 1980s and raised in the 1990s) rose at virtually the same pace in the Reagan years (16.1 percent) as they have in the Bush-Clinton years (16.8 percent).

Table 6.2
Reagan Tax Cuts vs. Bush-Clinton Tax Hikes: Overall Real Revenue Growth (billions of 1990 dollars)

After Reagan Tax Cuts			After Bush-Clinton Tax Hikes		
Year	Revenue Growth	(%)	Year	Revenue Growth	(%)
1982	738		1990	914	
1983	684	−7.3	1991	895	−2.1
1984	730	6.7	1992	895	0.0
1985	777	6.4	1993	922	3.7
1986	790	1.7	1994	982	6.5
1987	854	8.1	1995	1,034	5.3
1988	877	2.7	1996	1,082	4.6
1989	916	4.4	1997	1,090	0.7
Total		24.1	Total		19.3

SOURCES: *Historical Tables: Budget of the United States Government, Fiscal Year 1997* (Washington: Government Printing Office, 1996); and Congressional Budget Office, August 1996 revenue forecast (for growth in 1996, 1997, and Bush-Clinton total).

Nondefense Spending Has Rapidly Accelerated in the 1990s

It is a widespread myth that federal outlays on civilian programs have been constrained as a result of the 1990 and 1993 budget deals. *Federal spending on civilian programs now accounts for a larger share of national output (18 percent) than at any previous time in American history.* In 1995 dollars, federal nondefense spending has surged by $250 billion since the end of the Reagan presidency.

Social Welfare Programs Are Growing at an Unsustainable Pace

In constant 1995 dollars, since 1989 real Medicare spending has grown by $75 billion, or 73 percent; Medicaid spending has grown by $47 billion, or 112 percent; and welfare spending has climbed by $93 billion, or 72 percent (see Table 6.3). If the current pace of growth in entitlement spending continues, by 2015 entitlements will eat up all federal revenues.

Table 6.3
Social Welfare Spending 1989–95
(billions of 1995 dollars)

	1989	1995	Growth 1989–95 (%)
Low-income support			
Aid to Families with Dependent Children	13	18	38
Child nutrition programs	8	9	12
Earned Income Tax Credit*	6	15	150
Food stamps	17	26	53
Housing assistance	12	21	75
Medicaid	42	89	112
Supplemental Security Income	15	24	60
Unemployment compensation	17	21	26
Total low-income support	130	223	72
Medicare	103	178	73
Social Security	210	252	20
Total	443	653	48

SOURCE: Cato Institute calculations based on data from *Historical Tables: Budget of the United States Government, Fiscal Year 1996* (Washington: Government Printing Office, 1995), Table 8.6, p. 108.
*Includes only outlay portion of EITC.

The Temporary Reduction in the Deficit Has Been Almost Exclusively a Result of Post–Cold War Reductions in the Military

Defense spending now constitutes a smaller share (17 percent) of the federal budget than at any time in American history. Over the past eight years the Pentagon budget has fallen by almost $110 billion in real terms. That's almost precisely how much the real budget deficit has fallen over that period. The defense cutbacks, which ought to be continued, have helped camouflage the large nondefense spending increases in the 1990s.

The 1990 and 1993 Budget Deals Were Failures

Table 6.4 shows that, from 1990 to 1995, the national debt was $622 billion higher than anticipated in January 1989 when Reagan left office. As a share of GDP, the budget deficits were nearly 2 percentage points higher than anticipated. Measured in real dollars, the 1990–94 period showed the worst five-year deficit performance in the post–World War II era.

The budget picture has clearly brightened in the short term under Bill Clinton. The 1996 budget deficit came in at a 20-year low of $107 billion and 1.9 percent of GDP. That was good news. Most of the improvement was a result of the (temporary) spending restraint imposed by the 104th Congress and the shutdown of the government in late 1995. In April 1995, just before the 104th Congress's budget was drafted, the Congressional Budget Office predicted a Clintonomics baseline deficit for 1996 of $210 billion.

Table 6.4
Deficits in the 1990s
Reagan Baseline vs. Actual Performance

	CBO 1989	Actual	Difference
	Billions of Dollars		
1990	141	221	80
1991	140	269	129
1992	135	290	155
1993	129	255	126
1994	122	203	81
1995	110*	161	51
Total	777	1,399	622
	Percentage of GDP		
1990	2.6	4.0	1.4
1991	2.4	4.7	2.3
1992	2.2	4.9	2.7
1993	2.0	4.1	1.9
1994	1.7	3.1	1.4
1995	1.5*	2.4	0.9
Average	2.1	3.9	1.5

SOURCES: Congressional Budget Office, ''Economic and Budget Outlook,'' January 1989; and Congressional Budget Office, ''Economic and Budget Outlook,'' March 1990 (for 1995 projections).

Economic Growth Is a Necessary Condition for Deficit Reduction

The U.S. GDP has grown at an average rate of just 1.8 percent in the 1990s. That compares with a 3.2 percent growth rate in the 1980s and a 4.9 percent growth rate in the 1960s. Even during the cyclical recovery since the end of the 1990–91 recession, economic growth has averaged below 3 percent per year. If economic growth in the 1990s had kept pace with growth in the 1980s, national output would be $510 billion higher today and the budget deficit $100 billion lower. If current trends continue, the 1990s will produce the largest budget deficits and the slowest economic growth rate of any decade in the past half century.

The Fiscal Legacy of the 104th Congress

The 104th Congress promised a dramatic change in budget and tax policy in Washington. Was that promise kept? The first-year budget enacted by the GOP-controlled Congress for FY96 was an impressive accomplishment by Capitol Hill standards. The 1996 budget deficit was chopped to $107 billion—$100 billion less than the Clinton budget plan would have produced. Federal spending grew by only 3 percent—the slowest rate of increase since 1982.

But the 1997 budget was an embarrassing fiscal retreat for the GOP. Most of the spending programs whose budgets were cut in 1996 saw spending restored in 1997. Congress added about $15 billion of spending to accommodate Clinton administration demands. The power of the purse in 1997 was handed to the White House.

In sum, two years after the Republicans took control of Congress, the budget closely resembles the one the GOP inherited. Congress still is appropriating funds for failed social programs, such as the Legal Services Corporation and the Low-Income Home Energy Assistance Program; for programs that politicize our culture in ways that many Americans find objectionable, such as the Corporation for Public Broadcasting and bilingual education; for corporate welfare handouts including the Export-Import Bank and the Small Business Administration; for New Deal–era programs that lost their purpose in life at least a generation ago, such as the Rural Electrification Administration, the Tennessee Valley Authority, and the Davis-Bacon Act; and for Clinton's new generation of muddle-headed social policy initiatives, such as midnight basketball, the Goals 2000 program intended to federalize public school standards and curricula, and the $7.25 an hour Americorps "volunteer" program. Not a single cabinet-level agency was shut down.

Even the 1996 progress in deficit reduction appears to be short-lived. The CBO reported in August that, after 1997, the budget outlook steadily deteriorates in every year for the next decade and the deficit reaches $350 billion. Then the outlook really turns grim, as runaway entitlement expenditures—particularly for Medicare and Medicaid—hemorrhage. The CBO predicts that, unless income transfer payments are curtailed, the nation faces a future of "unsustainably high levels of federal borrowing," with the national debt ascending relentlessly from 60 percent of national output today to 150 percent by 2025.

13 Steps to Smaller Government

The fight in recent years in Washington over how to balance the budget has been a diversion from the vital task of cutting back on the size of government and giving more money and power back to workers, businesses, and families. "The true cost of government," Milton Friedman reminds us, "is not the amount it borrows, but the amount it spends." Around the world we see governments—out of economic necessity— shedding their most burdensome and unproductive state activities. In the United States today, we have a moral, constitutional, and economic imperative to reduce the size and scope of government. That can be accomplished through 13 steps.

Enact a Balanced-Budget Amendment to the Constitution

Why is it necessary to amend the Constitution and command Congress and the president to do what they once felt honor bound to do?

There are many flawed arguments for a balanced-budget amendment. For example, Republicans were wrong when they argued in 1995 that deficits per se crowd out private investment and lead to higher interest rates. In the 1980s the deficit rose rapidly and nominal interest rates fell rapidly. In the Clinton years the deficit has fallen and interest rates have risen. *Government spending, not government borrowing, crowds out private saving and investment.*

Many liberals, including just-retired Democratic Sen. Paul Simon of Illinois, argue that the budget should be balanced because federal interest payments are crowding out other expenditures in the budget. There is no evidence of that crowding-out effect. Federal spending has been climbing rapidly over the past six years even as interest expenditures have continued to reach all-time highs. If it were true that interest expenditures crowded out other spending in the budget, that would be a benign impact of budget deficits.

Conservative and liberal arguments *against* the desirability of requiring a balanced budget are even more fallacious. One flawed argument against balancing the budget offered by many liberal economists is that a balanced-budget requirement would prevent Congress and the president from using fiscal policy as a tool for stabilizing the economy. The evidence over the past 40 years suggests that fiscal policy has been more destabilizing than stabilizing. Even under the Keynesian model, the idea is to run budget deficits during recessions and surpluses during recoveries. Over the past quarter century Congress has run record deficits in good times and bad.

Many conservatives are misguided when they claim that a balanced budget would lead to higher taxes. The flaw in the thinking here is that it ignores the fact that the deficit *is* a tax. Deficits are simply deferred taxes. If conservatives truly believe that government is too big and costs too much, then it is very unlikely that voters will be willing to pay $200 billion more in taxes each year—or roughly $2,000 per household—to pay for the $1.6 trillion federal budget. More likely, they will demand substantial reductions in federal spending. (The tax consumers in Washington fully understand that, which is why every spending constituency from the Children's Defense Fund, to the American Association of Retired Persons, to major defense contractors opposes the balanced-budget amendment.) And if the balanced-budget amendment leads to less spending, then the true tax burden on the American economy will decline, not rise.

There are two reasons why budget deficits should be eliminated and then permanently constrained via a constitutional prohibition, one practical and one moral. The practical reason why budget deficits are harmful is that deficit finance is a hidden form of taxation. Federal borrowing injects a huge pro-spending bias into the budget process by allowing politicians to pass out a dollar of government spending to voters while only imposing 80 cents of taxes on them. Because the deficit is largely an invisible tax, voters demand more government than they otherwise would. Outlawing federal borrowing means that Congress has to raise a full dollar of taxes today for every dollar of spending it undertakes. That will substantially increase voter hostility to government spending.

The moral argument for requiring a balanced budget is that federal borrowing is a form of fiscal child abuse. Current deficit spending must be paid for eventually by future generations—that is, by those who have no say in the current political process. In sum, a balanced budget should

become a constitutional requirement, because running deficits is the ultimate form of taxation without representation. That is why Thomas Jefferson argued that "each successive generation ought to be guaranteed against
the dissipations and corruptions of those preceding, by a fundamental
provision in our Constitution."

Many contemporary critics of the balanced-budget amendment contend
that the amendment is not needed to balance the budget, just greater
political will power. But it is precisely because Congress will never exhibit
such will power that we need the amendment.

The unwillingness of Congress in modern times to balance the budget
is not so much a result of malevolent behavior on the part of legislators
as it is a rational response to the rules of the budget game. Those rules
establish incentives that offer political rewards for spending money, which
far outweigh the political rewards for saving money. The benefits of
government spending are provided to narrow interests, but the cost of any
individual government program is so widely disbursed that the burden on
any individual taxpayer is unnoticeable. For example, during the 104th
Congress, the advocates of public broadcasting lobbied furiously and
effectively to save their program from the budget knife by arguing that
those funds cost the average household just X per month. (Of course,
there are thousands of similar programs, each of which individually costs
the American household *just* X per month.) But the cost of spending
programs is even more politically inconsequential when it can be shifted
to future generations who cannot vote. (That is also a practical argument
for term limits.)

So it should be clear, given the fiscal outcomes of the past quarter
century, that without a balanced-budget amendment, there will probably
never again be a balanced budget. Every other device that has been tried
to eliminate federal red ink has failed: four budget deals since 1980,
Gramm-Rudman-Hollings I and II, and the 104th Congress's short-lived
crusade. The balanced-budget amendment is dismissed by some as a
gimmick. If that were true, Congress would have adopted it long ago.

One final note on the amendment. It would be best to include a provision
that would limit taxation or require a supermajority vote of Congress to
raise taxes, but with or without such a provision, the amendment is urgently
needed. If the only remaining objection is that Social Security is now
included in the unified budget, then for purposes of getting the amendment
passed, Social Security should be excluded. That is a concession worth
making in order to secure final passage, especially because excluding the
Social Security system would only require even deeper spending cuts.

Enact a Six-Year Spending Freeze

In 1997 the federal budget will reach $1.65 trillion. That is the most ever spent by any government in world history. This *Handbook* contains a series of budget recommendations that altogether would cut the budget roughly in half. That may seem unimaginable, but even if the budget were halved tomorrow, the federal government would still consume a greater share of national output (12 percent) than it has throughout most of American history.

One common-sense tactic for beginning to limit federal spending is to at least stop its growth. For the past quarter century the federal budget has grown on average by more than 7 percent per year—or about twice as fast as inflation. Even the first Republican Congress in 40 years, elected on the promise of smaller, less intrusive government, approved budgets that grew by 4 percent per year.

Given the federal government's nearly bankrupt state and the low rate of return Americans receive from their tax dollars sent to Washington, why should government grow at all over the near term? If the federal budget cannot be cut in absolute terms, as it should be, Congress should at least place a ceiling on total expenditures at the current level. Figure 6.2 and Table 6.5 show that the cumulative savings for the next six years from a budget freeze would be $1.3 trillion relative to the budget path that we are now on.

Locking in a spending freeze, as has been proposed by the National Tax Limitation Committee, would certainly force tough choices on Congress. Lawmakers would have to establish spending priorities and live within a genuine budget—as most Americans define the term. A freeze would invoke fierce but healthy competition among agencies for federal dollars and create a kind of "reverse log-rolling" effect in Congress. Outlays for favored programs could be increased, but other agencies would have to be cut or eliminated to accommodate the expansion. Many obsolete programs would almost certainly have to be abolished altogether to force spending under the ceiling. Legislators would be compelled to tame the huge entitlement programs of Social Security, Medicare, and Medicaid, because if those programs were not restrained, all other programs in the budget would have to shrink rapidly.

The spending constituencies in Washington would, of course, loudly protest a spending freeze. They would argue that it requires a scorched-earth budget policy, squeezing out funding for vital programs. Fiscal conservatives will need to make the case that the government should be

75

Figure 6.2
Savings from Proposed Spending Freeze

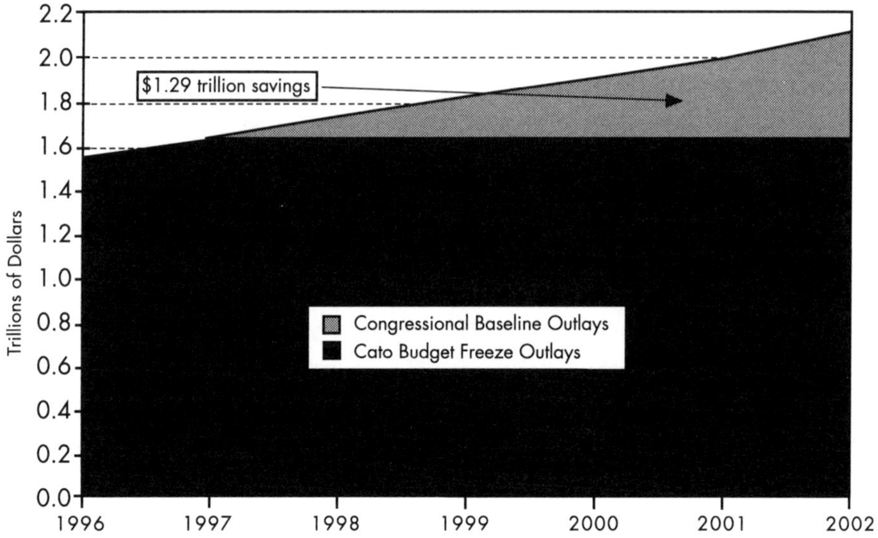

SOURCES: Congressional Budget Office, "Economic and Budget Outlook Update," August 1996; and Office of Management and Budget, July 1996 revenue forecasts.

Table 6.5
Savings from Proposed Spending Freeze
(trillions of dollars)

	1996	1997	1998	1999	2000	2001	2002	Total
Baseline outlays	1.57	1.65	1.72	1.81	1.90	1.99	2.11	12.75
Budget freeze outlays	1.57	1.64	1.65	1.65	1.65	1.65	1.65	11.46
Savings	0	.01	.07	.16	.25	.34	.46	1.29

SOURCES: Congressional Budget Office, "Economic and Budget Outlook Update," August 1996; and Office of Management and Budget, July 1996 revenue forecasts.

easily capable of doing everything it is supposed to do with $1.65 trillion a year. Most businesses and households have managed to do more with less for the past five years as budgets have been pinched. Why should government be immune from the belt tightening?

But can it really be done? Contrary to the conventional wisdom, there is no law of nature, or economics, or politics that requires the federal government to grow every year. During most postwar eras in the United States (we are in one now), the federal budget has declined in size. For example,

- In 1919, the last year of World War I, the federal budget climbed to $18.5 billion. By 1926 it had fallen to $2.9 billion.
- In the seven-year period from 1945 (the peak of spending for World War II) to 1951, the U.S. government's budget tumbled by half, from $93 billion to $42.4 billion.
- During the Korean War the federal budget rose to $76 billion in 1953. By 1955 it had fallen to $68 billion.

The typical pattern in each of those postwar eras was the same: as military expenditures fell, wartime tax burdens were cut and the budget was moved quickly back into balance. We even ran budget surpluses to begin paying off the wartime debt. None of those things has happened since the Berlin Wall came down and the Soviet Union was dissolved. There has been no tax cut, no retirement of the debt, and no balanced budget. Contrary to historical precedent, since the Berlin Wall came down, the federal budget has actually increased by $350 billion. A spending ceiling would end the insidious practice of using defense savings to hike the budgets of domestic agencies.

Enact a $1 Trillion "Peace Dividend" Tax Rate Cut

The total savings of $1.3 trillion from a spending freeze would produce a balanced budget by 2002 and provide a fiscal dividend large enough to pay for a $1 trillion tax cut, as shown in Table 6.6. But a large tax cut should be enacted irrespective of what steps Congress pursues on the expenditure side of the budget.

Seven years after the Cold War ended, it is time for the peace dividend tax cut that Americans should have received in the early Bush years. A six-year $1 trillion tax cut is roughly 1.5 percentage points of GDP, or about half the savings already generated from the military downsizing since 1987 (3 percentage points of GDP).

A $1 trillion six-year tax cut would reduce static revenue collections by 10 percent, or $1 trillion out of a $10.03 trillion tax take over the next six years. That is more than twice as large as the Republican tax proposal and five times as large as the president's.

A large tax cut is critical to any government downsizing strategy. Every dollar of taxes that is not sent to Washington is one less dollar for Congress

77

Table 6.6
Spending Freeze with Tax Cut Would Balance the Budget

	1996	1997	1998	1999	2000	2001	2002	Total
	Trillions of Dollars							
Outlays with budget freeze	1.57	1.64	1.65	1.65	1.65	1.65	1.65	11.46
Revenues with tax cut	1.46	1.35	1.38	1.43	1.50	1.56	1.67	10.35
Deficit	.11	.29	.27	.22	.15	.09	−.02	1.11
	Percentage of GDP							
Outlays	21.0	21.0	20.8	19.9	18.9	18.0	16.8	
Revenues	19.1	17.0	16.6	16.4	16.4	16.3	16.8	
Deficit	1.9	4.0	4.2	3.5	2.5	1.7	0.0	

SOURCES: Congressional Budget Office, "Economic and Budget Outlook Update," August 1996; and Office of Management and Budget, July 1996 revenue forecasts.

to spend. The evidence of the past 40 years indicates overwhelmingly that an increase in federal revenues incites more government spending, not less government debt. Federal revenues are *positively* correlated with the subsequent size of the deficit rather than negatively correlated. If taxes are cut, spending will be more restrained than otherwise. Richard Vedder has shown in a Joint Economic Committee study that every dollar of new taxes in the post–World War II era has led to $1.59 in new spending. Paradoxically, large tax cuts will facilitate the long-run effort to balance the budget, rather than impede it.

Reductions in marginal tax rates can also improve the performance of the economy and thus reduce the relative burden of government spending and deficits on the productive private sector. Marginal tax rate cuts in the 1920s, 1960s, and 1980s corresponded with substantial increases in growth and employment. Since faster economic growth is virtually a precondition for balancing the budget—if the economic growth rate were increased by 1 percentage point between 1997 and 2002, half of the budget deficit would automatically disappear—pro-growth tax cuts will enhance the prospects for a balanced budget that remains in balance. The converse is also true. If the economy continues to trudge forward at 2 to 2.5 percent per year, the federal budget may never reach balance.

The tax cut should not be a $500 tax credit, as has become part of Republican dogma in recent years. Rather, it should be aimed at reducing income or payroll tax rates, or both. That might involve one of three choices:

- an across-the-board 30 percent reduction in personal income tax rates;
- an income tax credit for all payroll taxes paid by the employee, as proposed by Sen. John Ashcroft (R-Mo.); or
- a flat tax or a national sales tax to replace the income tax at a rate below 20 percent.

Replace Foreign Aid with Free Trade

The federal government officially spends about $14 billion a year on bilateral and multilateral aid to other nations. Much of that money is contributed to the United Nations, the World Bank, and the International Monetary Fund. Israel and Egypt each receive more than $2 billion a year in U.S. foreign aid—even though Prime Minister Benjamin Netanyahu recently hinted to Congress that Israel might be better off without the crutch of welfare checks from the U.S. government.

Supporters of aid programs argue that the price tag is less than 1 percent of the total U.S. budget and thus fiscally inconsequential. But $14 billion is more than is paid in federal taxes by every family in the states of Delaware, Kansas, Maine, and New Hampshire. Moreover, the real foreign aid budget is probably closer to $100 billion—when much of the cost of NATO and other Pentagon "peacekeeping" activities that are wholly unrelated to protecting national security is factored in.

After tens of billions of dollars of U.S. taxpayer funding of aid programs over the past 40 years, there is not a scintilla of evidence that they have had any positive effect in promoting economic development. Much of the money is devoted to causes, such as population control, that are at best irrelevant to economic development. Cato scholars Doug Bandow and Ian Vásquez argue persuasively in their book *Perpetuating Poverty* that America's foreign aid programs do real harm to developing countries by rewarding economic failure and diverting policymakers' attention from the real path to prosperity, which is to adopt free-market reforms. Misguided IMF policy advice led up to the peso devaluation in Mexico. In other developing nations the IMF and the World Bank have urged policymakers to raise taxes to close budget deficits—which is exactly the wrong fiscal prescription.

All U.S. bilateral and multilateral foreign aid should be terminated immediately. Private capital will flow to nations that lower tax rates, promote free trade, shed the welfare system, deregulate, and protect private property rights. U.S. economic development assistance to developing coun-tries should be based on a simple principle: trade, not aid. We should be exporting our products and our democratic institutions to poor nations, not our tax dollars.

End Corporate Welfare As We Know It

The federal government currently spends $75 billion a year on direct subsidies to business. If all federal assistance to business were purged from the budget, deficit spending could be cut in half. Alternatively, if Congress were to eliminate all corporate spending subsidies, the savings would be large enough to entirely eliminate the capital gains tax and the federal estate tax. Reducing the deficit or eliminating those anti-growth taxes would do far more to benefit American industry and U.S. global competitiveness than asking Congress to pick industrial winners and losers. Then-senator Bill Bradley's attack on the corporate welfare state was accurate: "The best way to allocate resources in America is through a market mechanism. Tax and direct-spending corporate subsidies impede the market's functioning for non-economic, special interest reasons."

Last year both Congress and the Clinton administration pledged to shrink the corporate safety net. Those promises went largely unfulfilled. In 1995, for example, the corporate welfare budget was reduced by just 16 percent. In 1996 the cuts were even smaller.

Most expensive corporate subsidy programs continue to receive gener-ous allotments of taxpayer dollars. Those programs include the Agricultural Research Service; the Conservation Reserve Program; the International Trade Administration; fossil energy research and development; the Bureau of Reclamation; the Office of Commercial Space Transportation; the Over-seas Private Investment Corporation; the Export-Import Bank; the Agricul-ture Department's Market Promotion Program, which subsidizes the for-eign advertising of U.S. corporations such as Pillsbury, Dole, and Jim Beam; and techno-grant programs, such as the Advanced Technology Program.

The villain in corporate welfare is government *spending,* not tax deduc-tions. Tax provisions that are universally available to all companies and industries, such as faster write-offs of capital equipment or the advertising deduction, are *not* corporate welfare at all. To the extent the tax code contains unjustified tax favors carved out for specific industries or firms, the loopholes should be closed in conjunction with overall reform or elimination of the income tax.

The 105th Congress should immediately enact a budget rescission spending bill, perhaps titled "The Corporate Welfare Elimination Act," terminating a minimum of 40 to 50 business subsidy *spending* programs and close down the Departments of Commerce and Energy. Savings of at least $200 billion over six years should be targeted. The bill should be crafted in a bipartisan fashion by identifying those programs that have been recommended for extinction by groups such as the Cato Institute, the Heritage Foundation, the Progressive Policy Institute, and even in some cases the Nader group Essential Information. Many Republican deficit hawks, such as Rep. John Kasich of Ohio, Sen. John McCain of Arizona, and Sen. Spencer Abraham of Michigan, have made reductions in corporate subsidies a crusade. They should join with prominent Democrats who have also made good-faith efforts to reduce business aid, including Sen. Russ Feingold of Wisconsin and Reps. Charles Schumer of New York and Joe Kennedy of Massachusetts.

A fair and balanced budget-downsizing strategy should not spare politically well connected K Street special interests. Eliminating aid to dependent corporations adds credibility to Congress's equally vital agenda for ending failed social welfare programs. Both the social welfare and corporate welfare states need to be eliminated.

Gradually Convert Medicare into a Catastrophic Insurance Program

There is a health care crisis in America, but it is a crisis primarily driven by the runaway inflation of the two major government programs, Medicare and Medicaid, that provide subsidized health care to more than 60 million Americans. Since 1988 Medicare and Medicaid have been growing at a 12 percent annual rate. The CBO predicts a 10 percent growth rate in federal health spending over the foreseeable future. Medicare and Medicaid will consume nearly $400 billion by 2000. This stampede of government health inflation has occurred even as the rate of increase in private-sector health costs has fallen in recent years as employers have demanded greater cost sharing by their employees.

Admittedly, revamping Medicare and Medicaid won't be easy to do politically. Republicans in the 104th Congress stepped on a hornets' nest when they proposed relatively modest cost-saving reforms to Medicare. The tragedy of the GOP misadventure with Medicare in 1995 and 1996 is that Gingrich and company took the heat for trying to fix the program, but they endorsed solutions that did not fundamentally scale back the program in ways that would have gradually reduced senior citizens' reliance on government for health care.

Even more than Social Security, Medicare is a national financial time bomb. Its rapidly escalating costs will add $100 billion to the deficit by 2000 alone. The long-term unfunded liability of the system is $7.9 trillion—larger than the national debt and larger than the celebrated liability of Social Security.

The long-term goal for Medicare should be to convert what is now an unjustifiably generous, first-dollar-coverage prepaid health plan for seniors into a catastrophic insurance "safety net" program. The Part B deductible for Medicare (physician costs) is currently an absurdly low $100. If that had been indexed to medical inflation since the program was created 30 years ago, the deductible would be $400 today. The deductible for Part A (hospital stays) is $716, but most seniors have medigap insurance to cover the deductible and other copayments, so their out-of-pocket costs are often negligible.

The way to convert Medicare into a catastrophic coverage plan is to raise the Part A and B deductibles over time. Seniors should be responsible for covering the cost of routine medical expenses by paying out of pocket or purchasing medigap insurance. (Ideally, when medical savings accounts, described below, are made available to all workers, seniors too should be permitted to create tax-free accounts for expenses up to $3,000.) The goal for Medicare should be to increase the combined deductible to $3,000 in 1996 dollars as quickly as possible.

One way to make the restructuring of Medicare politically salable is by income testing. For example, the combined payments under Part A and Part B of Medicare could first be set at 1.5 percent of adjusted gross income (AGI) and then increased 1.5 percentage points each year for four years. Thus, beginning in 2001, the deductible would be 7.5 percent of AGI, the same rate that is now in the individual income tax code. Payments above the deductible, in most cases, would be fixed payments to the patient per illness or accident. A senior with an income above $40,000 would pay a total deductible of $3,000. Seniors would have the security of being financially protected for the cost of major illnesses or extended hospital stays. But a basic inequity in the health care system would be redressed. Mostly nonworking, senior citizens—the wealthiest age group in America—would no longer receive a Cadillac health insurance plan paid for out of the paychecks of relatively lower income working Americans.

Change the Tax Treatment of Health Insurance to Allow Tax-Free Medical Savings Accounts (MSAs) as a Way to Reduce the Inflation in Private and Public Health Care

In 1994 President Clinton's national health plan was soundly rejected by the voters and by Congress. Yet in the last two years, Clinton and the Republican Congress moved us incrementally toward a national health system. Unless an alternative free-market health plan is embraced soon by Congress, America will end up with a Clinton-style socialized medicine plan by the end of the century.

Thirty years of experience have taught us that a larger direct federal role in health care will almost certainly have three effects: (1) it will send medical costs soaring for everyone; (2) it will lead to a deterioration in the quality of care to which Americans have access; and (3) it will bust the federal budget.

Probably the only viable defense against a national health insurance system—under which all Americans are required to purchase uniform insurance directly or via the government and under which those with healthy lifestyles are forced to subsidize those with unhealthy lifestyles— is to make tax-free medical savings accounts (MSAs) widely available as quickly as possible. The Kennedy-Kassebaum law enacted last year provides for a limited MSA pilot project. MSAs should be made available to all individuals and businesses that wish to participate.

MSAs have the ultimate effect of personalizing health insurance. Under this plan, each worker is allowed to put, say, $3,000 per year tax-free into an MSA, which works much like an individual retirement account for health care. (This could be implemented at the same time that conventional employer-provided health insurance tax incentives are limited or eliminated altogether.) The worker (through the employer or on his or her own) then purchases a catastrophic health insurance plan for expenditures above $3,000. For expenditures below $3,000 the worker pays the hospital or doctor directly out of his or her MSA. If the patient incurs more than $3,000 in health costs during the year, then his catastrophic insurance coverage kicks in to pay the rest. If the worker spends less than $3,000, he gets to roll the money into a regular individual retirement account, and the savings can be spent upon his retirement.

MSAs would once again make patients cost-conscious health care consumers. The primary reason that medical costs have been rising so rapidly is that the share of health care costs paid directly by the patient has declined from about 50 percent to about 20 percent since 1960. Over the same time period, total expenditures for medical care have increased from about 5 percent to 14 percent of GDP. That is no coincidence. Given the dominance of third-party payments, neither patients nor physicians have an adequate incentive to control the costs of medical care.

Where MSAs have been tested, they have reduced health costs because patients are now spending their own dollars when they go to the doctor or the hospital. Workers are rewarded for staying healthy and for avoiding placing extraneous demands on the health care system. If made available to all workers, MSAs would reduce the growth of the demand for medical care, the relative inflation of the price of medical services, and total private and public medical expenditures.

Raise the Retirement Age for Social Security and Medicare and Fix the Consumer Price Index

Social Security and Medicare, the two massive income redistribution programs for America's senior citizens, face a combined unfunded liability over the next 75 years of more than $13 trillion—according to the government's own trustees. That's twice the size of the current national debt. The combined annual budget for Social Security and Medicare is now more than half a trillion dollars. Social Security has passed defense to become the largest single program in the federal budget.

Over time, Social Security and more recently Medicare have been interpreted as a political contract between the working-age population and people who are now retired. That constrains the possibility of large savings—other than those described above—in the two programs in the near term. But it should not cause us to defer dealing with the long-term problems of the system—particularly because they are so massive and beyond dispute.

The ultimate solution for Social Security is to convert the government's one-size-fits-all program into a system of personal retirement accounts (PRAs) as described in Chapter 23. While that is being done, the 105th Congress should move immediately to accelerate the increase in the retirement age that is already scheduled for Social Security. Beginning in 1997 the retirement age (and early retirement age) should be raised by three months per year for the next 24 years. That would mean that the age at which one would receive full retirement benefits would be 66 in 2000, 67 in 2004, 68 in 2008, until the retirement age reached 71 in 2020. Workers could still retire at 65 but with reduced benefits.

Because of a quirk in current law, the Medicare retirement age is not scheduled to increase at all—despite the program's massive future deficits.

Without question, any increase in the retirement age for Social Security should apply to Medicare as well.

Incrementally increasing the age for receiving full benefits under those two old-age programs would be an equitable step toward cushioning the impact of the demographic time bomb that will explode in the next 20 years when the baby-boom generation begins to retire. Without a change in retirement age, the ratio of workers to retirees is expected to fall to less than 2 to 1 by the year 2030. Such a dependency ratio would place considerable strain on the economy and a larger burden on today's children—the next generation of workers. It is worth noting that if the retirement age for Social Security had been indexed to the increase in life expectancy since 1935, when the program was created, the age for receiving full benefits would today be 72.

Congress should also move immediately to fix the overstatement of inflation in the Consumer Price Index. A national commission headed by economist Michael Boskin will report soon that the CPI is overestimated by as much as one full percentage point a year. That means that increases in federal benefits, most important Social Security, that are indexed to inflation are exceeding the actual increase in the cost of living. The Boskin commission's recommendations for fixing the CPI should be adopted by Congress.

Devolve All Federal Welfare Programs to the States and Private Charities

Thirty years ago, when President Lyndon Johnson launched the War on Poverty, he declared that "the days of the dole are numbered." We have now surpassed day 10,000. Over that period, some $5 trillion has been spent on this war—more in current dollars than the cost of fighting World War II.

The federal government, along with the states and cities, spends an estimated $300 billion per year on anti-poverty programs. That is almost three times the amount that would be needed to lift every poor family above the poverty level. Still, the poverty rate in the United States remains extremely high and is no lower than when the avalanche of spending to prevent poverty began. As Charles Murray of the American Enterprise Institute emphasizes, "The tragedy of the welfare state is not how much it costs, but how little it has bought." The system does not work well for either the poor or the taxpayer.

The welfare state is fundamentally flawed because it rewards bad behavior—illegitimacy and family breakup and discourages good behavior—

work, marriage, and individual responsibility. A recent Cato study shows that welfare benefits are so high for the nonworking poor, and taxes are so high for the working poor, that a typical female head of a household that is on welfare and receiving public housing would, in most states, have to find a job that paid total benefits of $8.50 an hour to compensate for the loss of welfare benefits. By not working, the poor are not being lazy—they are simply responding to the monetary incentives that the welfare state has created.

The 104th Congress took the first positive step in 30 years to end the welfare state. The primary cash assistance program—Aid to Families with Dependent Children—will now be run by the states. The entitlement feature of the program has been ended in favor of an annually appropriated block grant. Eventually Congress should end the block grant and leave the funding to the states and the private sector. The bill also technically requires work after two years of assistance—but it remains to be seen whether the work requirement will be enforced and, more important, whether it will discourage illegitimacy and entry into the welfare system in the first place.

But AFDC is just one small brick in the modern welfare edifice. Washington now offers more than 60 means-tested programs to help the poor. Three of the most expensive "anti-poverty" programs are Medicaid, food stamps, and public housing. They too should now be returned to the states and, to the fullest extent possible, private charities.

Devolving welfare to the states would be advantageous for several reasons. First, it would allow states full flexibility in serving as innovators and laboratories to devise welfare programs that provide a basic safety net without rewarding destructive behavior. State governments have already begun to experiment with promising reforms in welfare. The most ambitious of those experiments, designed to get people off welfare and into jobs, have been adopted in Wisconsin under Gov. Tommy Thompson and in Michigan under Gov. John Engler. Devolution of welfare to the states would help quickly sort out approaches that work from those that do not. Second, interstate competition would force states to control bureaucratic costs, hold down benefit levels, and impose meaningful restrictions on eligibility—all things Washington has failed to do. Third, states are more likely to see the role of government as one of augmenting successful private charitable support systems, rather than supplanting them.

If welfare is not fully devolved to the states, a second-best option is to completely abolish all forms of welfare for able-bodied recipients—AFDC, food stamps, public housing, Medicaid, Supplemental Security Income, and the rest—and repeal the minimum wage and use part of the savings to expand the Earned Income Tax Credit. The EITC is the least harmful income support program because—unlike almost all other welfare assistance, which is predicated on the recipient's not working—the tax credit goes only to those who work. The EITC has the added benefit that it does not require a large welfare industry to deliver the benefits. Welfare providers have been the primary beneficiary and advocate of federal welfare programs.

Terminate Hundreds of Low-Priority Domestic Programs

Nearly $100 billion a year is spent on domestic programs that have been identified as candidates for termination by such independent agencies as the Congressional Budget Office, the General Accounting Office, the Grace Commission, and even by President Clinton himself in the budget submissions during his first term. They survive, not because they serve any national interest, but because of political or parochial considerations.

As noted above, the 104th Congress eradicated very few of those agencies. Although the House Appropriations Committee lists hundreds of programs terminated in 1995 and 1996, most were of minor budget consequence: the world-famous $500,000 daily ice delivery to the House of Representatives, the $12.5 million Cattle Tick Eradication Program, the $4.3 million Nutrition Education Initiative, the $148,000 House barber shop, the $30 million we've been spending each year for consumer and homemaker education, $1 million for Native Hawaiian and Alaskan cultural arts, and other such absurdities. The bigger fish got away. The original budget resolution crafted by House Budget Committee chairman John Kasich would have terminated 300 programs and closed down the Departments of Education, Energy, and Commerce. Unfortunately, Congress retreated from the plan.

The appendix to this chapter contains a list of recommended program terminations with a total annual taxpayer savings of $170 billion per year. What has been missing in recent years is a political strategy for eliminating those programs. In addition to attacking corporate welfare and foreign aid, as mentioned above, here are six more strategies that should be pursued:

Start with the Easy Targets. Many programs have almost no constituency outside of Washington, D.C., and thus should be relatively painless to zero out. Virtually all of the programs within the Department of Energy fall into that category, for example. Programs that incite public hostility, such as the National Endowment for the Arts and Goals 2000, also should be targeted for elimination.

Approve the Spending Cuts Contained in President Clinton's Budget. President Clinton's budgets have been lean in the spending reduction department, but they do call for the elimination of or substantial funding reductions for low-priority programs with annual savings of nearly $10 billion a year. Those programs include

- wastewater treatment grants
- nuclear reactor research and development
- HUD special purpose grants
- Small Business Administration grants and loans
- Impact Aid
- uranium enrichment programs
- selected student loan programs
- Agency for International Development
- international security assistance
- Appalachian Regional Commission

End Welfare for the Affluent. Many federal domestic programs primarily benefit Americans with above-average incomes. Examples:

- An estimated 40 percent of the $1.4 billion sugar price support program benefits the largest 1 percent of sugar farms. The 33 largest sugar cane plantations each receive more than $1 million. One family alone, the Fanjuls, owners of several large sugar farms in the Florida Everglades, captures an estimated $60 million a year in artificial profits thanks to price supports and import quotas (and to generous campaign contributions to both political parties).
- The wool and mohair subsidy program (now called the National Sheep Industry Improvement Center) at the USDA is supposed to help herders of small herds of sheep. The *Wall Street Journal* reported in 1995 that the third largest recipient of wool and mohair subsidies in Lincoln County, New Mexico, is none other than ABC's Sam Donaldson. Each year $97,000 in subsidy checks is delivered to his house in suburban Virginia. The *Journal* reported that millions of dollars of farm price support checks are delivered to "farmers" who live in cities.

- Amtrak riders—particularly on the Northeast Corridor routes—have average incomes far higher than the national median.
- Much of the money spent on the National Endowment for the Arts finances operas and art exhibits for wealthy clienteles in affluent areas. The beneficiaries can afford to pay for those programs themselves if they have value.

End Welfare for Lobbyists. Many federal programs fund nonprofit organizations that then use those tax dollars to lobby for more taxpayer dollars. Examples include the Legal Services Corporation, which funds legal aid centers that lobby for a larger LSC budget, and the Title X program, which funds Planned Parenthood. The American Association of Retired Persons, which has endorsed nearly $1 trillion in new federal spending, receives some $80 million a year in federal grants. And perhaps the worst abuser of all, the National Council of Senior Citizens, receives 96 percent of its budget from grants from the Environmental Protection Agency and other federal agencies, according to the Heritage Foundation's Government Integrity Project. To end the practice of taxpayer funding of lobbyists, Congress should enact legislation sponsored by Rep. Ernest Istook (R-Okla.) that would prevent organizations that receive any federal grants from lobbying. That restriction should apply to for-profit companies and nonprofit groups.

Create a Constituency for Spending Cuts by Coupling Tax Relief with Budget Reductions. Income tax cuts for families should be combined with cutbacks in programs and regulations designed to "help" families, such as day-care subsidies, Head Start, sex education funding, school lunch programs, the "family leave" bill, and so forth. A reduction in the capital gains tax should be paired with elimination of business subsidies.

Challenge the Constitutionality of Federal Spending Programs. Where in the Constitution does it say anything about Congress's having the power to spend money on swimming pools, Beef Jerky TV advertisements, parking garages, and midnight basketball leagues? The U.S. Constitution confines Congress's spending authority to a select few areas. The enumerated powers of the federal government to spend money are defined in the Constitution under article I, section 8. They include the right to "establish Post Offices and post roads; raise and support Armies; provide and maintain a Navy; declare War"; and fund other mostly national-defense-related activities.

The Constitution grants no authority for the federal government to run the health care industry, impose wage and price controls, provide job training, subsidize electricity and telephone service, lend money to business or foreign governments, require businesses to give their employees leave when they have a child in the hospital, or build football stadiums and tennis courts.

Much of this spending is erroneously defended under the general welfare clause of the Constitution. But as Cato constitutional scholar Roger Pilon explains, it is clear from a reading of history that the general welfare clause "was not meant to be a carte blanche for Congress to spend money, but rather was meant as a restrictive clause to prohibit any special interest spending which did not 'promote the general welfare.' " Thomas Jefferson was concerned that the general welfare clause might be perverted, and so to clarify its meaning he wrote in 1798, "Congress has not unlimited powers to provide for the general welfare, but only those specifically enumerated."

Members of Congress take an oath to uphold the Constitution. They should start taking that oath seriously. When dubious spending programs come before them for funding, they should first ask, Is there constitutional authority for Congress to appropriate this public money? In that way, Congress should establish a "constitutional veto" on federal spending that is clearly outside the bounds of the Constitution. For too long, Congress has simply asserted an unlimited power of the purse. That attitude has undermined the role of the Constitution. It has also helped inflame our current fiscal crisis.

Close the Department of Transportation and Repeal the Federal Gas Tax

The original rationale for the U.S. Department of Transportation was to build the interstate highway system. That was a legitimate federal function, since all U.S. citizens benefit from a coordinated network of interstate highways. The interstate highway system was completed 10 years ago. The vast majority of DOT funding is now spent on noninterstate highways, local roads, and urban transit systems. It makes no sense to collect the federal gasoline tax, send it to Washington, D.C., pass it through a federal bureaucratic maze at DOT, and then send it back to the states where the funds originated.

In transportation policy, the federal government has become not just a costly and unnecessary but also a meddlesome middleman. Until last year, states were forced to comply with a federal 55-mile-an-hour speed limit in order to get back their gas tax revenues from Washington. Federal highway funds come with other strings attached that inflate construction costs: the Davis-Bacon Act (requiring union wages on federal highway projects), minority set-aside programs, and buy-American provisions. Those add about 30 percent to the cost of federal construction projects and thus contribute to the decay of America's public infrastructure. Moreover, increasingly Congress uses the DOT budget as a pot of money from which to deliver pork-barrel projects that states would rarely fund if they were spending their own taxpayers' money.

All of the inefficiency and redundancy could be ended by closing down the DOT and repealing the 18.4 cent federal gasoline tax. States could then raise the gas tax themselves (as much as they wished) to pay for whatever road building and repair were needed. Eliminating the cost of the federal bureaucracy of 65,000 workers in Washington will cause construction and maintenance costs for highways, bridges, and transit systems to fall. Many governors have endorsed this idea as consistent with federalism and the Tenth Amendment.

Privatize Federal Assets

Government owns about one-third of all the land in the United States—and in most years it adds to its holdings by purchasing or confiscating properties. Under the Clinton administration, for example, hundreds of thousands of acres in California and Utah have been seized by Uncle Sam. Yet only a tiny fraction of the vast federal land holdings are of environmental or historical significance.

The market value of oil lands alone is estimated to be roughly $450 billion. Government also owns tens of billions of dollars worth of other assets, including mineral stockpiles, buildings, and other physical capital. Most of those assets are not put to productive use and thus yield little or no return to the taxpayers. Federal holdings that should be transferred to private ownership include

- nonenvironmentally sensitive federal lands
- federal oil reserves
- certain Amtrak routes
- the $250 billion federal loan portfolio
- the federal helium reserve
- public housing units
- federal dams

- the Naval Petroleum Reserve
- the air traffic control system

The 105th Congress should begin a campaign to privatize those and other unneeded federal assets with a goal of raising $25 billion a year. The funds raised from asset sales should be dedicated to retiring the national debt and reducing federal interest payments.

Conclusion

The Economist recently assessed the accomplishments of the 104th Congress. "Mr. Gingrich saw 1994 as marking a change in direction," the magazine wrote. "But the pattern of the half century argues otherwise. It shows a series of expansions of government's reach, punctuated by conservative pauses and corrections." Then government resumes its relentless rise.

Despite some notable early successes, the Republican-controlled 104th Congress made only slight progress in reversing the underlying trend toward bigger government in America shown in Figure 6.1. The federal government still consumes nearly one-quarter of national output. In the end, big government survived the GOP assault almost unscathed.

The challenge for the 105th Congress is to end the federal government's relentless rise in the 20th century. The goal is not primarily to balance the federal budget—though that is worth doing. The goal is to greatly shrink the federal budget—through a combination of tax and spending cuts.

The budget alternative presented here would dramatically reverse the trend of government expansionism. Table 6.6 shows that government spending and taxes as a share of national output would shrink to below 17 percent of output by 2002. In future years federal spending would be reduced to roughly 15 percent of GDP when all the budget recommendations were fully implemented. This is a budget blueprint that would make America freer and more prosperous entering the 21st century.

Appendix: Cato Institute List of Recommended Federal Program Terminations, FY96

Program	Amount (millions of dollars)
U.S. Department of Agriculture	
Economic Research Service	50
National Agricultural Statistics Service	80
Agricultural Research Service	800
Cooperative State Research, Education and Extension Service	900
Animal and Plant Health Inspection Service	400
Food Safety and Inspection Service	600
Grain Inspection, Packers and Stockyard Administration	20
Agricultural Marketing Service	500
Conservation Reserve Program	1,800
Federal Crop Insurance Corporation	2,000
Agricultural commodity price supports and subsidies	10,000
Natural Resources Conservation Service	1,100
Rural Housing and Community Development Service	1,700
Rural Business and Cooperative Development Service	100
Rural Electrification Administration subsidies	1,000
Foreign Agricultural Service	800
Market Access Program	100
Food stamps	
Children's nutrition subsidies for the nonpoor	1,000
Special Supplemental Food Program for Women, Infants, and Children	3,700
Commodity Credit Corporation export credit	200
Food donations programs for selected groups	200
Export Enhancement Program	400
P.L. 480	300
USDA land acquisition programs	100
Forest Service, renewable resource management	600
Forest Service, road and trail construction	100
Forest Service, forest and rangeland research	200
Forest Service, state and private forestry	150
Total Department of Agriculture	54,900
Department of Commerce	
Economic Development Administration	400

Economic and Statistical Analysis	50
International Trade Administration	200
Export Administration	40
Minority Business Development Agency	40
National Ocean Service	200
National Marine Fisheries Service	350
Oceanic and Atmospheric Research	200
Fishery products research, development, and promotion	20
Advanced Technology Program	250
Manufacturing Extension Partnership	100
National Institute of Standards and Technology	300
National Telecommunications and Information Administration	90
Total Department of Commerce	2,240
Department of Education	
Goals 2000	500
School-to-Work Programs	200
Elementary and Secondary Education Grants	7,100
Impact Aid	800
School Improvement Programs	1,200
Safe and Drug-Free Schools Act	400
Office of Vocational and Adult Education	1,500
Office of Bilingual Education	150
College Work-Study Grants	600
Office of Educational Research and Improvement	500
Direct Student Loan Program	500
Office for Civil Rights	60
Total Department of Education	13,510
Department of Energy	
General Science and Research activities	1,000
Solar and Renewable Energy, research and development	300
Nuclear Fission, research and development	200
Magnetic Fusion, research and development	300
Energy Supply, research and development	3,400
Uranium Supply and Enrichment activities	50
Fossil Energy, research and development	400
Naval Petroleum and Oil Shale Reserves	200

Energy conservation programs	400
Strategic Petroleum Reserve	300
Energy Information Administration	70
Economic Regulatory Administration	20
Clean Coal Technology	160
Power Marketing Administration subsidies	200
Departmental administration	300
Total Department of Energy	7,300

Department of Health and Human Services	
Health Professions Curriculum Assistance	300
National Health Service Corps	100
Maternal and Child Health Block Grant	700
Healthy Start	100
Title X Family Planning Program	200
Indian Health Service	1,900
Substance Abuse Block Grant	1,200
Mental Health Block Grant	300
State day-care programs	1,300
State welfare administrative costs	1,700
State child support administrative costs	1,900
Low-income home energy assistance	1,200
Refugee assistance programs	400
Family preservation and support grants	100
Payments to states for Job Training (JOBS)	1,000
Child Care and Development Block Grant	900
Social Services Block Grant	3,200
Head Start	3,300
Child Welfare Services	300
Community Services Block Grants	400
Child Abuse Grants to States	20
NIH overhead cost reimbursements	100
Total Department of Health and Human Services	20,620

Department of Housing and Urban Development	
Public Housing Programs	4,200
College Housing Grants	20
Community Development Grants	5,100
HOME Investment Partnerships Program	1,200

Community Planning and Development	500
Low-Income Housing Assistance (Sec. 8)	10,000
Rental Housing Assistance	600
Fair Housing Activities	20
Federal Housing Administration	300
Total Department of Housing and Urban Development	21,940
Department of the Interior	
Bureau of Indian Affairs	1,700
Bureau of Reclamation water projects	500
U.S. Geological Survey	600
Helium fund and reserves	20
Migratory Bird Conservation	40
North American Wetlands Conservation	10
Cooperative Endangered Species Conservation	30
National Wildlife Refuge Fund	20
Sport Fish Restoration Fund	200
National Park System, fee collection support	10
Land Acquisition programs	150
Total Department of the Interior	3,280
Department of Justice	
Community Oriented Policing Services	1,800
Violence against Women Act	120
Byrne Law Enforcement Grants	140
Correctional Facilities Grants	600
Substance Abuse Treatment for State Prisoners	20
State and Local Law Enforcement Assistance	100
Weed and Seed Program	20
Antitrust Division	20
Drug Enforcement Administration	700
Interagency Crime and Drug Enforcement Task Force	200
Total Department of Justice	3,720
Department of Labor	
The Job Training Partnership Act	1,000
Adult Training Grants	800
Dislocated Worker Assistance	900
Youth Training Grants	100
Summer Youth Employment and Training Program	600

School-to-Work Programs	100
Job Corps	1,100
Migrant and Seasonal Worker Training	60
Community Service Employment for Older Americans	400
Trade Adjustment Assistance	300
Employment Standards Administration	200
Total Department of Labor	5,560
Department of State	
United Nations organizations	600
Inter-American organizations	100
North Atlantic Treaty Organization	40
Organization for Economic Cooperation and Development	60
United Nations peacekeeping activities	200
International Fisheries Commissions	20
Migration and Refugee Assistance	700
Foreign aid to Egypt	2,000
Foreign aid to Israel	3,000
Narcotics control assistance to foreign countries	100
Agency for International Development	2,900
Total Department of State	9,720
Department of Transportation	
Motor Carrier Safety Grants	60
Highway Traffic Safety Grants	200
Federal Railroad Administration	20
Amtrak subsidies	600
Federal Transit Administration	4,500
Grants-in-Aid for Airports	1,500
Payments to air carriers program	20
Maritime Administration	500
Cargo Preference Program	500
Transportation Systems Center	200
Partnership for a New Generation of Vehicles	200
Total Department of Transportation	8,300
Department of the Treasury	
Presidential Election Campaign Fund	100
Customs Service, Air and Marine Interdiction Program	60

Interagency Crime and Drug Enforcement Task Force	60
Total Department of the Treasury	220
Department of Veterans Affairs	
VA benefits for non-service-related illnesses	200
VA health care facilities construction	600
Total Department of Veterans Affairs	800
Other Agencies and Activities	
African Development Foundation	20
Appalachian Regional Commission	200
Consumer Product Safety Commission	40
Corporation for National and Community Service	600
Corporation for Public Broadcasting	300
Davis-Bacon Act	1,000
Equal Employment Opportunity Commission	200
EPA Wastewater Treatment Subsidies	2,400
EPA Superfund	1,400
EPA Environmental Technology Initiative	60
EPA Science to Achieve Results grants	80
Export-Import Bank	500
Federal Labor Relations Board	20
Federal Trade Commission	40
High-Performance Computing and Communications	800
Inter-American Foundation	20
International Monetary Fund	40
International Trade Commission	20
Legal Services Corporation	300
NASA International Space Station Program	2,000
NASA New Millennium Initiative	400
NASA Reusable Launch Vehicle Technology Program	100
NASA Aeronautics Initiative Research Partnerships	300
National Endowment for the Arts	200
National Endowment for Democracy	40
National Endowment for the Humanities	200
National Flood Insurance	200
National Labor Relations Board	100
National Science Foundation Program to Stimulate Competitive Research	40

Neighborhood Reinvestment Corp.	40
Office of National Drug Control Policy	40
Office of Science and Technology Policy	20
Overseas Private Investment Corporation	40
Peace Corps	200
Securities and Exchange Commission	100
Service Contract Act	600
Small Business Administration	800
Tennessee Valley Authority, development activities	100
Trade and Development Agency	40
U.S. Global Change Research Program	1,700
U.S. Information Agency	1,200
World Bank	40
Total other agencies and activities	16,540
Total Cato budget savings	168,650

Suggested Readings

Congressional Budget Office. *Reducing the Deficit: Spending and Revenue Options.* Washington: CBO, August 1996.

Hodge, Scott A. *Rolling Back Government: A Budget Plan to Rebuild America.* Washington: Heritage Foundation, 1995.

Moore, Stephen. *Government: America's #1 Growth Industry.* Lewisville, Tex.: Institute for Policy Innovation, 1993.

—Prepared by Stephen Moore

7. The 1998 Defense Budget

Congress should

- reduce the budget authorization for the Department of Defense from the present $243 billion to $154 billion (in 1997 dollars) in increments over the next five years;
- make it clear that this defense budget reduction must be matched by a narrowing of America's national strategy from the present "two major regional contingencies" to one;
- encourage a shift in military missions from extensive use of ground forces to punitive long-range attack;
- cut the active general purpose force structure to 6 Army divisions, 2 Marine divisions with their air wings, 10 Air Force tactical air wings, and 6 Navy aircraft carrier battle groups with 5 Navy air wings;
- ensure that smaller general purpose forces are equipped with the most effective weapons and information technology and are fully funded;
- require accelerated reduction in strategic nuclear offensive weapons, down to the START II targets of 3,500 countable weapons; then require further negotiations with Russia to bring the strategic offensive nuclear forces of both sides down to about 2,000 warheads;
- accelerate research and development of strategic defense for the territorial United States against ballistic and cruise missiles and aim for the beginning of deployment about a decade from now;
- mandate the effective detection and suppression of terrorism against American society, while making special efforts to avoid intrusions on the lives and property of American citizens; and
- overall, shift the emphasis of American defense away from alliance commitments, collective security, and "extended deterrence" and toward the protection of the American homeland and society against direct external assaults.

How to Think about Defense Policy

To understand defense policy, we need a theory that relates a country's role and objectives in the world all the way "down" to the resources that are required for such a stance. Otherwise, everything done for defense looks arbitrary, expensive, and even wasteful. Thus, this chapter will end up with some prescriptions for defense policy that are part of a comprehensive scheme. That means that reforms in the defense program will imply some larger changes in the way America does its security business, and its foreign policy business, in the world.

You can't comment usefully on the defense budget unless you can trace the connections among foreign policy (the way that our national society orients itself to the international system); national strategy; military missions; force structure, major weapons systems, and operational doctrine; and resources of money and military personnel. Those constitute levels in a "hierarchy of concerns." Together, they are the linkage between the geopolitics of the U.S. situation in the international system and the nation's political economy.

You also can't make reliable comments about the defense budget unless you know what the various items cost, particularly combat forces in their entirety (including their supporting units and structures and their weaponry). We have to reconstruct the "full-slice" costs of those forces.

We can read the foreign policy pronouncements of an administration, not for the words or the tone, but for the operational implications—in terms of the ensuing strategies that must be adopted, the military missions that will be generated, the forces and weapons that will become necessary, the needs for budgetary dollars and recruitment of military personnel. That is the logic of foreign policy.

We must judge foreign policy pronouncements by those tangible requisites and by whether this country, as a political economy, can, and will, meet the requisites—that is, will give the policy and its consequences (the entailed contingent actions) steady, reliable support and will provide the revenues, from the public wealth, and make them available to the government to fund those actions. That is the logistics of foreign policy.

If we find, by applying those operational tests, that the nation cannot or will not support the professed objects of the nation's foreign policy, then "something has to give." There will have to be some feedback in the model, in the levels of the hierarchy of concerns.

A Rational Model of Defense

We have posited a rational model, in which national defense is (1) related to the external situation of this country in the international system and (2) rooted in, and ultimately constrained by, the multifaceted political economy of this country: economic, social, and political (including constitutional). Though we might disagree with the substance of America's present defense policy, we find it consistent with the level of defense output that is required to support America's present national strategy and foreign policy.

That means that critics cannot take credit for any significant efficiencies (better cost-effectiveness ratios). For one thing, presumed savings from the elimination of ''waste'' cannot be used in any realistic future calculation. For another thing, the so-called building blocks of force that the Pentagon has decreed appropriate to each of the two planned ''major regional contingencies'' are largely correct; indeed, if anything, they are the minimal requisites to fight and win each of the regional contingencies, say, a desert war in the Persian Gulf and an encounter with North Korea.

But this estimate of the necessary building blocks has been challenged by ostensibly knowledgeable military analysts. The effect of their critiques—if believed—is to dilute the relationship between military missions and military forces and to make it seemingly feasible for the United States to do more with less. The reality is different: To fight Desert Storm in 1991, the United States had, in and close by the theater, forces that represented 45 percent of its (then) active worldwide force structure—and that structure was considerably larger than it is now.

I suppose the critics could argue that all that force was redundant. But that would be a tenuous argument. That is because of ''the American way of war.'' It is a sociological fact that Americans will fight only with marked technological superiority on any battlefield and with grossly disproportionate superiority of force, and, moreover, they will insist on quick victory, with a minimum of casualties.

I will advocate radical savings in the defense budget, but not through sleight of hand, or sleight of rhetoric—only through reductions in forces, which demand commensurate reductions of the objects of America's national strategy and foreign policy.

The Demands of Foreign Policy

Analysis of the defense budget must start with an operational interpretation of America's foreign policy and national strategy. That interpretation can be construed from a reading of the secretary of defense's annual "posture statement" in conjunction with the White House document, *A National Security Strategy of Engagement and Enlargement.*

The quickest rendering of those documents is "world's policeman." "Engagement" entails the propensity to involve the United States, even militarily, in a large list of contingencies in the world—not very different from the Bush administration's "new world order," which was literally universal, and almost abstract, to the point of presence and intervention in the interest of "stability," more or less for its own sake. "Enlargement" (of democracy in the world) offers an expansion (if that is possible) of the occasions for American intervention, because of the addition of that functional object of our foreign policy.

The judgment of "world's policeman" obtains, despite the obligatory official disclaimers and protestations of "selectivity" and "restraint." Operationally, there is no middle ground between being the world's policeman and not being the world's policeman.

Certainly, from a budgetary standpoint, there is no middle ground. The cost of this nation's foreign policy is not its "international affairs budget" (at approximately $16.5 billion a year, expensive but ludicrously insignificant as a target of partisan critics) but rather our defense budget of $243 billion. Thus, the larger question that we are asking is, Can the United States afford its foreign policy?

Critical Analysis of the U.S. Defense Budget

The basic document elucidating U.S. defense expenditures is the *Annual Report to the President and the Congress* by the reigning secretary of defense—in this case, William J. Perry's February 1996 report for fiscal year 1997.

First, we have to be clear about what set of figures we are going to use. For FY97, the budget authority originally requested by the secretary of defense, for the Department of Defense itself (line item 051), is $242,632,000; we will round that figure to $243 billion.

The report of the secretary of defense is complete, truthful, accurate, and informative. The problems with the report, from the standpoint of defense analysis, are that the numbers

1. are stated, and aggregated, in ways that do not, in themselves, reveal the "full-slice" costs of keeping the combat forces in the force structure for one year and

2. do not, without further rearrangement, throw light on the costs, to the United States, of defending key regions of the world.

Without such insights, we cannot relate defense costs to foreign policy objectives.

There seems to be a popular fascination—an obsession, even—with the cost of individual items of hardware, say, the unit cost of the next air superiority fighter plane or the cost of one Seawolf attack submarine. Ironically, those are just pieces of larger systems and, more important, forces that cost even more—in fact, dozens of times more than the "big ticket items" themselves.

So we perform an "anatomy" and regroup the officially stated costs in categories that will give us more insight into two kinds of matters: the functional split of the entire defense budget of $243 billion and the "full-slice" costs (including all support costs and overhead costs) of the combat units of the four (splitting the Marine Corps from the Navy) military services.

Functional Split

The functional split of the entire defense budget is presented in two ways, by combat outputs and by regional attribution. The split by combat outputs is given in Table 7.1. Strategic nuclear forces and general purpose forces are the *only* true outputs of the Department of Defense—all the rest of the "program categories" of that department are not outputs in themselves but inputs of support and overhead into the combat outputs.

The second way the functional split of the entire defense budget is presented is by regional attribution. The active-duty general purpose forces (10 Army divisions; 3 Marine divisions, each with its organic double-strength air wing; 13 Air Force tactical air wings; 11 Navy aircraft carrier

Table 7.1
Combat Outputs

Combat Output	Cost ($ billions)	Percentage of Budget
Strategic nuclear forces	26	11
General purpose forces (and special operations forces)	217	89

battle groups with 10 Navy air wings) are "attributed" to the geographical regions of the world, as defined by the Department of Defense. The regional attribution of those forces is given in Table 7.2.

The cost to the United States of defending the regions of the world in FY97 is given in Table 7.3.

Table 7.2
Attribution of Ground Forces

Region	Army Divisions	Marine Divisions
Atlantic		
Europe	3	0
Persian Gulf/Middle East	4	1
Total	7	1
Pacific	3	2
Total	10	3

NOTE: Since the calculation and attribution of all the general purpose forces "pivots" on the ground forces, in this table they are used to represent the other forces as well.

Table 7.3
Cost of Regional Defense

Region	Cost ($ billions)
Atlantic	
Europe	53
Persian Gulf	82
Total	135
Pacific	82
Total	217

"Full-Slice" Costs

The "full-slice" costs (including all support costs and overhead costs) of the combat units of the four (splitting the Marine Corps from the Navy) military services are given in Table 7.4.

Table 7.4
"Full-Slice" Costs of Combat Units

Unit	"Full-slice" Cost per Unit ($ billions)
Army division (averaging the various types of division: armored, mechanized, infantry, light infantry, air assault, airborne)	7.05
Marine Corps (3 division-wing teams)	24.7
Air Force tactical air wing	2.29
Navy aircraft carrier battle group kept forward (since the best rotation plan that can be carried out, over an intermediate period, is 3 total carrier groups to "generate" 1 carrier group constantly on a forward battle station)	3.8 x 3 = 11.4

Proposals for Reform

Our rational model of defense policy leads us to discount heavily—to reject totally, in some cases—theories, prototheoretical assertions, and even atheoretical insinuations to the effect that (1) the defense program and defense budget (aggregate spending, what we buy, what we plan to use it for) are the results of organizational momentum, bureaucratic aggrandizement, corporate greed, unaccountable waste, mindless administration, perceptual panic, and other "explanations" that would cut the linkage between national requirements and requisite resources and that, therefore, (2) since there is "no reason" for what we are now doing, we can make, with impunity, purely arbitrary cuts and "transfers" from the defense budget.

That is not the case. Of course, there is, as in any human enterprise, some distortion of means, but that, in a proper model of defense planning, constitutes the "noise," not the signal. The signal is that, for the most part, we have to pay for what we get, more or less at the going rates. If we want to save considerable amounts from the defense budget, we will have to slight some elements of our national strategy, and we will have to give up some objects of our foreign policy.

107

There should also be some other, independent, criterion—not just dollar savings—for determining what kind of defense program we will have. That criterion would be the "appropriateness" of defense policy: appropriateness to our irreducible security requirements—safeguarding the lives and domestic property of our citizens, the national territory, and the autonomy of our political processes—and, beyond that, perhaps appropriateness for supporting larger defined interests of the country in the world.

Threats and Missions

If one had to identify developments in the world that might present real threats to American society in, say, the next two decades, the first task would be to identify what should *not* be on that list:

- The narcotics trade and criminal syndicates, as fields for the employment of the military.
- Political practices, including human rights pressures, in other countries. This is not to say that American groups and individuals cannot speak out, and even wage a form of "private diplomacy." But the American government should stay out of such quarrels. It may "react" to practices in some regimes by thinning out, or cooling off, official relations, but it should not adopt trade sanctions, blockades, armed assaults, and the like in order to change other countries' political practices.
- "Economic warfare." The United States happens to have the assets of economic redundancy and diversity and "scale," even in an age of supposed "interdependence." Though we would not want to do so, we could ride out, passively, a fair number of foreign attempts at deprivation of resources, trade, and investment.
- Aggression by regional powers, in their own regions. The United States also has the asset of tremendous strategic depth (a fact that was first officially noted by President George Washington in 1796). There is a larger point involved here: Even a country like China—and, arguably, already a country such as Russia—will be seen to have lapsed into "macroregional" status, and therefore to have failed to present a *global* challenge to the United States. Therefore, we (that is, American arms makers) may provide weaponry and supplies to "decent" countries in other regions who wish to enhance their defensive potential. But the United States, as a government, should, over

a reasonably short time, absolve itself of guarantees for and sponsorship of other countries in other regions of the world.

In the following subsections I will discuss the kinds of matters that *should* be the concerns of American security policy.

Dealing with Powers in Other Regions

As an item of foreign policy, the United States should adopt a noninterventionist stance, leaving events in other regions of the world to work themselves out according to the play of power and diplomacy of the nations in those regions.

Yet it is not unimaginable that circumstances could arise that would suggest a military mission into some other region, against some regional power or coalition of powers. Therefore, our national strategy must encompass the possibility of our waging an other-regional strike.

And so, our mission-planning assumption will pivot on the capability to wage one ("simultaneous") large-scale attack on a "major" regional power, but without the prospect of taking and holding territory beyond, perhaps, the immediate bases necessary to sustain the military strikes, and without the prospect of continuing a conflict long enough to require a "mobilization base" for our deployed forces.

Well within the force requirements for such a state of affairs would be a modest American engagement in some true peacekeeping (not peace-enforcing) mission in some rare situation that met stringent requirements of advancing our own diplomatic aims. Such a mission would be subject to the stricture that an American deployment would be designed to be of very short duration (a feature that would practically rule out most such missions).

That planning assumption will, in turn, carry over into our design of force structure and weapons and operational doctrines. Thus, to implement this very guarded kind of "hedged noninterventionist" strategy and possible missions, we would have to prepare to wage, not sustained interventions, but punitive strikes.

A punitive strike might be less than decisive. It would virtually have to be executed by "stand-off" forces. The "fires" would become the attack, rather than, as in the military operations we have ordinarily waged, support for the attack by our maneuver units. (There would still be some "plausible" function for ground forces, if they fit into a basically punitive doctrine. Ground forces can "fix" and "channel" an enemy, force an enemy to mass and sometimes dismount, and so on.)

The habitual distinction between long-range and short-range delivery of fires would be collapsed; with very precise, and terminal, guidance, virtually the same accuracy could be obtained from any distance.

There would be more emphasis on the projectiles than the platforms. That would imply increasing use of unmanned and perhaps expendable platforms, too; indeed, the distinction between platform and projectile might well be lost.

As for targets, we could punish an enemy force, but the very distinction between force-targets and value-targets would be blurred. We might seek to destroy an enemy force as an item of value.

Warding Off Direct Assaults on the United States

We are left with the threat of direct assault on the United States. Such a threat consists, actually, of two problems, at opposite ends of the scale of "delivery" of destruction—but, in the future, perhaps with converging scales of violence:

1. long-range attacks on the United States with weapons of mass destruction, particularly nuclear weapons, and
2. terroristic delivery of the entire range of weapons, from small arms and conventional explosives to weapons of mass destruction, including nuclear bombs, chemicals, and biological agents.

Those threats are tangible and real, and they can occur even without our (immediate) intervention in quarrels in other regions of the world. They are, however, still "on the horizon," though that horizon is now probably less than 10 years, in terms of the sheer technical and physical capability of antagonists. Those potential attacks have to be physically interdicted.

An enemy's potential long-range delivery of highly lethal munitions calls for active defenses. It is probably the case that present "off-the-shelf" missile interception technology is not adequate to the task—certainly not to the task of thinning out, satisfactorily, a "barrage" attack and perhaps not even to the task of reliably and nearly perfectly interdicting a "limited" missile attack by hostile regional powers. (Note that the only power, now and foreseeably, able to unleash a barrage attack is Russia, but Russia is, of course, an unlikely aggressor against the United States.)

But at some point, (1) this country will need strategic societal defenses; (2) the American public will insist on whatever degree of strategic societal defense we can feasibly deploy; (3) the incremental physical protection afforded, though not perfect, will appear to dwarf the arms-control complications (if any still exist by that time, since the Russians—the only arms control partner that we must take into account—themselves will be amenable to deploying some strategic defense); and (4) a prediction could be made, with some confidence, that technological progress will converge on a set of capabilities that will translate into an effective missile-acquiring and missile-killing defense system.

Targeting and Firing Offensive Nuclear Weapons

Nuclear threats must also continue to be deterred. That is why, in the impending "multinuclear world," the United States must retain a pared-down, but still potent, and varied, retaliatory force of nuclear offensive weapons. Targeting would be primarily military and military-logistical. That equates to a "counterforce" doctrine, though not in the narrowest sense of targeting only the offensive nuclear forces of potential enemies. As for the doctrine of precedence of use, we would contemplate the possibility of preemption, in an advanced crisis, and upon reliable indication that a regional enemy, in a situation of hostilities, was preparing a nuclear strike (or a strike with other weapons of mass destruction) against our deployed conventional forces, our theater-deployed nuclear assets, and, probably, some of our allies' forces and logistical, economic, and societal targets. (In the "New Paradigm," and against lesser-than-Russian regional nuclear adversaries, the putatively destabilizing aspects of counterforce and its presumption of preemptive first strike are no longer overriding. However, to the extent possible, we would want to assign preemptive tasks to conventional munitions.)

In the case of terroristic delivery of lethal devices into the American homeland, what is required is not strictly military measures, let alone measures that would have any appreciable impact on any sector of the federal budget, military or otherwise. What is needed is intelligence, and police work and border control.

In specifying those measures, one encounters inevitable contradictions with the civil liberties of American citizens, which are already severely affected by the ambitious use, by agencies of government, of laws adopted under the rubric of "money laundering," "drug enforcement," and the like. We must strain all the harder, therefore, to maintain safeguards against government abuse of the privacy of the lives, and the transactions, of American citizens.

Reducing the Defense Budget

Correct policy would limit the objectives of U.S. foreign policy and national strategy to the essential minimum; then, from that low base, it would hedge a bit against the unexpected or the miscalculated; and then it would make sure that the objectives, the strategies, and the military missions were adequately supported—with forces and weapons, the requisite degree of readiness, and the proper funding.

Conventional Forces

With regard to conventional forces, preparing to fight only one "major regional contingency"—and that only as a hedge against provocations that are not even actually projected—would *save*, from current (1997) general purpose force levels,

- 4 Army divisions—down to 6,
- 1 Marine division (land force component)—down to 2,
- 3 Navy aircraft carrier battle groups (ships)—down to 6,
- some Navy amphibious shipping—roughly, down to 1 "set,"
- 7 Air Force tactical air wings—down to 10,
- 2 (equivalent) Marine air wings—down to 4 (equivalent),
- 5 Navy air wings—down to 5.

Strategic Nuclear Forces

The country should implement, on an accelerated basis, the START II strategic offensive ceilings on nuclear forces, bringing countable U.S. forces down to about 3,500 warheads; then we should negotiate a further reduction to approximately the 2,000 level (including theater as well as strategic weapons). But we should not disarm, strategically, below that level, in a threat climate that will, predictably, include a half-dozen potentially hostile regional nuclear (or other mass-destruction) powers with longer range delivery systems. With such a force, the United States would, of course, avoid any commitments to "extended deterrence."

I suggest an (almost) dyad of offensive nuclear forces: stand-off bombers and submarine-launched missiles, along with some shorter range theater missiles (including cruise missiles) capable of being fired from bases, including offshore naval vessels such as cruisers or attack submarines, within a regional theater of conflict. The almost-dyad might or might not retain a number of our land-based intercontinental ballistic missiles. It is no longer so important to eliminate land-based missiles, and they are relatively cheap and relatively secure from a command-and-control standpoint.

Roughly, only two of the various categories of nuclear powers of the future would have to be "addressed" by U. S. nuclear strategy: (1) the objectively powerful Russian force and (2) the overtly hostile forces of an Iraq, Iran, Libya, or North Korea. With a force of 2,000 warheads, distributed roughly between submarine-launched and other-based weapons, the United States could deal flexibly with such potential adversaries. My objective U.S. offensive nuclear force is given in Table 7.5.

A slight acceleration of those offensive nuclear weapon reductions, and a reduction to lower levels, even beyond the schedule initiated by the Bush administration and continued into the Clinton administration, should provide the savings needed to supply the relatively (in absolute dollar terms) small additional amounts to support an enhanced development program on the strategic defensive side. We now spend, on missile defense (strategic as well as theater, nuclear as well as conventional, research as

Table 7.5
Suggested Offensive Nuclear Force

System	Warheads
8 Trident submarines, each carrying 20 D-5 missiles, each with approximately 6 to 8 warheads	960–1,280
24 B-52H bombers equipped with (10 notional) air-launched cruise missiles	240
16 B-2 (penetrating stealth) bombers carrying (10 notional) gravity bombs	160
[optional] 100 land-based ICBMs, each carrying one warhead	100
400 (theater-range) cruise missiles	400
Total	1,860–2,180

well as some production) something like $3 billion a year. (Cumulatively, we have already spent about $40 billion.)

Actual deployment of a strategic defensive shield would cost an indeterminate amount, since the location of the platforms, and even some of the ultimate physical principles, are in the shadow of uncertainty. But one can posit a range of another $100 billion to $120 billion for the remaining development and deployment. (I have, skeptically, added some to the Congressional Budget Office's estimate of $31 billion to $60 billion for both the remaining research and the deployment of the "Dole/Defend America" version of strategic defense, over 13 budget years through 2010.) Deployment should not start until the design of the system is firmly in place, and that cannot be before 10 years from now; deployment would take place over a minimum of a decade from that time. Therefore, we are talking about deployment costs of $5 billion to 7 billion a year, starting a dozen years from now.

Meanwhile, we would have to accelerate research and development, and even the engineering and testing phase. So we would have to figure on spending, on these earlier phases of strategic defense, something like $5 billion a year, up to the time that deployment was agreed and began to take place.

Finally, we should invest the relatively insignificant monetary amounts necessary to ward off and curtail terrorism.

This dramatically revised national security program can be obtained at an eventual annual budgetary expenditure of $154 billion (in 1997 dollars), instead of the planned expenditure of $243 billion. From the 1997 base— allowing about five years for the phaseouts, and allowing some inflation— by 2001 our alternative would cost about $173 billion a year, in contrast to the administration's $270 billion.

Thus, the above principles lead to a defense budget that would save some $89 billion to $97 billion a year from present and planned spending.

A National Security Strategy of Disengagement and Independence

By avoiding other-regional intervention with ground forces and enhancing the protection of our society by accelerated strategic defense and some carefully placed efforts against terrorism, we would achieve a cheaper defense that would be more appropriate to the American situation, both internationally and domestically.

Such a stance would amount to "strategic disengagement" and "strategic independence." The two formulas are complementary, and both are needed to bracket the strategy. ("Strategic independence" is a term coined by Ted Galen Carpenter, especially in *A Search for Enemies: America's Alliances after the Cold War.* "Strategic disengagement" is the designation of Earl C. Ravenal in, for example, the *Foreign Affairs* article "The Case for Strategic Disengagement.") "Independence" connotes autonomy of national decisionmaking. "Disengagement" represents, more concretely, a defensive stance in the world, even with geographical resonances. It combines the notions of distance and insulation (as much as can be realized in the age of military technologies of long-range destruction and instantaneous information).

Both elements of national strategy anticipate the situation, as well as counsel the role, of the United States in the world that impends.

Suggested Readings

Carpenter, Ted Galen. *A Search for Enemies: America's Alliances after the Cold War.* Washington: Cato Institute, 1992.

Perry, William J. *Annual Report to the President and the Congress.* Washington: Government Printing Office, March 1996, for fiscal year 1997.

Ravenal, Earl C. *Defending America in an Uncontrollable World: The Military Budget, 1997–2002.* Washington: Cato Institute, forthcoming, 1997.

———. *Designing Defense for a New World Order: The Military Budget in 1992 and Beyond.* Washington: Cato institute, 1991.

White House. *A National Security Strategy of Engagement and Enlargement.* Washington: Government Printing Office, February 1996.

—Prepared by Earl C. Ravenal

8. Pentagon Pork

Congress should

- eliminate any military construction add-on projects that are not essential; doing so in the FY97 defense budget would have saved at least $600 million;
- reduce the number of general and flag-rank officers by 25 percent;
- remove all nondefense spending (e.g., providing security for sporting events, such as the Olympic Games, and research on breast cancer) from the Pentagon budget; either eliminate such programs or transfer the spending to the proper budget classification;
- end subsidies to arms producers, which currently total more than $7.6 billion per year; and
- refrain from spending more money on the purchase of weapons not requested by the administration, such as additional B-2 bombers.

After the 1994 election, the Republican-controlled 104th Congress promised to eliminate unnecessary and wasteful government spending, especially blatant pork-barrel spending. Although that is a familiar refrain during campaign season, there was some hope that the Republicans—presumably more willing than Democrats to reduce government spending—would actually deliver the promised cuts. But when it came to Department of Defense spending, the pork not only remained untrimmed, it actually grew larger.

There is no single accepted definition of what constitutes pork-barrel spending in the defense budget. Sometimes the defense budget is used as a massive federal jobs program that particularly favors the states or districts of members of Congress who sit on the relevant committees. The pork can include such items as unnecessary weapons programs and military bases that are not needed for national security but remain open to provide economic benefits to the surrounding communities. Corporate welfare, in the form of subsidies to defense contractors, is another example of pork-barrel spending. In addition, the defense budget includes programs that are not even marginally related to national security, which should either be eliminated or moved to the relevant budget classification.

Above and beyond the Call of the Pentagon

The 104th Congress added $6.9 billion in additional appropriations to the Pentagon's fiscal year 1996 budget and $11 billion more than the $254 billion the Clinton administration requested to the FY97 military budget. According to an assessment by the Pentagon comptroller, only about half the extra dollars Congress has added for weapons purchases accelerate programs already budgeted in long-range service plans. Of the remainder, about $3.3 billion, or 46.6 percent, qualifies as pork for programs not budgeted beyond FY97.

Much of the extra money was added to weapons systems the Pentagon did not request. Despite the fact that the administration does not want more funding for the B-2 bomber, for example, the FY97 authorization act added $212 million for it. Congress also added $539 million for the Aegis destroyer and $799 million for the New Attack Submarine.

The FY97 authorization act also added $82 million to the administration's request for B-1B bomber upgrades. That is a particularly wasteful expenditure. The Pentagon considers the B-1B's current capability sufficient to interdict enemy targets. Moreover, the General Accounting Office and the Air Force estimate that the modified B-1B would strike only a very small percentage of the Air Force's designated targets, and Unified Command officers have said they would use far fewer B-1Bs than even the Pentagon says are necessary.

Bringing the Bacon Home

Like their Democratic colleagues, most Republicans are reluctant to cut pork-barrel spending that benefits their constituents. In 1996 the services produced, at the request of the House National Security Procurement Subcommittee, chaired by Rep. Duncan Hunter (R-Calif.), a telephone book–sized list of military programs and the congressional districts that benefit from them. Such documents enable members of Congress to determine exactly how many jobs are created or preserved by proposed increases in military spending. Spending on the Javelin hand-held, anti-tank missile built by Texas Instruments in Lewisville, Texas, for example, would help preserve 556 jobs in the district of Rep. Dick Armey (R-Tex.), the House Majority Leader. Even the most ardent budget cutters find projects that so clearly benefit their districts almost irresistible.

Pushing pork into the Pentagon budget is not a practice reserved solely for Congress. Presidential candidates can be equally enthusiastic proponents of pork-barrel spending, especially in states rich in electoral votes. In 1992 Clinton promised to fund the V-22 tilt-rotor aircraft—which the Pentagon itself recommended killing—and carried Pennsylvania, the state in which it is produced and which has 23 electoral votes. Clinton also promised funding for the Seawolf submarine, which the Bush administration had tried to kill. Construction of the Seawolf is important to jobs in Connecticut and Rhode Island, two states that Clinton needed to carry and did. Nineteen ninety-six was no different. Clinton traveled to California to promise full funding for the C-17 cargo aircraft, a major jobs program in Southern California, while Bob Dole barnstormed California promising to build an additional 20 B-2 stealth bombers.

Wasteful military spending is hardly a new topic, but its perennial appearance in the DoD budget is embarrassing for the Republicans to explain—especially when they defend pork-barrel programs even as they argue that national defense is underfunded. One of the few legislators willing to blow the whistle on such hypocrisy is Sen. John McCain (R-Ariz.), who, along with Rep. David Minge (D-Minn.), chairs a congressional porkbusters coalition. McCain notes that Congress has added nearly $1 billion per year in unrequested military construction projects since FY90. The FY97 military construction appropriations bill exceeded the administration's request by $900 million in the House version and by $700 million in the Senate. Representative Minge points out that the House version of the bill included $300 million for 42 projects not on the Pentagon's long-range plan. Sen. John Glenn (D-Ohio) states, "Most of these things . . . do not even deserve to be talked about . . . as being necessary. Most of them are add-ons that are favors to particular Members, and we know it, and anybody who works on this legislation knows it."

At a minimum, Congress needs to take seriously its own criteria for considering military construction projects. Only projects that the armed services consider mission-essential—that address a serious quality-of-life issue or a significant operational deficiency—should be considered for funding. And even those projects should receive appropriations only after the project is programmed and a site identified. Other military construction add-ons are most likely pure pork.

Thus far, however, there has been precious little real debate on the use of the Pentagon budget as an all-purpose pork barrel. When the House of Representatives brought the defense authorization bill to the floor for a vote, not a single amendment was permitted that would have cut either overall spending or funding for a specific weapons program. (Instead, the debate centered around such "vital" issues as the sale of pornography in military compounds.)

Nondefense Spending

One major source of pork-barrel spending in the military budget is the array of items that have nothing to do with defense. The FY97 DoD appropriations conference agreement includes numerous examples of nondefense spending.

Nondefense Spending in DoD Budget

- $1 million for the Harnett County School Board in Lillington, North Carolina
- $3.4 million for medical research performed by "private-sector or nonfederal physicians who have used and will use the antibacterial treatment method based on the excretion of dead and decaying spherical bacteria"
- $1 million for an off-island leave program for Johnston Atoll employees
- $8 million for mitigation of environmental impacts on Indian lands
- $2 million for the National Automotive Center
- $100 million for breast cancer research
- $45 million for prostate cancer research

Many of the nonmilitary items in the Pentagon budget do not merit federal funding at all. Even items that constitute the legitimate use of taxpayer funds, however, should not be included in the military budget unless they are defense related.

Prime Porkers

The uses and abuses of military pork range from the merely ridiculous to the utterly outrageous. Some of the more prominent recent items are discussed next.

Civilian Marksmanship Program

The Army continues to spend from $2 million to $4 million per year on the 100-year-old civilian marksmanship program, which now subsidizes National Rifle Association shooting competitions. Instead of terminating the program, as the Army recommended, Congress plans to help establish the Corporation for the Promotion of Rifle Practice by giving away $80 million worth of Army rifles, ammo, cars, computers, and a one-time cash infusion. Congress should terminate Army sponsorship of the program.

Operational Support Airlift

Operational Support Airlift, the Pentagon's VIP air fleet, is far larger than any conceivable wartime need requires. That leads to frequent abuse of the approximately 500-craft fleet, which costs $378 million per year to maintain. The most famous example is Air Force Gen. Joseph Ashy's 1994 flight, with an aide and a pet cat, on a military transport from Italy to Colorado, at a cost of $120,000. The trip would have cost no more than $5,300 on a commercial carrier. Also popular are helicopter rides from Andrews Air Force Base to the Pentagon (a 20- to 30-minute cab ride) at a cost of $400 to $1,600 per flight. Both the General Accounting Office and the 1995 Roles and Missions Commission have documented that the size of the fleet is excessive even for wartime needs. The OSA should be reduced by at least 25 percent.

Grade Creep in the Services

There appears to be a trend in the services toward adding general and flag-rank officers, despite a reduction in military personnel overall. In July 1996, for example, the Marine Corps succeeded in getting 12 new general officer positions authorized—giving them a total of 80 generals for 174,000 Marines—despite the opposition of Sen. Charles Grassley (R-Iowa), who noted that the Marine Corps used to manage 199,000 troops with only

121

70 generals. (Indeed, the 1996 increase gives the Marine Corps one more general than it had at the end of World War II, when there were 495,000 Marines.) More generals mean more desk jobs, more support staff, more bureaucracy, more perks, and, of course, the spending of more taxpayer money.

According to a Senate Armed Services Committee report, the Marines argued that they needed to add 12 more flag officers in order to "have greater representation at the general officer level on the Department of Navy/Secretariat staff and in the joint arena." In other words, the new generals are not intended for combat leadership but to do battle for programs and money at the Pentagon and other joint service headquarters.

Now the race is on. An unidentified Pentagon official has said that the current 865 generals and admirals are not enough to do the Pentagon's work. While the Army and Air Force have not weighed in yet, the Navy's personnel chief told Congress his service needs 25 to 30 more admirals to avoid gaps in flag positions. Without more admirals, however, the Navy would have to put captains in admirals' slots—which would save money because captains are paid less than admirals. It would also ensure that prospective flag officers could perform as admirals before being promoted.

Instead of permitting such self-serving institutional grade creep, Congress should cut the number of current top brass by 25 percent, as called for in the FY97 Defense Authorization Act. That would help rectify the problem of top-heavy services, which has emerged since overall active-duty forces have been reduced by more than one-third since 1991.

National Defense Sealift Fund

Another prime example of pork is the National Defense Sealift Fund, a little-known account that is emerging as a major source of business for Gulf Coast and southern California shipyards. The account finances construction and conversion of vessels on which the military can preposition weapons and materiel around the world for rapid deployment. Beginning in 1994, Congress, on its own initiative, began adding funds for a prepositioning force of three ships not requested by the Pentagon but strongly backed by the Marines and a number of shipyards. The *Washington Post* reported in June 1996 that the House Appropriations Committee added another $250 million to the Pentagon budget for work on the ships for the Marines. The committee also doubled the request for Army sealift, approving $1.2 billion to pay for four ships in FY97, instead of the two the administration had requested. In the FY98 budget the funds for this account should be returned to 1996 levels.

Pork to the Private Sector

Although, strictly speaking, federal subsidies to arms contractors who sell their weapons overseas are not entirely Pentagon pork—as some of the subsidies come from the budgets of departments such as State and Commerce—the DoD is the main justification for and the prime protector of the subsidies. The United States is the number-one subsidizer of arms exports in the world, employing nearly 6,500 full-time personnel to promote and implement overseas arms sales.

A recent study by the World Policy Institute detailed the cost of providing such welfare to weapons dealers. The study found that subsidies for arms exports totaled more than $7.6 billion in 1995—an increase of nearly 10 percent over 1994—making them the second largest subsidy for business in the entire federal budget. That figure includes loans, grants, giveaways, and promotional activities.

Welfare for arms dealers includes such items as the establishment of a Center for Defense Trade at the State Department; the Commerce Department's Office of Strategic Industries, which helps U.S. military contractors market their wares around the world; the financing of exhibitions for U.S. contractors at overseas air shows; Foreign Military Financing of $3.1 billion per year; Excess Defense Articles giveaways; waivers for research-and-development recoupment fees; the newly established Defense Financing Facility, which gives loan guarantees to foreign customers who purchase U.S. weapons; and Economic Support Funds of $2.1 billion per year.

The cost of those programs equaled more than one-half of the value of all U.S. arms exports in 1995. Moreover, subsidies are scheduled to increase; thus the majority of U.S. weapons sales for the rest of this century will be paid for by American taxpayers, not foreign customers.

Even worse, many of the subsidies support sales of weapons to countries that cannot pay for them, meaning that American taxpayers pick up the whole tab. Since 1991, for example, the U.S. government has written off nearly $10 billion in arms-related loans to such nations as Egypt, Iraq, Niger, and Senegal. Such arms subsidies are one of the most egregious examples of pork-barrel defense spending. Instead of increasing, such subsidies should be eliminated immediately. That would save taxpayers billions of dollars per year. Moreover, it would most likely slow regional arms races and reduce the likelihood that U.S. troops will in the future face enemies that possess American weapons courtesy of U.S. taxpayers.

Suggested Readings

Capaccio, Tony. "Half of Hill's Weapons Adds Could Qualify as 'Pork.' " *Defense Week,* June 17, 1996.

"Congressional Summer Games: Members of Congress Go for the Gold-Plated Pork in the Pentagon Budget." Council for a Livable World Education Fund Online, August 1996. At http://www.clw.org/pub/clw/ef/follies/bloat.vot.html

Diamond, John. "Report Reveals Where GOP 'Pork' May Go." *Army Times,* June 17, 1996.

Evans, David. "Business as Usual." *Proceedings*, October 1995.

The FY 1996 Military Construction Budget: Business As Usual? Washington: Business Executives for National Security, July 28, 1995.

"The Military Budget." In *Cato Handbook for Congress: 104th Congress.* Washington: Cato Institute, 1995.

Morgan, Dan. "Defense Budget Additions Buoy Sun Belt Shipyards." *Washington Post,* June 30, 1996.

Pincus, Walter, and Dan Morgan. "Defense Budget 'Add-Ons' (or Pork and Pet Projects) Manage to Survive." *Washington Post,* July 19, 1996.

—Prepared by David Isenberg

9. Corporate Welfare

Congress should

- terminate programs that provide direct grants to businesses;
- eliminate programs that provide research and other services for industries;
- end programs that provide subsidized loans or insurance to businesses;
- eliminate trade barriers designed to protect U.S. firms in specific industries from foreign competition at the expense of higher prices for American consumers;
- base defense procurement contract decisions on national security needs, not on the number of jobs created in key members' districts; and
- eliminate the income tax loopholes carved out solely for specific companies or industries and substantially lower the tax rate so that there is no net revenue increase.

The federal government currently spends roughly $75 billion a year on programs that provide subsidies to private businesses. Two years ago both Congress and the Clinton administration pledged to attack that pervasive corporate safety net. They have had very little success. Virtually every corporate welfare program that existed in 1994 is still squandering taxpayer dollars today. Many have had their budgets increased. If the size and cost of the federal government are ever going to be reduced, those taxpayer rip-offs must be eliminated.

What Is Corporate Welfare?

It seems as if everyone is opposed to corporate welfare. The problem is that not everyone defines it in the same way. Corporate welfare should be carefully defined as any government spending program that provides unique benefits or advantages to specific companies or industries. That includes programs that provide direct grants to businesses, programs that provide research and other services for industries, and programs that provide subsidized loans or insurance to companies.

There are more than 100 such corporate subsidy programs in the federal budget today, with annual expenditures of roughly $75 billion. Terminating those programs could save taxpayers more than $400 billion over the next five years.

Some analysts employ a broader definition of corporate welfare that includes targeted corporate tax loopholes. But allowing corporations to keep more of their own earnings is not a form of welfare. It is their money, after all. To label such loopholes as welfare, one essentially must maintain that all money belongs to the government, and thus any portion that government allows you to keep is a gift.

Furthermore, simply closing tax loopholes without simultaneously reducing tax rates would put billions more dollars into the hands of the federal government. American businesses are certainly oversubsidized, but they are also overtaxed and overregulated. The last thing we need is a tax hike.

Nevertheless, targeted tax breaks are certainly bad policy. Because they provide special treatment for politically powerful industries, such tax breaks run counter to the notion that all taxpayers should be treated the same.

Furthermore, targeted tax breaks create distortions in the workings of the economy. Government steps in and creates an uneven playing field by granting tax breaks to particular industries. As a result, our economy's resources do not go toward their most efficient use, which makes it more difficult for America's businesses to be successful.

While targeted tax breaks are not corporate welfare, they are bad policy and should be eliminated. However, such tax reform should only be done on a revenue-neutral basis, or preferably as a net tax cut. That is, since closing loopholes broadens the tax base, tax rates must be correspondingly reduced to avoid an overall increase in taxes.

Categories of Corporate Welfare

Working from the definition of corporate welfare as ''any government spending program that provides unique benefits or advantages to specific companies or industries,'' we identify three main categories of corporate welfare.

Direct Grants to Businesses

Perhaps the most egregious example of corporate welfare is the Agriculture Department's $100 million a year Market Access Program (formerly Market Promotion Program). Created in 1985, MAP gives taxpayer dollars to exporters of food and other agricultural products to offset the costs of their overseas advertising campaigns. Though there is an amendment offered to defund this program every year, it has somehow managed to survive.

Another example is the Commerce Department's Advanced Technology Program ($200 million a year), which gives research grants to consortiums of some of the nation's largest high-tech companies. Those grants allow private companies to use taxpayer dollars to help them develop and bring to market profitable new products.

Programs That Provide Research and Other Services for Industries

The Agriculture Department's Agricultural Research Service ($700 million a year) conducts research focused on increasing the productivity of the nation's land and water resources, improving the quality of agricultural products, and finding new uses for those products. Those activities enhance the profitability of one specific private industry, the agricultural industry.

The Energy Department's Energy Supply Research and Development Program ($2.7 billion a year) aims to develop new energy technologies and improve on existing technologies. Its activities include applied research-and-development projects and demonstration ventures in partnership with private-sector firms.

The Commerce Department's National Oceanic and Atmospheric Administration ($1.9 billion a year) provides services such as mapping, charting, and weather forecasting that are beneficial to specific private industries. Furthermore, those services are already being provided by the private sector.

Programs That Provide Subsidized Loans or Insurance to Businesses

The Export-Import Bank ($700 million a year) uses taxpayer dollars to provide subsidized financing to foreign purchasers of U.S. goods. Its activities include making direct loans to those buyers at below-market interest rates, guaranteeing the loans of private institutions to those buyers, and providing export credit insurance to exporters and private lenders.

Similarly, the Overseas Private Investment Corporation ($70 million a year) provides direct loans, guaranteed loans, and political risk insurance to U.S. firms that invest in developing countries.

---

12 Worst Corporate Welfare Programs

- Market Access Program (Agriculture Department)
- Advanced Technology Program (Commerce Department)
- Technology Reinvestment Project (Defense Department)
- Export Enhancement Program (Agriculture Department)
- Maritime Administration Operating-Differential Subsidies
- Forest Service road and trail construction
- Export-Import Bank
- Overseas Private Investment Corporation
- International Trade Administration
- Small Business Administration
- Energy Supply Research and Development
- Agricultural Research Service

The Problem with Corporate Welfare

Corporate welfare programs are often purported to be pro-business. They are not. Such programs do nothing to promote a freer economy. They make it less free. Here are seven reasons why such policies are misguided and dangerous:

1. **The federal government has a disappointing record of picking industrial winners and losers.** The average delinquency rate for government loan programs (8 percent) is almost three times higher than that for commercial lenders (3 percent). The Small Business Administration delinquency rate reached over 20 percent in the 1980s, and the Farmers Home Administration delinquency rate has approached 50 percent.

2. **Corporate welfare is a huge drain on the federal treasury.** Every year $75 billion of taxpayer money is spent on programs that subsidize businesses. Meanwhile, politicians proclaim that we can't afford a tax cut.

3. **Corporate welfare creates an uneven playing field.** By giving selected businesses and industries special advantages, corporate subsidies put businesses and industries that are less politically well connected at a disadvantage.

4. **Corporate welfare fosters an incestuous relationship between business and government.** All too often, the firms and industries that contribute the most to political campaign coffers are the largest recipients of government handouts.
5. **Corporate welfare programs are anti-consumer.** For instance, the Commerce Department has estimated that the sugar subsidy program costs consumers several billion dollars a year in higher prices.
6. **Corporate welfare is anti-capitalist.** As Wall Street financier Theodore J. Forstmann has put it, corporate welfare has led to the creation in America of the "statist businessman," who has been converted from a capitalist into a lobbyist.
7. **Corporate welfare is unconstitutional.** Corporate subsidy programs lie outside Congress's limited spending authority under the Constitution. Nowhere in the Constitution is Congress granted the authority to spend taxpayer dollars to subsidize the computer industry, or to enter into joint ventures with automobile companies, or to guarantee loans to favored business owners.

The central premise behind corporate welfare programs is that the best way to enhance business profitability is to do so one firm at a time. In fact, the best thing government can do to promote economic growth is to simply get out of the way and let private entrepreneurs with their own capital at risk determine how the economy's resources will be directed. That means creating a level playing field, which minimizes government interference in the marketplace, and dramatically reducing the overall cost and regulatory burden of government. Terminating the dozens of ridiculous corporate welfare programs and reforming the tax code are essential parts of bringing that about.

Suggested Readings

Moore, Stephen, and Dean Stansel. "Ending Corporate Welfare As We Know It." Cato Institute Policy Analysis no. 225, May 12, 1995.
_____. "How Corporate Welfare Won: Clinton and Congress Retreat from Cutting Business Subsidies." Cato Institute Policy Analysis no. 254, May 15, 1996.
Shapiro, Robert. "Cut and Invest: A Budget Strategy for the New Economy." Progressive Policy Institute Policy Report no. 23, March 1995.

—Prepared by Dean Stansel

10. Replace the Tax System

Congress should

- repeal the capital gains tax, or at least index gains for inflation;
- abolish the federal estate tax;
- outlaw the passage of all retroactive taxes;
- end the withholding tax;
- send an annual tax disclosure form to all taxpayers;
- require a supermajority vote to raise taxes;
- abolish the Internal Revenue Service's lifestyle audit;
- enact a 25 percent "alternative maximum tax" for individuals and businesses; and
- replace the income tax with a national sales tax and close down the IRS.

Perhaps the single most urgent policy initiative for the 105th Congress is to replace America's arcane, anachronistic, and anti-growth tax code. Jimmy Carter had it right 20 years ago when he described the U.S. income tax system as a "disgrace to the human race."

The income tax system is unsalvageable. We have to start all over. Congress has "reformed" the tax system 31 times in the past 40 years—or once every 1.3 years on average. The code remains as unwieldy today as ever. Hundreds of thousands of small businesses pay more in tax preparation costs than they pay in taxes. Dale Jorgenson, chairman of the Economics Department at Harvard, calculates that moving to a flat rate tax on consumption would raise as much revenue as the current income tax system while increasing economic growth by more than $200 billion. That translates into an increase in average household income of more than $2,000 a year.

The personal income tax, the corporate income tax, the estate tax, and the capital gains tax would be replaced with a simple flat rate national retail sales tax. A sales tax rate of 15 percent could fully replace all of the revenues from the current income tax. With increased economic growth and appropriate spending cuts, the sales tax rate could be reduced to 10 to 12 percent after five years.

Defects of the Current Tax System

The current federal income tax system is harmful to our economy and our civil society in a variety of ways.

First and most obviously, taxes are too high. A founding principle of this nation was the idea of "no taxation without representation." The tragedy is that today we have immeasurably more taxation with representation than we ever had without representation. In 1900 the average U.S. household surrendered $1,500 a year in taxes. In 1950 that figure had risen to $7,000. In 1995 the average household paid nearly $20,000 in taxes.

The share of workers' paychecks devoted to federal, state, and local taxes rose from about 11 percent in 1930 to about 23 percent in 1950 to just shy of 40 percent in 1995. Figure 10.1 from the Tax Foundation shows that taxes now take a larger share of family income than food, clothing, and medicine combined.

Second, economically destructive tax rates are discouraging savings, investment, and work. George Hatsopoulos, chairman of Thermo Electron Corporation in Massachusetts, summarized the problem concisely: "The tax system of the United States is a major contributor to three of the most important economic problems confronting our country: (1) a disastrous rate of national savings, (2) a non-ending trade imbalance, and (3) a declining rate of investment."

It was never supposed to be this way. The very first income tax in 1913 had rates ranging from 1 to 7 percent—with the highest rate applying only to Americans who had the equivalent of a $5 million or more income today. Table 10.1 compares the original income tax with what it has become today. A proposed provision of the Sixteenth Amendment to cap the tax rate permanently at 10 percent was defeated on assurances that the language was unnecessary because the tax rate would never exceed that amount. As early as 1917, the start of World War I, the top marginal rate was raised to 67 percent, although it fell after the war. In 1944, during World War II, the top marginal rate was raised to 94 percent. In other words, the government took 94 cents of every additional dollar earned and the worker kept 6 cents. Today, the top tax rate stands at 42 percent.

Figure 10.1
Representative Budget of Two-Income Family, 1995

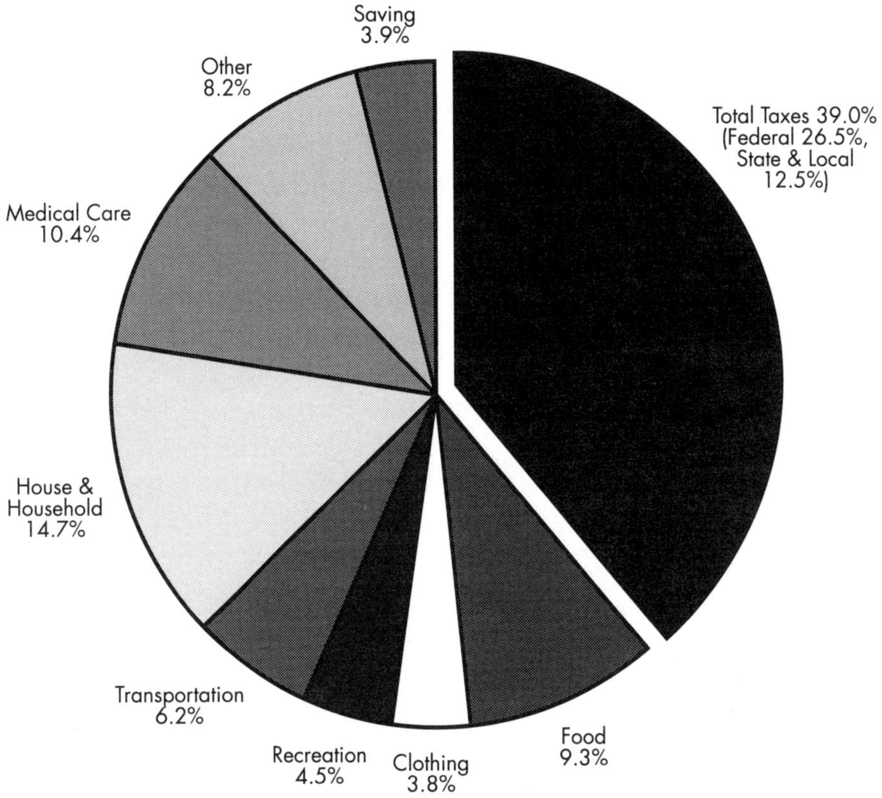

Saving
3.9%

Other
8.2%

Total Taxes 39.0%
(Federal 26.5%,
State & Local
12.5%)

Medical Care
10.4%

House &
Household
14.7%

Transportation
6.2%

Recreation
4.5%

Clothing
3.8%

Food
9.3%

SOURCE: Tax Foundation, 1996.

Some economists resist the notion that high tax rates are economically harmful, but it was President John F. Kennedy who eloquently warned of the perils of soak-the-rich tax policies some 30 years ago when he unveiled his own tax cut plan:

> An economy hampered with restrictive tax rates will never produce enough revenue to balance the budget, just as it will never produce enough jobs.

It is instructive to note that America has experienced three periods of very strong economic growth in modern times: the 1920s, the 1960s, and the 1980s. Each of those growth spurts coincided with reductions in marginal tax rates. In 1923, after the end of World War I, President Calvin Coolidge cut income tax rates. In 1964 the Kennedy tax cut lowered the

Table 10.1
The First and Last Income Tax

	1914	1994
Income taxes paid (billions of 1994 dollars)	$6.7	$683.4
Per capita income taxes (1994 dollars)	$69	$2,622
Individual tax filers	360,000	113,829,000
Percentage of population filing returns	0.5%	45%
IRS budget (millions of 1994 dollars)	$110	$7,100
IRS employees	4,000	110,000
Pages of federal tax law	14	9,400
Pages of IRS forms	4	4,000
Top tax rate	7%	40%
Tax rate on median family	0%	28%

SOURCES: Cato Institute and *Harper's Magazine*, April 1977, p. 22.

top income tax rate from 91 percent to 70 percent. In 1981 Ronald Reagan cut tax rates 25 percent across the board, chopping the top tax rate from 70 to 50 percent (which was then lowered to 28 percent in 1986). What was the result?

- In the six years after the 1923 tax cuts, the American economy grew by 5 percent per year, and tax revenues nearly doubled.
- In the seven years after the Kennedy tax cuts, the economy grew by 5 percent per year, and income tax revenues climbed by 80 percent.
- In the seven years after the 1981 Reagan tax cuts, the economy grew by 4 percent per year, and federal revenues grew by 75 percent. The percentage of households with incomes above $50,000 rose from 18 percent to 23.5 percent.

After both the Kennedy and the Reagan tax rate cuts, federal revenues paid by the wealthiest Americans actually *increased.* After the Kennedy tax cuts in 1963, which lowered the top income tax rate from 90 to 70 percent, taxable income reported by the richest Americans rose by 40 percent. Between 1980 and 1990, the top income tax rate was chopped from 70 percent to 28 percent. Over that same period, the share of income taxes paid by the wealthy increased from 18 percent of the total in 1980 to 26 percent in 1990. In fact, real federal revenues increased by 24 percent in the seven years after the Reagan tax cuts (1982–89). They will have increased by only 20 percent in the seven years after the Bush and Clinton tax hikes (1990–97). That suggests that tax rates today are too high to expand the economy and to balance the budget.

The economic evidence suggests that nations with flat and low marginal income tax rates outperform neighboring countries with steeply progressive tax systems. Economists at the World Bank, hardly a bastion of supply-side orthodoxy, examined evidence dating back to 1870 and discovered "a negative association between economic growth and . . . the marginal tax rate." The world's fastest growing economy over the past 20 years, Hong Kong, has the lowest marginal tax rates (15 percent maximum) on labor and capital.

A third defect of the tax system is that it has become a labyrinth of complexity. Jack Valenti, president of the Motion Picture Association of America, recently complained, "No other nation relies on such a cluttered mess of rules and regulations that are both contradictory and abrasive. We have given birth to a priesthood of lawyers and accountants who gravely inspect the entrails of our tax system and then charge outrageous prices for the knowledge they alone possess."

Just how unfathomable is the tax system? David Brinkley, in his recently published memoirs, cited this example from an instruction booklet for tax-payers:

> Subparagraph B in Section 1 G 7, relating to income included on parents' returns, is amended (1) by striking $1,000 in clause i and inserting twice the amount described in 4 A ii and (2) by amending subclause capital (II) of clause small ii. . . .

That tortured language is surely not English. It is perhaps comprehensible to a small handful of lawyers on Capitol Hill and well-paid accountants and tax attorneys. But it is gobbledygook to most other Americans.

That is just one tiny example. Here's another. During a 1995 hearing before the House Ways and Means Committee on the U.S. income tax system, the chief tax counsel for Mobil Oil Corporation brought to the House office building a six-foot-high stack of bound papers. They weighed 150 pounds. They were Mobil Oil's tax forms for fiscal year 1993. It cost Mobil an estimated $15 million and more than 100 full-time man-years just to figure out how much they owed in taxes. Mobil is not unique. In 1994 the Internal Revenue Service received nearly 1 billion form 1099s as part of the government's effort to track income from dividends and interest and other forms of business income. Dick Armey has calculated that "the IRS sends out eight billion pages of forms and instructions each year, which if you laid them end to end would stretch 28 times the circumference of the earth."

Economist James L. Payne, author of *Costly Returns,* has calculated that American workers and businesses spend at least 5.4 billion man-hours a year figuring out their taxes. That is more man-hours than it takes to build every car, van, and truck manufactured in the United States. Sen. Richard Lugar (R-Ind.), an advocate of the national sales tax, reports that more man-hours are used each year to figure out taxes than are worked by every resident of his state of Indiana. Estimates of the dead-weight economic loss attributable to the complexity of the tax system range from $75 billion to $200 billion a year, or as much as $2,000 for every household in America.

Despite countless efforts at tax "simplification," most Americans do not view the tax code as user friendly. The *average* fee for preparation of a tax return is now almost $200. IRS data confirm that in 1992 more than 50 million individual returns were done by tax preparers at an average fee of $200. Eighty percent of those using professional preparers have incomes below $50,000 of adjusted gross income, according to tax litigation consultant Dan Pilla, author of *How to Fire the IRS. Money* magazine discovered in 1991 that 70 percent of the members of Congress on the two major tax-writing committees—House Ways and Means and Senate Finance—could not figure out their own returns and used professional tax preparers. All told, Americans spend about $30 billion a year for the services of tax accountants and lawyers. Those services do not add to the nation's wealth; they deplete it.

Perhaps the most troublesome consequence of our modern income tax system is the enormous investigative and prosecutorial powers we have conferred on the IRS. Constitutional rights to privacy are routinely subverted by the IRS. Today, without a search warrant, the IRS has the right to search the property and financial documents of American citizens. Without a trial, the IRS has the right to seize property from Americans—and it does so routinely. In 1994 the IRS was forced to acknowledge that hundreds of auditors were illegally scouring through the returns of American citizens. Congress has done nothing; our elected officials routinely turn a blind eye to the IRS's abuses.

136

No campaign against the excesses of big government in Washington is complete without a revamping of the IRS. Investigative reporter David Burnham reports, "The IRS is twice as big as the CIA and five times larger than the FBI. The IRS controls more information about more Americans than any other governmental agency. . . . With its unequaled authority to seize property and its unparalleled access to financial records, the IRS has become the nation's single most powerful instrument of social control."

The IRS has broad prosecutorial powers and can gain access to the most personal and private financial information of Americans. Today banks, investment houses, and employers are required to report 81 specific types of personal financial transactions.

Unfortunately, the IRS is one of the most error prone of all federal agencies. A recent Cato Institute study by Daniel Pilla finds that IRS information supplied to taxpayers is wrong about 20 percent of the time. When challenged, the IRS has been found to overcharge taxpayers an average of $2,000 per return. Yet in tax court the burden is on the individual to prove that the government is wrong in its assessment and fines.

No other institution is as great a threat to our civil liberties as the IRS. Its abuses will surely continue as long as we retain an income tax system.

Tax Reform in the 105th Congress

To make the tax system fairer, simpler, less intrusive, and more pro-growth, Congress should adopt nine reforms.

Abolish, or at Least Index, the Capital Gains Tax

The capital gains tax is an assault on the American dream. It is a tax penalty imposed on those who risk their money to start a business, operate a farm or ranch, invest in stocks, or build a better life for themselves and their families.

The capital gains tax also places the United States at a huge competitive disadvantage in the global race for capital compared to most of our international rivals. Almost no other developed nation punishes investment and capital formation as much as the United States. For example, the long-term capital gains tax rate in the United States is 28 percent; in Japan it is 20 percent; in France it is 18 percent; and in Germany it is 8 percent.

Although many Democrats complain that a capital gains tax cut is an "unfair" benefit to the rich, the truth is that 70 percent of the tax returns that show capital gains are from Americans with adjusted gross incomes below $70,000.

The capital gains tax is a grossly unfair tax for another reason as well. More than two-thirds of the taxes paid are on gains due purely to inflation. To understand the extent of the capital gains inflation penalty, consider the following hypothetical case. If an investor purchased $10,000 of stock in 1970 as a nest egg for retirement, and that stock appreciated in value at the same rate as the Dow Jones industrial average over the next 20 years, then by 1992 it would have had a value of roughly $31,000. Yet just to keep up with inflation over that 20-year period, the stock would have had to have been worth $34,000 in 1992. In other words, when inflation is accounted for, this investor suffered a real loss of $3,000 ($31,000 − $34,000). But Uncle Sam requires this investor to pay a $5,700 capital "gains" tax on his investment, *even though it lost money relative to inflation.* Hence, the real tax rate on the investment is over 100 percent! At the very least, such unfairness should be ended by indexing capital gains for inflation.

But ultimately, the tax on capital formation should be eliminated. That would liberate capital that could be reinvested in entrepreneurial, start-up businesses—the very kinds of businesses that might just be the next Microsoft or find a cure for AIDS.

Eliminate the Estate Tax

The U.S. estate tax is even more indefensible than the capital gains tax. The tax today brings in only $12 billion—or less than 1 percent of total federal revenues. Yet taxpayers spend many times that amount of money in estate planning to avoid paying the tax. The major victims of the 55 percent estate tax are small business owners, farmers, and others with medium-sized estates. Often family businesses have to be dismantled or sold to meet estate tax obligations. A 1993 study by economist Richard Wagner of George Mason University calculates that the federal government would collect more tax revenue over time if it simply abolished the estate tax altogether.

Outlaw the Passage of All Retroactive Taxes

One of the most offensive features of the 1993 Clinton tax hike was the retroactivity of the income and estate tax increases. Those kinds of unannounced retroactive tax hikes amount to nothing more than a partial government taking of private property. One might expect such seizures of money and property from the governments of authoritarian nations, but not in a constitutional democracy like the United States. James Madison described retroactive laws as "contrary to the principle of the social compact." Congress should consider legislation, introduced in 1995 by Sen. Paul Coverdell of Georgia, that would permanently ban the imposition of retroactive taxes.

End the Withholding Tax

The withholding tax was introduced in 1943 as part of the war effort to facilitate the collection of taxes at a time when even clergymen and Disney's Mickey Mouse were enlisted by the U.S. government to increase Americans' tax payments. Legislators spoke openly of taxes that needed to be "fried out of the taxpayers." One senator cheered the provision as a way to "get the greatest amount of money with the least amount of squawks."

Withholding was of dubious constitutionality during a period of crisis, such as war, but during normal times it is clearly an excessive power of government. The central objection to withholding is that it is the ultimate hidden tax. People don't miss what they don't see. Many Americans even regard the check they get that refunds excess money withheld as a gift from government. Income taxes should be paid monthly, or at the end of the year, by the earner's writing a check to the IRS, as proposed by Rep. Cliff Stearns (R-Fla.). That would allow Americans to calculate on a regular basis whether they are getting their money's worth from government.

Send an Annual Tax Disclosure Form to All Taxpayers

Each year when the IRS sends its tax forms to American families, it should be required to send a tax disclosure form listing all federal taxes and estimating all state taxes paid by the family in the previous year. The taxes listed would include federal income taxes; Social Security taxes (both employer and employee share); and estimates of state income, sales, and gas taxes. That also would allow Americans to see how much they pay each year for government.

Require a Supermajority Vote to Raise Taxes

Several states, including Arizona, California, and Nevada, have adopted measures requiring that any tax increase by the legislature pass by a two-thirds vote in both houses. Such a measure is needed at the federal level. It should apply to *all* tax increases, not just income tax hikes. A two-thirds-vote requirement for tax increases would allow Congress to raise taxes during time of war or national crisis but would help prevent the routine tax hikes that have been enacted in Washington over the past 20 years.

End the IRS's Lifestyle Audit

No feature of the IRS's broad investigative powers is more of an assault on privacy rights than the lifestyle audit, first launched in 1994. Under the new auditing procedure, the tax collectors will now ask taxpayers intimate questions about their lifestyles and spending behavior that have little or nothing to do with the financial information contained on the tax forms. What schools do your children attend? Where did you go for vacation last year? How often do you go out for dinner? What's your credit card balance?

As part of those audits, IRS examiners are now creating dossiers that profile the economic position of all American tax filers. In IRS training Aid 3302-102, titled "Components of Economic Reality," some 47 different aspects of a person's life are identified as elements of the dossier. Included are neighborhood, home, investment income, recreational vehicles, college tuition, trips, club memberships, weddings of children (perhaps Ross Perot wasn't so paranoid after all), and hobbies. Also included in the list are "level of sophistication and cultural background."

The IRS has no intention of relying solely on the citizen's own statements in creating the dossier. The IRS is lining up informants who may have information about the citizen under audit. Informants include landlords, employers, business and personal associates, ex-spouses, even next-door neighbors. In some cases the informants will be paid if the information leads to higher tax collections. The lifestyle audit is attempting to create a nation of snitches. Congress should terminate it immediately.

Enact an Alternative Maximum Tax

A March 1996 GrassRoots Research poll indicates that, by a two-to-one margin, Americans favor a constitutional amendment that would prohibit federal, state, and local taxes from taking a combined total of more than 25 percent of anyone's income.

That can be ensured through legislation creating an "alternative maximum tax." Until the income tax system is ended entirely and the Social Security system is privatized, the federal government should allow workers and businesses the option of bypassing the 9,000 pages of tax laws and instead complying with a postcard tax return with no deductions, no loopholes, and no credits. The taxpayer would simply be assessed a flat rate tax of 25 percent on total gross income as a substitute for income and payroll tax liability. Many millions of Americans who cannot take advantage of the myriad loopholes in the system now unfairly pay an average income/payroll tax rate of more than 25 percent. For millions of others, who might even pay slightly more tax under the alternative maximum tax, the savings in tax preparation costs and the lessened aggravation would make the alternative tax an attractive option. Hong Kong's highly successful flat tax is very similar in concept to this alternative maximum tax concept.

Replace the Income Tax with a National Sales Tax

There is a great debate brewing across America about whether a national sales tax or a flat tax, as Rep. Dick Armey (R-Tex.) and Steve Forbes have proposed, would be the ideal substitute for our current failed income tax system. Unquestionably, either would be vastly superior to what we have now.

But the flat tax suffers from one critical defect: it is still an income tax. As such, it does not eliminate the IRS from our lives (though it should reduce the IRS's role). It would still be the business of the government to monitor our incomes—thus impelling the government to continue to pry into the most private aspects of Americans' financial affairs. Although simpler, it would still require workers and businesses to fill out tax forms each year.

The best replacement for the income tax would be a national retail sales tax on all final-use goods and services. The retail sales tax is far preferable to the value-added tax (VAT), which is supported by many business groups in Washington and is the centerpiece of a bipartisan tax reform proposal by Sens. Pete Domenici (R-Nev.) and Sam Nunn (D-Ga.). European-style VATs have been disasters in virtually every nation in which they have been enacted. They have not increased savings rates. The tax rates have been continually raised. And, most important, they have served as engines of growth of government. That is because the VAT is a tax that is hidden from the consumer—imbedded in the costs of goods and services consumers purchase.

A recent Cato study by tax expert David Burton outlines the features of a national sales tax plan. The four components of the plan are as follows:

- **A 15 percent sales tax, which would eventually fall to 10 percent, on the final purchase of goods and services at the retail level.** The sales tax would be similar to the familiar state sales tax collected at

141

the cash register in 45 states and the District of Columbia. Intermediate purchases would be exempt. The individual and corporate income tax, the estate and gift tax, and most non-trust-fund excise taxes would be repealed. The rate should decline in future years to 10 to 12 percent as economic growth allows more revenues to be raised at a lower rate and as government spending is reduced.

- **A universal rebate for every household exempting all consumption up to the poverty level.** A national sales tax need not be regressive. By allowing the first $18,588 of consumption each year for a family of four to be tax-free, the system protects low-income families from the tax. The rebate could be provided as a credit against the payroll tax, allowing all workers to be reimbursed for any sales tax paid on consumption up to the poverty level.
- **Reimbursement to states and retailers for the cost of collecting the national sales tax.** The national sales tax should provide an administrative credit to retailers to compensate them for the cost of collecting and remitting the tax. A credit of one-half of 1 percent would reimburse retailers about $4 billion for their compliance and collection costs. In a national system administered by the states, states should be compensated for their costs.
- **Abolition of the Internal Revenue Service.** The states should be primarily responsible for administering the national sales tax since they have the most expertise in sales tax administration. The IRS would be abolished, and a much smaller, less intrusive federal excise tax bureau would collect trust fund excise taxes such as the gasoline tax. The Social Security Administration would enforce and collect payroll taxes.

Boston University economist Laurence Kotlikoff has estimated the impact of a revenue-neutral replacement of the income tax with a retail sales tax. He calculates that, after just five years, the national savings rate would rise to two and a half times its current anemic level; the capital stock would grow by 8 percent above the level attained under the current tax system; output would be 5 percent, or $500 billion, higher than otherwise.

The abolition of the income tax should no longer be viewed as a utopian fantasy but as a viable plan that is rapidly gaining political momentum. Last year Reps. Dan Schaefer (R-Colo.), Billy Tauzin (R-La.), and Dick Chrysler (R-Mich.) introduced a national sales tax bill that adopts many of the provisions noted above. Senator Lugar is likely to lead a parallel effort in the Senate.

Conclusion

The American public has quite correctly come to regard the current tax code as an arcane and unwieldy mess and the IRS as an intimidating nuisance in their lives. Almost no one—other than accountants, tax lawyers, and lobbyists, all of whom profit from the current convoluted mess—defends the tax code we now have in place.

To compete and win in the 21st century, America needs a tax system that is fair, simple, and pro-growth. The tax code ought to promote the national interest over special interests. It should be user friendly. And it ought to reward rather than punish work, saving, risk taking, and economic success. All of those objectives could be accomplished by abolishing the income tax and replacing it with a low national sales tax.

Suggested Readings

Adams, Charles. *For Good and Evil: The Impact of Taxes on the Course of Civilization.* Lanham, Md.: University Press of America, 1992.

Burton, David. ''Emancipating America from the Income Tax: How a National Sales Tax Would Work.'' Cato Institute Policy Analysis, forthcoming.

Kotlikoff, Laurence. ''The Economic Impact of Replacing Federal Income Taxes with a Sales Tax.'' Cato Institute Policy Analysis no. 193, April 15, 1993.

Lindsey, Lawrence. *The Growth Experiment: How the New Tax Policy Is Transforming the U.S. Economy.* New, York: Basic Books, 1990.

Moore, Stephen, and John Silvia. ''The ABCs of the Capital Gains Tax.'' Cato Institute Policy Analysis no. 242, October 4, 1995.

—Prepared by Stephen Moore

FEDERAL AGENCIES: THE ABOLITION AGENDA

11. Department of Education

Congress should

- abolish the Department of Education and
- return education to the state, local, or family level, as provided by the Constitution.

Education is a perfect example of one major theme of this *Handbook:* that even many vitally important things in American society are not the province of the federal government. No one questions the importance of education in a complex modern society. Education is the process by which we impart moral values to our children, make them part of our particular culture, develop their ability to think, and give them specific kinds of information that they will need to be productive adults, good citizens, and civilized human beings.

Today there is great concern about the quality of American education. Every month brings another study on how poorly American students fare in international competition. The Third International Mathematics and Science Study, released in November 1996, found that U.S. eighth-graders scored below the average of students from 40 nations on math and just above average on science. U.S. students scored lower than students from Singapore, Korea, Japan, Hungary, and other countries.

But neither the importance of education nor its poor quality means that education is an important function of the federal government. In fact, education is not mentioned in the Constitution of the United States, and for good reason. The Founders wanted most aspects of life managed by those who were closest to them, either by state or local government or by families, businesses, and other elements of civil society. Certainly, they saw no role for the federal government in education.

Once upon a time, not so very many years ago, Congress understood that. The *History of the Formation of the Union under the Constitution,* published by the United States Constitution Sesquicentennial Commission, under the direction of the president, the vice president, and the Speaker of the House in 1943, contained this exchange in a section titled "Questions and Answers Pertaining to the Constitution":

Q. Where, in the Constitution, is there mention of education?
A. There is none; education is a matter reserved for the states.

The greatest service the 105th Congress could perform for American education would be to rekindle the original understanding of the delegated, enumerated, and thus limited powers of the federal government and to return control and financing of education to states, localities, and families.

This argument is not based simply on a commitment to the original Constitution, as important as that is. It also reflects an understanding of *why* the Founders were right to reserve most subjects to state, local, or private endeavor. The Founders feared the concentration of power. They believed that the best way to protect individual freedom and civil society was to limit and divide power. Thus it was much better to have decisions made independently by 13— or 50—states, each able to innovate and to observe and copy successful innovations in other states, than to have one decision made for the entire country. As the country gets bigger and more complex, and especially as government amasses more power, the advantages of decentralization and divided power become even greater.

The science of economics was in its infancy when the Constitution was written, and modern management theory had not even been imagined. But two centuries later we can make even stronger arguments against a federal role in education. Not only is freedom safer when power is divided, we now recognize that progress is far more likely under decentralized and competitive systems than under central direction.

After state test results showed that the vast majority of California public school students could not read, write, or compute at levels considered proficient, Superintendent of Public Instruction Delaine Eastin appointed two task forces in 1995 to investigate reading and math instruction. The task forces found that for 10 years there had been a wholesale abandonment of the basics—such as phonics and arithmetic drills—in California class-rooms. It was bad enough that California taxpayers had spent more than $200 billion to impose such disastrous "reforms" on more than 4 million students. But imagine how much worse the problem would have been if the U.S. Department of Education had been able to impose such a scheme on the whole country.

Origins of the Department

Defenders of the federal role in education insist that the department has no power to impose anything on the nation's schools. It can only study, advise, inspire, and offer supplemental funding. Of course, our folk wisdom tells us that he who pays the piper calls the tune—as federal money increases, so does federal control.

When the Education Department was created in 1979, many critics warned that a secretary of education would turn into a national minister of education. Rep. John Erlenborn (R-Ill.), for instance, wrote, "There would be interference in textbook choices, curricula, staffing, salaries, the make-up of student bodies, building designs, and all other irritants that the government has invented to harass the population. These decisions which are now made in the local school or school district will slowly but surely be transferred to Washington." Dissenting from the committee report that recommended establishing the department, Erlenborn and seven other Republicans wrote, "The Department of Education will end up being the Nation's super schoolboard. That is something we can all do without."

Such concerns were not limited to Republicans. Rep. Patricia Schroeder (D-Colo.) predicted, "No matter what anyone says, the Department of Education will not just write checks to local school boards. They will meddle in everything. I do not want that." David W. Breneman and Noel Epstein wrote in the *Washington Post,* "Establishing a cabinet-level department is a back-door way of *creating* a national education policy." And Richard W. Lyman, president of Stanford University, testified before Congress that "the two-hundred-year-old absence of a Department of Education is not the result of simple failure during all that time. On the contrary, it derives from the conviction that we do not want the kinds of educational systems that such arrangements produce."

A *Washington Post* editorial raised the fear that "by sheer bureaucratic momentum, [a department of education] would inevitably erode local and state control over public schools." Another *Post* editorial reminded us, "Education remains a primary function of the states and localities, which is surely one reason this country has not had a national ministry of education as part of its political tradition. We think it is a tradition worth holding on to."

The Department Today

Eighteen years after its founding, what has the Department of Education achieved? Although its advocates promised that a cabinet-level department would be leaner and less expensive than the previous federal education programs scattered through many agencies, the department's budget has more than doubled, from $14.5 billion to $31.1 billion. John Berthoud of the Alexis de Tocqueville Institution points out that

> in the decade prior to the establishment of the Department of Education, [federal] spending on education rose at only about half the rate of the rest of the non-defense discretionary budget (35% versus 65.4%). In the period since the establishment of the department, *education* spending has risen at a rate over three times as fast as non-defense discretionary programs (29.5% versus 7.9%).

It's no wonder that the National Education Association and other professional educationists wanted to see a cabinet department for education.

It's much less clear that the department has had any positive effect on education. After a blue-ribbon commission reported in 1983 that "a rising tide of mediocrity" threatened American education, more than 250 state task forces swung into action to improve the schools. Many states adopted "comprehensive" reform packages. Almost all involved higher taxes. Indeed, there were many reforms in school *inputs:* stricter attendance rules, minimum grades required for permission to participate in extracurricular activities, longer school days, more competence testing, more homework, higher teacher pay, a longer school year—and of course more money. Yet test scores remain far lower than they were in 1963, when the long slide began.

A survey released in the fall of 1995 found that U.S. students were woefully ignorant of American history. Results of the 1994 National Assessment of Educational Progress showed that 57 percent of high school seniors scored below the "basic" level of history achievement. To achieve the "basic" level, students had to answer only 42 percent of the questions correctly. Bad as the overall results were, some of the findings raise questions about just what our teachers are trying to teach. For instance, only 39 percent of fourth-graders knew who said, "This government cannot endure half slave and half free" (Abraham Lincoln), only 41 percent knew that the Pilgrims and Puritans came to America for religious freedom, but 69 percent knew that Susan B. Anthony was famous for helping women win the right to vote. Only 47 percent of high school seniors knew that containing communism was the most important goal of U.S. foreign policy between 1945 and 1990, but nearly 70 percent knew that infectious diseases brought by European settlers were the major cause of death among American Indians in the 1600s. One might suspect that our teachers are more determined to teach feminist history and the sins of America and its Founders than the basic facts of American history and American achievements. It's fair to assume that the Department of Education has—at best—done nothing to improve that situation.

Goals 2000

The centerpiece of the Clinton administration's education efforts has been Goals 2000, a comprehensive plan to encourage states to meet eight ambitious goals originally developed by the nation's governors. The Goals 2000: Educate America Act of 1994 and its supporters repeatedly promise that it is not intended to control or direct education, only to support and encourage reform. But as Lance Izumi and Natalie Williams point out in a paper published by the Pacific Research Institute and the Claremont Institute, the Goals 2000 Act uses the word "will" at least 45 times in describing what states and local districts are expected to do to accomplish the act's goals. The more permissive "should" is used only three times. For instance, one finds such dictates as

- States and school districts will create integrated strategies. . . .
- Schools . . . will offer more adult literacy, parent training and life-long learning opportunities. . . .
- Every local educational agency will develop a sequential, comprehensive kindergarten through twelfth grade drug and alcohol prevention education program. . . .

To get federal money, states must prove that they have in place a plan that incorporates all those requirements.

Goals 2000 creates a plethora of new federal bureaucracies, including the National Education Standards and Improvement Council, the National Education Goals Panel, the National Skills Standards Board, the National Educational Research and Policy Priorities Board, the National Library of Education, the National Occupational Information Coordination Committee, and the National Education Dissemination Committee. It also provides for a network of regional educational laboratories.

The act doesn't stop at prescribing actions for states and schools. It also declares, "Every parent in the United States will be a child's first teacher and devote time each day to helping such parent's preschool child learn." A worthy goal indeed, but does the federal government intend to investigate—or require that states investigate—whether every parent in America is "devoting time each day to helping such parent's preschool

149

child learn''? Sheldon Richman writes in a study for Colorado's Independence Institute that the entire Goals 2000 program is based on the discredited philosophy that ''high-quality education in the United States requires planning and coordination by the federal and state governments.''

Discussing Goals 2000 and H.R. 6, another education bill passed by the 103rd Congress, former secretaries of education Lamar Alexander and William Bennett argue, ''It becomes plain that their authors want to substitute decisions made in Washington for decisions made by individual households and communities. . . . They use federal funding in a deceptive way that is designed to elicit the behaviors that other parts of the legislation declare to be 'voluntary.' ''

Former Department of Education official Diane Ravitch explains that the new federal standards ''would permit federal regulation of curriculum, textbooks, facilities and instructional methods. . . . The bill describes the federal 'opportunity-to-learn' standards as 'voluntary,' but litigation would quickly turn them into mandates.''

New Directions

As the world is turning away from central planning and government mandates, U.S. education policy is moving in just the opposite direction. A legitimate concern about the quality of education has been co-opted by the education establishment and turned into an excuse for more funding and more federal regulation. Amazingly, the 104th Congress actually appropriated more money for the Department of Education in fiscal year 1997 than President Clinton had requested. In a memo to department employees, Secretary of Education Richard W. Riley and Deputy Secretary Marshall S. Smith called their new budget ''a truly remarkable turn of events for the Department of Education.'' Not only did Congress give the department $26.3 billion in discretionary funds, $743 million more than the president had requested, it managed to increase funding over FY96 for several much-criticized programs:

- Goals 2000, up 40 percent
- Concentration Grants to Local Educational Agencies, up 46 percent
- Safe and Drug-Free Schools State Grants, up 26 percent
- Bilingual and Immigrant Education, up 40 percent

If money could solve the problems of American schools, surely it would have done so by now. Every legislator and education policymaker should memorize Figure 11.1. Remember, the dollars in the figure are adjusted for inflation. We're spending five times what we did 50 years ago, and more than twice what we spent, per pupil, 30 years ago when test scores started to slide.

The problem with U.S. schools is not lack of funding. The problem is that the schools are run by a bureaucratic government monopoly, which is increasingly isolated from competitive or community pressures. We expect good service from businesses because we know—and we know that they know—that we can go somewhere else if we're not happy. We instinctively know we won't get good service from the post office or the division of motor vehicles because we can't go anywhere else.

So why, on the eve of the 21st century, are we still running our schools like the post office instead of Federal Express? We need to open education to competition and let parents choose the schools they think will be best for their children, without making them pay once for government schools and again for an independent school.

You can bet that if schools had to depend on satisfying customers, there wouldn't be many that decided to skip phonics and math for 10 years—

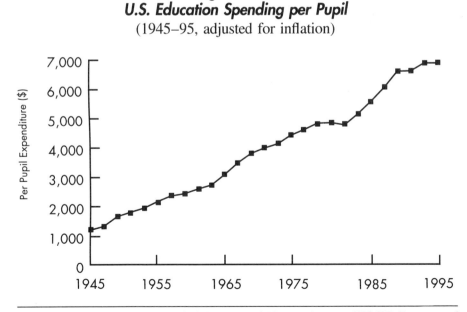

Figure 11.1
U.S. Education Spending per Pupil
(1945–95, adjusted for inflation)

Source: National Center for Education Statistics, *Digest of Education Statistics, 1995*, U.S. Department of Education, p. 163.

as California's schools did—and then say, "We made an honest mistake"—as California's superintendent of public instruction did. Long before 10 years had passed, the students and their families would have departed.

The way to improve American education is to open the system to choice and competition: Give parents the freedom to send their children to schools that they choose. Get the dynamism and innovation of the for-profit sector looking for ways to deliver more education for less money. Let a thousand experiments bloom—from charter schools to vouchers to tax credits to private management to full separation of school and state—and let families and school systems emulate the successful ones.

But here's the urgent warning to well-meaning members of Congress: *Don't do any of this at the federal level.* Don't reform education. Don't change the rules. Don't set up a demonstration project. Don't impose national standards. And by all means, don't set up a national voucher plan.

Just eliminate the Department of Education, end its meddlesome subsidies and regulations, and return its $30 billion budget to the American people in the form of a tax cut. Then let 260 million Americans decide how best to spend that money. The question isn't whether Americans will spend lots of money on education. The question is *who* will spend that money: Congress and the federal bureaucracy, state bureaucracies, local school districts, or families. The closer to the family the decisionmaking is, the more dynamic, competitive, and innovative the educational system will be.

Congress should affirm the wisdom of the Founders in not granting the federal government any power over education and return the vital function of education to the states, localities, and families where it can be managed best.

Suggested Readings

Boaz, David, ed. *Liberating Schools: Education in the Inner City.* Washington: Cato Institute, 1991.

Goldberg, Bruce. *Why Schools Fail.* Washington: Cato Institute, 1996.

Izumi, Lance T., and Natalie Williams. "Goals 2000 and California Education: Devolution in Retreat?" San Francisco: Pacific Research Institute, 1996.

Lieberman, Myron. *Public Education: An Autopsy.* Cambridge, Mass.: Harvard University Press, 1993.

Richman, Sheldon. "Why Colorado Should Drop Out of Goals 2000." Denver: Independence Institute Issue Paper, 1996.

—Prepared by David Boaz

12. Special-Interest Departments: Commerce and Labor

Congress should

- eliminate corporate subsidies provided by the Commerce Department's Economic Development Administration as well as allied independent bodies like the Small Business Administration, the Export-Import Bank, and the Overseas Private Investment Corporation;
- dismantle programs designed to inhibit trade, whether managed by the International Trade Administration or the independent International Trade Commission;
- end racial spoils programs, such as the Minority Business Development Agency;
- privatize weather forecasting and similar activities conducted by the National Oceanic and Atmospheric Administration;
- cut information collected by the Census Bureau back to the necessary minimum;
- dismantle the Commerce Department and manage the Census Bureau and Patent Office through a much smaller independent agency;
- eliminate federal training programs and the federal role in unemployment insurance;
- repeal federal regulations governing hours and wages, leaving Americans free to bargain over their terms of employment;
- take a position of neutrality between business and labor, ending restrictions on employee-employer cooperation and negotiation;
- eliminate federal oversight of the workplace, relying instead on the combination of tort law, workers' compensation programs, and market incentives to promote safety;
- merge statistical operations of the Department of Labor with the Census Bureau; and
- close down the Labor Department, shifting any remaining functions to a revamped National Labor Relations Board.

The federal government was originally conceived as an institution with limited, enumerated powers. However, over time, interest groups and politicians have cooperated in vastly expanding federal powers. The result is a growing Leviathan with a bloated bureaucracy of some 14 cabinet departments and 3 million federal employees. Indeed, raising agencies to cabinet level has become a favorite tactic for conferring political status upon influential interest groups, such as business and labor.

The Departments of Commerce and Labor are essentially payoffs to two major interest groups—businesses and labor unions. The Bureau of Labor was established in 1884, from which sprang the Department of Commerce and Labor in 1903, which was split into two separate departments a decade later. Neither reflects an appropriate use of federal power.

Department of Commerce

The Commerce Department has rightly become a symbol of corporate welfare—federal subsidies for business. Among the most egregious are the Economic Development Administration and the Advanced Technology Program. EDA is an old congressional standby, through which Congress funnels money to businesses and localities in the name of promoting economic growth in distressed areas. Yet 80 percent of the country is eligible for agency subsidies, and major retailers and hoteliers have been prime EDA beneficiaries. EDA loans have proved to be about the worst paper available: of $471 million loaned during the 1970s, only $60 million has been recovered. The agency has sought congressional approval to sell off some of its bad loans for less than a dime on the dollar.

ATP, one of the fastest growing Commerce Department programs, represents corporate welfare reinvented. ATP is supposed to promote new technological developments, as if potential sales in a $6 trillion domestic economy alone did not provide corporate America with sufficient incentive to invest in promising new technologies. The United States has been the global leader in pharmaceuticals, for instance, without government handouts. This nation also dominates the computer and software industries and has played a leading role in the information age without needing assistance from Washington.

In contrast, government has demonstrated a remarkable ability to choose losers over winners. From the old Supersonic Transport to high-definition television, U.S. politicians backed losing technologies. In fact, American firms have leapfrogged French and Japanese efforts to create HDTV, leaving those nations with billion dollar bills for useless government research.

Moreover, ATP transfers provide a Who's Who in corporate welfare—BP Chemicals, Caterpillar Inc., DuPont Fibers, IBM, Texas Instruments, 3M, Xerox, and more. All received millions of dollars toward the development of products that they already had an incentive to produce. Such transfers would be unjustified were Uncle Sam flush with cash; they are scandalous at a time when Washington is running $150 billion annual deficits.

Independent bureaucracies like the Export-Import Bank, the Overseas Private Investment Corporation, and the Small Business Administration play much the same role but without even a pretense of promoting new, improved technologies. Instead, those programs underwrite American business doing what all businesses do—borrowing, investing, and trading.

Also deserving elimination are the Commerce Department's protectionist trade activities, administered by the International Trade Administration and the independent International Trade Commission. Tariffs are nothing but taxes on American consumers that enrich domestic producers and reduce the competitiveness of U.S. exporters. The anti-dumping laws, though promulgated with the rhetoric of fairness, are barely disguised protectionism—economically unsustainable regulations twisted to the advantage of domestic producers.

Like so many other federal agencies, the Commerce Department also promotes a racial spoils system. For instance, the Minority Business Development Agency uses taxes collected from all citizens to serve a small percentage of minority-owned businesses. Amazingly, in past years the agency has even given grants for "decreasing minority dependence on government programs." The best way to reduce such dependence would be to kill the agency, while improving the overall business climate through lower taxes and less regulation.

In recent years, the Commerce Department has become a symbol of something besides corporate welfare—political fundraising. Presidential campaign managers used to become postmasters general, in which position they hired campaign workers across the country for postal jobs. Now they become secretaries of commerce and work—organizing trade junkets, for instance—with all the party's funders. In the past eight years, the secretaries of commerce have included the finance chairman of President Bush's campaign, the chairman of the Democratic National Committee, and the chairman of President Clinton's campaign.

When he moved from the DNC to the Commerce Department, Ronald H. Brown took with him several campaign fundraisers, including T. S. Chung, Melinda Yee, and Melissa Moss. It's remarkable that so many people had skills that were useful both in political fundraising and in managing the weather service and the Census Bureau. Brown's most celebrated hire, who made the reverse trip from Commerce to the DNC, was John Huang. Huang's duties at Commerce seem to be shrouded in mystery, but they enabled him to raise an impressive $2.5 million for the DNC within a year after leaving his government job. Of course, that total should be reduced by the amount that had to be given back to the donors—$725,000 at this writing.

Although the Commerce Department has become a taxpayer-funded sinecure for political fundraisers, the National Oceanic and Atmospheric Administration and the National Institute of Standards and Technology do provide some valuable services, such as weather forecasting. However, the private sector is capable of handling such tasks. Privatization could be achieved either directly or through a more gradual process beginning with contracting out.

The Census Bureau must keep track of population movements for the fair apportionment of Congress, but sophisticated statistical analysis obviates the need for the traditional decennial head count, and there is no justification for many of the agency's intrusive questions, which serve illicit political purposes (apportioning grants along ethnic and racial lines) or business goals (de facto marketing research for which companies should pay).

Department of Labor

Congress should be equally tough with the Labor Department. The agency's training programs have, in the main, proved to be abject failures. Scores of government efforts have had only minimal success in providing workers with more remunerative and permanent work. Whatever training Washington wishes to provide should be contracted out to private firms with appropriate incentives to ensure more positive results before payment.

Unemployment insurance discourages not only work but also private savings to cushion a period of joblessness. The program should be left with the states, which could decide if they wanted to create a substitute, experiment with different approaches (such as granting funds only after a period of unemployment during which workers would have to rely on their own resources, or offering a lump sum option to encourage recipients to consider furthering their education or creating a small business), or dispense with the program altogether. One of the virtues of federalism is allowing different communities to handle problems like unemployment differently.

Congress should also roll back federal regulation of the labor market. The minimum wage destroys jobs, since it prices out of work anyone who lacks sufficient education, experience, and skills to earn the minimum. Were that not the case, the government could make everyone rich by imposing a minimum of $100 or $1,000 an hour. Similar in effect is the Davis-Bacon Act, which requires the payment of union scale wages on federally funded construction projects.

Restrictions on overtime and other terms of employment are equally misguided. Employees and employers should be free to bargain over the terms of employment. Different workers are likely to prefer different packages of benefits; there is no reason for Washington to decide, say, the right overtime pay rate.

Similarly, the government should not be in the business of promoting labor unions or aiding corporations. Early in its history Washington favored the latter; more recently it has leaned toward the former. But, again, federal regulation, though justified as helping working people, actually interferes with the right of employees to choose the working conditions that they prefer. At the same time, restrictive regulations bar workplace flexibility— which benefits employees and employers alike—and penalize blameless companies for transgressing rules designed to give organized labor an unfair boost in representation elections. Among the reforms that are necessary are measures ending exclusive representation by one union, restrictions on labor-management cooperation, and the requirement that firms hire union organizers as employees.

Congress should also dismantle the Occupational Safety and Health Administration. Despite imposing annual costs estimated to run between $11 billion and $34 billion on the economy (the agency's nitpicking regulation is legendary), OSHA has not improved U.S. workplace safety. The rate of employee fatalities has been falling for six decades and is affected more by workers' compensation laws and tort litigation than by OSHA. (After all, it is not good business for companies to end up with dead or injured workers.) At the same time, there has been little drop in workplace injuries since the creation of OSHA. The most realistic assessment of the maximum benefit of OSHA regulation is about $4 billion, which falls somewhere between one-third and one-ninth of the cost imposed by the agency on the U.S. economy. Repeal, not reform, is warranted, leaving workplace safety constrained by a variety of more cost-effective mechanisms, including state workers' compensation statutes, private lawsuits, and market pressure.

Necessary tasks performed by the Department of Labor, such as collecting statistics and figuring the rate of inflation (Bureau of Labor Statistics), could be transferred to an independent Census Bureau. Oversight of private pensions (Pension Benefit Guarantee Corporation, a quasi-independent body) could be shifted to the Department of the Treasury, with the agency stripped of its role as guarantor—which poses multi-billion-dollar liabilities for taxpayers—and focused instead on ensuring that private companies fulfill their contracts with former employees.

The federal government has grown dramatically and inexorably because politicians desiring to expand their power have joined with interest groups desiring to benefit from that expansion of political power. Both the Commerce and Labor Departments are examples of government bureaucracies—amalgams of special-interest subsidies, officious government interference, and a few legitimate tasks—that should not exist. Congress should act accordingly.

Suggested Readings

Bandow, Doug. "Corporate America: Uncle Sam's Favorite Welfare Client." *Business and Society Review*, no. 55 (Fall 1985): 48–54.

———. *The Politics of Envy: Statism as Theology*. New Brunswick, N.J.: Transaction Publishers, 1994.

———. *The Politics of Plunder: Misgovernment in Washington*. New Brunswick, N.J.: Transaction Publishers, 1990.

Bovard, James. *The Fair Trade Fraud: How Congress Pillages the Consumer and Decimates American Competitiveness*. New York: St. Martin's, 1991.

Dickman, Howard. *Industrial Democracy in America: Ideological Origins of National Labor Relations Policy*. La Salle, Ill.: Open Court, 1987.

Moore, Stephen, and Dean Stansel. "Ending Corporate Welfare As We Know It." Cato Institute Policy Analysis no. 225, May 12, 1995.

———. "How Corporate Welfare Won: Clinton and Congress Retreat from Cutting Business Subsidies." Cato Institute Policy Analysis no. 254, May 15, 1996.

Reynolds, Morgan. "Labor Reform: A Blip on the Radarscope." In *Assessing the Reagan Years*. Edited by David Boaz. Washington: Cato Institute, 1988.

———. *Making America Poorer: The Cost of Labor Law*. Washington: Cato Institute, 1987.

———. *Power and Privilege: Labor Unions in America*. New York: Universe, 1984.

—Prepared by Doug Bandow

13. Department of Energy

Congress should

- eliminate the U.S. Department of Energy;
- create a national nuclear weapons agency (NNWA), under the direction of a civilian official in the Department of Defense, to supervise the nuclear weapons program, civilian radioactive waste, and weapons cleanup undertakings; the new agency should operate under the budget and weapons program review of DoD;
- renegotiate nuclear weapons cleanup programs assumed by the NNWA to reflect prioritization of containment and neutralization of risk rather than removal and return of sites to pristine conditions;
- privatize all laboratories managed by the DOE except two of the three weapons laboratories;
- eliminate all research and development programs overseen by the DOE;
- eliminate all energy conservation and renewable fuel subsidies;
- sell the assets held by the power marketing administrations to the highest bidders;
- sell the Strategic Petroleum Reserve, the Naval Petroleum Reserve, and all oil shale reserves; and
- eliminate the Energy Information Administration, the Energy Regulatory Administration, the Home Weatherization Program, and all university and science education programs managed by the DOE.

The Department of Energy is a large department by any measure. It has 20,000 employees and a budget of $14.7 billion per year. Another 150,000 workers are employed at DOE's national laboratories, cleanup sites, and other facilities. Yet fully 69 percent of its budget is directed at nuclear weapons or nuclear cleanup activities. Less than 4 percent of its budget is actually related to energy activities. The remaining 27 percent is devoted to research and development.

DOE's management of federal power marketing administrations, uranium enrichment activities, and oil and gas holdings provides a total revenue of about $5 billion to the federal government ($1.5 billion in net "profits"). If DOE's nondefense programs were privatized as a whole, the resulting private corporation would number 177 on the *Fortune* list of the 500 largest corporations in America.

Energy is no different from any other commodity in the marketplace. Energy production and distribution are better directed by market forces than by government planners and bureaucrats. Likewise, weapons maintenance and related nuclear activities are better directed by defense, than by energy, personnel. There is no more reason for a department of energy than for a department of automobiles.

First, Eliminate the Department

Even if few of the actual functions of the DOE are eliminated, eliminating the department and transferring its programs to other agencies would be a worthwhile undertaking. Maintaining a cabinet-level energy department is risky because it provides a ready structure for the reintroduction of direct federal energy market interventions—a perfect command post from which some future "Energy Czar" could once again punish energy producers and consumers in the event of some temporary energy "emergency." Elimination of the DOE would make it very difficult for government to launch any future interventions in the energy marketplace.

In the event of a new energy crisis, Congress would be best advised to ensure energy supplies and fuel diversity by allowing markets to work unimpeded by bureaucratic second-guessing. The existence of an energy department presents too strong a temptation for intervention, which is widely acknowledged to have been disastrous in the past.

Reorganize the Military-Industrial Complex

Nuclear weapons production, maintenance, and related activities cost taxpayers about $5 billion annually, or 34 percent of DOE's budget. The department's various cleanup programs—another $5 billion annually— are necessitated by the environmental mismanagement of the nuclear weapons complex. Although the stockpile maintenance and cleanup operations certainly need to be continued, the agency responsible for those activities hardly needs to be represented at the president's cabinet table. There is no compelling reason for those activities to be under the administrative umbrella of an "energy" department, since "energy" has virtually nothing to do with either administrative function.

It makes far more administrative sense for those activities to be assumed by the Department of Defense. As the National Defense Research Institute of the RAND corporation recently pointed out, "It is questionable whether there remains any reason to continue the separation of nuclear responsibilities between DoD and DOE." Likewise, a 1995 General Accounting Office survey of 37 academic experts and former DOE officials found overwhelming support for removing DOE from the business of nuclear weapons development, stockpile maintenance, and arms control verification responsibilities.

A national nuclear weapons agency (NNWA) should thus be established, under the direction of a civilian official at DoD, to supervise the nuclear weapons program and related cleanup undertakings. The weapons-related activities of Los Alamos, Lawrence Livermore, and Sandia should be reduced to reflect post–Cold War realities, consolidated within two of the three aforementioned national laboratories, and placed under the direction of the NNWA.

Reform Federal Environmental Cleanup Programs

Federal nuclear weapons facilities such as Rocky Flats, Colorado, and Hanford, Washington, are expected to take 30 years or more to remediate. Current cleanup standards negotiated by the DOE with state and local communities establish rigorous protocols, based on the federal Superfund statute, that are aimed at returning sites to near-pristine conditions. Estimates of the ultimate cost of such cleanups vary dramatically, but even the most conservative estimate of $200 billion rivals the cost of the savings-and-loan bailout. Other estimates peg ultimate cleanup costs as high as $1 trillion.

While cleaning up those sites is certainly a federal responsibility, the cleanup standards adopted by the DOE are unachievable as well as inordinately costly. Although that is widely understood within the scientific community, the point was perhaps best made in a report issued in 1995 by an advisory board appointed by DOE to study the national laboratories:

Probably the most important reason behind the slow pace of assessment and cleanup is the low quality of science and technology that is being applied in the field. Many of the methods, such as "pump and treat" for contaminated groundwater remediation, cannot provide the claimed benefits. There is a lack of realization that many—and most experts believe most— existing remediation approaches are doomed to technical failure. Others would require unacceptable expenditures and much extended time to reach their stated objectives.

If the nuclear weapons complex is transferred to the Department of Defense, it makes sense to transfer cleanup operations there as well. RAND notes that "under the assumption that DOE continued to manage environmental cleanup, there would arise the issue of who was responsible for new environmental problems created by a DoD organization. It is not clear that bifurcating responsibility for nuclear waste cleanup—between old and new, or between that from weapons programs and that from other sources—would be prudent." Accordingly, it makes sense to also give the proposed NNWA this authority. The aforementioned GAO survey of energy experts likewise found an overwhelming consensus for transferring civilian nuclear disposal; nuclear weapons waste management and cleanup; and all matters of environmental, safety, and health oversight out of the Department of Energy.

Current standards for cleanup of nuclear sites negotiated by the DOE are, even if desirable, untenable both economically and politically. Moving to a standard of risk neutralization allows far more sites to be cleaned up and correspondingly speedier health protection for the general public. Most environmental engineers believe that such a change in cleanup protocols on federal sites would cut total remediation costs by at least 50 percent.

Privatize the National Laboratories

The DOE maintains 10 major laboratories and 18 minor ones with a joint annual budget of $6 billion and a 50,000-employee payroll. The taxpayers' "investment" in those laboratories has truly been staggering— over $100 billion since the creation of the DOE. The national laboratories today are no longer focused exclusively on weapons programming; they have branched out to include environmental, commercial, and various other research activities now that the Cold War is over. For example, 40 years ago, 90 percent of Lawrence Livermore's budget was devoted to defense activities. Today, only 40 percent of its budget is so targeted.

More than 50 reports and audits over the last several decades have warned of ongoing administrative, managerial, and cultural problems at the laboratories, yet the GAO notes that "none of those past studies and reviews has resulted in overall consensus about the future missions of the multi-program laboratory system, raising questions about DOE's capacity to provide a vision for this system."

Perhaps the most compelling recent analysis of the national laboratories is the February 1995 Galvin Report, the product of a corporate-academic task force appointed by the secretary of energy, that trumpeted "one critical finding" as "so much more fundamental than we anticipated that we could not in good conscience ignore it. The principle behind that finding is: government ownership and operation of these laboratories does not work well." The prescription?

> The principal organizational recommendation of this Task Force is that the laboratories be as close to corporatized as is imaginable. We are convinced that simply fine-tuning a policy or a mission, a project, or certain administrative functions will produce minimal benefits at best.

Accordingly, Congress should float stock for each separate laboratory for purchase by any interested party. If there is insufficient commercial interest in any particular facility, the federal government should turn that facility over to the management agent currently under contract to the federal government to operate the facility. That agent would then retain full ownership rights to the laboratory and be free to operate it as it wished, contracting with public and private entities in the free market. The federal government would retain full liability for environmental contamination at all the privatized laboratories and would be responsible—through the NNWA—for remediating any environmental contamination that threatened public health.

Eliminate Energy Research and Development

The DOE spends approximately $5 billion annually on research and development. Over the past four decades, the federal government has poured $17 billion into general nondefense nuclear science and $63 billion into general energy research and development, 70 percent of which since the mid-1980s has been devoted to applied energy R&D. Clearly, federal energy R&D expenditures are not trivial.

Secretary Hazel O'Leary argues that DOE's R&D programs are important because they "are so high-risk and so expensive that no one company's board of directors will agree to invest in it [*sic*]." Yet when a particular research activity involves high risk and minimal return due to scientific uncertainty or low energy prices, or both, the market does not "fail" by not investing in the project; it operates rationally.

Perhaps the most serious examination of federal R&D programs—conducted for the Brookings Institution by economists Linda Cohen of the University of California at Irvine and Roger Noll of Stanford University—found that energy R&D has been an abject failure and a pork barrel for political gain. MIT's Thomas Lee, Ben Ball Jr., and Richard Tabors likewise observed in *Energy Aftermath* that "the experience of the 1970s and 1980s taught us that *if a technology is commercially viable, then government support is not needed; and if a technology is not commercially viable, no amount of government support will make it so*" (emphasis in original).

Even the Galvin Report concluded that the DOE's laboratories—the main tool by which the department forwards its R&D agenda—"are not now, nor will they become, cornucopias of relevant technology for a broad range of industries."

The reason that energy R&D has such a disappointing track record is that politicians and bureaucrats are charged with deciding which industries, technologies, and projects to support on the basis of political, not economic or scientific, considerations. As former senator William Proxmire once remarked, "Money will go where the political power is. Anyone who thinks government funds will be allocated to firms according to merit has not lived or served in Washington very long." Eric Reichl, former director of the Synthetic Fuel Corporation and long-time member of the DOE's Energy Research Advisory Board, agrees: "The more R&D dollars are available, the more of them will go to some marginal [ideas]. The high-merit ideas will always find support, even from—or particularly from—private industry. In general, then, government R&D dollars will tend to flow to marginal ideas. Exceptions always exist, but they are just that, exceptions."

Federal energy R&D expenditures should be immediately eliminated. The argument that they have provided a net social benefit to the economy is simply dogma masquerading as fact. On the contrary, available evidence suggests that federal energy R&D has proven a waste. Any research the government might need done in order to accomplish otherwise constitutional ends—such as the cleanup of federal facilities—should be bid out to private-sector entities under the direction of the newly created NNWA at the Department of Defense.

Eliminate Subsidies for Energy Efficiency and Renewable Energy

The DOE funds numerous programs that are designed to directly and indirectly subsidize the adoption of energy-efficient technologies and the use of renewable fuels. Favored industries receive federal money for technical assistance, information programs, grants, export subsidies, and demonstration projects. More directly, the DOE—under direction of the 1992 Energy Policy Act—pays utilities 1.5 cents per kilowatt hour for power generated from solar, wind, geothermal, or biomass conversion facilities. Those programs should be removed root and branch from the federal budget and all enabling legislation amended or repealed as necessary.

A massive, 10-year experiment with state mandatory energy conservation programs (termed ''demand-side management'' or ''integrated planning'') has proven a multi-billion-dollar bust with few efficiency gains and significant rate increases for electric power customers. State renewable fuel subsidies and mandates in California—the state most aggressive in promoting such programs—have resulted in electricity rates twice the national average and have sparked a counterrevolution to free electric power companies from monopoly regulation. Clearly, where federal policy has been most aggressively amplified, the result has been a disaster for energy consumers.

In fact, a recent study by Resource Data International prepared for the Center for Energy and Economic Development calculates that current policies will only increase the market share of renewable fuels from today's 2 percent to 4 percent of the market by 2010—at a cost to ratepayers of $52 billion. Once fossil fuels become relatively more scarce, markets will turn to alternative fuels and more energy-efficient technologies and practices on their own volition out of economic self-interest. Subsidies and mandates are simply unnecessary.

Privatize the Power Marketing Administrations

In 1994 the DOE sold $2.9 billion worth of electric power, a total of 8 percent of the nation's annual power production. The facilities that generate that power are mostly dams: Hoover, Grand Coulee, and 129 other smaller dams operated by the Army Corps of Engineers and the Bureau of Reclamation. The DOE's five power marketing administrations (PMAs)—the agencies that deliver public power wholesale (with the exception of the Bonneville Power Administration, which also sells power retail) to publicly owned utilities and rural power cooperatives—are together as large as major private power companies.

The PMAs were originally justified on two premises: first, that monopoly electricity corporations would not find enough profit in electrifying rural America and thus government must step in and provide the power and, second, that government could provide power to consumers at less cost than could private companies because it could do so "at cost" without worrying about capital costs or profit margins. The former premise is now irrelevant. Rural America is thoroughly electrified and would remain so with or without the PMAs. Moreover, 60 percent of rural America is already served by investor-owned utilities. The latter premise—cheap federal power—was a socialist chimera. Public electricity generation has proven to be far more costly than private power.

All five of the PMAs should be privatized by asset divestiture and sold to the highest bidder by an asset privatization working group under the management of the Treasury Department. The divested assets should include the right to market power produced at federal facilities (without any price constraint) and the generation equipment associated with energy production at those facilities (owned primarily by the Army Corps of Engineers and the Bureau of Reclamation). The privatization of PMAs should grandfather in existing operating conditions at hydroelectric generating facilities, including minimum flows from the dams, and provide a "preference" to current customers that would relieve them from current contract requirements if they so desire. Sale of the four PMAs proposed by the Clinton administration is estimated to bring in between $3.4 billion and $9 billion to the federal treasury, with Bonneville likely to bring in approximately $9 billion.

Although there might not be a market for the largest federal dams, such as Hoover or Grand Coulee (although that remains to be seen), there are more than 100 smaller dams that would find ready buyers. More than 2,000 hydropower facilities are owned by the private sector (compared to 172 facilities owned by the public), and 56 percent of the nation's hydropower is generated by private companies. Those facilities are not necessarily small generators. The Conowingo Dam, a 500-megawatt facility in Maryland's Susquehanna River, and the Brownlee Dam, a 585-megawatt facility on the Snake River, are both owned by nonfederal power companies.

Indeed, current PMA customers complain that the Army Corps of Engineers and the Bureau of Reclamation are failing to maintain power facilities or upgrade them. Both organizations are under orders not to expand power facilities so that federal dollars can be used for other priorities. Sale of those facilities would mobilize private capital for maintenance and upgrading.

Most retail consumers of public power would experience no rate increases under privatization. The reason is that, even though public power is sold to intermediary wholesale purchasers at between 1 to 3 cents per kilowatt hour, those wholesalers (rural electric cooperatives and municipal utilities) typically resell that power to their customers at market rates— 6 to 8 cents per kilowatt hour. In other words, the retail customers of public power do not receive the public subsidy; the rural electric cooperatives and municipal utilities do.

Governments around the world, including those of Poland, Hungary, Spain, Italy, Argentina, and Peru, are privatizing government-operated power systems. In fact, the United States budgets $400 million annually to encourage other countries to adopt market-based economic policies and to advance the privatization of industrial assets. It is indeed ironic that, thus far, the United States refuses to take its own advice.

Sell the Oil Reserves

The federal government maintains a 591-million-barrel Strategic Petroleum Reserve of unrefined, generally high-sulfur crude oil in five caverns in Texas and Louisiana and a Naval Petroleum Reserve consisting of major oil and natural gas fields in Buena Vista, California (the Elk Hills facility), Teapot Dome near Casper, Wyoming, and Naval Oil Shale Reserve Number 3 near Rifle, Colorado. Today, the NPR includes some of the largest oil fields in the lower 48 states, producing about 60,000 barrels of crude oil a day.

The various oil reserves of the federal government should be privatized immediately. There is simply no reason for the federal government to own productive oil or shale fields. Nor can any petroleum reserve, no matter how large, insulate the United States from the effects of international supply disruptions. Selling the SPR would bring anywhere from $7 billion to $10 billion in revenue to the treasury, while sale of the NPR would, according to the Office of Management and Budget, bring another $1.6 billion into the treasury.

The SPR is not large enough to meet America's oil demand even in the short term and could never provide significant help in the (extremely unlikely) event of wrenching supply disruptions. The effective withdraw capacity of the SPR is only about 2 million barrels a day, enough to replace but 25 percent of America's daily oil imports for approximately 90 days. Fortunately, however, that will make no difference for the military in the event of a complete cutoff of foreign oil. Joshua Gotbaum, assistant secretary for economic security at the Department of Defense, testified before the Senate on March 29, 1995, that the military could fight two major regional wars nearly simultaneously while using only one-eighth of America's current domestic oil production.

No serious energy economist expects oil prices to ever equal, on a sustained basis, the price of putting a barrel of oil—approximately $45— in the SPR. If one thinks of the SPR as the functional equivalent of an insurance policy, then the premium on the policy exceeds the benefits under the policy.

Short of a seamless naval embargo, no oil boycott could prevent the United States from purchasing oil in the international marketplace. As noted by MIT economist Morris Adelman, the dean of energy economics, "The danger is of a production cutback, not an 'embargo.' The world oil market is one big ocean, connected to every bay and inlet. For that reason the 'embargo' of 1973–74 was a sham. Diversion was not even necessary, it was simply a swap of customers and suppliers between Arab and non-Arab sources."

The NPR doesn't even pretend to operate for a "rainy day"; instead it amounts to straightforward federal ownership of productive oil and gas lands. There is no economic rationale for such an arrangement, no military need for the fields, and no credibility to the argument that federal ownership of the means of production is superior to private ownership.

Conclusion

The plethora of minor DOE undertakings buried in the budget should all be eliminated. As discussed in Chapter 40, the Federal Energy Regulatory Commission should be dismantled. The Home Weatherization Program is nothing but welfare with extremely high overhead, and welfare policies are properly addressed elsewhere in the budget. The Energy Information Administration subsidizes the collection of market information for an industry that scarcely needs taxpayer help.

The above views may be rare in Washington, but they are orthodox among serious economists. As noted by Richard Gordon, professor of mineral economics at Pennsylvania State University and recent recipient of the International Association of Energy Economists' Outstanding Contributions Award, "The dominant theme of academic writings is that governments have done more harm than good in energy," a view "almost universally supported by academic energy economists, whatever their political outlook."

Eliminating the Department of Energy would lead to lower energy prices and a strengthened energy industry and go a long way toward closing the federal budget deficit.

Suggested Readings

American Petroleum Institute. *Reinventing Energy: Making the Right Choices.* Washington: American Petroleum Institute, 1995.

Block, Michael, and John Shadegg. "Lights Out on Federal Power: Privatization for the 21st Century." Washington: Progress and Freedom Foundation, October 1996.

Bradley, Robert L. Jr. *Oil, Gas and Government: The U.S. Experience.* Lanham, Md.: Rowman & Littlefield, 1996.

Kealey, Terrence. *The Economic Laws of Scientific Research.* New York: St. Martin's, 1996.

Lee, Thomas, Ben Ball Jr., and Richard Tabors. *Energy Aftermath.* Boston: Harvard Business School Press, 1990.

Stelzer, Irwin. "The Department of Energy: An Agency That Cannot Be Reinvented." Washington: American Enterprise Institute Studies in Policy Reform, 1996.

Taylor, Jerry. "Mighty Porcine Power Rangers: The Case against DOE." Cato Institute Policy Analysis, forthcoming.

—Prepared by Jerry Taylor

14. Cultural Agencies

> **Congress should**
> - privatize the National Endowment for the Arts,
> - privatize the National Endowment for the Humanities, and
> - defund the Corporation for Public Broadcasting.

In a society that constitutionally limits the powers of government and maximizes individual liberty, there is no justification for the forcible transfer of money from taxpayers to artists, scholars, and broadcasters. If the proper role of government is to safeguard the security of the nation's residents, by what rationale are they made to support exhibits of paintings, symphony orchestras, documentaries, scholarly research, and radio and television programs they might never freely choose to support? The kinds of things financed by federal cultural agencies were produced long before those agencies were created, and they will continue to be produced long after those agencies are privatized or defunded. Moreover, the power to subsidize art, scholarship, and broadcasting cannot be found within the powers enumerated and delegated to the federal government under the Constitution.

The National Endowment for the Arts, an "independent" agency established in 1965, makes grants to museums, symphony orchestras, and individual artists "of exceptional talent" and organizations (including state arts agencies) to "encourage individual and institutional development of the arts, preservation of the American artistic heritage, wider availability of the arts, leadership in the arts, and the stimulation of non-Federal sources of support for the Nation's artistic activities." Among its more famous and controversial grant recipients were artist Andres Serrano, whose exhibit featured a photograph of a plastic crucifix in a jar of his own urine, and the Institute of Contemporary Art in Philadelphia, which sponsored a traveling exhibition of the late Robert Mapplethorpe's homoerotic photographs. (Thanks to an NEA grantee, the American taxpayers once paid $1,500 for a poem, "lighght." That wasn't the title or a typo. That was the entire poem.) The NEA's fiscal 1996 budget was $100 million, reflecting cuts made by the 104th Congress.

The National Endowment for the Humanities, with a fiscal year 1996 budget of $110 million, "funds activities that are intended to improve the quality of education and teaching in the humanities, to strengthen the scholarly foundation for humanities study and research, and to advance understanding of the humanities among general audiences." Among the things it has funded are controversial national standards for the teaching of history in schools, the traveling King Tut exhibit, and the documentary film *Rosie the Riveter*.

The 27-year-old Corporation for Public Broadcasting—FY96 budget, $275 million—provides money to "qualified public television and radio stations to be used at their discretion for purposes related primarily to program production and acquisition." It also supports the production and acquisition of radio and television programs for national distribution and assists in "the financing of several system-wide activities, including national satellite interconnection services and the payment of music royalty fees, and provides limited technical assistance, research, and planning services to improve system-wide capacity and performance." Some of the money provided local public radio and television stations is used to help support National Public Radio and the Public Broadcasting Service.

Note that the amount of arts funding in the federal budget is quite small. That might be taken as a defense of the funding, were it not for the important reasons to avoid *any* government funding of something as intimate yet powerful as artistic expression. But it should also be noted how small federal funding is as a percentage of the total arts budget in this country. The NEA's budget was barely 1 percent of the $9.68 billion in private contributions to the arts from corporations, foundations, and individuals in 1994. According to the chair of the American Arts Alliance, the arts are a $37 billion industry. Surely they will survive without whatever portion of the NEA's budget gets out of the Washington bureaucracy and into the hands of actual artists or arts institutions.

The 104th Congress voted to phase out the NEA over three years. The 105th Congress should honor that commitment and also end federal involvement with the NEH and the CPB.

Poor Subsidize Rich

Since art museums, symphony orchestras, humanities scholarship, and public television and radio are enjoyed predominantly by people of greater-than-average income and education, the federal cultural agencies oversee a fundamentally unfair transfer of wealth from the lower classes up. *Newsweek* columnist Robert J. Samuelson is correct when he calls federal cultural agencies "highbrow pork barrel." As Edward C. Banfield has written, "The art public is now, as it has always been, overwhelmingly middle and upper-middle class and above average in income—relatively prosperous people who would probably enjoy art about as much in the absence of subsidies." Supporters of the NEA often say that their purpose is to bring the finer arts to those who don't already patronize them. But Dick Netzer, an economist who favors arts subsidies, conceded that they have "failed to increase the representation of low-income people in audiences." In other words, lower income people are not interested in the kind of entertainment they're forced to support; they prefer to put their money into forms of art often sneered at by the cultural elite. Why must they continue to finance the pleasures of the affluent?

Corruption of Artists and Scholars

Government subsidies to the arts and humanities have an insidious, corrupting effect on artists and scholars. It is assumed, for example, that the arts need government encouragement. But if an artist needs such encouragement, what kind of artist is he? Novelist E. L. Doctorow once told the House Appropriations Committee, "An enlightened endowment puts its money on largely unknown obsessive individuals who have sacrificed all the ordinary comforts and consolations of life in order to do their work." Few have noticed the contradiction in that statement. As author Bill Kauffman has commented, Doctorow "wants to abolish the risk and privation that dog almost all artists, particularly during their apprenticeships. 'Starving artists' are to be plumped up by taxpayers. . . . The likelihood that pampered artists will turn complacent, listless, and lazy seems not to bother Doctorow." Moreover, as Jonathan Yardley, the *Washington Post*'s book critic asked, "Why should the struggling young artist be entitled to government subsidy when the struggling young mechanic or accountant is not?"

173

Politicizing Culture

James D. Wolfensohn, former chairman of the Kennedy Center for the Performing Arts, has decried talk about abolishing the NEA. "We should not allow [the arts] to become political," he said. But it is the subsidies that have politicized the arts and scholarship, not the talk about ending them. Some artists and scholars are to be awarded taxpayers' money. Which artists and scholars? They can't all be subsidized. The decisions are ultimately made by bureaucrats (even if they are advised by artists and scholars). Whatever criteria the bureaucrats use, they politicize art and scholarship. As novelist George Garrett has said, "Once (and whenever) the government is involved in the arts, then it is bound to be a political and social business, a battle between competing factions. The NEA, by definition, supports the arts establishment." Adds painter Laura Main, "Relying on the government to sponsor art work . . . is to me no more than subjecting yourself to the fate of a bureaucratic lackey."

Mary Beth Norton, a writer of women's history and a former member of the National Council on the Humanities, argues that "one of the great traditions of the Endowment [for the Humanities] is that this is where people doing research in new and exciting areas—oral history, black history, women's history to name areas I am familiar with—can turn to for funding." When the NEH spent less money in the mid-1980s than previously, Norton complained, "Now, people on the cutting edge are not being funded any more." But if bureaucrats are ultimately selecting the research to be funded, how cutting-edge can it really be? How can they be trusted to distinguish innovation from fad? And who wants scholars choosing the objects of their research on the basis of what will win favor with government grant referees?

Similar criticism can be leveled against the radio and television programs financed by the CPB. They tend (with a few exceptions) to be aimed at the wealthier and better educated, and the selection process is inherently political. Moreover, some of the money granted to local stations is passed on to National Public Radio and the Public Broadcasting Service for the production of news programs, including *All Things Considered* and the *MacNeil/Lehrer Newshour*. Why are the taxpayers in a free society compelled to support news coverage, particularly when it is inclined in a statist direction? Robert Coonrod, the executive vice president of CPB, defends his organization, saying that "about 90 percent of the federal appropriation goes back to the communities, to public radio and TV stations, which are essentially community institutions." Only 90 percent? Why not leave 100 percent in the communities and let the residents decide how to spend it? Since only 21 percent of CPB revenues come from the federal government, other sources presumably could take up the slack if the federal government ended the appropriation.

It must be pointed out that the fundamental objection to the federal cultural agencies is not that their products have been intellectually, morally, politically, or sexually offensive to conservatives or even most Americans. That has sometimes, but not always, been the case. Occasionally, such as during the bicentennial of the U.S. Constitution, the agencies have been used to subsidize projects favored by conservatives. The brief against those agencies would be the same had the money been used exclusively to subsidize works inoffensive or even inspiring to the majority of the American people. The case also cannot be based on how much the agencies spend. In FY95 the two endowments and the CPB were appropriated less than $650 million total, a mere morsel in a $1.5 trillion federal budget. (The Kennedy Center for the Performing Arts and the Endowment for Children's Educational Television get $23.5 million more.) The NEA's budget is less than 5 percent of the total amount spent on the arts in the United States.

No, the issue is neither the content of the work subsidized nor the expense. Taxpayer subsidy of the arts, scholarship, and broadcasting is inappropriate because it is outside the range of the proper functions of government and it needlessly politicizes, and therefore corrupts, an area of life that should be left untainted by politics.

Government funding of anything involves government control. That insight, of course, is part of our folk wisdom: "He who pays the piper calls the tune." "Who takes the king's shilling sings the king's song."

Defenders of funding for the arts seem blithely unaware of that danger when they praise the role of the national endowments as an imprimatur or seal of approval on artists and arts groups. Jane Alexander says, "The Federal role is small but very vital. We are a stimulus for leveraging state, local and private money. We are a linchpin for the puzzle of arts funding, a remarkably efficient way of stimulating private money." Drama critic Robert Brustein asks, "How could the NEA be 'privatized' and still retain its purpose as a funding agency functioning as a stamp of approval for deserving art?"

The politicization of whatever the federal cultural agencies touch was driven home by Richard Goldstein, a supporter of the NEH. Goldstein pointed out,

The NEH has a ripple effect on university hiring and tenure, and on the kinds of research undertaken by scholars seeking support. Its chairman shapes the bounds of that support. In a broad sense, he sets standards that affect the tenor of textbooks and the content of curricula. . . . Though no chairman of the NEH can single-handedly direct the course of American education, he can nurture the nascent trends and take advantage of informal opportunities to signal department heads and deans. He can "persuade" with the cudgel of federal funding out of sight but hardly out of mind.

The cudgel (an apt metaphor) of federal funding has the potential to be wielded to influence those who run the universities with regard to hiring, tenure, research programs, textbooks, curricula. That is an enormous amount of power to have vested in a government official. Surely, it is the kind of concentration of power that the Founding Fathers intended to thwart.

Separation of Conscience and State

We might reflect on why the separation of church and state seems such a wise idea to Americans. First, it is wrong for the coercive authority of the state to interfere in matters of individual conscience. If we have rights, if we are individual moral agents, we must be free to exercise our judgment and define our own relationship with God. That doesn't mean that a free, pluralistic society won't have lots of persuasion and proselytizing—no doubt it will—but it does mean that such proselytizing must remain entirely persuasive and reactions to it entirely voluntary.

Second, social harmony is enhanced by removing religion from the sphere of politics. Europe suffered through the Wars of Religion, as churches made alliances with rulers and sought to impose their theology on everyone in a region. Religious inquisitions, Roger Williams said, put towns "in an uproar." If people take their faith seriously, and if government is going to make one faith universal and compulsory, then people must contend bitterly—even to the death—to make sure that the *true* faith is established. Enshrine religion in the realm of persuasion, and there may be vigorous debate in society, but there won't be political conflict—and people can deal with one another in secular life without endorsing each other's private opinions.

Third, competition produces better results than subsidy, protection, and conformity. "Free trade in religion" is the best tool humans have to find the nearest approximation to the truth. Businesses coddled behind subsidies and tariffs will be weak and uncompetitive, and so will churches, synagogues, mosques, and temples. Religions that are protected from political interference but are otherwise on their own are likely to be stronger and more vigorous than a church that draws its support from government.

If those themes are true, they have implications beyond religion. Religion is not the only thing that affects us personally and spiritually, and it is not the only thing that leads to cultural wars. Art also expresses, transmits, and challenges our deepest values. As the managing director of Baltimore's Center Stage put it, "Art has power. It has the power to sustain, to heal, to humanize ... to change something in you. It's a frightening power, and also a beautiful power. . . . And it's essential to a civilized society." Because art is so powerful, because it deals with such basic human truths, we dare not entangle it with coercive government power. That means no censorship or regulation of art. It also means no tax-funded subsidies for arts and artists, for when government gets into the arts-funding business, we get political conflicts. To avoid political battles over how to spend the taxpayers' money, to keep art and its power in the realm of persuasion, we would be well advised to establish the separation of art and state.

Suggested Readings

Banfield, Edward C. *The Democratic Muse.* New York: Basic Books, 1984.

Boaz, David. "The Separation of Art and the State," *Vital Speeches*, June 15, 1995.

Grampp, William. *Pricing the Priceless.* New York: Basic Books, 1984.

Kauffman, Bill. "Subsidies to the Arts: Cultivating Mediocrity." Cato Institute Policy Analysis no. 137, August 8, 1990.

Kostelanetz, Richard. "The New Benefactors." *Liberty,* January 1990.

Lynes, Russell. "The Case against Government Aid to the Arts." *New York Times Magazine,* March 25, 1962.

Samuelson, Robert J. "Highbrow Pork Barrel." *Newsweek,* August 21, 1989, p. 44.

—Prepared by Sheldon Richman and David Boaz

15. Costly Agencies

> **Congress should**
>
> - eliminate the Departments of Agriculture, Interior, Transportation, and Veterans Affairs;
> - close down major independent agencies such as NASA, the Tennessee Valley Authority, the Small Business Administration, the Corporation for National and Community Service, the Legal Services Corporation, and the Appalachian Regional Commission; and
> - terminate obscure independent agencies like the Advisory Council on Historic Preservation, the Japan–United States Friendship Commission, the Marine Mammal Commission, the National Education Goals Panel, the State Justice Institute, and the U.S. Institute of Peace.

Abolishing cabinet-level departments and independent agencies is an essential element of a return to constitutional government. Previous chapters in this section have called for the abolition of four cabinet agencies. That should not be construed as an endorsement of the other nine departments. At least four of those—the Departments of Agriculture, Interior, Transportation, and Veterans Affairs—should be on the chopping block as well. Among the nearly 100 independent agencies that squander billions of taxpayer dollars every year, there are dozens of additional candidates for elimination.

Famed corporate turnaround artist Albert J. Dunlap criticized the 104th Congress for targeting only three cabinet-level departments for elimination. He feels that there are only four departments that should *not* be eliminated: Defense, State, Justice, and Treasury. "The rest of them are useless," Dunlap said. We agree. The time is right for a return to a federal government with only those powers specifically enumerated in the Constitution. Closing down costly cabinet departments and independent agencies is an essential part of that process.

Department of Agriculture

The U.S. Department of Agriculture pays farmers not to grow crops on their land in order to keep their selling prices high, then turns around and doles out food stamps so that consumers can afford to pay those inflated prices. Though the portion of the population that farms has declined, the USDA bureaucracy has not. There is now roughly one bureaucrat for every six full-time farmers. The USDA should be eliminated, freeing farmers to grow whatever quantity of whatever crops they see fit and to sell them at whatever price the market will bear.

Department of the Interior

The Department of the Interior is responsible for managing the hundreds of millions of acres of land owned by the federal government—one-third of the land in the United States. Mismanagement of those lands has caused significant environmental damage—for example, to the Florida Everglades and the old-growth timber of the Pacific Northwest. Given his poor track record, Uncle Sam is uniquely unqualified to serve as a landlord. The Interior Department should be abolished, and those lands that have recreational or historical value should be sold or given to private conservation groups such as the Nature Conservancy or the Audubon Society. Such groups would surely do a better job of preserving those lands than has the federal government. Lands that have commercial value—such as timber and grazing lands—should be sold to the private business concerns that currently lease them from the federal government or to environmentalists who wish to buy them for conservation purposes.

Department of Transportation

The Department of Transportation functions largely as a money launderer, in the process creating jobs for Washington bureaucrats at the expense of taxpayers everywhere else. The federal government collects taxes from all of us and turns some of that money over to the Transportation Department, from which it is then sent back to states and localities to fund local highway and mass transit projects. Surely we would all be better off if we got rid of the middleman. Furthermore, all taxpayers should not be required to fund local mass transit systems in the first place.

Government has proven its ineptitude in that area; virtually all of those systems are huge money losers. Other DOT activities include subsidizing the shipping industry and endangering the safety of our airways through mismanagement of the Federal Aviation Administration's air traffic control system. In honor of its 30th anniversary in 1997, the DOT should be put out to pasture.

Department of Veterans Affairs

The former Veterans Administration was elevated to cabinet status in 1989. It is our newest cabinet agency. DVA is responsible for administering the programs that serve our military veterans, a job it does quite poorly. The Veterans Health Administration, our separate federal hospital system for veterans, routinely provides lower quality care at a higher price than would the private sector. Veterans wait hours and sometimes months to receive medical treatment. Taxpayers are asked to subsidize such treatment with billions of their tax dollars every year and are also held accountable for the hundreds of millions of dollars worth of medical malpractice claims filed against VHA personnel. Roughly 90 percent of eligible veterans choose private alternatives over VHA care. We should trust their judgment. The VHA should be abolished and veterans should be integrated into the mainstream health care system. DVA's remaining functions could be handled by an independent agency.

Major Independent Agencies

In addition to the 14 cabinet-level departments, there are nearly 100 independent agencies in our federal government. They range in size from the $350 billion Social Security Administration to the $200,000 Commission for the Preservation of America's Heritage Abroad. Some of the larger ones that should be targeted for elimination are described below.

National Aeronautics and Space Administration

Although the image of the United States leading the world in space travel has been a source of patriotic inspiration for many Americans, it has come at a very high price. NASA's current annual budget is about $13 billion. Individuals who wish to contribute their money to space exploration activities and private businesses that wish to engage in such activities should do so. Overtaxed Americans struggling to make ends

181

meet should not be forced to join in. NASA should be abolished, and the American people should have their taxes reduced accordingly.

Federal Emergency Management Agency

Any time there is a natural disaster FEMA is trotted out as an example of how well government programs work. In reality, by using taxpayer dollars to provide disaster relief and subsidized insurance, FEMA itself encourages Americans to build in disaster-prone areas and makes the rest of us pick up the tab for those risky decisions. In a well-functioning private marketplace, individuals who chose to build houses in flood plains or hurricane zones would bear the cost of the increased risk through higher insurance premiums. FEMA's activities undermine that process. Americans should not be forced to pay the cost of rebuilding oceanfront summer homes. This $4 billion a year agency should be abolished.

U.S. Information Agency

The USIA spends $1.2 billion a year and employs 7,000 bureaucrats in an effort to inform citizens of other nations about the policies of the United States. To monitor its progress, the USIA commissions public opinion surveys about the United States and its policies in nearly every country. It supports public-access libraries in developing countries and overseas performing and fine arts programs and international broadcasting activities such as Voice of America and Radio Marti. None of those activities is a justifiable expenditure of taxpayer dollars. The USIA should be terminated.

Tennessee Valley Authority

The Tennessee Valley Authority is a government-owned corporation, established in 1933, that had net outlays of $1 billion in 1996. Its primary activity is to operate a multi-billion-dollar electric utility that is the sole supplier of electric power to an 80,000-square-mile area in the seven states along the Tennessee River valley. Other TVA activities include maintaining a system of dams, reservoirs, and navigation facilities that benefit the private shipping industry; managing 300,000 acres of public land and 11,000 miles of shoreline; conducting environmental research; and funding a variety of local economic development projects. TVA's activities and assets should be privatized.

182

Small Business Administration

The $700 million a year Small Business Administration provides direct loans and loan guarantees to small businesses, as well as administrative counseling and disaster relief. Those loan programs assist fewer than 1 percent of all small businesses. To qualify for an SBA loan a business must have been turned down for a loan by at least two banks. Not surprisingly, the SBA has a terrible record in selecting businesses to support—as many as 20 percent of its loans go sour in any given year.

Corporation for National and Community Service

People working together, volunteering their own time and resources, to solve problems within their communities are part of what makes America unique. The AmeriCorps program, operated by the Corporation for National and Community Service, perverts that notion by paying "volunteers" $7 an hour—plus educational vouchers to be used to retire student loan debts—to do community service. Furthermore, it is sometimes difficult to describe those activities as "community service." For instance, a nonprofit group in Colorado forced AmeriCorps members to draft and distribute political fliers attacking a city councilman who was up for reelection. Other AmeriCorps members were bused to an Earth Day rally in Maryland last year. The $500 million a year Corporation for National and Community Service and its thousands of paid volunteers should be taken off the dole immediately.

Legal Services Corporation

The LSC distributes tax dollars to local nonprofit organizations to fund free civil legal assistance to those in poverty. Unfortunately, all too often those tax dollars are instead used to fund lobbying and other political advocacy activities. That is an inappropriate use of taxpayer funds. The $400 million LSC should be abolished. Those who wish to help the indigent obtain legal assistance should do so directly, rather than by funneling their dollars through the federal bureaucracy.

Appalachian Regional Commission

The Appalachian Regional Commission was established in the 1960s to help reduce poverty and geographic isolation in the 13 states of the mostly rural Appalachian region. The largest share of ARC's budget goes toward highway development grants to state governments. Over the years those dollars have financed the construction of more than 2,000 miles of

183

local roads. ARC also provides money for construction of basic infrastructure (e.g., water and sewer systems), housing project financing, business development grants, and efforts to increase access to health care. Since ARC's activities are clearly local in nature, they should not be funded by the federal government. The $200 million ARC should be abolished.

Peace Corps

Technically, the Peace Corps is not an independent agency. It gets its money from the "funds appropriated to the president" account. Nevertheless, it too is a prime candidate for elimination. The Peace Corps spends $230 million a year to provide support for volunteers working to reduce poverty, hunger, disease, and illiteracy in other countries. Such activities are not within the proper purview of government. They would be more appropriately, and no doubt more effectively, conducted by private charitable organizations.

Obscure Independent Agencies and Commissions

In addition to the major independent agencies, there are dozens of smaller, obscure agencies and commissions with budgets of less than $50 million a year. While that may be small in federal budget terms, to most taxpayers it is a substantial sum. Some of the more egregious examples and their annual budgets are listed below.

- Advisory Council on Historic Preservation, $3 million
- Architectural and Transportation Barriers Compliance Board, $3 million
- Commission for the Preservation of America's Heritage Abroad, $200,000
- Federal Financial Institutions Examination Council Appraisal Subcommittee, $2 million
- Institute of American Indian and Alaska Native Culture and Arts Development, $11 million
- Japan–United States Friendship Commission, $2 million
- JFK Assassination Records Review Board, $1 million
- Marine Mammal Commission, $1 million
- National Capital Planning Commission, $5 million
- National Commission on Libraries and Information Science, $1 million
- National Education Goals Panel, $1 million

- Neighborhood Reinvestment Corporation, $40 million
- Office of Government Ethics, $8 million
- Office of Navajo and Hopi Indian Relocation, $27 million
- Ounce of Prevention Council, $1 million
- State Justice Institute, $13 million
- United States Institute of Peace, $12 million

Although cabinet-level departments are politically attractive targets for elimination, there are dozens of smaller, more obscure independent agencies that are often overlooked. They, too, are a drain on federal tax dollars. Reducing the size and cost of the federal government requires going after all costly agencies with equal fervor.

Suggested Readings

Bauman, Robert. "70 Years of Federal Government Health Care: A Timely Look at the U.S. Department of Veterans Affairs." Cato Institute Policy Analysis no. 207, April 27, 1994.

Bovard, James. *The Farm Fiasco.* San Francisco: Institute for Contemporary Studies, 1989.

Fitzsimmons, Allan. "Federal Ecosystems Management: A 'Train Wreck' in the Making." Cato Institute Policy Analysis no. 217, October 26, 1994.

Hess, Karl Jr., and Jerry Holechek. "Beyond the Grazing Fee: An Agenda for Rangeland Reform." Cato Institute Policy Analysis no. 234, July 13, 1995.

Love, Jean, and Wendell Cox. "False Dreams and Broken Promises: The Wasteful Federal Investment in Urban Mass Transit." Cato Institute Policy Analysis no. 162, October 17, 1991.

Luttrell, Clifton B. *The High Cost of Farm Welfare.* Washington: Cato Institute, 1989.

Murray, Charles. *What It Means to Be a Libertarian.* New York: Broadway, 1997.

—Prepared by Dean Stansel

185

THE GROWING THREATS TO CIVIL LIBERTIES

16. Civil Liberties in America

> **Congress should**
> - before passing any law, ask whether the Constitution grants Congress the power to pass the law;
> - if so, ask further whether the proposed law violates the enumerated or unenumerated rights guaranteed in the Bill of Rights or unreasonably intrudes into individual, family, and community decisionmaking; and
> - begin to repeal existing laws that infringe on the liberties of Americans.

The United States is the freest country in the world, yet American liberties are increasingly violated, limited, or circumscribed by government as it expands into every corner of civil society. As the chapters in this section point out, the federal government today limits our political speech, subjects us to more wiretapping than ever before, criminalizes more activities every year, interferes with the content of broadcasting, and assumes unprecedented police and prosecutorial powers.

Because the narrowing of our liberties takes place gradually, and always for noble-sounding reasons, many Americans don't realize just how many freedoms they have lost. Yet it would take a book to list them—James Bovard made a start in his *Lost Rights: The Destruction of American Liberty.*

Freedom is often threatened by people who seek power—as an end in itself, as a means to wealth or other goods, or to further some noble purpose. The American Constitution was designed to direct, limit, and constrain the use of power in order to protect liberty. But as the Founders knew, and as has become even more clear in modern times, liberty can be threatened by well-meaning people who seek only to do good. Justice Louis Brandeis put it well: "Experience should teach us to be most on

our guard to protect liberty when the government's purposes are beneficent.
. . . The greatest dangers to liberty lurk in insidious encroachment by men
of zeal, well-meaning but without understanding.''

The greatest threat to the civil liberties of Americans is one that is so
obvious it is often ignored: the increase in the size and scope of the federal
government. Drawing on their experience with the British government,
their knowledge of history, and their understanding of the relationship
between civil society and the state, the Founders wrote a constitution that
carefully limited the powers of the federal government. They declared that
government could have only those powers that were explicitly delegated to
it by the people; they enumerated those powers in our written Constitution;
and they made clear in the *Federalist Papers* and elsewhere that the federal
government was limited to its enumerated powers. They also established
an amendment process in case future generations should decide to change
those arrangements.

When a Bill of Rights was first proposed, Alexander Hamilton wrote,
''Why declare that things shall not be done which there is no power to
do?'' But to satisfy those who feared that the government might nevertheless expand its power—and ''for greater caution,'' as James Madison put
it—Congress and the states did adopt 10 amendments known as the Bill
of Rights. The first eight specify particular rights that individuals hold
against the federal government; the Ninth Amendment declares that individuals have more rights than are named in the other amendments; and
the Tenth Amendment says that all powers not granted to the federal
government are reserved to the states or the people.

Today, when a new federal law is proposed, many freedom-loving
people on both the right and the left look to the Bill of Rights to see
whether the law will violate any constitutional rights. As a first step,
however, we should look to the enumerated powers to see if the federal
government has been granted the power to undertake the proposed action.
Only if it has such a power should we move on to ask whether the
proposed action would violate any protected right.

Much, perhaps most, of what the federal government does today is not
authorized by the Constitution. The federal government has assumed many
powers that were never delegated by the people and are therefore not
enumerated in the Constitution. It would be hard to find in the Constitution
any authority for economic planning, aid to education, a government-run
retirement program, farm subsidies, art subsidies, corporate welfare, energy
production, public housing, or mandated V-chips in television sets.

It is an old maxim that "ignorance of the law is no excuse." But how can anyone keep up with the law today, when the *Federal Register* publishes 60,000 pages of regulations annually and legislative bodies at all levels enact 150,000 laws a year? Many federal agencies have the power to arbitrarily ensnare, intentionally or not, almost any business or individual.

If we believe not only that the federal government should legislate on any matter that seems to us to require political solution but also that it can do so notwithstanding its constitutionally limited power, then we had better accept that violations of our civil liberties will come with the territory. For the first violation—the violation of the basic principle that the government has only the power we have given it—will soon be followed by a second violation—the violation of our right to plan and live our own lives, free from government's planning them for us.

Of course, not all violations of civil liberties are innocent by-products of well-intentioned legislation. Henry Adams observed that "politics, as a practice, whatever its professions, has always been the systematic organization of hatreds." Unscrupulous politicians will always seek to gain power and position by scapegoating some citizens and pandering to others. Gays and immigrants, Japanese and Arabs, straight white men and the very rich have all served recently as pretexts for ill-advised legislation.

Perhaps even more often, politicians target a truly reprehensible group in order to pass laws that have far broader effects. When we give the government broad wiretapping powers to fight terrorists, or keys to everyone's computers to combat child pornographers, we play into the hands of those who willingly disregard individual rights.

In the past few years, the federal government's intrusion has accelerated. We could point to examples in a wide variety of areas.

Privacy

Privacy has long been respected as a fundamental right of free people. Jurisprudence on the right to privacy has become entangled in a vague web of emanations and penumbras. A better foundation would be the old doctrine, "A man's home is his castle." That's the principle that underlies the Fourth Amendment and other parts of the Constitution. But some people in the government have used the specter of terrorism, child pornography, and organized crime to chip away at our right to privacy.

The Clinton administration set a record in 1995 (probably broken in 1996) for the most crime-related wiretaps in a year and for the most "national security" wiretaps without establishing probable cause for believing that a crime had been committed or was about to be committed. President Clinton asked Congress for the authority to conduct "roving wiretaps"—that is, wiretaps not on a particular phone but on any phone used by a particular individual—without court approval. Although that specific provision did not pass, the 1996 terrorism bill did expand the government's wiretapping authority.

Important messages are increasingly sent electronically. Thus the privacy of electronic communications is a growing concern. No one expects us to write all our letters on postcards so postal workers can read them, and if we write letters in code, that's none of the government's business. But the federal government has tried to restrict our ability to keep our electronic communications private. It has banned the export of the most effective encryption technology. It has repeatedly proposed a Clipper Chip system under which the government would hold a key to all the data in all the computers in the United States. Of course, the government promises never to misuse its power. One might consult the innocent Americans caught in everything from Filegate to Watergate to the Tuskegee experiment about the reliability of such promises. Louis Freeh, director of the Federal Bureau of Investigation, seems to want to go further than Clipper Chip and ban encrypted communications entirely.

Widespread drug testing is a particularly ugly intrusion into privacy rights. President Clinton and his Republican opponents have competed to see who could demand drug testing of more Americans. The president may have won the latest round by proposing to mandate that states require teenagers seeking driver's licenses to submit to drug tests. Such a law would presume every teenager guilty and subject him to an intrusive search, without any evidence of wrongdoing.

Freedom of Speech

As Bradley A. Smith writes in Chapter 18, limits on campaign spending restrict the ability of individuals to advance their political ideas. Whatever the Founders might have thought about obscenity or commercial speech, the First Amendment was certainly intended to protect political speech. Yet today's edifice of campaign finance regulations is designed to limit the very speech that is essential to democracy. It may be no coincidence that the reelection rate for incumbents has skyrocketed since the 1974 Federal Elections Campaign Act.

Now the Federal Election Commission is trying to go beyond even the unfortunate speech restrictions included in that law. As former attorney general William P. Barr wrote recently, the FEC "has mounted a sustained assault on First Amendment freedoms. It has persistently attempted to expand its authority over campaign spending limits into a sweeping license to suppress issue-oriented speech by citizens' groups." Among its most notorious cases are the lawsuits against the Christian Coalition and the National Right to Work Committee, both of which distribute voting guides that offer information about candidates for office. In retaliation, some Republicans and conservatives have pressed the FEC to harass the AFL-CIO as well. A better solution would be to abolish the FEC and allow every American to contribute money to advance his own political ideas in a robust debate.

The FEC is not the only government agency that has a chilling effect on free speech. The attempt to enforce increasingly restrictive "civil rights" laws has led to free-speech restrictions as well. The Fair Housing Act Amendments of 1988 make it illegal to advertise a dwelling in any way that indicates a preference for a particular kind of buyer or tenant, and the Department of Housing and Urban Development takes a very expansive view of what that means. HUD regulations note, "References to a synagogue, congregation or parish may . . . indicate a religious preference. Names of facilities which cater to a particular racial, national origin or religious group such as country club or private school designations . . . may indicate a preference." In other words, it's illegal to advertise a small apartment as "ideal for couple" because that might indicate a bias against singles. It's illegal to advertise "walking distance to synagogue"—an important selling point for Orthodox Jews—because that indicates a bias against Gentiles. HUD is also prosecuting developers whose ads don't picture the right racial mix of people. Real estate agents cannot legally tell their clients about the racial, ethnic, or family makeup of a neighborhood.

During the Clinton administration, HUD began investigating and threatening community activists who objected to shelters and public housing units in their neighborhoods. In New York, Berkeley, Seattle, and other places HUD enforcers demanded correspondence, minutes of meetings, flyers, and lists of contributors on the grounds that the activists were engaged in illegal racial harassment. The government's own harassment of people for exercising their First Amendment rights surely has a chilling effect on other Americans who might consider expressing their views of the federal government's plans.

The most notorious infringement on free speech in 1996 was the Communications Decency Act, passed by Congress, signed by the president, and defended in court by the Justice Department. That act criminalizes any use of a computer network to display "indecent" material, unless the content provider uses an "effective" method to exclude people under 18. There is no centralized, affordable, effective way to restrict children's access to particular sites on the Internet. If this law is upheld by the Supreme Court, Congress will have mandated that the greatest communications tool in history be restricted to material that would be appropriate for kindergartners. Of course, since Congress's authority does not extend to content providers in Denmark, the Cayman Islands, or Hong Kong, what the law may do is move the discussion of "inappropriate" topics outside the United States—a poor way to enhance U.S. leadership in software and information.

Another threat to free speech is the continuing campaign to outlaw the desecration of the American flag. As outrageous as flag burning is, the test of our commitment to freedom of speech is our willingness to tolerate offensive speech. The Founders put freedom of speech in the Constitution because they knew that we would all be tempted at one time or another to ban some kind of speech or expression, so it's best that everyone be unable to do so. It's interesting to speculate whether the flag-bedecked ties, hats, and other paraphernalia sported by Pat Buchanan and the delegates at the Republican National Convention would be legal under the flag-desecration amendment they favor.

Prevented by the courts from banning flag burning by statute, some members of Congress want a constitutional amendment to forbid desecration. Some advocates of campaign finance regulation likewise understand that such restrictions fall afoul of the First Amendment and want a new amendment to bring about *their* preferred exception. Maybe those new amendments should be numbered Amendment I(a), Amendment I(b), and so on, to keep all the exceptions in close proximity to the original First Amendment.

The Federalization of Almost Everything

President Clinton proclaims that "the era of big government is over." Former senator Bob Dole waved the Tenth Amendment at campaign rallies. Yet members of both parties have been quick to pass federal laws to deal with whatever seemed to capture the voters' imagination, regardless of whether the Constitution authorized federal activity in that area or whether centralized decisionmaking was appropriate. One of the great advantages of a federal system is that different solutions to problems can be tried; good solutions can be copied, and bad choices have limited impact.

The impulse to impose uniform solutions or eliminate "inequities" among regions is strong. President Clinton said in 1995, "As president, I have to make laws that fit not only my folks back home in Arkansas and the people in Montana, but the whole of this country. And the great thing about this country is its diversity, its differences, and trying to harmonize those is our great challenge." A *Washington Post* columnist says that America "needs badly . . . a single education standard set by— who else?—the federal government." Kentucky governor Paul Patton says that if an innovative education program is working, all schools should have it, and if it isn't, none should.

But why? Why not let local school districts observe other districts, copy what seems to work, and adapt it to their own circumstances? And why does President Clinton feel that his challenge is to "harmonize" America's great diversity? Why not enjoy the diversity? The problem for centralizers is that appreciating diversity means accepting that different people and different places will have different situations, different approaches, and maybe even different values. A fundamental question is whether centralized systems or competitive systems produce better results—that is, arrive at more solutions that, although not perfect, are better than they might have been. Our experience with competitive systems—democracy, federalism, free markets, or the vigorously competitive Western intellectual system—shows that they find better answers than do imposed, centralized, one-size-fits-all systems.

The Constitution specifically establishes only three federal crimes, yet today there are more than 3,000 federal crimes—and Congress keeps adding more. Congress has declared such clearly local crimes as carjacking, stalking, and church burning to be federal offenses. Why? Are local police incapable of handling such crimes? No, Congress's impulse seems to be to respond to popular pressure rather than fulfill its constitutional responsibility and engage voters in a discussion of the Constitution, federalism, and the role of Congress.

In 1995 the Supreme Court ruled that the passage of the Gun-Free School Zones Act exceeded the constitutional authority of the federal government. Banning the possession of a gun on or near school grounds probably makes sense—which is why almost all states did it before Congress made such possession a federal crime. But after the Supreme Court struck down the law, Congress—despite its rhetoric about the Tenth

Amendment—passed the law again, claiming to find authority in the much-abused commerce clause.

Local crimes weren't the only things Congress tried to federalize in the last session. The Defense of Marriage Act for the first time declared that the federal government would define marriage, rather than deferring to the several states. (It also declared that each state could refuse to recognize same-sex marriages performed in other states, probably in violation of the full faith and credit clause of the Constitution.) If the principle of federalism means anything, it means that on matters like marriage, the people most directly concerned with the issue should decide. In the case of American federalism, that means that marriage should be defined by the states or even by local communities, not by a federal override of state prerogatives.

From crime to welfare, from health care to marriage to environmental policy, Congress has increasingly usurped local decisionmaking and imposed uniform national rules on a large and diverse country.

Unequal Rights

One of the fundamental principles of the rule of law is equal treatment under the law for all citizens. Justice doesn't require equality of outcomes— indeed, only massive injustice could seek to achieve such a result—but it does require equal legal rights. "Civil rights" should certainly mean equality under the law. No one should be given legal preferences or disadvantages on the basis of such characteristics as race, gender, religion, or sexual orientation.

A Congressional Research Service study found in 1995 that there were 160 federal programs that offered preferences on the basis of race. The commitment of President Clinton and Congress to eliminating racial preferences from the law resulted in repeal of only 1 of those 160 laws. Congress should heed the message of the California Civil Rights Initiative—which is the message of Thomas Paine, William Lloyd Garrison, Frederick Douglass, *Brown v. Board of Education,* and Martin Luther King Jr.— and repeal all laws that consider race, religion, or gender in granting or denying federal benefits or contracts.

The debate over the Defense of Marriage Act showed Congress's confusion about equal rights. While 85 senators voted to deny equal marriage rights on the basis of sexual orientation, at the same time 49 senators voted to forbid private employers from discriminating on the basis of sexual orientation. Although such discrimination is usually irrational, it is very dangerous to inject the clumsy hand of government in the complex web of relationships that make up the American economy. We have learned from the well-intentioned effort to outlaw discrimination on the basis of race, religion, and gender that the attempt to enforce such a law easily leads to investigations, quotas, and an explosion of litigation. All taxpayers have a right to an efficient government that hires on the basis of job-related characteristics alone, so the federal government should not discriminate in its own hiring and contracting decisions on the basis of race, religion, gender, or sexual orientation; but we should be very cautious about extending the regulatory apparatus of anti-discrimination law to voluntary association.

The War on Drugs

Those who prosecute failing wars often tell us that there is light at the end of the tunnel, and so it is with the long-running war on drugs. If a government is involved in a war and isn't winning, it has two basic choices: de-escalation and withdrawal or escalation. We've seen quite a bit of the latter in the war on drugs. The federal government spends some $12 billion a year on the drug war—more than 10 times as much, adjusted for inflation, as it spent on the prohibition of alcohol. We make more than 1 million drug arrests a year. The president's Office of National Drug Control Policy boasts that we interdict more drugs entering this country every year, and yet "there has been no direct effect on either the price or the availability of cocaine on our streets."

The desperate attempt to "win" the drug war has led to increasing restrictions on individual rights. A law review article a few years ago was titled "Crackdown: The Emerging 'Drug Exception' to the Bill of Rights." Continuing frustration leads public officials to propose or enact laws that would require such things as random drug testing of federal employees, mandatory drug testing of all teenagers seeking driver's licenses, surveillance flights over private property, and even shooting down unidentified planes that might be carrying drugs.

One of the most notorious escalations of the war on drugs has been the increased and expanded use of "civil forfeiture." Forfeiture law currently enables law enforcement personnel to stop motorists and seize their cash on the spot and to destroy boats, cars, homes, airplanes, and businesses in often fruitless drug searches. The law is based on the idea of a legal proceeding against *property* that "facilitates" the commission of a crime. Thus when law enforcement personnel doubt that they can prove a defendant's guilt beyond a reasonable doubt, they can still seize his property

195

under the much weaker standard appropriate to civil proceedings. Even without the horror stories and abuses that have become rampant as a result of such forfeiture, this doctrine is a signal example of a government out of control and unbound by the rule of law.

Congress should reconsider the constitutionality and effectiveness of the entire war on drugs. But pending that, it should at the least reform civil forfeiture law. Congress should also refrain from trying to override or undermine the decisions of the people of Arizona and California to alter our current prohibition policies ever so slightly by allowing sick people to use marijuana medicinally on the advice of a doctor and by substituting treatment for incarceration of first-time drug offenders.

Conclusion

As the following chapters demonstrate, the largest and most complex government in history has broadened its reach far beyond what either the Constitution allows or prudence would recommend. No government can wield so much coercive power in so many different ways without intruding into more and more aspects of individual liberty. From wiretapping to data collection, from Internet regulation to the growing militarization of federal law enforcement, Congress should carefully examine the impact on civil liberties of its laws and those who enforce them. The best way for Congress to protect civil liberties is to rein in its breathtaking view of the scope and power of the federal government and begin to return the federal government to its constitutional limits.

Suggested Readings

Bolick, Clint. *Grassroots Tyranny: The Limits of Federalism.* Washington: Cato Institute, 1993.

Bovard, James. *Lost Rights: The Destruction of American Liberty.* New York: St. Martin's, 1994.

Heilemann, John. "Big Brother Bill." *Wired,* October 1996.

Hyde, Henry. *Forfeiting Our Property Rights.* Washington: Cato Institute, 1995.

Lynch, Timothy. "Dereliction of Duty: The Constitutional Record of President Clinton." Cato Institute Briefing Paper, forthcoming.

Pilon, Roger. "Discrimination, Affirmative Action, and Freedom: Sorting Out the Issues." *American University Law Review,* February 1996.

—Prepared by David Boaz

17. The Expanding Federal Police Power

> ## Congress should
>
> - repeal all federal criminal statutes that involve conduct that takes place solely in one state, unless the conduct involves uniquely federal concerns, such as destruction of federal property; and
> - tighten the Posse Comitatus Act so that it proscribes all use of military personnel and equipment, including the National Guard.

Since the 1980s the federal government has prompted the militarization of federal, state, and local law enforcement. That militarization has led not only to well-publicized disasters, such as Waco and Ruby Ridge, but to a widespread increase in violent law enforcement, which has played a major role in alienating Americans from their government. Such baleful consequences are the result of another dangerous trend, the expansion of the power of federal criminal justice far beyond its legitimate constitutional limits. Law and order begin at the top; the most important criminal justice reforms that Congress can enact are those that return federal law enforcement to its constitutional role.

The Constitution specifically authorizes federal enforcement of only three types of laws, all of which involve uniquely federal concerns. The first is based on the congressional power "To provide for the Punishment of counterfeiting the Securities and current Coin of the United States." The counterfeiting enforcement power immediately follows the delegation of power to Congress to "coin Money, regulate the Value thereof, and of foreign Coin."

The second congressional criminal power is "To define and punish Piracies and Felonies committed on the high Seas, and Offences against the Law of Nations." The third is, "Congress shall have Power to declare

Punishment of Treason.'' Although counterfeiting, treason, and piracy clearly involve areas of federal, not state, concern, it is notable that, even in those cases, the authors of the Constitution felt a need specifically to authorize congressional law enforcement.

While the body of the Constitution grants only narrow criminal powers to the federal government, the Bill of Rights, in the Tenth Amendment, specifically reserves to the states all powers not granted to the federal government.

Even the *Federalist Papers,* which were, after all, a defense of increased federal power, made it clear that criminal law enforcement would not come within the federal sphere under the new Constitution. James Madison wrote that federal powers ''will be exercised principally on external objects, as war, peace, negotiation, and foreign commerce. . . . The powers reserved to the several states will extend to all objects which, in the ordinary course of affairs, concern the lives, liberties, and property of the people, and the internal order, improvement, and prosperity of the state.''

Likewise, Alexander Hamilton, the most determined nationalist of his era, explained that state governments, not the federal government, would have the power of law enforcement and that that power would play a major role in ensuring that the states were not overwhelmed by the federal government: ''There is one transcendent advantage belonging to the province of the State governments, which alone suffices to place the matter in a clear and satisfactory light—I mean the ordinary administration of criminal and civil justice.''

Madison, Hamilton, and Jefferson were right to recognize that law enforcement is properly a local matter. As former attorney general Edwin Meese put it, ''Federal law-enforcement authorities are not as attuned to the priorities and customs of local communities as state and local law enforcement. In the Ruby Ridge tragedy, for example, would the local Idaho authorities have tried to apprehend Weaver in such an aggressive fashion? . . . More fundamentally, would Idaho officials have cared about two sawed-off shotguns? In the Waco situation, would the local sheriff's department have stormed the compound, or instead have waited to arrest David Koresh when he ventured into town for supplies, as he did frequently?''

Local law enforcement agencies spend local tax dollars and are directly accountable to local voters. In contrast, federal law enforcement agencies spend from a vast pool of ''other people's money'' and are subject, at most, to very indirect democratic control. It should be no surprise that so much federal spending on crime goes to programs like Drug Abuse Resistance Education and the McGruff Crime Dog, which sound good on the Senate floor but have been proven to be failures by social scientists.

The bulk of federal law enforcement activities is not aimed at stopping the crimes against persons and property that concern most Americans. Instead, federal enforcement involves primarily statutory offenses: controlled substances, firearms, gambling, and the like. In many cases, the federal laws regarding victimless crimes are much more severe than state laws, as if the people of the 50 states were of such poor moral fiber that they are not "tough enough" on marijuana cultivation or possession of unregistered firearms.

The misuse of two constitutional powers has been the basis for the overexpansion of federal criminal power. The enumerated powers of Congress "to lay and collect taxes" and "to regulate Commerce . . . among the several States" have been turned by specious interpretation into congressional powers over issues that have nothing to do with taxes or with interstate commerce.

Recently, in *United States v. Lopez,* the Supreme Court reminded Congress that the interstate commerce clause is not a grant of general police powers and that "states possess primary authority for defining and enforcing the criminal law." Even after the *Lopez* decision, though, the huge infrastructure of federal criminal law remains in place. Today, there are more than 50 different federal law enforcement agencies, 200 federal agencies with some law enforcement authority, and more than 3,000 federal crimes.

Guns and drugs (two quintessentially nonfederal concerns) have been the primary engines for a massive expansion of federal law enforcement. From 1980 to 1992, the number of criminal cases filed in federal courts rose 70 percent; drug cases and firearms cases both quadrupled.

One key reason for growth of federal criminal powers beyond constitutional boundaries has been the gullibility of the media and the public in regard to various frauds and panics fomented by persons with an interest in centralizing more power in Washington. During the 1930s J. Edgar Hoover, director of the Federal Bureau of Investigation, falsely told the American people that an unprecedented wave of child kidnappings was in progress, and the FBI was rewarded with substantial attention and funding. In the 1980s a very different FBI earned itself more funding by putting out phony claims about a wave of serial killers of children.

In 1996 an organization named the Center for Democratic Renewal began making claims about an alleged wave of white-supremacist arson attacks on black churches in the South. In fact, some of the "arsons" never took place, other "arsons" were accidental fires, and many white churches in the South have also been burned. Of the more than 90 fires at black churches, only 3 were set by racists. But the CDR's exaggerations fit the media's preconceptions about white racism, and so the "fact" of widespread racist church arsons became the pretext for yet more federal criminal power. The federal law against arson (which, of course, is illegal and vigorously prosecuted in every state under state law) was expanded even more.

Too often, the partisan debate on crime control misses the larger issue of the proper scope of federal power. Yes, it is true that President Clinton's plan to give local governments the money to put "100,000 new police on the street" actually provides funding for far fewer. But the more fundamental point is that federal control inevitably accompanies federal dollars. The trend toward centralization of criminal justice authority in Washington is a trend toward a de facto national police force, an entity of unparalleled danger to civil liberty. We should be thankful that the federal government has actually funded far fewer than 100,000 local police.

Likewise, use of federal funds to bribe states to enact particular types of laws regarding parole, juvenile justice, sex offender notification, or drug testing for drivers' licenses erodes the value of our federal system, whereby the 50 states can experiment with a variety of policies and serve as social laboratories. Instead, the diverse lessons from the 50 states are smothered by a national uniformity, often based on little more than what sounds good on the network news.

Perhaps the most dangerous effect of overfederalization of criminal law has been militarization of law enforcement. The Posse Comitatus Act of 1878 was passed to outlaw the use of federal troops for civilian law enforcement. The law made it a felony to willfully use "any part of the Army . . . to execute the laws," except where expressly authorized by the Constitution or by act of Congress.

An army's mission is to rapidly destroy enemies of a different national-ity, while law enforcement is supposed to serve and protect fellow Ameri-cans, who are guaranteed presumptions of innocence and other rights. The military operates on principles of authoritarian control, with no room for dissent, for waiting for a consensus to form, or for democracy. Military training is antithetical to the values of due process and diversity on which civilian law enforcement must be founded.

As one modern court stated, the Posse Comitatus Act "is not an anachro-nistic relic of an historical period the experience of which is irrelevant to the present. It is not improper to regard it, as it is said to have been regarded in 1878 by the Democrats who sponsored it, as expressing 'the inherited antipathy of the American to the use of troops for civil purposes.'"' Indeed, during the debate over ratification of the Constitution, the *Federalist Papers* assured Americans that the military would never be used against the American people.

Use of the military in domestic law enforcement has repeatedly led to disaster. In 1899 the Army was used to break up a miner's strike at Coeur d'Alene, Idaho, arrest all adult males in the area, and imprison the men for weeks or months without charging them. The area was under martial law for two years. During and after World War I, the Army was used to break peaceful labor strikes, to spy on union organizers and peaceful critics of the war, and to respond to race riots by rounding up black "Bolshevik agitators." Historian Jerry M. Cooper observes that the Army's efforts "substantially slowed unionization for a decade." One of the most egregious abuses of power in American history—President Truman's illegal seizure of the steel mills—was carried out with the military, which obeyed an unconstitutional order in seizing the mills. During the Vietnam War, military intelligence was again deployed against domestic dissidents. "Military investigation of civil protest activity was precisely the kind of abuse of standing armies that eighteenth-century antimilitarists had feared," Cooper observes. The 1970 killings of student protesters at Kent State University were, of course, carried out by a National Guard unit.

Judicial interpretation and acts of Congress have diluted the Posse Comitatus Act's narrow limitations. For one thing, the prohibition on the use of military personnel and equipment does not mean those personnel cannot be used to assist law enforcement, only that they cannot be used directly for enforcing the law itself. In addition, the proscription of use of the military is limited to personnel; military equipment can be used, as long as the civilian agency pays rent for it. In drug cases, the military equipment is free.

The drug enforcement exceptions, added to the Posse Comitatus Act by amendment beginning in 1981, have been very effective at undermining the honesty of law enforcement. The U.S. Marshals Service falsely claimed a possible drug problem with the Weavers at Ruby Ridge in order to get military reconnaissance flights over the cabin. (The "hot spot" from the alleged drug lab turned out to be a doghouse.) And the bureau of Alcohol, Tobacco and Firearms invented a phony drug nexus at Waco in order to obtain massive assistance from the U.S. Army, the Texas National Guard, and the Alabama National Guard.

Because of modern drug-war exceptions to the original Posse Comitatus Act, every region of the United States now has a Joint Task Force staff in charge of coordinating military involvement in domestic law enforcement. In region six, the JTF's *Operational Support Planning Guide* enthused, "Innovative approaches to providing new and more effective support to law enforcement agencies are constantly sought, and legal and policy barriers to the application of military capabilities are gradually being eliminated." Civilian agencies routinely obtain free military support by lying about drugs; because there is no sanction for lying, obvious falsehoods are accepted by the military as a pretext for intervention.

In addition to the direct use of the military in law enforcement, many federal law enforcement agencies have created their own paramilitary units. The most well known of those is the infamous FBI Hostage Rescue Team, which has spent considerable time in recent years holding hostages and has not even attempted to rescue a hostage for several years. There are also 56 FBI SWAT teams.

Abandoning J. Edgar Hoover's principle that FBI agents should be well-trained generalists, the FBI SWAT units specialize in confrontation, rather than investigation, even though investigation is, after all, the very purpose of the bureau. Whereas Hoover's agents wore suits and typically had a background in law or accounting, SWAT teams wear camouflage or black ninja clothing and come from a military background. They are trained killers, not trained investigators.

The rest of federal law enforcement seems determined to match the FBI swashbucklers. The U.S. Marshals Service has its own 100-man Special Operations Group. The SOG is located at the William F. Degan Memorial Special Operations Center in Louisiana, which is named after one of the men involved in the senseless shootout in which nonsuspect 14-year-old Sammy Weaver was shot in the back as he attempted to flee to his cabin, in Ruby Ridge, Idaho.

The BATF, meanwhile, has its Special Response Teams, which are recruited by, in the words of one ex-BATF agent, "hand-picking these superhormone guys." Like other agencies, BATF has stepped up the training of its field commanders in military tactics, under the supervision of the Army. Even the National Park Service and the Department of Health and Human Services have their own SWAT teams.

Absolute discipline and adherence to orders may be a virtue in the military, but not in civilian law enforcement. Perhaps if the members of the three SRTs that were used in the Waco raid had included a larger

Federal Police Power

share of older, slower, and wiser agents, someone would have spoken up when the raid commanders yelled "He knows we're coming" and "Let's go." Rank-and-file defiance of the order to launch a surprise attack with no element of surprise would have saved the lives of the four BATF agents and the Branch Davidians. As Jim Jorgenson of the National Association of Treasury Agents points out, agents who can run fast while carrying a submachine gun are no substitute for agents with the maturity to know where to go, when to fire, and when not to fire.

Besides setting a bad example, the federal government actively works to militarize local law enforcement. For example, Mark Lonsdale, director of the federal government's Special Tactical Training Unit, writes that there are various governmental programs, including those run by the federal Drug Enforcement Agency, "available to local law enforcement" for marijuana control. "The thrust of this training is towards developing more of a military approach to tactics."

One morning the residents of Cass Corridor (a poor neighborhood in Detroit) were startled by the sounds of explosives and massive gunfire. While many residents hid, the few who dared to look outside found an 80-man Detroit Police Department practice assault in progress on a vacant four-story building in the neighborhood. The deputy police chief in charge of the practice assault accurately explained that such drills are routinely performed by police agencies in conjunction with the U.S. Army and other federal agencies.

The federal government's Advanced Research Projects Agency supervises a Joint Program Steering Group for Operations Other than War/Law Enforcement, which brings Defense Department and Justice Department officials together in order to find civilian law enforcement applications for military technology. The U.S. Army Aviation & Troop Command is selling surplus OH6-A helicopters to state and local governments for use in drug law enforcement.

While the drug war has been the primary vehicle for expanding use of the federal military in domestic law enforcement, other uses of the military are also becoming common. As illegal immigration has become an increasingly important political issue, the U.S. Army and Marines have been deployed along the Mexican border to assist federal and local border patrol.

The blurring of the distinction between civilian law enforcement and martial law has taken America a long way from the standards of the Constitution. Ever since Sen. Estes Kefauver discovered juvenile delinquency in the 1950s, some persons have found political advantage in

203

demanding ever-greater use of coercive federal power for domestic law enforcement. The framers of our Constitution were right to recognize the profound threat to civil liberty posed by a centralized, increasingly militaristic federal police force. If Congress is serious about restoring the rule of law, it should restore law enforcement to its proper custodians, the states.

Suggested Readings

Calabresi, Steven G. "A Government of Limited and Enumerated Powers: In Defense of United States v. Lopez." *Michigan Law Review* 94 (1995): 752–831.

Kopel, David B., and Glenn H. Reynolds. "Shirt-Pocket Federalism." Available from http://i2i.org/CrimJust.htm.

Reynolds, Glenn Harlan. "Kids, Guns, and the Commerce Clause: Is the Court Ready for Constitutional Government?" Cato Institute Policy Analysis no. 216, October 10, 1994.

—Prepared by David B. Kopel

18. Restrictions on Political Speech

Congress should

- reject so-called "voluntary" spending limits;
- significantly raise or abolish limits on individual political contributions;
- abolish limits on contributions by political parties;
- reject efforts to require any given percentage of contributions to come from within a member's district;
- reject calls to abolish political action committees;
- deny expanded enforcement powers to the Federal Election Commission; and
- adopt a clear statutory definition of "express advocacy," which provides maximum protection to political speech.

Americans sometimes debate whether or not the First Amendment's right to free speech extends to pornography, hate speech, or flag burning, but virtually no one would contend that First Amendment protection does not apply to political speech. Yet for the past 22 years, since the 1974 amendments to the Federal Elections Campaign Act (FECA), Congress and its regulatory creation, the Federal Election Commission, have attempted to regulate, channel, and thwart political speech and participation by American citizens. This effort to police citizen participation in politics has been a disaster. It has directly contributed to government gridlock; helped to entrench incumbents in office and increased the influence of special interests; required members of Congress to devote enormous amounts of time to fundraising; cut off grassroots political participation; and, most important, deprived Americans of their civil right to engage in political speech. Is it any wonder that many Americans feel more distant from Washington than ever before?

Spending Limits

Recognizing that virtually all forms of mass communication in a modern society require the expenditure of money, the Supreme Court has, on First Amendment grounds, steadfastly rejected efforts to place mandatory limits on political spending. Such limits, the Court has recognized, directly restrict the amount of political speech in which candidates and individuals may engage.

Nevertheless, in recent years numerous proposals have been made to impose "voluntary" caps on campaign expenditures through a mixture of subsidies for candidates who agree to limit their spending and penalties for those who do not agree to arbitrary spending limits. Most of those proposals so severely tip the scales against any candidate who rejects the "voluntary" limits as to be, in effect, mandatory. As such, they would still be subject to constitutional challenge on First Amendment grounds. However, even setting aside such constitutional difficulties, efforts to limit spending are bad public policy.

Total political spending for all local, state, and federal races and ballot issues is approximately 0.05 percent of the nation's gross domestic product, only slightly more than what was spent 20 years ago. Studies have shown that voter interest in and knowledge of issues increase when more money is spent on a campaign. Yet total spending on congressional races in 1994 amounted to just $3.74 per eligible voter. We spend far more money on items that most Americans would agree are far less important—for example, potato chips. It is hard to argue that America spends too much on campaigns (see Table 18.1).

In addition to reducing the information available to voters, spending limits unfairly benefit incumbents. Limits on campaign spending make candidates more dependent on free media coverage. In most cases, incumbents, through the use of their offices, will find it easier to attract free coverage. In addition, incumbents usually begin a campaign with a high level of name recognition and an established political base. Challengers, on the other hand, need to spend more money to make themselves and their message known. Thus, spending limits benefit incumbents, as can be seen in the McCain-Feingold reform bill, filibustered in the 104th Congress. In both 1994 and 1996 every Senate challenger who spent less than the "voluntary" ceiling included in the McCain-Feingold bill lost, but every Senate incumbent who spent less than the "voluntary" ceiling proposed in the bill won.

Table 18.1
Campaign Spending in Perspective

Total congressional campaign spending, 1993–94: **$724 million**	Annual sales of Barbie Doll line: **$1 billion**
Cost of Michael Huffington's 1994 campaign for U.S. Senate in California: **$29 million**	Amount budgeted by Sony Music International to promote latest Michael Jackson CD release: **$30 million**
Total PAC contributions in federal elections, 1993–94: **$189 million**	Cost of producing the 1995 movie *Waterworld*: **$180 million**
Budget for Republican and Democratic Parties' 1996 presidential general election: **$62 million**	Amount spent in 1995 to promote syndicated reruns of the comedy "Seinfeld": **$100 million**
Total political spending in the United States, 1991–92 election cycle: **$3.2 billion**	Total amount spent annually on potato chips: **$4.5 billion**

SOURCE: Compiled from news reports.

Spending limits, including most proposals for "voluntary" limits, violate the First Amendment, are inherently unfair to challengers, limit the flow of information to voters, and should be rejected by Congress.

Contribution Limits

The 1974 FECA amendments limited individual campaign contributions to just $1,000, an amount that has never been adjusted. Had that amount been indexed for inflation, it would now be approximately $3,300.

Like spending limits, limits on campaign contributions benefit incumbents. Historically, most challengers relied on a small number of supporters to launch their campaigns. However, the $1,000 contribution limit requires candidates to raise sums in small amounts. That benefits incumbents, who are more likely to have a database of past contributors, broad name and issue recognition among other potential donors, and a longer time period in which to raise contributions.

At the same time, the $1,000 contribution limit has forced members of both houses to devote inordinate amounts of time to fundraising. Unable

207

to raise money in large amounts, candidates must attend a constant stream of fundraisers and spend hours on the telephone raising the money needed to finance a campaign for public office. Voters are quite right to be critical of the amount of time legislators spend raising campaign funds. However, that time commitment is a direct result of FECA's $1,000 campaign contribution limit.

Supporters of contribution limits argue that strict limits are needed to prevent the buying and selling of votes in exchange for campaign contributions. However, systematic studies of legislative voting records show that campaign contributions have far less effect on legislative voting patterns than do personal ideologies, constituent desires, and political party affiliations and agendas. Furthermore, by restricting the supply of campaign funds, contribution limits increase the relative value of each potential donation. A candidate who is unable to get campaign funds from political supporters (because they have already contributed the legal maximum) may feel added pressure to please potential new donors. Thus, in certain situations, contribution limits may actually increase the influence of campaign donors.

At a minimum, the limit on individual donations should be raised to $3,500 and indexed for inflation; a significantly higher limit, or the complete abolition of any personal contribution limit, would be preferable.

One "reform" idea popular in recent years has been to limit contributions received from sources outside a legislator's state or district. That idea is also misguided. It would prevent candidates from raising money, for example, from friends and family members outside the district. It would tend to increase the power of local media outlets and special interests in campaigns, by cutting off outside sources of financing. It would promote legislative gridlock by emphasizing the local nature of representation rather than the greater good of the country when legislative votes are cast. Finally, such proposals may be unconstitutional, as they constitute a complete ban on the political speech of the individuals involved. A legislator's vote affects all citizens, not just those in his or her district. Outsiders may not have the right to vote in local elections, but they do have the right to attempt to persuade and educate those who do vote.

Another popular proposal is to ban political action committees (PACs). PACs, however, provide a valuable public service by monitoring the activities of legislators and reporting the information to interested individuals. PACs mobilize small contributors and increase the importance of their contributions by combining them with those of like-minded individuals.

A ban on PACs would eliminate one of the most important forms of political access available to small contributors. It would violate not only the right to free speech but also the rights of individuals to associate and to petition government for redress of grievances.

In addition to raising or abolishing individual contribution levels, Congress should abolish limits on political party contributions to candidates. Parties serve to mediate disputes between interests and to form governing coalitions. Restricting financial support from the party to a candidate means that party support is of little more importance to a candidate than the support of any single interest group. Such a scenario naturally increases a candidate's reliance on special interests. Furthermore, by weakening the bond between candidate and party, FECA makes it more difficult for voters to hold one or the other party accountable for legislative action. In that way, FECA contributes to legislative gridlock and to the type of incumbent protection that has fueled demand for term limits. Parties exist in order to elect candidates to office; efforts to limit their ability to do so are counterproductive. Restrictions on party contributions should be repealed.

The Threat to Free Speech and Grassroots Politics

In addition to the negative consequences discussed above, FECA has placed barriers in the way of grassroots political participation and encroached on First Amendment rights.

Most obviously, of course, limits on campaign contributions infringe on the right of individuals to become involved in politics. Imagine the outcry if newspaper columnists were restricted to, say, two or three political columns per year, lest they gain "too much influence." The effort to prevent people from spending their own money to promote their political beliefs is contrary to the founding principles of this country. The Founders, after all, pledged their "lives," "sacred honor," and "fortunes" to the creation of our nation. They did not pledge their fortunes "up to $1,000 per annum."

In addition to that direct limitation on free speech, the complex regulations issued by the FEC to enforce FECA hamstring grassroots involvement in politics in a variety of other ways. For example, a 1991 *Los Angeles Times* investigation found that most individuals who violated FECA's complex provisions on total political expenditures were "elderly persons . . . with little grasp of the federal campaign laws." As election law attorneys Allison and Steve Hayward have pointed out,

If you set up a pornographic site on the World Wide Web, the government cannot regulate you in any way. But if you set up your own "Vote for Bill Clinton" site on the Web (or simply print your own bumper stickers), and spend more than $250 on the project, you become subject to FEC reporting requirements.

Even large, sophisticated groups have been hamstrung by the FEC in attempting to communicate with their members. For example, before the 1994 elections, the FEC adopted a restrictive rule that prevented the United States Chamber of Commerce from distributing candidate endorsements to over 220,000 dues-paying members and the American Medical Association from distributing endorsements to over 44,000 of its members. Most of those members were small business persons and self-employed professionals who often join such organizations precisely to obtain that type of political information. Although the Chamber and the AMA felt that the rule was unconstitutional, they were unwilling to risk fines by publishing endorsements before the election. Fortunately, like so many FEC rules, this rule was eventually found unconstitutional in federal court, but only after it had muzzled the Chamber and the AMA in the 1994 election.

The FEC has doggedly attempted to limit political speech through a doctrine known as "express advocacy." Under FECA, corporations, labor unions, and issue groups such as the Christian Coalition and the National Organization for Women may spend money to inform voters about issues but may not make expenditures "relative to a clearly identified candidate." The Supreme Court has held that such a limitation may apply only to communications that "in express terms advocate the election or defeat of a clearly identified candidate for federal office." The Court explained that such communications must include words such as "vote for," "elect," "support," "defeat," and "reject," relative to specific candidates. Any lesser standard, the Court has noted, is an unconstitutionally vague restriction on the right to communicate with the public on political issues. Yet despite repeated admonitions by both the Supreme Court and lower federal courts, the FEC has consistently attempted to expand the definition of "express advocacy" to include any communication that "encourages" actions to defeat or elect certain candidates. In other words, under the definition for which the FEC has fought, a voter guide that states, "Protect the Environment," and then compares the voting records of candidates on various environmental issues might be construed as express advocacy, if the candidates had different voting records on environmental issues.

Although the FEC has lost a steady string of court cases, it continues to press for an expanded definition of "express advocacy" that would allow it to regulate most political speech by unions, corporations, associations, and advocacy groups, from the National Rifle Association and the Christian Coalition to Planned Parenthood and Handgun Control, Inc. And though the FEC does, in fact, regularly lose in court, its actions have forced groups to spend tens of thousands of dollars in legal bills and had a chilling effect on speech generally, as can be seen in the Chamber of Commerce example described above.

Public Citizen and other "reform" groups have also called for stricter disclosure of the donors to issue advocacy groups. Here again, Congress should proceed cautiously and reject disclosure rules that would burden Americans' First Amendment rights. Most issue advocacy poses no danger of political corruption—money is not given to or spent directly on behalf of candidates, so disclosure serves less purpose than in the case of direct contributions to candidates. Furthermore, disclosure can have a chilling effect on individuals seeking to promote an unpopular position. The Supreme Court has long recognized that there is a right to anonymous speech and that groups that legitimately fear harassment may not be required to reveal their membership or donor lists. Requiring broad disclosure from issue advocacy groups would serve little purpose and come at a high price in added reporting and burdens on free, uninhibited speech.

If Congress is unwilling to repeal FECA in its entirety, it at least needs to make certain that the FEC is limited to its intended role of regulating campaign contributions, not controlling political speech. Thus Congress should amend the statute by writing into law a definition of "express advocacy" that mirrors that set forth by the Supreme Court in *Buckley v. Valeo*. Congress should also deny any added enforcement powers to a bureaucracy that has so consistently thumbed its nose at the Constitution, the courts, and the rights of the American people to participate in political activity.

Finally, Congress should not let the recent revelations of large foreign donations, some possibly made in the names of others, stampede it into hasty reforms. Contributions from foreign corporations and foreign citizens living abroad are already illegal. Similarly, it is already illegal to make a donation in the name of another person or entity. All that is needed is to enforce those laws. Although it is possible to extend those laws to prohibit contributions by U.S.-incorporated subsidiaries of foreign corporations, or by permanent legal alien residents of the United States, it must be remembered that those entities and individuals are subject to the same laws as are domestic corporations and U.S. citizens. That they have no right to vote is obvious. However, it is less obvious that they should be deprived of any legal means of participating in political debate in the country in which they are domiciled.

Conclusion

Efforts to ''fix'' the campaign finance system have been bad for government and bad for American citizens, who have a right to speak and be active in public affairs. The clear failure of FECA's regulatory scheme has led many to propose still more regulation and more bureaucracy to fix the problems that FECA has created or exacerbated. Congress should reject such calls for more regulation and instead focus on deregulating the system to fix the damage FECA has done.

Suggested Readings

Fair Government Foundation. *The FEC's Express War on Free Speech: An Examination of the Federal Election Commission's Lawless Regulation of Political Advocacy.* Washington: Fair Government Foundation, 1996.

Hayward, Steven, and Allison Hayward. ''Gagging on Political Reform.'' *Reason*, October 1996.

Sabato, Larry, and Glenn R. Simpson. ''Campaign Reform: A Better Way.'' *Wall Street Journal*, June 14, 1996.

Samuelson, Robert J. ''The Price of Politics.'' *Newsweek*, August 28, 1995.

Smith, Bradley A. ''Campaign Finance Regulation: Faulty Assumptions and Undemocratic Consequences.'' Cato Institute Policy Analysis no. 238, September 13, 1995.

—Prepared by Bradley A. Smith

19. Freedom on the Internet and Other Computer Networks

Congress should

- repeal the Communications Decency Act and reject "harmful to minors" substitutes;
- lift restrictions on the export of strong cryptography;
- reject mandatory key recovery;
- reject hasty amendments to the copyright law, such as those suggested in the Clinton administration's "White Paper on Intellectual Property"; and
- reject attempts to restrict anonymous computer communications.

In responding to the many voices that speak through the Internet and other computer networks, the United States can set the entire world an example of commitment to freedom of speech and privacy rights. From Argentina to Zambia, governments have recognized information provided over the Internet as a powerful threat to their oppressive regimes. Singapore and China, among others, have moved aggressively to censor newsgroups and Web sites.

It would be shameful for the United States to follow such examples. This Congress has the opportunity to reverse a number of unfortunate policies that make it appear that the United States is not, in spite of our heritage, a champion of liberty online.

Computer Networks—Past, Present, and Future

The Internet sprang up from a rudimentary Department of Defense network known as the ARPANET (ARPA stands for the Advanced Research Projects Agency). By the 1980s hundreds of universities, corporations, and governmental agencies around the world were connected to

ARPANET. ARPANET expired in 1989, but the Internet remained. Federal support for Internet backbones was phased out (except for vBNS, restricted to scientific uses); private commercial providers such as UUNET and Sprint have taken over the Internet backbone business. Today, over 40 million people are connected to the Internet, almost entirely over private or university networks, and the number is expected to grow to over 200 million by the end of the century.

Other computer networks, such as bulletin boards, have sprung up. A bulletin board is a conference and message exchange system usually devoted to a particular topic. The board is operated from a personal computer with one or more modems connected to it. Users access the service by dialing it on their own modems. Commercial online services like Prodigy, CompuServe, and America Online constitute yet another type of computer network.

One primary reason networks like the Internet have grown as fast as they have is freedom from regulation. Computer equipment manufacturers and designers were never burdened with the archaic regulatory structures all too familiar to telephone companies and broadcasters. Competition was fierce. Costs were forced down, making switches, servers, and software cheap enough to permit fast growth. The technology leapt ahead. And the network was simple to hook up to, because the engineers were free to make it so. They were not forced to design content controls or any other social policy into the network. That kept it cheap, and kept it growing.

From that foundation of economic liberty sprang powerful instruments of political freedom and free speech. Those include electronic mail (e-mail), the speedy equivalent of post office mail in the nonelectronic world. Discussion groups such as the ''listserv'' allow users to subscribe to a list devoted to discussion of a particular topic; any message posted to the list is distributed automatically to other users, usually without being reviewed by a human moderator. Newsgroups are another important forum; they permit users to access information at any time, without a subscription. Information can also be distributed using a home page on the World Wide Web, to which other documents on the Web can be linked. Yet another popular form of computer network speech is the chat room, an electronic forum set up to admit a limited number of speakers. Chats take place in real time and are spontaneous, like a face-to-face chat around a backyard barbecue.

For the ordinary person, computer networks are not just a source of information. They are a source of listeners and readers and viewers.

They transform the ordinary person into a speaker capable of reaching an audience of millions. Computer networks are nothing less than a vast engine of free speech with the potential to transform the entire "marketplace of ideas."

Computer networks can transform markets for goods and services as well. For many commercial and banking transactions, and in the areas of medicine and education, computer communications can substitute for ventures onto crowded highways. Unfortunately, computer networks also can provide new sites for crime. But overreacting to the perceived danger of crime on the net could kill the online commerce goose before it lays any golden eggs. Perhaps the greater danger, however, is that the government will leverage regulation of the network infrastructure into a system that allows it to invade our privacy at will.

The Communications Decency Act and Possible Successors

The Communications Decency Act (CDA), passed as part of the Telecommunications Act of 1996, criminalizes the use of any computer network to display "indecent" material, unless the content provider uses an "effective" method to restrict access to that material to people over the age of 18.

Two panels of judges, convened in New York and Philadelphia, have found there is *no* affordable, effective way for nonprofit or small business providers to restrict children's access to such material. Even if services like credit card authorization were much cheaper and were available for noncommercial transactions, however, the content providers would lose their audiences. No one will cruise the Web if he has to enter a personal identification number or credit card number every time he moves from one Web page or chat room to another. No one is going to bother to obtain a PIN or give his credit card number to view a handful of amateur photos or poems. Even large commercial sites would be affected by the decrease in traffic. *Thus, the statute effectively bans much speech from the Internet and other networks.* Proposed amendments to the statute that would revise it to cover only material that is "harmful to minors" would not substantially improve matters.

The Internet promised the ordinary citizen a low-cost method of reaching an audience beyond immediate family, friends, and neighbors. Legislation like the CDA betrays that hope and is also clearly unconstitutional.

Indeed, no regulation of computer network indecency, however carefully tailored, should pass constitutional scrutiny. Content control is not within the federal government's enumerated powers. And no legislator has been able to define indecency coherently. Such regulation is inherently unfair, especially as applied to spontaneous, casual speech of the sort that the Internet facilitates between unsophisticated and noncommercial speakers.

Finally, the federal government cannot legitimately claim that it has any interest in content control, when civil society has solved the perceived problem on its own. Private-sector solutions include both software filters that parents can use to screen out offensive material and Internet service providers who provide access only to child-safe materials.

One proposed amendment to the CDA that Congress should reject would have the effect of making the site-rating labels that work with filters such as SurfWatch mandatory for many sites. Mandatory labeling is forced speech. And labeling will not work at all with the most casual, spontaneous computer speech, including e-mail and individual statements posted to newsgroups, lists, and chat rooms. Also, making labeling mandatory will result in labels being applied carelessly or under protest. Voluntary systems will be more carefully administered, and therefore more helpful to parents who want to restrict their children's access to sexually oriented or violent materials.

Congress should repeal the Communications Decency Act and reject all proposed substitutes. The federal government has no legitimate interest in regulating sexually oriented material on the Internet.

Encryption and the First Amendment: Export Controls

Encryption software uses a code to scramble bits of the data sent over computer networks, so that only those with the key to the code can decipher it. The key is a string of numbers. The longer the string, the harder it is to break. The standard key length today is 56 bits. Stronger encryption technology is essential if citizens are to preserve their privacy and security when using computer networks. Otherwise, medical records, credit card numbers, trade secrets, and personal communications relayed over computer networks are not safe from prying eyes. A working group of respected cryptographers recently announced that 56-bit keys are insecure and that keys of at least 90 bits are required to secure information for the next 20 years.

Currently, regulations promulgated under the Arms Export Control Act and the International Emergency Economic Powers Act, as well as the International Traffic in Arms Regulations, hold back the use of strong encryption. There are no restrictions on the domestic use of strong encryption technology, but until recently, encryption software that uses a key length of more than 40 bits could not be exported without special permission. In the fall of 1996 the Clinton administration announced that it would allow companies to export key lengths of up to 56 bits, under licenses reviewed every six months, if the companies agreed to produce key recovery plans within two years. After two years, nothing stronger than 40 bits will be exportable without key recovery features.

Export controls interfere with the marketing and sale of powerful encryption technology. Software makers must develop one product for sale nationally and another for sale internationally, which is often prohibitively expensive. In developing a product for international sale, they must choose between two unpalatable and unprofitable options. The first is to sell a product internationally that offers only weak cryptographic protection. The second is to sell (or try to sell, after lengthy delays in the licensing process) a product that forces key recovery on their customers. Export controls have severely hampered U.S. software companies' serving world markets for encryption software.

Export controls violate the First Amendment. The export controls sometimes require academic research papers, discussions clearly protected by the First Amendment, that discuss ideas about cryptography to be submitted to the government for review. And, as one court recently held, software expresses ideas in language and is also protected by the First Amendment. No other holding would have made sense; a source code printed in a book is clearly protected by the First Amendment—the same source code stored on a computer disk should be equally protected. Because of export controls, some professors refuse to allow foreign students to take their classes, fearing reprisals from International Traffic in Arms enforcers.

The theory behind export controls is that they prevent strong encryption from falling into the hands of terrorists and criminals. But export restrictions will not keep strong encryption out of the hands of evildoers, since the technology is already widely available. If U.S. companies are forbidden to satisfy the worldwide demand for encryption, companies based in other countries will. A determined organization could, with the aid of a community of mathematicians, develop its own system of encryption using published mathematical models.

Finally, as computers become faster, codes that use keys of 56 bits or even 75 bits will become much easier to break. Software companies should feel free to develop encryption technology as strong as the industry needs. A communication encrypted today might need to remain private for years to come.

Encryption export controls should be lifted. Restricting the mass of users to keys of short bit length merely makes the network insecure; if a code can be broken by law enforcement personnel, it can be broken by hackers.

Encryption and the Fourth Amendment

At the time the Constitution of the United States was written, a group of people could enjoy a completely private conversation by going to the middle of a plowed field, where they could be certain that no one could overhear them. Today, electronic eavesdropping methods allow law enforcement officers to invade even that zone of privacy. New encryption technology will let privacy catch up, although no encryption technology is totally foolproof.

Under mandatory key recovery proposals, encryption software could not be used (either at home or abroad) unless arrangements were made that would enable either the government or a third party to access or reconstruct a key that would decode the message. Encryption without government access to keys would either be outlawed completely or made much less convenient to use. For example, use of public key cryptography often requires a ''certification authority.'' The certification authority is a third party who certifies that the user of a certain public key is in fact a certain individual. Sometimes, the certification authority might be a government agency. Government agencies could refuse to certify the identities of people who would not give access to their private keys.

Such mandatory key access proposals should be rejected. First, the federal government has no constitutional authority to require key access. Imagine a law requiring citizens to escrow their house keys with a third party, so that the police could enter their homes if necessary. Clearly, the Fourth Amendment requires that a warrant be issued on probable cause before the government is entitled to obtain the key to someone's house. There is no exception to the Fourth Amendment for locks that are difficult to pick. Demands for mandatory key escrow constitute an unprecedented power grab on the part of law enforcement officials. The police have always had rights, limited by the Fourth Amendment, to intercept private communications and read them, *if they could*. The police have never had the right to demand that people change the language in which they communicate to make themselves easier to understand.

Second, the security of a cryptographic system rests on the security of the keys, especially the keys used for signatures and identity authentication.

Requiring secret keys to *ever* leave their users' secure environment endangers the security of the network. So does the collection of large data banks of sensitive key information. Furthermore, third-party storage of private keys is incompatible with super-secure techniques intended to prevent the theft of keys, such as "perfect forward secrecy." And no one understands exactly how key access plans will work; uncertainty about the security of such systems will slow the development of electronic commerce and distort the development of software.

Third, the argument that mandatory key recovery is necessary for data recovery is a pretext. Individuals and firms should decide whether they would prefer a system in which lost keys mean lost data or one in which keys can be recovered. And keys used only for conversations communicated instantaneously need not be stored anywhere. Finally, a system in which keys are stored by a third party is unlikely to be useful for data recovery. Elaborate procedures would be necessary to ensure that the user was indeed entitled to recover the key.

Finally, the gains to law enforcement and national security from key recovery would be minimal. Criminals and terrorists could use multiple encryption to defeat the system; the outer encryption layer would use key recovery, to avert suspicion. The inner layer would not.

Congress should reject attempts to impose key recovery or similar schemes on users of encryption technology.

Conclusion

One of the most common reasons for which people give up their precious civil liberties is fear. Fear of new technology like the Internet is often born of misinformation. There is no more reason for a citizen of the United States to fear the Internet than to fear a printing press or a pen. Information is still information, however it is transmitted. And the First Amendment and the Fourth Amendment remain two important guardians of our civil liberties.

Suggested Readings

Bernstein, Solveig. "Beyond the Communications Decency Act: Constitutional Lessons of the Internet." Cato Institute Policy Analysis no. 262, November 4, 1996.

Corn-Revere, Robert. "New Age Comstockery: Exon vs. the Internet." Cato Institute Policy Analysis no. 232, June 28, 1995.

Keyworth, G. A. II, and David E. Colton. "The Computer Revolution, Encryption and True Threats to National Security." *Future Insight,* June 1996.

National Research Council. *Cryptography's Role in Securing the Information Society.* Washington: National Academy Press, 1996.

Post, David. " 'Clarifying' the Law of Cyberspace." *American Lawyer,* April 1996.
Samuelson, Pam. "Legally Speaking: The NII Intellectual Property Report." *Communications of the ACM* 37 (December 1994).

—Prepared by Solveig Bernstein and Lawrence Gasman

20. Broadcasting

Congress should

- prohibit the Federal Communications Commission from controlling the content of broadcasts,
- privatize the electromagnetic spectrum,
- repeal the Children's Television Act of 1990, and
- repeal the V-chip requirements.

Soon after printing presses were introduced to England, Henry VIII resolved to control the new medium by requiring that printing presses be licensed. Foreign books could only be distributed by the King's Stationer. Next, the government tried to ban unlicensed books. It lost that battle. Today we reap the benefits of privately owned, unlicensed presses and publishers everywhere in the Western world. In the United States that freedom is secured by the First Amendment, which declares that Congress "shall make no law . . . abridging the freedom of speech, or of the press."

The language of the First Amendment does not distinguish one medium of speech from any other. Despite that, the Supreme Court has held that broadcasters should receive less protection than the print media. And broadcasters, like the print media under Henry VIII, are licensed. The federal government's control over broadcasters' economic fortunes is easily leveraged into content controls. It is time to end this state of affairs.

Broadcasters' First Amendment Rights

Several unpersuasive arguments have been presented as to why broadcasters should not get full free speech rights. First, it is argued that broadcasters use public property. But so do speakers in public parks, and so do newspapers, which are delivered through the public streets and printed on paper made from trees that grew on federal lands. Furthermore, there is no sound reason that the electromagnetic spectrum should have been seized by the government. Government ownership of the spectrum is inefficient and unnecessary.

As argued in Chapter 33, the spectrum should be auctioned off to private owners. If declaring the spectrum public property means that broadcasters cannot enjoy free speech rights, that is itself an excellent reason to privatize the spectrum.

Some also claim that broadcasters cannot enjoy full First Amendment rights because broadcasting is too powerful and too pervasive to be free. But broadcasters are hardly more powerful than newspapers were in the 19th and early 20th century. And broadcasting faces competition from a growing number of other media outlets, from cable television to Direct Broadcast Satellites, the Internet, movies, VCRs, and, as always, the print media. Furthermore, television and radio are pervasive only when we want them to be; nobody is forced to own a radio or television set, or to turn it on. Finally, *if we fear the power and pervasiveness of broadcasting, we should especially fear the power of government control of broadcasting.*

Ending the FCC's Power over Content

The Communications Act of 1934 gives the Federal Communications Commission power to regulate broadcast licensees in the "public interest." Over the years, the FCC has employed that broad, undefined power to enact an extraordinary series of content controls.

Early in the 1940s the FCC actually forbade broadcasters to editorialize. Then, from 1949 until 1987, the Fairness Doctrine was imposed on radio and television stations. Broadcasters covering controversial issues of public importance were required to offer their facilities to those with opposing views. So broadcasters stayed away from controversy. The FCC repealed the Fairness Doctrine in 1987. Since then, there has been a stunning increase in the amount of informational programming on radio and television.

The FCC also controls "indecency" on radio and television. Indecent material is defined as that which is "patently offensive." What does that mean? No one knows. D.C. Circuit Court of Appeals Judge Patricia Wald found that the definition could include programs on childbirth, AIDS, abortion, or almost any aspect of human sexuality. The FCC has admitted that it cannot describe exactly what material is "indecent," explaining that indecency rulings must be made on a "a case-by-case basis." In other words, something is indecent if it offends a majority of FCC commissioners.

It would be unthinkable for any agency to impose either the Fairness Doctrine or the vague, arbitrary indecency regime on newspapers. And newspapers, of course, would fight back with court challenges. But broadcasters are reluctant to protest, for they are economic hostages of the FCC. When the FCC (or the White House) suggests new content controls (such as the new rules mandating quotas of children's television), broadcasters fear to assert their First Amendment rights for fear of reprisals at license renewal time or in spectrum allocation proceedings.

Congress should privatize the electromagnetic spectrum, so no federal power can control the content of broadcasts by threats of economic deprivation. As an interim measure, Congress should remove the power to review any aspect of broadcast content from the FCC's jurisdiction.

Repealing the Children's Television Act of 1990

The Children's Television Act of 1990 requires the FCC to consider whether a broadcast licensee has served the educational needs of children in license renewal proceedings. Under this law, the FCC has determined to force-feed children three hours of "educational" programming a week. When the government rates speech, approving some speech and disapproving other speech, all of us are endangered, children as well as adults.

Children's vulnerability to what they read and see and hear is often cited as a reason to allow the government *more* control over speech directed at young audiences. In fact, that vulnerability makes any measure of government control over speech directed at children very dangerous. Children are susceptible to propaganda. Totalitarian governments from Hitler to Stalin have known that; the dictator's picture hangs on the walls of the classroom.

It seems like a long journey from Nazi Germany to today's child-friendly FCC. But hundreds of years of world history teach that powers given to government agents to do good can just as easily be used to do bad. We do not know what changes the future will bring in terms of personnel and policies.

The danger is underscored by pointing out how arbitrary the judgment to require "educational television" in the public interest really is. Psychologists have argued for years about how children learn best and what they should learn, and how much time they should spend "learning" as opposed to just having fun. The federal government is not well equipped to supply the answer to those questions. And rating certain material as "educational" misleadingly implies that parents need not be concerned if their children sit staring at it for hours; kids are probably better off reading or playing outside. The Children's Television Act essentially allows the FCC to experiment on children, without any real evidence that it will do any good.

Fortunately, the First Amendment to the United States Constitution was written without special exceptions that permit controls on speech to children. The Children's Television Act of 1990 should be repealed.

Repealing V-Chip Requirements

The Telecommunications Act of 1996 requires the FCC to set a date by which manufacturers of television sets must begin installing "V-chips" capable of blocking violent programming in new sets. If the national networks fail to establish a satisfactory violence rating system on their own, the FCC is to establish an advisory committee to help them. Once ratings are established, the commission is empowered to require broadcasters to transmit them.

The V-chip regime represents a disingenuous attempt to evade the First Amendment. The law might look like the usual exercise of federal power over equipment, licensing, and transmissions, but it has one central purpose: to discourage the viewing of programming with a certain type of content. Clearly, it would be unconstitutional for Congress to direct the FCC to rate violent programming and refuse to renew the licenses of broadcasters who broadcast too much violence. The Supreme Court has declared government rating systems for movies unconstitutional. The V-chip regime uses subterfuge and threats to indirectly accomplish the same illegal objectives.

The V-chip does not restore civil society and private choice. Some advocates of the V-chip pretend that it is "voluntary." If that were true, the law would be unnecessary, and repealing the law would change nothing. But the system is not voluntary. Equipment manufacturers cannot choose whether to foist V-chips on consumers. Broadcasters cannot choose whether to have a ratings system, and whether to transmit it. Broadcasters who refuse to participate enthusiastically in the rating plan face reprisals at license renewal time.

The rating system the V-chip regime requires will offer parents little help in controlling what their children see and hear. There can be no consensus about what "violent" programming is. The news can be violent, as can reality-based shows like *Rescue 911*, slapstick humor like *I Love Lucy* and *The Three Stooges*, cartoons, social commentary like *Schindler's List,* and tales of heroes like Hercules and Xena. Even if violence could be meaningfully classified, there is simply too much television programming to rate carefully. Political works like *Das Kapital* have probably caused more violence in the 20th century than the most explicitly violent television program; controls on violence are closely akin to political censorship.

Imagine a law that required printers to encode on the spines of books a bar code that could be used to record ratings for violent content. If, within a year, publishers and authors had not come up with a rating system for book violence, a federal agency would be empowered to craft guidelines on their behalf. Publishers would be required to attach a rating to all the books they published. No one would pretend for a moment that such a system was voluntary.

The V-chip requirements of the Telecommunications Act of 1996 should be repealed.

Conclusion

Most of the restrictions on broadcast speech have been ostensibly imposed to protect children. But we do not help children by letting parents think that the government can substitute for supervised television viewing. We can best set an example for children by showing them that the First Amendment is much more than a bothersome obstacle to government, to be gotten around by indirect threats and economic pressure.

Suggested Readings

Corn-Revere, Robert. " 'V' Is *Not* for Voluntary." Cato Institute Briefing Paper no. 24, August 3, 1995.

Emord, Jonathan W. "The First Amendment Invalidity of FCC Content Regulations." *Notre Dame Journal of Legal Ethics & Public Policy* 6 (1992).

Weinberg, Jonathan. "Vagueness and Indecency." *Villanova Sports & Entertainment Law Journal* 221 (1996).

—Prepared by Solveig Bernstein and Lawrence Gasman

21. Terrorism

Congress should

- repeal the Antiterrorism and Effective Death Penalty Act of 1996,
- resist efforts to expand wiretapping,
- remove all export controls on encryption, and
- enact appropriations bills forbidding any executive branch official from spending money to promote the Clipper Chip.

From the Alien and Sedition Acts of 1798 to the Palmer Raids of 1919 to the McCarthy era to the present, proponents of restrictions on civil liberties have made exaggerated claims about various threats posed by American political dissidents and the necessity of a federal "crackdown." Indeed, proponents of a crackdown have often claimed that anyone who is skeptical of their exaggerated assertions must be sympathetic to the enemies of America.

Any violent crime is terrible, but terrorism is extremely rare in the United States. The risk that any given American will be killed by a terrorist is about the same as the chance that a randomly selected high school football player will one day be a starting quarterback in the Super Bowl. One's chance of being killed in a terrorist attack is many times less than one's chance of drowning in a bathtub or being killed by a fall from scaffolding or a ladder. We would not adopt the "if it saves one life" theory to justify a ban on bathtubs, even though hundreds of lives would be saved each year. Accordingly, America should reject terrorism legislation that will probably not save any lives and that demands that Americans give up things far more important than bathtubs.

Terrorists cannot destroy a free society, but they can scare a free society into destroying itself. In 1974 Irish Republican Army terrorists bombed pubs in Birmingham, England, killing 21 people. Home Secretary Roy

227

Jenkins introduced the Prevention of Terrorism (Temporary Provisions) Bill. Approved without objection in Parliament, the bill was supposed to expire in one year, but it has been renewed every year.

Under the Prevention of Terrorism Act, and subsequent British terrorism legislation, the police may stop and search without warrant any person suspected of terrorism. They may arrest any person they "reasonably suspect" "supports an illegal organization." An arrested person may be detained without court approval for up to a week. It is illegal even to organize a private or public meeting addressed by a member of a proscribed organization, or to wear clothes indicating support of such an organization.

In Britain wiretapping does not need judicial approval. If committed pursuant to an order from a secretary of state, acts such as theft, damage to property, arson, procuring information for blackmail, and leaving planted evidence are not crimes.

A suspect's decision to remain silent during interrogation may now be used against him in court. Although terrorism in Northern Ireland was the stated reason for the change, the change also applies in England and Wales. No one who has seen what is happening in Great Britain can feel confident that repressive measures introduced solely to counter terrorism will not eventually creep into the ordinary criminal justice system.

The Birmingham bombings that led to the Prevention of Terrorism Act resulted in the conviction of a group of defendants called the Birmingham Six, whose confessions were extracted under torture and who were convicted on what was later admitted to be the perjured testimony of a government forensic scientist. Eventually, they were freed, although if Britain had a death penalty, they would have been executed.

To state the obvious, all the repressive legislation has hardly immunized Britain from terrorism. To the contrary, British citizens are as vulnerable to an IRA car bomb as they were in 1974, and they are at much greater risk of being terrorized by the state itself. For centuries, "the rights of Englishmen" were proudly held up in contrast to the absolutism of the Continent. Far from being an exemplar to the world, the modern "anti-terrorist" United Kingdom has been found guilty of human rights violations under the European Convention on Human Rights more often than any other member of the Council of European States. As Britain's recent history illustrates, no matter how great a country's tradition of freedom, freedom can be lost in less than a generation if public officials, and the public, allow terrorism to destroy their traditional way of life.

To study the terrorism agenda being pushed in the United States these days is to study a series of assaults on the Bill of Rights. Despite the First

Amendment, some members of Congress have announced their dismay that explosives recipes (usually incomplete or otherwise erroneous) and other instructions for making products that are illegal without a special license can be found on the Internet. First of all, it is legal in the United States, and always has been, to publish information about how to make firearms, or explosives, or other weapons.

The fact that some such information is being distributed electronically, by phone lines, rather than in printed form by mail order, hardly changes its secure status within the protection of the First Amendment, any more than did the fact that *The Anarchist Cookbook* in the 1960s was printed with a high-speed modern printing press rather than a Franklin press. The government may not punish people for possessing knowledge or for reading about breaking the law. Indeed, a rule that outlaws speech because a criminal could learn something from it puts one on the way to banning crime novels and police training manuals, which, after all, contain detailed examples of how to commit various crimes.

Taggants

The main terrorism legislation threat to the Second Amendment is the Clinton administration's "taggants" proposal, under which literally millions of Americans would be classified as felons. A taggant is a chemical marker that can be placed in explosives. Even after the explosive is detonated, the taggant can identify the factory the explosive came from and perhaps the batch.

Whatever the possible value of taggants for commercial high explosives, taggants can be of no use for crimes involving black powder and smokeless powder. Those consumer products are sold in one- or five-pound bags. Smokeless powder and black powder are used in the home manufacture of ammunition (hand loading) by literally millions of families in the United States. Since one batch of factory powder may eventually be sold to tens of thousands of consumers, there is no realistic possibility that a taggant could lead to the solution of a crime. Instead, taggants legislation would create millions of crimes, since the Clinton proposal would criminalize the possession of black powder or smokeless powder without taggants, making the existing supplies of the millions of hand loaders a federal felony.

Taggants for gunpowder would have forensic value only if all powder purchases were registered and if each individual one-pound box of powder had its own individual taggant, a very expensive proposition. Even then, a person could obtain untagged powder by purchasing ammunition, disassembling it, and removing the powder. Thus all ammunition purchases would have to be registered.

A study from the Office of Technology Assessment suggests that taggants could destabilize smokeless powder and black powder. Although Switzerland is frequently cited as a model for the use of taggants, that country does not require taggants in smokeless powder and black powder.

Finally, according to the Office of Technology Assessment, taggants are easy to remove from gunpowder by sifting, or by viewing the powder under black light and picking the taggants out with tweezers. Other taggants can be removed with a magnet. In short, taggants in gunpowder are a stalking-horse for ammunition registration, with no real crime-fighting value.

Wiretapping

The Fourth Amendment has also come under severe attack, as the Federal Bureau of Investigation and other federal agencies have used terrorism as a vehicle to push existing plans for significantly expanded electronic surveillance. For example, the original Clinton and Dole terrorism bills defined almost all violent and property crime (down to petty offenses below misdemeanors) as "terrorism" and then allowed wiretaps for "terrorism" investigations. (Those provisions did not become law.)

Terrorists are, of course, already subject to being wiretapped. Yet, as federal wiretaps set record highs every year, wiretaps are used overwhelmingly for gambling and drugs. From 1983 to 1993, of the 8,800 applications for eavesdropping, only 16 were for arson, explosives, or firearms.

Wiretaps are currently authorized for the interception of particular speakers on particular phone lines. If the interception target keeps switching telephones (for example, by using a variety of pay phones), the government may ask the court for a "roving wiretap," authorizing interception of any phone line the target is using. Although roving wiretaps are currently available when the government shows the court a need, there is a campaign to allow roving wiretaps *without* court approval. In other words, the FBI would be on the honor system for conducting wiretaps according to the Constitution. The Fourth Amendment, however, mandates that an essential part of the system of checks and balances is that intrusive surveillance of Americans citizens must not take place without prior judicial authorization. Moreover, the FBI's recent record of lawlessness—from Ruby Ridge to Waco to Travelgate to Filegate, and all of the associated coverups—hardly inspires confidence that independent supervision of the bureau should be curtailed.

The final terrorism bill, while deleting provisions for warrantless roving wiretaps, did significantly expand wiretapping authority. The Electronic Communications Privacy Act outlaws wiretapping by the government or by private parties, with certain exceptions (such as when a warrant is obtained). The terrorism bill narrowed the type of communication interceptions that are considered to be wiretapping and thereby greatly expanded the scope of communications that can legally be intercepted by private actors, as well as by government officials who lack both probable cause and a search warrant. Wireless transmission of computer data is now subject to search without a warrant.

Encryption

If a person writes a letter to another person, she can write the letter in a secret code. If the government intercepts the letter, and cannot figure out the secret code, the government is out of luck. That basic First and Fourth Amendment principle has never been questioned. But, if instead of being written with pen on paper, the letter is written electronically, and sent over a computer network rather than by postal mail, do privacy interests suddenly vanish? According to FBI director Louis Freeh, the answer is yes.

Testifying before the Senate Judiciary Committee, Freeh complained that people can communicate over the Internet ''in encrypted conversations for which we have no available means to read and understand unless that encryption problem is dealt with immediately.'' The supposed encryption problem (i.e., people being able to communicate privately) could only be solved by outlawing high-quality encryption software like Pretty Good Privacy.

First of all, shareware versions of Pretty Good Privacy are ubiquitous throughout American computer networks. The cat cannot be put back in the bag. More fundamentally, the potential that a criminal, including a terrorist, might misuse private communications is no reason to abolish all private communication.

Although Freeh apparently wants to outlaw encryption entirely, the Clinton administration has been proposing the Clipper Chip as a first step. However, the Clipper Chip provides a low level of privacy protection against casual snoopers, and some computer scientists have already announced that the chip can be defeated. Moreover, the ''key''—which allows private phone conversations, computer files, or electronic mail to be opened by unauthorized third parties—-will be held by the federal government or a third party approved by the government. The federal government promises that it will keep the keys carefully guarded and use them only to snoop when absolutely necessary.

Proposals for the federal government's acquisition of a key to everyone's electronic data, which the government promises never to misuse, might be compared to the federal government's proposing to acquire a key to everyone's home. Currently, people can buy door locks and other security devices that are of such high quality that covert entry by the government is impossible; the government might be able to break the door down, but the government would not be able to enter quietly, place an electronic surveillance device, and then leave. Thus, high-quality locks can defeat a lawful government attempt to bug a home, just as high-quality encryption can defeat a lawful government attempt to read a person's electronic correspondence or data.

While wiretaps or government surveillance of computer communications may be legal, there should be no obligation for individuals or businesses to make wiretapping easy. Simply put, Americans should not be required to live their lives so that the government can spy on them.

Thus, although proposals to outlaw or emasculate computer privacy are sometimes defended as maintaining the status quo (easy government wiretaps), the true status quo in America is that manufacturers have never been required to make products that are custom designed to facilitate government snooping. The point is no less valid for electronic keys than it is for front-door keys.

Efforts to limit electronic privacy will harm, not just the First and Fourth Amendments, but also American commerce. Genuinely secure public-key encryption gives users the safety and convenience of electronic files plus the security features of paper envelopes and signatures. A good encryption program can authenticate the creator of a particular electronic document— just as a written signature authenticates (more or less) the creator of a particular paper document. Public-key encryption can greatly reduce the need for paper. With secure public-key encryption, businesses could distribute catalogs, take orders, pay with digital cash, and enforce contracts with verifiable signatures—all without paper.

Conversely, the Clinton administration's weak privacy protection (giving the federal government the ability to spy everywhere) means that confidential business secrets will be easily stolen by business competitors who can bribe local or federal law enforcement officials to divulge the "secret" codes for breaking into private conversations and files or who can hack the Clipper Chip.

Aliens

Although the United States has suffered exactly one alien terrorist attack in the last 11 years, special, harsh rules for aliens were at the top of the Clinton terrorism agenda. The new Clinton-Dole terrorism law allows secret evidence in alien deportation cases in which the government asserts that secrecy is necessary to national security. Georgetown University law professor David Cole calls the secret court the new "Star Chamber," because its powers resemble those of the inquisitorial court that the British monarchy, in violation of the common law, used to terrorize dissident subjects.

Modern Star Chamber proceedings are to be before a special court (one of five select federal district judges), after an ex parte, in camera showing that normal procedures would "pose a risk to the national security of the United States." After further ex parte, in camera motions, evidence that the government does not wish to disclose may be withheld from the defendant, who will instead be provided a general summary of what the evidence purports to prove. In other words, secret evidence may be used. Of course any of the "showings" that the government makes in camera and ex parte may be based on the unreviewable claims of a secret informant. No evidence may be excluded because it was illegally obtained, no matter how flagrantly the law was broken.

Legal aliens do not, of course, have the full scope of constitutional rights guaranteed to American citizens; for example, they cannot exercise rights associated with citizenship, such as voting or serving on a jury. But the Fifth Amendment's guarantee of due process protects "all persons," not "all citizens."

The argument for allowing secret evidence in deportation proceedings is that otherwise the identity or operational mode of a confidential informant might be jeopardized. First of all, the very purpose of the Sixth Amendment's confrontation clause is to prevent people's lives from being destroyed by secret accusations. Moreover, the argument against endangering the secrecy of confidential accusers in deportation cases proves too much. The very same argument applies in every other type of case in which informants are heavily used, including tax evasion, drug sales or possession, and gun laws. Obeying the confrontation clause may impede the short-term interests of law enforcement, but the Constitution makes it clear that a criminal justice system without a right of confrontation poses a far greater long-term risk to public safety than does requiring the government to disclose the reason why it wants to imprison, execute, or deport someone.

Some persons may accept the Star Chamber for legal resident aliens under the presumption that such procedures would never be used against American citizens. Yet if there is anything the experience of Great Britain proves, it is that special, "emergency" measures implemented in a limited jurisdiction soon spread throughout the nation. Cancers always start small. If one international terrorist incident in 11 years is sufficient to justify a Star Chamber for aliens, then it is hard to resist the logic that crimes that actually are widespread (such as homicide, rape, or sales of controlled substances) should be entitled to their own Star Chamber.

Everything that terrorists do is already illegal. Current laws already provide ample authority for investigations of potential terrorists, including persons who have done nothing more than talk big. The Oklahoma City and World Trade Center bombings were both solved under existing laws. While the 1995 terrorism bill, one of the most repressive measures ever enacted by the U.S. Congress, was promoted as a response to the Oklahoma City bombing, not a single item in the entire bill would have prevented that heinous crime or assisted in its solution. The tiny but sensational threat of terrorism should not be used as a pretext for stripping fundamental freedoms from the American people. As the Founders of the American Republic understood, public safety in the long run is best protected by vigorous enforcement of the Constitution, not by giving more power to federal agencies that abuse the powers they already have.

Suggested Readings

Kopel, David B., and Joseph Olson. "Preventing a Reign of Terror: Civil Liberties Implications of Terrorism Legislation." *Oklahoma City Law Review* 21, forthcoming.
Office of Technology Assessment. *Taggants in Explosives.* Washington: Government Printing Office, 1988.

—Prepared by David B. Kopel

22. The Ominous Powers of Federal Law Enforcement

Congress should

- shield the citizenry from abusive prosecutors by enacting an "ignorance-of-the-law" defense,
- restore the constitutional immunity against double jeopardy by abolishing "dual prosecution" by federal and state prosecutors,
- restore the constitutional right of trial by jury by abolishing "real-offense" sentencing, and
- halt the deputization of private industry by repealing the Bank Secrecy Act of 1970 and the Communications Assistance for Law Enforcement Act of 1994.

Federal law enforcement agencies have assumed extraordinary police and prosecutorial powers over the American people during the last 30 years. In some cases the government can now circumvent basic constitutional guarantees such as trial by jury and the prohibition against double jeopardy. The government is also employing disturbing surveillance strategies, such as enlisting the help of private industries to spy on American citizens. It is no overstatement to say that our national government is taking on too many attributes of a police state. The 105th Congress should reverse those ominous trends by restoring our constitutional safeguards against an overweening government.

Our Unavoidable Ignorance of the Law

History is filled with examples of tyrannical governments that were able to persecute unpopular groups and innocent individuals by keeping the law's requirements from the people. The Roman emperor Caligula, for example, posted new laws high on the columns of buildings so that they could not be studied by ordinary citizens. The Framers of the U.S. Constitution recognized that this type of rank injustice could arise even under a democratic form of government. As James Madison noted, "It will be of little avail to the people that the laws are made by men of their own choice if the laws be so voluminous that they cannot be read, or so incoherent that they cannot be understood; if they be repealed or revised before they are promulgated, or undergo such incessant changes that no man who knows what the law is today, can guess what it will be tomorrow." Unfortunately, Madison's vision of unbridled lawmaking is an apt description of federal regulatory policy in the 1990s. The Environmental Protection Agency, for example, set up a special hotline to answer legal questions from citizens. But the EPA does not guarantee that the information given over the hotline is correct—and reliance on incorrect information will not constitute a defense in a government enforcement action.

The sheer volume of modern law makes it impossible for an ordinary American household to stay informed—and yet the U.S. Department of Justice vigorously defends the old legal maxim that "ignorance of the law is no excuse." That maxim may have been appropriate for a society that simply criminalized inherently evil conduct, such as murder, rape, and theft, but it is wholly inappropriate in a labyrinthine regulatory regime that criminalizes activities that are morally neutral. It has been estimated that the number of new enactments by legislative bodies ranging from city councils to Congress is 150,000 per year. At that rate, a conscientious citizen would have to study 410 laws each and every day all year long—a full-time task, to say the least.

It is simply outrageous for the U.S. government to impose a legal duty on every American citizen to "know" all of the mind-boggling rules and regulations that have emanated from Washington over the years. The 105th Congress can remedy that unjust situation by passing a law that would require U.S. attorneys to prove that regulatory violations are "willful" or, in the alternative, permit a good-faith belief in the legality of one's conduct to be pleaded and proved as a defense. The former rule is already in place for our complicated tax laws; it should shield unwary Americans from all of the other regulations as well.

An Ever-Expanding Double Jeopardy Loophole

The Fifth Amendment's double jeopardy clause bars government from subjecting any person to multiple prosecutions for the same offense. But the Supreme Court has interpreted that clause in a way that allows separate state and federal prosecutions for the same conduct. That legal doctrine, which is known as the "dual sovereign" exception to the double jeopardy principle, gives federal prosecutors the power to retry thousands of state cases in federal court.

The double jeopardy principle has been recognized as one of the great bulwarks against government oppression. Without that protection, the government could use its vast resources to wear down political dissidents and others with repetitive prosecutions. Multiple prosecutions also allow government attorneys to hone their trial tactics before new juries, which only increases the risk of an erroneous conviction. To guard against that danger, the Framers of the Constitution explicitly incorporated the immunity against double jeopardy into the Bill of Rights in 1791.

The Bill of Rights, however, constrained only the federal government until the ratification in 1868 of the Fourteenth Amendment, which affords citizens the protections in the Bill of Rights against state government actions. Because federal criminal prosecutions were few and far between for much of our history, the question of how the double jeopardy principle fit into our federalist system remained a theoretical issue for many years. American courts were vexed early on, for example, by the question of whether the state and federal governments could make the same conduct a crime. The powers of the federal government are set forth in article I, section 8, of the Constitution, and the Tenth Amendment makes it clear that the "powers not delegated to the United States by the Constitution" are reserved to "the States respectively, or to the people." Early American courts believed that, by virtue of the separation of powers and the creation of separate jurisdictions, "double trials would virtually never occur in our country." In the rare instances of concurrent jurisdiction, the courts expected the prosecutors themselves to respect the double jeopardy principle. In *Jett v. The Commonwealth* (1867), for example, the Supreme Court of Virginia stated, "We must suppose that the criminal laws will be administered, as they should be, in a spirit of justice and benignity to the citizen, and that those who are entrusted with their execution will interpose to protect offenders against double punishment, whenever their interposition is necessary to prevent injustice or oppression; and that if, in any case, they should fail to do so, the wrong will be addressed by the pardoning power."

As long as the concurrent jurisdiction of the federal and state governments was limited, the potential for prosecutorial mischief was relatively minor. But the legal landscape was drastically altered after the turn of the century as the federal government expanded its criminal jurisdiction beyond "the unique areas of national concern listed among its constitutionally enumerated powers." Attorney Daniel A. Braun writes,

> The criminal legislation enacted during this century, especially the sweeping crime control measures passed since the 1960s, has greatly increased the quantity of substantive criminal offenses covered by parallel federal and state statutes. The criminal codes of the states and the nation presently identify many of the same wrongs and share many of the same goals. For this reason, an individual who violates the criminal law of a state stands a considerable chance of violating a provision of the federal code as well.

The Supreme Court has repeatedly upheld successive state and federal prosecutions. The Court's legal analysis typically emphasizes the law enforcement interests of government over the potential abuse of individual defendants. A common argument is that one sovereign might try to subvert the policies of the other. A state, for example, might try to undermine a national law by enacting a similar statute with a very light penalty so that defendants would rush to plead guilty in state court and thereby avoid a stiffer punishment under federal law. Although there may be some merit to that argument, the Court all but ignores the risks associated with its current rule, namely, that federal and state authorities may join forces to pursue common governmental interests. Justice Hugo Black, among others, insisted on viewing the legal issue "from the standpoint of the individual who is being prosecuted." In a biting dissent, Black observed, "If danger to the innocent is emphasized, the danger is surely no less when the power of State and Federal Governments is brought to bear on one man in two trials, than when one of these 'Sovereigns' proceeds alone."

It is imperative that the mischievous "dual sovereign" loophole in double jeopardy law be closed immediately. A number of state governments have, to their credit, restricted their prosecuting officials from initiating a criminal case against anyone who has already undergone a federal prosecution for any particular incident. The 105th Congress should restrain federal prosecutors with a similar rule.

Bypassing Trial by Jury

The Sixth Amendment says that any person accused of a crime "shall enjoy the right to a speedy and public trial, by an impartial jury." Trial by jury, however, is increasingly being bypassed by a concept known as "real-offense" sentencing. As unbelievable as it may seem, our courts can now punish an individual for an offense even after the jury has unanimously rendered a "not guilty" verdict. That pernicious doctrine is nothing less than an assault upon our entire constitutional system of justice.

When America declared independence from England, the jury trial was regarded as one of the most important safeguards against arbitrary and oppressive governmental policies. Thomas Jefferson, for example, considered the jury trial "the only anchor ever yet imagined by man, by which a government can be held to the principles of its constitution." During the contentious ratification debates, Alexander Hamilton pointed out that the right to jury trial was a subject that everyone could agree upon. In *Federalist* no. 83 Hamilton wrote, "The friends and adversaries of the [proposed constitution], if they agree in nothing else, concur at least in the value they set upon the trial by jury; or if there is any difference between them it consists in this: the former regard it as a valuable safeguard to liberty; the latter represent it as the very palladium of free government." Those firmly held convictions of America's early leaders were undoubtedly formed as a result of their colonial experience. Because colonial juries routinely refused to convict citizens who were prosecuted under oppressive British laws, Americans saw the jury as an indispensable "check" upon government abuse.

When the time came to form a new American government, the Framers of the U.S. Constitution placed the jury at the heart of our criminal justice system. They did that for a very specific reason: the Framers did not want the federal government to have the power to unilaterally brand a citizen as a criminal. In America prosecutors must first persuade a jury of laymen that the accused is a criminal who must be punished. The jury's unanimous assent to the government's indictment was to be a prerequisite to punishment.

Real-offense sentencing, however, undermines the constitutional safeguard of trial by jury in at least two ways. First, if the prosecutor fails to persuade a jury of the defendant's guilt at trial, he can now ask a judge for a second opinion. For example, *United States v. Rodriguez-Gonzales* (2d Cir. 1990) involved a jury trial for several counts of drug dealing and one count of "carrying a firearm during a drug trafficking offense." The jury convicted the defendant of the drug charges but acquitted him of the firearms charge. At sentencing, the judge found that "a firearm was possessed" and punished the defendant accordingly. As bizarre as it may sound, the defendant will serve 110 months in prison for the acquitted conduct.

Second, U.S. attorneys can withhold shaky evidence on some allegations until the sentencing phase by filing an indictment with a single charge. If the government is able to secure a conviction on the charge set forth in the formal indictment, prosecutors can then seek "enhanced penalties" for offenses the jury never heard about. The government has a strong incentive to employ that strategy against defendants because the evidentiary standards before a sentencing judge are well below those required at trial. Prosecutors only have to prove "sentencing factors" by a preponderance of the evidence instead of the traditionally high standard of "beyond a reasonable doubt." And because the Federal Rules of Evidence do not apply at sentencing, federal judges can add years to a defendant's sentence on the basis of flimsy hearsay evidence.

Justice Department officials defend real-offense sentencing by claiming that no person is being punished for unconvicted criminal conduct; some individuals are merely being punished more severely because of the factual circumstances surrounding the crime of which they were convicted. That is a dangerous play on words. For if the connection between trial and sentencing procedures is severed, Congress can simply manipulate the statutory maximum penalties for the thousands of actions that are now criminal. Such manipulation would effectively obviate the government's burden to prove the bulk of criminal activity before juries by proof beyond a reasonable doubt. Law professor Elizabeth Lear observes that "under the current regime of nonconviction offense sentencing, only the judge and the prosecutor need approve the bulk of punishment decisions." Such unbridled governmental power, Lear concludes, "eviscerates the jury's ability to control executive and judicial abuse."

The 105th Congress should not allow prosecutors to bypass the constitutional safeguard of trial by jury. Congress should jettison the present real-offense sentencing paradigm and move to a "conviction-offense" model. That would not be a move into unchartered territory. The state of Minnesota has been operating on a conviction-offense model for several years, and it is among the most respected of the state systems. Congress should adopt the wisdom of the Minnesota model.

The Deputization of Private Industry

Perhaps the most disturbing legal trend in recent years is the extent to which the federal government is compelling private organizations to assist in law enforcement investigations. Banks, for example, are legally required to spy on their customers and make periodic reports to the police. Telephone companies must open their records and facilities to government agents and give them whatever technical assistance they need to conduct their electronic surveillance. And, with those precedents firmly in place, the federal government is now seeking to expand its network of private informers by deputizing the hotel, airline, and financial services industries. The American tradition of voluntary cooperation with the police is being perverted into an insidious system of compulsory cooperation.

That trend began with the Bank Secrecy Act of 1970. The Department of Justice and the Internal Revenue Service convinced Congress that they could launch a more effective attack on organized crime if our domestic banks could be made to provide greater evidence of financial transactions. The result was a massive imposition of reporting and record-keeping requirements on America's banking institutions.

Under the Bank Secrecy Act, banks must spy on their customers and report any transaction involving more than $10,000 to the police. Every bank must also microfilm or copy every check drawn on it or presented to it for payment. That record-keeping requirement is extremely burdensome. A 1970 report from the House Committee on Banking and Currency estimated that a minimum of 20 billion checks have to be photocopied every year. Congress made no attempt, however, to compensate banks for that unfunded mandate.

The Supreme Court upheld the constitutionality of the Bank Secrecy Act in a six-to-three decision in 1974. The Court found no Fourth or Fifth Amendment violation and did not find the cost burden to be unreasonable. But Justice Thurgood Marshall took issue with the Court's Fourth Amendment analysis in a dissenting opinion: "By compelling an otherwise unwilling bank to photocopy the checks of its customers, the Government has as much a hand in seizing those checks as if it had forced a private person to break into the customer's home or office and photocopy the checks there." Justice William O. Douglas expressed his discomfort with the act by extending the government's logic beyond the context of banking: "It would be highly useful to government espionage to have like reports from all our bookstores, all our hardware and retail stores, all our drugstores. These records too might be 'useful' in criminal investigations." Like Marshall, Douglas believed the act to be unconstitutional.

Unfortunately, Justice Douglas's dissenting opinion has proven to be prescient. After the banks, the government deputized the telephone industry. For many years the regional Bell companies had been quietly cooperating with law enforcement investigations, but in 1976 the New York

Telephone Company refused to give the Federal Bureau of Investigation "the facilities and technical assistance necessary" for it to determine the numbers dialed by certain gambling suspects. The case wound its way through the courts and the Supreme Court ultimately ruled against New York Telephone. Turning the right to be left alone on its head, the Court said the telephone company had no "substantial interest in *not* providing assistance" to the FBI. Federal district courts can now compel innocent third parties to render assistance in law enforcement.

In 1992 the FBI took its notion of civic responsibility even further. When the telephone companies began developing new technologies such as fiber optics and cellular phones, the FBI complained that the new technology was outpacing its eavesdropping abilities. Congress yielded to the FBI's "top legislative priority" by passing the Communications Assistance for Law Enforcement Act of 1994 (CALEA). That act is forcing every telephone company in America to make its networks more accessible to police wiretaps. The cost of the necessary technology makeover is expected to be several billion dollars. Any communications carrier that fails to meet the standards of the attorney general can be fined up to $10,000 per day.

CALEA is a truly ominous precedent for America. The subordination of private industry to the directives of a national police agency is an authoritarian concept that is completely at odds with the philosophical underpinnings of the U.S. Constitution. Unfortunately, that disturbing legal trend shows no sign of abating. Recent "anti-terrorism" proposals seek to draw the airline, hotel, and financial services industries into the government's network of private informers and data gatherers. Such proposals will probably resurface in the near future.

A free society should never allow "crime reduction" to become an end in itself. When that happens, government tends to destroy the rights and liberties that it was supposed to maintain. That is precisely the dynamic that is at work in modern America. The 105th Congress must recognize that dynamic for what it is and take corrective action. Laws such as the Bank Secrecy Act and CALEA should be taken off the books. The American tradition of voluntary cooperation with law enforcement should be restored.

Suggested Readings

Bovard, James. *Lost Rights: The Destruction of American Liberty*. New York: St. Martin's, 1994.

Braun, Daniel A. "Praying to False Sovereigns: The Rule of Successive Prosecutions in the Age of Cooperative Federalism." *American Journal of Criminal Law* 20 (1992): 1–78.

Cass, Ronald A. "Ignorance of the Law: A Maxim Reexamined." *William and Mary Law Review* 17 (1976): 671–99.

DeLong, James V. "The Criminalization of Just About Everything." *American Enterprise*, March–April 1994, pp. 26–35.

Lear, Elizabeth T. "Is Conviction Irrelevant?" *UCLA Law Review* 40 (1993): 1179–1239.

Lynch, Timothy. "Polluting Our Principles: Environmental Criminal Prosecutions and the Bill of Rights." Cato Institute Policy Analysis no. 223, April 20, 1995.

Parent, Dale G. "What Did the United States Sentencing Commission Miss?" *Yale Law Journal* 101 (1992): 1773–93.

—Prepared by Timothy Lynch

DOMESTIC POLICY

23. Social Security

Congress should allow young workers to redirect the retirement portion of their payroll taxes to individual accounts that can be invested in private capital markets.

Social Security is going broke. The federal government's largest spending program, accounting for nearly 22 percent of all federal spending, faces irresistible demographic and fiscal pressures that threaten the future retirement security of today's young workers. Only by moving to a system of privately invested, individually owned accounts can a system of secure retirement be preserved.

According to the 1996 report of the Social Security system's Board of Trustees, the retirement system will be insolvent by 2029, down from 2030 in last year's report. This is the eighth time in the last 10 years that the insolvency date has been brought forward.

But focusing exclusively on that date is misleading. The implication is that Social Security's financing is fine until 2029, at which point benefits will suddenly stop. The reality is more complex and much more immediately dangerous.

Currently, Social Security taxes bring in more revenue than the system pays out in benefits. The surplus theoretically accumulates in the Social Security Trust Fund. As Figure 23.1 shows, the situation will reverse as early as 2012. Social Security will begin paying out more in benefits than it collects in revenues.

To continue meeting its obligations, the Social Security system will have to begin drawing on the surplus in the trust fund. However, at that point we will discover that the trust fund is really little more than a polite fiction. For years the federal government has used it to disguise the actual size of the federal budget deficit, borrowing money from the trust fund

Figure 23.1
Social Security Revenues versus Outlays

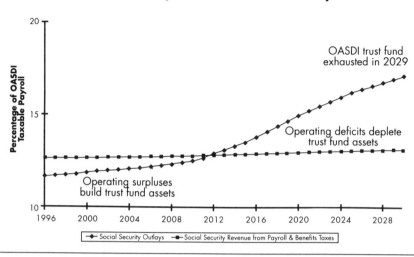

SOURCE: Derived from *1996 Annual Report of the Board of Trustees of the Federal Old-Age and Survivors Insurance and Disability Trust Funds* (Washington, D.C.: Social Security Administration, 1996), Table II.F13, p. 108.

to pay current operating expenses and replacing the money with government bonds.

Beginning in 2012, Social Security will have to start turning in those bonds to the federal government to obtain the cash needed to finance benefits. But the federal government has no cash or other assets with which to pay off those bonds. It can obtain the cash only by borrowing and running a bigger deficit, increasing taxes, or cutting other government spending. All those options pose obvious problems.

Even if Congress can find a way to redeem the bonds, the trust fund surplus will be completely exhausted by 2029. At that point, Social Security will have to rely solely on revenue from the payroll tax. But such revenues will not be sufficient to pay all promised benefits. Either payroll taxes will have to be increased to as much as 28 percent, more than double today's 12.4 percent rate, or benefits will have to be reduced by as much as one-third. (If taxes needed to fund Medicare are included, the total FICA payroll tax may have to be increased from today's 15.3 percent to as much as 40 percent!)

Social Security's financing problems are a result of its fundamentally flawed design, which is comparable to the type of pyramid scheme that is illegal in all 50 states. Today's benefits to the old are paid by today's taxes from the young. Tomorrow's benefits to today's young are to be paid by tomorrow's taxes on tomorrow's young.

Because the average recipient takes out more from the system than he or she paid in, Social Security works as long as there is an ever-larger pool of workers paying into the system compared to the pool of beneficiaries taking out of the system. However, exactly the opposite is happening.

Life expectancy is increasing, while birth rates are declining. As recently as 1950 there were 16 workers for every Social Security beneficiary. Today there are only 3.3. By 2025 there will be fewer than 2 (Figure 23.2). The Social Security pyramid is unsustainable.

Moreover, even if Social Security's financial difficulties can be fixed, the system remains a bad deal for most Americans, a situation that is growing worse for today's young workers. Payroll taxes are already so high that even if today's young workers receive the promised benefits, those benefits will amount to a low, below-market return on payroll taxes. Studies show that for most young workers such benefits would amount to a negative return on the required taxes. Those workers can now get far

Figure 23.2
Support/Benefit Ratio: Workers per Social Security Beneficiary

SOURCE: *1995 Annual Report of the Board of Trustees of the Federal Old-Age and Survivors Insurance and Disability Insurance Trust Funds* (Washington: Government Printing Office, 1995), page 122.

higher returns and benefits through private savings, investment, and insurance.

Privatizing Social Security

There is a better alternative. Social Security should be privatized, allowing people the freedom to invest their Social Security taxes in financial assets such as stocks and bonds. A privatized Social Security system would essentially be a mandatory savings program. The 10.52 percent payroll tax that is the combined employer-employee contribution to the Old-Age and Survivors Insurance portion of the Social Security program would be redirected toward a personal security account (PSA) chosen by the individual employee.

PSAs would operate much like current individual retirement accounts (IRAs). Individuals could not withdraw funds from their PSAs before retirement, determined either by age or PSA balance requirements. PSA funds would be the property of the individual, and upon death, remaining funds would become part of the individual's estate.

PSAs would be managed by the private investment industry in the same way as 401(k) plans or IRAs. Individuals would be free to choose the fund manager that best met their individual needs and could change managers whenever they wished. The government would establish regulations on portfolio risk to prevent speculation and protect consumers. Reinsurance mechanisms would be required to guarantee fund solvency.

The government would continue to guarantee a minimum pension benefit. The minimum pension could be set to a benchmark such as the minimum wage. If upon retirement the balance in an individual's PSA were insufficient to provide an actuarially determined retirement annuity equal to the minimum wage, the government would provide a supplement sufficient to bring the individual's monthly income up to the level of the minimum wage.

Given historic rates of return from the capital markets, even minimum wage earners would receive more than the minimum from the new system if they participated their entire working lives. Therefore, in the absence of a major financial collapse, the safety net would be required for few aside from the disabled and others outside the workforce.

The Chilean Example

The idea of privatizing a public pension system is neither new nor untried. Where privatization has been properly implemented, it has been remarkably successful. One of the best examples is the experience of Chile.

Chile's social security system predated ours, having started in 1926. By the late 1970s its benefit payments were greater than its taxes and it had no funded reserves. On the advice of Milton Friedman and other free-market economists, Chile decided to privatize its system.

The success of Chile's public pension privatization can be measured in many ways. Chile's private savings rate is 26 percent of GDP, compared with 4 percent in the United States. The infusion of capital into the private sector has contributed in large part to Chile's phenomenal 7 percent annual economic growth rate over the past 10 years, double ours.

But most important, beneficiaries are receiving much higher benefits. Since the privatized system became fully operational on May 1, 1981, the average rate of return on investment has been more than 14 percent per year. As a result, the typical retiree is receiving a benefit equal to nearly 80 percent of his average annual income over the last 10 years of his working life, almost double the U.S. replacement value.

Chile's reforms are seen as such a huge economic and political success that countries throughout Latin America, including Argentina, Peru, Colombia, Uruguay, and Mexico, are beginning to implement similar changes. In Europe, Britain provides a low minimum benefit through its traditional pay-as-you-go social security system, but that country has also allowed people to opt out of its benefits above that minimum through contributions to an expanded IRA. Nearly 70 percent of Britons have done so. Even Italy has begun to privatize some aspects of its social security system.

Solving the Problems of Privatization

Obviously, privatization of Social Security would not come without questions and problems.

First, the current Social Security system involves several elements of social insurance that make it much more than a simple retirement system. For example, portions of the payroll tax support the Disability Insurance and Medicare programs. Transferring those programs to the private sector is both possible and desirable but entails considerably more difficulty than privatizing the retirement portion of Social Security. Their fate should be decided separately.

Social Security also currently provides survivors' benefits that would disappear under a privatized system. But that would be largely offset because privatization would make benefits part of an individual's estate.

In addition, it would be relatively easy to use a portion of PSA funds to purchase life insurance.

Finally, it's important to recognize the redistributionist aspect of Social Security. Benefit formulas are calculated on a progressive basis that provides a relatively higher return to low-income workers than to people with higher incomes. A privatized system would generally reverse that. High-wage individuals would receive a higher total return on their investment, which would lead to greater income inequality.

Still, and far more important, low-wage workers would likely receive far more in benefits than they do under the current system. Because low-income workers are far more likely than the wealthy to rely on Social Security for all or most of their retirement income, the current system's low rate of return actually hurts them the most. Indeed, some studies show that because of the regressive nature of the payroll tax and the shorter life expectancy of the poor, they are the major victims of today's system.

The most difficult issue associated with any proposed privatization of Social Security is the transition. Put quite simply, regardless of what system we choose for the future, we have a moral obligation to continue benefits to today's recipients. But if current workers divert their payroll taxes to a private system, those taxes will no longer be available to pay benefits. The government will have to find a new source of funds. The Congressional Research Service estimates that cost at nearly $7 trillion over the next 35 years.

While that sounds like an intimidating figure, much of it is really just making explicit an already existing unfunded obligation. As noted above, the federal government already cannot fund as much as $4.9 trillion of Social Security's promised benefits. Those who claim we cannot afford to finance the transition have yet to explain how they will fund benefits for our children.

Even so, proponents of privatization have an obligation to explain how they would fund the transition. The reality will probably involve some combination of four approaches. The first is a partial default. Any change in future benefits amounts to a default. That could range from such mild options as raising the retirement age, reducing cost-of-living allowances, or means testing benefits to ''writing off'' obligations to individuals under a certain age who opt into the private system. For example, any individual under the age of 30 who chose the private system might receive no credit for past contributions to Social Security.

The second method of financing the transition is to continue a small portion of the current payroll tax. For example, instead of privatizing the entire OASI portion of the payroll tax, workers would be allowed to invest 6 or 8 percentage points, with the remainder temporarily continuing to fund a portion of current benefits.

Third, Congress can identify additional spending cuts and use the funds to pay the transition cost. Steve Entin, an economist with the Institute for Research on the Economics of Taxation, estimates that fully funding the transition would require slowing the rate of growth in federal spending by an additional ½ percent beyond currently envisioned cuts, eventually reaching a reduction of from $60 billion to $70 billion per year.

The final proposal often suggested for funding the transition is for the government to issue bonds to current system participants and taxpayers. The present value of the actuarially determined annuity due each system participant may be easily calculated and each system participant could be issued zero-coupon T-bonds maturing at the participant's projected retirement date. The bonds would be placed in each individual's PSA. However, while that has the virtue of making explicit the government's long-term obligations, it is really just an accounting gimmick. Ultimately, the government will still have to find the funds to make good on the bonds.

Social Security privatization is an idea whose time has come. For our children's sake, it can't come too soon.

Suggested Readings

Beard, Sam. *Restoring Hope in America: The Social Security Solution.* San Francisco: Institute for Contemporary Studies, 1996.

Borden, Karl. "Dismantling the Pyramid: The Why and How of Social Security Privatization." Cato Institute Social Security Paper no. 1, August 14, 1995.

Carter, Marshall, and William Shipman. *Promises to Keep: Saving Social Security's Dream.* Washington: Regnery, 1996.

Shipman, William. "Retiring with Dignity: Social Security vs. Private Markets." Cato Institute Social Security Paper no. 2, August 14, 1995.

Tanner, Michael. "Privatizing Social Security: A Big Boost for the Poor." Cato Institute Social Security Paper no. 4, July 26, 1996.

Weinberger, Mark. "Social Security: Facing the Facts." Cato Institute Social Security Paper no. 3, April 10, 1996.

—Prepared by Michael Tanner

24. Health Care

Congress should

- expand medical savings accounts;
- allow Medicare recipients the freedom to choose private options such as private insurance, managed care, and medical savings accounts;
- gradually increase Medicare deductibles;
- return control of Medicaid to the states through block grants; and
- allow states to opt out of Kennedy-Kassebaum provisions.

The central issue in health policy is who has the ultimate power and control over your health and its care—you or the government? Who ultimately decides what health services and treatments you receive, what doctors you see, what hospitals provide you critical care?

The Clinton health plan of 1993–94 came down squarely on the side of government control. Although the Clinton administration attempted to sell the plan as expanding health coverage and care to include everyone, in reality, the plan was a massive government rationing scheme that would have ultimately denied care and greatly depreciated the quality of care for the middle class in order to control costs.

The Clinton administration supported cost control as a way of obtaining funds to expand health care for the low-income population, essentially redistributing health care from the middle class. They also saw the middle class as consuming overly lavish health care and wanted to clamp down on such consumption to obtain resources for other, supposedly more urgent, "social needs."

The Clinton plan would have achieved rationing through a system that would ultimately have forced everyone into heavily regulated health maintenance organizations (HMOs), which would have enjoyed the ultimate power to decide what health care patients would receive and from whom. The HMOs would then have carried out the government's rationing policies. In hiding behind private, government-controlled megacorporations to perform such hideous rationing—under which the government and its big corporate deputies would have decided who lived and in what condition and who died and when—the Clinton plan was in its essence classic Italian fascism.

Fortunately, the American people rejected the idea of government-run health care. In the end, the Clinton health plan didn't receive a single vote in Congress.

Given that decisive debate and turn in American politics, the direction of health care reform in the future should be the opposite of the Clinton direction—power to the people. There are four major issues that the new Congress needs to address, applying that principle: medical savings accounts (MSAs), Medicare, Medicaid, and federal health insurance regulation.

Medical Savings Accounts

MSAs are the centerpiece of market-oriented health care. With MSAs, only a modest portion of health funds is paid to the insurer for catastrophic insurance covering all expenses over a high deductible, perhaps $3,000 per year. The rest, perhaps $2,000 per year, is paid into an individual account for each worker. The worker can then use the funds in the account to pay medical bills below the deductible amount. The funds can be used for whatever medical services or treatments the worker chooses. Whatever account funds the worker doesn't spend on health care can be withdrawn at the end of the year and used for any purpose.

With MSAs, therefore, workers would effectively be spending their own funds for noncatastrophic health care. As a result, they would have full market incentives to control costs for such care. They would seek to avoid unnecessary care or tests, look for doctors and hospitals that would provide good-quality care at the best prices, and consider whether the health care or service was worth the cost. That, in turn, would stimulate true cost competition among doctors and hospitals. Since consumers would be choosing among them on the basis of cost as well as quality, as in a normal market, providers would compete to minimize cost as well as maximize quality.

MSAs are already becoming popular. Some insurance brokerage firms now specialize in selling only MSA-type plans. As a result, over 3,000 companies in the United States now have MSAs for their workers, and the number is growing. Their experience is confirming the above analysis—MSAs are consistently reducing health costs by 30 percent or more. A growing body of actuarial data, as well as economic studies, confirms that result.

MSAs are just the opposite of the Clinton health plan. They shift power and control over health care away from government and third-party insurance bureaucracies to the individual patients and consumers themselves. That is why there is an unholy alliance against MSAs between the left-wing advocates of government-run health care and big corporate insurers.

Legislatively, the goal is to provide MSAs the same tax-exempt treatment afforded other forms of employer-provided insurance. Employer payments into an MSA plan should be deductible to the employer and not included in the employee's income. Interest or other returns earned on MSA funds should not be taxed until withdrawn. Funds withdrawn for health care should not be subject to tax. Funds withdrawn for any other purpose should be included in taxable income. Because individuals who purchase health insurance directly should have the same tax advantages as those who receive their insurance from their employers, the same tax treatment should be extended to individual contributions to MSAs.

Late in the last session of Congress, an MSA bill was finally enacted into law. Those who fought vigorously for MSAs, including prominently Ways and Means Committee chairman Bill Archer, should be commended for their efforts. But the truth is that the bill that finally passed was badly compromised and flawed. Consequently, the next Congress should quickly pass a new MSA bill that would fix those problems and finally offer sound MSAs to everyone.

The enacted MSA legislation would allow MSAs to only the first 750,000 workers who are either in small businesses of less than 50 workers or self-employed. The 750,000 limitation is administratively unworkable and would deny the new MSAs to most Americans. Moreover, even the permitted 750,000 MSAs are limited to four years. Those limitations will probably discourage all but a few insurers from offering MSAs, leaving workers without a real market in MSAs. The legislation contains numerous further complex restrictions and limitations that will probably discourage all but a few small employers from offering MSAs.

Another major problem with the legislation is that it provides for a 15 percent penalty on MSA withdrawals for non-health-care expenditures.

That is a crippling provision whose perverse impact is not well understood. The whole point of MSAs is to give people full market incentives not to spend money unnecessarily on health care. A penalty on non-health-care expenditures runs exactly contrary to that goal, penalizing people unless they do spend the money on health care. The current penalty is a distorting 15 percent bias toward spending money on health care unnecessarily, sharply undermining the MSA incentives to control costs.

Indeed, with the 15 percent penalty most workers with MSAs are worse off with the new MSA legislation than without it. Without the new law, all MSA funds, whether used on health care or not, are fully taxable, but there is no penalty for non-health-care withdrawals. With the legislation, MSA expenditures for health care are not taxed, but non-health-care expenditures are both taxed and subject to a 15 percent penalty. So the majority of workers who would not spend most of their MSA funds in a year are worse off.

Congress should pass a new bill providing for full MSAs. That would involve applying the tax treatment described above to MSAs and offering them to all workers, without a penalty on non-health-care withdrawals.

Medicare

Those who have not enjoyed the recent debate over Medicare should consider this: the fun has just begun. Until Medicare is fixed, this issue will be with us, growing bigger and bigger.

Medicare has a fundamental structural problem. It makes grand promises but does not have revenue sources anywhere near sufficient to finance them. The government's own projections show that over the long run the program's current revenue sources will finance only about a third of future expenditures.

Medicare Part A, the Hospital Insurance program, is financed by a flat payroll tax of 2.9 percent on wages. The latest projections by the trustees show that, under intermediate assumptions, paying all benefits to today's young workers in retirement will require a Medicare payroll tax rate of almost 9 percent. Medicare Part B, the Supplementary Medical Insurance program, pays doctors' bills and other health care charges. Monthly premiums paid by the elderly finance only about a third (31.5 percent) of the costs of this program. Taxpayers finance the rest out of general revenues.

By the time today's young workers retire, keeping the premiums at about one-third of Part B expenditures would require increasing premiums about four times (in 1996 dollars), again under intermediate projections.

That means current monthly premiums of almost $50 per person and $100 per couple would be increased to the equivalent of almost $200 per person and $400 per couple. Meanwhile, the Medicare Part B deficit financed by general revenues would alone be larger in constant 1996 dollars than the entire federal deficit today.

And those projections may well be overoptimistic. They assume, for example, that the rate of increase in life expectancy over the next 75 years will be substantially less than it has been over the last 50 years, while current and prospective advances in modern medical technology seem to suggest the opposite. Longer life expectancies, of course, would mean higher Medicare expenditures because retirees would be collecting benefits longer. The projections also assume that real wages will be growing twice as fast over the next 75 years as they have over the past 25 years. But if real wages continue to grow at the slower pace, the payroll tax will generate less revenue than expected.

Congress must be honest with the American public. The current system is unsustainable, and fundamental reform is necessary. It is a betrayal of congressional responsibility to allow this issue to become a partisan football or to allow fear of the seniors' vote to forestall needed changes.

Over the long run, Medicare must be transformed into a system that grants each retiree his share of whatever Medicare funds are available each year to use to purchase any of the full range of coverage options in the private sector. Those available funds would be the payroll tax revenues generated with the current 2.9 percent rate, and the premium payments and general revenue contributions would be limited to increase no faster than income and economic growth. Medicare would then continue to grow sustainably at the rate of economic growth, however fast that may turn out to be, but no faster. If necessary, the poor could be provided additional supplements to purchase private coverage.

The great criticism of this plan is that the Medicare funds granted to each retiree would not be sufficient over time to pay the full costs of coverage. But current Medicare revenue sources growing at the rate of economic growth represent all that society can devote to pay the medical expenses of retirees who are not poor. If retirees must make some contribution to the costs of their own coverage, that would not be unreasonable.

However, the cost-controlling incentives and efficiencies of private MSAs offer the prospect of keeping private coverage for the elderly near the amount of available Medicare funds described above. As noted previously, MSAs can be expected to reduce health costs by 30 percent.

257

At the same time, MSAs would provide even better benefits than Medicare, broader freedom of choice, and improved quality. That is why MSAs as one of the private options are so essential for such reform to work.

Moreover, another component of private-sector reform offers the prospect of completely closing the remaining long-term gap. Workers could be allowed to withdraw what they and their employers pay into Medicare each year and invest it through their own individual retirement accounts. In retirement, they would use the saved funds in those accounts to pay for their private health coverage. Because the saved funds would earn full market investment returns over the years, by the time the owners retired, they would be able to pay far more than Medicare. Indeed, on the basis of studies done on Social Security taxes and benefits, we can estimate that for the average worker the private savings account would pay three times what Medicare would pay.

Consequently, with this complete private-sector reform, retirees would have three times what Medicare Part A, the Hospital Insurance program, would pay, and they could use that money, along with the rest of their Medicare funds, to buy private coverage that would cost about one-third less than Medicare.

Congress should also investigate the possibility of allowing young workers to divert their 2.9 percent Medicare payroll tax to the purchase individual private insurance that would "kick in" at age 65. An early study by Professor Thomas Saving of Texas A&M University indicates that such insurance could be purchased by most young workers for far less than the current payroll tax. Of course, as with Social Security privatization, there are important transition questions—including how to continue paying current beneficiaries. There are other issues that remain unresolved as well, but this idea clearly deserves further consideration.

At the same time, Medicare benefits under both Part A and Part B should be subject to an increased deductible, adjusted each year to be large enough to keep Medicare expenditures no greater than Medicare revenues. That amount would be modest in the first year and would grow slowly over time. Several decades down the line, the deductible would be several thousand dollars per year. At the same time, limits on Medicare reimbursements should be removed so that the program would cover catastrophic expenses without limit. In the end, Medicare would be transformed from a first-dollar insurance plan to a back-up catastrophic program.

This private-sector reform is the only hope for solving the otherwise intractable Medicare financing crisis. Such reform would again shift more power and control to the people, allowing them to gain greater control over their Medicare funds and use them to buy the health coverage and services that best suited their needs and preferences.

Medicaid

Medicaid is another runaway entitlement program, with costs that have been rising by 10 to 15 percent per year for some time now. Indeed, the National Entitlement Commission, co-chaired by Sen. Robert Kerrey (D-Neb.) and now-retired Sen. John Danforth (R-Mo.), found that if no reforms are adopted, then in just 15 years all federal revenues will be consumed by just five federal obligations: Social Security, Medicare, Medicaid, federal employee retirement, and interest on the national debt. No revenue would be left for any other federal function, including national defense, welfare, and federal law enforcement. Those programs and any other federal spending would all have to be financed through bigger deficits. Obviously, fundamental reform of major entitlement programs is urgently needed.

State governments should be given complete responsibility for—and control over—Medicaid. Ideally, that should be done by returning responsibility for the program, along with the tax sources needed to fund it, to the states, thus eliminating any federal role. However, it may be necessary to begin the transition more gradually by block granting the federal share of the program's funding to the states. Each state would then be free to use the funds to address the health needs of the poor through whatever means best suited local conditions. The amount of the block grants would be limited, however, to grow no faster than the rate of economic growth. That would limit the program to sustainable levels; it would continue at the same size, relative to the nation's economy, as today.

States could then best use those funds by providing low-income beneficiaries vouchers that they could use to buy coverage, including MSAs, in the private sector. The cost-saving incentives of the private alternatives would enable the beneficiaries to get better benefits with the available funds. And such reforms would once again shift maximum power and control away from federal bureaucrats to the beneficiaries themselves.

Federal Regulation of Health Care

Last year Congress passed the ill-advised Kennedy-Kassebaum bill. That legislation will come back to haunt its supporters the same way the Medicare catastrophic health act of the late 1980s did.

259

The law runs flatly contrary to the principles of the Republican majority, by centralizing power once again in Washington, rather than devolving power to the states and the people. Indeed, it begins the process of federalizing health insurance regulation that was formerly the province of the states.

Moreover, the law will serve only to increase the cost of health insurance. Contrary to popular claims for it, the legislation does not allow workers to keep their current health insurance when they leave their jobs. Rather, it provides for guaranteed issue by forcing new insurers to accept them under either an individual policy between jobs or the group policy offered by their new employers.

Guaranteed issue will have a potentially catastrophic cost-increasing effect on the individual health insurance market, where workers pay for their coverage directly themselves. Only about 10 percent of workers are in that market, compared to 90 percent in the big group insurance market where employers pay for the coverage.

Consider a worker who has been healthy for 30 years, with the employer paying his premiums to a big group insurer all of that time. Now suppose he gets cancer, or heart disease, or AIDS and has to quit work as a result. Under the law, he can now force any individual insurer to cover him, even though he never paid any premiums to that insurer when he was healthy. His premiums now will cover only a small fraction of his costs, imposing huge losses on the insurer he chooses.

As a result, under the law, all of the sickest, highest cost workers in the big group market will now be dumped on the much smaller individual market. Insurers in that market will have to sharply increase their premiums as a result. That in turn will cause many low-cost, healthy workers to drop their coverage, forcing insurers to raise their premiums even higher. Eventually, this process may cause individual health insurance to become unmanageably expensive.

Indeed, individual insurers may simply withdraw from the market altogether in the face of this danger. Workers will then be unable to get insurance unless their employers buy it in the big group market. That will almost certainly result in pressure for the government to step in and provide them coverage.

Those provisions were sold to Congress on the basis of studies that concluded that the resulting cost increase for insurance would be small. But the studies unreasonably assumed that states would allow insurers to charge the sick high enough premiums to cover most of their high costs. On the contrary, states will likely force companies to charge the sick little or no more than the healthy. Otherwise, the law will be ineffective, as it would only offer workers coverage that is too expensive to buy. That would cause initial rate increases of at least 30 percent, and probably more after the healthy workers start dropping out.

A better approach would be to rely on guaranteed renewability and state risk pools. Guaranteed renewability would require insurers to continue to renew coverage for all who desired it, even those who left their jobs, with the same standard rate increases for everyone. That would effectively enforce the insurance contract, as insurance that allows the insurer to drop beneficiaries after they become sick is not insurance against anything at all; it simply misleads buyers. This would actually do what the recently enacted legislation was wrongly advertised as doing—allow workers who leave their jobs to take their insurance with them. Moreover, instead of forcing insurers in the much smaller individual market to cover all of the sickest workers from the big group market, this approach would require insurers in the big group market, who received the premiums when those workers were healthy, to continue to cover them when they became sick. This workable approach is already in effect for all individual health insurance and would have little effect on cost.

Those who had coverage would then all be assured of keeping it. For those who didn't buy coverage and became too sick to buy it later, each state should set up its own risk pool. The pools would charge above-market prices, perhaps 50 percent more than standard rates, to help cover the higher costs of those sick people. But to keep the insurance affordable, states would subsidize the pools from general revenues to cover remaining costs. The states could provide further subsidies for those who were too poor to pay all of the premiums.

Such risk pools are in fact already in effect in almost 30 states and have been shown to be workable. Only about 1 percent of the working-age population is uninsurable, so the cost of such pools is not great. Through such pools, necessary subsidies can be channeled to the small number who are truly in need, keeping costs low and avoiding disruption of the market for everyone else.

States under the Kennedy-Kassebaum legislation are supposed to be free to opt out of the onerous guaranteed issue provisions noted above and adopt other means of achieving the goals, such as the above-described guaranteed renewability and risk pools. But whether states will actually be able to do that under the law as passed is highly dubious.

The new Congress should repeal the dangerous Kennedy-Kassebaum legislation. But, if that is impossible, it should at least enact changes to ensure that states can choose the better reforms. Legislation should provide that governors can certify that their states have passed legislation to satisfy the goals of Kennedy-Kassebaum, and such certification would avoid all further requirements of that legislation. Each state could then hold its own governor accountable for his or her actions.

The 104th Congress also passed several other measures interfering in the operation of private insurance markets, including a mandate that insurers pay for a minimum of 48 hours of hospital maternity care and a requirement for parity in coverage of mental illnesses. Both provisions will lead to increased premiums and should be repealed. In the future, Congress should avoid the temptation to become the national insurance regulator.

Conclusion

The nation's major health care problems must be quickly addressed by taking an approach that is the opposite of that taken by the Clinton administration in 1993 and 1994. Ultimate control over the health care of workers and their families should not be shifted to the government and third-party insurance bureaucrats; control must be fully restored to the workers and their families themselves.

Suggested Readings

Ferrara, Peter. "More Than a Theory: Medical Savings Accounts at Work." Cato Institute Policy Analysis no. 220, March 14, 1995.

———. "The Establishment Strikes Back: Medical Savings Accounts and Adverse Selection." Cato Institute Briefing Paper no. 26, April 24, 1996.

Goodman, John, and Gerald Musgrave. *Patient Power: Solving America's Health Care Crisis.* Washington: Cato Institute, 1992.

Liebowitz, Stan. "Why Health Care Costs Too Much." Cato Institute Policy Analysis no. 211, June 23, 1994.

Saving, Thomas. "Medicare Reform: In Search of a Permanent Solution." Private Enterprise Research Center, Texas A&M University, College Station, Texas, November 15, 1996.

Tanner, Michael. "Medical Savings Accounts: Answering the Critics." Cato Institute Policy Analysis no. 228, May 25, 1995.

Tanner, Michael, and Doug Bandow. "The Wrong and Right Ways to Fix Medicare." Cato Institute Policy Analysis no. 230, June 8, 1995.

Wasley, Terree. *What Has Government Done to Our Health Care?* Washington: Cato Institute, 1992.

—Prepared by Peter Ferrara

25. Welfare Reform

> **Congress should**
> - end all federal funding of welfare, sending responsibility for both welfare programs and tax sources back to the states; and
> - tear down barriers to economic growth and entrepreneurship.

From across the political and ideological spectrum, there is now almost universal acknowledgement that the American social welfare system has been a failure. Since the start of the War on Poverty in 1965, the United States has spent more than $5.4 trillion trying to ease the plight of the poor. What we have received for that massive investment is—primarily—more poverty.

Our welfare system is unfair to everyone: to taxpayers, who must pick up the bill for failed programs; to society, whose mediating institutions of community, church, and family are increasingly pushed aside; and most of all to the poor themselves, who are trapped in a system that destroys opportunity for them and hope for their children.

Consider the results of our welfare system:

- **Illegitimacy.** In 1960 only 5.3 percent of births were out of wedlock. Today nearly 32 percent of births are illegitimate. Among blacks, the illegitimacy rate is over two-thirds. Among whites, it tops 23 percent. There is strong evidence that directly links the availability of welfare with the increase in out-of-wedlock births.
- **Dependence.** Nearly 65 percent of the people on welfare at any given time will be on the program for eight years or longer. Moreover, welfare is increasingly intergenerational. Children raised in families on welfare are seven times more likely to become dependent on welfare than are other children.
- **Crime.** The Maryland NAACP recently concluded that "the ready access to a lifetime of welfare and free social service programs is a

major contributory factor to the crime problems we face today." Welfare contributes to crime by destroying family structure and breaking down the bonds of community. Moreover, it contributes to the social marginalization of young black men by making them irrelevant to the family. Their role has been supplanted by the welfare check.

The 1996 Welfare Reform

Faced with the welfare state's dismal record, Congress finally took the first tentative steps toward eventual welfare reform in 1996. However, the 1996 welfare reform legislation falls far short of the reform needed to truly end this destructive program.

The law does contain one important reform: it ends welfare's status as an entitlement. Under an entitlement program, every individual who meets the program's eligibility criteria automatically receives the program's benefits. Spending on the program is not subject to annual appropriation but rises automatically with the number of people enrolled.

Ending welfare's entitlement status has two important effects. First, it allows states to impose a variety of conditions and restrictions on receipt of benefits. Second, it makes welfare spending subject to annual appropriation. Therefore, Congress can assert greater control over the growth in spending. However, except for that change, the law is woefully inadequate.

At the heart of the new law is a plan to shift control of welfare to the states through block grants. The theory is that, while the federal government will continue to provide funding, states will be free to experiment more widely. However, there is something less than clear logic in the idea of sending money from the states to Washington, having Washington take a cut off the top, then sending the money back to the states.

In addition, the history of block grants is not a pretty one. Tales of mismanagement, waste, and abuse in past or existing block grant programs are legion. Most audits have shown little or no increase in administrative efficiency. Although supporters of block granting welfare have suggested that administrative savings could be as high as 20 percent of program costs, past block grant programs have seldom achieved savings of more than 5 percent. And the tensions between state and federal government were often merely shifted to a battle between local and state governments.

Block grants reduce accountability by separating the revenue collector from the spender of the money—never a wise practice. Congress can blame the states for not spending the money wisely, while the states can blame Congress for failing to provide enough money to do the job.

Moreover, as Norman Ornstein of the American Enterprise Institute has pointed out, from Richard Nixon's "New Federalism" to Ronald Reagan's "New New Federalism" to Newt Gingrich's "New New New Federalism," the federal government has talked about shifting power to the states, giving them more money and more flexibility. But reality has seldom matched the rhetoric. Reality has usually meant less money *and* less flexibility.

That pattern appears to hold in the new law as well. The block grants will include numerous federal "strings" and other restrictions. Indeed, in many cases, Congress has simply replaced liberal mandates with conservative ones.

The biggest single mandate on the states is a requirement that welfare recipients participate in "workfare" in exchange for benefits. That requirement is behind all the rhetoric of "promoting work not welfare." The belief is that such jobs will give the recipient both work experience and incentives to get off welfare.

But the types of jobs envisioned under most workfare programs are unlikely to give recipients the work experience or job skills necessary to find work in the private sector. For example, Mayor Rudolph Giuliani of New York City wants welfare recipients to perform such jobs as scrubbing graffiti and picking up trash from city streets. It is difficult to imagine graffiti scrubbers learning the skills needed to put them in demand by private employers.

The idea of providing an incentive for recipients to get off welfare is largely based on the stereotypical belief that welfare recipients are essentially lazy, looking for a free ride. But the choice to go on welfare is more likely a result of a logical conclusion that welfare pays better than low-wage work. Most welfare recipients, particularly long-term recipients, lack the skills necessary to obtain the types of jobs that pay top or even average wages. Those individuals who do leave welfare for work most often start employment in service or retail trade industries, generally in such occupations as clerks, secretaries, cleaning persons, sales help, and waitresses.

A 1995 study by the Cato Institute revealed that the value of the total benefit package received by a typical welfare recipient averaged more than $17,000, ranging from a high of over $36,000 in Hawaii to a low of $11,500 in Mississippi. In 9 states welfare pays more than the average first-year salary for a teacher. In 29 states welfare pays more than the average starting salary for a secretary. In 47 states welfare pays more than

265

a janitor makes. Indeed, in the 6 most generous states, benefits exceed the entry-level salary for a computer programmer.

Since taking an entry-level job will mean an effective pay cut for many welfare recipients, most will fall back on public service jobs. But public service jobs are not free. It is estimated that it will cost at least $6,000 to $8,000 over and above welfare benefits for every workfare job created, a cost that will be borne by the states.

Moreover, there is no evidence that workfare programs work. The Manpower Demonstration Research Corporation conducted a review of workfare programs across the country and found few, if any, employment gains among welfare participants. Economists at the University of Chicago's Center for Social Policy Evaluation reviewed the major studies of workfare and welfare-to-work programs and found a consensus in the literature that "mandatory work experience programs produce little long-term gain."

There seems to be little difference, therefore, between that type of work program and the type of government-guaranteed jobs program traditionally decried by conservatives. Indeed, there is ample experience with government-created public service jobs. The Comprehensive Employment Training Program is perhaps the best example. CETA was established in 1973 to provide public service jobs for the economically disadvantaged. At its zenith, as many as 750,000 Americans were working in CETA jobs, approximately 12.5 percent of all those unemployed at the time. Jobs were funded by the federal government, but the program was administered by state and local governments. CETA quickly became one of the most wasteful and scandal-ridden government efforts in recent years. Make-work projects and political patronage were the norm. Its effect on earnings was marginal, and few participants moved to employment in the private sector. Would a conservative CETA really be better?

Martin Anderson, former senior economic adviser to President Reagan, sums up the simple illogic of workfare:

> If people are on welfare, then, by definition, those people should be unable to care for themselves. They can't work, or the private sector can't provide jobs enough. That is supposed to be the reason they are on welfare. What sense does it make to require someone to work who cannot work?
>
> The idea of making people work for welfare is wrongheaded. If a person is capable of working, he should be ineligible for welfare payments. Instead of requiring men and women who are receiving fraudulent welfare payments to work, we should simply cease all payments.

Workfare does not address the most serious social consequence of welfare—children growing up in single-parent families. The growing rate of illegitimacy, and its attendant problems such as crime, is one of the most serious social problems of our time. Not only does workfare not deter out-of-wedlock births, it doesn't even prevent additional births to program participants. A study by the Manpower Demonstration Research Corporation found that more than half of all welfare mothers became pregnant again after enrolling in workfare. The social pathologies associated with out-of-wedlock births will not disappear simply because the mothers are put to work in public service jobs.

The welfare reform law does make a half-hearted attempt to deal with illegitimacy—allowing states to end benefits to teen mothers and to women who have additional children while on welfare. But the far larger number of women over age 18 will still be eligible for welfare benefits if they give birth out of wedlock.

Because it allows states to exempt 20 percent of their welfare population from the five-year time limit, the law will actually apply to few welfare recipients. Most welfare recipients leave the program in far less than five years. The small minority of long-term recipients would be exempt. Thus, the law gives the illusion of forcing people off welfare without actually doing so.

Moreover, the time limit applies to only 1 of 77 federal welfare programs. Individuals who exceed the time limit will still be eligible to receive Medicaid, food stamps, public housing, the Special Supplemental Nutrition Program for Women, Infants, and Children, and a host of other benefits. Virtually no one will ever be required to simply leave the public dole.

End Federal Funding of Welfare

Instead of making block grants, Congress should eliminate federal funding for the entire social welfare system for those individuals able to work. This includes the new block grants for Temporary Assistance to Needy Persons (which replaced Aid to Families with Dependent Children), as well as Medicaid, food stamps, housing assistance, and the rest. This can be done by reviving a Reagan-era reform known as "turn-backs," in which specific federal aid programs (in this case welfare programs) are terminated and specific federal taxes are repealed. Responsibility for both collecting the revenue and spending the money is turned back to state and local governments. Turn-backs would eliminate the federal middleman altogether.

267

Those states that wish to continue welfare programs would be free to do so, but they would be required to finance those programs themselves. However, it would be preferable for most to follow the federal government's lead and return charity to the private sector, which is far better able to provide for the needs of the poor.

Tear Down Barriers to Economic Growth and Entrepreneurship

Almost everyone agrees that a job is better than any welfare program. Yet for years this country has pursued tax and regulatory policies that seem perversely designed to discourage economic growth and reduce entrepreneurial opportunities. Government regulations and taxes are steadily cutting the bottom rungs off the economic ladder, throwing more and more poor Americans into dependency.

Someone starting a business today needs a battery of lawyers just to comply with the myriad government regulations from a virtual alphabet soup of government agencies: OSHA, EPA, FTC, CPSC, and so on. Zoning and occupational licensing laws are particularly damaging to the types of small businesses that may help people work their way out of poverty. In addition, government regulations such as minimum wage laws and mandated benefits drive up the cost of employing additional workers. For a typical small business, the tax and regulatory burden for hiring an additional worker is more than $5,400.

Economist Thomas Hopkins estimates that the current annual cost to the economy of government regulations is more than $600 billion. That is $600 billion that cannot be used to create jobs and lift people out of poverty.

At the same time, taxes have both diverted capital from the productive economy and discouraged job-creating investment. Harvard economist Dale Jorgenson estimates that every dollar of taxes raised by the federal government costs the economy an additional 18 cents, leading to an annual loss of $200 billion from our gross national product. Moreover, tax rates are already so high that new taxes will cause even greater losses to the economy. Jorgenson estimates, for example, that the 1994 Clinton tax hike will cost the economy more than $100 billion over five years.

Those figures do not include the estimated $600 billion that the American economy loses every year because of the cost of complying with our dizzyingly complex tax system. In 1990 American workers and businesses were forced to spend more than 5.4 billion man-hours figuring out their taxes and filing the paperwork. That was more man-hours than were used to build every car, truck, and van manufactured in the United States.

A 1993 World Bank study of 20 countries found that countries with low taxes had higher economic growth, more investment, greater increases in productivity, and faster increases in living standards than did high-tax nations. Perhaps that should be a lesson for the United States. Elsewhere in this book there are detailed discussions of priorities for regulatory and tax relief. But as a general matter, instead of worrying about how to make poverty more comfortable, the 105th Congress should concentrate on tearing down the regulatory and tax barriers that help trap people in poverty.

Conclusion

In 1996 Congress took the first tentative steps on the road to welfare reform, but that is not enough. Congress should build on its efforts and end federal involvement in charity, returning responsibility for caring for the poor first to the states, then to the private sector. The civil society, or private charitable activity, is far better at meeting the real needs of the poor. At the same time, Congress should continue to tear down barriers to economic growth and entrepreneurship.

Suggested Readings

Murray, Charles. *Losing Ground: American Social Policy 1950–1980.* New York: Basic Books, 1984.

_____. *In Pursuit of Happiness and Good Government.* New York: Simon and Schuster, 1988.

Olasky, Marvin. *The Tragedy of American Compassion.* New York: Basic Books, 1992.

Tanner, Michael. *The End of Welfare: Fighting Poverty in the Civil Society.* Washington: Cato Institute, 1996.

Tanner, Michael, Stephen Moore, and David Hartman. "The Work vs. Welfare Trade-Off: An Analysis of the Total Level of Welfare Benefits by State." Cato Institute Policy Analysis no. 240, September 19, 1996.

—Prepared by Michael Tanner and Naomi Lopez

26. Urban Policy

Congress should

- downsize the federal government, starting with spending programs that are most irrelevant to cities—such as the Departments of Agriculture, Commerce, Energy, and Labor;
- end failed urban aid spending programs and use the savings to cut taxes;
- eliminate the capital gains tax as a means of luring capital back to cities;
- implement a policy of no net new mandates imposed on cities;
- identify and eliminate existing federal mandates that impose severe fiscal burdens on cities;
- replace the welfare state with a system that stresses moral values, work, family, private charities, and personal responsibility;
- shut down the U.S. Department of Education and return public schools to state and local control;
- shut down the Department of Housing and Urban Development (HUD) and devote any remaining funds to a program of housing vouchers for low-income families and transfer ownership of the existing public housing stock to the residents;
- decriminalize drugs to end the culture of crime and terror in our inner cities; and
- promote free trade and more liberal immigration policies.

Since Lyndon Johnson declared war on poverty 30 years ago, more than $2.5 trillion of federal money has been funneled into America's cities. Yet most objective measures of the livability of inner cities indicate more urban despair and decline. The single greatest indication of the deterioration of America's once mighty industrial centers—New York, Chicago, Cleveland, Buffalo, Detroit, St. Louis, and others—is that Americans are voting with their feet against the social conditions and economic policies of those cities. Between 1965 and 1994, 15 of the largest U.S. cities lost a total of 4.2 million people, while the total U.S. population rose by 60 million.

Much of the urban lobby today is predictably demanding even fatter checks from Washington as the cure for the problems of the inner cities. Fortunately, an increasing number of reform-minded mayors are beginning to publicly acknowledge the futility of that approach. As John Norquist of Milwaukee recently stated, "We need to return to a more traditional American paradigm of government, where power is retained as close to the people as possible. Washington can best help, by leaving us alone." That is still a minority view among urban advocates, but skepticism about the effectiveness of federal aid is growing.

A new urban policy should be based on the realization that conventional strategies for helping cities by expanding the federal budget cannot solve the problems of our inner cities (and arguably have made those problems worse). What is needed from Congress is a new economic development strategy based on the principle of "markets, not mandates."

The Comparative Advantage of Cities

Throughout most of American history, cities were the very symbol of the nation's industrial might and economic progress. One needed only to travel to the neighborhoods and business districts of New York, Chicago, Los Angeles, Cleveland, Detroit, Dallas, Milwaukee, and other cities to see the marvels of the marketplace at work—markets where industrious people came to earn good wages, where businesses and trade flourished, and where wealth was created.

Sadly, in recent decades the economic environment of many of America's largest cities has atrophied. Today, many cities have high levels of poverty, excessive crime rates, poor schools, joblessness, and—perhaps the most visible sign of decline—flight. As Table 26.1 shows, since the mid-1960s cities such as Cleveland, Detroit, Pittsburgh, and St. Louis have lost more than one-third of their population. What began as white flight has now become middle-class minority flight. One consequence of the migration from central cities is that urban America is losing economic and political clout to the suburbs.

Yet, as Jersey City's mayor Bret Schundler has emphasized, "There is no inevitability to the decline of America's central cities." Indeed,

Table 26.1
America's Shrinking Cities

City	1994 Population (thousands)	Estimated 1965 Population (thousands)	Change, 1965–94	
			Thousands	Percent
New York	7,333	7,839	−506	−6
Chicago	2,732	3,460	−728	−21
Philadelphia	1,524	1,976	−390	−23
Detroit	992	1,592	−600	−38
Baltimore	703	922	−219	−24
Cleveland	493	813	−307	−39
Washington, D.C.	567	760	−193	−25
Milwaukee	617	729	−112	−15
St. Louis	368	686	−318	−46
Boston	548	669	−121	−18
New Orleans	484	610	−113	−21
Pittsburgh	359	562	−203	−36
Denver	494	504	−36	−2
Buffalo	313	498	−185	−37
Minneapolis	355	459	−104	−23
15-city total	17,881	22,081	−4,200	−19
Total U.S. population	260,341	191,313	+69,028	36

SOURCE: U.S. Census Bureau.
NOTE: Numbers may not add to total due to rounding.

the demise of central cities seems to be almost uniquely an American experience.

America's cities still command substantial intrinsic economic advantages over suburbs. Those comparative advantages include

- Their physical location. Cities did not grow where they did by accident. They are typically strategically located at ports of entry and have an integrated transportation infrastructure.
- Their high population density. Their density creates market opportunities not generally available outside cities.
- Their vitality as centers of intellect and culture. Most of the top universities, museums, theaters, opera houses, sports stadiums, and restaurants are in central cities.
- Their status as magnets of regional clusters. Cities are critical to the well-being of surrounding suburbs; they define the identity, architecture, culture, and civic life of their regions.

273

It is also important to emphasize that although many American metropo-
lises are losing people, businesses, and capital, not all are suffering decline.
Dozens of the nation's largest cities—many on the West Coast, in the
Sunbelt, and in the Southeast—have been steadily prospering for at least
the past 20 years. Las Vegas, Nevada; Phoenix, Arizona; Arlington and
Austin, Texas; Sacramento and San Diego, California; Raleigh and Char-
lotte, North Carolina; and Jacksonville, Florida, all have rapidly rising
incomes, populations, and employment and low poverty and crime rates.

Meanwhile, many of the downtown areas of the older northeastern and
midwestern cities are starting to be rebuilt as well. Baltimore, Chicago,
Cleveland, and Pittsburgh, for example, have enjoyed a healthy renaissance
in their downtown business districts in the 1980s and 1990s. Unfortunately,
the decaying social conditions and the culture of poverty in those cities
continue unabated even as surrounding suburbs flourish.

How Washington Harms Cities

Although there is little if any objective evidence that the federal government's multi-billion-dollar spending policies have improved the livability
of urban America, many federal actions actually erode the natural comparative economic advantage of cities. Here are eight prominent examples:

- Economic instability fostered by years of reckless federal fiscal and
  monetary policies has wreaked havoc on cities. The massive federal
  budget deficit is sapping the American economy of its vitality and
  crowding out private investment that could be taking place in cities.
- Environmental regulations insensitive to market forces have reduced
  reinvestment in cities. For example, Superfund legislation discourages
  business development in cities because of potential liability costs.
- Labor rules, such as the Davis-Bacon Act and the Service Contract
  Act, have added unnecessary costs to city services. The minimum
  wage prices low-skilled inner-city residents out of jobs.
- The welfare state has disconnected the poor from the larger urban
  economy and disrupted the patterns of upward mobility that traditionally characterized the urban marketplace.
- Federal maritime policies have destroyed the value of one of our
  cities' oldest industries, shipping. The Jones Act and related protectionist laws have reduced the value of American ports.
- Federal mandates on cities have inflated and destabilized city budgets.

- Public housing programs have contributed to urban blight and have trapped the urban poor in an environment of poverty, fear, and hopelessness.
- Education grants have been designed to benefit the education establishment more than children. Federal education dollars have only propped up failing school systems and discouraged innovation.
- The federal government's failed war on drugs has converted our cities into America's equivalent of Beirut, as drug warlords create a climate of terror and lawlessness.

Are Cities Underfinanced?

For the past 30 years federal aid programs have been tragically predicated on a false premise: that declining cities are starved for resources. The truth is precisely the opposite. A recent Cato Institute Policy Analysis found that spending and taxes are much higher in declining inner cities than in growing inner cities or in suburbs. Table 26.2 highlights the huge disparities between the fiscal policies of the 10 cities with the greatest population growth in the 1980s and the 10 largest urban population losers. It shows the following:

- For every $1.00 spent per person in the high-growth cities, the shrinking cities spend $1.71. Expenditures in the high-growth cities average $673 per person and 5.7 percent of personal income versus $1,152 and 11.8 percent in the shrinking cities.
- A typical family of four living in one of the shrinking cities pays $1,100 per year more in taxes than it would if it lived in a high-growth city. A family of four pays $2,352 in taxes in shrinking cities and $1,216 in high-growth cities.
- Shrinking cities are much more likely to impose an income tax on residents than are high-growth cities. None of the 15 highest growth cities has an income tax, whereas 10 of the 15 lowest growth cities do. With very few exceptions, every city in America with a city income tax is getting poorer.
- Shrinking cities have bureaucracies twice as large as those of growth cities. The high-growth cities have 99 city employees per 10,000 residents; the shrinking cities have 235.
- Cities with high spending and taxes in 1980 lost population in the 1980s; cities with low spending and taxes gained population. High spending and taxes are a *cause*, not just a consequence, of urban

275

Table 26.2
Spending and Taxes in the 10 Highest Growth and 10 Lowest Growth Cities, 1980 and 1990

City	Percentage Change in Population, 1980–90	City Tax Revenue per Capita, 1980	Expenditures* per Capita, 1980	Expenditures* as Percentage of Money Income, 1990	City Tax Revenue per Capita, 1990	Expenditures* per Capita, 1990	Expenditures* as Percentage of Money Income, 1990	City Employees per 10,000 Residents, 1990
Highest growth cities								
Mesa	89%	$153	$547	5%	$149	$649	6%	81
Las Vegas	79%	$252	$547	4%	$213	$829	7%	74
Arlington	63%	$212	$385	3%	$323	$580	4%	68
Fresno	62%	$296	$645	6%	$279	$514	5%	82
Santa Ana	44%	$236	$446	4%	$329	$526	5%	69
Stockton	42%	$284	$860	8%	$305	$574	6%	75
Aurora	40%	$332	$501	4%	$369	$668	5%	84
Raleigh	38%	$249	$560	5%	$322	$734	5%	131
Austin	35%	$250	$529	5%	$365	$924	8%	215
Sacramento	34%	$309	$748	6%	$388	$732	6%	115
Average	53%	$257	$577	5%	$304	$673	6%	99
Lowest growth cities								
Newark	−16%	$508	$843	12%	$307	$1,117	15%	184
Detroit	−15%	$476	$1,300	13%	$507	$1,328	14%	215
Pittsburgh	−13%	$433	$953	9%	$601	$936	9%	159
St. Louis†	−12%	$687	$1,102	12%	$725	$1,205	12%	195

Cleveland	−12%	$386	$937	10%	$530	$959	11%	175
New Orleans†	−11%	$396	$1,047	10%	$547	$1,275	14%	197
Louisville	−9%	$377	$815	8%	$524	$1,144	12%	168
Buffalo	−8%	$439	$1,106	12%	$376	$1,083	12%	400
Richmond†	−7%	$882	$1,092	10%	$1,189	$1,502	12%	503
Chicago	−7%	$389	$756	7%	$574	$971	9%	149
Average	−11%	$497	$995	10%	$588	$1,152	12%	235

SOURCE: U.S. Census Bureau.

*Do not include expenditures on health, education, and welfare.

†County-type area without any county government.

decline. The fastest growing cities in the 1980s had very low spending—$577 per resident—at the start of the period. The cities with the most severe population losses had average spending in 1980 of $995 per resident. Taxes were $257 in the growth cities and $497 in the shrinking cities in 1980 (see Figure 26.1).

Expenditures are high and rising in large central cities primarily because their governments generally have above-average unit costs of educating children, collecting garbage, building roads, policing neighborhoods, and providing other basic services. For example, in 1989 the shrinking cities spent roughly $4,950 per pupil, whereas the high-growth cities spent $3,600. That $1,350 cost differential cannot be explained by better schools in places such as Detroit and Newark.

The influence of municipal employee unions also accounts for higher costs in declining central cities. Compensation for unionized local employees tends to be roughly 30 percent above wages for comparably skilled private-sector workers. In New York City the average school janitor is paid $57,000 a year. In Philadelphia, when Ed Rendell became mayor in 1991, the average municipal employee received more than $50,000 a

Figure 26.1
Relationship between 1980 City Taxes and 1980–90 Population Growth

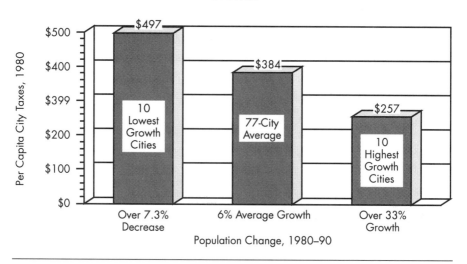

SOURCE: Cato Institute, based on data from U.S. Census Bureau.

year in salary and benefits. According to the Census Bureau, cities with populations over 500,000 pay their mostly nonunionized workers more than 50 percent more than do cities with populations under 75,000. In short, thriving cities are places where costs are lower, bureaucracies are smaller, and services are better.

The good news is that many cities are beginning to reform themselves. City leaders are starting to understand that, to compete effectively with surrounding suburbs, they need to follow the basic strategy of an effective and profitable business: deliver quality services at lower cost.

Mayor Norquist of Milwaukee often states that "America's cities will never be rebuilt on pity." Urban renewal will only occur when city officials begin to fully implement more intelligent, market-based policies—and when Washington begins to do the same.

Defining a Federal Role in Urban Renewal

The federal government is a creation of the states. The cities are creations of the states. A proper adherence to the constitutional principles of federalism would dictate that the federal government have almost no direct relationship with cities. Federal aid, to the extent that it continues at all, should be provided to the states. To the extent that cities and other jurisdictions of the states are in need of financial aid, it should be provided by the state legislatures.

Probably the only truly effective federal agenda for aiding the cities is to promote national economic growth. The lesson of the past three decades is that central cities' economic fortunes often turn with the national economy. In the slow-growth, high-inflation 1970s cities rapidly deteriorated; in the prosperous 1980s cities partially revived; but in the slow-growth 1990s cities are again financially strapped.

By far the most vital step is to create an overall policy climate in America that maximizes freedom, growth, and prosperity. That involves fixing the tax code, eliminating the capital gains tax, balancing the budget, reversing the regulatory reign of terror in Washington, privatizing Social Security, maintaining a noninflationary monetary policy, ending the war on drugs, and undertaking the other policy prescriptions detailed in this book. Each of those policies will promote the livability of cities much more effectively than the targeted urban aid policies that Washington has implemented with such futility over the past 30 years.

Federal Spending and Urban Revival

One of the most constructive steps that Washington could take to help cities would be to eliminate federal agencies that are inconsequential to cities. Currently hundreds of billions of dollars are spent on such agencies. The Departments of Agriculture, Commerce, Energy, and Labor, for example, have virtually no impact on the financial well-being or livability of cities. Yet city residents pay billions of dollars in taxes each year to pay for those departments. Cities are often the victims of government expansionism in Washington because many urban areas are actually losers in the game of federal roulette. For example, a Manhattan Institute study has shown that New York City's residents send more money to Washington than they retrieve in federal aid.

Even for cities that receive more federal assistance dollars from Washington than their residents and businesses pay in taxes, the funding is so encumbered with mandates and restrictions that only marginal benefits are produced. Indianapolis mayor Steve Goldsmith reports that there are now more than 500 federal programs providing aid directly to cities like Indianapolis or to disadvantaged populations living in cities. The aid comes with so many federal strings attached, he says, that "it is practically useless."

The urban lobby disagrees and insists that federal handouts to cities should be expanded. The U.S. Conference of Mayors has been demanding a new "Urban Marshall Plan" for cities with as much as $35 billion more spending each year. But the $2.5 trillion of federal checks delivered to cities over the past 30 years—the equivalent of 30 Marshall Plans—stands as a monument to the futility of that approach. Many cities are visibly worse off today than they were before the expenditure campaign began. Virtually all of the federal aid programs invented in the 1960s and 1970s turned out to be expensive failures. For example, Urban Development Action Grants, which were finally abolished in 1987, subsidized the construction of major chain hotels, such as Hyatts, and luxury housing developments with health spas and tennis courts in Detroit.

Despite federal grants totaling over $50 billion for urban transit since the mid-1960s, total transit ridership has declined. The federal government spent over $2 billion to build Miami's Metrorail, which Miamians call "Metro-fail"; today it has less than 20 percent of predicted ridership, and its operating subsidies are in the hundreds of millions of dollars a year. Before he retired from the Senate, William Proxmire presented his "Golden Fleece" award to the federal transit agency for "playing Santa Claus to America's cities" and for being "a spectacular flop." Similarly, a Congressional Budget Office audit of federal wastewater treatment grants to cities found that construction costs were 30 percent higher when plants were built with federal funding than when local taxpayers footed the bill.

Even cities that have been saturated with federal aid have not been able to leverage those funds to resuscitate their economies. In one famous experiment, from 1968 to 1972 Gary, Indiana, received more than $150 million for urban renewal—or about $3,000 per resident in today's dollars—yet Gary's deterioration continued.

Even the *New York Times* conceded in 1992, "Despite trillions of dollars spent over the years on thousands of different government social programs, politicians are no clearer today than they were a generation ago about the best ways to lift people out of poverty and make the cities a better place to live."

If trillions of dollars in spending and thousands of social programs won't revive inner cities, what will? Probably the most promising economic redevelopment strategy is a general tax rate cut to help lure investment back to capital-starved cities. In the 1980s after income tax rates and the capital gains tax were reduced, the number of inner-city minority-owned businesses tripled, according to statistics gathered by the U.S. Civil Rights Commission. Investigative reporter Joel Garreau, author of *Edge City*, has documented that in the 1980s dozens of downtown areas of industrial cities flourished as businesses returned. The lesson: pro–capital investment policies are pro-city.

Regulations and Mandates

Washington has proven over the past 30 years that it is incapable of balancing its budget, and through unfunded federal mandates it is now intent on making sure that states and cities can't balance theirs. Unfunded mandates are a popular method used by federal lawmakers to intervene in the affairs of state and local governments and thereby add huge costs to their budgets. Some cities, such as Columbus, Ohio, have calculated that federal mandates raised city costs by more than $1 billion over 10 years, or about $850 per household per year. The problem is getting worse each year. Currently, more than one-third of many city budgets is devoted to complying with federal mandates. Enough is enough.

Congress should promote urban renewal by shedding unnecessary regulations and mandates imposed on state and local governments. Increasingly, federal regulations are imposed on our cities without consideration of the costs of compliance. An agenda that would identify strategies for reducing regulatory costs to cities is long overdue.

One possibility would be the creation of an independent commission, modeled after the Military Base Closing Commission, to identify counterproductive or excessively expensive mandates imposed on cities. Easing the cost of mandates would allow cities to reduce local tax burdens and spend city revenues more productively.

Ending Welfare

The culture of poverty perpetuated by the current welfare state is—perhaps more than any other single factor—devastating the physical, economic, and moral infrastructure of cities. In many of our cities, we are now witnessing a third generation of Americans trapped in poverty. Thirty million Americans still live in poverty. Most of them reside in inner cities. The welfare bill passed by the 104th Congress is a start at ending the failed welfare state, but much more change is needed.

One of the most pernicious effects of welfare is that all too often it has become a deterrent to work. A recent Cato study shows that, in many cities, a typical welfare recipient living in public housing would have to find a job that paid upward of $10 an hour to replace lost welfare benefits. Table 26.3 shows that in New York City, a welfare mother would have to find a job paying at least $13 an hour to make work pay better than government income support programs. We have essentially priced low-wage workers out of the market. As discussed in Chapter 25, the way to improve the lot of the poor is to end the welfare system that traps people in the culture of poverty.

All income assistance for employable adults should be predicated on the recipient's working. One option to consider would be replacing all federal cash welfare programs, food stamps, and Medicaid for employable adults with a refundable tax credit (up to the amount of Social Security payroll taxes paid) for low-income families, if at least one adult in the household works at a full-time job. The idea behind the tax credit is that every family with a full-time worker should be able to afford the basic costs of food, shelter, child rearing, and other necessities. (Such a tax credit system could be made compatible with a flat tax.) If we guaranteed all working Americans a livable income, but ended all means testing of federal benefits, the work and marriage disincentive of the current welfare system would disappear and the dignity of work and family would be elevated. Finally, because that scheme would de-bureaucratize welfare, it

Table 26.3
Value of Welfare in Selected Cities, 1995

City, State	Pretax Income Equivalent*	Hourly Equivalent**
New York, NY	$,30,700	$14.76
Philadelphia, PA	$25,900	$12.45
Baltimore, MD	$23,600	$11.35
Los Angeles, CA	$23,500	$11.30
Detroit, MI	$22,700	$10.91
Indianapolis, IN	$21,100	$10.14
Akron, OH	$20,100	$9.66
Toledo, OH	$20,100	$9.66
Cleveland, OH	$20,000	$9.62
Pittsburgh, PA	$20,000	$9.62
Lexington, KY	$19,800	$9.52
Cincinnati, OH	$19,800	$9.52
Columbus, OH	$19,500	$9.38
Chicago, IL	$19,400	$9.33
Louisville, KY	$18,600	$8.94
Kansas City, MO	$17,700	$8.51
St. Louis, MO	$17,450	$8.39
Birmingham, AL	$15,300	$7.36
Houston, TX	$15,200	$7.31

Source: Michael Tanner, Stephen Moore, and David Hartman, "The Work vs. Welfare Trade-Off," Cato Institute Policy Analysis no. 240, September 19, 1995.
*Includes federal, state, and local income taxes and FICA taxes.
**Based on a 2080-hour work year.

would ensure that virtually all expenditures wound up in the pockets of the intended recipients.

Housing

HUD seems to exist more for the benefit of bureaucrats in Washington, D.C., than for that of America's inner cities. Currently, HUD has 15,000 federal employees. That's roughly 150 federal workers for every central city in America. But most of those federal employees have never set foot in our cities. They, and the vast programs they administer, are only marginally important to city development.

HUD should be abolished. The major beneficiaries of HUD are, not the inner-city poor, but federal workers, urban lobbyists, government contractors, mortgage bankers, and the construction industry. The urban aid programs have produced no positive results in revitalizing inner cities.

The construction of public housing should be terminated entirely. The strategy of spending billions of dollars over the past 40 years to segregate the poor in public housing projects has been a distinct and widely recognized failure. But for inexplicable reasons the strategy continues. Construction companies seem to be the sole advocates of the program.

Congress should recognize that most of the low-income housing supply problems are a result of misguided local housing regulations, such as restrictive building codes; prohibitions against inexpensive, prefabricated housing; zoning; and rent control.

One final responsibility of HUD is mortgage financing, handled primarily by the Federal Housing Administration. Increasingly, FHA does not serve lower income minority homebuyers, and it certainly does not boost homeownership in cities. Only 18 percent of FHA loan applications in 1993 were for homes in low- or moderate-income census tracts. Some low-income areas seem to be virtually quarantined by FHA. For example, a recent study found that 94 percent of the mortgages in south central Los Angeles were conventional, not FHA, mortgages. Instead, the FHA has aggressively moved into more upscale housing markets. Today, with its $153,000 mortgage cap—up from $67,500 in 1980—the FHA is serving wealthier families. Those markets are already well served by private mortgage insurers.

Even when the FHA does subsidize homebuyers in low-income neighborhoods, the assistance may be more of a burden than a benefit. Over the past 10 years more than 700,000 families suffered the trauma of losing their FHA-insured homes. FHA foreclosures often contribute to the deterioration of low-income neighborhoods. Gail Cincotta, head of the National Training and Information Center in Chicago and a long-time slum fighter, says, "The number 1 problem in revitalizing neighborhoods is FHA." She notes that in many low-income neighborhoods, FHA's default rate is 28 percent. Private insurers are much more likely to work with a financially distressed homeowner to refinance the mortgage and make other accommodations to keep the family in the home. A privatized FHA would, on balance, benefit cities.

Education Reform

In 1978 the federal government created the U.S. Department of Education. Since then the quality of inner-city schools—indeed almost all public schools—has visibly deteriorated. As former Dallas mayor Steve Bartlett laments, "If the Department of Education—and the $300 billion it has spent over the past fifteen years—has had any positive effect on the learning going on in classrooms in our cities—we have not seen it."

Cities are not inherently unsuitable environments for learning. After all, some of the best universities in the world are located in or around inner cities—the University of Chicago, the University of California at Los Angeles, Marquette, Harvard, Yale, Johns Hopkins, the University of Pennsylvania, the University of Minnesota, Columbia, and so on. Why then are those very same cities also home to some of the world's worst elementary and secondary schools?

The principal answer is that in the first case, the students and their families have a choice of schools. In the second, they do not. We know that monopolies don't work well in the private sector: they don't control costs, they aren't responsive to customer needs, and they are slow to change. We should not be surprised that monopoly systems work with equal inefficiency in the public sector.

The Education Department should be abolished. Education is a state and local responsibility. Congress needs to be frank with the American public by declaring that virtually any federal involvement in their local schools is likely to make them worse, not better. If states and cities are serious about improving their schools, they should break up the monopoly structure of inner-city schools through a means-tested voucher program that empowers parents and students, not teachers' unions, school boards, school districts, and PTAs. The vouchers could then be used by low-income parents to send their children to whatever school, public or private, they chose. Today, in most inner cities—including Washington, D.C., New York, Chicago, and Jersey City—children can receive a better education at half the cost of the public school monopoly in private schools.

In Milwaukee an experimental state voucher program is already in place and has generated widespread enthusiasm on the part of participating families. The children are experiencing greater academic success. In other cities, such as Dallas and Indianapolis, successful privately funded voucher programs have been launched. Most of the families served are low-income minorities.

Empowering parents with a choice about where they can send their children to school, perhaps more than any other single reform, would bring American families back to cities. Ultimately, the fate of this critical school reform rests in the hands of state and local governments—not in Washington.

Crime and Drugs

High crime rates in cities are one of the primary factors driving middle-income families out to the suburbs. Washington, D.C., with more than 500 homicides in 1993, has become derisively labeled the "murder capital of the world." Cities like Atlanta, Detroit, and Miami have crime rates that are as high as Washington's.

As is education, fighting crime is a state and local responsibility. The federal crime bill of 1993 was one of the most misguided pieces of legislation to pass Congress in many years. The $30 billion bill attempts to combat crime with $8 billion to $10 billion of new social spending—on arts and crafts programs, federally funded job training, self-esteem classes, and, of course, midnight basketball leagues. Yet if social spending were the antidote to high crime in cities, East Los Angeles and the Bronx would have the safest streets in the world. Another $10 billion is now being spent on Bill Clinton's 100,000 cops on the street program. Yet, it turns out, not surprisingly, that the cops will be primarily added, not in areas with significant crime rates, but rather in politically crucial areas where votes might be bought from appreciative voters with "free" federal dollars. In any case, there is no conceivable reason why cities and states cannot pay for their own police. The 1993 crime bill ought to be immediately repealed in its entirety.

The most critical step that the federal government could take to reduce crime in cities would be to end the war on drugs. Prohibition hasn't ended and won't end the use of marijuana, cocaine, and heroin, but it does make the drugs 10 to 100 times more expensive on the street than they would be on legal markets. The higher price means that users often commit crimes to pay for a habit that would be more affordable if drugs were legal. It has been estimated that at least half the property crime in major cities is a result of drug prohibition.

An even more frightening level of crime results from the fact that drug warlords (the modern-day Al Capones) now rule many of our inner cities. Participants in the drug trade have no peaceful means of settling disputes between buyer and seller or between rival sellers. A few years ago police estimated that 60 to 80 percent of Washington's murders were drug related. Law-abiding residents of inner cities are often caught in the cross-fire of the drug war.

The federal role in ending drug prohibition should be similar to the federal role in the repeal of alcohol prohibition in the early 1930s. The Twenty-First Amendment did not legalize alcohol sale and consumption;

rather it returned to the states the authority to set alcohol policy. The Controlled Substance Act of 1971, which makes drugs illegal, should be amended to eliminate the federal prohibition against psychoactives. Then states could establish their own policies. Many states would probably choose to treat marijuana and cocaine the way states now treat alcohol: sale to adults but not to children is legal, and taxes are high. That reform would take the astronomical profits out of drug trafficking and destroy the illicit drug trade that terrorizes so many of our cities. Not only would there be much less crime in inner cites, but police time could be freed to deal with other serious criminals. It is noteworthy that after alcohol prohibition was overturned in 1933, the crime rate fell for 10 straight years in the United States as the bootlegging industry collapsed.

Trade and Immigration

In general, America's cities are the beneficiaries of free trade and open immigration. Historically, cities prospered precisely because of their roles as trading centers. For example, many large American cities have ports that were hubs for international commerce until increased trade protectionism reduced their use. Moreover, immigrant businesses, which are flourishing in cities, are typically tied to imports to and exports from home countries. Many of the large American cities that are booming today—Miami, San Diego, San Francisco, Seattle, to name a few—owe much of their growth in enterprise to international trade. For example, the Miami area now accounts for nearly one-quarter of all U.S. trade with South America. Miami—with its flourishing financial services and communications industries—is now considered the capital of Central America. As Joel Kotkin, senior fellow at the Center for the New West, notes, "Global trade is critical to urban America's quest to regain its full economic potential."

Milwaukee mayor John Norquist says that "free trade can only be a huge asset to American cities." He is right. A vital pro-urban policy for the 105th Congress to adopt is tearing down restrictions on free trade.

Another huge asset for cities is immigration. That runs contrary to the views of many restrictionists and urban leaders, who argue that immigrants impose a burden on cities. The argument is made that states and especially localities with very large concentrations of immigrants are increasingly incapable of absorbing the large numbers of newcomers and that U.S.-born citizens, particularly low-income minorities, living in those areas and competing with foreign workers for jobs, are the victims.

Immigrants are also said to be changing the face of America's cities in ways that many Americans find deeply disturbing. For example, *Newsweek* recently raised the alarm for Californians with a frightening headline: "Los Angeles 2010: A Latino Subcontinent." Within a generation, predicts the article, "California will be demographically, culturally, and economically distinct from the rest of America." Gordon J. McDonald, former chief of the U.S. Border Patrol, is even more blunt in his assessment of the urban impact of immigrants. "Major cities have already been turned into extensions of foreign countries," he warns. Urban unrest, such as the 1990 rioting in Los Angeles, is said to be a sign of black rage resulting from job displacement by immigrants.

It is true that immigrants disproportionately affect our urban areas. Over half of all immigrants reside in just seven cities: Los Angeles, New York, Chicago, Miami, San Diego, Houston, and San Francisco. Most of the rest of the nation is negligibly touched by immigration. But the facts show very clearly that, on balance, the migration of foreign workers, businesses, and families into cities provides an economic vitality to those areas. The cities that attract immigrants tend to be much more economically successful than cities without immigrants. Moreover, the argument that American's inner-city underclass is hopelessly burdened by the presence of immigrants is refuted by the fact that America's most depressed urban areas—Detroit, St. Louis, Buffalo, Newark, Philadelphia, for example—have virtually no immigrants.

A recent study by the Alexis de Tocqueville Institute contrasted the economic conditions of the cities with the most immigrants and those with the fewest immigrants over the period 1980–92. The study examined seven variables measuring the prosperity of cities—from population growth, to poverty rates, to income growth, to crime, to taxes—and found that cities with large foreign-born populations fared much better than cities with few immigrants. The institute concluded, "Immigrants appear to be a primary catalyst for rebuilding and revitalizing America's inner cities."

James Madison once observed, "That part of America that has encouraged [foreigners] has advanced most rapidly in population, agriculture, and in the arts." That appears to be as true today as it was 200 years ago. Restrictionist immigration laws—which were considered by the 104th Congress and may be revisited by the 105th—will only deny cities the human capital so essential to their resurgence while exacerbating their fiscal problems.

Conclusion

The primary impetus for rebuilding cities has to come from city residents themselves. Much of the decline of America's once-mighty industrial cities

10 Most Burdensome Federal Regulations Imposed on Cities

- Davis Bacon Act
- Service Contract Act
- Superfund
- Clean Air Act amendments
- public housing admission and occupancy standards
- Fair Labor Standards Act
- 14(c) transit policy
- Jones Act
- Community Reinvestment Act
- minimum wage

has been a result of misguided policies—most important, soaring taxes and runaway municipal budgets—that cities have imposed on themselves. For too many years our cities have operated as if their primary clientele were government employee unions and big-business campaign contributors, not the residents themselves.

But Washington shares some of the blame for the collapse of cities, and thus a part of the responsibility for helping rebuild urban communities. The way for the federal government to help revitalize America's cities is to abandon one-size-fits-all bureaucratic dictates from Washington. Allow inner-city residents the maximum freedom to solve their own problems their own ways. In the past, federal aid to cities seems to have been predicated on the baffling notion that federal lawmakers have a better idea of what's best for cities than do the residents themselves.

The basic tenets of a sound and effective urban development strategy include reducing federal taxes and deficit spending; calling a "time-out" on unfunded mandates; devising policies that maximize the free choice of even the poorest residents of cities; ending drug prohibition; and, finally, upending federal policies such as the current welfare trap that reward bad behavior and punish the virtues of work and family.

If Washington were to start following those simple principles, the federal government could begin to be a constructive partner in rebuilding America's cities.

Suggested Readings

Boaz, David, ed. *The Crisis in Drug Prohibition.* Washington: Cato Institute, 1993.

Moore, Stephen, and Dean Stansel. ''The Myth of America's Underfunded Cities.'' Cato Institute Policy Analysis no. 188, February 22, 1993.

Staley, Sam. ''Bigger Is Not Better: The Virtues of Decentralized Local Government.'' Cato Institute Policy Analysis no. 166, January 21, 1992.

Tucker, William. *The Excluded Americans: Homelessness and Housing Policies.* Washington: Regnery, 1989.

—Prepared by Stephen Moore

27. A Federal Privatization Agenda

Congress should

- sell all federal energy enterprises;
- convert air traffic control, public broadcasting, and various research and development laboratories to self-supporting non-profit corporations;
- privatize Amtrak and the U.S. Postal Service via worker-management buyouts;
- gradually sell off commercial lands and buildings;
- auction off all remaining nonmilitary frequency spectrum;
- sell federal loan portfolios; and
- sell remaining commodity stockpiles.

Over the past decade governments worldwide have sold off more than $500 billion in assets and enterprises. Many additional billions worth of state assets have been given to citizens of former communist countries via privatization voucher programs. Privatization has dramatically improved the performance of former government enterprises, while improving the financial health of the governments involved. In private hands, former government assets no longer get taxpayer subsidies; indeed, they become net taxpayers. And the one-time proceeds from asset sales are used either to help meet budget-balancing goals or to pay down excessive levels of government debt. The United States has only begun to tap the potential of a serious program to divest federal enterprises and assets.

Sale of Federal Enterprises

Table 27.1 lists some federal enterprises that are potential candidates for privatization as going concerns.

Table 27.1
Salable Federal Enterprises

Asset	Sales Revenue ($ billions)	Annual Savings ($ billions)
Tennessee Valley Authority	8.5	1.0
5 power marketing administrations	14.0	1.2
Dams*	10.0	?
Energy facilities**	10.0	?
U.S. Postal Service	8.1	–
Air traffic control	3.5	–
Global Positioning System	7.0	?
U.S. Enrichment Corp.	1.0	?
National Weather Service	2.5	0.4
U.S. Geological Survey	0.5	0.6
4 NASA aeronautics labs	5.6	0.3
USDA Agricultural Research Centers	4.0	?
Department of Energy labs	6.1	?
Amtrak	–	1.0
CPB	0.3	0.3
Total	81.1	4.8

*Under the Army Corps of Engineers and the Bureau of Reclamation.
**Under the General Services Administration, Veterans Administration, and Department of Defense.

Electricity

The first four items in the table are all parts of federal energy systems. Worldwide, electric utility systems worth some $13 billion were privatized in 1995. Investment bankers and accounting firms have been analyzing and carrying out such transactions around the globe for the past 10 years, and a wealth of expertise is available on structuring such deals and coping with the inevitable political concerns, such as possible rate increases for electricity users. While privatization will mean the loss of tax subsidies for the utilities in question (thereby tending to increase rates), investor ownership will provide strong incentives for cost cutting (thereby tending to permit lower rates). With electricity deregulation fast approaching, it may well be a matter of survival for government-owned electric utilities to develop a truly commercial, entrepreneurial corporate culture (as has occurred via privatization overseas—in Argentina and Britain, for example).

One way of easing rate shock for consumers is to offer them shares in the enterprise on a preferential basis, as was done in most of the utility privatizations in the United Kingdom. That way, their gains as shareholders (dividends, capital gains) will help to offset any increases in their utility bills.

Postal Service

The most important reason to privatize the U.S. Postal Service is, not to raise money, but to improve the organization's ability to survive and thrive in a rapidly changing world. Because its monopoly status lets the USPS subsidize new services with profits from monopoly functions, competitors rightly object to any proposed new ventures by the USPS. Second, the corporate culture of the USPS is still that of its predecessor government agency. Lacking shareholders that can hold management accountable for truly commercial performance—and constrained by its mountain of procedural rules and red tape—the USPS is simply unable to operate like a real business. Sweden and the Netherlands have already privatized and deregulated their postal services; Argentina, Germany, and Malaysia are planning to do so; and Britain and Canada are considering the idea.

The best way to address the concerns of postal workers and management is to give them partial ownership of the privatized firm. Earmarking for workers and managers a meaningful fraction (10 percent or more) of the shares in a firm being privatized has become routine around the world, especially for large firms and especially for those that are labor intensive. Turning workers and managers into shareholders is one of the best known ways to change the corporate culture of a bureaucratic enterprise, giving every individual a tangible stake in its success as a profitable private enterprise.

Air Traffic Control and the Global Positioning System

For these two high-tech functions, the imperative to privatize is to permit users to realize the full potential of their vital 24-hour-a-day services. Current governmental personnel, procurement, and budgeting systems fatally hamstring the performance of the nation's air traffic control (ATC) system. It cannot retain sufficient highly experienced controllers in the most demanding locations because of civil service. It cannot procure state-of-the-art computers and electronic systems because, by the time the procurement process is completed, the systems have already become obsolete. And it cannot rationally plan and implement a modernization program on a year-by-year pay-as-you-go basis. As of 1996, 16 other countries—

293

including Australia, Britain, Canada, and Germany—had converted their ATC systems to user-funded corporations, independent of government procurement, civil-service, and budgetary systems. In Canada, a user-owned not-for-profit corporation—NavCanada—purchased the ATC system in 1996 for over $1 billion. A larger scale version could be applied in the United States.

Much the same analysis can be applied prospectively to the Global Positioning System, the complex of satellites that provide real-time position locating worldwide. Developed originally for defense purposes, the system has now been opened to civilian users. Full use of the GPS's tremendous capabilities over the next several decades promises huge benefits—to aviation, ocean shipping, trucking companies, fleet managers, individual drivers (navigation systems), hunters, backpackers, and others. But continued Department of Defense operation and management of the system will fail to realize the full range of the GPS's potential. A federally chartered corporation (like Comsat) could buy the system from the government and operate it on a user-fee basis.

Research and Development Agencies

The next items on the list are all involved in science-based activities for which commercial markets exist, and in which the agency's ability to operate commercially is often restricted by the constraints of being a government agency. Both the National Weather Service and the U.S. Geological Survey generate information products whose commercial value is potentially quite large. But their status as government agencies has required them to give away or sell for token amounts much of that valuable information. They are also plagued by budgetary constraints, which make it difficult for them to afford state-of-the-art computer systems that are critical to their success in processing the large volumes of information inherent in their work. As commercialized entities they would be free to borrow in the capital markets to modernize their equipment, demonstrating the soundness of those investments in terms of future sales of enhanced information products.

The National Aeronautics and Space Administration's aeronautical laboratories (Ames Dryden, Langley, and Lewis) are in a slightly different situation. The market for their aeronautical research and development is limited principally to the producers of aircraft and aircraft engines, along with the military. The labs' findings are provided at no charge to those firms and the Department of Defense. Hence, taxpayer support for those labs amounts to a subsidy to a specific industry and to the DoD. Privatizing those labs would be a way to end an industry-specific subsidy and would require those firms to purchase the valuable information and incorporate the cost into the ultimate prices of their products. The DoD would become responsible for funding that portion of the labs' work that it finds valuable. Much the same is true for many of the R&D labs of the U.S. Department of Agriculture and the Department of Energy.

Worker-management buyouts would be one form of privatization suitable for the various R&D labs. In the past five years, Britain has privatized a number of labs of this sort, dealing with research in agriculture, chemistry, construction, engineering, physics, and transportation.

Amtrak

Amtrak will be difficult to privatize in anything like its current form. Were the company to be put up for sale, with all current laws and provisions unchanged, it is doubtful that a single serious bid would be received, since Amtrak covers neither its operating nor its capital costs from its fares. Even the Northeast Corridor, where Amtrak enjoys its heaviest patronage, is a money-losing proposition.

The only way in which viable bids might be received for Amtrak is if Congress enacted major changes in the law that would permit dramatic reductions in Amtrak's costs. Such measures might include repealing the Federal Employers' Liability Act (at least as it applies to Amtrak), amending the Railway Labor Act to reduce severance pay from the equivalent of six years' to that of six months' normal pay, repealing statutory requirements for various types and levels of Amtrak service so as to permit it to discontinue specific routes or trains, and reforming Railroad Retirement and Unemployment Insurance.

Corporation for Public Broadcasting

Abundant cable and satellite television has greatly weakened the original case for taxpayer support of public broadcasting. Cultural and educational programming, once considered commercially inviable, is now available on competing commercial channels. And tentative offers from private firms indicate that the Corporation for Public Broadcasting and the Public Broadcasting System have developed programming with real market value. Privatizing the CPB would depoliticize it, thereby ending once and for all the controversies between liberals and conservatives over program content. If Congress judged none of the bids for the CPB acceptable, an alternative would be to earmark several billion dollars of the proceeds from the sale of broadcast frequencies as an endowment fund for the CPB, sufficient to end its dependence on annual appropriations. The CPB could then become an independent, nonprofit corporation, deriving its annual budget from earnings on its endowment fund, fundraising and sponsorship, and revenues from licensing and commercial spinoffs (e.g., *Barney*).

Sale of Federal Assets

Much larger than the potential value of federal enterprises is the potential value of other federal assets. Table 27.2 indicates that just eight categories of those assets might be worth as much as $444 billion.

Electromagnetic Spectrum

Thus far the Clinton administration has auctioned off over $10 billion in previously unallocated spectrum, thereby setting an important precedent— namely, the acknowledgment that frequencies are a form of property, an essential component of the means of production of communications ser- vices. But the current spectrum auctions fall short in two ways. First, auctions have been used only for a few frequency bands that were pre- viously unused. Second, what has been auctioned off is only a temporary right to use the frequency, not a true property right. The principle needs to be expanded in both of those areas.

Private ownership is equally valid for all civilian frequency bands, not just for those currently unoccupied. Among the most important bands are

Table 27.2
Salable Federal Assets

Asset	Sales Revenue ($ billions)	Annual Savings ($ billions)
Spectrum	150.0	?
Commodity lands (Forest Service, BLM)	160.0	3.0
Loan portfolio	108.0	2.0
Naval Petroleum Reserve	1.6	?
Federal Helium Reserve	–	?
Defense stockpile	1.0	?
Strategic Petroleum Reserve	13.0	?
Govt. bldg. & land	10.0?	?
Total	443.6	5.0

those used by broadcasters. Current license holders exist in a kind of twilight zone, in which their studios, antennas, broadcast equipment, and all the other means of production are privately owned, but the frequency— without which they cannot broadcast—is held at the sufferance of a federal agency that can rescind the right to use it in response to interest-group opposition to the content of current broadcasting.

Moreover, the Federal Communications Commission has decreed that certain frequency bands must be used only for the purposes that the commission has specified—even if alternative uses would be far more valuable. Many ultra-high television frequencies, for example, are worth relatively little in that use; the same frequencies could be worth vastly more if repackaged for other uses.

In a recent Reason Foundation study, communications attorney David Colton sets forth a three-phase program for dezoning, privatizing, and protecting spectrum bands. On the basis of careful analysis of recent auction prices, Colton estimates that privatization of all nonmilitary spectrum could yield between $100 billion and $300 billion. To be conservative, we have used $150 billion for this line in Table 27.2.

Commodity Lands

The next item is commodity lands—commercial timberlands owned and operated by the Forest Service and grazing lands owned by the Bureau of Land Management. A 1989 Reason Foundation study, making conservative assumptions, estimated that those lands are worth some $160 billion at market value. The Forest Service and the BLM are poor stewards of those lands. (The Forest Service is notorious for spending hundreds of millions of dollars on logging roads in forests the timber harvests from which do not produce sufficient revenues to recover the costs.) The BLM's policies encourage overgrazing. Both environmental and multiple-use goals can be secured as part of privatization. Deed restrictions, for example, can require the purchasers of forest lands to continue to provide access for multiple uses—hiking, fishing, hunting, and forestry. Especially environmentally sensitive BLM and Forest Service lands (where commercial operations cannot be economically self-supporting) can be set aside for sale to environmental groups.

Loan Portfolio

The federal government is the nation's largest lender—to homeowners, college students, and small businesses in particular. Unfortunately, the various agencies involved do a relatively poor job of collecting on those loans. A loan portfolio is an asset that can be sold for a percentage of its face value to a buyer that believes it can do a better job of collecting on the loans than the seller is doing. During the 1980s federal loan asset sales demonstrated that the federal government could receive up to 80 cents on the dollar for its loan assets. Assuming a sale price of between 60 and 80 cents on the dollar, the government's current $155 billion portfolio could yield between $93 billion and $124 billion.

Defense Reserves

During the Cold War, the government built up a huge variety of reserve stocks of various commodities. One of the oldest of those is the Naval Petroleum Reserve, at two sites in California and Wyoming. Those stocks of oil no longer have strategic value, and the oil is, in fact, sold into the commercial market today. Congress approved the sale of the California reserve in 1996. Another obsolete reserve is the Federal Helium Reserve, which accounts for 90 percent of the nation's helium sales. That reserve has a market value of between $1.0 billion and $1.5 billion; unfortunately, its borrowings from the Treasury, plus accumulated interest, total $1.4 billion, making net proceeds from the sale a wash. But at least the sale would provide a ready means of paying off the reserve's debt. In addition to oil and helium, the Defense Department acquired immense stockpiles of other commodities during the Cold War, much of which it is no longer necessary to maintain. Those stocks should be sold off over a period of years (so as not to greatly depress the market price of each commodity).

Strategic Petroleum Reserve

As a result of the oil embargoes of the 1960s and 1970s, the federal government created a huge civilian reserve stock of petroleum. While the reserve could prove valuable in a future situation of unexpected supply shortages, it is the existence of the reserve, rather than its ownership, that is critical. Private institutions could buy out the function of operating the reserve, and there is some reason to believe that the release of stocks from the reserve in response to market price increases would be more timely and less subject to arbitrary constraints than would releases under the current political management. The Congressional Budget Office has estimated the market value of the SPR at $13 billion and included its possible privatization in a recent options paper.

Government Buildings and Land

The federal government is the nation's largest owner of real property. Not only does it own one-third of the country's land area (the commodity lands discussed above, as well as national parks and wilderness areas), but it also owns huge amounts of valuable urban land and buildings. Moreover, the government owns some $12 billion of real estate overseas. It is high time Congress reviewed the General Services Administration's detailed inventory of federal real estate for the purpose of identifying salable properties, both domestic and foreign. A significant fraction of those holdings appears to be surplus by any reasonable definition. And for that real estate required for ongoing governmental functions, the government should consider the option of sale and leaseback. Many state and municipal governments are discovering that their in-house costs of operating and maintaining office space are as much as double those of the private sector. Rather than battle endlessly over whether or not to contract out selected operating and maintenance tasks, the GSA could realize savings by selling many buildings to professional real estate management firms and leasing back needed space at rates that reflect private-sector efficiencies.

Achieving Fiscal Benefits

As shown in Table 27.3, a serious privatization agenda could produce $525 billion in one-time proceeds, which should be earmarked for paying down the national debt. In addition, three other impacts would reduce the government's annual budget deficit. First, elimination of current operating costs or subsidies, or both, would yield nearly $10 billion per year in savings. Second, federal corporate income taxes on the privatized federal

Table 27.3
Overall Savings from Privatization ($ billions)

Type of Sale	One-Time Proceeds	Annual Deficit Reduction		
		Interest Savings*	Subsidy Elimin.	Fed. Corp. Tax**
Enterprises	81.1	6.08	4.8	2.76
Assets	443.6	33.27	5.0	15.08
Total	524.7	39.35	9.8	17.84

*Interest calculated at 7.5 percent on Treasury bonds.
**Federal corporate tax rate of 34 percent on revenue equal to 10 percent return on asset value.

299

enterprises would generate an estimated $18 billion per year. Third, the reduction in the national debt (thanks to the proceeds of the sale of assets) would lead to annual interest savings in the vicinity of $39 billion. Together, those three savings total $67 billion per year in permanent deficit reduction.

Those numbers may understate the full potential savings from federal privatization. Tables 27.1 and 27.2 are incomplete in two ways. First, some of the annual savings estimates are not included, because hard numbers are unavailable at this time. Second, other assets and enterprises can undoubtedly be added to these lists, producing further sales proceeds and associated annual savings. So the total proceeds and annual savings from a full-fledged federal privatization agenda would be larger than what is shown in these preliminary tables.

While the totals are large, most of the individual items are rather small. With each individual federal asset or enterprise defended by a well-established constituency with strong ties to the congressional committees that have historically dealt with that asset or enterprise, the gains from each isolated privatization may appear to not be worth the cost of the struggle to bring it about. That problem is analogous to that faced by advocates of closing surplus military bases in the 1980s. Rep. Dick Armey (R-Tex.) proposed the breakthrough solution of a Base Closing Commission, which had carte blanche to identify, on the merits, a whole set of bases that were good candidates for closure. Congress agreed to bind itself to accept or reject the entire package of recommendations in an up-or-down, no-amendments-possible vote. That mechanism permitted members of Congress to do what was right despite the potential of short-term pain in their individual districts.

A similar mechanism might prove useful in the case of privatization. A privatization commission could be charged with identifying, each year until a balanced budget had been achieved, a package of federal assets and enterprises to be privatized. The independent, bipartisan commission would produce an annual list of proposals that would be voted on as a package, without amendment, in an up-or-down vote. That approach has the best chance of overcoming what Milton Friedman has called "the tyranny of the status quo."

Suggested Readings

Anderson, Terry. "Rekindling the Privatization Fires: Political Lands Revisited." Policy Study no. 108. Los Angeles: Reason Foundation, 1989.

Colton, David. "Spectrum Privatization." Policy Study no. 208. Los Angeles: Reason Foundation, 1996.

Gibbon, Henry. "A Guide for Divesting Government-Owned Enterprises." How-to Guide no. 15. Los Angeles: Reason Foundation, 1996.

Houston, Douglas A. "Federal Power: The Case for Privatizing Electricity." Policy Study no. 201. Los Angeles: Reason Foundation, 1996.

Hudgins, Edward L., ed. *The Last Monopoly: Privatizing the Postal Service for the Information Age.* Washington: Cato Institute, 1996.

Poole, Robert W. Jr., and Viggo Butler. "Reinventing Air Traffic Control." Policy Study no. 206. Los Angeles: Reason Foundation, 1996.

—Prepared by Robert Poole

28. Crime

Congress should

- respect the Tenth Amendment of the Constitution by leaving the task of crime fighting to state government;
- pending complete federal withdrawal, halt the federal funding of state and local police, courts, and prisons; and
- pending complete federal withdrawal, repeal the federal drug laws and abolish the Drug Enforcement Agency.

In modern political discourse, the distinction between a national problem and a widely publicized local problem is about as clear as mud. It seems as if no area of our lives, no social problem, is beyond the purview of some federal agency. Whether the topic is teenage pregnancy, drug use, literacy, or the price of a gallon of gasoline, Washington's politicians and bureaucrats claim to have an answer. Crime is no different. Despite some tactical differences, the conventional wisdom in both of our major political parties is that the federal government should take a more active role in combatting crime. The conventional wisdom, however, is based on a set of assumptions that are both constitutionally dubious and resistant to empirical evidence.

The Modern Trend: Big-Government Law Enforcement

The Constitution delegates only a limited set of powers to the federal government. Contrary to popular belief, the Constitution does not authorize the Federal Bureau of Investigation, or any other federal agency, to combat intrastate crimes such as murder, rape, and theft. The Tenth Amendment leaves primary jurisdiction over criminal matters with state government.

In fact, the Constitution specifically mentions only three federal offenses: treason, piracy, and counterfeiting. And we know from the ratification debates that the question of whether Congress could create other federal offenses was raised more than a few times. Those who opposed the ratification of the Constitution warned that the proposed central government might try to define and enforce an expansive national code of offenses. Proponents of the Constitution responded to those dire predictions by assuring the public that the Constitution vested no such power in the central government. When that point of contention arose in the Virginia ratification debate—to cite just one example—Gov. Edmund Randolph declared that Congress would have no "cognizance over any other crime except piracies, felonies committed on the high seas, and offenses against the law of nations." Because that type of warranty was repeated over and over again by the salesmen of the Constitution, Thomas Jefferson would later maintain that our fundamental legal charter should be interpreted "according to the true sense in which it was adopted by the states, that in which it was advocated by its friends, and not that which its enemies apprehended."

Unfortunately, our original constitutional arrangement has almost completely unraveled. The contemporary debate among Justice Department officials and legislators revolves largely around the question of which crimes, if any, are *beyond* the authority of Congress. In a 1994 Supreme Court case, *United States v. Lopez*, President Clinton's solicitor general went so far as to attempt to persuade our highest court that Congress has plenary authority to create federal offenses.

The constitutional principle of federalism is easy to proclaim but often hard to uphold in the political arena. In recent years, Congress has yielded to popular pressure to make local offenses, such as carjacking, wife beating, stalking, and church burning, federal crimes. That disturbing trend will only continue unless congressional leaders make a serious effort to defend the Constitution against demagoguery.

While it is true that the state governments continue to handle over 90 percent of the criminal cases in America, the expanding role of the federal government is nonetheless remarkable. Consider the following historical developments:

- When the Constitution was ratified in 1787, there were only three federal crimes. Today there are over 3,000.
- In 1930, at the height of alcohol prohibition, there were about 400 FBI agents. Today the federal government employs over 69,000 full-time personnel who are authorized to make arrests and carry firearms.
- The budget for the Department of Justice has ballooned over the years. Ten years ago its budget was $3.9 billion. Today its budget

is over $13.7 billion. That phenomenal growth shows no sign of abating. The Clinton administration has requested $18.6 billion for 1997.

- An expansive federal criminal code has led to widespread federal electronic surveillance. Nineteen ninety-five marked the first year that federal law enforcement agents conducted more wiretaps than the police in the 50 states combined.
- Federal prisons are overflowing with inmates. In 1980 there were 24,363 federal inmates. By 1995 that number had quadrupled to 100,250. Despite an enormous prison expansion program, the Justice Department's own figures show that the federal prison system is operating at 26 percent over capacity.

Has big-government law enforcement reduced the level of crime in American society? One would think that, with such an enormous deployment of federal resources, the average American family would be feeling safer in their home and neighborhood. Sadly, the opposite is true. Millions and millions of citizens are touched by violent crime every year. A generation ago it was thought to be unwise to take shortcuts down dark alleys in cities. Today it is considered risky in most American cities to leave your own home after nightfall. And well-publicized crimes—such as the killing of Polly Klaas—have shown middle-class suburban residents that they are not as secure as they once believed.

Respected criminologists, such as Princeton professor John J. DiIulio Jr., have acknowledged the ineffectual results of federal intervention:

> Since 1968, Washington has spent scores of billions of dollars on crime and corrections, passed many get-tough crime bills, and spent trillions of dollars on anti-poverty programs. Crime rates have been largely unaffected by any of this.

Despite the paltry results, some Washington policymakers insist that the crime rate can be reduced by higher levels of spending and increased coordination between federal and state officials. The 105th Congress should resist that siren song.

Since there is very little evidence about what policies will actually reduce crime, we should *decentralize* decisions on public safety and study the successes and failures in various localities. After all, a crime-fighting strategy like community policing might work in San Francisco, but not in Miami.

Our constitutional system provides a continuous natural policy experiment for the states if the federal government will just respect the boundaries of its lawmaking authority. As Justice Louis Brandeis observed, "It is one of the happy incidents of the federal system that a single courageous State may, if its citizens choose, serve as a laboratory; and try novel social and economic experiments without risk to the rest of the country." The last thing the federal government should be doing is harmonizing the criminal justice policies of the 50 states through billion-dollar spending schemes. The 105th Congress should put a stop to federal meddling and get the national government back within its limited constitutional sphere without delay.

First Step: End the Federal Drug War

The single most important law that Congress must repeal is the Controlled Substances Act of 1970. That law is probably the most far-reaching federal statute in American history, since it asserts federal jurisdiction over every drug offense in the United States, no matter how small or local in scope. Once that law is removed from the statute books, Congress should move to abolish the Drug Enforcement Administration and repeal all of the other federal drug laws.

There are a number of reasons why Congress should end the federal government's war on drugs. First and foremost, the federal drug laws are constitutionally dubious. As previously noted, the federal government can only exercise the powers that have been delegated to it. The Tenth Amendment reserves all other powers to the states or to the people. However misguided the alcohol prohibitionists turned out to be, they deserve credit for honoring our constitutional system by seeking a constitutional amendment that would explicitly authorize a national policy on the sale of alcohol. Congress never asked the American people for additional constitutional powers to declare a war on drug consumers. That usurpation of power is something that few politicians or their court intellectuals wish to discuss.

Second, drug prohibition channels over $40 billion a year into the criminal underworld. Alcohol prohibition drove reputable companies into other industries or out of business altogether, which paved the way for mobsters to make millions through the black market. If drugs were legal, organized crime would stand to lose billions to legitimate businesses in an open marketplace.

306

Third, drug prohibition is a classic example of throwing money at a problem. The federal government spends over $12 billion to enforce the drug laws every year—all to no avail. For years drug war bureaucrats have been tailoring their budget requests to the latest news reports. When drug use goes up, taxpayers are told the government needs more money so that it can redouble its efforts against a rising drug scourge. When drug use goes down, taxpayers are told that it would be a big mistake to curtail spending just when progress is being made. Good news or bad, spending levels must be maintained or increased.

Fourth, the drug laws are responsible for widespread social upheaval. "Law and order" politicians too often fail to recognize that some laws can actually cause societal disorder. A simple example will illustrate that phenomenon. Right now our college campuses are relatively calm and peaceful, but imagine what would happen if Congress were to institute military conscription in order to wage a war in Bosnia or fight a dictator in the Middle East. Campuses across the country would likely erupt in protest—even though Congress did not desire that result. The drug laws happen to have different "disordering" effects. Perhaps the most obvious has been the turning of our cities into battlefields. Because drugs are illegal, participants in the drug trade cannot go to court to settle disputes, whether between buyer and seller or between rival sellers. When black-market contracts are breached, the result is often some form of violent sanction, which usually leads to retaliation and then open warfare in our city streets.

Our capital city, Washington, D.C., has become known as the "murder capital" even though it is the most heavily policed city in the United States. The violence reached such horrific levels in 1993 that Mayor Sharon Pratt Kelly asked President Clinton to deploy National Guard units. The idea of military troops occupying the capital city of the leader of the free world ought to give pause to reasonable people in both of our major political parties. Make no mistake about it, the annual carnage that stands behind America's soaring murder rates has nothing to do with the mind-altering effects of a marijuana cigarette or a crack pipe. It is instead one of the grim and bitter consequences of an ideological crusade whose proponents will not yet admit defeat.

Students of American history will someday ponder the question of how today's elected officials could readily admit to the mistaken policy of alcohol prohibition in the 1920s but recklessly pursue a policy of drug prohibition. Indeed, the only historical lesson that recent presidents and

Congresses seem to have drawn from the period of alcohol prohibition is that government should not try to outlaw the sale of booze. One of the broader lessons that they should have learned is this: prohibition laws should be judged according to their real-world effects, not their promised benefits. If the 105th Congress will subject the federal drug laws to that standard, it will recognize that the drug war is not the answer to problems associated with drug use.

Conclusion

The growing role of the federal government in everyday law enforcement is a deeply disturbing development. Fundamental constitutional principles such as federalism, the separation of powers, and the division of authority between the police and the military have been under a sustained attack. Those are the festering problems that Congress should be looking to address. It is imperative that the 105th Congress not only halt unconstitutional encroachment but consciously and deliberately roll it back until our written Constitution is once again the law of the land.

Suggested Readings

Baker, John S. Jr. "Nationalizing Criminal Law: Does Organized Crime Make It Necessary or Proper?" *Rutgers Law Journal* 16 (1985): 495–588.

Boaz, David. "A Drug-Free America—Or a Free America?" *U.C. Davis Law Review* 24 (1991): 617–36.

Brickey, Kathleen F. "Criminal Mischief: The Federalization of American Criminal Law." *Hastings Law Journal* 46 (1995): 1135–74.

Buckley, William F. Jr., et al. "The War on Drugs Is Lost." *National Review,* February 12, 1996.

Decker, Jarett B. "The 1995 Crime Bills: Is the GOP the Party of Liberty and Limited Government?" Cato Institute Policy Analysis no. 229, June 1, 1995.

Meese, Edwin III, and Rhett DeHart. "How Washington Subverts Your Local Sheriff." *Policy Review,* January–February 1996.

Niskanen, William A. "Crime, Police, and Root Causes." Cato Institute Policy Analysis no. 218, November 14, 1994.

Ostrowski, James. "The Moral and Practical Case for Drug Legalization." *Hofstra Law Review* 18 (1990): 607–702.

Packer, Herbert. *The Limits of the Criminal Sanction.* Stanford: Stanford University Press, 1968.

—Prepared by Timothy Lynch

29. Immigration

Congress should

- remove the new one-year time limit on filing for political asylum;
- expand or at least maintain current legal immigration quotas;
- repeal employer sanctions;
- stop the move toward a computerized national identification system and the use of government-issued documents, such as birth certificates and Social Security cards, as de facto national ID cards; and
- increase the number of H-1B visas and deregulate employment-based immigration to facilitate the entry of skilled immigrants and nonimmigrants.

Freedom of opportunity is the cornerstone of American society, and immigrants and those fleeing persecution desire that freedom. People continue to come from every corner of the globe to help build the strongest nation on earth. And for over 300 years immigrants and refugees, fleeing persecution and tyranny and seeking opportunities, not guarantees, have brought to America their talent, energy, and ideas.

Congress should reform the current immigration system so we can welcome more, not fewer, hard-working and talented individuals to this country. Additional immigrants can certainly be admitted through the employment-based portion of our immigration system, which allows us to bring in highly talented and motivated people from elsewhere in the world. Immigrants should be welcomed here so long as they do not burden taxpayers or commit crimes.

The overriding impact of immigrants is to strengthen the culture, increase the total output of the economy, and raise the standard of living of American citizens. Immigrants are advantageous to the United States for several reasons: (1) Since they are willing to take a chance in a new land, they are self-selected on the basis of motivation, risk taking, work ethic, and other attributes beneficial to a nation. (2) They tend to come to the United States during their prime working years (the average age is 28), and they contribute to the workforce and make huge net contributions to old age entitlement programs, primarily Social Security. (3) They are more likely to start new businesses than are native-born Americans—in 1995, 12 percent of the *Inc.* 500, the fastest growing companies in America, were started by immigrants. (4) Many immigrants arrive with extremely high skill levels or, regardless of skill level, a strong desire to work. (5) Their children tend to reach high levels of achievement in American schools and in society at large.

Today, approximately 7.5 percent of the U.S. population are legal immigrants and 9 percent are foreign born, which is significantly lower than the proportion—13 percent or higher—during the period from 1860 to 1930. The most recent Immigration and Naturalization Service data show that recent immigrants are dispersed over many more states than they used to be and that the proportion heading to California, Florida, and Texas declined from 1992 to 1995.

Immigration: Myths and Reality

Research demonstrates that the major arguments offered against immigration are not supported by the facts. The evidence supports the following conclusions.

1. **Immigrants typically more than cover the cost of public services used.** Economist Julian Simon calculates that native-born Americans receive more in annual government expenditures than do immigrants. The Urban Institute estimated in 1994 that immigrants pay $25 billion to $30 billion more in taxes than they receive in services each year. With immigrants now ineligible for public assistance programs under the recent welfare reform legislation, the net positive fiscal impact of immigrants will only increase.

2. **Immigrants create at least as many jobs as they fill.** Economists Rachel M. Friedberg of Brown University and Jennifer Hunt of Yale University wrote recently in the *Journal of Economic Perspectives* that ''despite the popular belief that immigrants have a large adverse impact on the wages and employment opportunities of the native-born population, the literature on this question does not provide much support for this conclusion.'' By starting businesses and spend-

ing their money on products made by Americans and immigrants alike, immigrants create at least as many jobs as they fill. Simply put, immigrants increase the supply of labor, but they also increase the *demand* for labor.

Although a few studies have attempted to show that immigrants in the short term may hurt the wages of some less skilled workers in some areas, those same data paradoxically say that other groups, such as women, see their wages rise as a result of immigration. A study by MIT economist Paul Krugman and Bar-Ilan University economist Elise S. Brezis concludes that, by encouraging increased investment, over time immigrants "may well tend to *raise* wages."

3. **Immigrants are not eroding America's culture.** While advocates of multiculturalism are misguided, there is no evidence that they are affecting the assimilation of immigrants in the United States. Critics of immigration often cite polls, but a unique CNN/*USA Today* poll found that more immigrants than natives believe that hard work and determination are the keys to success in America. And fewer immigrants than natives believe that immigrants should be encouraged to "maintain their own culture more strongly." In San Diego 90 percent of second-generation immigrant children speak English well or very well, according to a Johns Hopkins University study. In Miami the figure is *99 percent*. A recent report by the Manhattan Institute reveals that immigrants are more likely than are the native born to have intact families and a college degree and be employed, and they are no more likely to commit crimes. Over 60,000 immigrants serve in the nation's armed forces; nearly 7 percent of U.S. Navy personnel are immigrants, according to the Defense Department.

4. **The "new" immigrants are not less skilled or educated than the old.** Average education levels have risen each decade, though in recent decades immigrants' relative levels compared with those of natives have declined because of rapid increases in the educational achievement of natives.

5. **Immigrants do not harm the environment.** Assertions that immigrants will harm the environment by increasing the country's population growth rate contradict the experience of the past 50 years, which has seen environmental indicators improve while the population has increased.

That is not to say that immigrants do not impose some costs on the rest of us, that *all* immigrants who come are beneficial, or that our current immigration policy could not be improved. In the short term, immigrants do cause more crowding in our hospitals and schools. But an honest appraisal of the facts shows that the benefits far outweigh the costs.

How Does the Legal Immigration System Work?

Current legal immigration is tightly regulated and limited by numerical quotas and per country ceilings that prevent people from a few countries from obtaining all the visas. Only refugees, close family members, and individuals with a company to sponsor them can immigrate. A limited number of "diversity" visas are also distributed to immigrants from "underrepresented" countries. All categories are numerically restricted, except for the "immediate relatives" of U.S. citizens, whose totals changed little between 1986 and 1995.

Under U.S. law, an American citizen can sponsor (1) a spouse or minor child, (2) a parent, (3) a married child or a child 21 or older, or (4) a brother or sister. A lawful permanent resident (green card holder) can sponsor only a spouse or child. *No "extended family" immigration categories exist for aunts, uncles, or cousins.* Three-quarters of all family immigration visas in 1995 went to spouses and children. The other one-fourth went to the parents and siblings of U.S. citizens.

In 1997 Congress will reauthorize the Refugee Act, and, as it did in 1996, it should reject any refugee "cap." Such a cap is designed to slash the number of refugees admitted and would prevent flexible responses to emerging world situations. The annual number of refugees is set each year by consultations between the president and Congress. While U.S. programs to settle refugees from Southeast Asia are winding down, America certainly can accept refugees from other nations in their place.

Unlike refugees, who are accepted for admission while still outside the United States, people seeking political asylum must first enter the country and then request permission to stay. Contrary to the popular impression, it is quite difficult to obtain political asylum. Only 22 percent of the claims considered in 1994 were approved. There was no need to impose a time limit that requires individuals to file for asylum within one year of arriving in the United States, as Congress did in the 1996 immigration bill. Many victims of torture and persecution take time to heal from their emotional wounds and view asylum as an inevitable break with their followers back home. If a one-year time limit had been in effect in past years, 62.5 percent of those who later received asylum as legitimate refugees would have been denied asylum.

Recent INS reforms have corrected the system's key problems (asylum applicants can no longer receive work papers and disappear into the workforce). The number of first-time claims has dropped dramatically, and almost all new cases are completed within 180 days of filing. Congress should further reform the provision of the 1996 immigration law that allows low-level INS officials to prevent those arriving without valid documents from receiving a full hearing of their asylum claims. It is not difficult to understand why people fleeing torture or other forms of persecution often cannot obtain valid travel documents from their own governments. The "extraordinary circumstances" exception to the one-year time limit and the summary proceedings established to screen those entering without valid documents do not ensure a high enough standard of procedural protection for people with legitimate claims. It is a human rights imperative that both measures be changed.

Employment-Based Immigration

Immigrants are hired *in addition to*—not at the expense of—native-born Americans. There is not a fixed number of jobs in America, so by permitting employers to hire skilled foreign nationals we help companies grow and compete both here and abroad. The hostility of opponents of immigration to employment-based immigration indicates that some people do not want even highly skilled immigrants to come here. But these are the facts about employment-based immigration:

First, the numbers are tiny relative to the size of the U.S. workforce. The combined total of H-1B workers and employment-based immigrants (principals, not dependent family members) who received visas in 1995 came to approximately 99,000, or 0.079 percent of the American labor force.

Second, contrary to assertions that immigrant professionals are a source of "cheap labor," the median salaries of foreign-born engineers and scientists are *significantly higher* than those of their native-born counterparts who completed their Ph.D.s and master's degrees in the same year, according to National Science Foundation and National Academy of Sciences data.

Third, no correlation exists between unemployment rates and the presence of foreign-born people within a Ph.D. field. Fields in which many immigrant Ph.D.s are employed, such as math, engineering, and computer science, have unemployment rates of between 1 and 1.7 percent. Fields that attract relatively few immigrants, such as the geosciences and the social sciences, have unemployment rates between 2.3 and 2.8 percent.

Fourth, admission policies of American graduate schools favor U.S. minority applicants and U.S. citizens generally over foreign nationals, according to a joint study by the Association of American Universities and the Association of Graduate Schools.

Fifth, no evidence exists that the presence of foreign-born professionals prevents U.S. corporations from supporting efforts to improve education and train their workforces. American con ,anies spend $210 billion a year on training and donate $2.5 billion a year to colleges and schools.

Sixth, the Labor Department's Wage and Hour Division's Office of Enforcement can identify *just seven cases* in the past five years in which a U.S. corporation was even alleged to have used H-1B workers to replace laid-off Americans. And those seven cases are representative of the outsourcing trend—$28 billion annually in information technology alone—and would most likely have occurred regardless of U.S. immigration policy. Outsourcing has nothing to do with immigration.

Though overly bureaucratic, the system by which U.S. employers attract skilled foreign-born employees works fairly well. U.S. companies can hire skilled foreign nationals in a timely manner by using H-1B visas. Those visas are now generally approved within 60 days, though regulatory tie-ups may lengthen the time in the future. H-1B petitions are good for six years, but must be renewed after three years, and are granted to nonimmigrants after a company agrees to pay the new employee at least the "prevailing wage" paid in that industry and geographic area. Nonimmi-grants are not permanent residents and cannot progress toward citizenship.

Companies experience problems when they wish to sponsor existing employees or new hires for permanent residence. Since "labor certifica-tion" and other procedures take two or three years to complete, one key reason companies use H-1Bs is that few companies can afford to wait years to hire an individual.

Labor certification mandates such things as placing highly specific newspaper want ads to "test" the labor market. In effect, the Labor Department requires companies to engage in a new recruitment effort to replace a foreign national who was hired after a highly competitive recruit-ment process. At the very least, companies should be allowed to use current DOL rules—known as "reduction in recruitment"—and use the results of normal recruitment efforts to satisfy labor certification require-ments.

There are at least three reasons why an employer might wish to hire a foreign national: (1) the individual possesses unique knowledge; (2) the company is building a global workforce, in which case the individual would work in the United States for two to four years and then be employed by the company overseas, for example, in marketing in Venezuela; and (3) an employer needs to hire additional employees in certain positions to complement its U.S.-born workforce.

The Labor Department audit of employment-based immigration policy released in 1996 should not be the basis for reforming the system. That highly politicized report omits numerous facts that contradict its conclusions. For example, approximately half of U.S. companies' labor certification applications are denied (for a detailed analysis of the DOL report see *Interpreter Releases,* May 13, 1996). If there are companies that commit abuses that are not simply record compliance errors, DOL should target those companies, rather than restrict every corporation.

Immigration Today Is Low by Historical Standards

American Enterprise Institute scholar Ben Wattenberg uses this illustration to describe the current level of immigration: Imagine you are in a giant ballroom where 1,000 people are gathered for a Washington cocktail party. Champagne is being poured, waiters are carrying trays of hors d'oeuvres, and into the room walk three more people. Those three people represent the proportion of the U.S. population that immigrants add each year. They are not spoiling the party.

The United States maintained an unrestricted immigration policy during the 17th, 18th, and 19th centuries. Only the Chinese Exclusion Act of 1882 and some qualitative restrictions altered that policy. But in the 1920s Congress responded to rampant xenophobia and bizarre theories about racially "inferior" immigrants by establishing strict quotas. In 1965 Congress finally repealed such quotas and, in effect, increased the numerical limits. By 1990 Congress had raised the numbers and included more visas for employment-based immigrants.

Compared with other periods in American history, immigration is low today, not high. Figure 29.1 shows that immigrant arrivals as a share of the population—the most relevant measure of the impact of immigrants on our culture, infrastructure, and labor markets—are less than half the historical average. We can absorb, and have absorbed, far more immigrants than we do today.

315

Figure 29.1
Rate of Immigration by Decade, 1820–1990
(number of immigrants per 1,000 U.S. residents)

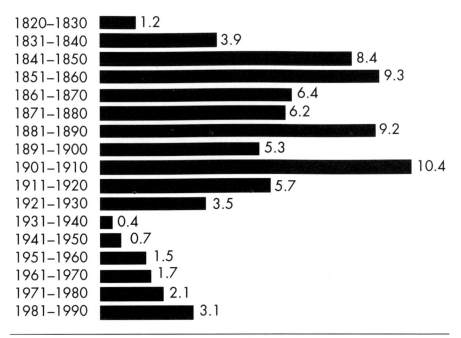

1820–1830	1.2
1831–1840	3.9
1841–1850	8.4
1851–1860	9.3
1861–1870	6.4
1871–1880	6.2
1881–1890	9.2
1891–1900	5.3
1901–1910	10.4
1911–1920	5.7
1921–1930	3.5
1931–1940	0.4
1941–1950	0.7
1951–1960	1.5
1961–1970	1.7
1971–1980	2.1
1981–1990	3.1

SOURCE: *Strangers at Our Gate: Immigration in the 1990s* (New York: Manhattan Institute, n.d.), p. 103.

Red Herrings in the Immigration Debate: Polls, Chain Migration, and "Increases"

Polls

For many decades people have told pollsters that they prefer fewer immigrants. That some polls still show that to be the case is a weak argument for reducing immigration, especially since people endorse the basic elements of current policy: Republican pollster Vince Breglio of RSM, Inc. found in a 1995 poll that Americans may favor cutting legal immigration generally, but by a two-to-one margin voters support allowing U.S. citizens to continue sponsoring their adult children and brothers and sisters. And a 1996 poll by Grassroots Research found that 61 percent of Americans agree with the statement: "Anyone from any country in the world should be free to come to America if they are financially able to provide for themselves and their family." That supports a policy of "immigrants yes, welfare no."

Chain Migration

The idea that an immigrant arrives and quickly starts sponsoring numerous relatives to begin an immigration "chain" is the reddest of herrings. Typically, if an immigrant decides to sponsor a family member he first becomes a citizen, which takes fives years or more. In fact, an average of *12 years* passes from the time an immigrant enters the United States and the time he or she sponsors a relative, according to the General Accounting Office. The term "chain migration" is meaningless since a *quarter of a century* would normally pass between the arrivals of the first and third immigrants in the supposed "chain." And most must enter through numerically restricted categories that are experiencing backlogs, which could mean many more years of waiting.

Numbers to Increase Temporarily

A statistical blip upwards in immigration totals that will appear for the next few years will probably be labeled a "surge" in immigration by its opponents. Do not be fooled. Immigration numbers predictably will increase—*and then decline*—as a continuing aftermath of the amnesty granted in the 1986 act.

Individuals to whom Congress granted amnesty in 1986—former undocumented aliens—are now becoming citizens and sponsoring their spouses and children. Those spouses and children are now physically in the country with their sponsors, either illegally or under the Family Unity provisions of the 1990 Immigration Act. *This increase in immigration is due primarily to the INS handing out green cards to spouses and children already physically here.* That accounting phenomenon is a blip that will disappear after a few years. By law, the addition of unused employment-based visas from 1995 also temporarily increased family immigration numbers in 1996.

Legal Immigration Reform: What Congress Should Do

In 1996 Congress followed the policy of immigrants yes, welfare no by overwhelmingly rejecting cuts in legal immigration (by 238 to 183 in the House of Representatives and by 80 to 20 in the Senate) and by passing a welfare bill that makes immigrants ineligible for public assistance. Immigrant welfare use, often overstated, is now off the table as part of the immigration policy debate. Near the end of the session, Congress passed a bill to address illegal immigration by increasing the number of border patrol personnel and making other reforms. Since illegal immigration is the main concern, and legal immigration is not a problem, it is not clear why Congress needs to make more than modest reforms to the current legal immigration system.

Congress should continue to keep the issues of legal and illegal immigration separate. For legal immigrants, Congress should at least maintain current family categories and quotas. Ideally, Congress should raise the current numbers by, among other things, setting aside separate visas for the one-third of spouses and children of lawful permanent residents in the immigration backlog who are physically separated from their sponsors. It should do so without tearing apart the current family immigration system, as the U.S. Commission on Immigration Reform recommended. In particular, Congress should resist attempts to stop brothers and sisters from immigrating simply because a backlog exists in that immigration category.

The INS should have fair naturalization procedures so that immigrants can enter fully into the civic life of the country. Although Congress has a legitimate oversight role in ensuring the quality of INS naturalization procedures, it should not erect new and onerous requirements that will impede naturalization under the guise of ''Americanization.''

Congress should raise the number of H-1B visas and deregulate employment-based immigration. In the future, to accommodate growth of the economy and companies' needs to expand, Congress should add at least 10 percent more H-1B visas annually over each prior year's usage. The Department of Labor must also streamline the labor certification process. The current regulatory scheme bears no relation to the competitive way companies recruit in the real world and should be eliminated or reformed to reflect market forces.

Illegal Immigration: What Congress Should Do

Illegal immigration is a problem that stems primarily from lack of economic opportunities in the countries below our southern border, not lack of INS authority.

The INS has the resources to control the border if it employs intelligent strategies to deter illegal immigrant crossings. In the 1996 immigration bill, Congress approved sanctions against the illegal immigrants themselves, including those who overstay visas for six consecutive months. Unfortunately, enforcement depends on an agency that few observers now consider competent to do its job.

Congress should repeal employer sanctions. Passed in 1986 and widely viewed as a failure, employer sanctions have made it a crime to ''knowingly" hire an illegal immigrant. The principle to follow is a simple one: It is the job of the federal government, not private business owners, to keep out of the country people who are not supposed to be here. The GAO has found that employer sanctions *have created a pattern of discrimination nationwide.*

Congress must oppose any further expansion of INS "pilot projects" to a full-fledged national computerized ID system. It should also prohibit any requirement that government-issued documents, such as birth certificates and Social Security cards, become de facto national ID cards, as was the intention of the 1996 immigration bill. Under the computer system scheme, an employer would check an individual's name and Social Security number against federal government databases. But there's no way for the employer (or the government) to know that the man standing before the employer is the real John Q. Smith. For such a system to have any chance of working, the government would have to require Mr. Smith to provide blood or a fingerprint, store that information in a government database, digitize it on a card (possibly a driver's license), and make it available to be matched every time Mr. Smith changed jobs or engaged in some other activity requiring federal government clearance. No one knows how those databases might be used in the future.

A national computerized ID system would be fraught with fraud and errors, and it would not deter illegal immigration. Ultimately, we must recognize that less than 1.5 percent of the U.S. population resides here illegally. Congress must reject efforts to "solve" the illegal immigration problem by discarding the principles of individual liberty upon which this nation was founded.

Conclusion

Few policies symbolize America's commitment to liberty as well as our willingness to accept immigrants. So long as immigrants are not burdening taxpayers—and the evidence is overwhelming that they are not—the rights of Americans are honored far more by permitting immigrants to work, reunite with their families, and find a safe haven from persecution than by closing the door.

Those who want to restrict legal immigration ask us to look to what they call America's last great "pause" in immigration. What they fail to disclose is that the last "pause" was one of the ugliest periods in American history. Spurred on by the Ku Klux Klan and bizarre eugenics theories about the racial inferiority of certain ethnic groups, in 1924 Congress enacted the "national origins" quotas that severely restricted the number of immigrants from certain nations, effectively barring those who were Asian born. As Sen. Spencer Abraham (R-Mich.), vice presidential candidate Jack Kemp, former education secretary William Bennett, and former senator Malcolm Wallop wrote in the *Wall Street Journal*, "These were sad chapters in America's past, not guideposts to its future."

Suggested Readings

Anderson, Stuart. *Employment-Based Immigration and High Technology*. Washington: Empower America, 1996.

Briggs, Vernon, and Stephen Moore. *Still An Open Door? U.S. Immigration Policy and the American Economy*. Washington: American University Press, 1994.

Handlin, Oscar. *The Uprooted: The Epic Story of the Great Migrations That Made the American People*. New York: Little Brown, 1973.

Simon, Julian L. *Immigration: The Demographic and Economic Facts*. Washington: Cato Institute and National Immigration Forum, 1995.

———. *The Economic Consequences of Immigration*. Cambridge, Mass: Basil Blackwell, 1990.

—Prepared by Stuart Anderson and Stephen Moore

REGULATION

30. Regulatory Reform: No Silver Bullet

Congress should

- focus its attention on substantive regulatory legislation,
- not renew the attempt to pass an omnibus regulatory reform,
- evaluate proposed regulations against a broad range of standards in addition to the benefit/cost standard,
- broaden the guarantee of just compensation to all property owners who are required by regulation to provide a public benefit, and
- reassert its authority to approve all pending regulations before they become law.

Federal regulations now impose direct compliance costs of about $500 billion a year. In recent years those costs have been a roughly stable share of gross domestic product, but that apparent stability masks two contrary trends. Federal economic regulation has been declining since the late 1970s. Over the same period, however, the cost of federal regulation of health, safety, and the environment has been increasing sharply. A reduction of the relative burden of federal regulation will require some combination of reducing the remaining economic regulations; major changes in the legislative authority for the regulation of health, safety, and the environment; and much more effective administration and congressional review of both existing and proposed new regulations.

The Clinton Record at Halftime

The regulatory record of the Clinton administration (so far) has been better than the Bush record, primarily because relatively little new regulatory authority has been approved on Clinton's watch. That is the good news. You already know the bad news: the Bush record was *awful*. The Bush administration endorsed more costly new regulatory legislation than any administration since Nixon. (Yes, dear reader, the modern regulatory state has largely been created during Republican administrations.) The Clinton record could have been much worse; Clinton's health plan of 1993 would have been the largest single expansion of regulatory authority since the New Deal, but that plan never reached a floor vote in a Congress controlled by the Democratic Party. And the Clinton record could have been much better if the administration had recognized that ''smart'' regulation, more often than not, means less regulation.

As it turns out, Congress has had a full regulatory·agenda during the Clinton years without much input from the administration. Most attention has been focused on the older forms of economic regulation. Congress initiated and approved the most important agricultural and telecommunications deregulation bills in 60 years. Other changes included ending the restrictions on interstate banking, deregulating intrastate trucking, and terminating the Interstate Commerce Commission. The only new laws that significantly increased regulation were the Family and Medical Leave Act and the minimum wage increase. The Safe Drinking Water Act and the comprehensive pesticide legislation were reauthorized without much change. The major regulatory controversy between the Clinton administration and the 104th Congress involved proposed changes in the regulatory review process. Clinton opposed a comprehensive regulatory reform bill but accepted most of its provisions as parts of other legislation.

The record of administrative regulation on Clinton's watch is more complex. Clinton issued a new executive order on regulation in September 1993 that is very similar to the two Reagan orders that it replaced, and in January 1996 the Office of Management and Budget issued more detailed guidelines on how to conduct economic and risk analyses consistent with the executive order. Those administrative measures would have provided an adequate basis for review of agency-proposed rules if reinforced consistently by the White House.

At the same time, however, several regulatory agencies aggressively pressed the limits of their statutory authority with the apparent approval of the White House. The Environmental Protection Agency sought authority to set pesticide standards without regard to the economic benefits of using pesticides and general authority to set cancer risk standards without a test of statistical significance. The Occupational Safety and Health Administration issued draft guidelines on how to reduce violent crime at retail establishments that are open at night, claiming that the ''general duty'' clause of its enabling legislation provides sufficient authority even without promulgation of a formal regulation. Most recently, the Food and Drug Administration announced major restrictions on tobacco marketing, the authority for which is now being challenged in court. The general lesson from those examples is that neither good executive guidance nor clear statutory language is sufficient to constrain an aggressive regulatory agency unless both the president and Congress reassert their joint authority to approve final rules. In the meantime, agencies are setting new records for excess regulation: a recent study estimates that the median cost per cancer averted by the Superfund program, for example, is $3.6 billion.

Next Steps

In the subsequent chapters, my colleagues summarize the many substantive changes in regulation that should be considered by Congress and the administration. My suggested next steps focus on the standards and process for reviewing and approving federal regulations. For years politicians and regulation analysts have been groping for some "bright line" standard, some procedure, some "silver bullet" to stop excessive regulation. For the most part, I suggest, that is wishful thinking; there is no substitute for the hard work necessary to revise the substantive regulatory legislation. Some changes in standards and procedures, however, can be helpful.

Standards

Scientists and economists, not surprisingly, have long promoted good science and good economics as the standards against which regulations should be evaluated. The scientists think that regulation should be considered only if there is a high level of statistical confidence in a scientifically plausible relation between cause and effect. The economists think that a regulation should be approved only if it generates the highest positive net benefits of any mutually exclusive alternative. Those standards have guided the White House regulatory review staffs beginning with President Ford and have been prescribed by executive order beginning with President Reagan.

As an economist, a former editor of the *Benefit/Cost Annual,* and the editor of *Regulation* magazine, I have also sung in that choir. Over time, however, I have come to believe that those standards are sometimes misleading and are seldom a sufficient screen against bad regulation. The crusade to regulate "by the numbers," I suggest, is similar to the crusade for scientific socialism—well-meant, naive, and ultimately futile.

Both the scientific and the economic standards are sometimes misleading. Careful scientific and statistical analysis is generally valuable, but it is not always appropriate to insist on a high level of statistical confidence. (The conventional standard is to reject any finding for which the probability of a zero relation is more than 5 percent.) If the cost of acting on false information is low relative to the benefits of acting on good information, it is rational to accept higher risks. In other words, the appropriate statistical standard is situation specific depending on the benefits and costs of the decision considered.

But the maximum net benefit standard itself is not a sufficient guide. Most important, the net benefit standard does not provide a rationale for a coercive transfer from some people to other people. That standard is appropriate, thus, only if its application *over a set of rules* generates expected net benefits for (virtually) everyone. Second, the net benefit standard does not provide a rationale for regulating the behavior of adults who bear the full marginal cost of their choices. More often than not, changes in personal behavior would increase safety at a far lower cost than would changes in environmental conditions, but this observation does not provide a basis for shifting the focus of regulation from environmental conditions to personal behavior. The net benefit standard may be the best basis for evaluating the regulation of risks to which people are involuntarily exposed. But the personal behavior of adults who bear the costs of their own choices should not be regulated at all, whatever the estimated net benefits.

And, for several reasons, those standards are seldom a sufficient screen against bad regulation. The authorizing legislation for much regulation preempts the standards by setting some other performance standard such as ''reasonable certainty of no harm'' or by directly setting technical standards that preclude the opportunity to choose the most efficient means to meet a performance standard. In several cases, the Supreme Court has overruled the net benefit standard when that standard was not specifically required by Congress. In those cases, Congress must bear the responsibility for the hard work to amend the authorizing legislation.

Moreover, the regulatory agencies have learned to play the numbers game. A pattern of potentially exaggerated estimates of physical effects, benefits, and costs is difficult to check because the regulatory agencies generate most of the relevant data. The draft EPA report on the costs and benefits of the Clean Air Act is only the most egregious recent example. There are still major disputes about the basic science on which much risk regulation is based; for example, there appears to be no nonarbitrary way to extrapolate from the carcinogenic effects of very high dose rates on test animals to the effects of very low dose rates on humans, but many billions of dollars have already been spent to reduce those potential effects.

For those reasons, even with the authority of an executive order that endorses the net benefit standard, the regulatory review agencies have had little success in rejecting proposed rules that do not meet the standard. The scientific and economic standards should be *supplemented* by different standards; one or two standards that have proved easy to evade are not enough. A proposed federal regulation, I suggest, should meet *each* of the following standards:

- Does the activity by some individual or firm impose significant (nonpecuniary) adverse effects on other parties?

  If not, no regulation of any type is appropriate. This standard alone would rule out all regulation of activities for which people bear the full cost of their own choices, all regulation of activities that have only pecuniary effects on other parties, and all regulations that require people to provide benefits to other people.

- Would regulation of activities with these adverse effects be more efficient than reliance on contract and tort law?

  If not, the proposed regulation should be rejected in favor of the common law. This is an important question to ask, because of the frequently too casual assumption that regulation is the only instrument for reducing adverse interpersonal effects. At the same time, one should recognize that the transactions costs of the tort law are now very high, especially when there are numerous tort feasors and tort victims.

- Does the conduct of this activity impose significant adverse effects on people in other states?

  If not, state governments have sufficient incentive and authority to control those effects, by either regulation or the common law, and no federal regulation is appropriate. The fact that activities with adverse effects may be nationwide is not a sufficient basis for federal regulation; potential multistate effects, not the multistate source of those effects, should be the focus of this standard. Not all nationwide problems require a federal response.

- Does federal statutory law provide authority for the proposed regulation?

  If not, the proposed regulation should not be approved even if potentially desirable. The Constitution vests all legislative powers in Congress, and regulatory agencies should not be allowed to define their own powers. If an agency contends that some new regulatory power is desirable, they should make their case to Congress.

- Does the Constitution provide authority for the proposed regulation?

  If not, of course, the proposed regulation should be rejected; the federal government does not have the authority to define its own powers. This is an awkward issue, however, because the federal government has effectively defined its own economic powers for over 60 years. The problem is that there is no effective procedure for challenging the authority of the federal government, given the Supreme Court's generally elastic interpretation of the Constitution.

- Does the proposed regulation generate the highest positive expected net benefit of any mutually exclusive alternative?

  If not, the proposed regulation should be rejected. It is most important to recognize that this net benefit standard is relevant only if the proposed regulation clears each of the prior five hurdles.

In summary, this approach does not replace the net benefit standard, but it focuses that standard and the necessary quantitative analysis on only those proposed regulations that meet five independent either/or tests. One side effect of this approach is that it shifts much of the burden for constraining federal regulation from scientists and economists to lawyers. So be it; there are more of them than there are of us.

Procedures

The regulatory reform movement has been dominated by the quest for some "silver bullet," some set of standards and procedures that would stop bad regulation. For several reasons, that goal has been elusive. The net benefit standard is not a sufficient basis for a redistribution of income, for the taking of private property to provide a public benefit, or for restricting the activities of individuals and firms that bear the full cost of their choices. Judicial review provides no protection against bad analysis; the courts will not accept the role of evaluating scientific and economic studies. Congress will not accept the regimen of an automatic sunset rule.

There is only one effective solution to this problem: Congress must take much more responsibility for the rules that are made with its authority. The necessary first step is careful drafting of the substantive legislation; much, maybe most, bad regulation is a faithful interpretation of bad legislation. If Congress is the problem, only a political or constitutional challenge can stop bad regulation.

One general rule would make both Congress and the agencies more responsible: The Fifth Amendment guarantee of just compensation should be broadened to include all property owners who are required by regulation to provide a public benefit. No compensation would be required, of course, for the costs of meeting regulations to reduce a public harm originating on the property. The distinction between providing a public benefit and reducing a public harm is one that courts made for many years and should be restored. A requirement to compensate property owners who provide habitat for endangered species, for example, would enormously improve the incentives of both property owners and the government.

In many cases, however, final rules go well beyond the intent of Congress. And Congress now has no effective procedure for vetoing those rules. After a brief preamble, the first words of the Constitution are "All legislative Powers herein granted shall be vested in . . . Congress." For 60 years or so, however, Congress has delegated the authority to approve final rules to regulatory agencies, subject only to the constraints of the substantive legislation and the Administrative Procedures Act. Moreover, since the 1983 *Chadha* decision, Congress may veto an agency rule only by a new law; agency-made rules, thus, become law even if endorsed only by the president and one-third of either house. The Constitution has been turned upside down.

One way or another, Congress must restore its authority to approve all final rules. A little-noticed amendment to the 1996 debt limit bill permits Congress to delay a final rule for 60 legislative days, but overriding the rule still requires a new law. The 105th Congress should first test this new authority by a very careful selection of pending rules to delay, with the objective of using the delay to organize a sufficient coalition to override them. Congress should also consider a resolution opposing the *Chadha* decision and some instrument to challenge that decision; the reasoning of the Court in that decision was about as dumb as that of any decision in the past 20 years, and there is reason to hope that the Court would change its position.

Congress may soon be ready for a more radical reassertion of its constitutional authority to approve all pending rules before they become law. Several bills with that objective were introduced in the 104th Congress and should be reconsidered. Congress could continue to delegate the *drafting* of rules to the regulatory agencies, but an affirmative vote would be required to approve a final rule. The regulatory agencies, thus, would be transformed from rule-making and rule-enforcing agencies into rule-drafting and rule-enforcing agencies. And the constitutional separation of powers would be restored.

On the basis of the reasonable expectation that Congress would not be willing to address as many new rules as are now approved every year, a case has been made that this procedure would overload Congress. But the number of new rules is neither optimal nor exogenous. New regulations, like any other types of new laws, should be limited to those that Congress is willing to address. More congressional responsibility will both improve the quality of regulation and reduce the number of new regulations.

Suggested Readings

McKinley, Vern. "Sunrises without Sunsets: Can Sunset Laws Reduce Regulation?" *Regulation,* no. 4 (1995).
Niskanen, William. "Clinton's Regulatory Record." *Regulation,* no. 3 (1996).
———. "Is Regulatory Reform Dead? Should Anyone Care?" *Regulation,* no. 3 (1995).
———. "Regulating by the Numbers." *Regulation,* no. 2 (1996).
Shapiro, Martin. "A Golden Anniversary? The Administrative Procedures Act of 1946." *Regulation,* no. 3 (1996).

—Prepared by William A. Niskanen

31. Financial Services

Congress should

- repeal the Bank Holding Company Act and merge the commercial bank and thrift charters,
- repeal the Glass-Steagall Act,
- privatize banking regulation and its attendant deposit insurance and systemic risks, and
- repeal the Community Reinvestment Act.

The Need for Banking Reform

In the 1980s Congress phased out depression-era controls on deposit interest rates, thus giving bank customers higher returns on their savings. And in 1997 the lifting of the remaining restrictions on interstate branching will give customers access to their accounts across state lines. But those boons are only a hint of the benefits to be reaped by peeling away remaining government banking regulations. Consumers could benefit from a system that more efficiently met their needs for borrowing to purchase houses, cars, and consumer goods; saving for their children's college educations or for their own retirement; and insuring themselves against accidents or illness. Businesses, too, will benefit from modernizing the financial system.

The computer and telecommunications revolution is changing the financial services industry by erasing the traditional lines of demarcation between various types of financial services providers. It has become increasingly difficult to differentiate banking, insurance, and securities products and services. The capacity to quickly acquire, process, and integrate economic and financial information will provide enormous benefits to consumers. For example, car loans and insurance could be packaged at a great savings in time and money for car buyers, just as buyers have long been able to purchase vehicles equipped with tires, batteries, and other accessories.

But outdated and costly regulations have spurred "regulatory arbitrage," the lawful yet often costly avoidance of obsolete regulations by innovators in the financial services industry. Regulatory reform clearly is needed.

Unfortunately, such reform went nowhere in the last Congress. The House Banking and Financial Services Committee attempted to launch the reform of the 1933 Glass-Steagall Act that separates commercial from investment banking. That bill would have allowed bank holding companies to further penetrate the securities business. That pleased some large banks, but others have little immediate interest in getting into the securities business and thus did not exert much political pressure in favor of this reform. Further, small banks wanted the freedom to offer insurance, but insurance agents strongly opposed that reform. The 105th Congress almost certainly will have to address those issues.

Repeal the Bank Holding Company Act and Merge the Commercial Bank and Thrift Charters

Commercial banks and thrift institutions (that is, savings-and-loan associations and savings banks) operate under separate charters. Both have been restricted in the kinds of services they can offer customers. Combining their charters would permit a depository institution to offer its customers a broad range of fully integrated banking products and services. Since 1989 Congress has eliminated most of the regulatory distinctions between banks and thrifts; marketplace distinctions between those two types of institutions also have diminished greatly.

But one big problem still remains. Today, commercial banks can be owned either by individual stockholders or by corporations. But corporations owning commercial banks must register with the Federal Reserve Board as "bank holding companies," or BHCs, under the Bank Holding Company Act. While stockholders can, as individuals, engage in any other business activities that they wish, BHCs can engage only in activities that are "closely related to banking," a term that the Fed traditionally has defined quite narrowly. Thus, neither General Motors nor Microsoft nor a major insurance company can own a commercial bank since their principal activities are not closely related to banking. (There are a few limited-use exceptions to this rule.) Only in recent years has the Fed permitted BHCs to begin to enter the securities business, but BHCs are still barred from offering most types of insurance as well as participating fully in other types of financial services activities. Most thrift institutions, on the other hand, operate under an entirely different holding company law that essentially permits anyone, including, for example, insurance companies, auto manufacturers, and day-care providers, to own a thrift.

Congress will be under political pressure to merge the bank and thrift charters, in part because it directed the Treasury Department to recommend how they could be combined. If those charters are not merged properly, the merger will force corporate owners of thrifts to qualify as BHCs or divest their thrifts. The merger presents Congress with a major challenge: does it charter up or charter down? Chartering up means creating a new depository institution charter that combines the best features of the bank and thrift charters, and then some; chartering down means imposing unnecessary restrictions on depository institutions. Thus, instead of allowing more financial institutions to offer more services to customers, regulatory changes could stifle competition and limit consumer choice.

Congress can avoid those problems, first, by repealing the Bank Holding Company Act, thus permitting anyone to own a bank regardless of the other businesses in which he or she may be engaged, and, second, by creating a new depository institution charter that combines the best features of the commercial bank and thrift charters. Interestingly, the elimination of federal restrictions on interstate banking, which becomes fully effective on June 1, 1997 (except in Texas), eliminated one of the initial rationales for the Bank Holding Company Act.

Repeal the Glass-Steagall Act

The debate over the future of bank and thrift charters as well as the holding company acts probably will be subsumed under a broader debate over financial services policy. The Glass-Steagall Act, passed as part of the Banking Act of 1933, separated commercial and investment banking. Ideally, Congress should repeal Glass-Steagall. But bank regulators are taking steps in that direction whether Congress acts or not. The Office of the Comptroller of the Currency regulates commercial banks registered at the federal level, called "national banks." It has just issued new rules to clarify long-pending questions concerning the powers of those banks, under the so-called operating subsidiary, or "op-sub," regulation. The "powers" debate addresses the activities in which a federally insured bank or thrift is permitted to engage. The "affiliations rights" debate addresses the question of who can own a depository institution and what else that owner can do. Currently, different affiliates of a bank holding company can offer commercial or investment banking services, but not both. However, a subsidiary of a commercial bank can offer only services "incidental to banking."

The comptroller's new op-sub regulation will permit national banks, or their subsidiaries, to seek permission from the comptroller to offer a broad range of financial services, notably insurance and securities, that in some cases are not even permissible to BHCs. In effect, a broad interpretation of existing banking law would permit the emergence in the United States of the "universal bank" like those now found in many other industrialized countries, including Germany and Great Britain. The Supreme Court, in four unanimous decisions within the last two years, has affirmed the comptroller's power to broadly interpret existing law when his office rules on applications by banks seeking to engage in new activities, provided the comptroller can make a "reasonable" case for his interpretation. Hence, the comptroller, if he so desires, could substantially repeal the Glass-Steagall Act by regulation.

The comptroller should enable commercial banks to shed the limitations that the Fed places on BHCs, because the universal bank form of organizational structure is more efficient for most banking organizations than the BHC form. Since almost all American commercial banks with more than $1 billion of assets are owned by BHCs, the comptroller could revolutionize the structure of the American banking industry within a few years.

But that new freedom will be a one-way street. While commercial banks will be free to offer many services, nonbank firms such as securities and insurance companies and mutual fund managers will be barred from directly entering the banking business.

Nonbanks will not want to own banks through a holding company structure because it would burden them with the inefficiencies associated with such a structure. Hence, the comptroller's broadening of the powers of national banks may force the 105th Congress to authorize the "universal financial services firm," which would permit securities, insurance, and mutual fund companies to directly own banks.

The Need for Further Reform

Permitting closer affiliations between banking and other types of financial services will force Congress to address several federal financial safety net issues. The federal financial safety net consists of federal deposit insurance; the Fed's role as lender of last resort to the entire financial system; and the central role that the Fed plays in the U.S. payments system, that is, clearing checks and electronic payments between banks. In addition, the states have created "guarantee funds" to protect insureds against insurance company insolvencies.

Depositors are protected by federal deposit insurance, up to $100,000, if their bank or thrift fails. In return, banks and thrifts are subject to heavy-handed government safety-and-soundness regulation, and they pay supposedly risk-sensitive deposit insurance premiums that in fact are not very risk sensitive.

Despite the savings-and-loan debacle, Congress did not reform deposit insurance when, in 1989, it committed taxpayer funds to clean up that mess. As an alternative to deposit insurance reform, in 1991 Congress toughened bank and thrift regulation. Those "reforms" represented an expansion of the federal government's police power over banks and thrifts; no attempt was made to introduce market-driven regulation or to privatize deposit insurance. Ironically, Congress also expanded the Fed's lender-of-last-resort function by making it easier for the Fed to lend to nonbank financial firms.

Permitting greater integration of financial services will overwhelm banking regulators. Their one-size-must-fit-all approach to regulation and compartmentalized structures are inappropriate for financial services firms pursuing widely varied business strategies that integrate the banking function with other types of financial services. Congress will be forced to consider more far-reaching concepts for ensuring the safe-and-sound operation of more varied financial institutions while maintaining stability in the financial system and providing loss protection for at least small depositors.

Privatizing Regulation

The financial markets already possess the means for self-regulation. One means is market-determined covenants and other contractual restrictions in bonds that corporations sell to investors, in loan agreements, and in insurance. Another means is risk-sensitive interest on loans as well as risk-sensitive premiums for insurance.

Congress could easily expand the use of contractual regulation. For example, it could require all financial services firms that accept deposits, provide insurance, or directly access the payments system to negotiate a "safety-and-soundness" contract with a private-sector entity that would monitor the financial services provider's compliance with the terms of its regulatory contract and protect depositors and insureds against any loss should the financial services firm become insolvent. Such a contract would specify the prudent practices to which the firm would agree to adhere in order to operate in a safe-and-sound manner. The monitoring firm's fee undoubtedly would be risk sensitive, reflecting the financial institution's probability of failure. The private sector could easily assume this most important function, which government bureaucrats have performed badly.

Shifting banks and other financial services providers to contractual regulation would benefit the American economy in two ways. First, individual firms would be able to negotiate prudent operating practices and safeguards tailored to their business strategies. Today, the business strategy of banks, thrifts, insurers, and other highly regulated firms is largely shaped by regulation. Tailor-made private regulations would make financial services providers more competitive and better equipped to serve their customers. For example, privately regulated financial firms would have sufficient operating flexibility to serve specialized markets, such as low-income and minority communities.

Contractual regulation also would benefit the economy by sharply lessening the herd tendencies of highly regulated banks, thrifts, and insurers that have created periodic financial disasters. Regulation, like taxation, greatly distorts business behavior because strategic planning in highly regulated firms is shaped to a great extent by what is permitted by government regulation. Contractual regulation, however, would give individual financial services firms much greater latitude to differentiate themselves from their competitors because they would be operating under regulatory strictures that they helped to design. Differentiation, which characterizes the strategies unregulated industries pursue, would produce fewer failures and lower insolvency losses because at any one time only a few firms, not an entire industry, would be pursuing business strategies that might eventually produce losses and even bankruptcy.

Privatizing Deposit Insurance

Requiring private-sector regulator-guarantors to protect depositors, insureds, and others would lead to the privatization of deposit insurance. Three aspects of this issue are worth considering.

First, a banking firm cannot switch to contractual regulation if it wants to operate without any deposit insurance. As a practical political matter, Congress will not allow any financial institution that takes deposits or provides insurance to operate without some kind of loss protection for depositors and insureds. Absent the alternative of no regulation, market-driven contractual regulation is, for all concerned, preferable to uninsured firms still subject to heavy-handed and increasingly counterproductive government regulation.

Second, the providers of contractual regulation could not attempt to shift some of the cost of their errors to large depositors and other creditors of the institutions they regulated. That is because any attempt at such cost shifting could trigger massive bank runs that would destabilize the financial system. Consequently, private-sector regulators should guarantee all deposits, and not just the first $100,000 per customer, which today is the limit for federal deposit insurance, unless a bank is too big to fail (TBTF). TBTF is a reality in the industrialized world because the sudden liquidation of a large bank, insurer, or securities firm could destabilize the financial system. In TBTF situations, other financial firms and even the general taxpayer are taxed to protect creditors who are not protected in smaller failures. Consequently, as a practical matter, deposit insurance limits apply today only to depositors in smaller banks, which is highly unfair. A private regulatory mechanism would allow protection of all deposits and insurance obligations in all financial firms and thus would eliminate that unfairness and ensure financial stability.

Third, any regulatory process—government or private—should protect taxpayers against losses arising from regulatory failures. That clearly did not happen in the S&L crisis, nor does it happen under government deposit insurance and insurance guaranty schemes when healthy institutions are taxed to pay for losses arising from regulatory failures. Consequently, Congress's modernization of the structure of the financial services industry must be accompanied by deposit insurance and regulatory reforms that provide failure-proof taxpayer protection.

One way that privatized regulation could ensure financial stability without taxpayer risk is through "cross-guarantees." Banks and thrifts could enter into regulatory contracts with ad hoc syndicates of private-sector guarantors, largely other banks and thrifts. Guaranteed institutions would pay a risk-sensitive premium to their guarantors for protecting depositors and others against loss should the guaranteed institution fail. The guarantors would then use an independent firm to monitor the guaranteed institution's compliance with the terms of its cross-guarantee contract. Risk-spreading rules applicable to each contract would protect taxpayers against deposit insurance losses even in conditions worse than the Great Depression.

As an added plus, cross-guarantees would liberate Congress from having to decide who could do what within the financial services arena. Instead, the activities and affiliations of individual guaranteed firms could be addressed

335

entirely through their cross-guarantee contracts. The commercial marketplace, not the political marketplace, would then shape the structure of the financial services industry.

No doubt there are other ways the private sector could guarantee deposits and privatize regulation. It is time for Congress to begin exploring such approaches.

Repeal the Community Reinvestment Act

Congress has loaded substantial welfare obligations on banking, notably through the Community Reinvestment Act. While the CRA reads fairly innocuously, regulations adopted under it increasingly compel banks and thrifts (but not untaxed credit unions) to subsidize their lending and other banking activities in low- and medium-income and minority communities.

Supporters of the CRA claim that it is fair because banks and thrifts receive federal deposit insurance, which the supporters claim is a subsidy that flows from taxpayers to banks and thrifts. In fact, federal deposit insurance has subsidized ineffective government regulation, and much of that subsidy has been paid by healthy institutions in the form of punitive regulation and higher deposit insurance premiums than they would pay in the commercial marketplace.

The CRA is not intended to deter discrimination against individuals. Instead, it is a credit allocation device designed to funnel loans into neighborhoods and communities thought to be underserved by banks and thrifts. However, any such market failure reflects the distortions caused by government regulation. Shifting banks and thrifts to private, contractual regulation would permit those institutions to adopt more differentiated business strategies than is possible today; consequently, some depository institutions would find it quite profitable to serve low-income and minority communities, thus obviating the need for the CRA. Furthermore, as technology fosters increased opportunities for regulatory arbitrage, it will become increasingly difficult for Congress to safely impose social welfare obligations on those institutions that it can still snare in its regulatory web.

Conclusion

Rapid technological change demands fundamental regulatory reform in the financial services industry, to reflect both the eroding distinctions among various types of financial products and financial services providers and the irreversible decline in the efficacy of traditional government safety-

and-soundness regulation. Financial stability and protection of the prover-
bial "widows and orphans" among depositors and insureds will continue
to be valid political concerns; however, government regulatory micromanagement of banks, thrifts, insurers, brokerage firms, and mutual funds
no longer can provide that stability and protection. Attempts to restore
the efficacy of government regulation will merely impair the efficiency
of financial services firms; Humpty-Dumpty cannot be put back
together. As part of broader privatization initiatives, the 105th Congress
should shift individual financial firms to private, contractual regulation,
thereby permitting the marketplace to determine what constitutes prudent banking as well as the specific activities in which individual firms
are engaged.

Stripping away government regulation of banking would help both
consumers and businesses. Consumers would be able to obtain a mix
of financial services tailored to their individual needs for less cost and
with greater security than is currently the case. Businesses could more
easily acquire loans, insurance, and capital, all necessary for operating
in a more competitive and integrated world economy.

But those benefits will only be realized if government steps aside
and allows banks and customers to manage their own affairs. Financial
institutions in other countries often are freer than those in America,
putting many foreign firms at a competitive advantage over American
ones. It is time to establish a level playing field by removing counterproductive regulation of American banks.

Suggested Readings

Ely, Bert. "Cross-Guarantees: Market-Driven Regulation for Banking." *TMA Journal,*
September–October 1994, pp. 38–40.

———. "Financial Innovation and Risk Management: The Cross-Guarantee Solution."
Jerome Levy Economics Institute of Bard College. Working Paper no. 141, May 1995.

———. "The Future Structure and Regulation of Financial Services." Presentation to
the National Policy Forum, May 14, 1996.

McKinley, Vern. "Community Reinvestment Act: Ensuring Credit Adequacy or Enforcing Credit Extortion?" *Regulation,* no. 4 (1994).

Petri, Tom, and Bert Ely. "Better Banking for America: The 100 Percent Cross-Guarantee
Solution." *Common Sense* (Fall 1995): 96–112.

———. "Cross-Guarantees: A Horse of a Different Color." *Bank Director,* Second
Quarter 1994, pp. 32–36.

—Prepared by Bert Ely

32. Food and Drug Administration

Congress should

- allow drug companies an "opt-out" option from FDA efficacy testing or repeal the FDA's authority to review efficacy,
- eliminate user fees,
- phase out FDA review of drug safety to increase patient access to potential medical breakthroughs,
- curb FDA authority to regulate marketing practices, and
- eliminate FDA regulations that undermine competitiveness and investment.

Federal Pharmaceutical Policy

Research in and development of innovative medical technology is literally a matter of life and death. But at a time when the United States is on the verge of revolutionary improvements in health, medical progress is under attack by excessive regulation by the FDA.

The 104th Congress considered some minor though welcome changes in the tangled and time-consuming regulations that govern the development, testing, and marketing of pharmaceuticals and medical devices. Unfortunately, no significant reforms were passed.

Currently, the federally mandated process for introducing a new drug to the retail market consists of three phases. Under Phase I, the FDA must be satisfied that the new drug is safe and will not harm patients. Under Phase II, the FDA must be satisfied that there is a correlation between the use of a product and the effect that the product is suppose to produce. Under Phase III, a company is required to run tests to demonstrate just how effective the product is.

339

That system has been built up over decades. Under the Food, Drug and Cosmetic Act of 1938, companies had to submit a new drug application (NDA) before selling a new medicine. The NDA was to contain evidence that the drug was safe to use. The FDA had 60 days in which to reject an application, otherwise it was automatically approved.

Today the FDA uses administrative means to prolong the time required to permit clinical use of medicines. According to Peter Barton Hutt, FDA's chief counsel during the 1970s, the FDA throws up several obstacles to access to drugs in the name of safety. The FDA

- requires unnecessary animal studies before permitting clinical investigation;
- requires a lengthy and complex investigation of new drugs before those drugs are allowed on the market;
- places "clinical holds" on human investigations to prevent immediate determinations of clinical value; and
- prohibits companies from charging for drugs used in clinical investigations, thus increasing the cost of development.

By a conservative estimate, FDA delays in allowing U.S. marketing of drugs used safely and effectively elsewhere around the world have cost the lives of at least 200,000 Americans over the past 30 years. That figure does not include deaths that might have been prevented by the use of drugs such as Prozac, which is associated with the decline in suicides of individuals suffering from depression. FDA regulations denying Americans timely access to new drugs have extracted a high cost in health and lives.

Five Cases of Tragic Delays

- Dr. Louis Lasagna, director of Tufts University's Center for the Study of Drug Development, estimates that the seven-year delay in the approval of beta blocker heart medicines cost the lives of 119,000 Americans.
- During the three and half years it took the FDA to approve the new drug Interleukin-2, 25,000 Americans died of kidney cancer even though the drug had already been approved for use in nine other countries. According to Eugene Schoenfeld, a cancer survivor and president of the National Kidney Cancer Association, "IL-2 is one of the worst examples of FDA regulation known to man."

- In 1985 the National Heart, Lung and Blood Institute of the National Institutes of Health stopped a study comparing a genetically engineered clot-busting drug called TPa because the study showed that TPa was so effective in reducing heart attack–related deaths that it would be unethical to withhold it from volunteer patients. Yet it took the FDA four years to approve the drug, despite the NIH decision. That delay cost 30,000 lives.
- Even though the generic Alzheimer's drug Tacrine was being safely used by humans here and around the world, it took the FDA seven years to approve the drug. The FDA claimed that because the drug caused temporary liver toxicity it was unsafe.
- The generic anti-cancer drug Flutamide was available in Europe for years and was proven safe, but the FDA failed to approve it. According to Dr. Bruce Chabner, director of the National Cancer Institute's Division of Cancer Treatment, "We're talking about delays of years." Subsequently the National Cancer Institute accused the FDA of being "mired in a 1960s philosophy of drug development, viewing all new agents as . . . poisons."

As a result of the lobbying efforts of AIDS activists, the FDA has moved quickly to approve NDAs for AIDS drugs since the early 1990s. Three protease inhibitors, a class of drugs that block the replication of the HIV virus nearly to the point of stopping progression altogether, were approved in less than three months. Although AIDS drugs are being approved more quickly than in the past, approval times for breakthrough drugs that could give hope to patients with other life-threatening diseases, such as cancer and brain diseases, remain astonishingly slow. The FDA takes an average of 14 months to review the NDAs for cancer drugs and 32 months for drugs designed to treat brain diseases such as ALS, Alzheimer's, and depression.

In 1962 Congress gave the FDA the power to require companies to demonstrate that their drugs were effective as claimed. At the time, drugs were a relatively new form of therapy; surgery and palliatives were still first-line therapy for most illnesses. Today, drugs are the first therapy physicians use before having to resort to surgery or giving up hope. In turn, insurers, physicians, and patients expect increasingly improved results from new drugs. Manufacturers must be able to demonstrate that their new products are more clinically effective than existing products or be faced with a limited market. The market is essentially doing the job the FDA was chartered to do more than 30 years ago.

In 1969 the Department of Health, Education and Welfare (now the Department of Health and Human Services) recommended evaluation procedures such as self-certification by companies and delegation of the approval authority to advisory groups made up of patients, specialists, and researchers. Such organizations would act like Underwriters Laboratories, a private, nonprofit organization that sets safety standards for various products, mostly electrical. Private alternatives to the FDA would ensure the safety of drugs and provide companies and consumers with a forum for establishing a drug's effectiveness using criteria selected by consumers rather than FDA bureaucrats.

The benefits of FDA efficacy regulation are paltry at best; the costs, however, are substantial. Efficacy regulation makes drugs more expensive and less accessible. According to the Center for the Study of Drug Development at Tufts University, the time required to get a new drug through the FDA approval process has been increasing since 1962. Today it takes an average of 15 years to get a drug reviewed by the FDA.

As a result, the cost of drug development has skyrocketed, increasing by over 400 percent in less than two decades. The Office of Technology Assessment has determined that the cost of developing a new drug is, on average, $394 million. Drug manufacturers now conduct an average of 60 clinical trials of each new drug for which they seek marketing approval and dozens more to extend approval of existing drugs that are effective in treating diseases other than those for which they were originally approved. Since 85 percent of the cost of pharmaceutical development goes to complying with FDA regulations, those regulations amount to a tax on investment in basic biomedical research.

The effect of FDA regulation on the price of drugs is profound. Assuming a 14 percent return on drug development, excessive FDA regulation increases the required break-even return on a drug by about 200 percent. Not only do such regulatory costs raise the price of new drugs, they also reduce basic research at a time when the opportunities for medical progress are increasing.

In the name of consumer protection, the FDA is retarding biomedical research and development. Just as control of information in despotic counties destroys creativity and innovation, the FDA's monopoly on the research, development, and use of new medical knowledge is choking off the next medical revolution. In the process it is raising the cost of essential drugs and denying sick people access to lifesaving medicines.

The Solution

A five-step process could free pharmaceutical manufacturers and biotech firms from the federal approval process.

Allow Drug Companies to Opt Out of FDA Efficacy Testing

A simple way to accelerate the approval process would be to allow manufacturers to not subject their products to the Phase III field test of efficacy. Companies could be required to label their products "Determined to be safe by the FDA, but the FDA has not reviewed the efficacy data and cannot make any claims to the efficacy of the drug as set forth in this product's label."

That approach would allow consumers the option of using safety-tested products far earlier than otherwise would be the case. Producers, of course, would seek to demonstrate the efficacy of their products to consumers. By giving producers a choice of ways to do that, the opt-out option would foster the development of independent certification labs, which would perform the functions that Underwriters Laboratories performs for electronic and other consumer products.

After this step, or perhaps even in place of it, Congress should repeal the FDA's authority to review drug efficacy. That would result in a number of benefits. It would reduce the amount of time and money research-based companies must spend on drug development. And it would mean that companies could invest more money in basic research, the source of future medical breakthroughs. Without the FDA, companies would still be forced to demonstrate their products' effectiveness to patients and physicians.

Reductions in development costs and time would accelerate new discoveries and their commercialization. As a result, more products would enter the market, forcing lower costs and greater price competition. Lower development costs and prices would encourage investors and researchers to put more money into basic research and development of new drugs.

The FDA has already proven the value of repealing efficacy authority. Manufacturers of generic drugs—copies of drugs whose patents have expired—need only show that the performance of a generic drug is similar to that of the pioneer drug. Generic drugs have been widely accepted by physicians and patients.

Further, under pressure from AIDS activists, the FDA has suspended the efficacy standard for some AIDS drugs. Instead, companies must show simply that drugs are safe and have a reasonable chance of being effective in terms set by patients themselves. As a result, the number of AIDS drugs in development has increased despite the fact that advances are hard to come by. In addition, the price of AIDS medicines, though high, has declined as a result of increased competition.

Eliminate User Fees

Much FDA regulation, particularly Phase III regulation and delays on new drug applications, is unnecessary. Supporters of the FDA claim that a lack of staff is forcing the agency to sit on approvals. In fact, the FDA has added nearly 1,000 staffers with $300 million raised by requiring companies to pay for the privilege of undergoing FDA scrutiny. Called "user fees," such charges are nothing more than a tax on innovation. Not only has the FDA failed to reduce approval times, it has actually expanded its regulatory sweep by proposing even more rules and regulations.

The FDA claims that user fees are allowing it to reduce the time it takes to approve new drugs. In fact, the FDA has manufactured an artificial reduction. It has transferred many aspects of review from one part of the approval process to another and counts as "approval time" only the reduced part of the process. Moving the goal posts makes the agency appear more efficient, but it does not reduce the 10 to 15 years a company must invest to move a drug onto the market.

User fees are an extraordinary burden on the hundreds of small biotechnology firms that are the source of many medical breakthroughs. Eliminating user fees would amount to eliminating an unfair tax on the most innovative and entrepreneurial high-tech firms. Supporters of the FDA might complain that the loss of user fee revenue would force the agency to slow down drug approvals. In fact, there is an alternative to feeding the FDA's regulatory addiction: allow less costly private certification of a product's efficacy.

Furthermore, the FDA has not yet been able to accomplish its main objective in creating user fees—to cut drug approval times in half in five years. The FDA testified before Congress in 1992 that the additional revenue from the user fees would enable the agency, by September 1997, to acquire the resources needed to approve breakthrough drugs in 6 months and all other drugs in 12 months. However, next year will mark the five-year anniversary, and reauthorization, of the User Fee Act. Perhaps that would be an opportune time to reexamine the, as yet, unmet goals of the legislation and begin, in earnest, the campaign to reform the FDA.

Phase Out FDA Review of Drug Safety

Even if the FDA's efficacy review authority were eliminated, the agency's control over pharmaceutical safety would still deny patients access to many important drugs, which costs billions in health care dollars, causes unnecessary suffering, and results in an untold number of lost lives. Over the past 30 years the FDA has gained nearly complete control over drug testing. But the FDA takes little account of the harm done by delays in introducing new products into the market. To ensure that patients have quicker access to safe drugs, Congress should legislate the following changes:

- The FDA should be permitted to require only nonclinical studies to ensure safety if it determines that the risk from a drug outweighs the risk from disease. Standards should be liberalized when there is no effective alternative therapy.
- Clinical holds should be limited to instances in which they are essential to public health. Patients and groups such as the American Heart Association and others focusing on cures for various diseases should be empowered to challenge a clinical hold by petition.
- Companies should be able to use well-controlled foreign studies or a definitive study at any phase to demonstrate safety.
- The FDA should not delay approval because of manufacturing process review unless it can prove in writing that the safety risk of a manufacturing process outweighs the risk of the disease.
- The FDA must review an NDA within 180 days, or the application will be deemed approved.

Those steps should only be interim measures en route to a completely private system for ensuring product safety.

Curb FDA Authority to Regulate Marketing Practices

Thanks to the FDA, we now live in a country where patients can use unapproved drugs to commit suicide if terminally ill but are not allowed to use off-label drugs to stay alive.

The FDA has far exceeded the bounds of its statutory authority to monitor the marketing practices of companies; it now asserts a right to control the flow of all new medical information. The FDA has gone beyond ensuring that companies provide truthful and scientifically supportable information; it now characterizes any discussion of or reference to a product—whether in an advertisement, article, or conference—as marketing. The FDA assumes that neither doctors nor patients can make reasonable choices among drugs and that it must control those choices through strict regulation.

Even though unapproved uses are regularly reported in the medical literature, the FDA prohibits companies from engaging in or supporting any form of public education about or providing any information on those uses. As a result, doctors and patients are prevented from obtaining useful information about unapproved uses of drugs for treating disease.

The FDA's regulation of marketing practices should be limited to ensuring that a drug is safe for use. The FDA should be able to review and approve labeling to ensure that it is consistent with findings of safety studies. Disputes about the truthful advertising and promotion of drugs should be resolved by other regulatory bodies or through litigation.

Companies should be permitted to discuss unapproved uses of drugs without fearing an investigation. They should be allowed to include information about unapproved uses in advertising and labeling as long as the use has been evaluated in well-controlled studies published in peer-reviewed medical literature. At present, the FDA requires companies to conduct expensive studies to demonstrate the effectiveness of unapproved uses of approved products. That requirement should be eliminated as long as other studies indicating the effectiveness of an unapproved use are available.

Eliminate FDA Regulations That Undermine Competitiveness and Investment

The FDA's regulation of other aspects of biopharmaceutical research, development, and manufacturing imposes unnecessary costs on consumers and affects the competitiveness of the nation's biomedical enterprises.

No new product can be approved until the FDA certifies that the manufacturing process is acceptable. The FDA has a stranglehold on manufacturers at the preapproval stage because it can impose any manufacturing requirements it wishes without fear of being challenged. The FDA hinders the use of new manufacturing methods by insisting that it approve every single manufacturing change. That forces companies that wish to use the latest manufacturing technology to move overseas. The FDA should be prohibited from delaying approval because of manufacturing unless it can show in writing that the risk outweighs the risk of disease.

The FDA denies companies the ability to export drugs to other countries where those drugs are already approved for marketing by making it difficult for companies to obtain export licenses. As a result, companies cannot sell products abroad before they are approved for marketing here and therefore must export their technology, build manufacturing facilities abroad, and emphasize foreign marketing. Congress should eliminate the export license requirement, and companies should be allowed to export if any of 21 developed countries has approved the drug.

Conclusion

FDA reform is truly a matter of life and death, not only for America's biotechnology industry, but for the billions of people around the world who wait and hope for cures and better treatments for major illnesses. Some of the FDA's critics suggest that while the agency needs fixing, its basic mission, protecting the public from unsafe and useless drugs, should be preserved. However, the FDA has not yet shown that it can achieve that goal without hindering consumers' access to much needed medicine. The solution to that problem is not to reinvent government regulations and agencies. Rather, it is to back the government out of the drug approval business, turning the task over to the private sector that has time and again proved its capacity to produce lifesaving and pain-reducing medicines.

Suggested Readings

Epstein, Ralph, et al. "The Future of Medical Innovation: Health, Safety, and the Role of Government in the 21st Century." Washington: Progress and Freedom Foundation, February 7, 1996. At www.pff.org/pff/mip/fdatac.html.

Gieringer, Dale H. "Compassion vs. Control: FDA Investigational Drug Regulations." Cato Institute Policy Analysis no. 72, May 20, 1986.

Goldberg, Robert M. "Breaking Up the FDA's Medical Information Monopoly." *Regulation,* no. 2 (1995).

Higgs, Robert. "FDA Regulation of Medical Devices." Cato Institute Policy Analysis no. 235, August 7, 1995.

Peltzman, Sam. *Regulation of Pharmaceutical Innovation: The 1962 Amendments.* Washington: American Enterprise Institute, 1974.

Siegel, Joanna E. "Reforming FDA Policy: Lessons from the AIDS Experience." *Regulation,* no. 4 (1991).

Ward, Michael R. "Drug Approval Overregulation." *Regulation,* no. 4 (1992).

—Prepared by Robert M. Goldberg

33. Telecommunications

Congress should

- establish full private property rights in the broadcast spectrum and end restrictions on the use of that spectrum;
- end FCC intervention in standard setting;
- repeal 47 U.S.C. §254, which forces telecommunications customers and businesses to subsidize universal service; and
- roll back the interconnection obligations imposed on phone companies.

Decades of experience with telecommunications regulation teach a simple lesson: regulation stifles competition and growth. By contrast, the computer and software industry, largely unfettered by regulation, is one of the most vibrant, competitive, and innovative sectors of the economy. In 1996 Congress tentatively deregulated some aspects of the telecommunications industry. But the work of deregulation is not done. The telecommunications industry should be free to build itself on a sound foundation of freedom of contract and property rights.

Recognizing That Regulation Doesn't Work

The rapid pace of change in the telecommunications industry makes regulatory micromanagement harmful for two reasons. First, regulators cannot adapt regulations fast enough to keep up with changes in the industry. Cellular phones were delayed for 10 years by the Federal Communications Commission, at a cost to the economy estimated by National Economic Research Associates to be $85 billion. Regulators' attempts to adjust to change create further uncertainty and delay.

Second, regulators are most friendly to familiar technologies and see new competition as an attack on regulatory goals. MCI had been using microwaves to send signals over long distances in competition with AT&T

for decades, although competition was long discouraged by the FCC. For years the FCC suppressed cable to protect television broadcasters.

In enacting the Telecommunications Act of 1996, Congress recognized that traditional regulation hurts business and consumers. Local and long-distance phone companies were permitted to enter one another's markets and to compete with cable television. Cable operators were freed from rate regulation. The antitrust consent decrees that had brought the business planning of the Bell Companies, AT&T, and GTE under the jurisdiction of the federal courts were terminated. But the act did not go far enough in freeing the industry to manage its own affairs.

Although the act did remove some statutory barriers to competition, the FCC retains the authority to impose formidable barriers of its own. The act delegated at least 80 matters to the FCC. A statute that makes it illegal for Company A to compete with Company B is not a good thing. But allowing competition only if Company A spends two years wrestling with regulators and subsidizes Company C is not much better. Regulatory discretion is not the same thing as freedom.

Setting the Market Free

Congress should do the following four things to move the telecommunications industry toward an efficient market structure.

Privatize the Electromagnetic Spectrum

Once mainly television and radio broadcasters and a few primitive point-to-point devices used the electromagnetic spectrum. Now the spectrum is used by satellites sending voice, data, and video communications and by cellular phones, personal communications services, pagers, and wireless local area networks. Perhaps in the future it will be used by wireless Internet access services. The wireless sector of the economy is ready to leap ahead into the 21st century.

But the current regulatory structure that governs spectrum allocation and assignment holds the industry back. Early in the history of broadcasting, government claimed the electromagnetic broadcast spectrum as public property. The only way to prevent interference, the theory was, was to have the government allocate blocks of spectrum to particular uses and then assign licenses to those frequencies within a certain area to individual users. For example, a certain range of frequencies is set aside for FM radio, and would-be broadcasters apply for licenses to provide FM service to a particular region or city. In 1993 spectrum licenses began to be distributed by auction, rather than by hearings or lotteries. That reform did not go far enough.

The government, not the marketplace, still decides which "blocks" of spectrum will be used for what services. The slowness of the process costs the economy tens of billions of dollars. A Progress and Freedom Foundation analysis estimates that a six-year delay in bringing personal communication service technology to the market cost the economy $9 billion.

Even if delays could be eliminated (history suggests they could not be), it makes no sense for government to dole out spectrum to some industries and close it off to others. Bureaucrats cannot know better than entrepreneurs how to use the spectrum. Consumers should not be forced to pay more for mobile phone service because the government thinks that the part of the spectrum that could be used for mobile telephony should be used only for advanced television.

Furthermore, the current spectrum allocation system allows citizens to benefit from the use of assigned portions of the spectrum only temporarily. Users of the spectrum get licenses, not full property rights. As residents of the former Soviet Union learned the hard way, private property rights are central to a thriving economy. Temporary licenses make investment in the industry more risky and less rewarding. David Colton, author of a report prepared for the Reason Foundation, cites estimates that auctioning off full property rights in the electromagnetic spectrum could raise from $100 billion to $300 billion in revenues.

Anyone (including foreign investors) should be able to use any part of the spectrum to provide any service, as long as he or she complies with rules against interference. Rights in spectrum should be full property rights, freely transferable.

End Government Intervention in Industry Standard Setting

Different bits of telecommunications hardware, such as switches, television sets, and telephones, need to be compatible with the rest of the telecommunications network. So the industry needs standards that operate well without being too expensive. Can government help? No. Government cannot do better than entrepreneurs in choosing industry standards.

Recognizing that, the FCC refused to decide whether digital phone systems should use time division multiple access or code division multiple access technology. Customers, engineers, and businesses will decide which is the better standard. The absence of mandated standards encourages companies to develop the best product they can, knowing the product will be tested in the marketplace, not in endless politicized hearings.

But the FCC has not consistently applied that wisdom. In the late 1980s the FCC began trying to pick a standard for high-definition television (HDTV). Almost a decade later, the FCC still has not chosen a standard. Representatives of the computer industry believe that the standard the FCC favors will not work well with computer graphics, which will keep computers from evolving into digital televisions and competing in new markets.

The FCC's venture into HDTV standard setting reveals two hazards of government involvement. First, government standard setting means delay. And, because the technology changes so quickly, the standard will need to be adjusted. That means more delay at every stage. Second, government standard setting becomes a political football, used to restrict competition.

In the land of opportunity, no federal commission should have the power to say to a business that technology it invested millions to develop may not be sold. Standard setting should be removed from the FCC's jurisdiction.

Repeal Universal Service Laws

Lawmakers erroneously enshrined an expansive concept of universal service in the Telecommunications Act of 1996, extending subsidies to cover advanced services for the first time. The universal service provisions are incompatible with competition and should be repealed.

The FCC first formalized a universal service policy in 1970. Revenues from artificially high prices on long-distance phone service subsidized artificially low prices for local phone service. That meant that the FCC could not allow competition because competition would force long-distance prices down. There would be no money left to subsidize local services.

When the FCC could hold back competition no longer, business users and intrastate long-distance customers paid more so local service could cost less. As competition grew between providers of local business phone service, the monies that had been siphoned from business users to residential users began to dry up.

The answer in the Telecommunications Act of 1996 was to make all telecommunications service providers pay something toward the universal service subsidy. But that will force all telecommunications customers to pay extra, in the form of a surcharge or a tax, for service. The extra charge will actually *slow* the spread of new services, hurting both consumers and the telecommunications industry. Businesses with the least healthy balance sheets will be hit the hardest.

It's unfair to ask some telephone customers to pay more so that other customers can have lower bills. Subsidizing service to rural areas is particularly unjust. Many rural telephone customers are wealthy. And people live in rural areas by choice. Some things cost more in urban areas (housing), and some cost more in rural areas (transportation). People living in those areas should bear the consequences of their decision to live where they do.

History suggests that competition will work better than subsidies to bring services to the poor and to rural areas. By 1920, after a period of competition between independent telephone companies, rural households in the United States had the *highest*, not the lowest, levels of telephone service. In Ohio, Indiana, Illinois, and Kansas, subscription levels ranged from 60 to 70 percent. More recently, intense competition in the computer industry has illustrated how quickly prices come down when free markets are unleashed. Competition, not subsidies, will make even advanced services accessible to the poor.

Finally, telecommunications service providers should be willing to offer services at reasonable prices to schools. LEXIS and Westlaw, for example, offer law students free use of their databases, hoping to win customers in the future.

Universal service subsidies impose a massive hidden tax on telephone consumers. The universal service provisions of the Telecommunications Act of 1996 should be repealed.

Reexamine New Interconnection Regulations

The interconnection obligations imposed on telephone companies by the Telecommunications Act of 1996 were drafted with the best of intentions. Unfortunately, good intentions do not necessarily make good law. Legislators should begin rolling back interconnection regulations.

Ordinarily, no one gets to use his competitor's facilities to help him compete. One moving company is not obligated to carry other companies' shipments on its own trucks. But that is precisely what interconnection obligations require. By comparison with almost every other industry, interconnection obligations are an extraordinary remedy.

Clearly, requiring one company to connect to its competitor violates the first company's property rights. And it is a subsidy to the second company. Let us assume that invasions of property rights can sometimes be justified to prevent monopoly (which was argued in the case of the companies that once formed the old Bell System). Even then, lawmakers should move carefully to make the invasion as limited as possible.

Instead of proceeding with caution, the Telecommunications Act of 1996 imposes interconnection obligations broadly on *all* telephone companies, regardless of whether those companies threaten to monopolize anything. Interconnection was assumed to be a cure-all for sick markets—all benefit and no cost—and the drawbacks of interconnection were never explored.

First, the interconnection obligations described in the act embroil telecommunications companies in an enormously complex political regulatory apparatus, embodied in the FCC's 700-page interconnection order. Connecting two communications networks requires businesspeople to wrestle with difficult issues of engineering, pricing, and billing. By giving the parties to the negotiations the option of playing political games in the federal or state regulatory arena, the act makes already uncertain negotiations less likely to proceed smoothly.

Second, the act gives interconnecting companies almost complete parity with the incumbent service provider. That gives interconnecting companies little incentive to develop their own networks. They can be parasites on the incumbent networks indefinitely. Incumbents are less likely to undertake the expense of building new networks, knowing those networks will be used by competitors. Too generous interconnection could diminish chances of facilities-based competition.

Third, mandated interconnection may be a form of subsidy; property is taken from one company to be used by another. The more generous the interconnection rights, the greater the subsidy. Expansive interconnection brings into existence a plethora of feeble competitors, all dependent on others' networks. Thus, expansive interconnection will lead to weak competitors who must use the political process to survive.

Because the costs of the interconnection regulatory apparatus probably outweigh the benefits, Congress should consider repealing the interconnection obligations entirely. Congress might also consider second-best alternatives. First, reform the interconnection laws so that companies that never had government help in maintaining monopoly power need not allow their networks to be used by competitors. Second, give companies that benefit from interconnection incentives to build their own networks, and make it harder for parasitic competitors to survive. Start by

- amending the interconnection provisions to sunset on a clear, certain date;

- reforming the law so companies need not offer complete parity in interconnection agreements; and
- discouraging companies entering interconnection negotiations from manipulating the regulatory process.

Conclusion

The regulatory strictures that have been placed on the telecommunications industry were put there with good intentions. But this regulatory regime and the litigation that goes along with it have severe consequences: The market works less efficiently. The uncertainty of the regulatory system deters investment. The regulatory system is used to impede and delay competition. Telecommunications entrepreneurs should be free to develop a communications infrastructure for the 21st century.

Suggested Readings

Colton, David. ''Spectrum Privatization: Removing the Barriers to Telecommunications Competition.'' Reason Foundation Policy Study no. 208, July 1996.

Gasman, Lawrence. *Telecompetition: The Free Market Road to the Information Highway.* Washington: Cato Institute, 1994.

Keyworth, G. A. II, et al. *The Telecom Revolution: An American Opportunity.* Washington: Progress and Freedom Foundation, March 1995.

Mueller, Milton. *Universal Service: Competition, Interconnection, and Monopoly in the Making of the American Telephone System.* Cambridge, Mass.: MIT Press, 1996.

—Prepared by Solveig Bernstein and Lawrence Gasman

34. Postal Service

Congress should

- privatize the U.S. Postal Service and
- repeal the Private Express Statutes that preserve the postal monopoly.

Although fast, efficient communications are vital for advanced industrial economies and societies, the United States is poised to enter the 21st century with a postal system established in the 18th.

It is a federal crime for private suppliers to transport and deliver messages on pieces of paper or other material media and charge prices as low as those of the U.S. Postal Service. Yet the problems with the USPS, which has the monopoly right to provide those services, are chronic. And the defects of the government system stand in contrast to the successes of the private-sector-created telecommunications revolution. Faxes and e-mail are becoming the preferred means of sending important and urgent messages or purchase orders. It is time for the federal government to abandon this last monopoly.

The Postal Monopoly

Mail delivery has not always been a government monopoly. In the early 1800s private railroads and steamboats gave rise to private companies offering mail delivery services. The Private Express Statutes of 1845 put an end to that service between cities. Private companies still delivered within cities until the Postal Code of 1872 barred them from doing so.

Today the USPS is a $55 billion per year operation employing approximately 800,000 workers. Nearly half of the mail handled by the Postal Service is advertisements. A little over 30 percent is business-to-business correspondence. Some 15 percent is household-to-business mail, that is, payment of bills. Only around 8 percent of the mail is household-to-household, such as letters and greeting cards sent between families and friends.

Chronic Problems

Periodically, the public hears horror stories about the inefficiency of the USPS that confirm what seems clear from personal experience. In 1994 inspectors at the South Maryland processing facility found 2.3 million pieces of bulk mail delayed for up to nine days and 800,000 pieces of first-class mail delayed for three days. In Chicago that same year, 5.9 million pieces of forwarded mail were delayed for a month. A hundred bags of months-old mail were found in one truck; 200 pounds of burned mail were found under a viaduct.

The USPS has made major efforts over the past two years to improve quality and cut costs, promising that efficiency savings would be passed along to businesses and balk mailers, the Postal Service's largest customers. But many mailers complain that the USPS has failed to deliver on that promise.

Recent quality improvements, in part the result of adding more manpower and thus increasing costs, simply are part of a striking pattern of roller-coaster drops and improvements in quality that the Postal Service has experienced for decades. Each postmaster general pledges to improve mail services and hold down costs. Some do, for a time. But problems always come back. That should come as no surprise. After all, a government monopoly that faces no direct competition has little incentive to improve the quality and costs of its services.

High Costs

The prices of goods and services drop when markets force suppliers to become more efficient. Airline deregulation since the late 1970s has cut ticket prices by from 10 percent to 30 percent. Deregulation of trucking has saved at least $100 billion over a decade. One estimate is that as much as $90 billion was saved in one year. That savings translates into lower prices for many consumer products. And as the power of personal computers has skyrocketed, costs have plunged. Yet the price for first-class mail has not gone down. Stamp prices have risen nine times since 1973, from 8 cents to 32 cents today.

High labor costs account for part of the price of stamps. The average wage and benefits package of Postal Service clerks and sorters is nearly $43,000, compared to about $35,000 for all private-sector workers. Pensions for postal workers are backed by the American taxpayers. And the Postal Rate Commission found recently that "nonproductive time" constitutes 28.4 percent of mail-processing labor costs. There is 1 manager for every 10 workers at the USPS, compared with 1 for every 15 workers at Federal Express.

In recent years the USPS has expanded contracting out for some services. In September 1996, for example, the USPS announced it would use 1,200 private operators to answer telephone inquiries. And the Postal Service has offered discounts for businesses that presort mail going to different cities and for bar-coded mail, and it allows transportation of such presorted bags by private trucks to post offices in the cities of destination.

Why not contract out all bulk shipments between major distribution centers, or all mail sorting to private suppliers, or simply allow the private sector to perform those functions entirely? By adopting private-sector techniques and assistance, the USPS is demonstrating that the private sector could handle mail delivery without a government monopoly. Of course, it is also certain that the 800,000, mostly unionized, postal workers will ensure that such progress goes only so far.

Nonpostal Service

The USPS also has attracted criticism for straying from its government-mandated and protected task of delivering first- and third-class mail. The Postal Service, for example, has gone into the business of marketing prepaid phone calling cards for long-distance calls, competing with private firms. That competition of a government monopoly with the private sector is manifestly unfair. Postal facilities and assets were acquired through monopoly power. The USPS now uses those facilities and assets to compete with the private sector.

The USPS has begun renting out space in the parking lots of its post offices for the erection of commercial antennas for cellular phone transmissions and other uses. In addition to running afoul of local regulations, that constitutes more unfair competition with the private sector. The Postal Service pays no property taxes on its real estate, whereas a private provider of space for broadcast operations would be subject to taxes.

In the early 1980s the Postal Service expressed initial interest in extending its monopoly over the emerging e-mail market. Fortunately, it failed at that attempt. Now, however, it is developing services to put electronic postmarks on e-mail and to guarantee e-mail security since mail fraud and tampering are federal crimes. Yet there already are private encryption software and services. And, no doubt, as the USPS uses its federal protection to keep e-mail secure, federal regulation of e-mail will follow.

Recent Developments

Despite recent improvements in the timeliness of mail delivery, the USPS continues to draw criticism. In September 1996 a study, *Postal Service Reform: Issues Relevant to Changing Restrictions on Private Letter Delivery,* was released by the General Accounting Office in response to a request by Sen. David Pryor (D-Ark.), the ranking Democrat on the Subcommittee on Federal Services, Post Office, and Civil Service of the Senate Government Affairs Committee. Remarkably, the report addressed the usually forbidden topic of repealing the Private Express Statutes. The report states that "it is not clear whether the underlying economic basis for the Statutes cited by the Postal Service . . . remains valid today."

Another indication of the need for change is found in the pronouncements of Murray Comarow, a former senior assistant postmaster general and, more important, the executive director of the presidential commission that devised the plan that in 1970 reorganized the Post Office into today's U.S. Postal Service. At that time he was critical of changes made by Congress to the original reorganization plan; those changes allowed binding arbitration of labor disputes and created the Postal Rate Commission to set prices. Comarow now believes that it is time to revisit the issue of the USPS, to appoint another commission to consider future arrangements, including a possible privatized system.

Two Approaches to Privatization

The real question is not whether the USPS should be privatized but rather how it should be done. Two actions are essential to accomplishing that goal:

- Privatize the Postal Service. The USPS, including its equipment, trucks, buildings, real estate, and other assets, along with its liabilities, principally worker pensions, should be sold off. The U.S. government should eliminate all official support for mail delivery.
- Repeal the postal monopoly. That would mean that any private provider could compete in any service currently offered by the USPS, principally delivery of first- and third-class mail.

Two approaches to the task appear to be politically possible.

Give the Postal Service to Its Employees under an Employee Stock Ownership Plan

The main barrier to postal privatization is the 800,000-person, mostly unionized, workforce whose members are found in every congressional district across the country. Union leaders have been vehemently opposed, not only to privatization, but to many of the reforms that would make the Postal Service more efficient. That suggests that postal workers will have to be given incentives to prevent them from blocking privatization. During the 104th Congress Reps. Dana Rohrabacher (R-Calif.) and Philip M. Crane (R-Ill.) introduced legislation (H.R. 2100) that would do just that.

The employee-stock-option-plan approach would proceed in three steps:

- First, both the assets and the liabilities of the USPS would be transferred to the employees.
- Second, the government would still guarantee current employees pensions comparable to what they might have expected without privatization. Pensions for new employees would be determined by, and be the responsibility of, the new private USPS.
- Third, the postal monopoly would be retained for a five-year period to give the Postal Service an opportunity to reorganize.

Some critics would contend that a USPS privatized intact would still have an unfair advantage over potential private competitors. Further, say critics, American taxpayers in effect currently own the Postal Service and should be beneficiaries of the privatization. Thus, an alternative plan could contain the following elements:

- First, the Postal Service would be broken up into five regional delivery companies, plus a package delivery division and a division to coordinate privatization.
- Second, the regional divisions would be sold off to any buyer. Some stock might be reserved for sale to postal workers at concessional prices to purchase their support.
- Third, when each division was privatized, the postal monopoly would be removed.

No doubt other, better approaches are possible. And no doubt the political battle that accompanies any major policy change will determine which approach is used. But the case for privatization is strong. So if Congress wishes to ensure an efficient and cost-effective communications system for the 21st century, it should repeal the last monopoly and allow private providers to compete.

Suggested Readings

Adie, Douglas K. *Monopoly Mail: Privatizing the United States Postal Service.* New Brunswick, N.J.: Transaction Publishers, 1989.

Ferrara, Peter, ed. *Free the Mail: Ending the Postal Monopoly.* Washington: Cato Institute, 1990.

General Accounting Office. *Postal Service Reform: Issues Relevant to Changing Restrictions on Private Letter Delivery.* 2 vols. Washington: General Accounting Office, September 1996.

Hudgins, Edward, ed. *The Last Monopoly: Privatizing the Postal Service for the Information Age.* Washington: Cato Institute, 1996.

Sidak, J. Gregory, ed. *Governing the Postal Service.* Washington: American Enterprise Institute Press, 1994.

—Prepared by Edward L. Hudgins

35. Labor Relations Law

Congress should

- eliminate exclusive representation, or at least pass a national right-to-work law, or codify the U.S. Supreme Court's 1988 decision in *Communications Workers of America v. Beck;*
- repeal section 8(a)2 of the National Labor Relations Act, or at least permit labor-management cooperation that is not only union-management cooperation;
- codify the Supreme Court's ruling in *NLRB v. Mackay Radio & Telegraph* (1938) that employers have an undisputed right to hire permanent replacement workers for striking workers in economic strikes;
- overturn the Supreme Court's ruling in *NLRB v. Town & Country Electric* (1995) that forces employers to hire paid union organizers as ordinary employees;
- protect the associational rights of state employees by overriding state and local laws that impose NLRA-style unionism on state and local government workers; and
- repeal the 1931 Davis-Bacon Act and the 1965 Service Contract Act.

In a market economy it makes little sense to distinguish between producers and consumers because most people are both. It also makes no sense, outside discredited Marxist theory, to distinguish between management and labor since both are employed by consumers to produce goods and services. Management and labor are complementary, not rivalrous, inputs to the production process.

Unfortunately, U.S. labor relations law is based on the mistaken ideas that management and labor are natural enemies; that labor is at an inherent bargaining disadvantage relative to management; and that only unions backed by government power, which eliminate competition among sellers of labor services, can redress that situation. The National Labor Relations Act, as amended, is based on ideas that might have seemed sensible in the 1930s but do not make any sense in today's information age. That act is an impediment to labor market innovations that are necessary if the United States is to continue to be the world's premier economy in the new millennium. The NLRA ought to be scrapped or at least be substantially amended so it reflects modern labor market realities.

The Labor Front Today

In 1995 only 10.4 percent of the private-sector workforce was unionized. That figure has been declining since 1953, and by the year 2000 it will be no higher than 7 percent—exactly where it was in 1900. Unions, at least in the private sector, are going the way of the dinosaur. They are institutions that cannot succeed in the competitive, global economy of the future. Firms and workers must be more innovative and have the freedom to adjust to changing market conditions if they are to reap the rich rewards of a more prosperous world economy.

Further, about half of union members now work for the public sector, that is, governments. They do not produce goods and services that are subject to market forces. Yet despite the decline of unions, the old regime that supports them is still in place.

Exclusive Representation

The principle of exclusive representation, as provided for in section 9(a) of the NLRA, mandates that if a majority of employees vote to be represented by a particular union, that union is the sole representative of all workers, whether an individual worker voted for or against it or did not vote at all. Individual workers are not free to designate representatives of their own choosing. While workers should be free, on an individual basis, to hire a union to represent them, they should not be forced to do so by majority vote. Unions are not governments; they are private associations. For government to tell individual workers that they must allow a union that has majority support to represent them is for government to violate those workers' freedom of association.

Union security is the principle under which workers who are represented by exclusive bargaining agents are forced to join, or at least pay dues to, the union with monopoly bargaining privileges. In the 21 right-to-work states such coercive arrangements are forbidden under state law. (Section 14[b] of the NLRA gives states the right to pass such laws.) The union justification for union security is that some whom they represent would otherwise get union-generated benefits for free. Note that if exclusive representation were repealed, only a union's voluntary members could get benefits from the union because the union would represent only its voluntary members. The right-to-work issue would be moot. Forced unionism would, at long last, be replaced by voluntary unionism.

The NLRA serves the particular interests of unionized labor rather than the general interests of all labor, and it abrogates one of the most important privileges and immunities of U.S. citizens—the right of each individual worker to enter into hiring contracts with willing employers on terms that are mutually acceptable. Unfortunately, no Court has had the courage to take up the issue since the 1930s. It is time for Congress to do so.

There are three options Congress might choose to remedy the current situation:

- Eliminate exclusive representation. Ideally, the current restrictions on the freedom of workers to choose who if anyone represents them should be eliminated. That might be politically difficult. Thus, several short-term options are available.
- Adopt a national right-to-work law. Under this option workers would still be forced to let certified unions represent them, but no worker would be forced to join, or pay dues to, a labor union. This is a poor second best to members-only bargaining.
- Codify the Supreme Court's 1988 decision in *Communications Workers of America v. Beck.*

In the *Beck* decision the Court declared that the dues of union members could not be used for purposes not directly related to collective bargaining, principally for political contributions. But the federal government has done little to protect this right of workers. Congress could do so by incorporating, for private-sector workers, the procedural and substantive protections that were granted to government workers who are forced dues payers in *Chicago Teachers Union v. Hudson* (1986). The Worker Right to Know Act, H.R. 3580, introduced in 1996 but never voted on, is an excellent model for codifying *Beck.*

The urgency of codifying *Beck* has been made clear by the National Labor Relations Board's decision in *California Saw and Knife Works* (1996). In that case the NLRB greatly circumscribed workers' *Beck* rights, even going so far as to say that unions could use their own staff accountants to determine how much of their expenditures were for non-collective-bargaining purposes.

Repeal Section 8(a)2 of the NLRA

This is the section that outlaws so-called company unions. More important, it is the section that unions have discovered they can use to block any labor-management cooperation that is not union-management cooperation. Labor-management cooperation is crucial to America's ability to compete in the global market. It must not be constrained to union-management cooperation.

Workers who want to have a voice in company decisionmaking without going through a union should be free to do so. A 1994 national poll of employees in private businesses with 25 or more workers, conducted by Princeton Survey Research Associates, revealed that 63 percent preferred cooperation committees to unions as a way of having a voice in decisionmaking. Only 20 percent preferred unions.

In the 1992 *Electromation* case, the NLRB declared that several voluntary labor-management cooperation committees, set up by management and workers in a union-free firm to give employees a significant voice in company decisionmaking, were illegal company unions. The Teamsters then argued that the only form of labor-management cooperation the government should allow was union-management cooperation. On the basis of that argument, the Teamsters won a slim majority in a certification election. As a result of the *Electromation* decision, Polaroid Corp. was forced to disband voluntary labor-management cooperation committees that had been in existence for 40 years.

In the 1993 *DuPont* case, the NLRB ruled that labor-management cooperation committees in a unionized setting were illegal company unions because they were separate from the union. The voluntary committees were set up to deal with problems with which the union either could not or would not deal.

The report that was issued by the Dunlop Commission on January 9, 1995, recommends "clarifying" rather than doing away with section 8(a)2. It says that voluntary worker-management cooperation programs "should not be unlawful simply because they involve discussion of terms and conditions of worker compensation where such discussions are incidental to the broad purposes of these programs." That will do little to solve the problem. What is "incidental"? Who will decide? Answer: the NLRB that has already given us the *Electromation* decision.

It is time for Congress to unequivocally state that employers and workers may formulate and participate in any voluntary cooperation schemes they like so long as any individual worker may join and participate in any union he or she chooses without penalty.

Short of repealing section 8(a)2, Congress should amend it to permit labor-management cooperation that is not union-management cooperation.

The Teamwork for Employees and Managers Act (H.R. 473 and S. 295), passed by Congress but vetoed by President Clinton in 1996, is an excellent model. Unions supported Clinton's veto because they do not wish to compete on a level playing field with alternative types of labor-management cooperation. The Employment Policies Foundation has demonstrated that productivity gains from employee involvement systems are typically in the 18 to 25 percent range. Under existing laws, union-free firms in America are not allowed to implement such systems unless they agree to accept the yoke of NLRA-style unions, and doing so usually reduces productivity in other ways.

Codify the Supreme Court's Ruling in NLRB v. Mackay Radio & Telegraph (1938)

Once and for all, it should be made clear that, although strikers have a right to withhold their own labor services from employers who offer unsatisfactory terms and conditions of employment, strikers have no right to withhold the labor services of workers who find those terms and conditions of employment acceptable. Strikers and replacement workers should have their constitutional right to *equal* protection of the laws acknowledged in the NLRA.

Overturn the Supreme Court's Ruling in NLRB v. Town & Country Electric (1995)

Section 8(a)3 of the NLRA makes it an unfair labor practice for an employer to discriminate against a worker on the basis of union membership. According to the Supreme Court, that means that an employer cannot refuse to hire or cannot fire any employee who is a paid union organizer. Unions send paid organizers (salts) to apply for jobs at union-free firms and, if employed, to foment discontent and promote pro-union sympathies. In the *Town & Country Electric* decision, the Court said that employers could not resist that practice by firing or refusing to hire salts. In other words, employers must hire people whose main intent is to subvert their business activities. That is like telling a homeowner that it is illegal to exclude visitors whose principal intent is to burglarize his home. Congress should allow employers to resist this practice.

Protect the Associational Rights of State Employees with a Federal Statute

Congress has constitutional authority under the Fourteenth Amendment to protect the privileges and immunities of citizens of the United States. Thus it is not necessary to undo the harm of government employee unionism state by state.

The principles of exclusive representation and union security abrogate the First Amendment rights of government employees who wish to remain union free. Government is the employer, hence there is sufficient government action to give rise to Bill of Rights concerns.

Under the Bill of Rights, government is not supposed to intrude on an individual citizen's right to associate or not associate with any legal private organization. A voluntary union of government employees is a legal private organization. But forcing dissenting workers to be represented by, join, or pay dues to such an organization is an abridgment of those workers' freedom of association.

Moreover, in government employment, mandatory bargaining in good faith (which is a feature of the NLRA) forces governments to share the making of public policy with privileged, unelected private organizations. Ordinary private organizations can lobby government, but only government employee unions have the privilege of laws that force government agencies to bargain in good faith with them. Good faith bargaining is conducted behind closed doors. It requires government agencies to compromise with government employee unions. Government agencies are forbidden to set unilaterally terms and conditions of government employment (questions of public policy) without the concurrence of government employee unions. Not even the Sierra Club has that special access to government decision-makers or that kind of influence over decisionmaking. In short, government employee unionism, modeled on the NLRA, violates all basic democratic process values. It should be forbidden. This is why Title VII of the 1978 Civil Service Reform Act greatly restricts the scope of bargaining with federal employee unions and forbids union security in federal employment.

It ought also to forbid exclusive representation and mandatory good faith bargaining in federal employment.

Repeal the 1931 Davis-Bacon Act and the 1965 Service Contract Act

The Davis-Bacon Act, passed at the beginning of the Great Depression, had two purposes: to stop prices and wages from falling and to keep blacks from competing for jobs that had hitherto been done by white unionized labor. Both of its purposes were wrong. Falling wages and prices were precisely what were needed to reverse the collapse of real income and employment in the early 1930s. (Both fell from 1929 to 1933, but prices fell by more than wages. Thus the real cost of hiring workers increased during that time period.) The purchasing power fallacy that misled first Herbert Hoover and later Franklin Roosevelt (e.g., the National Industrial Recovery Act) did as much to deepen and prolong the Great Depression as the Smoot-Hawley tariff.

The racist motivation behind the legislation is plain for anyone who reads the *Congressional Record* of 1931. For example, Rep. Clayton Allgood, in support of the bill, complained of "cheap colored labor" that "is in competition with white labor throughout the country."

While most current supporters of Davis-Bacon are not racists, the law still has racist effects. There are very few minority-owned firms that can afford to pay union wages. As a result they rarely are awarded Davis-Bacon contracts, and many of them stop even trying for those contracts.

Moreover, Davis-Bacon adds over a billion dollars each year directly to federal government expenditures, and billions more to private expenditures on projects that are partially funded with federal funds, by making it impossible for union-free, efficient firms to bid on construction contracts financed in whole or in part with federal funds. Today Davis-Bacon serves no interest whatsoever other than to protect the turf of undeserving, white-dominated construction trade unions.

The claim, on January 6, 1995, by Robert A. Georgine, president of the AFL-CIO Building and Construction Trades Department, that Davis-Bacon has long been supported by the GOP because it adheres to "free market principles by recognizing existing wages within each community set by the private marketplace, not by imposing an artificial standard or deleterious government interference," is self-serving nonsense. Prices set by the free market do not need any government enforcement at all. They are the prices at which the production and exchange plans of buyers and

369

sellers of inputs and outputs are coordinated with each other. They are the prices that would exist in the *absence* of any government involvement. The AFL-CIO and its constituent unions want government to impose prices that are more favorable to their members and officers than the marketplace would produce. The "prevailing wage" or "community wage" set by the Department of Labor under the Davis-Bacon Act is always the union wage—not the free-market wage. After all, unions are insistent that they make wages higher than market-determined wages. Only members of the GOP in thrall to unions' in-kind and financial bribes would support Davis-Bacon. No member of Congress, of either party, who supports the free market can be against repealing Davis-Bacon.

The Service Contract Act does for federal purchases of services what the Davis-Bacon Act does for federally funded construction. It wastes billions of taxpayer dollars for the sole purpose of attempting to price union-free service providers out of the market. Both acts should be placed in the dustbin of history along with the syndicalist sympathies that inspired them.

Conclusion

The more integrated global economy offers greater opportunities for American enterprises and workers to prosper. Greater productivity world-wide means more wealth for those who can trade their services to willing customers. But to do so, American workers and the enterprises that employ them must be empowered to act quickly to meet market demands. That means eliminating the laws and regulations that destroy jobs and make workers a burden rather than an asset to employers.

Suggested Readings

Baird, Charles W. "Are Quality Circles Illegal? Global Competition Meets the New Deal." Cato Institute Briefing Paper no. 18, February 10, 1993.
_____. "Outlawing Cooperation: Chapter Two." *Regulation*, no. 3 (1993): 12–15.
_____. "The Permissible Uses of Forced Union Dues: From *Hanson* to *Beck.*" Cato Institute Policy Analysis no. 174, June 30, 1992.
_____. "Toward Equality and Justice in Labor Markets." *Journal of Social, Political and Economic Studies* 20, no. 2 (Summer 1995): 163–86.
Bernstein, David. "The Davis-Bacon Act: Let's Bring Jim Crow to an End." Cato Institute Briefing Paper no. 17, January 18, 1993.
Nelson, Daniel. "The Company Union Movement, 1900–1937: A Reexamination." *Business History Review* 56 (Autumn 1982): 335–57.
Potter, Edward E., and Yi K. Ngan. *Estimating the Potential Productivity and Real Wage Effects of Employee Involvement.* Washington: Employment Policy Foundation, 1996.

Reynolds, Morgan O. *Making America Poorer: The Cost of Labor Law.* Washington: Cato Institute, 1987.

—Prepared by Charles W. Baird

36. Occupational Safety and Health Administration

> **Congress should** shut down the Occupational Safety and Health Administration (OSHA), or barring that, it should at least
>
> - reduce OSHA's enforcement budget;
> - further exempt from inspections companies with strong safety programs and reduce fines for firms making legitimate efforts to correct health and safety problems; and
> - repeal OSHA's "general duty" clause that allows inspectors to enforce regulations that are not published or are poorly understood by enterprises.

Labored Safety Agency

OSHA is charged with protecting workers from job-related injuries and illness. All Americans want safe jobs, just as they want a clean environment, no automobile deaths, and no crime. Unfortunately, a society free of risk is not realistic. People are generally unwilling to accept the severe restrictions on personal freedoms as well as the monumental economic expense needed to pursue the impossible task of eliminating all risks to personal health and safety. And attempts to eliminate one risk or danger often create other risks, some worse than the originals.

As it currently operates, OSHA does not increase worker safety in a cost-effective manner. The workers' compensation policies of state governments, for better or for worse, have the major effect on workplace safety. And minor reforms of OSHA probably will not better protect workers; they will simply add to the costs of doing business.

OSHA therefore should be shut down, or at least it should stop issuing mandatory workplace standards, stop inspecting firms for compliance with federal standards, and stop imposing fines for noncompliance.

OSHA's Effect on Workplace Safety

OSHA is the most recently constructed pillar of the U.S. safety policy system. That system also includes tort laws, state workers' compensation insurance programs, and research on and public education about the causes and consequences of work hazards by the National Institute of Occupational Safety and Health (NIOSH). Interwoven with the four pillars of safety policy are the labor market forces establishing compensating wage differentials, which are the wage premiums workers require to accept job-related health hazards.

How safe were workplaces before OSHA's creation in 1970, and how safe are they now? Figure 36.1 shows that the frequency of workplace deaths has declined dramatically over time. In 1933 for every 100,000 workers there were 37 annual workplace fatalities. By 1993 the rate of fatalities had fallen by about 80 percent, to 8 per 100,000 workers annually.

Figure 36.1
Workplace Fatalities, 1933–93

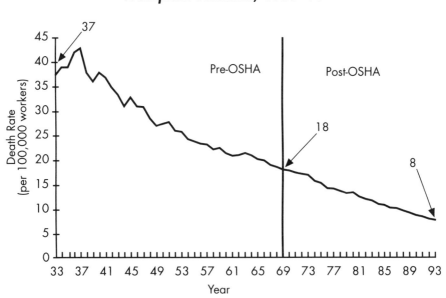

SOURCE: Authors' calculations based on National Safety Council, *Accident Facts, 1994* (Itasca, Ill.: NSC, 1994).

As points of reference, in 1993 the chance of dying in an accident at home was slightly greater (9 in 100,000 annually) and the chance of dying in a motor vehicle accident was two times greater (16 in 100,000 annually) than the chance of dying in an accident at work.

The time series of data on nonfatal workplace injuries and illnesses paint a somewhat different picture of improving workplace safety than do the data on fatal injuries. Figure 36.2 shows nonfatal workplace injuries and illness since 1973, the first year firms were required to report industrial accidents and diseases. Unlike death rates, injuries and illnesses do not show a marked decline over time.

Because of the drop in the rate of workplace deaths from 18 per 100,000 workers in 1970 to 8 per 100,000 workers in 1993, both Secretary of Labor Robert Reich and Assistant Secretary of Labor for Occupational Safety and Health Joseph Dear have credited OSHA with reducing workplace fatalities by 57 percent. To credit OSHA with all of the post-1970 drop in fatalities is similar to a physician's taking credit for the health of

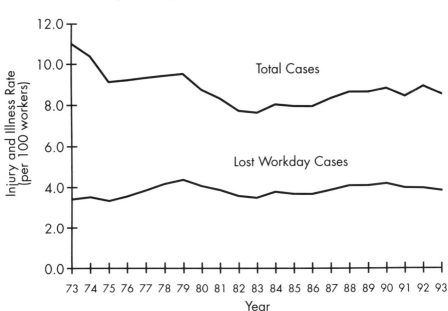

Figure 36.2
Workplace Injuries and Illnesses, 1973–93

SOURCE: U.S. Department of Labor, OSHA, "Occupational Injury and Illness Rates per 100 Full-Time Workers, 1973–94," at http://www.osha.gor/oshstats/bls/html.

375

a patient whom the doctor did not start treating until two weeks after the patient began recovering. The impact of the doctor, and the impact of OSHA, must be judged on the counterfactual evidence of what the pace of recovery would have been without any intervention.

Devising the counterfactual trend for OSHA is extremely difficult. Unlike medical interventions, there is no control group against which to compare workplace fatalities before and since OSHA. Simply looking at the raw data does not make one leap to the conclusion that OSHA has had a dramatic impact on workplace safety. Figure 36.2 shows no downward trend in either the total frequency of workplace injuries or the frequency of injuries resulting in at least one lost workday. Figure 36.1 shows that the workplace fatality rate began its downward trend well before the creation of OSHA. The trend was fueled not by OSHA but in large part by improvements in safety technology and changes in the occupational distribution of labor, for example, away from more dangerous assembly line work to white collar service jobs.

Richard Butler of the University of Minnesota, who studied National Safety Council data on workplace fatality rates, summarized his findings on OSHA: "Not only is there an absence of an OSHA shift in death rates as reflected in ... trends, there does not appear to be any shift after controlling for other factors. Generally, the OSHA variable is statistically insignificant."

While OSHA supporters cite a few studies suggesting that the agency improves workplace safety, the vast majority of studies has found no statistically significant reduction in the rate of workplace fatalities or injuries due to OSHA. It is thus hard to conclude that OSHA meets even the minimum criterion for any government program: Does it have any desirable effect on the problem it is supposed to solve? Even using the most optimistic estimates, OSHA would be responsible for lowering workplace injuries in the United States by no more than 5 percent.

Giving the agency the benefit of the doubt, other questions must be asked: Do OSHA's benefits outweigh its costs? Is the program economically efficient? A back-of-the-envelope calculation, using the range of estimates of OSHA's effectiveness in reducing injuries and the implicit value workers place on safety, indicates that OSHA produces annual safety benefits of from $0 to $4 billion. A study by Robert Hahn and John Hird published in 1991 in the *Yale Journal on Regulation* places the annual cost of OSHA's current health and safety standards at $11 billion, based on either changes in input productivity or expenditures on OSHA-mandated capital equipment. Using cost figures provided by OSHA, Harvey James of Washington University's Center for the Study of American Business recently estimated that the cost of complying with OSHA's regulations in 1993 was about $34 billion. Even with the most favorable of the above estimates, the benefits of OSHA, which may very well be zero, fall far short of its costs.

Chronic Problems with OSHA

OSHA in the future is unlikely to reduce workplace fatalities in a cost-effective manner no matter what reforms are implemented. The leading causes of work-related deaths are now highway motor vehicle accidents and murders by customers and coworkers. Those are difficult to control using workplace safety standards. Further, the self-employed suffer a disproportionate share of work-related deaths. OSHA's inspection-and-fine approach to safety is ill-suited to preventing accidents in one-person operations.

The general problem with OSHA's approach was aptly noted by the National Coalition on Ergonomics in its response to the proposed, and quickly withdrawn, ergonomic standard. The coalition statement said that OSHA "assumed that every workplace and every job is a potential disorder waiting to happen." Workplace standards impose costs on firms regardless of whether they have problems with safety and health or whether their problems can be successfully combated using the procedures mandated by OSHA.

OSHA is not ineffective because its budget is too small or because it has too few safety and health inspectors. A comparison of the United States and Canada suggests the likely impact of strengthening OSHA's enforcement powers. In the 1980s the government of the province of Quebec in particular began to pursue a much more interventionist policy to protect workers from injuries on the job. For instance, Quebec allows workers to refuse hazardous tasks, requires firms to establish joint workplace safety committees with labor representatives, and makes firms initiate accident prevention programs. The Commission de la Santé et de la Sécurité du Travail, Quebec's equivalent of OSHA, spends over four times more per worker on prevention activities than does OSHA. Even with more innovative safety measures and a much greater level of enforcement, the new Quebec system of workplace regulation has been no more effective in improving worker safety and health than was the old.

377

Alternatives to OSHA

In light of its ineffectiveness, giving OSHA more money, personnel, and power is not the way to cost-effective workplace safety. Most protection on the job comes from state workers' compensation insurance programs and market-determined compensating wage differentials.

State-run workers' compensation insurance programs are currently the most influential public attempt to promote workplace safety. Insurance premiums that take account of workplace safety encourage firms to establish safe and healthy work environments. As the frequency of claims rises, the price of workers' compensation insurance increases, thereby penalizing firms for poor safety records. Michael Moore of Duke University and W. Kip Viscusi of Harvard University estimate that, without workers' compensation insurance, the number of fatal accidents and diseases would be 48 percent higher in the United States.

Market forces also promote worker safety and health. Empirical studies show wages rising with workplace risk. All else being equal, the typical American worker in a job with a likelihood of injury earns, on average, 2 to 4 percent more than a person working in a safer job. The added compensation firms must pay to workers who accept more hazardous work is an incentive for firms to expand their investments in safety programs. Firms weigh the benefits of improved safety—smaller compensating wage premiums, lower costs of purchasing workers' compensation insurance, fewer work stoppages, and smaller fines for possibly violating OSHA health and safety standards—against the costs of expanded safety programs.

In 1993 firms paid more than $55 billion for workers' compensation insurance and an estimated $200 billion in wage premiums to workers for accepting some job hazards. OSHA, both federal and state, assessed fines of only $160 million in 1993. At a ratio of 1,594 to 1, the economic incentives to improve safety by reducing compensating wage differentials and workers' compensation insurance expenses far surpass the safety-enhancing incentives of the relatively small fines imposed by OSHA for violating its standards.

Reform for the New Congress

Rather than waste more resources on an agency that cannot be effective, Congress should shut down OSHA and allow state and local officials to use their own means to ensure worker safety. State policymakers should work to reform their workers' compensation insurance policies to allow market forces to fully operate. In addition, state policymakers should review and reform their tort law systems to allow workers to seek redress from employers in true cases of employer negligence and reckless endangerment.

If OSHA cannot be shut down soon, a good alternative would be to phase out OSHA while immediately revising its current approach to standard setting, inspections, and fines. In particular, Congress should

- Reduce OSHA's enforcement budget and redirect the funds to NIOSH. The reduction in the enforcement budget would of necessity force OSHA to abandon most heavy-handed dealings with business in favor of less coercive tactics. NIOSH research on improving workplace safety and health, and information and guidelines concerning threshold levels of exposure to dangerous substances or workplace practices, at least will do little harm to businesses and could be of some use. Workers do have a modicum of knowledge of risk, as demonstrated by the compensating wage differentials for exposure to risk. Ideally, such information could be collected and distributed by insurance companies or other private concerns.

- Further exempt from inspections companies with strong safety programs and reduce fines for firms making legitimate efforts to correct health and safety problems. In the face of congressional criticism over the past year, OSHA already has moved in that direction. In general, all fines, except ones for the most egregious violations of safety and health regulations, should be lowered and firms should be given the opportunity to correct alleged deficiencies before they are fined.

- Repeal the "general duty" clause of the Occupational Safety and Health Act. That clause mandates that employers furnish each employee a job "free from recognized hazards that are causing or likely to cause death or serious physical harm." Currently, OSHA inspectors can use the general duty clause to enforce unpublished and poorly understood regulations.

- Allow OSHA to investigate on a more selective basis worker complaints of health and safety concerns. OSHA must now evaluate every formal worker complaint filed against an employer. A majority of complaints are groundless, consuming staff resources without producing improvement in worker health and safety. Since 1989 more than half the complaint-initiated inspections have uncovered no serious violations of OSHA regulations, and nearly a third of the complaint-initiated inspections have uncovered no violations whatsoever.

Suggested Readings

Kniesner, Thomas J., and John D. Leeth. "Abolishing OSHA." *Regulation,* no. 4 (1995).
———. *Simulating Workplace Safety Policy.* Boston: Kluwer Academic Publishers, 1995.
Loeser, John D., Stephen E. Henderlite, and Douglas A. Conrad. "Incentive Effects of Workers' Compensation Benefits: A Literature Synthesis." *Medical Care Research and Review* 52, no. 1 (March 1995): 34–59.
Viscusi, W. Kip. *Fatal Tradeoffs: Public and Private Responsibilities for Risk.* New York: Oxford University Press, 1992.

—Prepared by Thomas J. Kniesner and John D. Leeth

37. National Aeronautics and Space Administration

> *Congress should* shut down the National Aeronautics and Space Administration (NASA). To that end, it should
>
> - scrap plans to build a space station or, failing that,
>   - upon completion, sell off the station to private purchasers and
>   - allow the private sector to provide and pay for all future travel to and from the station as well as station operations, maintenance, and expansion;
> - sell off the space shuttle or, failing that, turn over as much of shuttle operations as possible to the private sector;
> - build down government civilian space activities by
>   - barring NASA from building and operating launch vehicles and requiring NASA and all other nondefense government agencies to purchase future launch services from the private sector,
>   - requiring NASA to accept bids from private firms for the acquisition of scientific data including data traditionally collected by planetary probes, and
>   - eliminating Mission to Planet Earth or turning it over to other government agencies and contracting with private service providers for all data needs.

From Exploration to Freight Hauling

The possible discovery of extinct Martian life has renewed discussions of the future of America's space program. While the Clinton administration immediately used the discovery to justify NASA's budget, it fortunately has not pushed for a manned mission to Mars, though it is envisioning an unmanned landing and sample return mission for 2005. However, especially in recent decades, NASA actually has hindered the advance of space science as surely as economic planning in communist countries undermined prosperity. The federal role in civilian space ventures should be cut, not expanded.

The space program and NASA were born of the Cold War wish to wipe out the embarrassment of early Soviet space successes. While the government has a legitimate defense role in space, commercial ventures, and most scientific research and exploratory ventures, ideally should be carried out by the private sector. But in the late 1950s many Americans believed that only governments could undertake such endeavors. The lunar landings forever will be celebrated as great human and technological achievements. Yet today NASA is wasteful and ineffective, squandering the public's goodwill, enthusiasm, and tens of billions of dollars.

In the early 1970s, as NASA saw Moon landings curtailed and Moon bases ruled out, it sought to preserve its big budgets and staffs with another big project: the Space Shuttle, which was sold to policymakers as a reusable and thus cheaper way to put payloads into orbit than expendable launch vehicles. In effect, NASA's mission went from science and exploration to freight hauling.

If at that time NASA had begun to turn over space activities to the private sector, space stations and Moon bases might be a reality today. Market competition usually brings down the real price of goods and services. For example, the price of airline travel in constant dollars since the mid-1970s has been cut by as much as half. Shipping costs for oil have dropped by 75 percent. In 1981 a megabyte of computer memory, which was not even available in the first IBM personal computers, would have cost around $45,000. Today a megabyte can be had for only a few dollars. And in the communications satellite industry, the one space activity principally in the private sector, costs have dropped dramatically in real terms.

By contrast, as nearly as can be determined from impenetrable NASA accounting, the cost of putting payloads into orbit has skyrocketed. David Gump in his book *Space Enterprise* estimates that the cost in constant dollars went from $3,800 per pound with Apollo to $6,000 with the shuttle. Alex Roland of Duke University estimates that the cost of a shuttle flight, including development and capital costs, is not the $350 million claimed by NASA but closer to $2 billion, which works out to about $35,000 per pound.

As NASA developed and flew early shuttle missions, it had to fend off private competitors. In the late 1970s and early 1980s federal agencies were forbidden to contract with the infant private launch industry to put government payloads in orbit.

As it became apparent in the early 1980s that the shuttle was a costly white elephant, NASA needed a mission to justify the shuttle's continued existence. Regardless of any commercial or scientific benefits, an orbiting space station seemed to serve that purpose. But the cost of the station, initially named "Freedom," went from a promised $8 billion to nearly $40 billion before the current stripped-down $30 billion model, renamed "Alpha," was redesigned in 1993. A recent General Accounting Office report found that, through June 2002, the actual cost of designing, building, and launching the station will be $48.2 billion. The cost of operating the station after its assembly through 2012 will add another $45.7 billion to the price tag for a total station bill of $93.9 billion.

As NASA sought to protect its big budgets, it continued to ignore the private sector. For example, Space Industries of Houston in the 1980s offered to launch for $750 million a mini-station that could take government and other payloads a decade before the planned NASA station. The government would not contract with that private supplier.

NASA's projects and decisions continue to be driven by politics, and by the need to preserve the agency's budgets and scope of responsibilities. In a sense it now runs like its Soviet rival of three decades ago, attempting to impress the public with no regard for the economics of its operations, with politics rather than markets dictating decisions.

An indication of the unsound habits that still infest NASA is its preliminary consideration of a plan to use the shuttle to rescue a Chinese communications satellite, purchased from Hughes Satellite, that was launched into a useless orbit by a Chinese Long March rocket on August 18, 1996. The insured value of the launch and spacecraft is $102 million. The shuttle rescue would cost $400 million.

It is time for the federal government to follow a builddown strategy to extract itself from most civilian space ventures and let the private sector take over.

Scrap the Space Station

Estimates of the actual costs of completing the station range from around $18 billion to nearly $100 billion. Once built, the station will be operated by NASA at an annual loss of at least $2 billion in taxpayers' funds. Among the station's problems:

- There is no prospect of any profitable commercial venture coming from NASA's operation of the station. No customers are committed to paying the actual costs of renting space on the station. NASA will have to give away space at a loss. Because the station is to be run as a command economy, there are no opportunities for private companies to take over parts of the operation at lower costs.
- Costs are creeping up again. For example, two shuttle flights, planned for 1998 and 1999, respectively, that were supposed to use the station for experiments are now being used, along with at least $230 million in science funding, for station construction.
- A special Presidential Advisory Commission, chaired by Martin Marietta Corporation's CEO Norman Augustine, in 1991 stated, "We do not believe that the space station . . . can be justified solely on the basis of the (nonbiological) science it can perform, much of which can be conducted on Earth or by unmanned robots." That conclusion is hardly surprising. Building a station with a price tag of nearly $100 billion to handle scientific experiments valued in only hundreds of millions of dollars is like insisting on a chauffeur-driven limousine to go to the corner store for milk.

If the political will to scrap the station cannot be mustered, a second-best option would be to

- sell the station off to private purchasers upon completion and
- allow the private sector to provide and pay for all future travel to and from the station as well as station operations, maintenance, and expansion.

The station will have to be sold at a loss, but at least taxpayers will not continue to lose money on its operation. Under nonsubsidized private management, a real market will develop for use of the station based on the actual costs for private launchers to transport payloads and technicians to the station. The prices for use of the station will change with real costs. Thus, for example, the price for space on the station may start low, but as launch costs come down, greater demand for space will cause its value and prices to rise. Most important, station policy will not be determined by politics or bureaucratic power.

A variation of that approach is suggested by Rick Tumlinson, president of the Space Frontier Foundation. While still involving government funding, his "Alpha Town" approach contains elements to help create markets in space. One element would be tax and regulatory exemptions for space enterprise. Another would force NASA to sell off rather than scrap unused assets. For example, each shuttle flies 98 percent of the way to orbit with an external fuel tank the size of a 17-story building. Once the nontoxic liquid oxygen and hydrogen from those tanks burn off, they are dropped into the ocean. If they were placed in orbit, they could be sealed and "homesteaded" by private owners who could use them as platforms for experiments, space hotels, or any other activity of which an entrepreneur could conceive. But NASA currently has no incentive to create competition for its own space station by placing the tanks in orbit for private use.

Those approaches to privatization are similar to the approach used to privatize assets in communist countries. Putting assets in private hands best guarantees their profitable use. Thus, future expansion of the station would only occur in response to market demands rather than bureaucratic dictates and would be paid for by customers, not taxpayers. If done right, such a privatization would help create a true private market for space services.

Sell Off the Space Shuttle

Without a space station to build, there will be little reason to keep the overpriced shuttle in operation.

The Clinton administration announced a "privatization" of the shuttle in 1995, but what it actually meant was that the operation of the shuttle would be contracted out to a single private company at some set rate per flight. United Space Alliance will operate the shuttle for a price still being negotiated but probably around $400 million per flight on the basis of seven flights per year.

But the American taxpayers still will foot the bill. Without a station to build, the shuttle could be allowed to fly any science missions already scheduled. But no new mission should be accepted by NASA.

If NASA continues with station construction, as much of the shuttle's operations as possible should be turned over to the private sector. Perhaps NASA could allow the private operator of the shuttle to sell launch services to customers. United Space Alliance could seek paying customers and could "rent" the shuttle from NASA for such a profit-making venture. Since United Space Alliance would have to put some of its own money at risk, it would have an incentive to reduce the real costs of a shuttle flight.

That approach or some variation of it might help ensure that the life spans of the shuttles were determined more by economic than by political considerations.

Other reforms have been discussed on Capitol Hill by those seeking to break NASA's exclusive power to decide which experiments will be flown into orbit on each flight in cargo space not needed for station-construction activities. The current arrangement gives NASA no incentive to increase shuttle efficiency. Some people suggest that funds be given directly to perspective users, scientists and other experimenters, in the form of vouchers for the purchase of launch services. Proponents of that approach believe it could create more marketlike demand for launch services, forcing the operator of the shuttle to compete for business. Many questions are raised by that approach; for example, would such vouchers become a kind of high-tech entitlement for scientists? But the suggestion does demonstrate the wide recognition that the current NASA shuttle cannot be expected to give way to an efficient private space transportation system.

Build Down Government Civilian Space Activities

Congress should take the following steps to build down government civilian space activities.

Bar NASA from Building and Operating Launch Vehicles and Require All Other Nondefense Launches and All Nonemergency Defense Launches to Be Purchased from the Private Sector

The market for private-sector launch services has been actively discouraged by NASA in the past. And today, instead of contracting for launch services, NASA still is addicted to purchasing expensive hardware while spending very small amounts on actual science. As part of a builddown of government involvement in civilian space activities, NASA and all other government agencies should be required to contract out for all launches.

The telecommunications revolution has pushed up demand for communications media. Satellites now cannot be launched fast enough to meet demands for World Wide Web use, direct digital television, and other uses. American firms such as Boeing and Lockheed have entered partnerships with Russian suppliers to provide launch services. The French company Arianespace continues to be a world leader in space transportation.

The Pentagon ought not be exempt from the push to privatize. The Defense Department clearly should continue to own and control intercontinental ballistic missiles that might need to be launched at a moment's notice. But many defense functions, such as remote sensing with satellites that require launch services, are planned years in advance. There is no reason why launches for such systems could not be secured from the private sector. Yet the Defense Department, continuing to protect its budget, currently is spending $2 billion to develop a new expendable launch vehicle.

Market conditions are ripe for competition to help create more private-sector launch alternatives, which will bring down prices and provide better service. The U.S. government should not be in competition with the private sector in the provision of those services any more than it should be competing in trucking or air travel. If the government does have legitimate cargos to place in orbit, it should go to private providers.

Require NASA to Accept Bids from Private Firms to Acquire Scientific Data

NASA's scientific activities involve not just launches but data collection. Far more valuable from a scientific perspective than the space station and the shuttle have been the planetary probes overseen by the Jet Propulsion Laboratory in California, which is under NASA but has considerable independence. And while costs are not as high as those for the shuttle or station, the process is still wasteful and politicized. For example, 60 percent of the support contracts that the JPL issues to the private sector are reserved for minority contractors.

Rather than build their own probes, even if they are carried into space by private launchers, JPL and other NASA or government agencies should allow scientists to purchase data from the private sector. What that means, in effect, is that, as part of the builddown of NASA, certain data would be offered for a price and private suppliers would devise the most cost-effective ways of acquiring those data to secure contracts.

That approach was considered for one of the toughest possible projects. In 1987–88 an interagency U.S. government working group considered the feasibility of offering a one-time prize and a promise to rent to any private group that could deliver a permanent manned Moon base. When asked if such a station was realistic, private-sector representatives answered "Yes!" but only if NASA stayed out of the way and did not force the private providers to use the shuttle or proposed station. Needless to say, that approach never saw the light of day.

Eliminate Mission to Planet Earth or Turn It Over to Other Government Agencies and Contract with Private Providers for All Data Services

NASA in recent years has seen environmental projects as potential cash cows. It has fought with other agencies—through its Mission to Planet Earth, a project to study Earth's ecology—for jurisdiction over satellites to monitor the environment. Typical of its tactics, in February 1992 it made screaming headlines with its announcement that a huge ozone hole could be in the process of opening over the Northern Hemisphere. In fine print the data were skimpy at best. Still, the agency got the politically correct headlines as its funding was being debated. There were few headlines months later when no ozone hole developed.

The mission itself is of questionable value. It seems aimed more at selectively acquiring data to push politically correct agendas than at collecting information that is urgently needed by policymakers but cannot be acquired by other, less costly means.

Even if the mission is not shut down, it does not belong in NASA's portfolio. Some other department should direct the project. Further, government agencies should not be in the business of launching remote-sensing satellites into space or owning those satellites. There are private-sector providers that could collect the desired data; those providers would submit bids to the agency wishing the information.

Conclusion

NASA administrator Daniel Goldin has struggled to bring greater efficiency to his agency and find innovative ways to overcome bureaucratic inertia. In some cases he has made improvements. But he is like the former Soviet Union's Mikhail Gorbachev, trying to save his failed system by introducing limited market reforms when what is needed is a real free market.

Those who believe that mankind has a future in space should think deeply and seriously about how to ease the government out of civilian space activities. Only by approaching this challenge with the same honesty and clarity of mind that were needed to put men on the Moon can a landing on Mars and other future goals be attained.

Suggested Readings

Crawford, Alan Pell. "An 'Industrial Policy' for Space?" Cato Institute Policy Analysis no. 69, April 25, 1986.

388

Gump, David P. *Space Enterprise: Beyond NASA.* New York: Praeger, 1990.

Hudgins, Edward. Testimony before the U.S. House of Representatives, Committee on Appropriations, Subcommittee on VA, HUD, and Independent Agencies, February 2, 1995.

Meyers, Gene. *ET-Solutions.* West Covina, Calif.: Space/Life Project, 1990.

Tumlinson, Rick N. "The First Human Town in Space: Alpha Town." *Space Front* (Winter 1996).

—Prepared by Edward L. Hudgins

38. Transportation

Congress should

- close the Department of Transportation;
- eliminate the federal gasoline tax;
- end all federal transportation subsidies and entrust states and municipalities with maintaining infrastructure such as highways, roads, bridges, and subways;
- repeal the Urban Mass Transit Act of 1964;
- repeal the Railway Labor Act of 1926;
- privatize Amtrak;
- privatize the air traffic control system;
- remove all federal regulations that prevent airports from being privately owned or operated;
- lift the ban that prevents foreign airlines from flying domestic routes in the United States; and
- repeal the Jones Act.

Praise be to the conscientious members of Congress who last year removed federal speed limits and replaced the antiquated Interstate Commerce Commission with the Surface Transportation Board. A clear step toward less regulation, the Interstate Commerce Commission Termination Act required that at least one member of the new three-member board have private-sector business experience, limited terms of board members to five years, and limited the STB's ability to impose artificial labor protection when new railroads are formed. The STB already has allowed the merger of Union Pacific and Southern Pacific—a move that the Justice Department, staffed by a slew of trustbusters and regulation enthusiasts, would have thwarted. The 105th Congress should follow those exemplary actions with complete deregulation that will enable the transportation sector to meet commuter needs in the 21st century.

Competition in domestic transportation has put money back into the pockets of American consumers and producers since the most restrictive regulations were abolished in the 1970s and 1980s. The General Accounting Office reported in 1996 that the average airfare per passenger-mile had decreased 10 percent since deregulation. According to Clifford Winston and Steven Morrison of the Brookings Institution, deregulation has led to airfares 22 percent lower than they would have been had regulation continued. Other estimates of the savings are much higher. Deregulation of the trucking and railroad industries has achieved similar results—the combination of lower freight rates and reduced inventories has saved, by some estimates, as much as $100 billion annually. Deregulation has led to the opening of hundreds of innovative short-line railroads—most of them nonunion in an industry that was historically almost 100 percent unionized. Deregulation also has allowed open entry to the trucking business, which has resulted in thousands of start-up, nonunion, motor carrier companies that have broken the labor monopoly of the Teamsters Union. At the same time, the quantity and quality of transportation services have increased and accident rates have declined.

Despite deregulation's high returns, the government continues to meddle with transportation—shipping and urban mass transit, in particular, are both heavily subsidized and regulated at the federal level. While complete deregulation is a commendable goal, this chapter addresses only the most costly and inefficient regulations. Ultimately, however, Congress should completely deregulate transportation and return control to the private sector.

Infrastructure, Mass Transit, and Gasoline Taxes

The Department of Transportation should be abolished and public roads, national highways, and urban mass transit systems returned to the states and to the private sector. Whatever justification there may once have been for a national transportation department has disappeared; the goal of creating a national rail and road network was met long ago. Taxpayers currently send $14 billion a year to the DOT only to have their money returned with strings attached. People around the country should not have to send their money to Washington before it can be spent to construct local roads.

The Urban Mass Transit Act of 1964 should be repealed—its swamp of requirements fails to keep pace with urban change, preventing the efficient operation of urban mass transit systems. When the act was adopted, most commuters traveled from suburbs to cities; now, however, most trips are intrasuburban. Despite the shift in commuting patterns, the outdated transit act provides incentives to local governments to build urban rail and subway systems by providing up to 75 percent of construction funds, even though many cities need funds for suburban systems such as buses and car pool lanes. By subsidizing one form of transportation—in this case, the least needed and most inefficient form—the government encourages financially strapped localities to opt for subsidized systems despite their inability to meet commuter needs.

Safety and Savings: The Benefits of Deregulation

- Safer airways: Since deregulation in 1978, airline accidents have declined more than 50 percent.
- Safer roads: Airline deregulation has increased air travel 11.4 percent and reduced car travel 3.9 percent, resulting in 600,000 fewer automobile accidents annually.
- Passenger savings: Increased availability of airline flights has saved airline passengers $10.3 billion per year.
- Consumer savings: Deregulation of the trucking and railroad industries has saved as much as $100 billion annually. That represents $380 in savings for every person in America—an effective increase in disposable income of $1,500 for a family of four.

Section 13(c) of the Urban Mass Transit Act is particularly costly. To receive federal funding for local projects, local transit authorities must show that no transit workers will be adversely affected by the proposal; otherwise, the measure will not be implemented. Thus, proposals for improved efficiency, which often include recommendations for downsizing the workforce or cutting costs, are frequently thwarted in favor of protecting a costly but "job-saving" status quo.

In conjunction with abolishing the DOT and repealing the Urban Mass Transit Act, Congress should return the transportation tax base to the states by abolishing the federal gasoline tax—a primary source of funds for federally subsidized infrastructure projects. When states are allowed to assess and fund their own infrastructure needs, they will be able to select the transportation systems that best meet local demands and reintroduce gasoline taxes where appropriate.

Railroads

By loosening federal control of rail prices and services, the Staggers Rail Act of 1980 reduced real prices for most rail services 50 percent. The Railway Labor Act, however, continues to impede the development of high-quality, efficient rail service. The railroads have the most unionized workforce in the United States—union dues are compulsory and average wages for rail workers are in the top 1 percent of wages nationwide. The RLA effectively doubles labor costs and drives up freight rates 20 to 25 percent. In addition, rail unions are the only unions in the country that can use secondary boycotts to paralyze enterprises that are not direct parties to a labor dispute. The RLA should be repealed and labor issues resolved under the National Labor Relations Act, which regulates labor relations in the private sector.

For over 25 years Amtrak, the government's passenger rail service, has operated in the red at the expense of American taxpayers. Although its services are neither essential for social equity nor a result of market failures, nearly 40 percent of Amtrak's costs are taxpayer subsidized. In 1995 American taxpayers paid some $1 billion in taxes to cover Amtrak's operating cost—half of which is consumed by salaries and benefits for its overpaid employees. Amtrak's notoriously poor customer service, predictable tardiness, and clattery old coaches have caused it to lose its only legitimate source of funding—passengers. Since 1990 Amtrak has been losing passengers at a rate of 3 percent per year. Even Amtrak spokesman Clifford Black has said privatization is a good idea, "provided we're permitted to wean ourselves off of operating subsidies." Congress should give Amtrak a brief restructuring period and immediate regulatory relief, after which all subsidies should be terminated and the government's shares sold.

Air Travel

The competition unleashed by the Air Cargo Deregulation Act of 1977 and the Airline Deregulation Act of 1978 has led to substantially lower fares, better passenger service, and more flight options; yet the public has not been afforded the full benefits of complete deregulation. The federal government still owns, manages, or regulates the air traffic control system, airport facilities, and foreign carriers' access to U.S. routes.

The Federal Aviation Administration owns and operates the air traffic control system (ATC)—a high-tech operation that must operate reliably

24 hours a day, 365 days a year. The present ATC has proven consistently that it is not capable of keeping pace with the rapid advancements brought about by deregulation. First, civil service constraints bar the FAA from attracting and keeping the most experienced controllers. Second, ATC equipment is outdated and unreliable even though better equipment and technology have been available for years. According to the DOT, those systemic weaknesses result in flight delays that cost airlines and travelers $5 billion a year.

What is even less tolerable than the economic waste are the fatal airline accidents that have resulted from the ATC's ineptitude: a number of fatal collisions, including ground collisions at Detroit Metro and Los Angeles International airports, were caused by the ATC's malfunctioning ground radar system. The ATC must be freed from the bureaucratic constraints that make it both inefficient and dangerous. Privatizing the ATC would allow airlines to benefit from improved equipment thus enabling them to meet flight schedules (the majority of airline delays are due to ATC problems, not aircraft problems). The American public would benefit from improved arrival and departure times, as well as the increased safety that would result from better tracking and routing of planes.

A majority of airports are owned by local governments and operated by local administrators. Airport administrators are required to ration gate use to carriers according to strict federal regulations. If airports were privately owned, access to gates and flight frequency could be determined by market forces, which would result in a more efficient allocation of terminals and gates. For example, higher rates could be charged during rush hours and lower rates could be charged during lower use times. At the very least, if the government continues to own and operate airports, rights to gates should be auctioned off. That should only be an intermediate solution, however; the best solution would be to privatize the airports.

Congress should also lift the ban that prevents foreign airlines from flying domestic routes in the United States. Many foreign airlines have achieved a level of safety and service exceeding that of U.S. carriers, and the U.S. traveler should be afforded this option. Like domestic deregulation, enabling foreign airlines to compete with domestic airlines will lower prices, improve safety, and increase the quantity and quality of airline services.

Shipping

A hodgepodge of conflicting policies—subsidization, protectionism, regulation, and taxation—unnecessarily burdens the U.S.-flag fleet, forces

U.S. customers to pay inflated prices, and curbs domestic and international trade. The 1995 fiscal budget obligated $503 million for cargo preference programs alone. That figure excluded administrative costs, overhead, and an additional $214 million set aside for the Operating Differential Subsidy. And the passage of the Maritime Security Act of 1996 extended those subsidies for another 10 years. The list of rules and regulations governing shipping is too exhaustive to catalogue here, but one thing is clear: shipping policies must be thoroughly reviewed and revamped. Congress should pay particular attention to deregulation of ocean shipping and other trade- and consumer-oriented reforms.

In particular, the 105th Congress should repeal the Jones Act (section 27 of the Merchant Marine Act of 1920). The Jones Act prohibits shipping merchandise between U.S. ports "in any other vessel than a vessel built in and documented under the laws of the United States and owned by persons who are citizens of the United States." The act essentially bars foreign shipping companies from competing with American companies. A 1993 International Trade Commission study showed that the loss of economic welfare attributable to America's cabotage (the exclusive right of a country to operate traffic within its territory) amounts to $3.1 billion per year.

Because the Jones Act inflates prices, many businesses are encouraged to import goods rather than buy domestic products. For those reasons, Sen. Jesse Helms (R-N.C.) introduced legislation that would open domestic shipping to foreign-flag vessels. Helms called the Jones Act "a harmful anachronism that enables a few waterborne carriers to cling to a monopoly on shipping." He noted that the Jones Act has forced many North Carolina pork and poultry farmers to import grain from Canada rather than the Midwest, because certified shipping vessels are unavailable and rail is an inefficient alternative.

The primary argument made in support of the Jones Act is that we need an all-American fleet on which to call in time of war. But during the Persian Gulf War, only 6 older vessels of the 460 that shipped military supplies came from America's subsidized merchant fleet. Rob Quartel, then a commissioner at the Federal Maritime Commission, wrote, "In short, the success of the military sealift—a brilliant feat of logistics— occurred despite [rather than because of] 75 years of government subsidies, protectionism, regulation, and energy and management controls." Since the Jones Act requires American sailors to staff domestic vessels, it also has significant support from organized labor.

The Top Nine Costs of Transportation Regulation

- Mass transit operating costs have increased at five times the rate at which they did before federal subsidies, while costs in the private bus industry have declined.
- Taxpayers currently send $14 billion a year to the DOT.
- Time lost because of traffic congestion costs commuters $100 billion annually.
- Since 1964 inefficient, taxpayer-subsidized transit projects have cost taxpayers $43 billion.
- Labor restrictions stemming from the Railway Labor Act cost railroads and shippers $4 billion annually.
- In 1995 American taxpayers paid some $1 billion in taxes to cover Amtrak's operation cost—half of which is consumed by salaries and benefits for overpaid employees.
- Airline delays cost travelers $5 billion per year.
- The Jones Act costs America $3.1 billion per year.
- Taxpayers pay $100,000 annually to protect each U.S. seaman's job.

Repealing the Jones Act would allow the domestic maritime industry to be more competitive and would enable U.S. producers to take advantage of lower prices resulting from competition among domestic and foreign suppliers. Ships used in domestic commerce could be built in one country, manned by another, and flagged by still another. That would result in decreased shipping costs, with savings passed on to U.S. consumers and the U.S. shipping industry. The price of shipping services now restricted by the act would decline by an estimated 25 percent.

Suggested Readings

Cox, Wendell, and Jean Love. "False Dreams and Broken Promises: The Wasteful Federal Investment in Urban Mass Transit." Cato Institute Policy Analysis no. 162, October 17, 1991.

———. "Reclaiming Transit for the Riders and Taxpayers." In *How Privatization Can Solve America's Infrastructure Crisis*. Edited by Edward L. Hudgins and Ronald D. Utt. Washington: Heritage Foundation, 1992.

Ferguson, Allen R. "Reform of Maritime Policy: Building Blocks of an Integrated Program." *Regulation* 17, no. 2 (1994): 28–36.

General Accounting Office. "Airline Deregulation: Changes in Airfares, Service, and Safety at Small, Medium-Sized, and Large Communities." Chapter Report GAO/RCED-96-79, April 1996.

Love, Jean, Wendell Cox, and Stephen Moore. "Amtrak at Twenty-five: End of the Line for Taxpayer Subsidies." Cato Institute Policy Analysis no. 266, December 19, 1996.

Moore, Stephen, and Dean Stansel. "Ending Corporate Welfare As We Know It." Cato Institute Policy Analysis no. 225, May 12, 1995.

Morrison, Steven A., and Clifford Winston. *The Evolution of the Airline Industry.* Washington: Brookings Institution, 1995.

Poole, Robert W. "Privatizing Essential Services." In *Market Liberalism: A Paradigm for the 21st Century.* Edited by David Boaz and Edward H. Crane. Washington: Cato Institute, 1993.

Quartel, Rob. "America's Welfare Queen Fleet: The Need for Maritime Policy Reform." *Regulation* 14, no. 3 (1991): 58–67.

Reynolds, Morgan O., and D. Eric Schansberg. "At Age 65, Retire the Railway Labor Act." *Regulation* 14, no. 3 (1991): 85–90.

—Prepared by Darcy Ann Olsen and Edward L. Hudgins

39. Antitrust

Congress should

- repeal the Sherman Antitrust Act of 1890, especially section 2, and eliminate the Federal Trade Commission's power to act against ill-defined "unfair competition";
- repeal the Clayton Act of 1914, especially sections 2 and 7; and
- repeal the Robinson-Patman Act of 1936.

Antitrust as Anti–Free Market

Antitrust laws allow the federal government to regulate and curtail basic business activities, including pricing, production, product lines, and mergers, usually in the name of preventing monopolies and fostering competition. The irony is that the laws in fact impose arbitrary government limitations on competition, keep prices for consumers high, and weaken American industries. Massachusetts Institute of Technology economist Lester Thurow wrote in his 1980 book *The Zero-Sum Society* that "the time has come to recognize that the antitrust approach has been a failure. The costs it imposes far exceed any benefits it brings."

American industries, in today's more integrated global economy with low trade barriers, do not lack competition. Imports, which were valued at 3.9 percent of America's gross domestic product in 1970, are 9.6 percent today. Exports were 4.1 percent of GDP in that year and are currently 7.2 percent. That new situation makes the rationale for antitrust laws even more absurd than in the past.

A recent example of the potential abuses of antitrust laws was the threat by Anne Bingaman of the Clinton administration's Justice Department to stop the August 1995 release of Microsoft Corporation's Windows95 operating program for personal computers. Microsoft was also planning to run its own online Microsoft Network (MSN) Internet access service. To make it easier and more tempting for Windows users to subscribe to MSN, whenever a machine using Windows95 was switched on, an icon that would allow subscribers to connect with MSN with a single click of the mouse would appear on a computer's desktop screen.

Bingaman believed that that would give Microsoft's MSN an unfair advantage over other online services such as America Online, Compuserve, and Prodigy—in spite of the fact that the alleged unfair monopolistic competitor, MSN, literally did not exist at the time Bingaman was threatening to stop Windows95. Further, the supposed Microsoft "advantage" consisted of the fact that it would take two clicks of the mouse for users of Windows to sign on to competing online services. And in any case, with three or four clicks of the mouse, a Windows95 user could put an icon for a competing online service onto the desktop menu with the MSN icon.

Fortunately, the Clinton administration did not act against Microsoft in that case, though it has harassed Microsoft in other ways. But that kind of silly second-guessing of the markets has characterized the history of antitrust laws.

Antitrust laws are always enforced arbitrarily and sometimes capriciously, violating the due process of law and relying on ex post facto rulings.

A fundamental principle of Anglo-American law is that crimes must be clearly defined. But with antitrust the definitions are vague and constantly changing, depending on the whims of regulators and policymakers. Businesses rarely know in advance which practices may constitute price discrimination or "predatory" pricing or may "substantially lessen competition" in the eyes of the antitrust enforcers. As Alan Greenspan once observed, antitrust

> is a world in which competition is lauded as the basic axiom and guiding principle, yet "too much" competition is condemned as "cutthroat." . . .
> It is a world in which the law is so vague that businessmen have no way of knowing whether specific actions will be declared illegal until they hear the judge's verdict—after the fact.

Consequently, businesses do not compete and serve consumers as vigorously as they otherwise would, for fear of running afoul of new and creative interpretations of what constitutes an illegal business practice.

There can never be a precise definition of "competition," for competition, as a dynamic process, constantly leads to the discovery of new techniques for competing. The criteria the government has used in the past to try to define competition—size of firms, prices that are "too high" or "too low," closeness of substitute products, and the like—are all meaningless and arbitrary.

Antitrust laws are anachronisms whose time may never have come and is certainly gone today. Congress thus should do three things.

Repeal the Sherman Antitrust Act of 1890, Especially Section 2, and Eliminate the Federal Trade Commission's Power to Act against Ill-Defined "Unfair Competition"

The first federal antitrust law—the Sherman Act of 1890—is usually portrayed as a law that was necessary to prevent large enterprises or industries from restricting competition by cutting output and driving up prices. Section 1 prohibited "every contract, . . . combination, or conspiracy in restraint of trade," while section 2 made "monopolization" illegal. The Federal Trade Commission Act of 1914 gave the newly created FTC general powers to act against "unfair competition."

But at the time of the passage of the Sherman Act, the economics profession almost unanimously considered the act inherently incompatible with rivalrous competition. Having observed the merger movement of the late 1880s, economists "rejected the idea that competition was declining," notes historian Sanford D. Gordon, who surveyed economists' attitudes toward the late 19th-century trusts.

Monopolies supposedly restrict output and raise prices. But the trusts that were accused of monopolizing their industries in the late 1880s had been, in fact, increasing their output several times faster than the overall economy had been growing during the decade preceding the passage of the Sherman Act. Also, during that deflationary period, those industries had been dropping their prices faster than the general price level had been dropping. That behavior is contrary to any definition of monopoly.

Members of Congress at that time clearly recognized those facts, but they wanted to pass a law that would protect less efficient and higher priced businesses. "Trusts have made products cheaper, have reduced prices," complained Rep. William Mason during the House debates over the Sherman Act. Low prices, he said, "would not right the wrong done to the people of this country by the 'trusts' which have destroyed legitimate competition and driven honest men from legitimate business enterprises."

That curious opposition to low prices needs to be understood in the context of the trade debate occurring at the time. Without protectionism, trusts were reducing prices and driving out less efficient producers. The Sherman Act was passed as a smoke screen for the real cause of monopoly in the late 19th century: tariffs. Sen. John Sherman (R-Ohio) himself sponsored the 1890 McKinley tariff, passed just three months after the Sherman Act. "That so-called Anti-Trust law," the *New York Times* wrote on October 1, 1890, "was passed to deceive the people and to clear the way for the enactment of this ... law relating to the tariff." Senator Sherman attacked trusts because they "subverted the tariff system; they undermined the policy of government to protect American industries by levying duties on imported goods."

Protectionists did not want prices paid by consumers to fall. But they also understood that to gain political support for high tariffs they would have to assure the public that industries would not combine to increase prices to politically prohibitive levels. Support for both an antitrust law and tariff hikes would maintain high prices while avoiding the more obvious bilking of consumers.

Repeal the Clayton Act of 1914, Especially Section 7

The Clayton Act of 1914 restricted mergers between companies, but its result was to restrict price competition.

At a time when most industries face international competition or the threat of it, it is foolish and destructive to have laws, such as section 7 of the Clayton Act, that regulate mergers. Mergers usually occur because business partners believe the merger will create synergy—the value of the two companies combined will be greater than their individual values, which is to say that together they will serve consumers better. Mergers or takeovers are sometimes motivated by the belief on the part of the acquiring firm that the "target" firm is being poorly managed and that new management can improve efficiency and profitability. Such mergers facilitate the flow of productive assets into the hands of more efficient managers. Some mergers are simply alternatives to bankruptcy.

University of Chicago economist Yale Brozen concluded in his treatise *Concentration, Mergers, and Public Policy* that the regulation of mergers has "restrained output and the growth of productivity" and is "contributing to the deterioration of the competitive position of the United States" in international markets. That is a particularly telling point in light of the fact that Japan not only does not restrict mergers but actively encourages them, recognizing their importance to productivity and competitiveness. Under the Japanese *Keiretsu* system, literally hundreds of firms sometimes merge (often vertically) to form "export trading companies" that successfully compete in international markets. U.S. policy could encourage greater competitiveness by scrapping section 7 of the Clayton Act and all other laws that restrict mergers.

Repeal the Robinson-Patman Act of 1936

The Robinson-Patman Act, along with section 2 of the Clayton Act, effectively outlaws price cutting by permitting price discrimination (charging different prices in different markets) only if it can be justified by differential costs of serving different markets, or if a price reduction is made "in good faith" to meet the price reduction of a competitor. Any business that initiates vigorous price competition runs the risk of being sued for having not waited for a rival to cut its prices first and then met the price cut "in good faith."

In any case, economists and courts simply do not have the technical expertise to determine whether or not price differentials are justified by cost differences, given the difficulties inherent in cost accounting. And in most instances, firms prosecuted for price discrimination have been forced to raise their prices.

Conclusion

Economies go through cycles of business mergers and divestitures. Public opinion goes through cycles of concern that enterprises are too large and concentrated or too small and weak, unable to meet challenges from large foreign competitors. But the largest companies of yesterday, such as integrated steel producers, have been replaced at the top of the industrial ladder by the Microsofts of today. In the future, no doubt other industries and enterprises will rise to the top. The only danger from monopolies is from those created or fostered by the government, such as the monopoly on most mail delivery.

Antitrust laws that allow the federal government to second-guess markets and hold up or prohibit sound business practices have no valid place in a market economy. Congress can help ensure that America businesses will be able to adjust to changing market conditions by eliminating those laws.

Suggested Readings

Armentano, Dominick. *Antitrust and Monopoly: Anatomy of a Policy Failure.* New York: Wiley, 1982.

Brozen, Yale. *Concentration, Mergers, and Public Policy.* New York: Macmillan, 1982.

DiLorenzo, Thomas J. "The Origins of Antitrust: An Interest-Group Perspective." *International Review of Law and Economics* 5 (June 1985).

Greenspan, Alan. "Antitrust." In *Capitalism: The Unknown Ideal.* Edited by Ayn Rand. New York: Signet, 1966.

—Prepared by Thomas J. DiLorenzo

ENERGY AND ENVIRONMENT

40. Electricity Deregulation

Congress should

- repeal the Federal Power Act of 1935 and abolish the Federal Energy Regulatory Commission (FERC);
- repeal the 1935 Public Utility Holding Company Act (PUHCA) and the 1978 Public Utility Regulatory Policy Act (PURPA);
- privatize federal power marketing authorities, the Tennessee Valley Authority, and all federal power generation facilities;
- eliminate all tax preferences afforded municipal power companies and electricity cooperatives;
- eliminate all federal price subsidies, tax incentives, and regulatory preferences for renewable energy;
- declare that any state or municipal regulation of the generation, transmission, distribution, or retail sale of electricity sold across state lines interferes with interstate trade and is a violation of the U.S. Constitution's commerce clause; and
- require open, nondiscriminatory access to all federal public rights-of-way for electricity transmission and distribution services, except when such services present a public safety hazard.

The Dynamic of Deregulation

The rollback of regulations protecting "monopolistic industries" from competition has been one of the main legislative stories of the past 20 years. The trucking, railroad, airline, bus, banking, natural gas, and telecommunications industries have all been—to one degree or another—introduced to the world of economic competition. And now, after several years of regulatory skirmishes, interest-group posturing, political calculation, think-tank pontificating, and academic *Sturm und Drang*, the $200 billion electricity industry awaits its turn as the last great industry to receive federal regulatory parole.

The potential gains are great. A study by economists Michael Maloney and Robert McCormick of Clemson University estimates that freeing electricity markets would probably cut electricity prices by 25 percent or more, a substantial savings not only for residential electricity consumers but for consumers of products that require a great deal of energy to produce. Moreover, the electricity business is increasingly international in scope, and a lean, competitive American power industry would be better positioned in the global marketplace than the regulated, straightjacketed industry of today.

Before the 105th Congress begins to hammer out the interest-group compromises that typically constitute "deregulation," it would be wise to profit from the political and economic lessons of the past 20 years. To wit,

- Trusting the regulators to redesign the regulatory apparatus will probably perpetuate past regulatory errors and sabotage competition.
- "Deregulation" often serves as legislative cover under which new political coalitions seize regulatory control of an industry once it becomes clear that the old coalition of special interests can no longer sustain itself.
- Efficient market structures cannot be ascertained a priori by legislators or bureaucrats; only by letting markets spontaneously develop can we know the "best" industrial arrangements.

Unfortunately, the early debate over whether and how Congress should deregulate the electricity industry has been almost completely uninformed by the above observations. Most of the industry's would-be reformers seek to impose *their* vision of how the industry ought to be organized; delegate much if not most of the detail work of deregulation to federal and state regulators; and continue exercising political control over the transmission, distribution, and sale of electricity.

Managed Competition: Bad for Health Care, Good for Electricity?

The traditional argument for economic regulation of the electric utility industry is that it is a natural monopoly. Yet virtually all economists now agree that the generation of electricity is no longer characterized by sufficient economies of scale to warrant monopoly regulation. Thus, many economists are also convinced that the retail sale of electricity is sufficiently competitive to justify the end of protected service territories for electric utilities. While some continue to extol the virtues of monopoly regulation and the status quo, overwhelming evidence exists that consumers are paying far more for electricity than is necessary and that monopoly regulation is the reason.

The remedy for this situation is commonly believed to be mandatory retail wheeling, which means requiring electric utilities to turn their private transmission and distribution systems into public highways. An electricity consumer would have the right to choose the company from which he would like to purchase power, and the utility company would be required to deliver that electricity to the consumer at regulated, nondiscriminatory rates.

The current debate surrounding electric utility reform presupposes mandatory retail wheeling and concentrates on the economic, social, and political consequences of wheeling. How much of the current social and environmental regulatory regime surrounding electricity service should survive? What should the timetable be for transition? Do new environmental controls need to be imposed to counterbalance increased emissions that generating lower priced electricity might cause? How much leeway should states have to oversee electricity competition? Should the economic losses many utilities will undoubtedly experience due to uncompetitive facilities and uneconomic third-party power contracts ("stranded costs") be compensated by ratepayers, and if so, how?

In sum, managed competition—retail competition under the continuing watchful eye of regulators and a tightened regulatory grip on the grid— is the starting point for both reformers and their opponents. Congress can and should do better.

Free the Wires

Mandatory retail wheeling is the popular foundation of reform because few regulators or political decisionmakers believe that alternative transmission and distribution grids would arise to challenge today's interconnected grid. Consequently, absent regulation, it is feared that utilities would either close their transmission or distribution lines to competitors or use their monopoly status to "gouge" both independent generators and consumers. Yet there is little cause for such handwringing. Those sorts of arguments, which were marshaled energetically before and during the debates about restructuring trucking, airlines, natural gas, and railroads, have been proven wrong. Consequently, they should be met with skepticism today. Mandatory retail wheeling is *not* necessary for retail competition.

First, the possible emergence of alternative grids is not at all far-fetched. Investigations by economists have found little evidence of electricity businesses ever having "naturally" achieved monopoly status before the advent of public utility commissions, which implies that the "monopoly" grid is more an artificial product of regulation than of economic efficiency or market inevitability. In fact, the two main characteristics of natural monopolies—high fixed costs and economies of scale—are largely absent in modern utilities, which suggests that the grid is vulnerable to competition. Interestingly, the few communities that already have a choice of electricity providers—each with its own separate grid—pay rates below regional averages.

The concern that local zoning and land-use regulations would block the construction of alternative grids ignores the fact that multiple "rights-of-way" (telephone and cable lines, natural gas pipelines, and sewage lines, for example) already connect both retail and commercial establishments to outside service providers. Those providers could conceivably piggyback power lines on their current rights-of-way and directly enter the electricity distribution business with a minimum of local disruption. Alternatively, power lines could be buried. While more costly, buried lines haven't led to substantially higher rates in town such as Lubbock, Texas, where some degree of limited competition exists. Finally, the power of eminent domain allows states to address local intransigence to grid expansions if absolutely necessary.

Yet alternative grids are not necessary prerequisites to competition. First, electric utilities already "compete" with other utility companies (who threaten to lure away industrial consumers and thus, ultimately, residential consumers), self-generation (an option that is gaining popularity with industrial consumers and is increasingly affordable even for homeowners), and energy-efficient technologies (which become more attractive as rates rise). The demand for electricity is not inelastic. In fact, the dynamic of competition already present in the industry is chiefly responsible for the collapse of the regulatory status quo.

Second, deregulation of transmission and distribution might well lead, not to alternative grids, but to user-owned grids. Consumers, after all, would have an incentive to protect themselves against rate gouging, while electric utilities—faced with well-positioned competitors in a newly freed market—would have an incentive to sell grid rights in order to stabilize their customer base and raise capital. Jointly owned transmission and distribution lines are already common in the electricity business and numerous other businesses. Taxi dispatch services, natural gas pipelines, and large freight vessels, for instance, turn to user-owned arrangements as a market response where significant economies of scale exist.

Third, the electricity transmission and distribution network affords many paths around any bottlenecks that a monopolist might seek to exploit. As long as entry is not blocked, expansions or loops can be readily constructed and tied into the grid. Given the interconnectedness of the grid, no monopolist could survive under a system of transmission and distribution property rights.

Finally, the mere threat of—or potential for—competition is enough to force incumbent monopolies to act as if they were in competitive markets. As economist William Baumol and others have pointed out, as long as markets are contestable, monopolists typically act to deter entry by providing services at market rates and have little opportunity to extract monopoly profits should they behave otherwise. The relevant concern is not whether competitors do or do not exist in a given market. The real concern is whether entry to the market is open or closed. As long as entry is possible, there is little to fear from aspiring monopolists.

The most important reason, however, to discount the fear of price gouging on the grid is the inability of rate regulation——the remedy presupposed by mandatory retail wheeling—to make any difference in the price of services delivered to the consumer. As University of Chicago professor and federal judge Richard Posner observes, ''Relatively moderate errors, of the kind that regulatory agencies can scarcely avoid committing given the intractable problems involved in the computation of revenue requirements, can render profit regulation quite ineffectual.'' Empirical studies by such noted economists as Thomas Gale Moore, Walter Mead, and the late Nobel laureate George Stigler demonstrate the empirical truth of that observation. They and others have found that rate regulators are incapable of forcing utilities to operate at a specified combination of output, price, and cost. Thus, they are unable to control rates. The price an electric utility monopolist would charge for power absent governmental oversight is, according to their empirical studies, the *current* price (at least, for today's set of services).

The Dangers of Retail Wheeling

Turning the grid into a common carrier while regulating the rates charged to third parties is the central mistake of the present reform agenda, not only because such regulation is unnecessary for competition to emerge, but because it may sabotage economic gains that are otherwise within our grasp.

Retail wheeling presupposes the efficiency of the present ownership and operational structure of the transmission and distribution business: monopoly, preferably regulated. Yet the electricity industry has been subjected to so many decades of government planning, subsidy, and distortions that reformers are in no position to say with certainty what an efficient transmission and distribution system would look like. Would an efficient industry be better off with vertical disintegration, user-owned grids, competing grids, a small number of (relatively unregulated) monopoly providers, a pooling company arrangement (known in the trade as "poolco"), or more widespread self-generation? No one can possibly know for certain absent the discovery process unleashed by the spontaneous workings of the market.

Mandatory retail wheeling subverts the market order by discouraging (and in some plans, absolutely prohibiting) alternatives to the heavily regulated monopoly system. Compulsory access to the grid would lessen the incentives for third parties to form alternative networks or various user-owned arrangements. The market experiments necessary to discover more efficient institutional arrangements for the grid will proceed far slower and more haltingly under a regime of mandatory retail wheeling.

Moreover, mandatory retail wheeling threatens another round of stranded cost recovery at ratepayers' expense. Once more efficient arrangements are discovered by the market (as they inevitably will be, albeit at a slower pace under mandatory retail wheeling), consumers will leave the monopoly grid for those more efficient (hence, less costly) transmission and distribution arrangements. Utilities will again, with some justification, claim that they made certain investments in the grid either because utility commissions explicitly ordered them to do so or only because they were guaranteed cost recovery by the government. Consumers then might well be forced into a *second* multi-billion-dollar bailout of the electricity industry, but this time of stranded grid assets as opposed to today's bailout of stranded generating capacity.

The allocation of transmission and distribution resources under retail wheeling will be made, not on the basis of highest expected value of service (the standard by which most business decisions are made), but on the basis of nondiscriminatory access. Access is based on legal and political formulations without consideration of economic efficiency.

410

Retail wheeling, then, will inevitably weaken the economic vitality of the grid. Moreover, by definition, it significantly weakens grid ownership rights and brings us dangerously close to de facto government ownership of transmission and distribution with all the problems attendant to such socialist enterprises.

In essence, mandatory retail wheeling transforms a privately owned and operated (albeit heavily regulated) electricity roadway into a public highway. Under a strict reading of the Fifth Amendment to the Constitution, it's hard to ignore that mandatory retail wheeling amounts to a "taking" of private property for a public purpose—expedited competition. The cost of that taking must also be considered by reformers. Either the public will be forced to compensate utilities for their lost property rights (which might well amount to billions of dollars), or they will fail to compensate utilities, in which case the "cost" of retail wheeling will be borne by all property owners who will experience a marginal erosion of the protections against governmental power.

Finally, the expansion of micromanagerial regulation of the grid that mandatory retail wheeling requires threatens to offset whatever deregulatory gains are obtained through retail consumer choice. That is because utility regulators and their constituents will undoubtedly be tempted to capture some (or perhaps all) of the surplus wealth generated by lower retail prices. As Benjamin Zycher of the Milken Institute has pointed out, "The universal characteristic of regulation, regardless of industry, time, or place, is a redistribution of wealth from political losers to those favored by regulators and politicians." Allowing regulators to keep their seats at the industry table (albeit in a slightly different seating arrangement) might simply mean that any larger economic "feast" cooked up by retail wheeling would be offset by the growing appetite of one of the least desirable dinner guests.

Up from Ira Magaziner!

Since rate regulation is incapable of controlling rates—and since electricity transmission and distribution are probably not natural monopolies anyway—true reform should be directed, not at reinventing regulation, but at actually eliminating it; not at managing competition, but at freeing it from political control.

The Federal Power Act should be repealed and FERC abolished. FERC's main remaining responsibility is to oversee the regulation of interstate electricity commerce, an oversight role that has proven counterproductive and unnecessary. (FERC's other main responsibility—the regulation of interstate oil pipelines and gas markets—is even less necessary.)

PURPA should be repealed. Its main function is to force utilities to purchase power from third parties at avoided cost (as calculated by state public utility commissions), an unnecessary requirement that has done much to saddle utilities with uneconomic power contracts and consumers with excessive electricity rates.

Likewise, the archaic PUHCA should be repealed. By strictly controlling the ownership and management structures of electric utilities, PUHCA has crippled the industry by preventing market entry, prohibiting industry reorganization, and discouraging market discovery of new, more efficient ways of delivering electricity to consumers.

Congress should also ensure a level economic playing field by privatizing the federal power marketing authorities, the Tennessee Valley Authority, and all federal power generation facilities; and tax and fiscal preferences afforded municipal power companies and electricity cooperatives should be terminated. As Chapter 13 shows, public power generation facilities are in deteriorating condition and would be better off—as are all enterprises—were they owned by private businesses that should not be required to compete with their own government for customers. Subsidizing consumer power damages the economy and harms the environment. Similarly, tax and fiscal preferences afforded municipal power companies and rural electricity cooperatives presume that certain management and ownership structures should be encouraged at the expense of others. That bias against private, investor-owned businesses is inappropriate in a free-market economy and without any empirical merit.

All federal price subsidies, tax incentives, and regulatory preferences for renewable energy should also be eliminated. First of all, the environmental benefits of renewable energy are dramatically overstated. In fact, every single renewable energy source has drawn legitimate opposition from environmental organizations on various counts. Second, fossil fuel is far less expensive than renewable energy because it is both more abundant and less costly to deliver to consumers. If and when fossil fuels become more scarce, the electricity industry will turn to more abundant (i.e., cheaper) alternatives without prompting from government. Third, the price disparity between fossil and renewable fuels simply cannot be attributed to present or past subsidies. According to the Department of Energy's Energy Information Administration, federal subsidies account for only 4 percent of the total energy economy. Finally, renewable energy subsidies and preferences are one of the main reasons that electricity rates are far higher than they should be.

Yet the most damaging electricity regulations emanate from state public utility commissions, not FERC or Congress. Those bodies must be reined in by Congress in order for the full benefits of deregulation to be realized.

While many legislators are (rightly) reluctant to interfere in state regulatory affairs, the Constitution's celebrated commerce clause gives Congress the power to remove barriers to interstate trade erected by state lawmakers. Congress should therefore preempt all state or municipal regulations that control the generation, transmission, distribution, or retail sale of electricity sold across state lines. States would retain the right they have under the Tenth Amendment to regulate purely *intrastate* trade but would find that the interstate nature of electricity service would render such intervention rather ineffectual.

Conservatives predisposed to respect states' rights should recognize that states have no right to erect barriers to interstate commerce, which only serve to inflate electricity rates, limit consumer sovereignty, and damage the vitality of the nation's economy. Congress would be shirking its duty if it allowed such economic violence to continue indefinitely.

Finally, nondiscriminatory access to all federal rights-of-way should be provided for electricity transmission and distribution services, except when such services present a public safety hazard. Such a move would mitigate any efforts of those who might seek to block competitive transmission and distribution markets, and it would provide a revenue stream to the federal government, which might help to balance the budget.

Recipes for "Half a Loaf"

Given the ambitious nature of the reforms recommended in this chapter, it might be that the 105th Congress is reluctant to take such bold deregulatory steps. While one certainly wouldn't want the "best" to become the enemy of the "better," it is questionable whether mandatory retail wheeling—particularly as it is currently evolving—is any significant improvement over the status quo. Legislators should energetically resist attempts to impose new regulations of any kind—or to take utility property or uses without compensation—regardless of the rationale offered by even the best intentioned. Mandatory retail wheeling is simply *not* consistent with a deregulatory agenda.

Achieving "half a loaf" of reform is perhaps best done by piecemeal adoption of the agenda laid out above. Other, more ambitious second-best answers might include forcing utilities to initially divest either their generation or transmission assets as a precondition to deregulation, transforming FERC into a specialized antitrust body (akin to the Surface Transportation Board) to hear complaints in an otherwise deregulated industry, and capping rate increases for *present* electricity services for a short period of time after deregulation (a step that would prove largely superfluous since deregulated rates would go down for all but the most heavily subsidized). The virtue of the above reforms is that, while by no means perfect, they provide maximum freedom for electricity markets while addressing the real (yet unfounded) fear of monopoly power in the least damaging way possible.

Reforms other than the above threaten to prove counterproductive. The archaic regulatory structure in place is crumbling, and legislators must take care not to inadvertently arrest its collapse with measures that reinforce the political control of electricity. As Zycher has noted,

> Economic regulation carries the seeds of its own destruction, as market forces tend over time to find ways to provide services to the political losers at marginal cost, and so to deprive the winners of the largesse generated by political and social institutions. No stranger to this process, the electric utility sector is deregulating itself, as market forces yield a more competitive environment by circumventing the restrictions and inefficiencies imposed by traditional rate-of-return regulation.

Electricity deregulation would provide more, better, and cheaper electricity service to both commercial and residential ratepayers while increasing the vitality of an industry crucial to the economy of the next century. No greater deregulatory opportunity faces the 105th Congress.

Suggested Readings

Bradley, Robert L. Jr. "Is Renewable Energy for Electric Generation Really 'Green' and 'Almost Competitive'?" Cato Institute Policy Analysis, forthcoming.

———. "The Origins of Political Electricity: Market Failure or Political Opportunism?" *Energy Law Journal* 17, no. 1 (1996): 57–102.

Ballonoff, Paul. *Ending the Never Ending Energy Crisis.* Washington: Cato Institute, in press.

Gordon, Richard. "Deregulation and the New Competitive Order in Electricity Generation." Paper presented at the Cato Institute/Institute for Energy Research conference, "New Horizons in Electric Power Deregulation," Washington, March 2, 1995.

Posner, Richard. "Natural Monopoly and Its Regulation." *Stanford Law Review* 21, no. 3 (1969): 548–643.

Taylor, Jerry. "Electric Utility Reform: Shock Therapy or Managed Competition?" *Regulation,* no. 3 (1996): 63–76.

Zycher, Benjamin. ''Market Deregulation of the Electric Utility Sector.'' *Regulation* 15, no. 1 (1992): 13–17.

—Prepared by Jerry Taylor

41. Environmental Protection

Congress should

- eliminate federal subsidies that exacerbate environmental damage;
- restore federal common-law causes of action for interstate discharges;
- repeal the Endangered Species Act and replace it with a federal biological trust fund;
- repeal the Comprehensive Environmental Response, Compensation, and Liability Act (Superfund);
- amend the Clean Water Act to devolve regulatory authority for intrastate discharges to state and local governments, replace command-and-control technology dictates with general facility performance standards for interstate discharges, and eliminate all federal funding for water and sewage treatment programs;
- repeal all regulatory programs directed at wetlands preservation spawned by section 404 of the Clean Water Act;
- repeal the Clean Air Act save for those elements dealing with stratospheric ozone and vehicular emissions;
- repeal the Resource Conservation and Recovery Act; and
- eliminate standing for citizen enforcement suits not based on a showing of harm.

The Poverty of Environmental Politics

The political terrain on which the environmental debate is conducted today is defined almost entirely by the central premises of the environmental left. The green lobby maintains that ecological resources are by definition public property, or commons, that must be centrally planned and stewarded by bureaucratic agents lest they be recklessly despoiled by industry. Moreover, central planners must not only have nearly complete veto power over private actions that might affect the environment; they must also be empowered to stipulate how much pollution is acceptable and exactly how each business is to go about controlling emissions and even, in some circumstances, how products are manufactured. The inescapable differences among millions of pollution sinks, environmental carrying capacities, and manufacturing processes are inevitably blurred and ''averaged'' in one-size-fits-all regulations that—while not always efficient or environmentally optimal—at least have the virtue of requiring fewer than a million regulators.

It is on that intellectual terrain that environmental reform is debated. More moderate environmental groups and most business lobbyists accept that terrain but suggest the replacement of command and control by more flexible, market-oriented regulations that allow businesses more options for controlling pollution but retain limitations on overall discharges.

Some businesses and political conservatives go further, arguing that state and local governments should be provided waivers to adjust permissible pollution levels to accurately reflect local geography, environmental carrying capacities, and unique industrial circumstances. They also maintain that regulatory stewardship of the ecological commons does not occur in a vacuum and that the economic cost of various protection strategies must be part of the environmental policy equation.

And then, of course, there is the never-ending argument about whether pollutant x or phenomenon y truly presents a human health or ecological threat so great that government regulation is necessary. Unfortunately, political muscle, not scientific evidence, more often than not settles those sorts of debates.

The need for environmental regulatory reform is hard to ignore. The United States has invested almost $1.5 trillion in environmental protection over the past 25 years and will be spending more on the environment than on national defense by the presidential election of 2000. Environmental regulations now cost the average American household $1,800 annually. Yet continuing public anxiety over the health of environmental resources indicates that few Americans are satisfied that they're getting what they pay for. Regardless, anything on which the federal government currently spends $200 billion annually (albeit indirectly through regulatory mandates) deserves scrutiny. Even minor improvements in regulatory efficiency would produce significant gains for the American consumer.

An Alternative Agenda for Reform

While both the moderate and conservative proposals for reform have drawn considerable support from academics and policy analysts on both the left and the right, they are but reforms at the margins of the status quo. They hardly qualify as "anti-environmental." But when the topography of the debate is defined by the environmental left, they are easily construed as "law-gutting" operations because the public equates regulatory reach

---

Five "Brownest" Programs in the Budget

- Agricultural subsidies are responsible for excessive pesticide, fungicide, and herbicide use with corresponding increases in non-point-source pollution.
- Sugar import quotas, tariffs, and price support loans sustain a domestic sugar industry that might not otherwise exist; the destruction of the Everglades is the ecological result.
- Electricity subsidies via the power marketing administrations and the Tennessee Valley Authority artificially boost demand for energy and thereby are responsible for millions of tons of low-level radioactive waste and the disappearance of wild rivers in the West.
- Irrigation subsidies and socialized water-management programs have done incalculable damage to western habitat while artificially promoting uneconomic agriculture with all the attendant environmental consequences.
- Federal construction grant projects—such as river maintenance, flood control, and agricultural reclamation undertakings of the Army Corps of Engineers—allow uneconomic projects to go forward and cause an array of serious environmental problems.

---

with environmental protection. And why not? If all parties to the debate agree that centralized planning of the economy—or at least heavy direct intervention—is necessary to ensure protection of the environment, anything that would undermine federal command authority is perceived as anti-environment.

In truth, the fundamental premises of the environmental debate in Washington today are faulty. Rather than fine-tune the agenda of the environmental left, serious reformers should be guided by the following ideas.

Congress Should Take the Environmental Version of the Hippocratic Oath: "First, Do No Harm"

The biggest and worst polluter in America is the federal government, which subsidizes a host of activities that arguably cause more environmental damage than all the actors in the "unfettered" free market.

It makes no sense for the federal government to subsidize environmental destruction on one hand while establishing laws, regulations, and vast bureaucracies to mitigate it on the other. Reconsidering those subsidies would help not only the environment but the economy as well.

The "Greenest" Political Agenda Is Economic Growth

There are a number of reasons why economic growth is perhaps the most important of all "environmental" policies. First, it takes a healthy, growing economy simply to afford the pollution control technologies and weather the economic dislocations necessitated by environmental protection. A poorer nation, for example, could scarcely have afforded the $150 billion this nation has spent on sewage treatment plants over the past 25 years.

Second, growing consumer demand for environmental goods (parks; recreational facilities; land for hunting, fishing, hiking; urban air and water quality) is largely responsible for the improving quantity and quality of both public and private ecological resources. Virtually all analysts of this phenomenon conclude that, for the vast majority of consumers, environmental amenities are "luxury goods" that are in greatest demand in the wealthiest societies. Economic growth is thus indirectly responsible for improving environmental quality in that it creates the conditions necessary for increased demand for (and the corresponding increase in supply of) environmental quality.

Third, advances in technology, production methods, and manufacturing practices—both a cause and a consequence of economic growth—have historically resulted in less, not more, pollution. Even advances in nonenvironmental technologies and industries have indirectly resulted in more efficient resource consumption and less pollution.

Finally, there is a strong correlation between personal wealth and health, and, as noted in a 1993 article in the *New England Journal of Medicine*, "Economic factors are critically important in the prevention of illness." The study, conducted by researchers at the National Center for Health

Statistics, concluded that education and income are the most important factors in determining how long a person will live.

Since most federal environmental laws are concerned, not with ecological protection per se, but with protecting human health from ostensibly dangerous pollutants, particularly expensive environmental regulations can do more harm than good by lowering living standards below what they otherwise might be, which, in turn, increases an array of health risks. Several economists have estimated, in fact, that each $7.5 million in regulatory costs results in one additional "statistical" death, a finding that was adopted several years ago by the U.S. Court of Appeals for the District of Columbia in *UAW v. OSHA*. Even if that conclusion is off by an order of magnitude, it still calls into question a great deal of the federal regulatory code.

Local and Regional Pollution Problems Are Properly the Province of Local and State Officials

Most federal environmental regulations address discharges that affect localities, not interstate regions or the nation as a whole. The principle of subsidiarity—one of the foundations of this nation's political architecture—suggests that local problems are best dealt with by local officials, regional problems by state officials, and national problems by federal officials. The U.S. Constitution largely codifies that principle by placing limits on the reach of federal power (see Chapter 16), and the Supreme Court finally seems inclined, after a 60-year hiatus, to limit the reach of federal regulatory power to those areas that substantially affect interstate commerce.

Thus, Congress should carefully examine *United States v. Olin*, a May 1996 decision from the U.S. District Court for the Southern District of Alabama. In that decision, Judge W. Brevard Hand found unconstitutional (in part) a Superfund consent decree because the pollution being remedied not only failed to cross state lines but arguably failed to cross property lines. Nor was Judge Hand convinced that the pollution was a matter of "commerce" or that the discharges affected commerce at all, substantially or not. While the case is being appealed (and other federal district courts have been uniformly reluctant to apply the reasoning in *United States v. Lopez* to the world of federal environmental law, as discussed by Roger Pilon in Chapter 3), a nonpolitical examination of the commerce clause calls much of the federal environmental code into serious question.

There are not only good constitutional reasons to question the centralized regulation of local pollution; there are good practical reasons as well.

Environmental problems differ in each community, and each community ought to have the flexibility to set its own priorities when allocating resources for ecological and public health protection in the interests of addressing the most serious local problems first. Moreover, there is an incalculable value in regulatory competition. Allowing states—the "laboratories of democracy"—to experiment with a multiplicity of regulatory philosophies and structures will allow us to discover more efficient and effective regulatory regimes than those advocated by the stultified regulatory monopoly in Washington. "Letting a thousand regulatory experiments bloom" would be a wise and progressive fiscal and environmental policy, as well as a valuable exercise of the admonition to "think globally, act locally."

This environmental principle is a sharp departure from the status quo and accounts for most of the bold reforms recommended at the beginning of this chapter. Superfund addresses the contamination of soil and nearby groundwater aquifers, quintessentially local matters. Many sections of the Clean Water and Clean Air Acts are concerned with protecting local and regional pollution sheds or discharges that are more appropriately addressed by workplace safety standards. Water and sewage treatment grants subsidize expenditures that should be paid for by local taxpayers (or consumers of private services) and encourage unnecessarily large, uneconomic, and inefficient facilities. The Resource Conservation and Recovery Act imposes a mind-numbing command-and-control regimen to oversee the production, use, and disposal of hazardous wastes, the effects of which are almost entirely localized.

The standard objection—that state and local governments are incapable of protecting the environment—is more fable than fact. As David Schoenbrod, New York Law School professor and cofounder of the Natural Resources Defense Council, demonstrates, federalization of environmental protection actually slowed progress in pollution abatement and continues to provide suboptimal environmental protection.

Privatizing the Environmental Commons Is Preferable to Socializing It

Pollution should be thought of as a kind of trespass—the disposal of one's garbage or waste on the property of another. The fundamental premise of (both left and right) environmentalism is that it is the legislature's role to determine to what extent such trespass should be allowed, and it is the executive branch's job to enforce limitations on trespass. The implicit (and often explicit) assumption of modern environmentalism is that environmental property (air, water, and even land) is really public property, and the trespass that occurs is a trespass against society as a whole. Accordingly, remedies for those trespasses are matters of political, not private, concern.

Yet there is no reason why environmental resources cannot be owned by private parties. For example, the legal mechanics of private groundwater rights are conceptually no more difficult that the existing legal mechanics protecting private oil field rights. In England private organizations such as fishing clubs actually own stretches of rivers and streams. And the right to ownership of air above one's property is frequently legally recognized. Use of chemical "tracers" in pollution discharges (an increasingly common practice in various studies) allows even difficult-to-detect emissions to be "branded" or "fingerprinted" and thus traced back to their sources.

An alternative environmental paradigm would hold that, if pollution is essentially a trespass upon private property, the private property owner, not governmental agents, should determine what is or is not acceptable and under what circumstances (or contractual arrangements) such trespass is to be allowed. Disputes should be brought to civil courts, not politicized legislatures, for adjudication.

Pollution problems caused by discharges from multiple sources (which would make problematic the straight application of trespass law) have often been controlled by the "condominium" model of property ownership. For example, German communities currently maintain private associations for protecting the Ruhr, Wupper, and Emscher Rivers; polluters are required to hold shares in those associations and are assessed costs for maintaining water quality. That regime has worked admirably in terms of both economic efficiency and environmental quality.

While common-law environmental policies, like all pollution control strategies, are primarily matters for local and state officials, not the federal government, to adopt when appropriate, Congress must affirmatively act in order to allow this paradigm shift to occur. Numerous courts have held that regulatory standards preempt common-law actions since they implicitly "nationalize" (and thus remove from the realm of private tort action) resources that would otherwise be left to private parties to police. Repealing federal regulatory standards would remove what is, perhaps, the chief obstacle confronting states and localities interested in shifting from a regulatory to a common-law environmental paradigm.

When confronting pollution problems that cross regional boundaries, Congress should explicitly restore common-law causes of action for interstate discharges, remove regulatory controls when private actions appear to provide a reasonable alternative, and eliminate standing for citizen enforcement suits not based on a showing of harm. By doing so, Congress would demonstrate to states the viability of the common-law approach while vastly improving the economic and ecological consequences of environmental protection.

Carl Pope, president of the Sierra Club, believes that this sort of approach "would yield restrictions on pollution more stringent than those embodied in any current federal and state pollution laws." That's certainly true if a pollutant is truly harmful or a significant nuisance, since individuals, not governmental authorities, would have the final say over how much pollution they were willing to tolerate on their property or persons. It would also have the benefit of allowing an array of voluntary contractual relationships between polluter and polluted, internalize the cost of pollution, and minimize the transactions costs and inefficiencies caused by politicized rulemaking.

Pollution Is Most Efficiently Controlled by Businessmen, Not Centralized Regulators

Command-and-control regulations, which require regulators to determine exactly which technologies and what manufacturing methods are to be adopted for pollution control in every single facility in the nation, place an informational burden on public officials that is impossible to meet in the real world. Every facility is different. Every air and water shed has different carrying capacities for different pollutants. By necessity, central regulators must issue variations upon "one-size-fits-all" standards since there simply isn't enough manpower or expertise to carefully weigh the most efficient mandates for each plant in each pollution shed.

Both common sense and experience tell us that individual plant managers are better equipped to discover the most efficient ways to control pollution at their facilities than are Environmental Protection Agency technicians and consultants. That is the case, not only because those managers have more direct knowledge of their facilities and the technology of production, but because competition forces cost minimization, and even the most dedicated EPA official isn't going to lie awake nights searching for new solutions to pollution control problems.

Economist Tom Tietenberg reports that empirical studies show that "performance-based" standards—those that require regulators simply to decide how much pollution can be allowed from a facility and leave it to the facility to meet that standard in whatever way it desires—result in uniformly lower control costs. A 1990 joint Amoco-EPA study of a Yorktown, Virginia, oil refinery found that federal environmental standards could be met at 20 percent of current costs if the refinery were allowed to adopt alternatives to EPA mandates.

Wherever common-law remedies for interregional pollution problems seem problematic because of transactions costs, performance-based regulation should be substituted for the current command-and-control regime.

Land Is Better Managed by Private Owners Than by Government Bureaucrats

Fully 29 percent of all land in the United States—662 million acres—are owned by the federal government, and 95 percent of those acres are under the control of either the Department of the Interior or the Department of Agriculture. Those holdings are concentrated in 11 western states. For example, 82 percent of Nevada, 68 percent of Alaska, 64 percent of Utah, 63 percent of Idaho, 61 percent of California, 49 percent of Wyoming, and 48 percent of Oregon are owned by the federal government.

The federal government also owns a vast estate of commercially marketed resources: 50 percent of the nation's soft-wood timber, 12 percent of grazing lands, and 30 percent of all coal reserves. Approximately 30 percent of the nation's coal production; 6 to 7 percent of domestic gas and oil production; and 90 percent of copper, 80 percent of silver, and almost 100 percent of all nickel production are from federal lands.

That state of affairs is far more disturbing than most observers realize. First, as University of Colorado law professor Dale Oesterle observes, "The federal ownership of large amounts of land, much of it with significant commodity producing potential, puts the federal government at the core of our national market system, affecting the price in nationally significant markets and a myriad of down-stream products." Indeed, the federal government owns a very large slice of the country's means of production, which fundamentally subverts the free-market system.

Second, the federal government is an extremely poor manager of resources. The cost of its grazing, timber, and water management programs greatly exceeds the commercial revenues. And as virtually all ecologists (liberals and conservatives) concede, the federal government has been a horrible steward of environmental resources. Rampant subsidies for both commercial and recreational industries have distorted markets (sometimes dramatically) and done great harm to the ecosystems of the West.

Finally, when politicians are charged with allocating public resources, a ferocious political tug of war over who gets what is inevitable. Given the hundreds of thousands of jobs that are dependent on the outcome (and the millions of people who rely on those resources for recreational and aesthetic pursuits), it should be no surprise that political "losers" are tempted to take matters into their own hands and settle them by violent means if necessary. It is no exaggeration to note that the "war over the West" is literally tearing up hundreds of communities west of the Missouri River in a manner dangerously at odds with civil society.

Minor adjustments in resource management of public lands gingerly address the symptoms without getting at the disease: public ownership. Most Americans believe that private individuals—not the government— should own land whenever possible and simply have no idea that the federal government owns such a vast estate. Congress should stop the obsessive fine-tuning of socialist resource management plans and launch serious hearings designed to draw attention to the well-documented crisis of federal land mismanagement. Once serious, concerted effort has been made to highlight the problems of socialist land management, Congress should begin drafting divestment plans to rectify the situation.

Property Regulated for Species or Ecosystem Protection Is Being Taken for a Public Purpose and the Owners Should Be Compensated

As Chapter 30 argues, compensating property owners for takings meant to secure public goods such as endangered species or habitat is a simple matter of fairness and constitutional justice. But protecting property rights is also a necessary prerequisite for ecological protection. Property owners who expect to experience economic losses if their property is identified as ecologically important are tempted to destroy that habitat or species population before public officials become aware of its existence. Numerous analysts, from people at the National Wilderness Institute to ecological-economist Randal O'Toole, conclude that the "shoot, shovel, and shut up" dynamic largely explains why the Endangered Species Act has failed to either stabilize listed populations or return a single species to health.

The ESA, which restrains private property owners from certain uses of their land in order to secure the "public good" of species protection, should thus be repealed since it provides no compensation to landowners for public takings. Instead, a federal biological trust should be established that would be funded out of general revenues at whatever level Congress found appropriate. The trust fund would be used to purchase conservation easements (in a voluntary and noncoercive fashion) from private landowners in order to protect the habitat of endangered species. (Public policies for public land are another matter and are appropriately set at the discretion of the Department of the Interior and Congress.)

The virtue of such a system is that landowners would have incentives rather than disincentives to protect species habitat, and the "ranching" of endangered species for commercial purposes would be allowed. The ESA prohibits such practices out of a misguided belief that any commercial use of an endangered species inevitably contributes to its decline. Yet the experience of the African elephant and other threatened species belies that concern and strongly suggests that, if private parties are allowed to own and trade animals as commodities, commercial demand is a critical component of population protection.

Similarly, section 404 of the Clean Water Act—the provision that ostensibly empowers the EPA to regulate wetlands—should be repealed. Like the ESA, it takes otherwise inoffensive uses of private property for a public purpose and provides disincentives for wetland conservation. Protection of wetlands habitat should be left to the federal biological trust fund.

Environmental Regulations Should Be Approved by Congress before Taking Legal Effect

See Chapter 4 for discussion of this idea.

Translating Ideas into Action

The arguments laid out above are readily applicable to the most pressing environmental policy questions before the 105th Congress, and the agenda suggested at the beginning of the chapter will allow market liberals to both free the economy from unnecessary regulatory costs and improve environmental protection.

Yet the question arises, how politically viable is such an agenda, particularly given the perceived public backlash against milder reforms forwarded in the last Congress? First of all, it should be noted that, if even the slightest deregulatory action is going to be characterized as "gutting environmental protection" by the left, then only by dropping the entire subject—or adopting the green agenda—can congressional reformers escape such accusations. Second, if any positive reform is destined to be characterized in such extreme terms, then public opposition to dramatic reform will be no greater than public opposition to milder reform.

That said, the agenda laid out in this chapter has many more selling points than the milder reform agenda of the 104th Congress. Completely replacing one regulatory practice with another forces a more honest discussion about policy alternatives than do reforms that adjust the status quo at the margins. In no way can the former strategy be characterized as "watering down" the laws, whereas the latter approach is vulnerable to just such a charge.

Second, polls indicate that the American people are intuitively sympathetic to the agenda laid out above. According to a survey conducted by the Polling Company of 1,000 voters,

- 75 percent believe Congress should be required to approve newly written federal regulations before they are enacted;
- 67 percent support a "first, do no harm" federal environmental agenda;
- 65 percent believe state or local governments would do a better job of environmental protection than the federal government;
- 64 percent support compensating landowners when environmental regulation prevents them from using their property;
- 49 percent support a nonregulatory, incentive-based approach to endangered species conservation; and
- 45 percent support a nonregulatory, incentive-based approach to wetlands conservation.

Those findings are consistent with the findings of the few other surveys that have been conducted on these subjects. It's certainly true that most Americans consider themselves environmentalists and support policies to protect the environment. Yet it's clear from both surveys and voting behavior that Americans are not at all convinced that big, centralized, regulatory government is the best way to keep America green. They are right.

Suggested Readings

Anderson, Terry, and Donald Leal. *Free Market Environmentalism.* San Francisco: Pacific Research Institute, 1991.

Beckerman, Wilfred. *Through Green-Colored Glasses: Environmentalism Reconsidered.* Washington: Cato Institute, 1996.

Competitive Enterprise Institute. *Environmental Briefing Book 1996.* Washington: Competitive Enterprise Institute, 1996.

Meiners, Roger, and Bruce Yandle, eds. *Taking the Environment Seriously.* Lanham, Md.: Rowman & Littlefield, 1993.
Regulation, no. 4 (1996).

—Prepared by Jerry Taylor

42. Environmental Health Risks

Congress should

- repeal statutes that require government registration or notification before new chemical products are put on the market;
- pass the responsibility for the safety of chemical products to manufacturers; and
- examine the expected health benefits from current environmental protection laws and consider elimination of the laws that offer tiny, if any, benefits.

"Risk" has been the most potent word in the enactment of the federal environmental protection laws that now burden the country with more than $150 billion in annual regulatory costs. Risks of cancer, risks of birth defects, risks of other health effects, risks of ecological damage have all been paraded before Congress, and Congress has responded by passing laws that direct the Environmental Protection Agency to "go forth and eliminate risk."

"Risk assessment" is the term used to describe the assortment of animal tests, human studies, mathematical extrapolations, and conjectures that go into estimating risks from chemicals and radiation in the environment. Risk assessment, as practiced by the government, has been roundly criticized for depending on assumptions that guarantee exaggerated estimates of risk.

There have been two easy responses to the identified problems with risk assessment: better science and cost/benefit analysis. The fierceness with which proponents of the current system battle against both can be taken to indicate that better science and cost/benefit analysis would make a real difference if adopted. In fact, that's unlikely. Far more definite action is needed to improve risk assessment. That action is to take risk assessment out of the federal government and put it in the private sector.

Science and Risk

Science can't solve the problems because the problems are with risk assessment, not science, and risk assessment is not science. Science involves two processes. The first is proposing hypotheses about how a part of the physical universe works. The second is testing the hypotheses to see if they are indeed predictive. All kinds of hypotheses can be advanced, but a hypothesis without a test has little or no value. Scientists accept and rely on the hypotheses that survive tests, and they use information garnered in the testing of hypotheses in the formulation of new hypotheses. The process continues, and hypotheses that survive testing are used to make further predictions.

An example makes it clear why "better science" will have little effect on risk assessment. Based on information from laboratory animals that are exposed to very high levels of a chemical or, rarely, on the results of studies of workers exposed to high levels of a chemical in the workplace, the product of most risk assessments is a prediction that exposure to a chemical at a particular concentration over a specified length of time will cause an increase in disease. In the language of science, the risk assessment product is a hypothesis. But the hypothesis cannot be tested. It cannot be tested because the predicted risks of cancer or heart disease or neurological disease are such a tiny addition to the usual number of those diseases that the risk, even if realized, cannot be detected against the usual "background" number of cases. For instance, the EPA commonly proposes regulations of chemical exposures that are associated with a one-in-a-million chance of cancer, which is equivalent to three cancers each year in the United States. There in no way that that increase can be detected against the background of more than a million new cancers that occur each year.

The small risk that is predicted cannot be detected, so there is no way to test the prediction. For the same reason, any improvement in health that might accompany any intervention to reduce exposures can't be measured either.

Of course, science does have a role to play in bringing the best techniques and information to risk assessment (that is so even though most estimates of risk cannot be tested). As an example, some chemicals that are known to cause cancer interact directly with DNA and cause mutations, and some do not. There is no reason to think that the model used to predict cancer risks associated with chemicals that interact with DNA works equally well for other chemicals, and essentially all other countries in the world have always used different models for the two kinds of chemicals. Since its

432

inception, the EPA has resisted that idea and insisted on using a model that predicts the maximum risk for all chemicals. In its 1996 draft revised cancer guidelines, the agency acknowledges that two different risk assessment models are necessary to estimate the risks from the two classes of chemicals. Even so, its "new" model preserves essential characteristics of the old one. In time, the EPA might incorporate better science into its risk assessments, but science has a difficult time against what the EPA calls "science policy choices"—and others call assumptions. So long as the federal government holds a monopoly on risk assessment methods and interpretations, the EPA can brush aside even the most solidly based scientific information as it pursues regulatory aggrandizement.

Cost/Benefit Analysis

Similarly, few significant changes can be expected from requiring more cost/benefit analyses. Such analyses are very data intensive, and the way data are collected can influence the outcome of any assessment. Currently, and probably under any scheme, regulatory agencies gather the data. So long as they have that capacity, cost/benefit analysts will be at the agencies' mercy, whether the analysts are employed by the federal government or by the private sector.

What difference do cost/benefit analyses make, anyway? Regulatory programs of the Federal Aviation Administration, theoretically, provide an additional year of life to one person for every $23,000 in regulatory expenditures; the EPA requires an expenditure of 330 times as much, almost $7,600,000, for the same benefit. In fact, the discrepancy is far, far larger. The FAA calculations are based on information about real airplane accidents that killed real people; the EPA calculations are based on estimated rates of human disease that cannot be tested. Such information has not led to rollbacks in expensive regulations, and there is little reason to expect it to.

Current Regulations

The idea that "Washington knows best" has dominated Congress's efforts to deal with environmental risks. It has produced a patchwork of laws with different criteria, an ever-expanding EPA, increasing regulatory costs, and no demonstrated health benefit from regulating environmental chemicals. Only Congress can alter that course. Ideally, Congress will remove the government from risk assessment and leave it to manufacturers to certify the safety of their products and to the courts to provide compensation to persons who are injured by faulty products.

Congress can start that process with changes to the Federal Insecticide, Fungicide, and Rodenticide Act (FIFRA) and the Toxic Substances Control Act (TSCA). FIFRA requires that the manufacturer or importer of a pesticide provide the EPA with detailed results of tests for adverse effects on humans and other life forms in the environment, and the EPA then decides whether the agent can be licensed for particular uses. TSCA requires that the manufacturer or importer of any "new" commercial chemical product supply the EPA with whatever testing information is available, and then the EPA can decide whether additional tests are needed before the chemical is introduced into commerce.

Independent Certification

Congress can pass the responsibility for the safety of chemical products to the manufacturers. Most manufacturers would immediately seek expert opinions about the safety of their products as a protection against liability. To supply that need, third-party organizations for testing and certifying chemicals would spring up. Such organizations would be analogous to the Underwriters Laboratories, Inc., which certifies electrical devices as safe without any government intervention. Third-party testing laboratories can conduct and interpret animal tests, and councils of experts, such as the American Council of Government Industrial Hygienists, can provide recommendations about conditions for safe use of the substances. Larger, consensus organizations, such as the American National Standards Institute, would also probably be interested in providing the tests and analysis necessary to certify a substance as safe enough for use. The proper functioning of such a system will require a tort system that compensates people who might be injured.

There would be great differences between the current system in which government does risk assessments and a system from which the government was absent. The assumptions that are based on old information and exaggerate risks and dictate the results of EPA risk assessments would be lifted, and the newest information could be incorporated into risk assessments. More important, the people who carried out tests and did assessments would not be government employees subject to no penalties for foot dragging and sloppy work. They would be working on contract to the manufacturers, which would lead to their completing their work on time, and they would be well aware that sloppy work could result in their employers becoming known as unreliable and the loss of their own jobs. Wholesalers and retailers would find it in their interests to sell certified chemicals and to base their advertising on the certification. Formulators, who mix chemicals for specific applications, and food processors, who use chemicals, would choose certified chemicals to attract customers. It is entirely possible that some certification marks would come to be associated with more rigorous standards, and the buyer could choose between and among different products on the basis of certification, costs, and other factors.

How Large Are the Risks from Chemicals in the Environment?

Congress will hear that rates of cancer and other diseases will soar if the EPA backs off from its current regulatory course. Congress can take advantage of those claims to hold hearings to investigate just how big the risks are that the EPA is charged with controlling. If those risks are as small as almost all experts agree that they are, the entire panoply of environmental protection laws directed against chemicals can be reconsidered in light of their enormous expenses and tiny, and most uncertain, benefits.

Suggested Readings

Ames, Bruce N., Lois S. Gold, and Walter C. Willett. "The Causes and Prevention of Cancer." *Proceedings of the National Academy of Sciences* 92 (1995): 5258–65.

Environmental Protection Agency. *Unfinished Business: A Comparative Assessment of Environmental Problems.* Washington: Environmental Protection Agency, February 1987.

Gough, Michael. "How Much Cancer Can EPA Regulate Away?" *Risk Analysis* 10 (1990): 1–6.

Gough, Michael, and Steven Milloy. "EPA's Cancer Guidelines: Guidance to Nowhere." Cato Institute Policy Analysis no. 263, November 12, 1996.

Tengs, Tammy O., et al. "Five-Hundred Life-Saving Interventions and Their Cost-Effectiveness." *Risk Analysis* 15 (1995): 369–90.

—Prepared by Michael Gough

FOREIGN AND DEFENSE POLICY

43. NATO Expansion

Congress should refuse to approve the enlargement of NATO for the following reasons:

- NATO is a military alliance, whose purpose is to deter and fight wars, not merely an association for political cooperation.
- NATO expansion is motivated overwhelmingly by the fear of Russia that exists in the states clamoring for membership in the alliance; those states want reliable protection, not just paper guarantees.
- No Russian political figure of any significance welcomes NATO expansion, or even takes the Western justifications for it seriously.
- Russia, despite its weak conventional military forces, still possesses one of the largest nuclear arsenals in the world, making any NATO-Russian confrontation over Eastern Europe especially dangerous.
- The United States is obliged to use nuclear weapons, if necessary, to protect all the other members of the alliance; many of the proposed new members could not be defended by conventional means.
- NATO expansion risks dividing Europe and increasing the danger of major war in Europe.

NATO is a military alliance, not a political association. When World War II ended, the hope was that the United Nations would succeed where the League of Nations had failed. But collective security under the banner of the United Nations quickly became a victim of the Cold War. As hopes for a collective security system vanished, the United States decided to substitute a security guarantee to the nations of Western Europe, the North Atlantic Treaty Organization. Several years after the formation of NATO, the Soviet Union responded by creating its own alliance, the Warsaw Pact.

With the end of the Cold War, the Soviet Union dissolved the Warsaw Pact, but NATO, the alliance of the victors, survived. Without a clear adversary, however, it was an alliance in search of a purpose. The conflict in Bosnia gave it one mission: "out-of-area operations"—preserving peace in the portions of Europe that are not part of the alliance. Why have such a powerful armed force, people asked, if it cannot be used where peace is threatened?

NATO's involvement in Bosnia underlines its central purpose: to deter and fight wars. It is not surprising that the expansion of NATO's role in Bosnia has involved it in its first armed missions ever. What that signifies, however, is that the expansion of NATO's role carries with it the danger of even more armed conflict.

During the Cold War the Soviet Union typically backed down when confronted by the United States and its allies. But the United States made no effort to unilaterally challenge the Soviet Empire. Nevertheless, there were miscalculations that could have proved catastrophic, notably the Cuban missile crisis. And although it is sometimes said that the Cold War was won without a shot being fired, that statement ignores the veterans of Korea and Vietnam, whose sacrifice deserves greater recognition. Those wars were fought in large part to preserve the credibility of Washington's alliance commitments, including NATO.

In the debate over NATO expansion, that central purpose of a military alliance—to deter and fight wars—has been overlooked. To be sure, a military alliance can serve additional purposes, and NATO played a role in fostering democracy in its members. But other international institutions can also serve that purpose. As NATO's role in Bosnia reminds us, the distinctive features of a military alliance are its war-fighting capabilities and responsibilities.

Fear of Russia

Since the purpose of a military alliance is to deter and fight wars, the countries that want to join the alliance typically have a particular threat in mind. Alliances are different from collective security systems. Collective security is designed to be inclusive. Any country can join, and any country, even a member, can become an enemy that must then be disciplined by the other members. As noted, the United Nations was designed as a collective security system. After the Cold War ended and Iraq invaded Kuwait, the United Nations authorized military action against Iraq even though it was a UN member.

Alliances are very different. Unlike collective security systems, they are exclusive, because they have a particular enemy in mind. For NATO, that threat was the Soviet Union. During the Cold War it was inconceivable that the Soviet Union or the other members of the Warsaw Pact would have been allowed to join NATO.

With the Cold War over, why is a military alliance in Europe necessary? Why retain NATO, which even with expansion will remain exclusive— because it will inevitably exclude Russia?

That, of course, is the nub of the argument. Despite all the rhetoric about the end of the Cold War, a new NATO, and so forth, the fundamental purpose of NATO is to provide an American security guarantee to countries that are afraid of Russia. To be sure, those fears are not baseless. We cannot know how the political and economic turbulence in Russia will turn out, and certainly some statements by Russian leaders provide cause for concern.

But we should be honest about the motives of the Central and even the Western European nations that desire the expansion of NATO. If NATO expansion is not designed with Russia in mind as a likely adversary, why is Russia excluded from possible membership? When the United Nations was formed, nobody thought of excluding Russia. Russia was even given a veto in the Security Council, whereas now the common refrain is that Russia must not have a veto in Europe. The conclusion is inescapable: NATO expansion is motivated by fear of Russia, combined with the (somewhat contradictory) conviction that Russia is too weak to do anything to resist expansion of the alliance. And despite the sugary assurances issuing from Western capitals that an enlarged NATO is not directed against Russia, the Russians are not fooled.

Russia's Reaction

When Andrei Kozyrev was Russia's foreign minister, Western leaders thought some deal could be reached so that NATO could expand without antagonizing Moscow. Those expectations still exist, but now they are based on little more than wishful thinking. When foreign observers interpreted some remarks by Kozyrev's successor, Yevgeny Primakov, as moderating the Russian opposition to NATO expansion, he quickly shot them down.

Consequently, those promoting NATO expansion increasingly say that Russian opposition doesn't matter, that Russia will have to accept expansion because it has no other options. But that is not the way the Russians see it. Three possible responses, in particular, should be noted.

Alliance with China

Over the last few years, Russia's relations with China have been growing warmer. Although no one should desire hostility between two major powers, the basis of their rapprochement seems to be their mutual resentment of U.S. policy. NATO expansion is evidently one of the reasons Moscow is drawing closer to Beijing. "Various highly-placed Russian leaders began to talk about 'looking' for allies in the East in the second half of last year, purportedly in response to a possible expansion of NATO," the Athenian newspaper *New Europe,* which follows events in Russia closely, reported in May 1996. "The idea of the need for such an alliance is becoming more and more acceptable to Russia." In fact, when Russian president Boris Yeltsin was in Beijing in 1996, meeting with his Chinese counterpart Jiang Zemin, he declared that the Chinese leader "strongly supports Russia's stand that the eastward expansion of NATO to the Russian Federation's borders is unacceptable."

Pressure on Neighbors

If NATO expands to the east, Russia will probably respond by putting pressure on its closest neighbors. In December 1994, a Russian scholar at Moscow's USA and Canada Institute warned that "Russia may meet NATO's advance eastward with its own advance westward." Warnings like that, it must be stressed, come from Russians who want to prevent a confrontation and who are telling Americans what the reaction is likely to be in their country. "In these conditions, quite moderate politicians will favor a remilitarization of the country," argues Dmitri Trenin, a Russian foreign policy specialist at the Moscow office of the Carnegie Endowment for International Peace. "The formation of a military and political alliance within the [Commonwealth of Independent States] . . . will become a priority trend of post-Soviet integration."

Indeed, one Russian correspondent with close ties to the defense ministry has even reported that Russia might launch a preemptive attack if NATO deploys troops forward as part of any expansion:

> Russia's future reaction to any attempt to deploy foreign troops near its border (including such a move under the guise of conducting maneuvers) is quite predictable. It will be exactly the same as Washington's reaction in 1961 [*sic*], when our troops landed in Cuba. First there will be a blockade

(if the geographic location of the future conflict zone allows this), then an ultimatum demanding an immediate troop withdrawal and, if the ultimatum is not complied with, a preventive strike that would deprive the adversary of offensive capabilities.

The danger is especially great for the Baltic states. According to the Council on Foreign and Defense Policy, a working group on Russia's policy with respect to NATO, "the Baltic states' desire to join NATO . . . will create a potential source of real crisis in the center of Europe." Given the location of the Baltic states, it is doubtful that NATO could provide any effective conventional military assistance if they were threatened by Russia. And even though Russian forces did not perform well in Chechnya, they still pose a threat to the Baltic republics. As the Defense Intelligence Agency recently told Congress, "Through the next 5 years . . . Russia will retain the capability . . . to overwhelm any other former Soviet state with a conventional offensive, provided it has sufficient time to prepare." In these circumstances, the prospect of NATO membership for the Baltic republics will offer false hope, much like the British and French guarantee to Poland in 1939. Even worse, far from deterring Russian action, it could actually incite Russia to take the action we all seek to avert.

Repudiation of Arms Control

During the Cold War, the capstone of East-West negotiations was arms control, especially the agreements designed to limit the nuclear arms race. Given the disintegration of the Soviet bloc and the weakness of Russian conventional forces, people have tended to forget that Russia still possesses a vast nuclear arsenal capable of destroying the United States. Indeed, despite Washington's worries about security threats around the world, that arsenal still represents the only threat to America's national survival, and consequently it still deserves attention as our highest national security priority.

In early 1996 the Senate consented to ratification of the START II Treaty, which would dramatically reduce the arsenals of Russia and the United States and create a more stable balance. However, Russian political leaders have grown disenchanted with the treaty as overall U.S.-Russian relations have soured. In particular, they have begun to link NATO expansion with START II. In 1994 Duma Defense Committee chairman Sergei Yushenkov warned that NATO expansion would deliver "a probably fatal blow to arms limitation regimes." More recently, Sergei Karaganov, chairman of Russia's Council of Foreign and Defense Policy, told a conference sponsored by the Congressional Research Service that "almost inevitably, Russia will be pushed, whatever the government is, toward more emphasis on nuclear weapons in its strategic policy and in pushing the nuclear matter to the forefront of European politics."

Dangerous U.S. Obligations

As noted, the United States is obligated to defend any NATO member that is the victim of aggression. During the Cold War, the threat was the Soviet Union. That was why the United States had such a massive military presence in Germany, which was the major line of confrontation with Soviet forces in Europe. With the end of the Cold War, those forces have been significantly reduced, as have those of Washington's NATO allies. Given the even greater degradation of Russian conventional forces, those defense drawdowns do not undercut the security of existing NATO members even if relations between Russia and NATO deteriorate.

Expansion of NATO eastward, however, is something else altogether. The farther east one goes, the greater the potential Russian military threat and the harder the NATO conventional defense. As already noted, with regard to the Baltic states, it is difficult to imagine how NATO could mount an effective conventional defense at all. Thus, the paradox of NATO expansion is that those countries most likely to enter NATO in a first round of enlargement—the Czech Republic, Hungary, and Poland—are the least threatened because they are farthest away from Russia. Their entry, however, is likely to increase the threat to the most vulnerable countries. Moreover, their entry is also likely to increase the Russian nuclear threat to them. So long as they are not NATO members, they are not likely to be targets of Russian nuclear forces. But if Russia makes good on threats to increase reliance on nuclear weapons in response to NATO expansion, it is likely that the new members of NATO will be on the target list. And the United States cannot protect them against *nuclear* attack.

The extent of the U.S. obligation to defend its NATO allies should not be underestimated. If they are attacked, we *must* defend them, or we will be dishonored. And if we cannot defend them by conventional means, we shall have to initiate nuclear war. That is what NATO means. That is why we refused Soviet entreaties during the 1980s to adopt a policy of no first use of nuclear weapons. We did not want to initiate nuclear war, and we deployed large conventional forces in Europe to forestall the

442

Table 43.1
Results of Public Opinion Poll

	Czech Republic	Hungary	Poland
Support	8%	9%	23%
Oppose	85%	85%	67%

SOURCE: Stanley R. Sloan and Rosan Hollak, *NATO's Future and U.S. Interests: Edited Transcript of a Congressional-Executive Dialogue*, Congressional Research Service Report for Congress 96-400 F, May 3, 1996, p. 128.

possibility that we would have to initiate nuclear war. But we never disavowed the option. *The U.S. obligation under NATO involves the initiation of nuclear war if there is no other way to defend a NATO member under attack.* It should go without saying—but it nevertheless needs to be said, since advocates of NATO enlargement seem determined to ignore the point—that this is not a commitment to be extended lightly.

There is also the question of expense. According to the Congressional Budget Office, the cost of NATO expansion over a 15-year period would be $61 billion to $125 billion, with the United States expected to pay between $5 billion and $19 billion. "Such U.S. costs might be manageable," the CBO concludes, "but only if—as NATO and CBO assume—the Visegrad nations [Poland, Hungary, the Czech Republic, and Slovakia] themselves bear a substantial portion of the costs of expansion."

With all due respect to NATO and the CBO, that assumption is wildly unrealistic. Given the economic situation of the Visegrad states, and even of the existing NATO allies, they cannot be expected to come up with that kind of money. More to the point, their own citizens do not want to do so. In 1995 the U.S. Information Agency conducted a public opinion poll of citizens of the Visegrad countries to learn whether they were willing to increase defense expenditures as a condition of membership in NATO. The responses are given in Table 43.1. In short, if NATO expands, the United States will assume greater military risks and a vastly increased defense burden. No one else can make good on the security guarantee, and no one else can—or will—pay for it.

Provoking a New Cold War?

The end of the Cold War brought a sigh of relief throughout the world. The new relationship between Russia and the United States, in particular, provided assurance that the nuclear threat to civilization was vastly diminished. Democracy had won and Russia would be accepted as part of the West. There would be no Third World War to follow the First and Second.

Now those hopes are ebbing. Many in the West do not realize it yet, but there is a change in Russia, a change that has been inspired largely by our attitudes. And NATO expansion is a major reason for that change. "We had been very successful in changing the attitude toward NATO in Russia until the decision was made to enlarge NATO," Karaganov told the CRS conference. "NATO expansion, because of the reaction in the country, is killing the partnership."

The purpose of NATO expansion is misconstrued by its proponents. It is presented as an effort to overcome Yalta, but it will simply recreate Yalta by moving the frontier of "the democratic West" farther east. In NATO jargon, that new boundary does not mean creating a new division of Europe. Although Russia will not be allowed into the new NATO, it is to be offered a formal charter with NATO in compensation. American officials seem genuinely surprised that Russians are offended when they are told, as in the television commercial, that an imitation brand "is just as good as a Xerox."

We should have no illusions. NATO expansion will set back relations with Russia. There will be adverse consequences. Moreover, enlargement will not even provide greater security for those countries admitted to NATO. We risk repeating the empty guarantees of the 1925 Treaty of Locarno. Those who point to Munich and warn of appeasement if NATO does not expand should remember the empty British and French guarantee to Poland. As the historian A. J. P. Taylor asked, was it better to be a betrayed Czech or a saved Pole?

The arguments for NATO expansion have been characterized by naivete and dishonesty. When NATO expansion comes before the Senate, that body should engage in serious debate and not be rushed into a hasty decision. The NATO treaty involves a commitment to risk America's very survival in defense of other countries. That is not an obligation to be undertaken without the most careful consideration.

Suggested Readings

Brown, Michael E. "The Flawed Logic of NATO Expansion." *Survival* (Spring 1995).

Carpenter, Ted Galen. *Beyond NATO: Staying Out of Europe's Wars*. Washington: Cato Institute, 1994.

Carpenter, Ted Galen, ed. *The Future of NATO*. London: Frank Cass, 1995.

Kober, Stanley. "NATO Expansion and the Danger of a Second Cold War." Cato Institute Foreign Policy Briefing no. 38, January 31, 1996.

_____. "The United States and the Enlargement Debate." *Transition,* December 15, 1995.

Sloan, Stanley R., and Steve Woehrel. "NATO Enlargement and Russia: From Cold War to Cold Peace?" Congressional Research Service Report for Congress 95-594S, May 15, 1995.

Sieff, Martin. "Russians Feel Isolated as NATO Grows: Policy Could Push Ties to Iran, China." *Washington Times,* September 23, 1996.

—Prepared by Stanley Kober

44. The Balkan Thicket

Congress should

- call for the immediate withdrawal of all U.S. troops from Bosnia;
- refuse to appropriate funds for any further deployment of U.S. troops to Bosnia;
- urge the members of the European Union to expand their military presence in Bosnia, if they deem Bosnian stability important to their own interests;
- seek to reverse plans for the expansion of NATO or for NATO "out-of-area" operations; and
- urge the administration to reverse Washington's growing military and intelligence ties to Croatia, Albania, and other states in the Balkans.

For five years Bosnia has dominated the U.S. foreign policy agenda. Over that period the United States has committed enormous levels of political, diplomatic, military, and financial resources to the Balkans. Those commitments continue today in the form of the deployment of American military forces in the region and in pledges of financial support for the reconstruction of Bosnia.

At the beginning of 1997 there is still no certainty that that huge investment of time and effort will produce a stable settlement. One important lesson for post–Cold War foreign policy has, however, become unambiguously clear: disorder in Europe has an awkward habit of leading to U.S. engagement irrespective of considerations of national interest or the weight of public opinion.

Unfortunately, in the case of Bosnia, the strategic necessity to treat European security issues soberly was forgotten. A similar carelessness threatens to distort the lessons of the Bosnian experience. Bosnia is not, as many claim, a NATO-led success that paves the way for the United

States to take on new and costly commitments in Europe through an expansion of NATO. The real lessons lead in the opposite direction. To secure its interests in Europe, the United States, in concert with the West European powers, should devise credible and effective security structures under which Europeans take responsibility for safeguarding the stability of their region without direct U.S. intervention.

Bosnia: 1991–95

The most regrettable aspect of the Bosnian tragedy was that it was to a great extent avoidable. Despite historical and ethnic complexity, the essential elements of the Bosnian conflict were not hard to understand. They reflected a wish on the parts of the peoples of the constituent republics of the former Yugoslavia to form new states in which Slovenes, Croats, Serbs, Muslims, and Macedonians, respectively, would dominate the organs of government.

In Serbia, Slovenia, Croatia, and Macedonia that process was accomplished with varying degrees of difficulty. Bosnia, where no ethnic group represented a majority of the population, presented a geometric leap in the degree of challenge. An independent Bosnia based on a unitary central government would have turned both Bosnian Serbs and Bosnian Croats into minorities and was therefore unacceptable to them. Both Serbs and Croats made that fact clear in early 1990, well in advance of the outbreak of fighting in April 1992.

In the early stages of the Bosnian crisis, the European governments took the lead in the search for a solution, proposing a "cantonal" division of Bosnia under which the various ethnic groups would exercise local autonomy under a loose central government. The United States opposed that solution but did not have an alternative plan of its own. The Clinton administration appeared indecisive, at times arguing that vital American interests were at stake, on other occasions insisting that they were not.

There then followed a two-year interval of ill-concealed intra-NATO disarray. In general, U.S. policymakers favored the use of airpower to reverse Serb territorial gains, while the Europeans, who provided the main part of the UN peacekeeping forces in Bosnia, were reluctant to expose their forces to retaliation. They favored diplomatic means, using economic sanctions to pressure President Slobodan Milosevic of Serbia to force the Bosnian Serbs to make concessions. Meanwhile, the Serbs continued to control about 70 percent of Bosnia's territory.

Behind the scenes, however, an important change in the balance of power was taking place. In February 1994 the United States brokered a federation between Bosnian Croats and Muslims—and a loose confederation between Croatia and Bosnia—and a significant volume of arms, some from Iran, began to flow to the federation. By early 1995 the federation had gained enough strength to take advantage of Serb military overextension in eastern Bosnia and launched a counteroffensive. Serb-held areas in Croatia and western Bosnia were quickly retaken, causing massive flows of Serb refugees into Serbia. The Serb share of Bosnian territory slipped back to about 50 percent. The Muslim-Croat federation was resurgent, and the Serbs were forced to contemplate the prospect of defeat. That reversal of military fortunes set the stage for a political compromise.

The Dayton Agreement

The agreement reached at Dayton, Ohio, in November 1995 was in every sense a compromise. It was also a highly ambiguous document, allowing each side to emphasize the elements it liked and to disregard those it regarded as unpalatable. The agreement contained detailed provisions on military issues (cease-fire, disengagement of forces, withdrawal of weapons, etc.) but was crucially vague on measures to implement the civilian side of the agreement (elections, return of refugees, voter registration, war crimes trials, etc.). It also postponed consideration of some of the more contentious issues (land corridors linking various sectors of the ethnic political entities, for example). It should be no surprise, therefore, that military implementation has proceeded far more smoothly than civilian aspects of the agreement. Nor should it be any surprise that long-term stability in Bosnia is far from ensured.

The central ambiguity of the Dayton accord concerned the very issue over which the war had been fought: the relationship between the central government of Bosnia and the constituent ethnic communities. The agreement calls for a federal structure with a single international personality and a single currency. At the same time, however, it legally acknowledges the separate existence of the Serb and Croat political entities and holds out to them the prospect of forming "special parallel relationships" with neighboring states, that is, Serbia and Croatia. It may be seen, therefore, that while the official outcome of the Dayton negotiations was that Bosnia should emerge as a unitary state, the door was also left open to partition.

Future U.S. Policy

The single greatest positive achievement of the Dayton agreement was to bring the large-scale conflict to an end and to provide the conditions in which elections (albeit flawed) were possible. Nevertheless, given that the differences between the Bosnian parties remain great, a continuation of that state of relative tranquillity cannot be taken for granted. A misjudgment by U.S. or West European policymakers—or merely greed on the part of the parties—could still plunge Bosnia back into war.

A crucial mistake would be to misinterpret NATO's role in Bosnia. Although NATO troops performed admirably in providing the necessary security framework for the September election, the earlier NATO role in making a peace settlement possible was at best peripheral. The much-vaunted NATO airstrikes in August 1995 came *after* the Serbs had accepted most of the provisions later embodied in the Dayton agreement. The key elements leading to the signing of the Dayton accord were, first, the battlefield success of Croatia and, second, the vital (albeit tacit) political concession by the United States of accepting the possibility of Bosnian partition.

That insight has important implications for future U.S. policy. On the political side, the United States should avoid the temptation to become involved in nation building in Bosnia. The September 14, 1996, balloting was the third election there since 1990. In each case the ethnic separatist vote has been dominant. The message is clear: the maintenance of Bosnia as a unitary state will be highly problematic. If it is maintained, all well and good. If, however, the forces for partition prove overwhelming, the United States should not seek to resist them.

While it is clear that a continued strong international presence will be indispensable to ensure Bosnia's transition to independent status, or to a peaceful partition, that role is best filled by European forces. The Europeans have the greatest interest in a stable Balkan region. Given institutional reforms within NATO (the establishment of the Combined Joint Task Force concept that provides for European NATO forces to operate independent of U.S. forces) and within the EU (the strengthening of the Western European Union—the military alliance of West European states), the Europeans now possess the capability to carry out that task. Under no circumstances should the role of U.S. forces in Bosnia be prolonged. An extended U.S. role would simply replicate the confusion and intra-alliance struggles over policy of the past five years. It would also commit the United States to needless risk and expenditure. The former is significant, but the latter should not be minimized. The existing deployment cost American taxpayers at least $3.5 billion through the end of 1996.

The United States has also made a series of little-noticed commitments elsewhere in the Balkans. Not only has Washington undertaken to arm and train a new Bosnian (Muslim-dominated) army, it has reached military agreements with Croatia and Macedonia and continues to deploy troops as part of a UN peacekeeping force in Macedonia. An extensive network of intelligence ties has also developed between the United States and Croatia, Macedonia, and Albania. Such commitments dangerously expose the United States and should be abandoned or reduced as soon as possible. It would be folly for Washington to seek to make the congenitally unstable Balkan peninsula an American protectorate.

The Bosnian conflict also contains wider lessons for U.S. security policy. Since the fall of the Berlin Wall in 1989, NATO has been looking for a new role. NATO's supporters who hoped that the Bosnia crisis would provide just such a justification for NATO's continued existence—with a new role of dampening "out-of-area" conflicts—are likely to be disappointed. That is hardly surprising. NATO is configured to meet a massive conventional threat across agreed international borders, not to deal with civil wars. Most analysts agree, however, that, for the foreseeable future, conflict in Europe will most probably arise from Bosnia-like intrastate disputes. To deal with those eventualities, new security institutions, directed by the Europeans, are needed in Europe. The United States should have no desire to become entangled in future Bosnias.

Suggested Readings

Akhavan, Payam, and Robert Howse. *Yugoslavia the Former and Future: Reflections by Scholars from the Region.* Washington: Brookings Institution, 1995.
Carpenter, Ted Galen. "Holbrooke Horror: The U.S. Peace Plan for Bosnia." Cato Institute Foreign Policy Briefing no. 37, October 27, 1995.
Carpenter, Ted Galen, and Amos Perlmutter. "Strategy Creep in the Balkans." *National Interest* (Summer 1996).
Clarke, Jonathan. "Instinct for the Capillary: The Clinton Administration's Foreign Policy 'Successes.'" Cato Institute Foreign Policy Briefing no. 40, April 5, 1996.
———. "Rhetoric before Reality." *Foreign Affairs* (September–October 1995).
———. "The United States and Future Bosnias." Cato Institute Foreign Policy Briefing no. 36, August 8, 1995.
Owen, David. *Balkan Odyssey.* New York: Harcourt, Brace, 1995.
Woodward, Susan. *Balkan Tragedy.* Washington: Brookings Institution, 1995.

—Prepared by Jonathan G. Clarke

45. Reducing the Risk of Terrorism

The U.S. government should

- avoid entanglement in regional conflicts or civil wars that do not have a direct and substantial relevance to vital American security interests;
- focus the attention and resources of the intelligence agencies on terrorism and other serious national security threats instead of phony or exaggerated problems such as economic espionage; and
- consider state-sponsored terrorist attacks against American civilians acts of war, not a law enforcement issue, and respond, in cases where there is clear and compelling evidence, with a formal declaration of war.

The sabotage of Pan American flight 103, the bombing of the World Trade Center, and (possibly) the crash of TWA flight 800 make it clear that Americans have become targets of international terrorism. Unfortunately, that danger is likely to grow rather than recede in the coming years. Moreover, the potential for thousands, rather than dozens or hundreds, of casualties in any single incident is also rising.

In a speech to a recent conference on terrorism sponsored by the Cato Institute, former CIA director R. James Woolsey noted that a terrorist attack involving chemical or biological agents instead of conventional explosives would be vastly more destructive than the terrible events that have already taken place. For example, the introduction of anthrax, a deadly but easily cultivated bacterium, into an urban environment could kill tens of thousands of people in a matter of days. The quantity of anthrax needed to produce such a catastrophe could be carried in a briefcase.

It is imperative that Congress and the executive branch begin to examine ways in which to deal more effectively with the threat of international terrorism. Although, as noted in Chapter 21, it is not possible for a free society always to prevent determined terrorists from striking, there are policy changes that can materially reduce the risk that Americans will be the target of terrorist initiatives directed from abroad. Those changes will, however, require a radically different U.S. foreign policy as well as a refocused mission for the U.S. intelligence community.

What Terrorism Is—and Isn't

Most discussions of terrorism are surprisingly vague about the concept itself, and even prominent experts frequently fail to define the term. Their approach is reminiscent of Supreme Court Justice Potter Stewart's handling of obscenity. Stewart conceded that he could not define obscenity, but he assured his colleagues, "I know it when I see it."

If we are to deal intelligently with terrorism, a more rigorous approach is necessary. Terrorism is best defined as violence directed against innocent people for a political purpose. Both the "political purpose" and the "innocent people" components are crucial. The political purpose requirement is needed to distinguish terrorist incidents from ordinary crimes, however brutal those crimes may be. For example, the New York City nightclub arsonist and (probably) the Centennial Park bomber in Atlanta were common criminals, not terrorists.

The "innocent people" standard is more difficult to define with precision and is also more controversial. With rare exceptions, though, "innocent people" should mean civilians, not military personnel. That is especially true if targeted military forces are operating in another country and are parties to an armed struggle or ongoing political dispute. Indeed, attacks on military personnel should not be defined as terrorism even if the troops are operating in their own country, if there is no peaceful mechanism to remove the incumbent regime from power and the armed forces serve to prop up a dictatorship. Under those circumstances, attacks directed against such targets constitute guerrilla warfare, not terrorism.

The consequences of the attacks are, of course, no less terrible than terrorism would be for the victims and their loved ones. Nevertheless, it is important to make the distinction between guerrilla warfare directed against professional soldiers and wanton assaults on innocents who are in no way involved in the underlying disputes.

U.S. Foreign Policy: Making America a Target

The bombing of the World Trade Center and the other terrorist incidents that have victimized American civilians—as well as the attacks on U.S.

troops in Saudi Arabia—demonstrate that Washington's foreign policy has a direct bearing on the likelihood of violence against both American military personnel and American civilians. Such acts are hardly inexplicable. Perpetrators are not randomly selecting the United States out of a directory of members of the United Nations; they have rather specific grievances against America.

It might be tempting to conclude that those who attack American targets are simply fanatics who hate American values and culture. Many experts on terrorism have advanced that argument. University of California professor Ronald Steel, for example, contends that

> the United States is the locus of power in a "new world order" that would render irrelevant traditional faiths and even whole societies. Americans pride themselves on being in the forefront of the modern, in being the world's leader. But not everyone finds that world as appealing or even as inevitable as we do. To many it is deeply threatening. Naturally, the discontented of the world hold us responsible for their plight: their poverty, their ignorance, their weakness, their irrelevance.

Steel is not entirely wrong. There are certainly some terrorists who hate America because of the values it supposedly represents: especially modernity, secularism, and individualism. Nevertheless, it would be a mistake to conclude that most attacks on U.S. targets are motivated by a blind hatred of American values. City University of New York professor Yan Sun, responding to Steel's assertion, made a crucial distinction. Steel missed the point "of why certain segments of the rest of the world may harbor resentment of the United States," Yan Sun argued. "It is not American ways and values that threaten them," but "American insistence on imposing those on others."

It is even more accurate to say that terrorism is primarily a backlash against Washington's meddlesome global interventionist foreign policy—a policy that often has little, if any, connection with the values embraced by most Americans. U.S. leaders have chosen to interfere in an assortment of regional, subregional, and even internal quarrels around the world. Whether in Somalia, Haiti, Bosnia, the Persian Gulf, or the Taiwan Strait, U.S. leaders are willing to threaten to use or actually use military might to impose "made in Washington" solutions. Such interventions inevitably work to the advantage of certain countries or factions and to the decided disadvantage of others. We should, therefore, not be surprised that aggrieved parties may want to exact revenge against the United States.

Nowhere is that tendency more pronounced than in the Middle East. Washington's pervasive support of Israel and its policies is an obvious source of anti-American sentiment throughout the Islamic world, but it is not the only one. The increasingly extensive U.S. support of an array of "friendly" Arab dictatorships also inflames groups that want to oust those regimes. Washington's friends and allies in the region—Egypt, Algeria, Jordan, Saudi Arabia, Kuwait, and the other Persian Gulf states—have three characteristics in common. They are repressive, corrupt, and faced with growing domestic opposition.

The depth and intensity of popular bitterness toward the United States for being the patron of such autocracies would probably shock most Americans. Even relatively moderate opponents of the incumbent regimes increasingly regard Washington as an enemy. Mohammed Masari, the London-based Saudi exile who heads the Committee for the Defense of Legitimate Rights, typifies that attitude. Masari advocates democracy for Saudi Arabia and repeatedly condemns terrorist acts. Nevertheless, after the bombing of the American barracks in Dhahran, Masari told BBC radio that foreign troops in his country were "legitimate targets" and that the United States should expect similar incidents as long as its soldiers stay in the kingdom propping up the House of Saud.

If Washington insists on playing the role of global policeman, violent retaliation against American targets, both inside and outside the United States, will be one of the inevitable costs of that policy. And the cost appears to be rising. Incidents such as the bombing of the World Trade Center are especially significant. Even at the height of the Vietnam War, Hanoi's agents never dared attack Americans in the United States. The World Trade Center incident indicates that terrorists are becoming bolder.

Perhaps most ironic, some of the terrorists appear to be monsters of our own making. During the 1980s the U.S. government financed, trained, and equipped the Afghan *mujaheddin* in their armed struggle against the Soviet invader. The policy was a short-term success, as Afghan fighters tied down Soviet military units and inflicted numerous casualties. The war itself became so unpopular in the Soviet Union that it probably contributed to the political unraveling of the communist state.

Nevertheless, the policy has produced horrific side effects over the long term. Not only does the chaos in Afghanistan exceed that in such places as Somalia and Bosnia, but alumni of the Afghan war are showing up in insurgent forces and terrorist organizations throughout the Middle East and beyond. And the principal target of their animosity is their onetime patron, the United States. Such are the unintended consequences of an interventionist foreign policy.

A Policy for Dealing with Terrorism

A sustainable policy to deal with the threat of terrorism would have three key elements. First, the United States should stop meddling in conflicts and disputes that do not have a direct and substantial connection to the vital security needs of the American people. A global interventionist strategy was dangerous enough when the lives put in harm's way were primarily those of American military personnel. The strategy has now become prohibitively risky; the lives of thousands, or even millions, of American civilians could be threatened by terrorist attacks. No rational policymaker should want to run such risks except for the most crucial stakes.

Rescinding Washington's global interventionist policy would not be a case of appeasing terrorists, as proponents of interventionism habitually claim. Adopting a more restrained security strategy would be a wise move even if no terrorist threat existed. The present policy is far too expensive and entangles the United States in conflicts in strategically and economically insignificant countries such as Somalia and Bosnia. The danger of terrorism being directed at Americans is merely an additional reason for rejecting interventionism.

Second, the attention and resources of the intelligence agencies need to be focused on serious national security threats such as terrorism. They must not be distracted by inappropriate missions such as dealing with the "threat" of economic espionage. That does not mean that the budget of the intelligence community (nearly $30 billion annually) needs to be increased. The intelligence agencies do not need more money or personnel; they need to better utilize the money and personnel they now have. Indeed, a leaner, better focused intelligence apparatus might well be able to do its job on significantly less than $30 billion a year, and Congress should seriously consider that possibility.

Counterterrorism will pose a great challenge to the intelligence agencies. Monitoring terrorist organizations and assessing their capabilities and intentions is a crucial mission, but penetrating such cells will be exceptionally difficult. Many of them are small, free-lance, highly decentralized operations whose members are almost pathologically suspicious of outsiders. In addition to an extreme reliance on an "old boy network"—in which service in the Afghan war is often a key feature—the personnel are typically motivated by fanatical religious or ideological agendas. Bribes and other inducements that intelligence agencies use to recruit operatives are markedly less effective with such individuals than with officials of corrupt governments.

The decentralized nature of many terrorist organizations makes retaliation as difficult as penetration. Unlike their predecessors in the 1970s and 1980s, today's terrorists often do not boast of their deeds. That makes it difficult even to identify the perpetrators of a terrorist incident, much less to locate and either apprehend or eliminate them.

Nevertheless, the intelligence agencies have a vital role to play in the campaign against terrorism. They must be America's eyes and ears in a dangerous world. The agencies have a twofold mission—to identify international terrorist organizations and plans so they can be thwarted and, whenever those efforts fail, to locate the culprits so that retaliatory measures can be brought to bear.

Third, although many (perhaps most) current terrorist organizations are relatively small, free-lance operations, there are cases in which terrorist initiatives against Americans are directed or sponsored by other governments. Countering such state-sponsored terrorism is not a matter solely for the intelligence or law enforcement agencies. As syndicated columnist Charles Krauthammer argues, the United States has every right to consider such incidents acts of war against the American people and should respond accordingly.

Krauthammer's argument is conceptually correct. Evidence indicates, for example, that two agents in Libya's intelligence service planted the bomb that brought down Pan Am flight 103, killing 189 Americans. It is difficult to believe that those agents acted without the authorization of senior officials in the Libyan government. Therefore, if the evidence of Tripoli's complicity stands up to scrutiny, that incident constitutes an act of war just as surely as if Libyan ships had shelled an American city and inflicted those casualties.

Responding to such an outrage with a declaration of war might seem drastic, but one of the prime constitutional responsibilities of the federal government is to defend the American people from external attacks. It is supremely ironic that Washington is willing to use military force for an assortment of causes around the world, most of which have little if any relevance to the security of the American people, but has treated the slaughter of 189 Americans by the Libyan government as merely an extradition issue involving the two agents.

Issuing a declaration of war does not necessarily mean that U.S. bombers must immediately launch strikes against the target country or the Marines conduct an amphibious invasion. U.S. leaders would have a full range of options for implementing such declarations at times and places of their choosing. War aims could be set at whatever level was deemed appropriate. Options might range from a demand that the perpetrators of the terrorist attack be turned over to American authorities to the complete removal of the offending regime.

A declaration of war is important as a statement of national intent. It also puts the United States in a different position under international law. Imposing a naval blockade, for example, is illegal in peacetime but legal in wartime. Washington could then inform countries trading with America's enemy that a state of war exists and that their ships must remain outside the blockade zone or be subject to boarding or attack.

Although Krauthammer is correct that a state-sponsored terrorist incident is an act of war, not a law enforcement matter, some qualifications need to be attached to his proposal. Most important, there must be clear and compelling evidence of another government's complicity in the attack. When it is a question of the direct participation of government operatives, as was apparently the case in the Pan Am bombing, the issue is simply whether there is sufficient evidence. A trickier situation arises when the allegation is of government sponsorship, rather than direct involvement. In that case, the standard should be that the accused regime must have actively sponsored an organization or individual that it knew intended to attack American civilians. General financial support of, or military training and other assistance to, organizations with political agendas (such as overthrowing the existing government in their respective countries) is not a sufficient casus belli unless the organization has already committed terrorist acts against the American people and the regime has nevertheless continued its sponsorship.

As a matter of policy, Washington should consider a declaration of war only when state-sponsored terrorism has been directed against Americans inside the United States or in another locale where they have a reasonable expectation of safety. (Passengers aboard an airliner flying in international airspace certainly qualify.) American civilians who travel to areas where there is an armed conflict are in a different category. An attack on such civilians is no less an act of terrorism, but the American government and society cannot be expected to incur the risks entailed in prosecuting wars merely to avenge the deaths of their fellow citizens who have voluntarily put themselves in harm's way. Those civilians who insist on being in such places as Sarajevo, Mogadishu, or Kabul must do so at their risk.

Finally, in addition to the requirement for clear and compelling evidence of state complicity in a terrorist act, it is imperative that the evidence be presented to Congress along with a request for a formal declaration of war. A decision about whether the Republic goes to war is too important to leave in the hands of the president and his appointed advisers. The decision ought to be made—as the Constitution specifies—by Congress. Not only is that mandated by the Constitution—a fact that has largely been forgotten as chief executives have waged numerous presidential wars during the past half century—but it is an important check on rash action. The president may believe that the evidence of state-sponsored terrorism is compelling in a particular case, but others may conclude otherwise. It is important that the president's assessment be evaluated by an independent tribunal.

The policy outlined here for dealing with international terrorism is not a panacea, but it is prudent, balanced, and sustainable. We would not go around the planet looking for trouble, as Washington's current policy has us doing. But if trouble comes to us despite a policy of restraint, we will be prepared to use the intelligence agencies to identify and neutralize such threats whenever possible. We must also be willing to use the armed forces to punish those responsible for terrorist outrages that cannot be thwarted.

Suggested Readings

Bandow, Doug. "Terrorism Is a Result of U.S. Foreign Policy." *Conservative Chronicle,* August 28, 1996.

Carpenter, Ted Galen. "The Unexpected Consequences of Afghanistan." *World Policy Journal* (Spring 1994).

Kober, Stanley. "Why Spy? The Uses and Misuses of Intelligence." Cato Institute Policy Analysis no. 265, December 12, 1996.

Krauthammer, Charles. "Declare War on Terrorism." *Washington Post,* August 9, 1996.

Laqueur, Walter. "Postmodern Terrorism." *Foreign Affairs* (September–October 1996).

Rubin, Trudy. "Free-Lance Terrorism." *Journal of Commerce,* August 8, 1996.

Steel, Ronald. "When Worlds Collide." *New York Times,* July 21, 1996.

—Prepared by Ted Galen Carpenter

46. Persian Gulf Policy

The U.S. government should

- terminate formal and informal U.S. security commitments to Bahrain, Kuwait, Oman, Qatar, Saudi Arabia, and the United Arab Emirates;
- abandon the "dual containment" policy directed against Iran and Iraq;
- end U.S. participation in Operation Provide Comfort and Operation Southern Watch;
- withdraw U.S. military personnel and prepositioned equipment associated with U.S. security commitments to the southern gulf countries;
- encourage the southern gulf states to take responsibility for their own security by bolstering their national self-defense capabilities and enhancing regional defense cooperation through the Gulf Cooperation Council;
- provide limited U.S. assistance, especially advice on enhancing the effectiveness of national force structure and integrating southern gulf military capabilities, to the southern gulf states individually and to the GCC; and
- end its policy of trying to manage Persian Gulf security and instead act only as a balancer of last resort if developments in the region pose a serious threat to vital U.S. national security interests.

Since the 1990 Iraqi invasion of Kuwait, Washington has assumed almost total responsibility for Persian Gulf security. The twin pillars of U.S. Persian Gulf strategy are the deeply flawed "dual containment" policy—which seeks to contain Iran and Iraq simultaneously—and U.S. security commitments to the southern gulf states of Bahrain, Kuwait,

Oman, Qatar, Saudi Arabia, and the United Arab Emirates. It is a risky and expensive strategy that threatens to embroil the United States in myriad conflicts (including civil wars) in the perennially unstable gulf region. The strategy also is probably unsustainable over the long term.

U.S. Interests in the Persian Gulf Region

The United States has no vital national security interests at stake that justify attempting to manage Persian Gulf security. The end of the Cold War has reduced the strategic significance of the gulf region, and there is considerable disagreement about the nature and importance of the remaining American interests there. Proponents of an activist U.S. policy usually cite Persian Gulf oil as the primary reason to maintain current policy.

Unhindered access to gulf oil is desirable, but it is not so essential to the American economy that it rises to the level of a vital interest. The United States currently buys only $11 billion worth of gulf oil per year, yet U.S. taxpayers spend $40 billion to $50 billion (some analysts estimate as much as $70 billion) per year to defend the region. During the Cold War, the possibility that the Soviet Union could gain control of gulf oil was a formidable threat. Regional powers, however, depend too heavily on oil revenue to withhold supplies altogether and could raise prices only modestly. Moreover, Western Europe and Japan are much more dependent on gulf oil than is the United States; to the extent that outside powers should be concerned about regional contingencies, the West Europeans and the Japanese should play a leading role.

Dual Containment

Martin Indyk, the U.S. ambassador to Israel and the architect of the dual containment policy, set forth the following conditions in 1993 as essential to the pursuit of dual containment:

- cohesion of the gulf war coalition;
- cooperation of Israel, Egypt, Turkey, Saudi Arabia, and the other GCC states in U.S. efforts to preserve a regional balance of power favorable to the United States;
- continued U.S. military presence in the region; and
- successful restriction of Iraqi and Iranian military ambitions.

By the end of 1996, two of those conditions were clearly absent. The gulf war coalition began to unravel years ago, but its demise was undeniable after September 1996, when the United States launched cruise missiles against targets in Iraq in response to Iraqi participation in attacks against the Kurdish city of Irbil. Great Britain was the only enthusiastic backer of the U.S. action; Israel, Germany, Japan, and Kuwait offered only belated and lukewarm endorsements. All of the other gulf war allies either refused to endorse the operation—as such key U.S. allies as France and Saudi Arabia did—or denounced it outright—as Russia and China did.

The ability of the United States to rely on the cooperation of its major allies in the region (except perhaps Israel) to support U.S. efforts to influence the regional balance of power is likewise a thing of the past. Not only did U.S. regional allies fail to endorse Operation Desert Strike, but Turkey, Saudi Arabia, and Jordan refused to allow the United States to use air bases within their territory to conduct the operation.

Two of the four prerequisites for dual containment no longer exist, and the other two are increasingly precarious. The extent to which the United States has succeeded in restricting Iranian and Iraqi military ambitions is unclear. And the U.S. military presence in the region is increasingly the target of violent opposition, as the 1996 bombing in Dhahran, Saudi Arabia, and the 1995 bombing in Riyadh (which together killed 24 U.S. troops) suggest. In the conservative and xenophobic southern gulf societies, the American military presence is often a lightning rod for discontent.

Moreover, dual containment is a bad policy in any event. Though it seeks to avoid previous ill-fated attempts to cultivate one regime to counter the influence and power of the other, it invites even more problems. The consequences of isolating Iran and Iraq for the United States could be grave. An anti-U.S. alliance between Tehran and Baghdad is not inconceivable. And in the event of either regime's breakdown, many forces in the gulf region will seek to exploit the ensuing chaos, making a regional war—which the United States will have little hope of avoiding—nearly inevitable.

U.S. Security Commitments in the Southern Gulf

The other pillar of U.S. Persian Gulf policy is the network of formal and informal security commitments to the southern gulf states. The southern gulf is effectively a U.S. military protectorate. Regional sensitivities prohibit the United States from permanently basing U.S. military personnel in the gulf countries, but approximately 10,000 to 15,000 troops associated with the Fifth Fleet and rotational air force deployments in Saudi Arabia are in the region at any given time, plus troops participating in exercises.

The United States also has large amounts of prepositioned equipment in Kuwait and Qatar and is negotiating for permission to move additional equipment to the United Arab Emirates. Guaranteeing southern gulf security, however, is a risky undertaking and may ultimately prove an unsustainable policy.

There are numerous disputes between U.S. allies in the region. Although the U.S. military presence in the gulf is ostensibly intended to protect friendly countries from Iran and Iraq, many of the southern gulf countries fear threats from one another more than they fear Tehran's mullahs or Saddam Hussein. The smaller states are suspicious of Saudi Arabia. Ongoing feuds between the smaller states—Bahrain and Qatar, Oman and the UAE, and others—are also a source of tension.

The southern gulf monarchies also face serious internal problems. The fall in oil revenues has severely strained the region's cradle-to-grave welfare states. That economic pressure has tremendous political implications in countries where corrupt and authoritarian rulers have long relied on state largesse to pacify restive populations. Consequently, gulf monarchs face increasingly serious internal security threats. Major disturbances in Bahrain, for example, have prompted some experts to speculate that Bahrain may become the "next Iran." The comparison with Iran has also been applied to Saudi Arabia, where internal discontent also often has a strong element of anti-Americanism, as attacks on U.S. military installations in the kingdom have indicated.

Burden sharing is yet another major—and growing—problem. The American public has little tolerance for paying for the security of oil monarchies (or for transforming U.S. troops into mercenary forces at the service of sheiks, for that matter). Yet the southern gulf monarchies are increasingly unwilling or unable to pay the United States to defend them. The United States, if it is determined to continue guaranteeing gulf security, must plan on covering much, probably most, of the costs. Those costs are at least $40 billion per year and rising—an expense U.S. taxpayers cannot afford and should not be asked to pay.

A Way Out of the Persian Gulf Morass

Instead of devoting tremendous resources to a strategy that is probably unsustainable, the United States should rethink its Persian Gulf strategy. No policy will be risk free, but a lower profile and a more realistic strategy would probably be less risky and would certainly be less costly.

The United States should abandon the dual containment policy. According to the criteria set out by its own author, it is no longer a realistic policy (and many experts would argue that it never was). And instead of acting as the guarantor of Persian Gulf security, the United States should make clear to the southern gulf monarchies that they, not Washington, are primarily responsible for their own security.

That would restore the incentive for the GCC states to think seriously about security cooperation—not only with one another but perhaps with other Middle Eastern powers as well. The United States would still have the option to intervene in the region in the event of a threat to U.S. vital security interests, but U.S. involvement in regional crises would not be automatic. Unraveling the current tangle of U.S. security commitments to the southern gulf states would restore the full range of policy options instead of steering the United States into regional or civil wars.

Suggested Readings

Carpenter, Ted Galen. "Misguided Missiles." *New York Times,* September 12, 1996.

Carpenter, Ted Galen, ed. *America Entangled: The Persian Gulf Crisis and Its Consequences.* Washington: Cato Institute, 1991.

Conry, Barbara. "America's Misguided Policy of Dual Containment in the Persian Gulf." Cato Institute Foreign Policy Briefing no. 33, November 10, 1994.

———. "Time Bomb: The Escalation of U.S. Security Commitments in the Persian Gulf Region." Cato Institute Policy Analysis no. 258, August 29, 1996.

Gause, F. Gregory III. "The Illogic of Dual Containment." *Foreign Affairs* 73 (March–April 1994): 56–66.

Hadar, Leon. *Quagmire: America in the Middle East.* Washington: Cato Institute, 1991.

—Prepared by Barbara Conry

47. Toward a New Relationship with Japan

> **The U.S. government should**
>
> - inform the Japanese government that all U.S. military forces will be withdrawn from Japan in five years,
> - inform the Japanese government that the mutual security treaty will be terminated in seven years,
> - adopt a policy that encourages Japan to take primary responsibility for East Asian stability,
> - replace the U.S.-Japanese alliance with a more limited and informal security relationship,
> - redeploy approximately 50 percent of the U.S. air and naval units now stationed in Japan to Guam and other U.S. territories in the Central Pacific and demobilize the rest,
> - avoid the temptation to use the security commitment as bargaining leverage on trade issues, and
> - have as its fundamental goal the creation of a new relationship with Tokyo that treats Japan as a mature and responsible great power.

The U.S. military alliance with Japan no longer serves the best interests of either country. Washington subsidizes Japan's defense at the expense of American taxpayers. That subsidy, which has amounted to more than $900 billion (in 1996 dollars) since the early 1950s, is a powerful incentive for the Japanese government to continue free riding on the U.S. security guarantee. And Japan's much-touted host-nation support of $5 billion a year actually pays only a small fraction of the total cost of the U.S. security commitment.

Even worse, Washington's policy encourages a dependent mentality on the part of the Japanese and enables Tokyo to evade political and military responsibilities in East Asia even when Japan has important interests at stake. Japanese officials state repeatedly that, in the event of war, Japanese military units would not join U.S. forces in combat operations unless Japan itself were attacked.

U.S. leaders foolishly perpetuate Japan's security dependence. Washington's East Asian policy is held hostage to the exaggerated fears of Japan's neighbors, who oppose a more active military role for Tokyo. A lingering undercurrent of distrust toward Japan in U.S. policy circles has also been a major motive for Washington's "smothering" strategy.

A new policy is needed. It would seek a mature relationship between equals and recognize that Japan, as the principal great power in East Asia, must play a more significant role in the region's security affairs. The United States should withdraw its forces from Japan over the next five years and keep smaller forces based in Guam and other U.S. territories. The U.S.-Japanese alliance ought to be replaced by a more limited, informal security relationship.

The Illusion of Change at the Clinton-Hashimoto Summit

Instead of squarely addressing the need for fundamental change, leaders of both countries have engaged in misleading propaganda offensives to convince their own populations that meaningful change is already taking place. The strategy of fostering such illusions was most evident following the April 1996 summit meeting between President Clinton and Japanese prime minister Ryutaro Hashimoto. Media accounts, manipulated by U.S. and Japanese officials, portrayed the agreements that emerged from the summit as marking a historic change in the U.S.-Japanese alliance.

That portrayal was erroneous. Although the United States agreed to consolidate its military bases on Okinawa, overall U.S. troop levels in Japan will remain the same. There was no hint of an eventual drawdown of those forces, much less that Washington would insist that Japan assume responsibility for its own defense.

The two changes in Tokyo's policy were equally tepid. Japan merely agreed to sell nonlethal supplies to U.S. forces in peacetime; there was no commitment to provide military materiel, nor was there an obligation to provide even nonlethal items in wartime. Tokyo's promise to conduct a review of its defense policy to determine whether there can be greater bilateral cooperation to deal with situations "in the areas surrounding Japan and which will have an important influence on the peace and security of Japan" appears unlikely to produce meaningful changes in the country's military posture. At most, it might lead to Japanese logistical support for U.S. military operations during an East Asian crisis. Even that meager change is increasingly doubtful. In the months since the summit, Hashimoto and other officials have emphasized that the review will not lead to a lifting of Japan's constitutional ban on involvement in collective defense missions. There is no indication whatsoever that Japanese troops ever intend to fight alongside American forces, unless Japan itself comes under attack. Despite the official and media hype, the summit agreements do not alter Japan's status as a U.S. military dependent.

A new—really new—relationship is needed. The huge demonstrations against the U.S. military bases following the rape of a 12-year-old Okinawa girl by three American soldiers, and public opinion surveys showing that many Japanese respondents—especially those on Okinawa where a vast majority of U.S. military personnel are stationed—now oppose the troop presence, suggest that the security relationship is under stress. The results of a nonbinding referendum in Okinawa on September 8, 1996, in which some 90 percent of those voting endorsed a proposal to reduce the size and number of U.S. bases on the island, confirm that point.

Japan's Evasion of Security Issues

But there is a more fundamental reason to phase out not just the troop presence but the alliance itself. Keeping Japan a U.S. military dependent is not healthy for either country. It perpetuates an expensive and dangerous set of security obligations for the United States while it encourages the Japanese to act as though they can forever evade difficult political and military issues.

The Japanese justification for military inaction is the country's "Peace Constitution," which was virtually imposed by Gen. Douglas MacArthur's occupation government after World War II. Article 9 of that document renounces war and asserts that "land, sea, and air forces, as well as other war potential" will never be maintained. Thus, Japanese officials contend, Japan is precluded from playing an active military role in world affairs.

Whenever Japan's political elite has wanted to pursue a particular policy objective, however, it has been able to find sufficient elasticity in article 9. (For example, in the early 1980s Japan decided to build the naval forces needed to defend the sea lanes out to 1,000 nautical miles from the archipelago.) Conversely, when Tokyo wants to avoid undertaking security responsibilities, the Peace Constitution provides a convenient excuse.

469

Overcoming Unwarranted Suspicion of Japan

U.S. officials who favor keeping Japan militarily dependent rarely admit publicly that the United States simply does not trust Japan—although a number of indiscreet comments in recent years confirm that such distrust exists. Instead, they contend that any significant Japanese rearmament or a more assertive policy by Tokyo would alarm Japan's East Asian neighbors, thereby producing a regional arms race and dangerous instability.

The other East Asian nations do fear a resurgent Japan and want the United States to maintain a large military presence to contain potential Japanese power. Although it would be unwise to discount the apprehension with which Japan is still regarded throughout East Asia, the specter of a larger Japanese military role may be less traumatic than it might at first appear. With the collapse of the Soviet Union, Japan could probably protect its security interests with a modest increase in defense spending, say to the level of 1.5 percent of gross domestic product. Only the most paranoid would be alarmed by a buildup of that magnitude. Moreover, the East Asian countries have some cause to worry about China's ambitions in the coming years and might not be all that averse to a stronger Japan that could help constrain those ambitions.

Even if regional leaders do not prove to be that farsighted, both East Asian and U.S. officials need to outgrow the simplistic assumption that Japan's military role must inevitably be one of extremes—either the rampant expansionism of six decades ago or the self-effacing dependency of the post–World War II era. It is probable that modern, democratic Japan would play a prudent role somewhere between those two extremes. In other words, Japan would act as a typical prosperous, conservative great power in the international system.

Moreover, the pertinent question from the standpoint of U.S. foreign policy should not be whether the status quo is more comfortable for the regional states but whether it is in the best interests of the American people. It is difficult to justify preserving expensive and dangerous military commitments indefinitely merely to spare Japan and its neighbors the difficulties of confronting and overcoming old animosities. Washington cannot permit its policy in East Asia to be held hostage by the ghosts of World War II.

Washington needs to encourage Japan to assume a more responsible security role. America's overall objective should be a reasonably stable balance of power among the principal East Asian nations. An activist Japan is an essential part, indeed the single most important component, of that balance-of-power system. In particular, Japan is the only country—other than the United States—that will be capable of being a strategic counterweight to China in the coming decades.

The Current Relationship Is Unsustainable

U.S. policymakers ignore mounting evidence that a security relationship between America as patron and Japan as dependent is not sustainable in the long term. By clinging to the status quo, American leaders risk an abrupt and nasty rupture of the alliance that could poison American-Japanese relations and create the dangerous power vacuum in East Asia that Washington has tried so hard to prevent.

There are storm warnings in both countries. The outcry against the U.S. military presence following the rape incident in Okinawa and the results of the September referendum on the U.S. bases are only the most recent and spectacular examples of rising Japanese annoyance. Anger about escalating U.S. demands on the trade front is another, albeit less visible, manifestation.

Sentiment in the United States toward Japan has likewise become more confrontational. An especially lethal danger will occur if Americans who are angry about trade matters begin to link that issue to Japanese free riding on defense. There are indications that such a linkage is already taking place, as evidenced by the widely discussed *Foreign Affairs* article by Chalmers Johnson and E. B. Keehn that appeared in the summer of 1995.

Public discontent with alleged Japanese misdeeds on trade issues will eventually produce pressure to adopt the suggestion of Johnson, Keehn, and others to threaten the withdrawal of the U.S. military shield as bargaining "leverage." American advocates of a confrontational trade policy will not be content indefinitely to subsidize the defense of a nation that they believe engages in unfair trade practices. Even Takakazu Kuriyama, Japan's former ambassador to the United States, has stated that the greatest danger to the alliance is "spillover" from economic conflict.

The outbreak of an armed conflict somewhere in East Asia that did not include an attack on Japan could also fracture the alliance. Japanese officials have made it clear that their country would merely hold America's coat while U.S. forces intervened to restore the peace. Johnson and Keehn accurately judge the probable consequences of such inaction in the case of a conflict in Korea: "The Pentagon should ponder the specter of Japanese warships standing idly by while the United States takes major risks to defend South Korea. Popular support in the United States for any defense of Japan would instantly vanish.''

That scenario underscores the inherent fragility of the U.S.-Japanese security relationship. Its continued viability is contingent on the alliance's never being put to the test by a military conflict in East Asia. U.S. policymakers will of course argue that the principal purpose of the alliance is to deter such a conflict in the first place. That is undoubtedly true, and the strategic partnership probably does make the outbreak of combat in the region less likely. Nevertheless, it is dubious wisdom to invest *all* of one's hopes in the infallibility of deterrence. To be viable, an alliance must also be of unquestioned value to both parties if deterrence fails and a war has to be waged. An arrangement in which one party assumes most of the costs in blood and treasure while the other party reaps the benefits is unstable as well as unjust.

U.S. leaders need to foster a U.S.-Japanese relationship based on the realities of the post–Cold War world, not a bygone era in which Japan lacked the economic strength or the political confidence to play an assertive, independent role in international affairs and the emotional wounds of World War II were still fresh. The new goal should be a mature relationship between equals—a relationship that recognizes that Japan is a great power in every respect.

Toward a New Relationship

Several steps must be taken to implement substantive changes. First, the United States should inform Japan that it intends to withdraw its forces from Japanese territory over the next five years and that it will renounce the security treaty two years later. At that point, Japan will be expected to provide entirely for its own defense. Washington should implement its withdrawal strategy without rancor and state explicitly that the move is not motivated by traditional complaints about burden sharing or by the more recent tensions over trade disputes. Under no circumstances should the United States use the security commitment as a bargaining chip. That approach would be a blueprint for Japanese resentment, and the damage to U.S.-Japanese relations could last decades.

Second, Washington should indicate to Tokyo that it no longer objects to Japan's assuming a more active political and military posture in East Asia. Quite the contrary, U.S. officials ought to adopt the position that, as the principal democratic great power in the region, Japan has a moral obligation to help stabilize East Asia and contain disruptive or expansionist threats.

Third, discussions should begin immediately about a new, more limited security relationship. Japanese and American security interests are likely to overlap in the coming decades, and it is reasonable to explore avenues of cooperation in those areas where there is a sufficient convergence of interests. That cooperation should not, however, take the form of a new alliance. An ongoing security dialogue and occasional joint military exercises would be more appropriate. Elaborate, formal treaty commitments are a bad idea in general. They lock a nation into commitments that may make sense under one set of conditions but become dubious or even counterproductive when conditions change.

The United States has some important East Asian interests and cannot be indifferent to the region's fate. No reasonable person would suggest that the United States withdraw its forces to Seattle and San Diego and adopt a Fortress America strategy. But having some interests in the region and being willing to make a contribution to its stability are a far cry from volunteering to be point man in every crisis. America can still protect its core interests with a significantly reduced military presence based in Guam, Wake, Midway, and other locations in the central and west-central Pacific. There is no need to have large numbers of forward-deployed forces, much less units to serve as automatic tripwires if even a minor conflict erupts.

The United States should be the balancer of last resort, not the intervenor of first resort, in East Asia's security equation. And the most crucial step in adopting that strategy is to devolve primary regional security responsibilities to Japan, the region's leading power.

Suggested Readings

Bandow, Doug. "The Japan-U.S. Arrangement Is Unfair to Both." *Asian Wall Street Journal,* September 10, 1996.

Carpenter, Ted Galen. "Paternalism and Dependence: The U.S.-Japanese Security Relationship." Cato Institute Policy Analysis no. 244, November 1, 1995.

———. "Smoke and Mirrors: The Clinton-Hashimoto Summit." Cato Institute Foreign Policy Briefing no. 41, May 16, 1996.

Johnson, Chalmers, and E. B. Keehn. "The Pentagon's Ossified Strategy." *Foreign Affairs* 74 (July–August 1995).

Layne, Christopher. "Less Is More: Minimal Realism in East Asia." *National Interest* 43 (Spring 1996).

—Prepared by Ted Galen Carpenter

48. Dealing with a Resurgent China

The U.S. government should

- end the annual turmoil and acrimony over the trade relationship by granting China most-favored-nation trade status that does not require annual certification;
- press Beijing for more serious enforcement of the intellectual property rights of American companies and individuals;
- inform Taiwan that the United States will not intervene militarily if a conflict breaks out between the People's Republic of China and Taiwan;
- allow Taiwan to purchase the weapons it believes are necessary to defend itself from possible coercion by Beijing;
- encourage the development of a balance-of-power security system in East Asia, managed by the East Asian powers, with Washington playing a low-key supporting role; and
- reject suggestions to adopt a confrontational "containment" policy directed against China; instead, pursue maximum economic relations to have a liberalizing impact on China's political, economic, and social systems.

Relations between the United States and the People's Republic of China have become increasingly testy in recent years, with acrimonious disputes over a variety of issues, including human rights, trade, and the status of Taiwan. There is growing sentiment in Congress and elsewhere for a more hard-line U.S. policy toward Beijing. In its extreme form, that sentiment favors the adoption of a full-blown containment policy, treating China as the Soviet Union was treated during the Cold War.

It would be a mistake for the United States to embrace a containment policy. Such an approach could produce a self-fulfilling prophecy, as a cornered China lashed out against its superpower adversary, thereby becoming the aggressor that the containment policy was designed to prevent.

One cannot ignore, however, the fact that some of Beijing's actions are cause for concern. From the standpoint of American interests, the PRC's casual export of nuclear and ballistic missile technology to Iran and other countries ruled by unpredictable, unsavory, and rabidly anti-American regimes is troubling. That action clearly does not improve the global security environment. Similarly, Beijing's belligerent behavior toward Taiwan and other neighbors in East Asia raises serious questions about what kind of great power China intends to be.

The challenge for an effective U.S. policy toward the PRC is to avoid either provoking needless confrontations or allowing to develop a strategic environment in which Beijing can threaten important American interests. That goal requires Washington to establish clear priorities in its China policy—something that the Clinton administration has generally failed to do.

Trade Issues

U.S. policymakers need to understand that no country, even one as powerful as the United States, can dictate to other great powers. Washington's relations with China in recent years, however, seem to consist of a lengthy series of demands with little hope that Beijing will respond positively to any of them. Perhaps the least constructive aspect of the relationship has been the annual controversy about whether the United States should extend China's most-favored-nation (MFN) trade status for another year. Beijing's critics in Congress and elsewhere use the recertification requirement to mount campaigns to condition extension on improvements in the PRC's human rights record, reductions in the multi-billion-dollar bilateral trade deficit, greater protection for the intellectual property rights of American firms, and a host of other issues.

The annual spectacle does little except cause needless friction in U.S.-Chinese relations. The temptation to link trade and human rights is understandable, since Beijing's systematic brutality toward political dissidents offends anyone who values individual freedom. Such repression is all too common in the world, however, and the United States cannot allow moral outrage to govern its trade relations with foreign countries. Moreover, as noted in Chapter 54, the freedom to buy or sell products and services without arbitrary government interference is itself an important human right—for Americans as well as Chinese.

Conditioning MFN status on a reduction in the trade deficit is even less justified. The obsession with eradicating deficits with such countries as China and Japan is one of the more unfortunate features of Washington's trade policy. The notion that trade deficits injure the American economy while surpluses strengthen it is unsupported by either contemporary or historical evidence. Indeed, the United States ran sizable trade surpluses during much of the Great Depression in the 1930s, and the last surplus occurred in 1975, a recession year. The bilateral trade deficit should be a nonissue in U.S.-Chinese relations.

Concerns about Beijing's apparent indifference to the pervasive piracy of American intellectual property in China are more substantive. Yet it would still be a mistake to condition MFN status on a resolution of that problem. Instead, U.S. officials should redouble their diplomatic efforts to pressure the Chinese government to take action against such theft. Some progress has been made in recent months, and this is one issue on which the authorities in Beijing appear willing to respond to American concerns.

Americans who believe that obstructing trade relations will coerce the Chinese government into being more cooperative and democratic advocate precisely the wrong policy. Sanctions would injure primarily the sectors of China's economy that are the most dynamic and have the most extensive connections with the outside world. Those sectors are dominated by younger, cosmopolitan Chinese who view the aging communist autocrats in Beijing with thinly disguised distaste and impatience. We should want to strengthen the new centers of power and change in China, not weaken them by disrupting trade relations. Although there is an outside chance that a worst-case scenario—a powerful Chinese economy exploited by an authoritarian government with an aggressively expansionist agenda—will materialize in the coming decades, it is more likely that economic liberalization will be followed by political liberalization, as we have seen in South Korea, Taiwan, and other East Asian countries. Maintaining, indeed increasing, our economic relations with China maximizes the probability of that benign outcome.

Washington should end the annual squabbling by granting China unconditional and indefinite MFN status—which should be renamed "normal trade relations" to better reflect what MFN actually gives any nation so designated. To the extent that we want to address such issues as the treatment of political dissidents and the protection of intellectual property rights, those matters should be handled through diplomatic channels.

Beijing's Security Behavior

While Washington should defuse the confrontation over trade issues, U.S. officials need to express greater concern about other aspects of Beijing's behavior. For example, the PRC has increasingly exported sophisticated weapons, ballistic missile components, and even nuclear-related technology to a number of countries, including states with virulently anti-American agendas, most notably Iran. There are indications that the civilian authorities in Beijing may not be fully in charge of policy and that some of the sales were free-lance initiatives by the People's Liberation Army. Washington needs to press President Jiang Zemin and other leaders about those sales, especially since some of the transfers may violate Beijing's commitments under the Nuclear Nonproliferation Treaty and other international agreements. If the sales were made with the approval of the civilian leadership, Washington should clearly express its view that such actions are destabilizing and could pose a threat to America's security. If the PLA is operating on its own, there are even more serious concerns.

Another troubling aspect of Beijing's political and military behavior is its increasingly aggressive conduct toward its neighbors. Beijing's belligerent actions toward Taiwan in late 1995 and early 1996 received a considerable amount of attention in the United States, but the PRC has also engaged in a distressing amount of saber rattling on other issues during the past two years. It has shown a willingness to use its growing naval power to press territorial claims to the Spratly Islands in the South China Sea, which led to a serious confrontation with the Philippines, another claimant, in 1995. More recently, the PRC made threatening statements and gestures (including military exercises) toward Japan in the territorial dispute between the two countries over eight islands—known as the Diaoyu islands in China and the Senkaku islands in Japan.

The point is not that the United States has important interests at stake in such disputes. Whose claim to islands in the South China Sea is most valid ought to be a matter of indifference to Washington, and under no circumstances should the United States allow itself to be drawn into that multisided dispute if armed conflict erupts. Similarly, whether China or Japan has the better claim to the Diaoyu (Senkaku) islands should have no relevance to the United States. (Unfortunately, because of America's alliance with Japan, this country could become entangled in such a petty squabble—yet another reason to terminate the U.S.-Japanese security treaty.) Even Taiwan's continued de facto independence, while certainly desirable, does not constitute an interest sufficient to justify America's willingness to risk war.

The pertinent point for the United States is what Beijing's aggressive posture may be indicating about China's prospective behavior as a rising great power in the international system. If Beijing intends to pursue an aggressively expansionist agenda, that is a matter of concern to Washington. China's intentions become all the more important because of the government's concerted effort in recent years to build up its military power. Beijing is clearly modernizing its forces and seems determined to have both a first-class air force and a blue-water navy. Although one should not overstate the magnitude of that buildup—the PRC's expanded military spending started from a low base and is still only an estimated $30 billion to $40 billion a year—the trend bears watching. China is already a major power with a modest but potent nuclear arsenal and ICBMs capable of reaching American territory. Washington, therefore, cannot be indifferent to Beijing's conduct in the security realm.

The dilemma facing the United States is how to avoid becoming embroiled in China's disputes with its neighbors without having a power vacuum develop in East Asia that might prove irresistibly tempting to Beijing. The latter development could lead to China's domination of the region and the emergence of a serious security threat to the United States. Nowhere is the dilemma more acute than with regard to the chief flash point in U.S.-Chinese relations, Taiwan.

The Most Dangerous Issue: Taiwan

Beijing's missile tests and military exercises in the Taiwan Strait in early 1996 underscored the danger that the United States may someday be pressured to defend Taiwan, at considerable peril to the American people. Although the crisis has temporarily eased, my conversations with officials of the Republic of China on Taiwan suggest that the long-term trend is ominous. Beijing insists that Taiwan is merely a renegade province of the PRC, and communist officials brusquely refuse to renounce the use of force to achieve reunification. Leaders of the ROC, although officially endorsing the concept of one China, seek expanded international recognition of their government and exude the confidence that comes from Taiwan's burgeoning economic power and successful democratization.

Yet it is doubtful that Taiwan could successfully defend itself against a PRC attack. Although Beijing probably does not have the airlift and sealift capacity to launch a successful invasion, it does possess sufficient

479

air and naval power to blockade and bombard Taiwan—unless the U.S. Seventh Fleet intervenes. American intervention, however, would risk a clash between two nuclear-armed great powers.

Taiwan's de facto security dependence on the United States is dangerous for all concerned. Instead of pledging to intervene in the event of a PRC attack on Taiwan, as suggested by the ROC's "friends" in the United States, Washington should allow Taiwan to buy the weapons needed to become militarily self-sufficient.

Unfortunately, the Clinton administration continues to drag its feet on Taipei's requests. ROC policymakers stress that Taiwan urgently wants to upgrade its military capabilities. Although Washington has been responsive to some requests—F-16 fighters and Stinger anti-aircraft missiles—administration officials have thus far declined to approve sales of other crucial items. Specifically, the Taiwanese want to buy attack submarines and develop, with U.S. assistance, an anti-ballistic-missile system. Submarines are considered especially important, because, unless the ROC has at least a modest fleet of subs, Beijing's navy could easily dominate the Taiwan Strait.

Washington contends that approving the sale of submarines would violate agreements with Beijing under which the United States promised not to provide Taiwan with "offensive weapons" or to alter the military balance. That rationale is misplaced on two counts. First, the distinction between offensive and defensive weapons is largely fictional; much depends on the objectives of the regime using the weapons. An F-16, for example, can be used for an unprovoked attack or to repel aggression. Second, the PRC's military capabilities have expanded dramatically since the early 1980s; approving the sale of submarines and anti-aircraft missiles to Taiwan would arguably restore, rather than disrupt, the military balance.

Administration leaders ought to recognize that the alternative to Taiwan's military self-reliance will be growing pressure on the United States to shield the island from attack. Since Beijing has nuclear warheads mounted on ICBMs capable of reaching American cities, a commitment to defend Taiwan would be extremely dangerous.

It would also be a commitment with shaky credibility. The credibility of a promise to defend an ally or client from a nuclear-armed adversary depends primarily on the relative importance of the issue at stake to the guarantor power and to the challenging power. Lessons drawn from America's Cold War experience with the Soviet Union may lead us to make overly optimistic assumptions about the outcome of a confrontation with the PRC over Taiwan.

The Kremlin considered it reasonably credible that the United States would risk nuclear war to keep such strategically and economically important prizes as Western Europe and Northeast Asia out of the orbit of a totalitarian superpower. A threat to incur the same grave risk merely to keep the PRC from absorbing Taiwan—a political entity the United States does not even officially recognize—is less plausible. In December 1995 a PRC military official bluntly told a prominent American visitor that Beijing did not fear U.S. intervention because "American leaders care more about Los Angeles than they do about Taiwan." Perhaps that comment is mere bluster, but we must consider the consequences if it is not.

ROC officials also seem skeptical about the willingness of the United States to risk war with Beijing to defend Taiwan. They understand that there is no treaty commitment from the United States nor are there American troops stationed on Taiwan to guarantee U.S. entanglement in any conflict that might erupt. Most of the Taiwanese realize that only their own strong military forces can provide a reliable guarantee of the ROC's security.

A promise to risk the lives of millions of Americans to defend Taiwan is not credible to the PRC or the ROC, and it is a promise that rational Americans would never want their government to fulfill. We can avoid the odious alternatives of either honoring a perilous commitment or of abandoning a defenseless Taiwan in the midst of a crisis. A far better option is to let Taiwan buy the weapons it needs for its own defense.

America as East Asia's Lone Ranger

America's dominant position in East Asia has contributed to the region's stability, but the tensions between the PRC and Taiwan in late 1995 and early 1996 demonstrated that the policy has an alarming drawback. In essence, the United States has volunteered to be on the front lines of every regional military crisis. That is an exceedingly dangerous strategy.

Although the most recent PRC-Taiwan crisis has receded, there is a high probability of similar imbroglios in the coming years. Not only could the United States find itself entangled in a perilous military confrontation, it might have to wage the ensuing struggle virtually alone. Taiwan would undoubtedly contribute to its own defense, but the reaction in various East Asian capitals to Beijing's menacing behavior indicated that assistance from Washington's other "friends" would be problematic, at best.

Indeed, virtually all of the East Asian governments made a concerted effort to distance their policies from that of the United States as the Clinton administration dispatched two aircraft carriers to the western Pacific to demonstrate concern about the rising tensions in the Taiwan Strait. South Korea and the Philippines both stressed that their ''mutual'' defense treaties with the United States did not cover contingencies in the strait. Such countries as Malaysia, Indonesia, Thailand, and Australia contented themselves with the banal response of urging restraint on all sides, conspicuously declining to endorse Washington's moves. Indeed, they echoed Beijing's position that Taiwan is a renegade province. Even Japan, the principal U.S. ally in the region, merely expressed ''understanding'' of the Seventh Fleet's deployment.

That glaring lack of support demonstrates that Washington's encouragement of dependency on the part of the noncommunist East Asian countries has created a most unhealthy situation. Those nations seek the best of both worlds: they want the United States to protect them from Chinese aggression, if that problem should arise, but they do not want to incur Beijing's wrath (or even jeopardize their commerce with China) by allying themselves with a hard-line U.S. policy. That may be a good, albeit cynical, deal for them, but it puts the United States in a terrible position. If China does make a bid for regional hegemony at some point, there is literally no power other than the United States that is positioned to block that bid. That is a blueprint for a U.S.-Chinese war in which China's neighbors conveniently remain on the sidelines.

Instead of continuing to foster the dependence of Japan, South Korea, and other East Asian nations, U.S. policymakers should make clear that America will not risk its very survival to defend them and preserve the stability of their region. Since they have far more important interests at stake than we do, they ought to incur the costs and risks of that mission. Washington's goal should be the emergence of a reasonably stable balance of power in East Asia. China might well be the single most powerful nation in that setting, but Japan and an assortment of midsized powers would have the capability—and the incentive—to counterbalance China and put a limit on its ambitions. The United States should play the role of balancer of last resort in the unlikely event that the PRC or some other country disrupted the regional balance of power and achieved a ''breakout'' that threatened vital American security interests.

Such a policy would materially reduce the likelihood of a military collision between the United States and China. It would even reduce the number of occasions on which contentious issues between the two countries were likely to arise, thereby maximizing the chances of a cordial bilateral relationship. Eliminating some of those sources of friction would clear the path for continued economic and cultural engagement, a strategy that is most likely to promote the evolution of a more tolerant and democratic China.

Suggested Readings

Bandow, Doug. "Taiwan: Not Worth War but Well Worth Arming." *Christian Science Monitor,* October 2, 1996.

Carpenter, Ted Galen. "Move beyond Cold War Theories." *Los Angeles Times,* March 3, 1996.

Dibb, Paul. "Towards a New Balance of Power in Asia." Adelphi Paper no. 295, May 1995.

Glain, Steve. "U.S. Probably Shouldn't Count on Help from Japan in Resolving Taiwan Flap," *Wall Street Journal,* March 11, 1996.

Hadar, Leon T. "The Sweet-and-Sour Sino-American Relationship." Cato Institute Policy Analysis no. 248, January 23, 1996.

Kristof, Nicholas D. "The Rise of China." *Foreign Affairs* (November–December 1993).

Munro, Ross H. "Evesdropping on the Chinese Military: Where It Expects War—Where It Doesn't." *Orbis* (Summer 1994).

Witter, Willis. "U.S. Gets No Help from East Asians in Backing Taiwan." *Washington Times,* March 14, 1996.

—Prepared by Ted Galen Carpenter

49. Weaning South Korea

The U.S. government should

- withdraw all American forces from South Korea over the next four years;
- offer to sell Seoul whatever conventional weapons it wishes to purchase;
- announce its intention to terminate the mutual defense treaty by the end of the decade;
- continue improving relations with North Korea by meeting America's obligations under the nuclear agreement, formalizing relations between the two countries, and lifting restrictions on trade and investment;
- offer to help mediate territorial disputes between South Korea and neighboring nations;
- encourage South Korea to expand security cooperation with Japan; and
- promote South Korea's participation in regional political and security forums.

Washington continues to maintain a large military presence in East Asia despite the collapse of Soviet communism and the growing strength of America's allies. Particularly dramatic is the transformation of the Korean peninsula, where the United States spends between $15 billion and $20 billion a year to defend South Korea, a nation fully capable of defending itself.

In the aftermath of World War II, America's global interventionist foreign policy appeared to have a purpose: containment of the hegemonic threat posed by the Soviet Union and its satellites. Today, however, there is nothing left to contain. America's enemies are a handful of dismal, impoverished dictatorships.

485

In such a world, especially after the expenditure of more than $13 trillion (1996 dollars) on defense during the Cold War, one would expect Washington to reconsider its military policy. But no. In the Pacific and East Asia, explains the Defense Department, America's "bilateral commitments remain inviolable, and the end of the Cold War has not diminished their importance."

And not just commitments—*expanded* commitments. The United States is building security contacts with Singapore and seeking new multilateral ties throughout East Asia, though not at the expense of its bilateral commitments, the Department of Defense hastily assures us. Even North Korea, perhaps, if Pyongyang's recent comments to some American visitors are to be believed, would like American protection. Such is the lure of getting the globe's most trusted cop to walk yet another beat at his own expense.

The lack of an enemy should pose a problem for those committed to preserving and extending Cold War institutions. But as public-choice economists would have predicted, the collapse of hegemonic communism, a genuine threat to America, has spurred what the Cato Institute's Ted Galen Carpenter aptly calls a "search for enemies," and thus the development of a cottage industry generating new justifications for old policies and programs. That search is well under way in East Asia. In 1953 the Republic of Korea (ROK) was a wreck—impoverished, war-ravaged, and ruled by an unloved autocrat whose belligerence helped land his country in a disastrous war. Without an American security guarantee, South Korea would not have long survived. But fast forward four-plus decades. The South is prosperous and democratic. It has twice the population of North Korea and an economy 18 times larger. Its adversary is ruled by an eccentric, uncharismatic autocrat who lacks international friends. North Korea talks of avoiding absorption by Seoul, not of conquest. Why, then, are U.S. forces in South Korea still necessary?

Some ROK officials still point north. But there is no special gravitational field on the Korean peninsula that prevents those living in the South from constructing a military as powerful as—or even more powerful than—that possessed by the North. Rather, for years South Korea has *chosen* not to match the North's military effort; indeed, ROK defense outlays have been falling as a percentage of the government's budget and the country's gross domestic product. That is a curious way for a nation allegedly under siege to act.

Even many South Koreans recognize that to argue that the South needs Washington's help against the North is starting to sound ridiculous—

rather like the United States begging the Europeans for protection against Mexico. The growing implausibility of the old justification has led to a busy search for new threats requiring American attention. Not surprisingly, it didn't take long for Americans and South Koreans alike to find some: China and Japan, obviously, along with the ubiquitous demon of instability. Indeed, it has taken a century, but Seoul seems about to achieve its original objective in opening relations with the United States—finding a distant ally to guarantee its security from possible aggression by great powers in the region.

South Korea's Big Brother

South Korea's desire for a friendly big brother is understandable. After all, at different points in its history the peninsula has been dominated or occupied by Japan, China, and Russia. With the passing of the North Korean threat, a worried Seoul is again looking at its geographical position and for that distant ally. As the Ministry of National Defense stated in 1990, "The Korean peninsula is located in a strategically sensitive area where the interests of the four major regional powers—the United States, the Soviet Union, China and Japan—converge." Actually, America is not and never was a regional power in East Asia on the basis of geography, but that is what the ROK wants Washington to think. President Kim Young Sam told Congress during his trip to America in July 1995 that "to maintain peace in the Korean peninsula and to maintain stability in the Asia-Pacific region, the U.S. force in the Republic of Korea is necessary."

The ROK's desire for continued protection is certainly understandable, even though Seoul could build a military sufficient to make the cost of aggression too high for any of its neighbors. The pertinent question is whether South Korea's desire for protection is a valid basis for U.S. policy. In the absence of the hegemonic threat posed by Soviet communism, the defense of South Korea loses its connection to U.S. security, and the rationale for Washington to maintain a costly and dangerous military tripwire far from home disappears.

After all, it would be desirable, from America's standpoint, for South Korea to garrison South Florida. Japan could help patrol the Atlantic. German and French forces could guard Alaska. Britain could provide radar and air defense for the continental states. All of those steps would be beneficial, since they would allow Americans to devote more of their resources to other pursuits. Alas, the allies would probably not find an appeal for such assistance a persuasive reason for subsidizing America's defense.

Benefits to America

The United States should view the four-decade-old defense subsidy to South Korea in the same way. At the most basic level, U.S. policymakers need to ask, Does intervention in Korea benefit Americans, the people who will be paying for and dying in any war? That U.S. political elites enjoy greater influence (and travel opportunities) because of such an alliance and troop deployment is not enough. Common people, too, should benefit, and benefit enough to warrant the expense.

That expense, in the case of Korea, and more broadly East Asia, is not minor. It involves the risk of war resulting from disputes that no longer have relevance to America's security. Maintaining the forces necessary to police the region runs upward of $40 billion annually, about half of which is attributable to the defense of South Korea. As a result, Washington's security guarantees impose an onerous tax burden on all Americans and put U.S. firms at an economic disadvantage in the international arena. Moreover, the Mutual Defense Treaty with South Korea is one of many commitments that have forced America to adopt imperial rather than republican policies; imperial policies range from an outsized military to a secretive national security bureaucracy.

What are we getting in return, if no longer genuine defense? The principal answer is allies. In fact, if the United States wanted, it could have as allies most nations on earth.

But alliances are supposed to serve a purpose—enhancing not undermining America's security. Maintaining rigid alliances, security guarantees, and troop deployments for the sake of keeping allies is, not just costly, but dangerous, since the way we prove that we are a loyal ally is by participating in their conflicts, even those with no significant connection to U.S. security. Nowhere is that more obvious than on the Korean peninsula, the international flashpoint where the most Americans are at the greatest risk.

Another reason to preserve America's Cold War military posture in the region, explains the White House, is to contribute "to regional stability by deterring aggression and adventurism." But it would be dangerous to set stability as the lodestar for U.S. policy. It may conflict with other important goals, be irrelevant to American security, or be impossible to impose from outside. Or, in light of the changing balance of power, it may be enforceable by other states in the region. In the end, the chimera of stability is likely to lead Washington to risk thousands of lives day in and day out, and spend tens of billions of dollars year after year, in hopes of preventing events that are not only purely speculative but also tangential to U.S. security.

Finally, America's military presence in and treaty with the ROK are supposed to yield a host of other benefits—national credibility, open trading systems, cultural exchange, democratic education, and the like. Whether or not those benefits in fact result from U.S. military deployments in South Korea is open to question, and even if they do, they are at best fringe benefits. They do not justify commitments that are simultaneously expensive and dangerous.

Of course, some say that disengagement may be the right policy, but not just yet. One argument is that cutting the number of U.S. forces in Korea should be used as a "bargaining chip" to gain North Korean arms reductions. Other pundits propose waiting until the North Korean nuclear issue is definitively resolved, or the North's communist regime has fallen, or South Korea has matched Pyongyang's military, or rapprochement has occurred between the two Koreas. However, there will always be another plausible reason to hold off for a few years. In practice, "not yet" really means "never." The reason for creating the U.S.–South Korean alliance has disappeared; the conditions that once warranted its continuation have disappeared. Now the bilateral treaty and troop deployments should disappear.

And disappear completely. Disengagement must be total—all forces, all guarantees. To do otherwise, following the Carter administration's plan of withdrawal-lite (withdrawing ground forces but retaining air units and the security treaty), offers little if any advantage to America. As Professor Earl Ravenal of Georgetown University explains, such a strategy "promises perpetual involvement but invites recriminations by allies. It is the typical middle position, with all the obvious contradictions of that position and with few earmarks of definitive choice." But the end of the Cold War and South Korea's dramatic economic growth call out for definitive choice.

America should, of course, consult with Seoul about the details of the withdrawal process, so that the ROK can smoothly adjust as the United States disengages. Moreover, Washington should offer to sell the South almost any conventional arms that it desires. That is especially important in the areas of air and naval forces, where the ROK has chosen to rely on U.S. capabilities. Although South Korea today possesses an advanced domestic arms industry, the United States could ensure that the ROK has the opportunity to build whatever force it deems necessary to deter Northern adventurism.

An American withdrawal, even so configured, would undoubtedly worry many South Koreans. But today Seoul is capable of providing for its own defense—and of preparing for eventual reunification.

There's no doubt that many South Koreans hope for, and, indeed, expect, a North Korean collapse. To assume that will occur would, of course, be foolish. Still, the ROK should be prepared for such a contingency, since Romania proved that even the most brutal totalitarian system may actually be so fragile as to shatter after one good demonstration. Even under the best of circumstances (the "soft-landing" scenario) reunification will not be easy. In that endeavor the two Koreas are essentially on their own. The two superpowers may have been able to divide the peninsula after World War II, and the surrounding countries and the United States can help draw the North into the larger international community to maximize the chances of a soft landing, but they can't put the peninsula back together.

At the same time, Washington should help foster a more positive international environment in which the two Koreas could warm up today's very cold peace. First, the United States needs to improve its relations with the North, fulfilling the nuclear agreement, formalizing diplomatic relations, and ending restrictions on investment and trade. While promising Pyongyang a new nuclear reactor in return for abandoning the pursuit of an atomic bomb is hardly a fool-proof strategy, North Korea has so far kept its commitments, and critics have offered nothing better. The accord has the potential of keeping the peninsula nuclear-free, and therefore is worth its cost.

Second, opening full diplomatic relations and allowing private economic relations are relatively cheap steps that would simultaneously give America a window on the world's most closed society and reward the North for choosing a less belligerent course. Again, if such steps help induce Pyongyang to become a more normal member of the international community, they will be well worth taking.

Further, the United States should help encourage greater regional cooperation, particularly between the ROK and both Japan and the Association of Southeast Asian Nations. America's friends in East Asia have achieved dramatic economic success; now they need to forge stronger political and security ties. Washington's most important goal should be to encourage

Seoul and Tokyo, which have so many common interests, to cooperate. Unfortunately, Washington's seemingly permanent security guarantee has made it easy for both countries to behave irresponsibly, sacrificing the potential for improved military and political links to nationalistic squabbling over barren islands. The United States should emphasize the importance of nations in the region building multilateral agreements and institutions to deal with potential security threats, from whatever source.

Are there risks to American military disengagement from Korea and elsewhere in East Asia? Of course—anything is possible, however unlikely. But with the end of the Cold War, Washington need no longer take on the burden of other nations' mistakes.

In turn, South Korea would no longer have to help pay for America's mistakes. The ROK should ponder well the price of its continuing security dependence on the United States. Having such an "elder brother"—long Korea's goal—obviously has important advantages. But there are costs as well. First is the frequent negative social impact. The 1995 subway brawl between U.S. soldiers and Korean civilians may have been sensationalized, but it nevertheless illustrates an important cost of dependency.

Second is the question of respect accorded the ROK as a nation. "Most people in South Korea are beginning to feel more prestigious and self-confident," says newspaper columnist Kil Jeong Woo. "These kinds of things should be respected by our American friends, not ignored." But they will be ignored so long as the South relies on what amounts to U.S. military charity to guarantee its defense. Washington will not treat South Koreans with respect as long as it remains the security patron.

This issue may have consequences beyond simply wounding the ROK's national ego. While Washington is generally benevolent, there is no reason to expect it to put the South's interest before its own. Nor is that ever likely to change: the United States has yet to establish a security partnership among equals. Washington believes in being either a big brother or a passing acquaintance. The former might seem to be preferable to many South Koreans, but when the issue involves war—whether, for instance, to impose sanctions on or launch military strikes against the North over its nuclear program—the cost to Seoul could end up being enormous. Decisions involving South Korea's security should be made in Seoul, not Washington.

South Korea's Ministry of National Defense has already acknowledged the importance of developing "a future-oriented defense policy in preparation for the twenty-first century and the post-unification era." As South

Korea emerges as a significant international player in economic and political terms, it needs to begin planning to play an equally influential, and independent, military role as well.

In the end, however, Washington must take the initiative to terminate the Mutual Defense Treaty and return to its noninterventionist roots, and to do so on the basis of American interests. Seoul and its neighbors throughout East Asia will probably always want the United States to be prepared to fight to the last American for them. But Washington should risk the lives and wealth of its citizens only when something fundamental is at stake for their own political community. The lives of U.S. soldiers are not gambit pawns to be sacrificed in some global or regional chess game. It is time to bring American troops home from Korea.

Suggested Readings

Bandow, Doug. "A New Korea Policy for a Changed World." *Korean Journal of Defense Analysis* (Winter 1992).

_____. "North Korea and the Risks of Coercive Nonproliferation." Cato Institute Foreign Policy Briefing no. 24, May 4, 1993.

_____. *Tripwire: Korea and U.S. Foreign Policy in a Changed World.* Washington: Cato Institute, 1996.

Bandow, Doug, and Ted Galen Carpenter, eds. *The U.S.–South Korean Alliance: Time for a Change.* New Brunswick, N.J.: Transaction, 1992.

Carpenter, Ted Galen. "Ending South Korea's Unhealthy Security Dependence." *Korean Journal of Defense Analysis* (Summer 1994).

_____. *A Search for Enemies: America's Alliances after the Cold War.* Washington: Cato Institute, 1992.

Corbin, Marcus, et al. "Mission Accomplished in Korea: Bringing U.S. Troops Home." *Defense Monitor* 9, no. 2 (1990).

—Prepared by Doug Bandow

50. Cuba

Congress should

- repeal the Cuban Liberty and Democratic Solidarity (Libertad, Helms-Burton) Act of 1996;
- repeal the Cuban Democracy (Torricelli) Act of 1992;
- restore the policy of granting Cuban refugees political asylum in the United States;
- eliminate or privatize Radio and TV Marti;
- end all trade sanctions against Cuba and allow U.S. citizens and companies to visit and establish businesses in Cuba as they see fit; and
- move toward the normalization of diplomatic relations with Cuba.

In 1970, 17 of 26 countries in Latin America and the Caribbean had authoritarian regimes. Today, only Cuba has a dictatorial regime. Although the transition to market-oriented democracies, where individual liberty and property rights are protected under the rule of law, is far from complete in any of the region's countries, that transition is already leading to greater political stability and economic prosperity. Economic sanctions have not been responsible for the region-wide shift toward liberalization, however. They have, in fact, failed to bring about democratic regimes anywhere in the hemisphere, and Cuba has been no exception. Indeed, Cuba is the one country in the hemisphere against which the U.S. government has persistently and actively used a full economic embargo as its main policy tool in an attempt to compel a democratic transformation.

The failure of sanctions against Cuba should come as no surprise since sanctions, however politically popular, are notorious for their unintended consequences—harming those they are meant to help. In Cuba, Fidel Castro is the last person to feel the pain caused by the U.S. measures. If sanctions failed to dislodge the military regime in Haiti, the poorest and most vulnerable country in the region, it is difficult to believe that they could be successful in Cuba.

A Cold War Relic

The trade embargo against Cuba was first authorized under the Foreign Assistance Act of 1961, passed by the 87th Congress. President John F. Kennedy issued an executive order implementing the embargo as a response to Fidel Castro's expropriation of American assets and his decision to offer the Soviet Union a permanent military base and an intelligence post just 90 miles off the coast of Florida at the height of the Cold War. Castro's decision confirmed Cuba as the Soviet Union's main ally in the Western Hemisphere.

For three decades Cuba was a threat to U.S. national security. Not only did Cuba export Marxist-Leninist revolutions to Third World countries (most notably, Angola and Nicaragua), but, more important, it served as a base for Soviet intelligence operations and allowed Soviet naval vessels port access rights. However, with the collapse of the Soviet Union and the subsequent end of Soviet subsidies to Cuba in the early 1990s, that threat virtually ceased to exist. (There is, of course, always the slight possibility that Castro will do something reckless.) With the demise of the security threat posed by Cuba, all valid justifications for the embargo also disappeared.

Trade sanctions against Cuba, however, were not lifted. The embargo was instead tightened in 1992 with the passage of the Cuban Democracy (Torricelli) Act, a bill that former president George Bush signed into law. The justification for it was, not primarily national security interests, but the Castro regime's form of government and human rights abuses. That change of focus was reflected in the language of the act, the first finding of which was Castro's "consistent disregard for internationally accepted standards of human rights and for democratic values."

In 1996 Congress passed the Cuban Liberty and Democratic Solidarity (Libertad) Act, a bill that President Clinton had threatened to veto but signed into law in the aftermath of the downing of two U.S. civilian planes by Cuban fighter jets in international airspace.

The Unintended Consequences of a Flawed Policy

The Libertad Act, better known as the Helms-Burton Act, named after its sponsors Sen. Jesse Helms (R-N.C.) and Rep. Dan Burton (R-Ind.), is an ill-conceived law. It grants U.S. citizens whose property was expropriated by Castro the right to sue in U.S. courts foreign companies and citizens "trafficking" in that property. That right—not granted to other U.S. citizens who may have lost property in other countries—is problematic because it essentially extends U.S. jurisdiction to the results of events that occurred on foreign territory.

By imposing sanctions on foreign companies profiting from property confiscated by the Castro regime, the Helms-Burton Act seeks to discourage investment in Cuba. But fears that foreign investment there, which is much lower than official figures claim, will save the communist system from its inherent flaws are unfounded; significant capital flows to Cuba will not occur unless and until market reforms are introduced. While the Helms-Burton Act may slow investment in Cuba, U.S. allies (in particular, Canada, Mexico, and members of the European Union) have not welcomed that attempt to influence their foreign policy by threats of U.S. sanctions. Consequently—and not surprisingly—the European Union is contemplating retaliatory sanctions.

The ultimatum sent by some U.S. policymakers, best expressed by Rep. Ileana Ros-Lehtinen (R-Fla), who said, "Our allies have to choose whether to play footsie with Fidel or have access to the U.S. market," has been answered by those allies with another ultimatum: "The U.S. government has to decide whether to continue its current policy toward Cuba or trade with us." That confrontation risks poisoning U.S. relations with otherwise friendly countries that are far more important than Cuba to the economic well-being and security of the United States.

The stalemate also serves to divert attention, both inside and outside Cuba, from the island's internal crisis. At the same time, the embargo continues to be the best—and now the only—excuse that Castro has for his failed policies. Although the Soviet Union provided Cuba with more than $100 billion in subsidies and credits during their three-decade relationship, Cuban officials, who have estimated the cumulative cost of the embargo at more than $40 billion, incessantly condemn U.S. policies for causing the meager existence of the Cuban people. Elizardo Sánchez Santa Cruz, a leading dissident in Cuba, has aptly summed up that strategy: "He [Castro] wants to continue exaggerating the image of the external enemy which has been vital for the Cuban Government during decades, an external enemy which can be blamed for the failure of the totalitarian model implanted here."

As long as Castro can point to the United States as an external enemy, he will be successful in barring dissent, justifying control over the economy and flow of information, and stirring up nationalist and anti-U.S. sentiments in Cuba.

Cuba Must Determine Its Own Destiny

Perhaps the biggest shortcoming of U.S. policy toward Cuba is its false assumption that democratic capitalism can somehow be forcibly exported from Washington to Havana. That assumption is explicitly stated in the Helms-Burton Act, whose first purpose is ''to assist the Cuban people in regaining their freedom and prosperity, as well as in joining the community of democratic countries that are flourishing in the Western Hemisphere.''

But the revolution in democratic capitalism that has swept the Western Hemisphere has little to do with Washington's efforts to export democracy. Rather, it has to do with Latin America's hard-earned realization that the free-enterprise system is the only system capable of providing self-sustaining growth and increasing prosperity.

Now that the Cold War has ended, moreover, Cuba no longer poses a credible threat to the United States. Whether Cuba has a totalitarian or a democratic regime, though important, is not a vital U.S. national security concern. The transformation of Cuban society, as difficult as that may be, should be left to the Cuban people, not to the U.S. government. As William F. Buckley Jr. has stated, ''If the Cuban people overthrow Mr. Castro, that is the end for which devoutly we pray. But if they do not, he is their problem.''

Furthermore, there is little historical evidence, in Cuba or elsewhere, that tightening the screws on Cuba will produce an anti-Castro rebellion. On the other hand, Cato scholar James Dorn has observed that ''the threat of using trade restrictions to advance human rights is fraught with danger . . . [because] it undermines the market dynamic that in the end is the best instrument for creating wealth and preserving freedom.''

Even though Cuba—unlike other communist countries, such as China or Vietnam, with which the United States actively trades—has not undertaken meaningful market reforms, an open U.S. trade policy is likely to be more subversive of its system than is an embargo. Proponents of the Cuban embargo vastly underestimate the extent to which increased foreign trade and investment can undermine Cuban communism, even if that business is conducted with state entities.

Cuban officialdom appears to be well aware of that danger. For example, Cuba's opening of its tourism industry to foreign investment has been accompanied by measures that restrict ordinary Cubans from visiting foreign hotels and tourist facilities. As a result, Cubans have come to resent their government for what has become known as "tourism apartheid." In recent years Cuban officials have also issued warnings against corruption, indicating the regime's fear that unofficial business dealings, especially with foreigners, may weaken allegiance to the government and even create vested interests that favor more extensive market openings.

Further undercutting the regime's authority is the widespread dollar economy that emerged as a consequence of foreign presence and remittances from abroad (now banned by the Helms-Burton Act). The dollarization of the Cuban economy—a phenomenon now legalized by the Cuban regime as a result of its inability to control it—has essentially eliminated the regime's authority to dictate the country's monetary policy.

Replacing the all-encompassing state with one that allows greater space for voluntary interaction requires strengthening elements of civil society, that is, groups not dependent on the state. That development is more likely to come about in an environment of increased interaction with outside groups than in an environment of increased isolation and state control.

At present, there are signs that civil society is slowly emerging in Cuba, despite Castro's attempts to suppress it. For example, the Catholic Church, the main recipient of humanitarian aid from international nongovernmental organizations, has experienced a resurgence since the Archbishop of Havana was made a Cardinal.

The Concilio Cubano, an umbrella organization that comprises more than 130 reform groups, has also come into being. The downing of two planes operated by a Miami-based exile group in February 1996 may have been a message to the internal opposition, which has often been harassed by Castro's repressive apparatus. However, the mere existence of a broad-based internal opposition movement is highly significant, and if Concilio Cubano can survive official harassment during its formative stages, its role in the future may be similar to the one Solidarity played in Poland during the 1980s. Finally, there are the small-business owners who are able to earn a living in the small but growing nonstate sector.

Cuban exiles should also be allowed to participate in the transformation of Cuban society. However, their participation need not require active involvement of the U.S. government. Thus, Radio and TV Marti, government entities that broadcast to Cuba, should be privatized or closed down. If the exile community believes that those stations are a useful resource in their struggle against the Castro regime, they have the means—there are no legal impediments—to finance such an operation.

A New Cuba Policy Based on American Principles

Washington's policies toward Cuba should be consistent with traditional American principles. First, the United States should restore the practice of granting political asylum to Cuban refugees. The 1994 immigration accord between the Clinton administration and the Cuban government has turned the United States into Castro's de jure partner in oppressing Cubans who risk their lives to escape repression.

There is no reason to believe that Cuban refugees would not continue to help the U.S. economy as they always have. The 1980 boatlift, in which 120,000 Cuban refugees reached U.S. shores, proved a boon to the economy of South Florida. In addition, since the Cuban-American community has repeatedly expressed its ability and desire to provide for refugees until they can provide for themselves, such a policy need not cost U.S. taxpayers.

Second, the U.S. government should protect its own citizens' inalienable rights and recognize that free trade is itself a human right. As Dorn says, "The supposed dichotomy between the right to trade and human rights is a false one. . . . As moral agents, individuals necessarily claim the rights to liberty and property in order to live fully and to pursue their interests in a responsible manner." In the case of Cuba, U.S. citizens and companies should be allowed to decide for themselves—as they are in the case of dozens of countries around the world whose political and human rights records are less than admirable—whether and how they should trade with it.

Third, U.S. policy toward Cuba should focus on national security interests, not on transforming Cuban society or micromanaging the affairs of a transitional government as current law obliges Washington to do. That means lifting the embargo and establishing the types of diplomatic ties with Cuba that the United States maintains with other states, even dictatorial ones, that do not threaten its national security. Those measures, especially the ending of current sanctions, will ensure a more peaceful and smooth transition in Cuba. After all, as former Reagan National Security Council member Roger Fontaine explains, "It is not in our interest to acquire another economic basket case in the Caribbean."

Unfortunately, strengthening the economic embargo has left the United States in a very uncomfortable position. Washington has depleted its policy options for dealing with future crises in Cuba or provocations from Castro. Given the absence of other options, if chaos ensues on America's doorstep, U.S. officials will be under tremendous pressure to intervene militarily.

Some people claim that a relaxation of the embargo would deprive the United States of its most effective tool for effecting change in Cuba, but tightening the embargo has left the United States with only its most reckless one.

Conclusion

Rep. Robert G. Torricelli (D-N.J.) offered the following justification for U.S. policy after Helms-Burton was passed by Congress: "Different policies might have worked, might have been taken. But the die has been cast. Years ago we decided on this strategy and we are in the end game now. It is too late to change strategy." But it is not too late to change strategy and the "endgame" may yet take years to complete. Current policy, in any case, increases the likelihood of a violent Cuban transition into which the United States would unnecessarily be drawn.

A better policy would recognize that while Castro may be a clever political manipulator, his economic forecasting and planning have been dismal. Supporters of the embargo casually assume that Castro wants an end to the embargo because he believes that step would solve his economic problems. More likely, Castro fears the lifting of the U.S. sanctions. It is difficult to believe, for example, that he did not calculate a strong U.S. response when he ordered the attack on two U.S. planes in early 1996. It is time for Washington to stop playing into Castro's hands and instead pull the rug out from under him by ending the embargo.

Suggested Readings

Buckley, William F. Jr. "Castro and Pride." *Washington Times,* September 3, 1994.

Carpenter, Ted Galen. "Lift the Embargo, Clinch Democracy." *Insight,* April 25, 1994.

Melloan, George. "U.S. to Blame for Castro's Failure? Really Now!" *Wall Street Journal,* August 29, 1994.

Ratliff, William, and Roger Fontaine. "Foil Castro. Lift the Embargo." *Washington Post,* June 30, 1993.

Tanner, Mack, and Larry Grupp. "Viva la Evolution." *Reason* (August–September 1994).

Vásquez, Ian. "Washington's Dubious Crusade for Hemispheric Democracy." Cato Institute Policy Analysis no. 201, January 12, 1994.

—Prepared by L. Jacobo Rodríguez and Ian Vásquez

51. The United Nations

The U.S. government should

- withhold all payments to the United Nations until the new secretary-general demonstrates a commitment to reform;
- demand that the United Nations undergo a comprehensive audit and eliminate all programs and agencies that do not meet stringent criteria in terms of mission, organization, and performance;
- withhold all payments to the United Nations until such a comprehensive audit has been completed;
- announce that the United States will unilaterally reduce its contribution to the United Nations by 50 percent once current arrearages are paid in full; and
- pass legislation that prohibits the participation of U.S. troops in UN military operations.

The United Nations is a miasma of corruption beset by inefficiency, Kafkaesque bureaucracy, and misconceived programs. Numerous diplomatic efforts to encourage UN reform have failed. It is now obvious that the United States must use its financial leverage to force the UN bureaucracy and the arrogant General Assembly to reexamine their practices. The bottom line is that the UN will either be fundamentally reorganized or, in a relatively short time, it will cease to exist.

The Unholy Trinity: Waste, Fraud, and Abuse

After more than a half century, the verdict on the United Nations is in. The data on reform or lack thereof are available for all to see—and they are not a pretty picture. There is abundant evidence that waste, fraud, and abuse are rampant throughout the UN system.

The UN's astronomical personnel costs are one manifestation of the problem. Incredibly lucrative salaries are commonplace at the UN's New York headquarters. The average salary of a midlevel accountant at the UN is $84,000, compared to $41,964 for non-UN accountants. A UN computer analyst could expect to receive $111,500 per year, compared to $56,835 outside the UN bureaucracy. An assistant secretary-general receives $140,256; the mayor of New York gets $130,000.

Salary figures do not reflect the full disparity between UN and non-UN personnel costs, however. Salaries of UN diplomats are tax-free. Salaries of administrative staff include an "assessment" used to offset tax liability in most cases, so many of the staff salaries are tax-free as well. In addition, UN employees receive monthly rent subsidies of up to $3,800 and annual education grants of up to $12,675 per child. But such generous compensation does not translate into a productive workforce; former secretary-general Boutros-Ghali told the *Washington Post* that "perhaps half of the UN work force does nothing useful."

Widespread corruption is also a problem. Nearly $4 million in cash was stolen from UN offices in Mogadishu, Somalia. Other funds are not stolen outright but are spent for highly questionable purposes. The *New York Times,* for example, reported that $15,000 of $457,000 earmarked for a two-week conference on the Sustainable Development of Small Island States was spent flying representatives "of a national liberation movement recognized by the Organization of African Unity" to the conference. "In fact," the *Times* disclosed, "the movement was the Polisario from the Western Sahara, a desert region conspicuously short of small islands."

The Accountability Problem and Failed Attempts to Restore Responsibility

At the heart of the UN's problem is an almost total lack of accountability. Former U.S. attorney general Richard Thornburgh's 1993 report on UN mismanagement, along with subsequent investigations, charged that UN budgets, formed behind closed doors, are shrouded in secrecy. In addition, the actual performance of the myriad bureaucracies is rarely measured against criteria established at program inception. There is no way to tell whether the various, often overlapping agencies—for example, at least two dozen are involved in food and agriculture programs—are meeting their stated objectives.

Theoretically, the lack of accountability could in some ways be addressed by a comprehensive audit. Boutros-Ghali long resisted such an investigation, and, in fact, he reportedly had the Thornburgh report literally burned. Not until April 1994, when an impatient U.S. Congress demanded reform and threatened to withhold $420 million of the U.S. assessment from the UN coffers, was an independent inspector general—German diplomat Karl Paschke—named.

Paschke was short on funds, staff, and time. His independence was compromised when Boutros-Ghali inserted a "service at the pleasure of the Secretary-General clause" in his contract, which meant that Boutros-Ghali could dismiss him for virtually any reason. Nonetheless, Paschke produced an interim report in seven months—the first attempt at cost accounting at the United Nations in 50 years—which revealed, not surprisingly, that UN finances were a mess.

The new inspector general's first swipe at the Augean stables revealed some $16.8 million in outright fraud and waste. The report documented numerous examples, including the following:

- In Somalia, $369,000 was paid for fuel distribution services the contractor never provided.
- A project director of the UN Relief and Works Agency, which helps Palestinian refugees, kept $100,000 of agency money in his private bank account and failed to disclose a personal stake in the irrigation project under way.
- In Nairobi, a member of the UN Center for Human Settlements arranged loans worth $98,000 for a company of which she had been a partner and with whose director she was "closely associated."

By the time his report was out, however, Paschke had become part of the problem instead of part of the solution. His report contained the usual critique of poor management practices and abysmal personnel policy. But Paschke's overall conclusions proved more disturbing to the cause of real reform than any of his velvet-glove criticisms.

He said, "I have not found the UN to be a more corrupt organization, an organization that shows more fraud than any other comparable public organization." Members of Congress had hoped for an inspector general who would prove to be a junkyard dog, but U.S. ambassador to the United Nations Madeleine Albright—no UN basher—summed it up when she said that Paschke had thus far proved to be a "junkyard puppy." In short, the inspector general's effort devolved into a typical UN exercise in deflecting criticism without addressing the problems.

The New Secretary-General

Boutros Boutros-Ghali, the controversial secretary-general of the UN, was perhaps the foremost symbol of the problems associated with waste, fraud, and corruption at the UN, as well as one of the biggest obstacles to injecting accountability into the UN system. Instead of working to solve the UN's institutional problems, he thwarted U.S. efforts to do so.

At the same time, Boutros-Ghali was an aggressive proponent of expanding the mandate of the United Nations. In *Agenda for Peace,* his ambitious outline for the United Nations in the post–Cold War era, Boutros-Ghali called for the creation of a standing UN army. He was also one of the strongest advocates of the disastrous "nation-building" mission in Somalia.

There is some hope that with the election of Kofi Annan, the United Nations will no longer be run by a secretary-general who ignores or exacerbates the organization's deep-seated institutional problems while also trying to expand its mandate. Nevertheless, Congress should not casually assume that an era of reform has arrived. It should continue to withhold funds until Annan's promises of change result in meaningful deeds.

Power and the Purse

Until the mid-1950s the United States enjoyed the support of a majority of the 51-member General Assembly. That margin vanished forever when a momentary thaw in U.S.-Soviet relations after Stalin's death allowed the admission of 20 new members. Five years later the General Assembly had 82 members, nearly all former colonies of the European powers. By 1970 the number had jumped to 108; by 1980 it was 136; and by 1995 the General Assembly had a total of 185 member-states, each with one vote.

The vastly expanded General Assembly was soon dominated by non-Western states whose elites seldom shared the political culture of the democratic West. Despite their diverse interests, logrolling among UN members has historically resulted in General Assembly votes having a distinctly anti-American cast.

The Third World–dominated General Assembly also approves numerous programs and projects for which the vast majority of member-states contribute only a minuscule portion of the funding. In 1992, for example, the United States was assessed 25 percent of the general UN operating budget, while 79 member-states each paid 0.01 percent of the budget—

the minimum allowed. And another 9 each chipped in 0.02 percent. That means that a majority of the voting members of the General Assembly contribute less than 1 percent of the UN's general budget, while 14 members contribute 84 percent. A similar pattern is evident in the peacekeeping budget, to which the United States contributes 31 percent of the total.

That fundamental disconnect between power and purse is at the root of many of the UN's greatest problems. There is little hope of curtailing the proliferation of agencies and bureaucracy or significantly reducing corruption until the UN's major contributors wield more influence over the budget.

UN Military Operations

The United Nations is ill-equipped to conduct military operations. It has no general military staff—and therefore is incapable of integrating command-control-communications and intelligence with a planning function. There is no unified command. Personnel from different countries who serve in UN military missions do not reflect the same training and standards and judgment when it comes to putting people's lives in danger.

It should come as no surprise, then, that the UN's record in peacekeeping is a chronicle of failure. Operational ineptitude is only one problem. Perhaps the greater problem is the tendency of the United Nations to become a party to the conflict rather than to preserve its impartiality. In Somalia, the United Nations ended up on a manhunt for Mohammed Farah Aideed, the leader of one of the two main factions in the civil war. In Bosnia, the UN Protection Force was for all practical purposes at war with the Bosnian Serbs.

Under no circumstances should U.S. troops participate in UN military operations. In most cases, American participation in UN missions will not advance U.S. vital interests. Conversely, in the event that U.S. vital interests are at stake, allowing the United Nations to be involved in (much less lead) a military operation could have disastrous consequences.

Toward Constructive Internationalism

The United Nations can serve a modestly useful purpose. It is a valuable forum for international diplomacy, crisis management, and mediation. The UN also performs some important work in the humanitarian and assistance areas—although private organizations perform the same work more cost-effectively, since personnel costs account for 70 percent of UN operating expenses.

Without drastic reform, however, the United Nations will probably not exist for long. Rep. Joe Scarborough (R-Fla.) introduced legislation in the 104th Congress that would rescind the UN Participation Act, leading to the withdrawal of the United States from the United Nations and the relocation of the UN outside the United States. Although the measure did not become law, there was a surprising level of support both in Congress and among the general public for the initiative.

History has proven time and again t̶ ̶t the United Nations will not reform willingly. The only way the United Nations will engage in meaningful reform is if the United States uses its financial leverage. Congress needs to make clear to the United Nations that reforms must be forthcoming, and that it is prepared to put the United Nations into bankruptcy, if necessary, to force reform.

The use of such leverage, if joined with a Herculean effort to clean the Augean stables, would provide the foundation for a return to productive internationalism. The alternative is the end of the United Nations.

Suggested Readings

Bandow, Doug. "Do Not Endorse the Law of the Sea Treaty." Cato Institute Foreign Policy Briefing no. 29, January 27, 1994.
———. "Faulty Repairs: The Law of the Sea Treaty Is Still Unacceptable." Cato Institute Foreign Policy Briefing no. 32, September 12, 1994.
Carpenter, Ted Galen. "Foreign Policy Peril: Somalia Set a Dangerous Precedent." *USA Today Magazine,* May 1993.
Halper, Stefan. "A Miasma of Corruption: The United Nations at 50." Cato Institute Policy Analysis no. 253, April 30, 1996.
Helms, Jesse. "Saving the United Nations." *Foreign Affairs,* September–October 1996.
Hillen, John. "Killing with Kindness: The UN Peacekeeping Mission in Bosnia." Cato Institute Foreign Policy Briefing no. 34, June 30, 1995.
Phillips, James. "Needed at the UN: More Secretary, Less General." Heritage Foundation Executive Memorandum no. 455, June 1996.
Sheehy, Thomas P. "The UN's 50th Anniversary: Time for Reform, Not Celebration." Heritage Foundation Executive Memorandum no. 434, October 1995.

—Prepared by Stefan Halper

INTERNATIONAL ECONOMIC POLICY

52. Trade

The less government restricts Americans' access to the goods, services, labor, and capital of their choosing, the better for the nation as a whole. That is the history of the past 200 years.

Despite overwhelming support for free trade among economists, American political leaders sometimes overlook the benefits of international trade. That is because those benefits accrue almost imperceptibly to the many, while the short-term costs are highly visible to the few. International trade pits lower prices, higher quality goods, and a better standard of living against short-term job dislocation, even though such dislocation is necessary if the economy is to use its resources most effectively. Few gain from a static economy.

No misconception about international trade is greater than the belief that it "costs" America jobs and lowers our standard of living. As international trade flows have increased, the number of U.S. jobs has nearly doubled since 1960. Trade changes the mix of jobs and shifts people to different sectors, but overall it raises the economic well-being of individuals and families. The nation's businesses are able to specialize in the products and services they produce most efficiently.

Economics teaches that the best trade policy is one that allows U.S. companies and workers to make what we are best equipped to make at this stage in our development and to trade to obtain goods and services we *could* produce but are better off obtaining from other countries. To argue, as some do, that it is "unfair" that Mexicans work for lower wages and produce less expensive goods is no more valid than for Mexicans to complain that America possesses more highly educated workers who design and manufacture products in today's cutting-edge industries. Comparative advantage tells us that if Mexicans can produce some goods more cheaply than we can, we should buy those goods and make what our skills enable us to produce best.

Trade Deficits

Adam Smith wrote in 1776, "Nothing . . . can be more absurd than this whole doctrine of the balance of trade." Despite Smith's insight, the myth continues that "trade deficits" are inherently evil and reflect job losses. Trade deficits are only a problem if one believes that imports are bad and exports are good, even though in reality both exports *and* imports are good. The reason we engage in trade in the first place is to obtain imports, which raise our standard of living by furnishing a greater variety of goods and by providing needed competition to domestic producers. Goldman Sachs economist Ronald Krieger (see Table 52.1) succinctly presents the different views of economists, who view consumption as the end of economic activity, and noneconomists, particularly some politicians, who view production as the main goal. It is generally politicians, not economists, who support what is called a "mercantilist" trade policy that favors producers over consumers.

The irony is that even if achieving a trade balance were a worthwhile economic goal, making U.S. policy more protectionist would not accomplish it. The 1996 Economic Report of the President, which is produced by the Council of Economic Advisers, specifically states, "Trade policy . . . cannot significantly affect the overall trade balance. That is determined by domestic saving and investment and by government fiscal policy." Ten years earlier, the 1986 Economic Report of a Republican president

Table 52.1
Two Views of the World

Concept	Economist	Noneconomist
The purpose of economic activity is	consumer welfare	jobs and growth
The basic element of economic activity is	exchange	production
Work is a	cost	benefit
Imports are a	benefit	cost
Exports are a	cost	benefit
Cheap foreign goods are a	benefit	cost
The objective of trade is to	get goods cheaply	create jobs
Trade barriers hurt	domestic residents and foreigners	foreigners only

SOURCE: Ronald A. Krieger, "Economics and Protectionist Premises," *Cato Journal* 3, no. 3 (Winter 1983–84): 668.

said essentially the same thing, noting that the "current account balance is determined primarily by macroeconomic relationships."

The 1996 Economic Report makes an even more important point—namely, that maintaining a trade deficit with a particular nation is inconsequential. "Even if our overall trade were balanced, there is simply no reason to expect (or desire) . . . that our sales to Japan or Zambia will cancel out our purchases from those countries, in any given year or even over an extended period." That is worth keeping in mind when the monthly trade balance between the United States and such countries as Japan and China is reported.

The World Trade Organization

In the past five decades, the United States and other countries have negotiated successive rounds of the General Agreement on Tariffs and Trade. Those rounds have aided consumers by pushing down average tariffs worldwide from 40 percent to approximately 3 percent. But when Congress ratified the treaty from the Uruguay Round of GATT in 1994, critics raised concerns about the new World Trade Organization that it created.

The most prevalent misunderstanding is that the WTO threatens American sovereignty or that it may lead to world government. Though the organization would benefit from a less ominous-sounding name, its actual functions do not threaten American independence.

The WTO is not like the European Union, which does impinge on its members' sovereignty. In contrast to the EU, the main task of the WTO is to settle disputes between trading partners. When the United States or another nation alleges an unfair trading practice, the case is heard at the WTO by a three-judge panel, which is drawn from international trade experts from different nations. In addition, a type of court of appeals is made up of seven judges—three of whom are empaneled to hear an appeal—drawn from seven nations that currently include the United States and other friendly nations such as the Philippines, Egypt, and Germany.

The WTO dispute resolution mechanisms work as a type of binding arbitration, but the WTO does not possess a coercive power to enforce its rulings. If the United States decides not to abide by a WTO ruling, the other party to the dispute has the right to apply a trade sanction against U.S. products. And, of course, the United States might decide to retaliate for that sanction. All of that could happen, however, even if the WTO did not exist. The dispute resolution panels at least increase the likelihood that trade disagreements will be settled amicably.

In practice, domestic and international peace both benefit from mechanisms that resolve disputes on the basis of common rules rather than threats of aggression. If my neighbor and I disagree about who harmed whose property, is it better to escalate our argument into recriminations and violence or to submit our dispute to a civil court? In reality, the WTO does not threaten American sovereignty any more than the existence of arbitration or civil courts threatens individual liberty. The point is to take power away from politicians. Putting an end to midnight brinkmanship with Japan over trade disputes will benefit U.S. consumers by depoliticizing trade and moving it away from bilateral political fights and into multilateral forums based on the rule of law.

The second task of the WTO is simply to establish regular meetings to propose trade rule reforms, rather than waiting years to complete a round of GATT negotiations. Though each country has one vote on any reform, *no proposal from the WTO will become U.S. law if the U.S. Congress does not support it.* Cuba and Belize will not push around the United States, as some WTO critics allege, since our economy's might ensures us a virtual veto power over reforms that would damage important

American interests. In the face of a strong disagreement or WTO bias, the United States will always retain the right to leave the organization.

Export Control Laws

America's export control policies remain detached from the realities of the global marketplace. U.S. companies should be allowed to sell technologies that are being sold freely elsewhere in the world by their foreign competitors and the sale of which fails to present a clear danger to U.S. citizens or world peace. That is not the case today for many products, and much bureaucratic wrangling is needed before others can be exported.

For example, the Clinton administration's recent reforms of export control policy do not go far enough in permitting the export of strong cryptography and force unpopular "key recovery" procedures on users of the products. While the current policy on encryption is in flux, the U.S. government has restricted the export of strong encryption software despite the fact that competitors of American companies sell similar or even stronger encryption software abroad. That's just one example of the need to reform America's export control laws.

Fast-Track Authority

Congress should extend the president's "fast-track" authority, which will facilitate negotiations to include Chile in the North American Free Trade Agreement. In the Trade Act of 1974, Congress granted the president authority, with the support of implementing legislation, to negotiate and submit a trade pact to Congress, which then votes on it up or down without amendment. That procedure has helped prevent micromanaging from Capitol Hill and alleviated foreign concerns that an agreement made with a U.S. president could be reopened, picked apart, and returned in a different form.

Congress should not burden fast-track authority with such negotiating objectives as raising the labor and environmental standards of our trading partners. Forcing other countries to adopt U.S.-style labor and environmental laws is viewed internationally as an American attempt to rob other countries' workers of their comparative advantage.

Intellectual Property Rights

Unlike imposing new domestic laws on other nations, protecting the property rights of U.S. citizens is a legitimate function of government.

That is why defending the intellectual property rights of American producers whose materials are pirated abroad should be an important element of U.S. trade policy.

The U.S. government cannot abolish all piracy in this country, nor can a foreign government be responsible for every copyright or patent infringement in its territory. Nevertheless, where we see overwhelming evidence of government complicity or inaction in the face of substantial acts of piracy, it may be proper, as a last resort, for the U.S. government to apply targeted sanctions. In the long run, it is preferable to work with China and other nations on developing the proper institutions and policies to protect the intellectual property of U.S. nationals. China's eventual entry into the WTO would at a minimum allow such disputes to be settled in a less contentious forum.

Unilateral Free Trade

Removing all tariffs and nontariff import restrictions would improve consumer welfare far more than would any new initiative that emerges from a federal agency. In other words, U.S. policymakers need not wait for more trade agreements to sign. The net welfare gains to U.S. consumers if the United States simply eliminated all tariffs and quantitative restrictions on imports would be $15.62 billion a year, according to a U.S. International Trade Commission estimate for 1993. An additional $1.59 billion in net benefits would accrue from eliminating America's anti-dumping and countervailing duties. Permitting foreign airlines to operate without trade restraints in the U.S. domestic transportation market would yield additional standard-of-living improvements.

The phaseout of U.S. textile and apparel import quota rules—and the accompanying lower tariff rates under GATT—is a welcome step, though that measure will not be complete for a number of years. Other issues, though, need to be addressed. Today, many import restrictions are not tariffs per se but tariffs tied to numerical restrictions. For example, under the Uruguay Round Agreements of GATT, after a six-year period, no duties will be assessed on the country's first 20,000 metric tons of imported peanut butter and peanut paste. Yet imports over 20,000 metric tons will be dutiable at 131.8 percent ad valorem. Such restrictions increase prices below the quota as well as above by reducing the available quantity to be imported. The Uruguay Round Agreements also failed to eliminate America's restrictive import quotas on sugar. For dairy imports that come in "over" the established quotas, tariffs will merely replace blanket prohibitions. Higher tariffs also will be paid on cotton and meat imports that exceed a predetermined quota.

No economic rationale justifies numerical restrictions on imports. Only political influence can explain them. The same is true for provisions, often slipped into larger bills, that require certain products bought by the public or the U.S. government to contain a specific percentage of "domestic content." Such measures increase costs to taxpayers and consumers and distort the marketplace by mandating adherence to noneconomic factors of production. Another policy that serves no economic rationale is the Jones Act, under which U.S. domestic maritime shippers are protected from foreign competition at a cost of over $3 billion a year to the U.S. economy, according to the U.S. International Trade Commission. The Jones Act needlessly raises costs for agriculture, petroleum, and other industries that ship goods within the United States.

Anti-dumping and countervailing duty laws are another way government trade policy hurts consumers—and consumers include companies that import for manufacturing purposes. Anti-dumping laws are badly misused against foreign-made products, in part because the formulas employed are often biased in favor of the U.S. company filing the grievance. One major reform would be to make any case for anti-dumping duties pass a simple test: will assessing the duties benefit American consumers? The answer is likely to be no. Moreover, foreign companies should not be treated differently from domestic companies when evaluating claims of predatory pricing.

Anti-dumping orders can often be broad in scope and therefore frequently even include products that are not currently manufactured in the United States. For example, some anti-dumping orders have hurt high-tech companies seeking to import certain types of semiconductors. A bill introduced by Rep. Phil Crane (R-Ill.) would have temporarily suspended anti-dumping duties in situations in which the U.S. domestic user cannot obtain the product from a U.S. source.

Conclusion

International trade is not a war or even a contest between nations, which is why the "level playing field" argument for maintaining U.S. trade restrictions is inappropriate. Trade is a series of mutually beneficial exchanges between companies and individuals. Every distortion of those voluntary exchanges will probably lower the standard of living of Americans. While U.S. companies compete with their foreign competitors in the same industry, there is no case for government action to ensure that a particular company prevails or increases its sales.

Do other governments engage in protectionism? Yes, and such actions hurt their own citizens the most. We should address legitimate complaints of U.S. producers about lack of access to a foreign market through the dispute resolution panels established by the WTO. We must continue to move international trade away from highly politicized, bilateral confrontations and into a more depoliticized, multilateral arena where disputes can be settled judiciously. That course holds the most promise for expanding freedom and opportunity throughout the world.

Suggested Readings

Bhagwati, Jagdish, and Robert E. Hudec, eds. *Fair Trade and Harmonization: Prerequisites for Free Trade.* Cambridge, Mass: MIT Press, 1996.

Bovard, James. *Fair Trade Fraud.* New York: St. Martin's, 1991.

Kober, Stanley. "The Fallacy of Economic Security." Cato Institute Policy Analysis no. 219, January 24, 1995.

Lindsey, Brink. "Taking the Offensive in Trade Policy." In *Market Liberalism.* Edited by David Boaz and Edward H. Crane. Washington: Cato Institute, 1993.

Smith, Adam. *The Wealth of Nations.* 1776. Reprint, New York: Modern Library, 1937.

U.S. International Trade Commission. *The Economic Effects of Significant U.S. Import Restraints: First Biannual Update.* Publication 2935. Washington: U.S. International Trade Commission, December 1995.

—Prepared by Stuart Anderson

53. Unilateral Sanctions

Congress should

- require an analysis that measures the economic cost to the U.S. economy of all current and proposed economic sanctions;
- provide compensation to U.S. companies whose investments are lost or devalued because of a U.S.-imposed sanction;
- establish a time limit on any new economic sanction;
- require an explicit national security justification for any new economic sanction; and
- grant China, a frequent target of proposed sanctions, a multi-year waiver for most-favored-nation trading status and facilitate its entry into the World Trade Organization.

The attempt to punish foreign governments through unilateral sanctions and secondary boycotts is an unwelcome obstacle on the road to greater freedom of commerce. That development bodes ill for U.S. citizens, for America's diplomatic relations with our major trading partners, and for the poor of the targeted nations who are the most likely victims of economic sanctions. U.S. government restrictions send the wrong message about America's belief in the positive influence of private investment and fail to recognize that U.S. companies help foster greater economic and political freedom for people in developing nations.

Why Unilateral Sanctions Are Bad Policy

Unilateral sanctions simply do not work. There are no examples of U.S. unilateral economic sanctions changing the basic character or significant policies of a foreign nation. The 35-year economic embargo of Cuba, a tiny country less than 90 miles from our coast, is a monument to the ineffectiveness of unilateral economic sanctions as a foreign policy tool.

Yet, as Table 53.1 shows, the United States maintains sanctions against a number of countries, and several others are likely targets of future sanctions.

Supporters of sanctions often point to South Africa as a success story, but the facts tell a different tale. It is unrealistic to credit the U.S. congressional vote for sanctions in October 1986 with the overthrow of apartheid. It was not outside forces but powerful and well-organized domestic political forces that, after a three-decades-long struggle, achieved the peaceful overthrow of an anachronistic system that had no moral standing.

Because of the limited nature of the sanctions, the volume of U.S.–South African trade did change significantly, and many African governments

Table 53.1
U.S. Economic Sanctions

Countries in Which U.S. Economic Sanctions Are in Full Force— Total Embargo[a]	Countries on State-Sponsored Terrorism List— U.S. Restrictions on Financial Transactions	Countries on Drug De-certification List[b]	Likely Targets of Future Sanctions[c]
Cuba	Cuba	Afghanistan	China[d]
Iran	Iran	Burma (Myanmar)	Burma[e] (Myanmar)
Iraq	Iraq	Colombia	Nigeria
Libya	Libya	Iran	Indonesia
North Korea	North Korea	Nigeria	Mexico
	Syria	Syria	Pakistan
	Sudan		Angola
			Algeria
			Turkey
			Liberia
			Burundi

SOURCE: Personal communications with personnel at the U.S. Department of State.

[a]Legislation passed by Congress in 1996 places additional restrictions on foreign companies that invest in the energy sector in Iran and Libya or that use property confiscated in Cuba from American citizens.

[b]Countries that are decertified are not eligible for U.S. foreign assistance, except for anti-drug and humanitarian aid. The U.S. government is obliged to vote "no" on loan applications from these countries at multilateral development banks. National interest waivers have been granted to Lebanon, Pakistan, and Paraguay.

[c]These countries have been targeted for sanctions by lawmakers in recent bills or by the media.

[d]As an aftermath of the Tiananmen Square incident, the U.S. government restricts China's purchases of U.S.-made weapons and law enforcement materials.

[e]Sanctions are in place that deny U.S. visas to certain Burmese political leaders and that direct American votes against Burma in multilateral lending institutions; the executive branch decides on other actions.

that condemned apartheid continued to trade with South Africa behind the scenes. Disinvestment in South Africa led many Western companies to reduce their community-based funding of anti-apartheid organizations, according to the Investor Responsibility Research Center. After General Motors sold its plants, the new owners renewed sales to the South African military and police—which GM had ended—and reduced wages and total employment at the facilities.

To the extent that outsiders influenced developments in the country, it was through the discipline of market forces—banks were reluctant to make or renew loans in an unstable environment—and international expressions of opprobrium, such as banning South African participation in forums such as the Olympics. That helped shame the Afrikaner elite and, in combination with other forces, to lead to its abandonment of white-only rule.

It is also important to note that the economic sanctions against South Africa were multilateral, whereas all recent U.S. sanctions have been unilateral. In an effort to compel multilateral support from our allies, legislation passed by Congress in 1996 established secondary boycotts against firms doing business with Cuba, Iran, and Libya. Passed quickly in the wake of Cuba's shooting down of two airplanes flown by Cuban-Americans, the Cuban Liberty and Democratic Solidarity Act, sponsored by Sen. Jesse Helms (R-N.C.) and Rep. Dan Burton (R-Ind.), bars entry to the United States to CEOs of foreign companies that engage in commerce involving properties seized from Americans by Cuba many years ago. It also allows Americans to sue those foreign companies for triple damages in U.S. courts. Considering that South Africa is routinely cited by support-ers of sanctions, it is worth noting that Nelson Mandela announced his government's opposition to Helms-Burton.

Such sanctions harm our diplomatic relations with friendly countries, as evidenced by the threat of our major trading partners to retaliate against American measures that penalize their companies. Other nations object particularly to the extraterritorial authority the U.S. government assumed over citizens of foreign countries.

It is vainglory to believe that by adopting unilateral sanctions America is "leading by example," since nations throughout the world not only have refused to support recent U.S. sanctions but have actively opposed them. Leaders in France, Italy, Britain, Germany, and much of the rest of the world view economic sanctions as counterproductive and generally favor them only in extraordinary circumstances, such as war. Great Britain, for example, never supported the sanctions against South Africa and believes its constructive engagement policy was successful.

Without multilateral support, American trade sanctions can succeed only if a U.S. company is a monopoly supplier of a good or service to the targeted nation, which is not the case virtually anywhere in the world. In the absence of a monopoly, U.S. unilateral sanctions simply transfer business from an American company to a foreign competitor in the same market.

The goals of U.S. economic sanctions are often unrealistic. A bill seriously considered by Congress in 1996 would have banned all investment in Burma (Myanmar) unless the president of the United States certified "that an elected government of Burma has been allowed to take office." Clearly, the details of the situation in Burma differ from those of the situations in other nations, yet setting a standard that requires a trading partner to have an elected government is a dangerous precedent, since that would lead to questions about whether U.S. companies would some day be prevented from doing business in the vast majority of countries in Africa and the Middle East, and much of the rest of Asia, including China.

Our major trading partners are unlikely to support any future congressionally imposed ban on doing business in Burma. To have any hope of effectiveness, such a boycott would require the cooperation of China, Singapore, and other Asian nations, which is not likely to happen. In fact, Asian countries are choosing, not isolation, but closer engagement with Burma, having invited it to participate in the Association of Southeast Asian Nations. As has happened elsewhere in the world, U.S. unilateral sanctions against Burma will serve primarily to transfer business from American to foreign firms without accomplishing larger goals. To date, those U.S. corporations that have pulled out of Burma have seen their investments replaced by companies from Singapore and Western Europe.

As economic leaders, American companies should be encouraged to enter, not discouraged from entering, new markets. U.S. foreign investment not only is profitable for those companies that invest wisely; it also helps foster greater economic growth in developing nations. The companies help those nations advance their social, political, and economic institutions. The removal of American influence is often unfortunate because U.S. corporations tend to increase the wages and labor standards in the countries in which they operate. Companies engaged in long-term investments in Burma and elsewhere also build schools, hospitals, and roads that local governments often cannot afford. U.S. companies operating in Nigeria donate more money to help poor residents than does the U.S. government, according to the Corporate Council on Africa.

Common-Sense Criteria for Sanctions

All current and future U.S. sanctions should undergo an economic cost analysis to make clear that sanctions involve economic tradeoffs for the American people. A 1988 study from Johns Hopkins University estimates that over a 25-year period the embargo against Cuba cost American companies $30 billion in lost exports, while the diplomatic benefits gained by the United States were difficult to pinpoint. To avoid becoming entangled by new U.S. sanctions against energy investments *by any company* in Iran and Libya, many European oil companies and suppliers are likely to redesign their procurement policies to exclude American equipment makers. That will put at risk $600 million in U.S. exports and 12,000 export-related jobs, according to the Petroleum Equipment Suppliers Association.

The illusion that sanctions are cost free also necessitates reintroducing the concept of private property into the sanctions debate. It is one thing to stop sending U.S. government dollars to a distasteful regime; it is quite another to prevent private individuals and companies from legally using their own property in another country. All future sanctions bills should contain appropriations to compensate American companies and individuals for investments lost or devalued as a result of a U.S. economic sanction. For example, if a U.S. company is lawfully extracting natural resources from mines in Indonesia and Congress bans all investment there, that corporation should be compensated for its losses. Such a ban is a form of "takings"—within the meaning of the Fifth Amendment—and should be treated as such. That would make clear the real costs of sanctions and should encourage lawmakers to allow any ongoing company investment in a country to continue unmolested and to place no new restrictions on additional investment by such a company. Compensation should include the net present value of a company's investment plus a premium based on reasonable expectations of future profit. In the absence of compensation, the most any future U.S. sanction should be allowed to do is to block investments by new entrants into the targeted country's market.

Congress should also place time limits on economic sanctions so that the force of inertia does not allow such a significant foreign policy decision to continue indefinitely without being reexamined. The 1996 sanctions against Iran and Libya wisely carry a five-year sunset provision. Any sunset measure, however, should not interfere with the compensation paid to those whose investments are devalued by U.S. government action.

Congress should also require a finding that any sanction is in the "national security interest" of the United States. That finding ought to describe in specific terms how the conduct of the target country poses a threat to the security of the American people and how sanctions would materially reduce that threat. Such a requirement would not necessarily stop the use of sanctions, but it would raise the policy standard for sanctions beyond a show of distaste for another nation's domestic policies.

China and MFN Status

The annual ritual of attempting to deny China most-favored-nation (MFN) trading status serves no legitimate policy purpose and only reduces the stability of the U.S.-China relationship. MFN is itself a misnomer in that it does not grant China a "favored" trading position; it simply treats Chinese products the same as those from nearly all other countries in the world. Only seven countries do not have MFN status. It would be more appropriate to employ the term "normal trade relations." A measure to change MFN to "normal trade relations" was passed by the U.S. Senate in 1996 but did not become law.

The Clinton administration made a wise decision in 1994 when it de-linked human rights from trade and granted China its annual waiver for MFN. The next logical steps are to give China a multiyear waiver and to facilitate China's entry into the World Trade Organization. One emerging complaint against China is its significant trade "surplus" with the United States. Trade deficits, particularly between two nations, are not important economic indicators, do not represent job "losses," and should not be used to justify actions that restrict the flow of goods and services between nations.

Conclusion

The United States should maintain a flexible asylum policy to help victims of persecution from any country and should not provide financial assistance to oppressive regimes. But America cannot *force* other governments to become democratic, or even to treat their citizens humanely, though we should encourage, primarily through diplomatic means, moves toward more freedom.

Current sanction policies have hurt American companies while accomplishing little else. More engagement with the outside world, through increased tourism and a proliferation of trade and investment activity, is more likely to encourage the changes we would all like to see take place in Cuba, Burma, and elsewhere. Since dictatorships thrive by controlling the populace and finding scapegoats for domestic problems, greater interchange with the democratic, market-oriented United States would accomplish more than isolation.

Undoing current sanctions and refraining from imposing new unilateral sanctions against Burma, China, Nigeria, and other nations is the best policy course for the United States. Such sanctions are ineffective, eschew normal diplomatic channels, and undermine our international relations. U.S. companies are often hurt, not only directly, but indirectly because they gain a reputation as unreliable suppliers. Congress should at a minimum adopt reforms that make clear to the public the costs of such sanctions to individual companies and the U.S. economy as a whole. We should abandon the practice of attempting to improve the conduct of other nations by restricting the freedom of our own citizens.

Suggested Readings

Bartlett, Bruce. "What's Wrong with Trade Sanctions." Cato Policy Analysis no. 65, December 23, 1985.

Dorn, James A. "Trade and Human Rights: The Case of China." *Cato Journal* (Spring–Summer 1996).

Hufbauer, Gary Clyde, Jeffrey L. Schott, and Kimberly Ann Elliot. *Economic Sanctions Reconsidered*, 2d ed. Washington: Institute for International Economics, 1990.

Shin, Mya Saw, Alison Krupnick, and Tom L. Wilson. *"Burma" or "Myanmar"? U.S. Policy at the Crossroads*. Seattle: National Bureau of Asian Research, 1995.

—Prepared by Stuart Anderson

54. Trade and Human Rights

Congress should

- treat free trade as an important human right,
- decouple trade policy from human rights policy,
- repeal Jackson-Vanik and maintain a humane refugee and asylum policy, and
- open markets to promote prosperity and human rights.

Free Trade Is a Human Right

The proper function of government is to cultivate a framework for freedom by protecting liberty and property, including freedom of contract (which includes free international trade), not to use the power of government to undermine one freedom in an attempt to secure others. The right to trade is an integral part of our property rights and a civil right that Congress should protect as a fundamental human right.

Market exchange rests on private property, which is a natural right. As moral agents, individuals necessarily claim the right to liberty and property in order to live and to pursue their interests in a responsible manner. Congress should afford the same protection to economic liberties as to other liberties. Free trade is a right, not a privilege bestowed by government.

Protectionism Undermines Human Rights

Protectionism violates human rights. It is an act of plunder that deprives individuals of their autonomy. Controls on imports and exports impede not only the flow of goods and services but the exchange of information and the transmission of values that occur with free markets. When the market recedes, the government gains ground. People become more dependent on the state and more isolated when protectionism prevails.

A case in point is China. Before China's open-door policy, initiated in 1978, the Chinese Communist Party had a monopoly on economic, social, and political life. China isolated itself from the West and held the Chinese people hostage. The repressive system of collectivized farming prevented 80 percent of China's population from determining their own fate, and state enterprises locked in the urban population. The lack of any alternative to the centrally planned economy made China a giant serfdom where individuals had little hope of freedom. After 1978 China's open-door policy and the return of family farming (the so-called household responsibility system) freed millions of individuals from the grip of the CCP and allowed them to develop the nonstate sector. Today that sector dominates the economic landscape, and markets have largely replaced planning. With economic liberalization has come greater personal freedom—to choose one's job, to travel, to migrate from rural to urban areas, and to learn more about the West.

No one will deny that there are serious human rights violations in China, but it would be wrong to conclude that China has made no progress. As Jianying Zha writes in her book *China Pop,*

> The economic reforms have created new opportunities, new dreams, and to some extent, a new atmosphere and new mindsets. The old control system has weakened in many areas, especially in the spheres of economy and lifestyle. There is a growing sense of increased space for personal freedom.

Anyone who has visited China and seen the vibrancy of the market, the dynamism of the people, and the rapid growth of rural industry will concur with Zha's cautious optimism.

It also would be wrong to conclude that the solution to China's dismal human rights record is to deny China most-favored-nation (MFN) trading status or to use the blunt instrument of economic sanctions. Those actions would serve only to strengthen China's hard-liners and slow the process of liberalization.

Instead of imposing punitive tariffs on China by removing MFN trading status or using other restrictive practices to sanction China for human rights violations, Congress should decouple trade policy and human rights policy. Kate Xiao Zhou, in her recent book *How the Farmers Changed China,* shows beyond a doubt that "commercial activity is liberating" and "a major way out of governmental control." Congress should not lose that lesson in the pursuit of some "feel-good" policy that has little chance of changing China's political climate but will devastate its blossoming market sector. Keeping people in China and elsewhere in poverty by restricting their human right to trade is neither logical nor moral. Likewise, depriving Americans of the freedom to trade and invest in foreign countries violates their constitutional rights to life, liberty, and property.

A free-market approach to human rights policy, however, does not mean Americans should be indifferent to the use of slave labor, the abuse of child labor, or the use of political prisoners. Steps should be taken to restrict those practices. But blanket restrictions, such as the denial of MFN status or the use of sanctions not directly targeting the wrongdoers, should be avoided. The problem is that even limited actions are very difficult to enforce and unlikely to bring about political change in authoritarian regimes. The logical alternative is to use the leverage of trade to open nonmarket, nondemocratic systems to competition and let the rule of law and democratic values evolve spontaneously as they have in South Korea and Taiwan.

A Positive Program to Promote Human Rights

Congress should look to the U.S. Bill of Rights, not to the UN Declaration of Human Rights, for clarification of the nature of human rights. Only those rights that are consistent with individual freedom *and can be universalized*—that is, extended to everyone without violating the equal rights of others—can be justified. The fundamental right to be left alone to pursue one's happiness is inseparable from the rights to private property and free trade. If Congress is to uphold the Constitution, then the right to use one's property and to trade it for mutual gain needs to be given the same priority as the rights to free speech and association.

Many of the economic and social rights claimed in the UN Declaration of Rights are inconsistent with private property and individual freedom. Article 25 states that each person "has the right to a standard of living adequate for the health and well-being of himself and his family, including food, clothing, housing and medical care and necessary social services." If sanctions were imposed on China or other countries for failing to protect those alleged "human rights"—rights that lie outside the bounds of the U.S. Constitution, that cannot be universalized, and that cannot be implemented—the world would become less free and less prosperous. America would be putting up a "no exit" sign on the state sector and a "no entrance" sign on the emerging market sector in China and other Third World countries trying to make the transition from plan to market. Before acting too hastily, human rights advocates need to think more clearly about the nature of human rights and how best to help China and other countries along the path toward a free society.

A positive program for promoting human rights in China and elsewhere should include the following provisions:

1. Decouple trade policy from human rights policy. Grant China unconditional MFN trading status—which should be renamed "normal trade relations"—to open markets and to provide an outlet for the nonstate enterprises that are giving the Chinese people a window to the West. Hong Kong and Taiwan will benefit as well from the reduction in uncertainty in trade relations once China is afforded permanent MFN trading status.

2. Repeal the Jackson-Vanik amendment to the Trade Act of 1974 and maintain a generous refugee and asylum policy. The Jackson-Vanik amendment, which denies MFN status to communist countries if they do not allow relatively open emigration and necessitates the annual renewal of China's MFN status, was not an important factor in the collapse of the Soviet Union and is unsuitable for China. From a practical standpoint, no one believes that the United States is going to allow a billion Chinese into the country, so requiring China to have an open emigration policy is nonsensical as a condition for MFN status. To deny people the right to trade because their government denies them the right to emigrate is a dead-end policy for promoting human rights. The fall of the Soviet Union was not the result of sanctions; it was the result of the internal contradictions and weaknesses of the system of central planning and communism. The information revolution, the opening of markets, a strong U.S. national defense, and pressure from the West to conform to the rule of law were instrumental in ending the Soviet regime. Those same forces will help open China.

   Instead of focusing on emigration, Congress should focus on immigration and continue to provide a sanctuary for the victims of human rights violations in China and elsewhere. The number of refugees admitted into the United States each year is determined by consultation between the president and Congress. In that process, Congress should be open and generous. Providing an exit option for those fleeing tyrannical regimes will send a clear message that America is still the land of the free.

3. Open markets to promote prosperity and human rights. People must ultimately choose their own form of government and fight for free-

dom. The United States cannot change China or other repressive regimes by erecting trade barriers. Removing those barriers, however, would set in motion forces to undermine the ruling elites and increase the chances for democracy.

Free markets foster economic development and provide individuals with the means to liberate themselves from the state. A growing middle class will have a strong economic stake in determining its own political fate. The ground will then be prepared for constitutional change. As Taiwan's newly elected President Lee Teng-hui stated, "Vigorous economic development leads to independent thinking. People hope to be able to fully satisfy their free will and see their rights fully protected. And then demand ensues for political reform."

Congress's concern for human rights should be reflected in positive policies that remove impediments to the natural flow of goods, ideas, and people among nations. Traders have always been the carriers of culture as well as goods and services across national boundaries. The legitimate concern for human rights should not be allowed to degenerate into protectionism that denies Americans and foreigners their natural right to trade.

In the case of China, the U.S. government will have more leverage if it uses quiet diplomacy and expands trade than if it bashes that nation. Congress, however, should stand on principle and let China's leaders know that, to become respected members of the international community, they will have to accept rules of just conduct and let market institutions and the rule of law evolve. It is important for China to become a member of the World Trade Organization so that the nation's leaders have an incentive to adhere to the standards required of civilized nations.

Governments everywhere need to get out of the business of trade and leave markets alone. Western democratic governments, in particular, need to practice the principles of freedom they preach and recognize that free trade is not a privilege but a right. Using the threat of sanctions to promote human rights is illogical and risky. Freedom is better advanced by expanding international trade and cultivating market-liberalism at home.

Congress should not let the "feel-good" policy of linking trade and human rights raise a wall of protectionism that blocks out the light of liberty and impoverishes all nations.

Suggested Readings

Bastiat, Frederic. "Protectionism and Communism." In *Selected Essays on Political Economy*. Edited by G. B. de Huszar. Irvington-on-Hudson: Foundation for Economic Education, 1964.

Dorn, James A. "Trade and Human Rights: The Case of China." *Cato Journal* 16 (Spring–Summer 1996).

Lee, Teng-hui. "Taiwan's Quiet Revolution." Interview. *Wall Street Journal,* March 27, 1996.

Pilon, Roger. "The Idea of Human Rights." *National Interest* (Fall 1986).

Zha, Jianying. *China Pop.* New York: New Press, 1995.

Zhou, Kate Xiao. *How the Farmers Changed China.* Boulder, Colo.: Westview, 1996.

—Prepared by James A. Dorn

55. Rethinking the International Drug War

> **Congress should**
> - repeal the Anti-Drug Abuse Acts of 1986 and 1988 and all legislation requiring the United States to certify drug-source countries' cooperation in counternarcotics efforts,
> - declare an end to the international war on drugs, and
> - remove U.S. trade barriers to the products of developing countries.

Washington's international drug control campaign exhibits every flaw inherent to the worst forms of central planning. The war on drugs—a program whose budget has tripled over the last 10 years—has failed remarkably in all aspects of its overseas mission. Most telling, illicit drugs continue to flow across U.S. borders, unaffected by the more than $20 billion Washington has spent since 1982 in its supply-side campaign. The purity of cocaine and heroin, moreover, has increased, while the prices of those drugs have fallen dramatically during the same period.

The U.S. government has not only federalized the social problem of drug abuse by treating narcotics use as a criminal offense; it has intruded into the complex social settings of dozens of countries around the globe by pressuring foreign governments to adopt certain laws and policies. In the process, Washington has severely aggravated the political and economic problems of drug-source nations. Counternarcotics strategy thus conflicts with sound foreign policy goals, namely the encouragement of free markets and democracy in developing countries. For countless reasons, the international drug war is both undesirable and unwinnable.

Failure on Three Fronts

One component of the supply-side campaign, heavily emphasized by the Reagan and Bush administrations, has been interdiction of drug traffic coming into the United States. That approach has been ineffective at reducing the availability of cocaine and heroin because authorities seize only 5 to 15 percent of drug imports and because traffickers easily adapt to such disruptions by using new smuggling innovations and routes. In an implicit recognition of the failure of interdiction efforts, the Clinton administration began favoring strategies that focus on drug-producing countries. "It is more effective to attack drugs at the source of production where illicit production and transportation activities are more visible," former Clinton drug czar Lee Brown contended, "and thus more vulnerable."

Yet there was little reason to believe that an approach that emphasized eradication, crop-substitution, and interdiction efforts in drug-source countries would be more successful than interdiction of drugs along transit routes. Indeed, by early 1996, Gen. Barry McCaffrey, soon to become Clinton's new drug czar, conceded that the new strategy had not made "an operational difference."

A principal reason that supply reduction efforts cannot be expected to affect the use of cocaine, for example, lies in the price structure of the illicit drug industry. Smuggling costs make up only 10 percent of the final value of cocaine in the United States. Those costs, combined with all other production costs outside of the United States, account for only 13 percent of cocaine's retail price. Drug traffickers thus have every incentive to continue bringing their product to market; they view eradication and interdiction as a mere cost of doing business. Moreover, even if such efforts were successful at raising the price of coca paste or cocaine in drug-source countries, their effect on the final price of cocaine in the United States would be negligible. As analyst Kevin Jack Riley has observed, "Using source country price increases to create domestic scarcities is similar to attempting to raise glass prices by pushing sand back into the sea."

The efforts of international drug warriors are also routinely frustrated by drug traffickers' dynamic responses to counternarcotics policies. Already expecting interference in their business, traffickers build redundant processing facilities in case current ones are destroyed, for example, or stockpile their product inside the United States in case of smuggling interruptions. The massive resources available to the $300 billion global illicit drug industry also enable it to react to counternarcotics strategies with ease. At best, drug war "victories" are ephemeral as the industry accommodates itself to new conditions. That situation has reduced U.S. officials to citing drug seizure figures or expressions of political will by foreign governments as important gains in the U.S.-orchestrated war on drugs.

The evidence from the field is less compelling. According to the State Department's annual *International Narcotics Control Strategy Report*, the total area cultivated in coca from 1987 to 1995 grew from 175,210 hectares to 214,800. The area planted in opium poppy, mostly in South Asia, more than doubled from 112,585 hectares to 234,214 hectares during the same period. Eradication schemes—under which the U.S. government pressures source-country governments to eliminate drug crops by spraying pesticides, slashing illegal plants, or burning peasants' fields—appear to have had little effect on the spread of such crops.

Just as damning are the State Department's estimates of net production of illicit drug crops. From 1987 to 1995, coca leaf production increased from 291,100 metric tons to 309,400 metric tons, and opium production grew from 2,242 metric tons to 4,157 metric tons. Despite coercive drug control schemes, it is obvious that peasant farmers still view illegal drug cultivation as advantageous.

Less coercive schemes have also been tried. Crop-substitution and alternative development programs, for example, seek to encourage peasants to join the legal market in agriculture or other sectors. U.S. aid finances infrastructure projects, such as roads and bridges, and subsidizes the cultivation of legal agricultural goods, such as coffee and corn.

Here too, serious obstacles and unintended consequences undermine the best laid plans of Washington and the governments of drug-source countries. Coca plants, for example, grow in areas and under conditions that are thoroughly inhospitable to legal crops, making a switch to legal alternatives unrealistic. (Only 5 to 10 percent of the major coca-growing regions in Peru and Bolivia may be suitable for legal crops.)

Farmers can also earn far higher returns from illicit plants than from the alternatives. For that reason, even when they enter crop-substitution programs, peasants often continue to grow drug plants in other areas. Ironically, the U.S. government in such cases subsidizes the production of illegal drugs.

Indeed, programs that pay peasants not to produce coca can have other effects policymakers did not anticipate, as analysts Patrick Clawson and Rensselaer Lee point out: "The voluntary programs are similar to the crop acreage reduction program that the U.S. government uses to raise the income of wheat farmers. It is not clear why Washington thinks that a crop reduction program raises the income of Midwest wheat farmers but lowers the income of Andean coca farmers. In fact, in both cases, the crop reduction program really is a price support program that can raise farmer income.''

The drug industry also benefits from improved infrastructure. One World Bank report reviewed road projects, funded by the World Bank, the U.S. Agency for International Development, and the Inter-American Development Bank, in coca-growing regions in Peru. ''While the roads were useful in expanding coca production, they have severely hampered the development of legal activities.'' It is interesting to note that the major coca-growing regions in Peru and Bolivia—the Upper Huallaga Valley and the Chapare, respectively—have emerged at the sites of major U.S.-funded development projects of previous decades.

Finally, even if alternative development programs were able to raise the prices of legal crops so that they exceeded or were at least competitive with the price paid for illegal crops, that situation could not last. The cost of growing coca, for example, represents such a small fraction of the final value of cocaine—less than 1 percent—that the illicit drug industry will always be able to pay farmers more than the subsidized alternatives could command.

Coerced Cooperation

The main components of the international narcotics control campaign have produced dismal results and hold little promise of improvement. Although that reality may be well recognized by drug-source nations, U.S. law ensures that most of those countries' governments comply, however reluctantly, with U.S. demands. The Anti–Drug Abuse Acts of 1986 and 1988 condition foreign aid and access to the U.S. market on the adoption of narcotics control initiatives in foreign countries.

That legislation directs the president to determine annually whether drug-producing and drug-transit countries are fully cooperating in the U.S.-led drug war. The certification procedure employs a series of trade and aid sanctions and rewards intended to gain that cooperation. If the president decertifies a country, or if Congress rejects the president's certification, the United States imposes mandatory sanctions that include the suspension of 50 percent of U.S. aid and some trade benefits. Discretionary sanctions may include the end of preferential tariff treatment, limits on air traffic between the United States and the decertified country, and increased duties on the country's exports to the United States.

During the Clinton administration, more countries than ever (30) have come under the certification procedure, and a record number of countries (11 in 1995) have been decertified or granted national security waivers after failing to receive full certification. Most notably, Colombia was not certified in 1996.

U.S. Policy Is Not Just Ineffective

Efforts to "get tough" on drug-producing nations have caused an increase in violence and corruption, distorted economies, and undermined fragile democratic governments and elements of civil society. As long as drugs remain outside the legal framework of the market and U.S. demand continues, the enormous profit potential that results not only makes eliminating the industry impossible but makes the attempts to do so thoroughly destructive.

That Washington's prohibitionist strategy—and not the narcotics trade per se—may be responsible for the problems usually associated with drug trafficking, however, is not something U.S. officials care to acknowledge. Instead, patronizing statements are more typically heard. For example, Robert Gelbard, assistant secretary of state for international narcotics and law enforcement affairs, explained to a subcommittee of the House International Relations Committee in 1995 that, "thanks to U.S. leadership, more governments than ever are aware of the drug threat and have expressed their willingness to combat it."

In a perverse way, of course, Gelbard is right. To the extent that drug-source countries have engaged in the U.S.-led crusade against drugs, they have suffered the consequences. Colombia, the principal target of Washington's international drug control campaign, has over the years seen its judicial, legislative, and executive branches become steadily corrupted by the drug trade. Crackdowns on leading trafficking organizations have produced widespread violence and even dismantled cartels, but they have not affected the country's illicit export performance.

The pervasive influence of the illegal drug industry in Colombian society, and the Colombian government's apparently insufficient efforts to escalate the war against traffickers, led to Clinton's decertification of that country in 1996. Colombia's subsequent efforts to convince the United States it wishes to cooperate in the fight against narcotics led it to undertake coca eradication and other counternarcotic initiatives. Those initiatives have created resentment among peasant populations, who have consequently increased their support of major guerrilla groups, and have reinforced the business relationship between drug traffickers and the rebels who protect illicit drug operations. Indeed, Colombia's various guerrilla organizations earn anywhere from $100 million to $150 million from drug-related activities.

Furthermore, the escalation of the drug war has recently provoked a wave of guerrilla violence that has successfully displaced government authority in parts of the country. "If you can single out one act that has played a decisive role," Defense Minister Juan Carlos Esguerra explained, "I have no doubt that it is our frontal offensive against narco-trafficking in the southeast of the country." Guerrilla involvement in the narcotics trade has become so substantial that the government now refers to the country's largest rebel organization, the Revolutionary Armed Forces of Colombia, as the "third cartel," after the Medellín and Cali cartels, two previous drug war targets.

The United States has responded by increasing aid to the Colombian military, renowned for its human rights abuses and links to paramilitary groups. The U.S.-orchestrated drug war in Colombia and elsewhere has thus weakened civilian rule, strengthened the role of the military, and generated financial and popular support for leftist rebel groups. In Peru, for example, the Maoist Shining Path guerrillas received up to $100 million per year during the 1980s from their marriage of convenience with drug traffickers. That situation prompted Harvard economist Robert Barro to suggest that "the U.S. government could achieve pretty much the same results if it gave the aid money directly to the terrorists."

The crippling of the Shining Path came only after the Peruvian government suspended coca plant eradication programs and concentrated its efforts on anti-terrorist activities and market liberalization. Unfortunately, the administration of President Alberto Fujimori abrogated the constitution in 1992 in a move intended to fight the rebel groups and institutional corruption, problems nourished by the drug war. Peru has since reintroduced democratic rule and initiated further market reforms. Renewed U.S. efforts to get tough on Peru (the country did not receive full certification in 1994 or 1995), however, may compromise those successes. In early 1996, for example, Peru resumed coca eradication and other traditional anti-narcotics efforts despite Fujimori's 1993 statement that long-standing "Peruvian-American anti-drug policy has failed."

Latin American societies are not the only ones threatened by the global prohibitionist model. Illegal opium production takes place in Pakistan, Afghanistan, China, India, Thailand, Vietnam, Burma, and other countries in South and Central Asia. Many of those nations are struggling to become more market oriented and establish the foundations of civil society. As Gelbard has noted, "Most opium and heroin is produced in areas controlled by semi-autonomous, well-armed groups." U.S. supply-reduction efforts are increasingly focusing on countries that produce those drugs. Yet if aggressive prosecution of the drug war has managed to undermine relatively well rooted democracies such as Colombia's, there is every reason to believe that U.S. drug policy in Asia may be even more reckless.

Mexico provides perhaps the most urgent warning to leaders of Washington's anti-narcotics crusade. Major Mexican drug cartels have gained strength and influence as the U.S.-led interdiction campaign in the Caribbean has rerouted narcotics traffic through Mexico. Unfortunately, the result has been a sort of "Colombianization" of Mexico, where drug-related violence has increased in recent years. The 1993 killing of Cardinal Juan Jesús Posadas in Guadalajara, the assassinations of top ruling party officials, and the discovery of hundreds of millions of dollars in the overseas bank accounts of former president Carlos Salinas's brother all appear to be connected to the illicit drug business.

The destabilization of Mexico is especially unfortunate because of the country's efforts at economic and political liberalization. Unlike Colombia, however, Washington has granted Mexico full certification despite evidence of narcocorruption throughout the Mexican government. The inconsistency of U.S. drug policy toward the region is plain, but the internal contradictions of U.S. foreign policy would probably become too conspicuous were Washington to threaten sanctions against a partner in the North American Free Trade Agreement. An increasingly unstable Mexico also has serious implications for the United States. If Mexico experienced the level of social violence and volatility seen in Colombia or Peru, for instance, the United States would be directly affected—a development that would almost certainly provoke Washington's increased involvement in Mexico's complex domestic affairs.

Finally, Washington has not only created severe difficulties for drug-producing nations; its drug control efforts have helped disperse the narcotics industry to countries that might otherwise have avoided such penetration. Venezuela, Argentina, and Brazil, for example, have seen an upsurge in drug-related activity. Similarly, international disruptions in the various stages of illicit drug production have encouraged local traffickers to be self-sufficient in all stages of production. For example, the recent crackdown on Colombia's Cali cartel, which has temporarily depressed coca prices in

Peru, has prompted the Peruvian industry to enter more advanced stages of cocaine production.

Toward a Constructive Approach

Washington's international drug war has failed by every measure. Production of drugs in foreign countries has increased, and the flow of drugs to the United States has continued. Worse, U.S. narcotics control policies have severely aggravated political, economic, and social problems in developing countries. Attempts to escalate the drug war, even in a dramatic way, will do little to change those realities. Washington should instead encourage the worldwide shift away from statism and toward the creation of markets and civil society by ending its international crusade against drugs and opening its markets to drug-source countries' legal goods. Doing so will hardly affect U.S. drug consumption, but it would at least be a recognition that narcotics abuse is a domestic social problem that foreign policy cannot solve.

Suggested Readings

Boaz, David, ed. *The Crisis in Drug Prohibition.* Washington: Cato Institute, 1990.

Clawson, Patrick L., and Rensselaer Lee III. *The Andean Cocaine Industry.* New York: St. Martin's, 1996.

Duke, Steven B., and Albert C. Gross. *America's Longest War: Rethinking Our Tragic Crusade against Drugs.* New York: G. P. Putnam's Sons, 1993.

Riley, Kevin Jack. *Snow Job? The War against International Cocaine Trafficking.* New Brunswick, N.J.: Transaction, 1996.

Thoumi, Francisco. *Political Economy and Illegal Drugs in Colombia.* Boulder, Colo.: Lynne Reinner, 1995.

Vásquez, Ian. "Ending Washington's International War on Drugs." In *Market Liberalism: A Paradigm for the 21st Century.* Edited by David Boaz and Edward H. Crane. Washington: Cato Institute, 1993.

—Prepared by Ian Vásquez

56. Foreign Aid and Current Lending Fads

Congress should

- abolish the U.S. Agency for International Development and end traditional government-to-government aid programs;
- not use foreign aid to encourage or reward market reforms in the developing world;
- eliminate programs, such as enterprise funds, that provide loans to the private sector in developing countries and oppose schemes that guarantee private-sector investments abroad;
- privatize or abolish the Export-Import Bank, the Overseas Private Investment Agency, the U.S. Trade and Development Corporation, and other sources of corporate welfare; and
- end government support of microenterprise lending and nongovernmental organizations.

Foreign aid is among the most unpopular of all government programs with the American public. Although the public continues to place the alleviation of world poverty and the promotion of development in poor countries as priorities on its list of foreign policy concerns—a view consistent with the American tradition of generosity—it has lost confidence that the U.S. government is well suited to achieve those goals.

That apprehension is not unfounded, nor is it limited to average American citizens. Today, the failure of conventional government-to-government aid schemes is widely recognized and has brought the entire foreign assistance process under scrutiny. J. Brian Atwood, administrator of the U.S. Agency for International Development—the agency responsible for disbursing the bulk of Washington's bilateral development assistance—promised to improve his organization's performance, admitting that it was "on the road to mediocrity or worse."

That admission followed a Clinton administration task force's concession that "despite decades of foreign assistance, most of Africa and parts of Latin America, Asia and the Middle East are economically worse off today than they were 20 years ago." As early as 1989 a bipartisan task force of the House Foreign Affairs Committee concluded that U.S. aid programs "no longer either advance U.S. interests abroad or promote economic development."

Although a small group of countries in the developing world (some of which received U.S. aid at some point) has achieved self-sustaining economic growth, most recipients of U.S. aid have not. Rather, as a 1989 U.S. AID report suggested, aid has tended to create dependence on the part of borrower countries.

There are several reasons why massive transfers from the United States to the developing world have not led to a corresponding transfer of prosperity. Aid has traditionally been lent to governments, has supported central planning, and has been based on a fundamentally flawed vision of development.

By lending to governments, U.S. AID and the multilateral development agencies supported by Washington have helped expand the state sector at the expense of the private sector in poor countries. U.S. aid to India from 1961 to 1989, for example, amounted to well over $2 billion, almost all of which went to the Indian state. Ghanaian-born economist George Ayittey complained that, as late as 1989, 90 percent of U.S. aid to sub-Saharan Africa went directly to governments.

Foreign aid has thus financed governments, both authoritarian and democratic, whose policies have been the principal cause of their countries' impoverishment. Trade protectionism, byzantine licensing schemes, inflationary monetary policy, price and wage controls, nationalization of industries, exchange-rate controls, state-run agricultural marketing boards, and restrictions on foreign and domestic investment, for example, have all been supported explicitly or implicitly by U.S. foreign aid programs.

Not only has the lack of economic freedom kept literally billions of people in poverty; development planning has thoroughly politicized the economies of developing countries. Centralization of economic decision-making in the hands of political authorities has meant that a substantial amount of poor countries' otherwise useful resources has been diverted to unproductive activities such as rent seeking by private interests or politically motivated spending by the state.

Research by economist Peter Boone of the London School of Economics confirms the dismal record of foreign aid to the developing world. After reviewing aid flows to more than 95 countries, Boone found that "virtually all aid goes to consumption" and that "aid does not increase investment and growth, nor benefit the poor as measured by improvements in human development indicators, but it does increase the size of government."

It has become abundantly clear that as long as the conditions for economic growth do not exist in developing countries, no amount of foreign aid will be able to produce economic growth. Moreover, economic growth in poor countries does not depend on official transfers from outside sources. Indeed, were that not so, no country on earth could ever have escaped from initial poverty. The long-held premise of foreign assistance—that poor countries were poor because they lacked capital—not only ignored thousands of years of economic development history; it also was contradicted by contemporary events in the developing world, which saw the accumulation of massive debt, not development.

"New" Ideas

With the collapse of development planning and the worldwide shift toward liberalization, most advocates of foreign aid now acknowledge at least rhetorically the importance of markets and the private sector in economic development. U.S. AID, for example, emphasizes that it no longer lends mainly to governments.

Proponents of continued foreign assistance cite several noble-sounding goals to justify continued funding. They include efforts to advance market reforms, loans and guarantees to the private sector, active promotion of U.S. exports, and increased reliance on private voluntary organizations and "market-based" credit that reaches the poor.

Under a Democratic administration and a Republican Congress, appeals cloaked in market rhetoric have increased and are likely to persist. It is important, therefore, to separate fact from fiction and to examine cause and effect.

For example, a substantial amount of aid is still directed to the public sector. About 50 percent of U.S. economic aid goes to the Middle East; most of that aid is received by the governments of Egypt and Israel. It should not be surprising, then, that the region is notable for its low levels of economic freedom and almost complete lack of economic reform. In 1996 the Institute for Advanced Strategic and Political Studies, an Israeli think tank, complained, "Almost one-seventh of the GDP comes to Israel as charity. This has proven to be economically disastrous. It prevents reform, causes inflation, fosters waste, ruins our competitiveness and efficiency, and increases the future tax burden on our children who will have to repay the part of the aid that comes as loans.''

Promoting Market Reforms

Even aid intended to advance market liberalization can produce undesirable results. Such aid takes the pressure off recipient governments and allows them to postpone, rather than promote, necessary but politically difficult reforms. Ernest Preeg, former chief economist at U.S. AID, for instance, noted that problem in the Philippines after the collapse of the Marcos dictatorship: ''As large amounts of aid flowed to the Aquino government from the United States and other donors, the urgency for reform dissipated. Economic aid became a cushion for postponing difficult internal decisions on reform. A central policy focus of the Aquino government became that of obtaining more and more aid rather than prompt implementation of the reform program.''

Far more effective at promoting market reforms is the suspension or elimination of aid. Although U.S. AID lists South Korea and Taiwan as success stories of U.S. economic assistance, those countries began to take off economically only after massive U.S. aid was cut off. Indeed, the countries that have done the most to reform economically have made changes despite foreign aid, not because of it.

Moreover, lending agencies have an institutional bias toward continued lending even if market reforms are not adequately introduced. Yale University economist Gustav Ranis explains that with some lending agencies, ''ultimately the need to lend will overcome the need to ensure that those [loan] conditions are indeed met.'' In the worst cases, of course, lending agencies do suspend loans in an effort to encourage reforms. When those reforms begin or are promised, however, the agencies predictably respond by resuming the loans—a process Ranis has referred to as a ''time-consuming and expensive ritual dance.''

In sum, aiding reforming nations, however superficially appealing, does not produce rapid and widespread liberalization. Just as Congress should reject funding regimes that are uninterested in reform, it should reject schemes that call for funding countries on the basis of their records of reform. Indeed, had they received substantial foreign assistance as a reward for implementing far-reaching liberalization measures, it is unlikely that countries such as Chile or the Czech Republic would be as economically healthy as they are today.

Helping the Private Sector

Enterprise funds represent another initiative intended to help market economies. Under this approach, U.S. AID and the Overseas Private Investment Corporation have established and financed venture funds throughout the developing world. Their purpose is to promote economic progress and "jump-start" the market by investing in the private sector.

It was always unclear exactly how such government-supported funds could find profitable private ventures in which the private sector is unwilling to invest. Numerous evaluations have now found that most enterprise funds are losing money and many have simply displaced private investment that otherwise would have taken place. Moreover, there is no evidence that the funds have generated additional private investment, had a positive impact on development, or helped create a better investment environment in poor countries.

Similar efforts to underwrite private entrepreneurs are evident at the World Bank (through its expanding program to guarantee private-sector investment) and at U.S. agencies such as the Export-Import Bank, OPIC, and the Trade and Development Agency, which provide comparable services.

U.S. officials justify those programs on the grounds that they help promote development and benefit the U.S. economy. Yet the provision of loan guarantees and subsidized insurance to the private sector relieves the governments of underdeveloped countries from creating the proper investment environment that would attract foreign capital on its own. To attract much-needed investment, countries should establish secure property rights and clear economic policies, rather than rely on Washington-backed schemes that allow avoidance of those reforms.

Moreover, while some corporations clearly benefit from the array of foreign assistance schemes, the U.S. economy and American taxpayers do not. Indeed, subsidized loans and insurance programs merely amount to corporate welfare. The United States, in any case, did not achieve and does not maintain its status as the world's largest exporter because of agencies like the Export-Import Bank, which finances about 3 percent of U.S. exports.

Even U.S. AID claims that the main beneficiary of its lending is the United States because close to 80 percent of its contracts and grants go to American firms. That argument is also fallacious. "To argue that aid helps the domestic economy," renowned economist Peter Bauer explains, "is like saying that a shop-keeper benefits from having his cash register burgled so long as the burglar spends part of the proceeds in his shop."

Other Initiatives

The inadequacy of government-to-government aid programs has prompted an increased reliance on nongovernmental organizations (NGOs). NGOs or private voluntary organizations (PVOs) are said to be more effective at delivering aid and accomplishing development objectives because they are less bureaucratic and more in touch with the on-the-ground realities of their clients.

Although channeling official aid monies through PVOs has been referred to as a "privatized" form of foreign assistance, it is often difficult to make a sharp distinction between government agencies and PVOs beyond the fact that the latter are subject to less oversight and accountability. Michael Maren, a former employee at Catholic Relief Services and U.S. AID, notes that most PVOs receive most of their funds from government sources.

Given that relationship—PVO dependence on government hardly makes them private or voluntary—Maren and others have described how the charitable goals on which PVOs are founded have been undermined. The nonprofit organization Development GAP, for example, observed that U.S. AID's "overfunding of a number of groups has taxed their management capabilities, changed their institutional style, and made them more bureaucratic and unresponsive to the expressed needs of the poor overseas."

"When aid bureaucracies evaluate the work of NGOs," Maren adds, "they have no incentive to criticize them." For their part, NGOs naturally have an incentive to keep official funds flowing. In the final analysis, government provision of foreign assistance through PVOs instead of traditional channels does not produce dramatically different results.

Microenterprise lending, another increasingly popular program among advocates of aid, is designed to provide small amounts of credit to the world's poorest people. The loans are used by the poor to establish livestock, manufacturing, and trade enterprises, for example.

Many microloan programs, such as the one run by the Grameen Bank in Bangladesh, appear to be highly successful. Grameen has disbursed more than $1.5 billion since the 1970s and achieved a repayment rate of about 98 percent. Microenterprise lending institutions, moreover, are intended to be economically viable, able to achieve financial self-sufficiency within three to seven years. Given those qualities, it is not clear why microlending organizations would require subsidies. Indeed, microenterprise banks typically refer to themselves as profitable enterprises.

Furthermore, microenterprise programs alleviate the conditions of the poor, but they do not address the causes of the lack of credit faced by the poor. In developing countries, for example, about 70 percent of poor people's property is not recognized by the state. Without secure private property rights, most of the world's poor cannot use collateral to obtain a loan. The Institute for Liberty and Democracy, a Peruvian think tank, found that where poor people's property in Peru was registered, new businesses were created, production increased, asset values rose by 200 percent, and credit became available. Of course, the scarcity of credit is also caused by a host of other policy measures, such as financial regulation that makes it prohibitively expensive to provide banking services for the poor.

In sum, microenterprise programs can be beneficial, but successful programs need not receive aid subsidies. The success of microenterprise programs, moreover, will depend on specific conditions, which vary greatly from country to country. For that reason, microenterprise projects should be financed privately by people who have their own money at stake rather than by international aid bureaucracies that appear intent on replicating such projects throughout the developing world.

Conclusion

Numerous studies have found that economic growth is strongly related to the level of economic freedom. Put simply, the greater a country's economic freedom, the greater its level of prosperity over time. Those developing countries, such as Chile and Taiwan, that have most liberalized their economies and achieved high levels of growth have done far more to reduce poverty and improve their citizens' standards of living than have traditional foreign aid programs.

In the end, a country's progress depends almost entirely on its domestic policies and institutions, not on outside factors such as foreign aid. Congress should recognize that foreign aid has not caused the worldwide shift to the free market and that appeals for more foreign aid, even when intended to promote the market, will continue to do more harm than good.

Suggested Readings

Bailey, Ronald, ed. *The True State of the Planet.* New York: Free Press, 1995.
Bandow, Doug. "Uncle Sam as Investment Banker: The Failure of Washington's Overseas Enterprise Funds." Cato Institute Policy Analysis no. 260, September 16, 1996.
Bauer, P. T. *Dissent on Development.* Cambridge, Mass.: Harvard University Press, 1972.

Eberstadt, Nicholas. *Foreign Aid and American Purpose.* Washington: American Enterprise Institute, 1988.

Gwartney, James, Robert Lawson, and Walter Block. *Economic Freedom of the World 1975–1995.* Vancouver: Fraser Institute, 1996.

Lal, Deepak, and H. Myint. *The Political Economy of Poverty, Equity and Growth.* New York: Oxford University Press, 1996.

Lash, William H. III. "Who Needs an Eximbank?" Washington, Competitive Enterprise Institute, June 1995.

Maren, Michael. *The Road to Hell: Foreign Aid and International Charity.* New York: Free Press, 1997.

Osterfeld, David. *Prosperity versus Planning: How Government Stifles Economic Growth.* New York: Oxford University Press, 1992.

—Prepared by Ian Vásquez

57. Multilateral Lending Agencies

> **Congress should**
> - reject proposals for more aid funds and new lending institutions and initiatives;
> - terminate contributions to existing institutions, including the International Monetary Fund (IMF), the World Bank, and five regional multilateral lending agencies; and
> - push to privatize or close all seven institutions.

As World War II came to a close, the United States took the lead in creating the IMF and the World Bank. In succeeding years Washington supported the creation of five regional development banks modeled after the World Bank and has consistently been the largest contributor to all of them. Although the lending agencies were touted as the answer to Third World poverty, they have proved to be expensive failures, doing more to retard than to advance economic progress throughout the developing world. At the same time, they have wasted billions in U.S. tax dollars and created a well-funded lobby devoted to the expansion of failed foreign-aid programs.

The International Monetary Fund

Perhaps the most controversial lending agency is the IMF. Originally created to help nations suffering balance-of-payments difficulties, the fund moved into the development business after President Richard M. Nixon closed the gold window in 1971. Nixon's move ended the international system of fixed exchange rates, thus eliminating the fund's function of managing that system.

The IMF lends money to governments in support of economic adjustment programs, which are theoretically intended to promote economic development. Unfortunately, little development is evident after more than

50 years of fund lending. Perhaps the best test of the effectiveness of the IMF is the number of troubled developing countries that have "graduated" because of its loan programs, which entail both money and advice. (Causation, not correlation, is the relevant standard of proof, since the fund has lent to most developing nations at one time or another.) Even friends of the organization have trouble pointing to many success stories. The fund itself acknowledges a declining compliance rate in recent years.

That is not surprising, since the organization has been subsidizing the world's economic basket cases for years, without apparent effect. Through 1993, 11 nations, including Egypt, India, Sudan, and Turkey, had relied on IMF aid for more than 30 years; 32 had been borrowers for between 20 and 29 years; and 41, almost one-fourth of the world's nations, had been using fund credit for between 10 and 19 years. While the organization now says it is tougher about cutting off nations that take its money and violate its loan conditions, it continues to let politics trump economics. Russia barely waited for the ink to dry on IMF agreements before announcing that it did not intend to keep them, but the fund has continued to send money to Moscow.

Of course, the IMF is not the only aid agency to act as a permanent dole for economic failures, but it has increasingly taken the lead in international lending. There are several problems with IMF activities, including the organization's reliance on inappropriate conditions and lack of effective enforcement. The main problem, however, is that foreign loans, whatever the formal conditions accompanying them, effectively subsidize the cause of borrowers' poverty when their economic policies are badly distorted. Among the fund's major clients have been Argentina, Brazil, Mexico, and (the now dismembered) Yugoslavia, all of which have promulgated anti-growth, dirigiste policies for decades despite IMF loan programs. That fund officials lack either a conscience or common sense is evident from the organization's support of the odious Ceaucescu regime in Romania and the Mobutu dictatorship in Zaire.

The World Bank

The record of the World Bank is similar. The bank, established in the aftermath of World War II along with the IMF to reorder the global economic system, was envisioned as a "lender of last resort" to assist developing countries only when the global capital markets proved inadequate. But over the years the institution has become even more profligate than the IMF, lending over $20 billion annually to countries, irrespective of their economic worthiness.

The bank was originally intended to help countries finance the infrastructure necessary to encourage private investment. However, bank policy changed dramatically during the 1960s and 1970s when the organization increased its lending 13-fold under its president Robert McNamara. Admitted one bank official at the time, "We're like a Soviet factory. The push is to maximize lending. The . . . pressures to lend are enormous and a lot of people spend sleepless nights wondering how they can unload projects. Our ability to influence projects in a way that makes sense is completely undermined."

The institution became the chief financier of government-led economic programs. During the 1970s the bank committed roughly 80 percent of its funds to public enterprises. There were, in fact, few money-losing state enterprises in such heavy borrowers as Argentina, Brazil, India, and Mexico that were not subsidized year in and year out by the bank. Today, poor nations are left with the job of cleaning up the consequences of their statist economic strategies. Indeed, many new, market-oriented governments are now attempting to privatize old, bank-funded mistakes.

Moreover, the bank has long promoted development at any cost, whether to human rights or to the environment. Like the IMF, bank officials never met a dictator they didn't like; the bank has provided assistance to Ceausescu's Romania, Mengistu's Ethiopia, and communist China. Bank funds underwrote the worst forms of social engineering, such as Julius Nyerere's coercive *ujamaa* program, which brutalized tanzanian peasants and devastated the nation's agricultural economy. The bank also supported Indonesia's forced transmigration project.

Unfortunately, the environment has not escaped unscathed. Bank-backed water programs have disrupted local ecosystems and forced millions of farmers off their land without compensation. Bank lending underwrote the destruction of the Brazilian rain forest; other bank-subsidized development projects promoted deforestation, desertification, and flooding around the globe.

Given that record, it should not be surprising that bank-funded projects failed in their essential purpose: promoting development. An internal Operations Evaluation Department report in 1987 conceded that "the Bank's drive to reach lending targets" had led to "poor project performance." In the same year, auditors judged more than one-third of the bank's rural lending projects, accounting for roughly half of total bank

547

lending over the previous two decades, to be failures. Subsequent evaluations have documented a continuous record of projects that failed to meet expectations, were not sustainable, and left borrowing nations with little more than increased debt.

However, the bank's primary problem is not that it backs bad projects, though many are bad, but that it, like the IMF, has regularly underwritten governments that have had overall economic policies that preclude self-sustaining development. One bank evaluation found that 54 percent of agricultural projects studied were adversely affected by price controls and similar misguided regulations. Concluded the auditors, "It has become clear that it is not possible to implement viable projects in an unfavorable policy environment." Yet bank lending only increased in succeeding years.

To meet growing criticism of its record, in the 1980s the bank embarked on a program of so-called adjustment lending—policy-reform loans much like those offered by the IMF. But the bank is more interested in lending money than some nations are in borrowing it. A devastating internal study, the 1992 Wapenhans report, concluded that staffers were reluctant "to take a firm stand with Borrowers," preferring to ignore or waive noncompliance. As a result, "the high incidence of non-compliance undermines the Bank's credibility." Even bank senior vice president Ernest Stern was forced to admit that "time and again the best of policy intentions, the best of policy letters solemnly agreed to and signed by the finance minister and the Bank, broke down."

Of course, some countries have accepted bank adjustment loans and reformed their economies. But they received equally lavish funding before they reformed. In the end, countries will adopt politically painful reforms only if they possess the political will to do so. And they will generate that commitment only if forced to confront the high price of economic failure. For decades the bank has essentially handed alcoholic borrowers a fistful of $100 notes and told them to drink no more; after the money was squandered the bank demanded repayment. That policy has never worked, and it will not work in the future, even though bank officials now voice free-market rhetoric as readily as they issue checks.

A better reform model is provided by countries, such as the Soviet Union, that changed only when faced with the abyss of economic collapse. Countries determined to reform their economies don't need outside aid; those receiving outside aid will face less economic pressure to continue reforming. Sadly, the bank is not only wasting American taxpayers' money. It is hindering development in the very nations it says it wants to help.

The Regional Development Banks

Although the IMF and the World Bank are the leading lending agencies, five regional institutions have been created in the image of the latter: the African Development Bank, the Asian Development Bank, the European Bank for Reconstruction and Development, the Inter-American Development Bank, and the Middle East Development Bank. (The latter became operational only in November 1996.) Naturally, the United States is the largest contributor to every one.

The smaller development banks have all followed the same flawed lending policies as the World Bank. The African Development Bank wasted billions in some of the worst economic rat holes on earth while falling into administrative and fiscal chaos. The Inter-American Development Bank subsidized many of the same Latin American fiscal black holes underwritten by the IMF and the World Bank. The European Bank for Reconstruction and Development places greater emphasis on the private sector, but it spent most of its initial years of operation lavishing dollars on itself and has little to show for its efforts.

New Schemes

The fact that past lending has failed to promote economic growth has not slowed the profusion of plans for increased lending in the future. For instance, the G-7 has proposed creation of a new $50 billion fund, paid for by Western industrialized nations and run by the IMF, to subsidize nations, such as Mexico, that face financial crises. The multilateral lending agencies have developed a nearly $8 billion debt-relief initiative—which would require countries like the United States to forgive bilateral debt while the World Bank and the IMF offered new loans. Moreover, IMF head Michel Camdessus has proposed expanding borrowing rights from his organization by $36 billion and as much as doubling its capital, now $200 billion, and has pressed Washington to contribute $300 million for the fund's subsidized lending facility. The World Bank is preparing to push for another round of contributions to the International Development Association, a bank affiliate. The United States is committed to paying $234 million in arrears on a past capital increase for the Asian Development Bank and putting up 21 percent of the $1.25 billion in new capital for the Middle East Development Bank.

But none of those initiatives is likely to do any more good than did aid in the past. After all, there has been no shortage of foreign aid or commercial credit over the years, else poorer nations would not have been able to accumulate a $2.1 trillion debt. But that flood of cash has done nothing to promote development; to the contrary, much of the Third World has imploded while the number of development agencies has been increasing. Fully 70 developing states are poorer today than they were in 1980; 44 are worse off than they were in 1960.

Conclusion

Aid levels do not correlate with economic growth, and many recipients of the most foreign assistance, such as Bangladesh, Egypt, India, Sudan, and Tanzania, have been among the globe's worst economic performers. But the problem is not just that foreign assistance doesn't help. It almost certainly hurts. For years foreign aid from a multitude of sources has helped cover poorer countries' financial losses and sustain their economies, pushing off their days of reckoning. Today, Third World states are left with both huge debts and low growth. The answer is economic reform, not more foreign loans. Once reforms are in place, private credit and investment will follow naturally. The transition will, of course, be painful, but no amount of international lending, whether directly from the United States or from the IMF, the World Bank, or other development banks, can prevent that. Bad economic policies have to be made right.

Congress should end U.S. funding for all of those institutions. But that is not enough, since even without further American contributions the repayment of past loans would allow the lending agencies to continue lending tens of billions of dollars annually. Thus, the U.S. government also needs to push to privatize the organizations, like the IMF and World Bank, that might be viable and close down those, like the African Development Bank, that almost certainly are not.

Suggested Readings

Adams, Patricia. *Odious Debts: Loose Lending, Corruption, and the Third World's Environmental Legacy.* Toronto: Earthscan, 1991.

———. "The World Bank's Finances: An International S&L Crisis." Cato Institute Policy Analysis no. 215, October 3, 1994.

Bandow, Doug. "World Bank: Servant of Governments, Not Peoples." Chap. 13 in *The Politics of Envy: Statism as Theology.* New Brunswick, N.J.: Transaction Publishers, 1994.

Bandow, Doug, and Ian Vásquez, eds. *Perpetuating Poverty: The World Bank, the IMF, and the Developing World.* Washington: Cato Institute, 1994.

Hancock, Graham. *Lords of Poverty: The Power, Prestige, and Corruption of the International Aid Business.* New York: Atlantic Monthly Press, 1989.

Hoskins, W. Lee, and James W. Coons. "Mexico: Policy Failure, Moral Hazard, and Market Solutions." Cato Institute Policy Analysis no. 243, October 10, 1995.
Thibodeau, John. "The World Bank's Procurement Myth." Cato Institute Foreign Policy Briefing no. 43, September 4, 1996.
Walters, Alan. "Do We Need the IMF and the World Bank?" Institute of Economic Affairs Current Controversies no. 10, September 1994.

—Prepared by Doug Bandow

Contributors

Stuart Anderson is director of trade and immigration studies at the Cato Institute.

Charles W. Baird is professor of economics at California State University at Hayward.

Doug Bandow is a senior fellow at the Cato Institute and author of *Tripwire: Korea and U.S. Foreign Policy in a Changed World.*

Solveig Bernstein is assistant director of telecommunications and technology studies at the Cato Institute.

David Boaz is executive vice president of the Cato Institute and author of *Libertarianism: A Primer.*

Ted Galen Carpenter is vice president for defense and foreign policy studies at the Cato Institute and author of *Beyond NATO: Staying Out of Europe's Wars.*

Jonathan G. Clarke is a research fellow at the Cato Institute and coauthor of *After the Crusade: American Foreign Policy for the Post Superpower Age.*

Barbara Conry is a foreign policy analyst at the Cato Institute.

Edward H. Crane is president of the Cato Institute.

Thomas J. DiLorenzo is professor of economics at Loyola College's Sellinger School of Business and Management.

James A. Dorn is vice president for academic affairs of the Cato Institute and coeditor of *Economic Reform in China.*

Bert Ely is president of Ely & Company, Inc., and an adjunct scholar at the Cato Institute.

Peter Ferrara is an associate policy analyst at the Cato Institute and chief economist with Americans for Tax Reform.

Lawrence Gasman is director of telecommunications and technology studies at the Cato Institute and author of *Telecompetition: The Free Market Road to the Information Highway.*

Robert M. Goldberg is a senior research fellow at Brandeis University's Gordon Public Policy Center.

Michael Gough is director of science and risk studies at the Cato Institute.

Stefan Halper is a nationally syndicated columnist and a former White House and State Department official.

Edward L. Hudgins is director of regulatory studies at the Cato Institute and editor of *Regulation* magazine.

David Isenberg is a senior defense analyst at the Center for Defense Information.

Thomas J. Kniesner is professor of economics at Indiana University.

Stanley Kober is a research fellow in foreign policy studies at the Cato Institute.

David B. Kopel is research director of the Independence Institute and author of *The Samurai, the Mountie, and the Cowboy.*

John D. Leeth is associate professor of economics at Bentley College.

Naomi Lopez is an entitlements policy analyst at the Cato Institute.

Timothy Lynch is assistant director of the Center for Constitutional Studies at the Cato Institute.

553

Stephen Moore is director of fiscal policy studies at the Cato Institute and author of *Government: America's #1 Growth Industry.*

William A. Niskanen is chairman of the Cato Institute and author of *Reaganomics.*

Darcy Ann Olsen is managing editor of *Regulation* magazine.

Tom G. Palmer is director of special projects at the Cato Institute and an H. B. Earhart Fellow at Hertford College, Oxford University.

Roger Pilon is director of the Center for Constitutional Studies at the Cato Institute.

Robert Poole is president of the Reason Foundation in Los Angeles. He has advised the Reagan, Bush, and Clinton administrations and a number of state and city governments on privatization issues.

Earl C. Ravenal is Distinguished Research Professor of International Affairs at the Georgetown University School of Foreign Service and author of *Designing Defense for a New World Order.*

Sheldon Richman is vice president for policy affairs of the Future of Freedom Foundation.

Jacobo Rodríguez is assistant director of the Project on Global Economic Liberty at the Cato Institute.

David Schoenbrod, a former senior attorney and cofounder of the Natural Resources Defense Council and now a professor at New York Law School, is an adjunct scholar of the Cato Institute and author of *Power without Responsibility: How Congress Abuses the People through Delegation.*

Bradley A. Smith is professor of law at Capital University Law School in Columbus, Ohio.

Dean Stansel is a fiscal policy analyst at the Cato Institute.

Michael Tanner is director of health and welfare studies at the Cato Institute and author of *The End of Welfare: Fighting Poverty in the Civil Society.*

Jerry Taylor is director of natural resource studies at the Cato Institute.

Ian Vásquez is director of the Project on Global Economic Liberty at the Cato Institute and coeditor of *Perpetuating Poverty: The World Bank, the IMF, and the Developing World.*